FOURTH EDITION

Public

Policy

Perspectives and Choices

Charles L. Cochran and
Eloise F. Malone

LYNNE
RIENNER
PUBLISHERS

BOULDER
LONDON

Published in the United States of America in 2010 by
Lynne Rienner Publishers, Inc.
1800 30th Street, Boulder, Colorado 80301
www.rienner.com

and in the United Kingdom by
Lynne Rienner Publishers, Inc.
3 Henrietta Street, Covent Garden, London WC2E 8LU

Library of Congress Cataloging-in-Publication Data
Cochran, Charles L.
   Public policy : perspectives and choices / Charles L. Cochran and
      Eloise F. Malone. — 4th ed.
      p.   cm.
   Includes bibliographical references and index.
   ISBN 978-1-58826-674-3 (pbk. : alk. paper)
   1. Policy sciences. I. Malone, Eloise F. II. Title.
   H97.C6 2010
   320.6—dc22

                                                        2009026977

British Cataloguing in Publication Data
A Cataloguing in Publication record for this book
is available from the British Library.

Printed and bound in the United States of America

   The paper used in this publication meets the requirements
        of the American National Standard for Permanence of
        Paper for Printed Library Materials Z39.48-1992.

   5 4 3 2 1

To Dave Malone
who left this world a better place

Contents

Illustrations

Figures

Preface

Public policy should be one of the most stimulating and enjoyable areas of study in political science. Provocative issues of public policy—including environmental protection, energy independence, civil liberties, health care, immigration reform, homeland security, and how best to regulate the economy—are discussed in newspapers, television news, and Internet blogs every day.

The presidential election of 2008 energized the electorate and signaled an unusually intense struggle over the policy choices to be made over the next several years. For the first time in fifty-six years, neither candidate was an incumbent president or vice president. And for the first time ever, two sitting US senators challenged each other. Both candidates ran on a platform of change. An unpopular president, an unpopular and costly war, and an economy falling into a deep recession were the themes that dominated the political campaigns in the fall of 2008. Barack Obama became the first African American president of the United States, while Democrats increased their control in the House and Senate. Members of the Republican Party, who recently believed a permanent Republican majority had arrived, served notice that they intended to defend their conservative achievements against the Democratic Party's ambitious goals for progressive policy changes. The next several years promise to be fascinating for students of public policy and provide many lessons regarding successes and failures over public policy struggles.

Yet there is a widespread belief that US citizens are detached from public life, and that their interests are frequently drowned out by the clamor of special interest groups. A growing cynicism often results, leading to an ironic alliance between the average citizen, who comes to believe that the democratic process is largely a mockery, and the financial elites, who believe that it is best to entrust as little to government policymaking as possible. Attacks on the institutions of US government as *the problem* make it more difficult to craft the compromises needed to produce effective policies. Well-financed groups often resort to this tactic in an effort to block policies that may pose a threat to their interests. Growing economic inequality and the evolving political paradigm that supports it make up one of the most important trends in the modern United States. Often, the policies associated with support for the most well-to-do citizens negatively affect those who are less well-off.

Nevertheless, public policy as a discipline is optimistic. It is based on the profoundly significant belief that an understanding of the implications of public policy choices is essential for every citizen, and that the citizens in a democratic society can take responsible actions to improve the national well-being.

Why This Book?

The goal of this text is to bring the excitement of public policy as it is discussed in the public realm—and the optimism of the discipline as a whole—into the classroom experience. As with the preceding editions, our primary purpose is to tell the story of perspectives and choices in public policy in a clear, scholarly, balanced, and interesting manner. We believe that it is a narrative of great importance, one that sharpens our focus and clarifies our understanding of the society we live in and the rules that govern it.

Public policy continues to grow as a subfield of political science. At the same time, the study of public policy transcends the boundaries of academic disciplines and, in recent decades, interdisciplinary techniques have contributed important, but often controversial or competing, new perspectives. We have chosen to base our text on contributions from all the disciplines that are of concern to policy studies. We believe it is important for students to be thoroughly grounded in basic economic arguments such as market failures, free riders, externalities, economic rents, and moral hazards. We emphasize that practically everything is for sale in economic markets—but in a political society, many things should be beyond price. Relying too heavily on markets frequently produces results that offend our sense of justice and fairness. Other contributions such as democratic theory, rational public choice, international relations theory, and psychology are also necessary to understand the complexity of public policy problem solving.

Throughout the book, we try to integrate these relevant theories and approaches with the various analytical frameworks used in current struggles over policy issues and with empirical data from policy choices in practice. The path from understanding theory to understanding its application is often rocky, but we believe that it is also a stimulating, enjoyable path and one worth taking.

The Plan of the Fourth Edition

On the surface, this fourth edition follows the same successful organization as its earlier incarnations. The first five chapters provide a tour of the fundamental elements of a political scientist's way of thinking about policy issues and the policymaking process. We cover topics such as scarcity, rational self-interest, the tragedy of the commons, the free rider problem, and market and government failures as part of the essential core of public policy. In our experience, these are the subjects students will remember long after the course is over. We also develop the difference between the often idealistic goals of the policymaker and the reality of the circumstances in which public policy is hammered out; policy analysts, after all, are rarely constrained by the need to raise money and win votes, unlike the politicians who actually make public policy.

Making sense of these principles is important because, though fundamentally logical, they are often misunderstood. We do our utmost to explain public policy ideas clearly and in understandable language. At the same time, we try to avoid oversimplification and to elevate the policy problems by highlighting the political, philosophical, and economic issues that permeate even the most seemingly straightforward problems. We find that interweaving theoretical perspectives and real-life practical choices into our discussion offers the reader a well-rounded understanding of the policy issues at hand.

However, much has changed in the policy environment over the past several years: a new administration, a new balance of partisan power, and seismic shifts in the economy are all affecting the country's policy priorities. We have rewritten much of the text to take these changes into account, and new boxed features highlight contemporary case studies. These boxes also illustrate policy application and implementation and offer additional explanations of concepts and problems addressed in the text. In some instances, the boxed material serves as a medium for introducing or developing important ideas and issues that may be tangential to the main flow of a chapter and, therefore, are best treated separately.

In the aftermath of September 11, 2001, it became abundantly clear that what goes on in the rest of the world has a growing impact on policy issues in the United States. And with the more recent economic meltdown, our global interconnectedness is even more apparent. In this environment, we must be aware that other countries have faced the same policy dilemmas as the United States and often have made alternative choices that can inform our policy decisions. Consequently, we frequently compare US approaches to policymaking with those of other advanced countries, especially the nations of the Organisation for Economic Co-operation and Development.

Finally, we try to emphasize that the appeal to the individual of democratic decisionmaking is based on the ability of the collective to achieve goals that individuals cannot achieve acting separately. In this sense, democratic government is a necessary good in promoting the general welfare. Policy studies must inevitably raise issues about the ethical relationship between the individual and the collective. The study of public policy thus involves the thoughtful use of interdisciplinary insights and empirical evidence in pursuit of social justice. To achieve a humane society as well as an efficient economy, wise government involvement is inevitable.

Acknowledgments

We are indebted to so many people for their help in writing this book that it is difficult to know where to begin thanking them. Our parents imparted a strong sense of social justice and fairness to us. They also encouraged us to be informed about political issues and to be open to new ways of seeing things. This debt cannot be repaid, but only acknowledged. Throughout it all, Mimi Cochran was most important in encouraging us to press on and bring the project to a successful conclusion.

This past year was very difficult due to the death of Eloise's beloved husband, David Malone. Dave was a wonderful husband and a true friend, and he is sorely missed. And as a true scholar himself, he was always an encouraging presence in our every academic effort.

We also acknowledge debts to our colleagues and, especially, to our students. Our understanding of the material is more complete because of the thoughtful and challenging questions raised by students, which in turn has made us better teachers of public policy.

We owe special thanks to Glenn Gottschalk, Linda Hull, Barbara Breeden, and Florence Todd. Many other colleagues assisted by providing information, sources, and articles, and helped (frequently unknowingly) by way of conversations that stimulated new ideas or modifications of existing ones. The kind and patient guidance of Cindi Gallagher helped us to more clearly convey the information in the figures.

From the book's first incarnation to this current edition, reviewers—too numerous to name, but deeply appreciated nonetheless—read early drafts and offered invaluable comments. The entire staff at Lynne Rienner Publishers has been supportive, and all deserve acknowledgment. We call particular attention to Leanne Anderson and Claire Vlcek, who took a special interest in the project and saved us from public humiliation. For any other errors that remain, we blame each other.

—*Charles L. Cochran,*
Eloise F. Malone

1

Basic Concepts in Public Policy

As the 2008 campaign for president of the United States heated up, Democrat Barack Obama and Republican John McCain developed contrasting visions for the nation's future. Each staked out often stark positions to sharpen the differences between their views. Voters, increasingly fearful about their financial prospects during the economic downturn, were especially attentive to the candidates' appeals, which highlighted fundamental differences on public policy issues as well as their conception of government's role in each policy problem.

For example, although both Obama and McCain agreed that the health care system is not working and that there is a need to reduce the ranks of the 46 million uninsured Americans, their proposals for health care reform bore little resemblance to each other. McCain opposed publicly funded health care and mandates requiring everyone to obtain health insurance.[1] His proposal would replace the health insurance income tax break employees could receive when employers provide health insurance with a tax credit of as much as $2,500 for individuals and up to $5,000 for families. The credit would allow individuals to purchase coverage through their employers or via the individual market. McCain's position was that "we do not believe in coercion and the use of state power to mandate care, coverage or costs."[2] In contrast, Obama would require employers to provide health insurance or contribute to the cost of it, but exempt small businesses and reimburse all employers for catastrophic health costs. His plan would make insurance portable from job to job and prohibit insurance companies from denying coverage to individuals with preexisting health problems or from charging them higher rates.[3] Health issues will be discussed more fully in Chapter 10.

The candidates' positions on trade also revealed differing views. McCain strongly supported free trade, including the North American Free Trade Agreement (NAFTA) and US participation in the World Trade Organization (WTO).[4] McCain opposed the inclusion of labor conditions as part of trade agreements. Obama supported expanding trade only if the United States' trade partners include labor and environmental standards

1

that would "level the playing field" for US workers. He was critical of NAFTA for not including stricter labor and environmental standards for Canada and Mexico, and indicated his intent, if elected, to renegotiate the current agreement to include such standards.[5]

The titular leaders of the two political parties also clashed on their views of abortion and the role of government. McCain stated: "I do not support *Roe v. Wade*. It should be overturned."[6] He supported returning the issue of abortion to the states for disposition. Obama, on the other hand, believes that abortion is a woman's right and should be legally available in accordance with *Roe v. Wade*.[7]

The crisis that began in subprime mortgages and spread rapidly through the financial industry in September 2008 crystallized the candidates' views regarding deregulation. By way of background, the free market vision of the economy that rejected government regulation and oversight over financial markets had been encouraged by President Ronald Reagan. This view reached its zenith in the early years of the administration of G. W. Bush who rescinded many regulations and slashed regulatory funding. During the campaign, McCain indicated his long support for deregulation. In an article published in an actuarial journal in 2007, he had argued for deregulation, saying that "opening up the health insurance market to more vigorous nationwide competition, as we have done over the last decade in banking, would provide more choices of innovative products less burdened by the worst excesses of state-based regulation."[8] With the financial crisis growing daily, Obama relentlessly pressed McCain by arguing that it was the lack of regulation favored by Bush and McCain that brought on the disaster. McCain was forced to disavow his earlier position and claim that runaway greed brought on by "insufficient regulation" was the culprit. Although some conservatives in Congress resisted legislative efforts to rescue faltering institutions, claiming that the discipline of the marketplace should be the final arbiter, the prevailing sentiment was that government regulation is necessary when markets fail. Chapter 6 provides a more complete treatment of the financial crisis.

The candidates' contrasting views of the appropriate role of government raise the fundamental questions addressed by the branch of political science known as ***public policy***.* The goal of public policy is to understand how issues get on the policy agenda, what determines how policy choices are made, and how we are to understand the proper role of government in the policy process. Basic to public policy are the questions: What kinds of goods and services should the government provide? Why do we assume that the government should be the primary provider of highways, safety regulation of commercial aviation, unemployment compensation, and social security while goods and services such as food, clothing, and entertainment are left to the private sector? Essentially, why does the government engage in some policy activities and avoid others?

Since we must constantly be concerned with how to pay for the goods and services that the government provides, public policy must also address the problem of how

---

*Key concepts are indicated in boldface on first definition in the book.

the government raises the revenue to fund its policy expenditures. What kinds of taxes should be levied? Can the taxes serve other societal functions besides funding expenditures? Who should pay the taxes, and what effects do taxes have on encouraging or discouraging other activities in society? Could the government perform its policy and economic roles more efficiently? Can certain policy choices help us create a better society? How have these views changed over time? What are the major sources of public disagreement regarding what policies are appropriate for government to pursue?

This chapter begins with a review of the general issues that are addressed in public policy. It explains why public policy is an important field of study and introduces the vocabulary of public policy. The pages that follow define concepts needed to understand the policy process.

The driving forces behind public policies are **scarcity** and **rational self-interest**. In a diverse society that embraces different values and points of view, interests collide so compromises are unavoidable. Policy analysts must deal with practical questions of who will gain and who will lose by any given policy. Analysts consider whether government intervention improves on a market solution, and whether government intervention compromises values important to society in general.

What Is Public Policy?

Public policy emerged as a prominent subfield within the discipline of political science in the mid-1960s. In a broad sense, the analysis of public policy dates back to the beginning of civilization. Public policy is the study of government decisions and actions designed to deal with a matter of public concern. **Policy analysis** describes the investigations that produce accurate and useful information for decisionmakers.

The social sciences emerged from the humanities and the natural sciences during the latter part of the nineteenth century. The commitment to the methods of the natural sciences, with their concern for methodological and analytical rigor in the study of human behavior, has been critical to the development of social science. Social scientists share the conviction that rational scientific methods can be used to improve the human condition. The scientific method began to be applied to a wide range of social activity, ranging from the efforts of Frederick A. Taylor's studies on scientific management to the politics of the Progressives. Legislation in the Progressive era was delegated to "experts" in such new and presumably independent regulatory agencies as the Federal Trade Commission and the Federal Reserve Commission.

Policy Analysis and Value Neutrality

Although the social sciences emerged in an environment of social reform, by the early twentieth century there was a general retreat from any sort of policy advocacy. The social sciences in general adopted a value-neutral position under the guise of scientific objectivity. Scientific inquiry is probably one of the most prestigious activities in modern life. And those engaged in policy studies from a variety of social science disciplines were attracted to the idea that their studies would be more scientific if they eliminated values and merely focused on social behavior. As a result, many policy studies were confined to empirical descriptions. Such studies may prove useful in a variety of ways.

Positive Policy Analysis

Emphasis on value-free policy analysis is referred to as **positive policy analysis**, which is concerned with understanding how the policy process works. It strives to understand public policy as it is. It also endeavors to explain how various social and political forces would change policy. Positive policy analysis tries to pursue truth through the process of testing hypotheses by measuring them against the standard of real-world experiences. Positive policy analysis usually deals with assertions of cause and effect. A disagreement over such analysis can usually be resolved by examining the facts. For instance, the following is a positive statement: "If the US government raises interest rates, then consumers will borrow less." We can check the validity of this statement by measuring it against real-world observations. Other positive policy statements, such as "If long-term welfare recipients were required to finish their high school education as a condition of continuing to receive their welfare checks, a high percentage would develop employable skills and become self-sufficient," may be tested by setting up an experiment within a state. The results may confirm or refute the statement.

The attempt to become more scientific by excluding values has several major effects. First, by narrowing the focus to largely empirical studies, it reduced the relevance of policy analysis for policymakers, who must be concerned with preferred end-states such as "reduced ethnic antagonisms." Second, it reduced the importance of values in policy debates by shifting the discussion to cost-benefit analysis or the appropriate way to test a hypothesis. Finally, by glossing over the normative issues, the field of values was often abandoned to business interests and social conservatives. Applying models based on market efficiency while ignoring issues of "justice and fairness" played into the hands of business interests and social conservatives, who never stopped touting the values of right to property, and the virtues of self-reliance, independence, thrift, and hard work.

Normative Analysis

The Great Depression and Franklin Roosevelt contributed to a major change in policy approaches. The Roosevelt revolution swept aside any suggestion that promoting the general welfare could be divorced from normative goals. Nevertheless, there were many architects of the New Deal who preferred to think of themselves as a rather elite group of experts engaged in administering programs remaining above petty partisan bickering. Until the depression, during which 25 percent of the labor force was unemployed, many thought that unemployment was a personal problem, not a matter for government action. The Roosevelt administration changed that perception by fighting excessive unemployment through a variety of government policies. Government planning during the New Deal gave great impetus to operations research, systems analysis, and cost-benefit analysis as techniques for efficient management. After World War II, debates within the social sciences forced a search for more inclusive policy models. During the John F. Kennedy administration, new techniques such as the Planning, Programming, and Budgeting System (PPBS) were used by the "whiz kids" brought into the Pentagon by Secretary of Defense Robert McNamara.

The applied orientation of these techniques in the Department of Defense earned public recognition and acceptance of policy analysis while it encouraged debate among social scientists that they should become more active contributors to policy analysis and policymaking.[9] The techniques noted above, along with survey research, had wide applicability not only in public policy, but also in private industry. A debate arose between those in the social sciences who wished to maintain the more theoretical approach of positive analysis and those who wished to see the policy sciences applied to society's problems. In 1966, Hans J. Morgenthau, a well-known political scientist, summed up the views of those in favor of applying quantitative techniques to achieve practical outcomes, in a statement that could just as well apply to all the policy sciences:

> A political science that is neither hated nor respected, but treated with indifference as an innocuous pastime, is likely to have retreated into a sphere that lies beyond the positive or negative interests of society. The retreat into the trivial, the formal, the methodological, the purely theoretical, the remotely historical—in short, the politically irrelevant—is the unmistakable sign of a "noncontroversial" political science which has neither friends nor enemies because it has no relevance for the great political issues in which society has a stake.[10]

David Easton, in his presidential address to the American Political Science Association in 1969, signaled this momentum when he called for a "postbehavioral" approach that used techniques, methods, and insights of all relevant disciplines in dealing with social issues.[11]

Policy analysis, with a view toward resolving public issues, is *prescriptive* rather than *descriptive* when it recommends action to be taken rather than merely describing policy processes. It is referred to as **normative policy analysis**. Normative policy analysis is directed toward studying what public policy ought to be to improve the general welfare.

Normative analysis deals with statements involving value judgments about what *should* be. For example, the assertion that "the cost of health care in the United States is too high" is a normative statement which cannot be confirmed by referring to data. Whether the cost is too high or is appropriate is based on a given criterion, its validity depends on one's values and ethical views. Individuals may agree on the facts of health care costs, but disagree over their ethical judgments regarding the implications of "the cost of health care."

It is important to be aware of the distinction between positive and normative policy analysis, and not to substitute the goals or methods of one for those of the other. The value of policy analysis is determined by the accurate observation of the critical variables in the external environment. Only an accurate rendering of factual relationships can indicate how best to achieve normative goals. For example, a normative view that we should improve the educational system in the United States does not indicate how to achieve that goal most effectively or most efficiently. If we have limited resources to add to the education budget, how should we spend the funds? Would higher salaries attract more capable teachers? Should we extend the school year? Should we improve the teacher-to-pupil ratio by hiring more teachers? Should we add alternative educational programs? Only a rigorous study of the costs and benefits of various alternatives can indicate a preferred solution. In a republican form of government such as our own, such questions are settled by voting and through decisions made by those elected to run the institutions of government.

Frequently, however, normative statements can be used to develop positive hypotheses. Generally, most people do not feel strongly about the value of a capital gains tax cut. Their support or opposition to such a change in the tax law depends on a prescriptive belief about a valued end-state. Many politicians press to reduce the federal tax on capital gains. They argue that a reduction in the capital gains tax would increase incentives to invest in the economy and thus fuel economic growth. However, computer estimates have shown that this change in the tax structure would reduce government revenues after several years and raise the federal deficit. Estimates also have shown that upper-income groups would receive a significantly larger per capita benefit than would other income groups. The result of these estimates, when publicized, was a popular perception that the tax cut would be "unfair." Republicans have had difficulty in pressing the proposal for this reason.

In the decision to study public policy, there is an implicit ethical view that people and their welfare are important. We must try to learn about all the forces that affect the well-being of individuals and of society in the aggregate. The desire to improve the current system is the basis for public policy. To achieve that goal, as students of public policy we must first understand how the current system works.

In democratic societies, the decisionmaking authority is characterized by varying degrees of decentralization. When decisionmaking authority is distributed between different power centers, such as the different branches of government—executive, legislative, and judicial as well as local, state, or national levels and including various interest groups and the general public—no single group's will is totally dominant. Policy analysts therefore study how the actors in the policy process make decisions: How do issues get on the agenda? What goals are developed by the various groups? How are those goals pursued? Political elites must share power. They often differ concerning not only which problems must be addressed, but also how they should be addressed. The policy that results often reflects different powerful groups pulling in different directions and the outcome often differs from what anyone intended. Policy analysts therefore study how individuals and groups in the policy process interact with each other.

Policy analysts also attempt to apply rational analysis to the effort to produce better policy decisions. Thus, through empirical and rational analysis, a body of research findings opens up the possibility of policy analysts providing valuable input to promote the general welfare.

Decisions and Policymaking

Public opinion polls confirm that people worry about their economic well-being more than any other concern. People worry about educating their children and meeting mortgage payments. They worry about the high cost of health care, the needs of an elderly parent, and the threat of unemployment. These concerns cut across age groups. Students worry about finding a job when they graduate, paying their rent, making insurance payments. Many people express concern for economic problems like federal budget deficits, taxes, and inflation. Many are increasingly aware that personal well-being is somehow related to broader social trends. This relationship is the domain of public policy, though few really understand how the public policy process works or how it affects them personally.

Public policy comprises political decisions for implementing programs to achieve societal goals. These decisions hopefully represent a consensus of values. When analyzed, public policy comprises a plan of action or program and a statement of objectives; in other words, a map and a destination. The objectives tell us what we want to achieve with policy and who will be affected by policy. Public policy plans or programs outline the process or the necessary steps to achieve the policy objectives. They tell us how to do it. For example, a newly proposed public policy for national health care would include an objective statement explaining why a health care policy matters, along with a detailed health care program or procedure. The program might be "managed competition," or perhaps a "Canadian single-payer" program. Usually, the program stage provides the "moment of truth" and people are forced to face up to the values and principles they espouse.

Ultimately, public policy is about people, their values and needs, their options and choices. The basic challenge confronting public policy is the fact of scarcity, an ever-present aspect of the human condition. We cannot have everything we want. Unfortunately, available resources are limited while, for practical purposes, human wants are limitless. The combination of limited resources and unlimited wants requires that we choose among the goods and services to be produced and in what quantities. Because of scarcity, government may intervene to ration the distribution of certain goods and services thought to be in the public interest. Thus, because of scarcity, there is a need for governmental organizations (such as the Departments of Education, Energy, Defense, Health and Human Services, and Treasury) to allocate resources among competing potential users. Conversely, if there were no scarcity, we would not have to make choices between which goods or services to produce.

Poverty and *scarcity* are not synonymous. Scarcity exists because there are insufficient resources to satisfy all human wants. If poverty were eliminated, scarcity would remain. Because, even though everyone might have a minimally acceptable standard of living, society still would not have adequate resources to produce everything people desired.

Opportunity Costs

Public policy focuses on the choices individuals and governments make. Because of scarcity, people and societies are forced to make choices. Whenever we make a choice, costs are incurred. When the unlimited wants of individuals or society press against our limited resources, some wants must go unsatisfied. To achieve one goal, we usually have to forgo another. Policy choices determine which wants we will satisfy and which will go unsatisfied. The most highly valued opportunity forfeited by a choice is known as the **opportunity cost**. This cost equals the value of the most desired goods or services forgone. In other words, to choose one alternative means that we sacrifice the opportunity to choose a different alternative. For example, when you decide to enroll in college rather than get a job, the opportunity cost of college includes not only the cost of tuition and other expenses, but also the forgone salary.

People grouped in societies face different kinds of choices. The opportunity cost of any government program is determined by the most valuable alternative use. One tradeoff society faces is between national defense (guns) and social goods (butter). A fixed amount of money, say $100 billion, can be used to buy military goods, or an equivalent amount of social goods (education or health care), but it cannot be used to purchase both goods simultaneously. A decision to have more of one good is also a decision to have less of other goods. Another policy tradeoff society faces is between a cleaner environment and more income. Laws requiring reduced pollution result in higher production costs, which simultaneously squeeze profits, put a downward pressure on wages, and put an upward pressure on prices. Laws to reduce pollution may give us a cleaner, healthier environment, but at the cost of reducing corporate profits and workers' wages while raising costs for consumers.

The saying that there is no such thing as a free lunch indicates that, because of scarcity, choices must be made that preclude other alternatives.[12] This may seem an obvious point, but many often assume that there is a free lunch. For instance, many people speak of "free public schools" or the need for "free medical care" or "free highways." The problem is that "free" suggests no opportunities forfeited and no sacrifice. This is not the case, however, as the resources that provide education, health care, or highways could have been used to produce other goods. Recognizing that we face choices with tradeoffs, as individuals and collectively in society, does not tell us what decisions we will or should make. But it is important to recognize the tradeoffs in our choices because we can make astute decisions only if we clearly understand the options. The opportunity cost principle can be illustrated. Figure 1.1 summarizes the hypothetical choices in what political economists call a **production possibilities curve** (PPC). This production possibilities curve, or **production possibilities frontier** (PPF), provides a menu of output choices between any two alternatives. Think of it as a curve representing tradeoffs. It illustrates the hard choices we must make when resources are scarce, or the opportunity costs associated with the output of any desired quantity of a good. It also illustrates the indirect effect of **factors of production**, defined as land, labor,

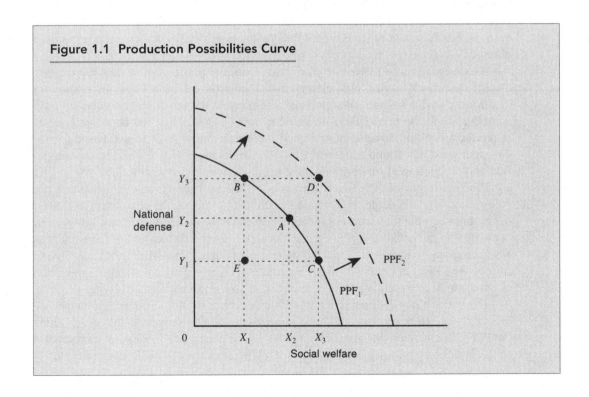

Figure 1.1 Production Possibilities Curve

and capital. Our ability to alter the mix of output depends on the ease with which the factors of production can be shifted from one area to another. For example, with the collapse of communism in Russia and Eastern Europe, the US government shifted some production from the defense industry to the civilian sector.

In Figure 1.1 the economy is at point A, but conservatives want to pull it to point B while liberals prefer point C, resulting in a political struggle. Both could get the quantity they want through economic growth (point D). Even at point D, both soon find that their wants are greater than the scarce resources available. And the tug-of-war would soon begin on the new PPF. Keep in mind that points on (not inside) the production possibilities frontier indicate efficient levels of production. When the economy is producing at point A, for example, there is no way to produce more of one good without producing less of the other. When a policy decision moves the production from point A to point B, for instance, society produces more national defense, but at the expense of producing less social welfare.

The economy cannot operate outside its production frontier with current resources and technology. It is not desirable to operate inside the frontier. Note that point E is a feasible output combination, but not a desirable one. Why? Because by moving to point B, for instance, the economy could produce as much social welfare as at point E, but it could also produce considerably more national defense. Or, by moving to point C, more social welfare could be produced without sacrificing the production of defense. Production at point E means that the economy's resources are not being used efficiently.

As we move more factors of production from the production of national defense toward social welfare, we must give up ever-increasing quantities of defense in order to get more social welfare, and vice versa. This is so universal a phenomenon that it is referred to as the **principle of increasing costs**. It states that the opportunity costs of producing additional units of one good increase as more resources are used to produce that good. Or, stated differently, in order to get more of one good in a given period, the production of other goods must fall by ever-increasing amounts.

Production potential is not fixed for all time. As more resources or better technologies become available, production possibilities increase. As population increases, the number of potential workers increases production possibilities. An improvement in the quality of the labor force, such as through improved education or investment in new plants and equipment, can also increase production possibilities. The outward shift of the PPF is at the heart of an expanding economy. This also means a reduction of opportunity costs and a potential increase in an overall standard of living.

The points along the production possibility curve or frontier indicate that many bundles of goods can be produced with the same resources. Consequently, movement along the PPF demonstrates that most changes in public policy are modest or **incremental** shifts. Policy changes are usually, but not always, relatively small, and are typically made with current conditions in mind. Hence, the best predictor of what the federal budget will be next year is the current budget. The decision to change the budget is made **at the margin**. Essentially, decisions at the margin mean that we focus on the effects of small changes in particular activities. Policymakers usually consider marginal not total benefits and costs; as a result, we are not faced with all-or-nothing choices. An important principle for anyone studying public policy is the significance of **marginal analysis**. Marginal analysis is a decisionmaking process that is concerned with the additional benefits that a plan of action will provide and the additional costs that will be incurred. A policy analyst would recommend that a proposed action be taken if, and only if, the marginal benefit of the action exceeds the marginal cost.

The PPF helps us see that choosing what mix of goods and services to produce is the essence of public policy considerations. A nation may face a guns-versus-butter choice in a period of high threats to national security, and environmental protection versus health care might come to the fore in peacetime. Shifts outward in the PPF represent growth; however, the production possibilities curve says nothing about the desirability of any particular combination of goods and services. To understand this, we have to know more than what choices have been made. We must also know why and how individuals and groups make choices and who benefits.

Social Choice

Resource scarcity sets up the conditions for social choice. It is important to emphasize that choices are ultimately made by individuals. The press may report that "the Congress passed a bill" or that "a divided Supreme Court decided," but these are summary expressions of a group decisionmaking process. Actually, a majority of the individual members of Congress voted for a bill, or a majority of the individual members of the Court decided a case before it. The mechanism for aggregating individual choices to arrive at collective decisions is democratic majority rule. The democratic process translates the private interests of individual human beings into group decisions. Interested individuals freely express their preferences and decide, in the aggregate, what the public policy decision will be. However, as we shall examine in Chapters 3 and 4, public opinion and the voting process may provide very weak guidance to political elites.

While individual choice is the basic unit of public policy analysis, there are often situations in which we treat an organization, such as a government agency, a lobbying group, or even a family, as a "black box"—a gadget whose output is known even though its internal workings are not completely known. Mechanisms such as television sets or computers are, for most, black boxes. In some instances, we will open the black box to examine how and why certain individual and group decisions are made. It is important that, as students of public policy, we understand what goes on within the black box of the "political system." We need to know how policy is produced within the institutional processes of the political environment and how voters, interest groups, and political parties behave.

More important, public policy originates in our understanding of the public interest. Appealing to that public interest is difficult because it mirrors the disagreement among competing concepts of social morality and justice. In many situations, there may be no conflict between acting in one's self-interest *and* the interest of others, or the common good, simultaneously. More frequently, however, if people act in their narrow self-interest, it becomes impossible to achieve the common good. A healthy public spirit, the social form of altruism, sometimes referred to as "social responsibility," is essential for a healthy democracy. A willingness to accept the general interest as one's own is what President Kennedy referred to when he said, "Ask not what your country can do for you, but what you can do for your country."

Social Justice

A fundamental problem is that there is no practical agreement on the meaning of justice. James Madison stated the dilemma in the *Federalist Papers* in describing individual differences and abilities of men. Different interests lead men to see the world differently. But "no man is allowed to be a judge in his own cause, because his interest would certainly bias his judgment, and, not improbably, corrupt his integrity."[13] The result is that conflict and not consensus is at the center of modern politics and public policy.

To illustrate the problem, consider a controversy between two individuals. One individual, Joan, is concerned with what she believes is the arbitrary nature of the distribution of wealth and income. She is particularly distressed over the accompanying inequality of power between those with considerable wealth and those without. She concludes that the poor are virtually powerless to improve their condition while the wealthy are able to increase their wealth and power with ease. The great inequalities in wealth and power are considered unjust by Joan. She concludes that government efforts to redistribute wealth in the direction of the poor through taxes are demanded by simple justice. Thus, help by government activity will lead to greater individual freedom and justice. Joan therefore decides to vote for political candidates who support such taxes and her notion of justice.

The second individual, Robert, has worked hard to achieve certain goals in life. These include financial independence that permits him to purchase a house, to travel, to send his children to college, and sufficient investments to permit a comfortable retirement. He now finds his goals jeopardized by proposals to raise taxes to reduce the deficit and to provide housing for the indigent. He regards these policies that threaten his goals as unjust because they deprive him of his financial resources against his will. He believes that justice demands the full entitlement of each person to the fruits of their own labor, and that each individual should have the complete right to use and control them.

If the economy is growing rapidly enough, Joan's projects may be implemented without threatening Robert's goals. In that case, they may both vote for the same political candidates. But if the economy is stagnant, and either Joan's or Robert's policies must be sacrificed to the other, it becomes clear that each has a view of justice that is logically incompatible with the other. In such cases, each will use their competing concepts of justice to promote incompatible social goals.

John Rawls, in his treatise *A Theory of Justice,* addressed the question of what constitutes a just distribution of goods in society.[14] He held that principles of just distribution may limit legitimate acquisition. If applying principles of just distribution requires a redistributive tax or the taking of property through eminent domain, that acceptance of the taking of property is the price that must be paid to achieve a broader justice in the community.

Robert Nozick argued in his book *Anarchy, State, and Utopia,* in response to Rawls, that each individual has a right in justice to the product of his or her labor unless or until that individual chooses to give some part of it to another person (or to a central authority for redistribution).[15] If the result of individual acquisition is a gross inequality between individuals, justice requires that the disparity be accepted.

The price to be paid for justice in each definition must be paid by another group. Neither of these contending principles of justice is socially neutral.[16] US culture has no accepted rational criterion for deciding between rights based on lawful entitlement versus claims based on need. However, Rawls and Nozick both suggest rational principles to appeal to the contending parties. Some, like Rawls, define justice in relation to an equitable distribution in society. For them, justice is based on a consideration of the present-day distribution. Justice should have priority over economic efficiency. This leads them to an appeal against absolute entitlement. Others, like Nozick, argue that legal acquisition of wealth and income in the past is alone relevant; present-day distribution is irrelevant.[17] They appeal against distributive rules to a justice based on entitlement.

Neither Rawls nor Nozick refer to what is deserved based on justice. But concepts of what is deserved or merited are implied. Nozick argues that individuals are entitled in justice to their wealth and property, and not that they deserve this wealth and property. However, groups supporting this position invariably argue that they are entitled to what they have acquired through their efforts, or the efforts of others who have legally passed title to them. Rawls protests on behalf of the poor that their poverty is undeserved and therefore unwarranted. The child born to the migrant worker is no less deserving than the child born to a family of wealth and privilege. Rawls called this the "natural lottery."

The debate over taxes further illustrates this difference in values between Rawls's distributive justice and Nozick's entitlement theory. The modern opposition to any tax increases or government expenditure policies originates in the strongly negative attitude toward taxation among those who must pay them. Taxes, they argue, are paid primarily by the haves while benefits accrue primarily to the have-nots. Many of the more fortunate members of society oppose all taxation, but their opposition to the redistribution of wealth through tax policy is not put so crudely.

A concern for liberty, the requirements of justice, efficiency, or the virtues of **laissez-faire** (noninterference) are the most frequently cited justifications. Indeed, it is perhaps naive to expect the privileged to respond sympathetically to policies that transfer resources from themselves to others, particularly since there is no community consensus on virtue. The affluent attack government as an arbitrary, profligate liability that is held in check only by relentless attention to its defects. Those with the temerity to promise increased services for the needy are promptly labeled "big spenders." The Rawls-Nozick philosophical debate is an extension of the economic and political rift between different groups in society. Not only is there no value consensus in public policy, but modern political competition is a less violent form of civil war.

Politics and Economics

How societies decide to utilize their scarce resources is determined by a variety of factors. Along with values, they include the history, culture, socioeconomic development, forms of government, and economic organization of those societies. The classic definition of **political science** is a study of "who gets what, when, and how in and through government."[18]

Robert Dahl reformulated the focus of political science in the first sentence of his classic work in the discipline as an insightful question: "In a political system where nearly every adult may vote, but where knowledge, wealth, social position, access to officials, and other resources are unequally distributed, who actually governs?"[19] Since Dahl posed the question, the United States has become a much more unequal society with a much larger share of income going to the most affluent. The point is that politics involves the struggle over the allocation of resources based on the values of the society. Public policy is the outcome of the struggle in government over who gets what.[20] **Economics** has been defined as "the science of how individuals and societies deal with the fact that wants are greater than the limited resources available to satisfy those wants."[21]

These definitions of the two disciplines of political science and economics have a great deal in common. Both are concerned with studying human behavior in competition for scarce resources. Public policy exists at the confluence of these disciplines (see Chapter 2). As such, any definition of public policy will reflect these origins. Most definitions of public policy are rather imprecise and we will offer only a working definition. For our purposes, public policy includes actions of government to convert competing private objectives into public commitments, and includes decisions not to take action. Public policies are purposeful decisions made by authoritative actors in a political system who have the formal responsibility for making binding choices among societal goals.[22] Policy choices are choices that a society must make *collectively*. For example, the decision to attempt to bail out financial institutions on the verge of collapse in 2008 was made by action taken in the House and Senate, with sharp disagreement from those voting in the minority, and signed by the president. Collective decisionmaking is complicated since, as has been noted, individuals may disagree about what is desirable. In private markets by contrast, consumers can express their individual preferences by buying the make, model, and color of a car of their choice.

The assumption voiced in the Declaration of Independence that individuals create government to secure their rights poses a paradox in contemporary US public policy. Men and women can advance their individual freedom only by giving up the anarchistic freedom of no government. Government policy must be coercive and constrain the individual in order to promote the general welfare and secure order and predictability through collective choices.

Three Basic Economic Systems

If political science is the study of who gets what, when, and how, then public policy may begin by examining the current state of affairs of who already has what, and how it was obtained. There are three basic types of economic organization. The oldest form of economic organization, with only a few examples still remaining throughout the world, is the traditional economy. **Traditional economies** are those in which economic decisions are based on customs and beliefs handed down from previous generations. In these societies, the three basic questions of *what, how,* and *for whom* to produce are answered according to how things have been done in the past. Today, in countries like Bolivia, the peasant economy outside of a city like La Paz is predominantly traditional.

Command economies (also known as planned economies) are characterized by government ownership of nonhuman factors of production. Since the government allocates most resources, it also makes most of the decisions regarding economic activities. In socialist economies, for example, the government may own most resources other than labor. Governments then decide what, how, and for whom goods are to be produced. The government determines to whom the goods will be distributed. Theoretically, in communist countries this was based on the principle: "From each according to their ability, and to each according to their needs." In practice, what was produced was often distributed according to political or party loyalty. Such governments generally follow policies resulting in wages being more evenly distributed than in capitalist economies.

Pure market economies (also known as capitalistic economies) are characterized by the doctrine known as *laissez-faire*. In this model, the government should leave the private sector alone and not try to regulate or control private enterprise. Unregulated competition would best serve the interests of society. In a market economy, *what* to produce is left up to entrepreneurs responding to consumer demand. *How* to produce is determined by available technology and entrepreneurs seeking the most efficient means of production in order to maximize their profit. And *for whom* the goods are produced is determined by consumer demand, or "dollar votes": if you have the money you can buy it. Prices are the signals in a market economy for what and how to produce goods. In a pure market economy, to whom the goods are to be distributed is completely ignored by the government. The goods are distributed to those possessing sufficient *rationing coupons* (in the form of dollar bills). If you have sufficient dollar bills, you can purchase whatever you demand in the marketplace: food, cars, health care, education, or homes. If you do not have these rationing coupons, the system will not recognize your needs since entrepreneurs respond only to demand (i.e., those willing and able to pay for the good in question). Thus, members of a pure market system with no government intervention would have to be willing to watch people starve to death in the streets, unless those starving could prevail on some private charity to provide minimum support.

Of course, the real world is much more complex than these simple definitions indicate; there are no examples of pure capitalism or pure command economic systems. While there are some examples that are closer to the definitions than others, it is not possible to draw a line between pure capitalism and pure command (or socialist) economies and place countries squarely on either side.

Mixed capitalism combines some features of both types of economic organization. It is a system in which most economic decisions are made by the private firms, but the government may also undertake certain economic activities. The government may also affect the behavior of the private sector through various regulations, taxes, and subsidies.

By comparison, the command form of economic organization proved significantly less efficient than economic systems that rely primarily on the market. Most noteworthy in this regard is the former Soviet Union, which became notorious for shoddy goods, shortages, and surpluses in the market; absenteeism among the labor force; and an overall lack of innovation in products and production techniques. Former Soviet president Mikhail Gorbachev finally proclaimed that he supported the dismantling of the command economy in favor of mixed capitalism. Today, most countries that undertook planned economies have abandoned this system in favor of mixed capitalism.

While command systems are very inefficient, pure market systems do not allocate resources in a way that most people are willing to tolerate. Hence, mixed capitalism in the United States, and increasingly in the rest of the world, is the basis for an increasing number of politico-economic organizations. John Maynard Keynes (see Chapter

5) was the theoretician of a partnership between government and private enterprise. In Keynesian economics, government is responsible for initiating policies that lead to full employment while ownership of the means of production, as well as profits, remain in private hands.

The perceived legitimate public policy role for government is much greater in those countries that are emerging from command economies, or other varieties of socialism, than in countries living under a mixed capitalism that evolved from more libertarian origins such as the United States. The US political and economic system begins with a bias in favor of a laissez-faire attitude, which has come to mean a minimal role for government in private lives and distributional policies. The history of the United States has forced a pragmatic reassessment of the role of government. For instance, 150 years ago, some highways, most schools, and all railroads were private; today, there are no major private highways, most schools are public, and interstate railroad passenger travel is overwhelmingly by Amtrak, a public enterprise.

Mixed economies are in a constant debate over the appropriate boundaries between government and private activities. There is now widespread agreement in the United States that private markets are essential to a successful economy, but government also has an essential role as a complement to the market. The precise nature of the role of government remains an ongoing source of contention that divides the two major political parties.

This is significant because, as we shall see, the existence of certain public policies that are taken for granted in many nations (such as a system of national health care) may be challenged by many in the United States as not being the legitimate domain of government.

Why Governments Intervene

If competitive markets usually provide the most efficient way to organize economic activity for society, why do governments sometimes intervene? Market forces do not always work as the theory would suggest. The two main reasons governments may intervene in market economies are due to **market failures**, or market problems that result in inefficient outcomes, and **redistribution**, or the shifting of resources from some groups to other groups in society.

Throughout this text, we will examine many market failures that impede the operation of market forces. The market mechanism works well as long as an exchange between a buyer and a seller does not affect a bystander, or third party. But all too often a third party is affected. Examples are everywhere. People who drive cars do not pay the full cost of pollution created by their vehicles. A farmer who sprays his crop with pesticides does not pay for the degradation of streams caused by the runoff. Factory owners may not pay the full cost of smokestack emissions that destroy the ozone layer. Such social costs are referred to as **externalities** because they are borne by individuals external to the transaction that caused them. In these cases, the government may improve the outcome through regulation.

Markets also fail in the face of excessive power through oligopolies or monopoly power. In such instances, the invisible hand of the market does not allocate resources efficiently because there is little or no price competition. For example, if everyone in a town needs water, but only one homeowner has a well with potable water, the owner of the well has a monopoly and is not subject to competition from any other source of drinking water. Government regulation in such cases may actually increase efficiency.

The economy may be represented as a pie. Market failures (inefficiencies) mean that there is potential for the government to step in and increase the size of the pie, or at least provide for what it deems is a more equitable distribution of the slices. For reasons we will discuss in Chapter 7, society may view the distribution of income or wealth to be unfair.

The market system certainly does not guarantee equality. To the contrary, the market ensures inequality. Many believe that the market is overly generous to those who are successful and too ruthless in penalizing those who fail in market competition. The society may decide that another dollar of consumption by a poor person would have higher utility than another dollar of consumption by a rich person. The government may intervene to redistribute some resources from those termed "very affluent" to groups that society has collectively decided are "too poor." The goal of many public policies is to provide a system that is closer to our ideas of social justice than capitalism provides.

Another area in which the market fails to perform adequately is in the provision of what are called **public goods**. Public goods have two characteristics. The first is referred to as **nonrival consumption**. Nonrival consumption means that another person's consumption does not affect your opportunity to also consume the good. If the government provides a national defense system that protects the nation from attack, then everyone living in the United States is protected. It is impossible to exclude someone living in the United States from protection even if they have not paid their fair share of taxes to provide the national defense network. The market mechanism works efficiently because the benefits of consuming a specific good or service are available to only those who purchase the product. A **private good** is a good or service whose benefits are confined to a single consumer and whose consumption excludes consumption by others. If a private good is shared, more for one must mean less for another. For example, the purchase of a hamburger by one individual effectively excludes others from consuming it. If the purchaser shares the hamburger with someone else, the portion shared cannot be consumed by the purchaser.

Certain other products in our society do not have the characteristic of private goods because they never enter the market system, so the market does not distribute them. These public goods are indivisible and nonexclusive—that is, their consumption by one individual does not interfere with their consumption by another. The air from a pollution-free environment can be inhaled by many people simultaneously, unlike a hamburger, which cannot be consumed simultaneously by many individuals. No one can be excluded from the use of a public good.

Another characteristic of public goods is that policy regarding them can be provided only by collective decisions. The purchase of private goods depends on an individual decision as to whether to spend one's income on hamburgers or swimming pools. But it is not possible for one person to decide to purchase national defense, dams, or weather services. The decision or agreement to buy a public good, and the quantity to buy, is made collectively. There are few examples of pure public goods, but clean air and national defense come as close to meeting the definition as any. **Impure public goods** satisfy the two public good conditions of nonrival and nonexcludability, though they do not meet the criteria as clearly. Examples include police protection and education. Police protection generally provides a safer environment for everyone living in an area, even if one does not contribute to the purchase of that protection. Cable television is an example of an excludable, but not a rival good. That is, the use of cable television by your neighbor does not diminish your ability to receive cable. However, it is possible to exclude a non-payer by not hooking them up to the system. Education is a similar good. The primary beneficiary of an education is the person educated. However, there are secondary benefits to society that result from a better-educated work force. Moreover, the amount of education allotted to one person does not affect the amount left for others. The same could be said for highway space or the administration of justice.

The communal nature of public goods leads to a major problem in public policy known as the **free rider**—someone who enjoys the benefits of someone else's purchase of a public good while bearing none of the costs of providing it. If two people both will benefit from national defense, good public education, or clean air, the question arises as to who should pay for it. Each individual has an incentive to avoid payment, hoping to take a free ride on other people's "purchase." As a result, all parties will profess little interest in purchasing the good, hoping others will step forward, demand the good, and pay for it. This is a rational response for individuals with limited resources. Everyone will benefit from the good by more than their proportionate cost, but they would benefit even more if others paid the entire cost. Thus, the good will not be purchased unless the government makes the purchase and requires everyone to pay his or her fair share through mandatory taxes.

How do we determine how many and what mix of public goods the government should purchase? By relying on a specific means of public decisionmaking: voting. Because voting is an imprecise mechanism that limits us to a yes or a no for candidates, it does not make any distinctions regarding the myriad of issues that must be acted on collectively. Nor does it register the intensity of preferences by various individuals or groups. Therefore, we sometimes find ourselves with an oversupply and other times with an undersupply of public goods.

Some conservatives tend to believe that certain public goods could be treated as private goods and brought into the market system, reducing the role of government. For example, tolls could be charged on all roads and bridges for their maintenance. This would limit the building and repair of highways to the amount of demand expressed by those paying the tolls. An admission fee to public parks might be charged to cover the services they provide—a fee that could simultaneously reduce congestion while funding maintenance and even development.[23] Public libraries could charge fees for their services to provide the budgets needed for salaries and the purchase of books and materials. Public transportation systems might charge fees necessary for them to operate profitably, or reduce their service and provide only the amount demanded by those paying the fares. According to conservatives, other areas of government operations could also be reduced through privatization. For example, the operation and maintenance of prisons may also be contracted out to private companies rather than being managed by public employees.

The privatization of public goods and services in this manner would certainly result in their being produced, more or less, as if they were private goods. However, there are many difficulties associated with this approach. First, there are the technical difficulties of making some public goods private. How do we make national defense a private good? Also, this approach offends our sense of justice and equity. Do we really think that national or state parks should exist to be enjoyed only by those with sufficient income to pay for their upkeep?

Imperfect Information

The market system is built on the assumption that individuals are rational and do not act capriciously, and that they have roughly accurate information about the market. Without adequate, correct information, people cannot make decisions in their rational self-interest. In fact, most people do not have adequate information to make rational decisions. Developing or finding the information has a significant opportunity cost associated with it. Very few people have the resources or time to do a complete research job.

Information, then, can be considered a public good, or a good with **positive externality**. When the information is provided, it can be shared by any number of people. Once in the public domain, it is impossible to exclude anyone from using it.

Manufacturers of consumer products, such as cigarettes, do not have an interest in advertising the health hazards associated with the use of their products. But ignorance about those hazards can be reduced by informing consumers, through mandatory labels on cigarette packages, that smoking is dangerous. The manufacturers may still advertise their cigarettes. But the mandatory labels attempt to mend omissions in the market system by introducing information so that individuals can make better choices.

Many people believe the government has a role in researching and disseminating various kinds of information relevant to consumer choices. For instance, the government might investigate and publicize information about the safety of different consumer products such as cars, drugs, food additives, microwave ovens, and other potentially dangerous products.

There is a debate regarding how this remedy for market failure should be applied. If one accepts the proposition that the individual is the best judge of his or her own welfare, then one may argue that governmental actions should be limited to the provision of information. The government, having produced the information, should not regulate the behavior of individuals, according to this view. Once people have been supplied with all the relevant information, they should be permitted to make their own choices—to consume dangerous substances (e.g., to purchase tobacco products) or to purchase potentially dangerous products. Only if the risks extend beyond the user—meaning that **negative externalities** exist involving third parties—may there be an argument for expanding the role of government beyond providing information. For example, those in favor of the right to a smoke-free work environment argue that the spillover effect of inhaling secondary smoke is hazardous to nonsmokers' health.

This view of the informational role of government is not followed consistently in practice. For example, the Pure Food and Drug Act prohibits the sale of certain harmful products, but does not provide the option of informing consumers of a product's harmful effects.

Equity and Security

Public goods, externalities, and ignorance all cause resource misallocation. They result in the market mechanism failing to produce the optimal mix of output. Beyond a failure of *what* to produce, we may also find that *for whom* the output is produced violates our sense of fairness.

These are situations, however, when markets fail to achieve the ideal economic efficiency. In a literal sense, in fact, markets always "fail" because economic efficiency is a fabricated definition based on a normative model of how the world *should* be. Market failure indicates that supply and demand forces have resulted in a mix of output that is different from the one society is willing to accept. It signifies that we are at a less than satisfactory point on the production possibilities curve. Some cases of market failure are so extreme, and the potential for corrective public policy action is sufficiently available, that most people would support some form of governmental intervention to achieve a better output mix. Because of these limitations, no country relies exclusively on the free market to make all of its socioeconomic policy decisions.

Not everyone agrees that turning the decisionmaking over to the public policy mechanism of government constitutes a good solution. Just as market failures can lead to outcomes that are inefficient or that society is not willing to tolerate, some government interventions may also result in *government failures*. Therefore, our examination of government intervention should consider the conditions under which government programs tend to not work well.

In general, the market mechanism answers the question of for whom to produce by distributing a larger share of output to those with the most rationing coupons (dollars). While this method is efficient, it may not accord with our view of what is socially acceptable. Individuals who are unemployed, disabled, aged, or very young may be unable to earn income and need to be protected from such risks inherent in life in a market economy. Government intervention may be sought for income redistribution through taxes and programs like unemployment compensation, Social Security, Medicare, and Temporary Assistance for Needy Families that shift those risks to taxpayers as a whole.

Redistribution of income to reduce inequities also falls under the theory of public goods because it adds to public security. Without some redistribution, we could expect more muggings and thefts to occur as people sought to escape the consequences of poverty. Moreover, leaving inequalities of wealth solely to market mechanisms would produce the phenomenon of the free rider again. Some individuals would no doubt contribute to charities aimed at reducing poverty, and everyone would benefit from somewhat safer streets. But those who did not so contribute would be taking a free ride on those who did. Society is therefore forced to confront tradeoffs between the inefficiencies of the market system and views of justice and equity. Every society has to deal with the question of what constitutes an equitable distribution of income. It is clear that no government policy is neutral on the question. Income distribution tends to reflect the biases of governments, ranging from traditional laissez-faire to planned economies. The political process by which any society governs itself must ultimately decide what constitutes an acceptable inequality of wealth and income.

Although government *can* improve on market outcomes, it is by no means certain that it always *will*. Public policy is the result of an imperfect political process. Unfortunately, policies are sometimes designed as a quid pro quo for campaign contributions. At other times, they merely reward society's elites or otherwise politically powerful individuals. Frequently, they are made by well-intentioned political leaders forced into so many compromises that the resulting policy bears little resemblance to the original proposal.

Public Policy Typology

One practical means of categorizing policies is based on the method of control used by policymakers. Control can be exerted through patronage, regulatory, and redistributive policies.[24]

Patronage policies (also known as promotional policies) include those government actions that provide incentives for individuals or corporations to undertake activities they would only reluctantly undertake without the promise of a reward. As distinct from policies that threaten punishment for noncompliance, this kind of policy motivates people to act by using "carrots." Not surprisingly, it is the recipients of the rewards who often convince the government to subsidize individuals or corporations to act. These promotional techniques can be classified into three types: subsidies, contracts, and licenses.

The use of **subsidies** has played a central role in the history of the United States. Alexander Hamilton wrote in his *Report on Manufactures,* one of the first policy planning documents in the administration of George Washington, that subsidies for US business should be provided by "pecuniary bounties" supplied by the government. Subsidies to business quickly became commonplace in the United States, ranging from land grants given to railroad companies, to cash subsidies for the merchant marine fleet, for shipbuilders, and for the airline industry.

Other subsidies to businesses have included loans to specific companies like the Chrysler Corporation or the more recent financial institution "bailout." Subsidies have also been provided to individuals through such policies as land grants to farmers in the nineteenth century, or through the current tax deductions allowed for interest on home mortgage payments.

Subsidies are typically made possible through the largesse of the US taxpayer. Since the cost is spread out among all the population, each person bears only a minuscule portion of the whole cost. There is little opposition to these kinds of subsidies, yet the threat of their removal can arouse intense reactions from their recipients, for whom their loss could entail significant financial hardship. Because subsidies are often attacked as "pork-barrel" programs, every effort is made to tie such projects to some "high national purpose" (such as military defense).

Contracts are also an important means of promoting particular policies. Contracts can be used to encourage corporations to adopt certain behaviors, such as equal employment opportunity, which they might otherwise find burdensome.

Through **licenses**, governments can grant the privilege of carrying on a particular activity. Licensing allows corporations or individuals to conduct a business or engage in a profession (e.g., a licensed pilot) that, without the license, is illegal. Licensing allows the government to regulate various sectors of the population and, indirectly, the economy.

Regulatory policies allow the government to exert control over the conduct of certain activities. If patronage policies involve positive motivation (the use of "carrots"), then regulatory policies involve negative forms of control (the use of "sticks"). The most obvious examples of regulation techniques include civil and criminal penalties for certain behaviors. The immediate example that comes to mind is regulating criminal behavior. Other forms of conduct are regulated, not to eliminate the conduct, but to deal with the negative side effects. For example, a public utility may provide a community with the "desired good" of electricity, but it can also seek monopoly profits. The conduct of the utility is "regulated" rather than "policed" in a criminal sense, in that the company is given an exclusive license to provide electrical energy to a given geographical area, but in return the government holds the right to regulate the quality of service and the rates charged.

Other forms of regulatory policies that generate more controversy include environmental pollution, consumer protection, or employee health and safety concerns. Tax policy often may have as its primary purpose not raising revenue, but regulating a certain type of behavior by making that behavior too expensive for most individuals or companies to engage in. By taxing a substance like gasoline, tobacco, or alcohol, the government encourages a reduction in the consumption of these products. Likewise, "effluent taxes" may raise the price of goods and services that pollute, which encourages companies to reduce their pollution to reduce or avoid the tax.[25]

Some environmentalists are critical of the use of market mechanisms to control pollution, even though they may reduce pollution efficiently. They feel that pollution is morally wrong and a stigma should be attached to the deed. If market mechanisms alone are used to reduce pollution, it is increasingly perceived as morally indifferent, a good to be bought or sold in the market like any other good. Environmental policy is thereby transformed from an expression of the current generation's trusteeship responsibility over the environment for future generations to an area where economic self-interest is the guiding standard. Regulatory decisions frequently reallocate costs for those affected. Unlike promotional policies that provide only benefits, regulatory policies are usually thought of in terms of winners and losers. The losses they cause are as obvious as their benefits.

Redistributive policies control people by managing the economy as a whole. The techniques of control involve fiscal (tax) and monetary (supply of money) policies. They tend to benefit one group at the expense of other groups through the reallocation of wealth. Changing the income tax laws from 2001 to 2003, for example, significantly reduced the taxes of upper-income groups compared to other income groups in society, although some of those at the very bottom were taken off the tax roles altogether. The result was a decline in the middle class.[26] Since those who have power and wealth are usually reluctant to share those privileges, redistribution policies tend to be the most contentious. Many past policies aimed at redistributing wealth more equitably, even when initially successful, faced severe obstacles in their long-term viability. The most obvious examples are those of the Great Society and War on Poverty programs of the 1960s. Programs with widely distributed benefits, such as Social Security, have enjoyed more success because of the larger number of people with a stake in their continuation.

Fiscal techniques use tax rates and government spending to affect total or aggregate demand. Each particular approach to taxing or spending can have a different impact on the overall economy, so political entrepreneurs often propose or initiate policies with the goal of achieving specific impacts. For example, in the late 1980s, President G. H. W. Bush, faced with a sluggish economy in an election year, proposed a policy of stimulating the economy by cutting taxes to increase demand (and, thereby, employment). He also proposed cutting taxes on capital gains, a policy that would have benefited primarily higher-income people, with the claim that it would encourage real investment.[27]

Monetary techniques, used by the Federal Reserve Board (the Fed), also try to regulate the economy by changing the rate of growth of the money supply or manipulating interest rates (for more on this, see Chapter 6).[28]

Conclusion

The crux of all our public policy problems is to be found in the hard reality of limited (scarce) resources. The free market has proven a superb device for efficiently producing goods and services, based on individual rational self-interest. Problems of scarcity, which are universal, require intervention. This suggests that solutions, whether left to market forces or government intervention, reflect values. There are a variety of possible solutions reflecting the biases and choices of the individuals proposing them.

People face tradeoffs when they make choices. The cost of any action, whether individual or collective, is measured in terms of what must be given up. People as well as societies tend to make decisions by comparing their marginal costs against their marginal benefits. People and societies will adjust their behavior whenever incentives change.

It is important to keep in mind that, although markets are a good way to organize many of society's activities, there are several areas where markets fail or produce outcomes unacceptable to society's collective values. In those cases, government can improve on market outcomes. Government efforts to relieve market imperfections (failures) by public policy may also be flawed, however. The question is whether government, which was created to "promote the general welfare," will provide solutions that will be less imperfect than market mechanisms.

Government may be the only actor that can improve market efficiency or alter economic and social costs, risks, and income distribution in a positive way. Some argue that these problems can be solved, but that most solutions mean someone must accept significant economic losses. No one willingly accepts a loss. So people struggle to veto any solution that would impact negatively on them, or at minimum have the cost transferred to someone else or another group. The effect is to produce "veto groups" waiting to aggressively fight any proposed public policy that would result in a loss to their position. Often, the political struggle that results causes a larger cost than gain for those attempting to effect the change. The result is often political and economic paralysis.

However, not all public policy solutions must be **zero-sum solutions**, where one group's net gains must be offset by another group's losses. There are non-zero-sum solutions, which usually involve increasing economic growth so there is more for everyone. But even this solution requires the intervention of government in the form of industrial policies, and many people see this as just another effort to have government provide a remedy no more promising than any the market itself can provide. The major economic competitors of the United States, including both Japan and Germany, have incorporated industrial policy as a key component of their public policies, but it is a controversial issue in the United States.

Questions for Discussion

1. If society desires health care and a clean environment for everyone, why does the free market not provide it?

2. Explain how scarcity, choice, and opportunity cost are related and make public policy inevitable.

3. What are the differing views concerning the appropriate role of government in intervening in the economy?

4. Should you consciously think about your values and goals when analyzing important tradeoffs and choices that you face? Why?

5. What are the major sources of disagreement among policy analysts concerning appropriate policies to pursue?

Notes

1. "McCain's Health Care Proposal," *Washington Post,* October 10, 2007.
2. Ibid.
3. Shan Carter, Jonathan Ellis, Farhana Hossain, and Alan McLean, "Election 2008: On the Issues: Health Care," *New York Times,* October 2, 2008, available at http://elections.nytimes .com/2008/president/issues/health.html (accessed October 2, 2008).
4. "John McCain on Free Trade," On the Issues, available at www.ontheissues.org/2008/ John_McCain_Free_Trade.htm (accessed October 3, 2008).
5. "Barack Obama on Free Trade," On the Issues, available at www.ontheissues.org/2008/ Barack_Obama_Free_Trade.htm (accessed October 3, 2008).
6. "John McCain on Abortion," On the Issues, available at www.ontheissues.org/2008/ John_McCain_Abortion.htm (accessed October 3, 2008).
7. "Barack Obama on Abortion," On the Issues, available at www.ontheissues.org/2008/ Barack_Obama_Abortion.htm (accessed October 3, 2008).
8. John McCain, "Better Care at Lower Cost for Every American," *Contingencies,* September–October 2007, p. 30.

9. Robert A. Heineman et al., *The World of the Policy Analyst: Rationality, Values, and Politics* (Chatham, NJ: Chatham House, 1990), p. 17.

10. Hans J. Morgenthau, "The Purpose of Political Science," in James C. Charlesworth, ed., *A Design for Political Science: Scope, Objectives, and Methods,* Monograph no. 6 (Philadelphia: American Academy of Political and Social Science, 1966), pp. 67–68.

11. David Easton, "The New Revolution in Political Science," *American Political Science Review* 63 (December 1969): 1051–1061.

12. The statement is accurate when referring to the market in the long run. However, it is not necessarily true in the polity in the short run. There are many public policies in which taxes paid by some people are redistributed to provide benefits for others. For example, middle-income taxpayers may provide funds for food stamps for the poor. Those providing the largesse for others usually want spending reductions while the recipients of the benefits favor more resources.

13. James Madison, *The Federalist* no. 10.

14. John Rawls, *A Theory of Justice* (Cambridge: Harvard University Press, 1971).

15. Robert Nozick, *Anarchy, State, and Utopia* (New York: Basic Books, 1974). Nozick's work is primarily a response to John Rawls. The extension of Nozick's thought leads to a view that the only form of economic life compatible with individualism is laissez-faire capitalism. Nozick's position is in the tradition of writers in the anarcho-capitalist tradition. His response to Rawls has attracted more comment than the writings of others with similar views.

16. See Alasdair MacIntyre, *After Virtue: A Study in Moral Theory,* 2nd ed. (Notre Dame, IN: University of Notre Dame Press, 1984), esp. chap. 17, "Justice as a Virtue: Changing Conceptions," for an excellent comparison of the theory of John Rawls and Nozick's countering view.

17. Nozick's critics point out that his thesis assumes that legitimate entitlements can be traced back to rightful acts of earliest acquisition. Based on that criterion, however, there are few legitimate entitlements, as most property has been inherited from those who originally used force or theft to steal the common lands of the first inhabitants.

18. Harold Lasswell, *Politics: Who Gets What, When, How* (Cleveland: Meridian Books, 1958).

19. Robert A. Dahl, *Who Governs? Democracy and Power in an American City* (New Haven, CT: Yale University Press, 1961), p. 1.

20. Thomas R. Dye, Harmon Zeigler, and S. Robert Lichter, *American Politics in the Media Age,* 4th ed. (Pacific Grove, CA: Brooks/Cole, 1992), p. 2.

21. Roger A. Arnold, *Macroeconomics* (St. Paul, MN: West, 1996), p. 6.

22. See Larry N. Gerston, *Making Public Policy: From Conflict to Resolution* (Glenville, IL: Scott, Foresman, 1979), pp. 4–6. See also Jay M. Shafritz, *Dictionary of American Government and Politics* (Chicago: Dorsey Press, 1988), p. 456.

23. See, for example, Dan Bechter, "Congested Parks: A Pricing Dilemma," *Monthly Review* (Federal Reserve Bank of Kansas City), June 1971. Overcrowding at public parks may reflect a distortion in the recreation market by charging too little for their use. It is argued that such low pricing amounts to a misallocation of resources. Raising the price would help "clear" the market and relieve congestion. If the price of visiting national parks were increased, more people would substitute other leisure activities.

24. See Theodore Lowi, "American Business, Public Policy, Case Studies, and Political Theory," *World Politics* 16 (July 1964): 677–715. See also Theodore Lowi, *The End of Liberalism: The Second Republic of the United States* (New York: W. W. Norton, 1979).

25. Taxation for the purpose of discouraging certain conduct or eliminating certain activities is often opposed on the grounds that the affluent can buy the right to behave in a manner that

is prohibitive to the less wealthy. The charge is correct in that the affluent may be less deterred by the higher price of gasoline, alcohol, tobacco, or other products that cause pollution than will the poor, who may be eliminated from the market by the repressive features of the tax. However, exercising the right to buy the products will make the wealthy poorer. Also, by discouraging the purchase of certain products, public health should improve and the environment should become cleaner. The repressive nature of the tax may also be beside the point if the extra amount that the affluent pay exceeds the value we place on the harm caused by alcohol or tobacco consumption, or if a cleaner environment caused by less consumption of gas or other products that cause pollution results in the transference of real income to the population as a whole.

26. See Richard Morin, "America's Middle-Class Meltdown," *Washington Post,* December 1, 1991, p. C1. Reporting on several studies, Morin stated that "the boom years of the 1980s were a bust for fully half of all Americans. At the same time, the safety net of social programs for the nation's poor was replaced by a safety net for the rich, speeding the decline of the middle class."

27. A **capital gain** is the realized increase in the value of an asset. **Real investment** refers to the accumulation of real capital, such as machinery or buildings, rather than financial investment (which refers to the acquisition of such paper instruments as bonds).

28. The Federal Reserve System's control over the money supply is the key aspect of US monetary policy. The Fed has three primary levers of power. The first concerns the reserve requirement. The Fed requires private banks to keep some fraction of their deposits in reserve. The reserves are held in the form of cash or as credits at its regional Federal Reserve Bank. By changing the reserve requirement, the Fed can directly affect the ability of the banking system to lend money. The second lever concerns the Fed's discount rate; the Fed changes the cost of money for banks and the incentive and ability to borrow. The third and most important lever involves the Fed's open market operations, which directly alter the reserves of the banking system. When the Fed buys bonds, it increases the deposits (reserves) available in the banking system. If the Fed sells bonds, it reduces the reserves and restricts the amount of money available for lending.

2

Methods and Models
for Policy Analysis

Although public policy has been recognized as a subfield of political science for only a few decades, the study of ways to "promote the general welfare" goes back centuries. Policy is made in the present, based on the past, with the purpose of improving the well-being of society's future. It utilizes both normative and scientific methodologies to achieve this. Public policy is action oriented. The purpose of studying public problems is to provide insight into a range of policy options in order to take some control over the future.

An Overview of Political Science Assumptions and Models

Every academic discipline has its own language and its own specialized way of thinking based on its specific subject matter and goals. Physicists analyze matter and energy and their interactions. Economists talk about inflation, unemployment, comparative advantage, and income distribution. Chemists examine the composition and the chemical properties and processes of substances. Psychologists talk about personality development, cognitive dissonance, and perception. Sociologists focus on the collective behavior and interaction of organized groups of human beings in social institutions and social relationships.

Political science is no different. Political scientists focus on people with conflicting interests competing for governmental power. As noted in Chapter 1, political science is about who gets what, when, and how. In other words, it focuses on what decisions are made by those in authority and why those decisions are made. Political scientists are concerned with the exercise of **political power**.

Aristotle put forward a biological explanation for political power when he said: "It is evident that the state is a creation of nature, and that man is by nature a political animal."[1] To Aristotelian thinkers, the state and political power are as natural and innate as the instinctual behaviors among herd animals. Refusal to accept prevailing authority, or even any governmental authority, has always been prevalent.

A number of political scientists have developed sociological explanations for the transmission of cultural values that hold a political society together, through child rearing, religious education, and socioeconomic class. These scholars see people in plastic terms. People are pliable and are molded by their social environment. Political power and even legitimacy are threatened when those in authority lose touch with the cultural values the masses have been taught to accept. Politicians frequently compete for power by claiming that their political opponents could destroy the cultural values on which society is built. For example, former president Bill Clinton maintained that Republicans had been working to embed negative stereotypes of Democrats in the nation's consciousness since the administration of Richard Nixon in 1968. In the 1994 elections, House Speaker Newt Gingrich tried to confirm the negative stereotypes of Democrats. Clinton wrote in his autobiography: "The core of his [Gingrich's] argument was not just that his ideas were better than ours; he said that his *values* were better than ours, because Democrats were weak on family, work, welfare, crime, and defense, and because being crippled by the self-indulgent sixties, we couldn't draw distinctions between right and wrong."[2]

Karl Marx and other political economists argued that the economic foundations of society determine the culture and what the law recognizes as legitimate. Some countries with similar cultures have developed very different political systems, undermining the Marxist claims about cultural development. Sigmund Freud suggested that culture is transmitted by the interactions between parents and children. Psychologist B. F. Skinner held that through "operant conditioning"—providing positive rewards for individuals engaging in behavior deemed "good," and negative rewards for behavior deemed undesirable—society improves. Finally, some Darwinian biologists see all human behavior as being driven by genes.

Political philosophers such as John Locke argued that human beings are rational. Individuals use their mental faculties to rise above mere conditioned behaviors or emotional attachment to past practices. Locke certainly agreed that the human mind is shaped as an individual grows and matures. Experiences which act on our senses develop the human capacity for reasoning. Subsequent behavior flows from these rational ideas. Locke was aware that most rulers, if not checked, would favor their own self-interests over the general welfare. Since everyone is equal, self-interested, and mostly rational, a social contract may be agreed on to limit power and ensure the general welfare. A government is formed to protect individuals and their property. Power resides with the citizenry who can dissolve the contract if the government abuses its authority.

It was only a small step from the political theory of the rational human being acting to promote the general welfare, to the theory of the modern economic human being who, while still rational, acts to promote his or her self-interest. This economic theory is now frequently applied to political, sociological, and psychological models of human nature as well.

Policy analysts recognize the complexity of human nature and avoid any attempt to analyze it using just one or two of these theories. For example, it is a mistake to reduce human beings, as some economists do, to actors who pursue material self-interest or, as some sociologists might, to actors completely defined by culture. A single theory of the individual, whether based in biology, sociology, economics, or psychology, results in a misleading oversimplification of human nature, although each theory may have an element of truth.

The purpose of this book is to introduce you to the political scientist's way of thinking. In particular, this book is about the political scientist as a **policy analyst**, someone who conducts investigations that produce accurate and useful information for decisionmakers. Learning to approach political problems as an analyst is a developmental process and does not occur quickly. This book will provide a combination of social science theory, case studies, and examples of notable public policy issues to help you to develop these skills. To begin, it is important to understand why the field of public policy is interdisciplinary, and why policy analysts must be eclectic in their methodology.

In the Middle Ages, all study was under the rubric of *philosophy,* which means "to seek wisdom." As shown in Figure 2.1, philosophy was divided into two parts: moral and natural. **Moral philosophy** focused on human existence and has evolved into the

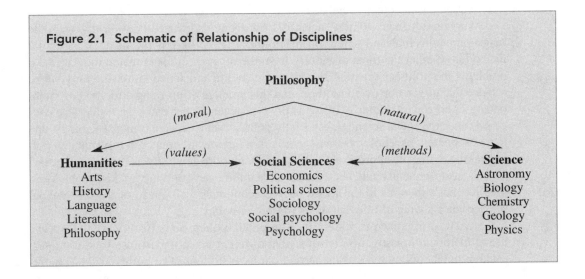

Figure 2.1 Schematic of Relationship of Disciplines

field that we today call the **humanities**. The subject matter of the humanities is our social world or, in other words, the human condition and human values. Because the social world is a projection of human nature, individuals can no more completely understand or control it than they can completely understand and control themselves. Indeed, it is the very intimacy of human involvement with the social world that inhibits both comprehension of and authority over it.[3]

Natural philosophy has evolved into the field that we today call the **natural sciences**. Since it is focused on aspects of the outside world that can be observed, weighed, and measured, it is viewed as being **value free**. It is a paradox that the natural world, which humans did not create, is much more susceptible to human understanding than is the social world, which is created by humans themselves. Through the discovery of the laws by which the universe is ordered, people can look back into the past and project into the future. Through this understanding, they can control and even harness the forces of nature as they wish.

More recently, a new set of disciplines existing between the humanities and the natural sciences, the **social sciences**, have matured and made significant contributions to our understanding of society through the systematic study of various aspects of the human condition. The social sciences have a split personality. They not only exist between the humanities and the natural sciences, but also borrow freely from both. The social sciences developed from the historical cultural values and conditions of the social community. At the same time, they adopted the methods of the natural sciences. Many believe that political science, of which the study of public policy is a subfield, exists at the confluence of the social sciences. It is not an independent discipline within the social sciences. In this view, a political scientist focuses on the political ramifications of the other social sciences.

As a consequence, political scientists use methods of investigation that span the range of intellectual and scientific disciplines. The criterion for using a particular method is whether the tools of inquiry from the other disciplines match the particular problems the political scientist is addressing. Political science is not the only social science that uses a borrowed toolbox, and this practice of utilizing a toolbox of methodologies borrowed primarily from the physical sciences has caused considerable concern.[4] Since the social sciences, especially political science, economics, sociology, and to a lesser extent psychology, are generally moving toward greater involvement in policymaking, it may be appropriate to think of them more generally as "policy sciences." This is most frequently said about economics. In the view of policymakers, John Maynard Keynes's theories in the 1930s moved economics well ahead of the other social sciences as a source of relevant ideas for public policy.

Statistical inference is widely used in public policy, as is historical inquiry. The use of historical investigation is somewhat different when undertaken by those interested in public policy than when carried out by historians. The policy analyst studies history to establish precedent, determine errors, or evaluate management.

The political scientist in the role of policy analyst must be increasingly prepared to work with specialists in the natural as well as the social sciences. There are increasing concerns in all levels of government for science policy. Issues regarding such questions as the environment, including the ozone layer, pollution, global warming, nuclear energy, and population issues, to name just a few, require the policy analyst to not only be cognizant of, but also take part in, scientific studies. Policy analysts today must have more than an appreciation of prevailing interpretations of scientific theory relevant to policy issues.

The political scientist's perspective, scholarly interests, and manner of thought are heavily influenced by the society of which he or she is a member. Every society has biases. However, the political scientist's obligation is to seek the truth, which will necessarily result in he or she being the messenger of things that society will not want to hear.

An existing political system is usually defended with the concession that it has problems, but that these problems can best be dealt with in terms of the existing system. Consequently, a society that styles itself as Marxist, like the People's Republic of China, cannot allow an investigation into the assumptions on which communist theory is based. Conversely, societies whose economies are basically capitalist in nature are biased against inquiries regarding the goal of equal distribution of property. A society based on a caste system, or some other type of ethnic or racial discrimination, cannot accept such issues as proper subjects for scientific inquiry. Likewise, in republican forms of government, it is taken for granted that the voting mechanism of the nation reflects fairly the "will of the people."

Since every society fosters support for the premises on which the community is based, a commitment to truth in studying a society leads to questions and controversy regarding its values and institutions. Thus, the influence of political scientists and economists on policymakers goes beyond their role as policy analysts. As Keynes wrote:

> The ideas of *economists and political philosophers,* both when they are right and when they are wrong, are more powerful than is commonly understood. Indeed the world is ruled by little else. Practical men, who believe themselves to be quite exempt from intellectual influences, are usually slaves of some defunct economist. Madmen in authority who hear voices in the air, are distilling their frenzy from some academic scribbler of a few years back.[5]

The Policy Analyst as Scientist

The **scientific method** was developed in the natural sciences as a way to help understand phenomena by using systematic inquiry to explain and predict. The same is true in the social sciences, of which political science and policy studies are a part. To those outside the social sciences, it may seem unnatural and even a bit pretentious to claim that political science is a science. After all, political scientists do not utilize the equipment and other trappings of science. The essential element of science, however, is found in the method of investigation. It requires the impartial construction and testing of hypotheses regarding the social world. The method of developing theories and testing them with regard to the effect of gravity on embryo development is just as applicable to studying the impact of a proposed tax subsidy to create additional housing.

Why Theory Development Requires Simplification

While policy scientists use theories and observation like natural scientists do, they face a complication that makes their effort especially difficult: experiments are sometimes impossible in the policy sciences. Biochemists testing a theory about the effect of pollutants on fish embryos can obtain many fish eggs to generate the data they need. In contrast to natural scientists, policy analysts usually do not have the luxury of being able to freely conduct experiments. At best, many social science experiments are difficult to carry out. People do not willingly let themselves become the laboratory subjects for someone else's experiment. For example, if policy scientists wanted to study the relation of imports to total employment, they would not be allowed to control imports to generate data. The risks and cost to society would be deemed too great. In this sense, policy scientists are not unlike astronomers in that although the latter can observe distant galaxies to generate data for analysis, their ability to conduct controlled experiments is very limited.

The difficulty in conducting controlled experiments in political science and public policy means that these social scientists will pay close attention to the events of history as a type of informal, spontaneous experiment. For example, turbulence in several Asian economies once vaunted as models of economic development causes concern in financial markets throughout the world. In affected Asian countries, it depresses living standards. For policy analysts, it poses difficult problems of how to respond to contain the problem and reverse the economic decline. But it also provides policy scientists with an opportunity to study the relationships between banking, barriers and subsidies to international trade, currency speculation, and domestic savings and consumption. The lessons learned from such as episode continue long after the particular crisis has passed. Such events provide important case studies that improve our theoretical understanding of critical variables and suggest ways to monitor and evaluate current economic policies.

Public Policy and Theory

The first step in the scientific method is to recognize, or identify, the problem to be addressed. Isaac Newton, a seventeenth-century mathematician, observed an apple fall from a tree. Newton's thinking over the problem of explaining "why" the apple fell led him to develop a theory of gravity that applies not only to apples, but also to other objects in the universe. Policy analysts must likewise identify the problem to be addressed such as how to improve the labor skills of the average worker.

Scientists must make **assumptions** to cut away any unnecessary detail. Assumptions are made to help us get to the heart of the problem by reducing its complexity. Assumptions help make a problem easier to understand. In Chapter 1, for example, we looked at a production possibilities frontier that assumed there were only two types of goods in an economy when in fact there might be dozens or even thousands. By assuming that there are only two types of goods, military and social, for example, we can concentrate on the relationship between them. Once the relationship is understood, we are in a better position to understand the greater complexity of a world with other goods.

A critical skill for anyone engaged in scientific inquiry is the ability to decide which assumptions to make. For example, suppose that we want to study what happens to the quality of health care provided to the indigent if Medicaid funding were increased. A key factor in the analysis would be how prices respond to increased funding. Since many Medicaid fee schedules are set by the government, we might assume that prices would not change in the short run. But in the longer run, we would expect physicians and other health care providers to demand higher prices or payments for their services covered under Medicaid. Thus, in the longer run, we would have to assume price increases. A physicist may assume away the effect of friction when dropping a feather and a baseball in a vacuum, but different assumptions would be necessary in calculating the effect of friction in the atmosphere when dropping a feather and a baseball over the side of a building; so too policy scientists must modify their assumptions when conditions change. Models and theories are similar to assumptions in that they also simplify reality by omitting many details. By refining our concentration, we can better understand reality.

If we wished to provide policymakers with a complete description of "income distribution," we could go out and collect all the data we could find, present it to decisionmakers, and "let the facts speak for themselves." But a complete description, gathering data from millions of households; thousands of separate federal, state, and local governments; and thousands of firms is unworkable and would be ineffective as a guide to public policy.

Theories help make sense of the millions of facts. Theories help explain how the political and economic aspects of society work by identifying how basic underlying causal relationships fit together. A **theory** in a scientific sense is a set of logically related, empirically testable hypotheses. Theories are a deliberate simplification of related generalizations used to describe and explain how certain facts are related. Their usefulness derives from this ability to simplify otherwise complex phenomena. Thus a theory is not a mirror image of reality.[6] A theory will usually contain at least one **hypothesis** about how a specific set of facts is related. The theory should explain the phenomena in an abstract manner. The inclination to abstract from nonessential details of the world around us is necessary because of the awesome complexity of reality. **Abstraction** is the process of disregarding needless details in order to focus on a limited number of factors to explain a phenomenon. As an abstraction, a theory is useful not because it is true or false, but because it helps analysts understand the interactions between variables and predict how change in one or more variables will affect other dependent variables.

Theories attempt to do the same thing—bring order and meaning to data that, without the theory, would remain unrelated and unintelligible. For example, a policy analyst might wish to explain why some people have very high incomes while others barely survive economically. To do so, the analyst must try to separate or abstract the meaningful data from the insignificant data. Thus, variables such as gender, age, education, and occupation may be considered meaningful. Other variables, such as parents' educational level or income, may be considered interesting, but less significant. Still others, such as eye color, height, or weight, may be considered unimportant and not be included among the explanatory variables. The theory developed by the analyst is built on all these assumptions and makes up a simplified, logical account of income inequality and its causes.

A theory must be consistent with the facts that it draws together. And the facts, in turn, must lend themselves to the interpretation that the theory puts upon them. Finally, the conclusions derived from the theory must flow logically from the theory's premises or assumptions.

The policy analyst, therefore, must determine which variables to include and which to ignore when conducting social analysis. Although events and forces in a socioeconomic setting reflect all the intrinsic ambiguity of human nature in motion, policy analysts assume that, under comparable circumstances, events and forces will appear in a similar manner. As Michel de Montaigne said:

> As no event and no shape is entirely like another, so also is there none entirely different from another. . . . *If there were no similarity in our faces, we could not distinguish man from beast; if there were no dissimilarity, we could not distinguish one man from another.* All things hold together by some similarity; every example is halting, and the comparison that is derived from experience is always defective and imperfect.[7]

From theories—interpretations of variables—we are able to formulate hypotheses: tentative statements that have not yet been tested. Because hypotheses, like theories, are abstractions, it is necessary to test them. The hypothesis must be stated as an affirmative proposition (i.e., not as a question) that is capable of being tested against empirical evidence. Accordingly, a hypothesis is most useful when it relates two or more variables in terms of a comparison. For example, we might develop a hypothesis such as: "Cost-control incentives in health care proposed by the private sector are more effective than those imposed by government agencies." The analyst will include only those variables in the hypothesis that are critical in explaining the particular event.

Hypotheses contain variables that can take on different values. A **value** is a measurable characteristic of a variable (such as "strong," "neutral," or "weak"). We might hypothesize: "Strong (value) support for a president will vary positively with low (value) inflation and low (value) unemployment." In this hypothesis, "support for a president" is the dependent variable. "Inflation" and "unemployment" are independent variables. The variables or values selected depend on the questions being asked or the problems to be resolved. Variables are the most basic elements in theories. A **variable** is a term in a hypothesis that can assume different values. In the hypothesis above, we could have substituted the variables "support for a member of the Senate" or "support for a member of Congress" for "support for a president." All this is part of the scientific method as applied to the social sciences, as shown in Figure 2.2.

The Scientific Method in the Social Sciences

The scientific method as applied to the social sciences progresses along the pathway of theory and observation suggested in Figure 2.2. The variables are defined, assumptions noted, and hypotheses framed. Various implications and predictions are deduced and stated from the hypotheses. These three steps make up building a theory. In the

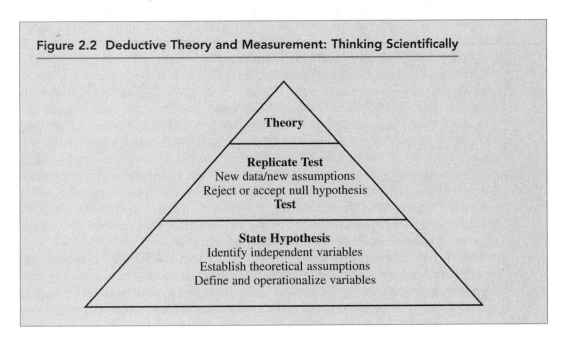

Figure 2.2 Deductive Theory and Measurement: Thinking Scientifically

Theory

Replicate Test
New data/new assumptions
Reject or accept null hypothesis
Test

State Hypothesis
Identify independent variables
Establish theoretical assumptions
Define and operationalize variables

fourth step, the theory is tested. The data either fail to reject or reject the theory. If the data fail to reject the theory, this still does not prove it true. It merely fails to disprove it. This can increase one's confidence in the theory, but a theory must continue to be evaluated by seeking additional tests. If, on the other hand, the evidence rejects the theory, there are two possibilities. Either the theory can be amended based on the evidence obtained from the test, or it can be abandoned altogether, in which case those who formulated the theory must return to the first step and start developing a new one. Usually, political scientists prefer simple theories to complicated ones. The preference for the simplest of competing theories over more complicated theories when both are consistent with the data is known as **Ockham's razor**, named after fourteenth-century philosopher William of Ockham who urged its use to "shave away" superfluous theoretical complexities.

Policy Theory

One of the most humbling aspects of the study of public policy is how complex it actually is. Dividing the policymaking process into stages of agenda setting, selection of an alternative, adoption, implementation, and evaluation simplifies it into workable segments for inquiry. Most researchers feel forced to concentrate their efforts on just one stage of the process, to reduce their studies to manageable size. In the past two decades, process studies have contributed to understanding of what goes on in policymaking, but by themselves do not show the causal relationships between the policymaking stages. There has been a considerable effort by those in the rational public choice school to develop a theory of policymaking within that tradition.[8]

Policy theory has developed a disreputable public image—partly because of its inability to predict future outcomes with the same precision as do the natural sciences, partly because of some theorizing that is irrelevant or trivial, and partly because many politicians have found it expedient to ridicule theory in policy analysis. We must distinguish between policy theory and actual public policy. **Policy theory** can develop rules and principles of policy that can serve as a guide for action in a given set of circumstances.[9] Public policy refers to the actual action taken. In an ideal world, public policy would always be consistent with the policy theory put forward. Policy problems and issues, by definition, have political ramifications. The result is that policy theory is modified by political realities. For instance, theory might indicate that we should raise taxes to reduce inflation but, during an election year. the theory may yield to political realities resulting in reduced taxes to win votes.

But it is exactly the importance of public policy that makes policy theory so critical. If there were no possibility of changing the general social welfare through public policy, political science and economics might both be disciplines asking merely historical questions. How did the US government react to the stagnant economy during the Great Depression of the 1930s? How have health or education policies changed since the mid-1970s?

Human Behavior and Predictability

The policy sciences deal with the behavior of people, which is not so neatly categorized as other phenomena. How does one find order given so many variables that cannot be isolated? A variation of this view holds that human beings are the least controllable or least predictable of subjects for scientific inquiry.[10] However, even if one accepts the argument of the great complexity of the social sciences, one cannot conclude that the discovery of relationships is impossible, only that there are more variables, which makes it more difficult to discover the critical ones.

Another argument runs that, while the natural sciences deal with inanimate matter subject to natural laws, the social sciences focus on humans with free will and passions not subject to such laws. Consequently, generalizations formulated in the social sciences lack predictive power. It is true that free will and passions like love, hate, pride, envy, ambition, and altruism are more unpredictable in their effects on human behavior than natural causes are on the behavior of atoms. All of these influences, which are extremely difficult to understand, interact within individual humans and affect their behavior. Nevertheless, having free will and passions does not mean that individuals do not act rationally on the basis of their values, disposition, character, and external restraints, and that these actions cannot be understood.[11]

For the natural sciences, if hydrogen and oxygen are mixed under specific conditions, then water will always result. However, for the social sciences, if the government decides for budgetary reasons to reduce welfare payments (and incidentally support the self-help work ethic), then some individuals will adopt the desired behavior pattern, but others will not. Some people, faced with reduced benefits, will work hard to find a job and become self-sufficient. Others, seeing few options, may adopt a life of crime as their avenue of escape. And the same individuals may react differently at different points in time.

The social sciences have developed ways to predict group behavior even though they cannot predict individual behavior. For example, social scientists cannot predict which particular individuals will be killed by handguns or automobile accidents on a given weekend, but they can predict with surprising accuracy the total number who will be killed. Pollsters are likewise able, through sampling techniques, to learn the major concerns of voters. Political candidates can use this knowledge to place themselves in a favorable position to gain the support of potential voters. This predictive ability is of course crucial for policymakers who wish to know how people will react to a change in, for example, the capital gains tax. One's reaction to a capital gains tax cut will depend on several factors such as income level, expectations regarding how one's own position will be helped or hurt by the proposed tax change, and awareness of the law and its effect. Some individuals will react in surprising ways, but the overall response will be predictable within a small margin of error.

Public policy analysis bases its predictive efforts on the assumption that individuals act so consistently in their rational self-interest that they can be said to obey "laws" of behavior. Several such generalizations provide a logical matrix for understanding human behavior similar to the laws used to account for events in the material world. But social scientific generalizations have their limitations. Human beings bent on maximizing their self-interest may behave in a number of different ways, depending on their understanding of their situation.

Nevertheless, the unpredicted or random movements—the errors—of individuals tend to offset each other. Knowledge of this fact makes possible the **statistical law of large numbers**, which states that the average error (irregularity) of all individuals combined will approach zero. Since the irregularities of individual behavior will tend to cancel each other out, the regularities will tend to show up in replicated observations.

The Policy Analyst as Policymaker

Policy experts are often asked to explain the causes of certain events. Why, for example, has violent crime declined in almost every US city in the past few years? At other times, policy analysts are asked to recommend policies to reduce crime. When social scientists are explaining why violent crime has declined, they are acting in their role as scientists. When they are proposing policies to reduce criminal activity, they are acting in their role as policymakers.

As noted in Chapter 1, it is important to understand the difference between positive and normative analysis. Positive analysis tries to explain the world as it exists. While policymakers may value scientific analysis, they have an additional goal. Someone involved in normative analysis is trying to bring about a different and presumably better end-state. For example, two individuals might be involved in a discussion of drug usage in the United States. The following exchange might be heard:

Jim: Current drug laws contribute to urban decay.
Colleen: Most drug laws should be rescinded.

The important distinction between the two statements is that the first is *descriptive* of a social condition, at least as perceived by Jim. The second is *prescriptive* in that it describes the legal order as it *should be,* that is, the law ought to be changed. We can gather evidence to support or counter Jim's positive statement. Colleen's normative statement about what the policy ought to be cannot be confirmed or refuted by merely gathering evidence. Deciding on the appropriate policy will involve our philosophical views and personal values. This is not to deny that our evaluation of the evidence about drug laws and urban decay will influence our value judgments about what the policy ought to be. Specialists in public policy spend a great deal of time trying to determine what the critical relationships are and exactly how society works. But the whole purpose of government, and public policy, is to improve society by promoting the general welfare.

Why Policy Analysts Disagree

The fact that policy is dependent on values results in the community of policy scholars being no more unified in outlook than is the political community. Policy scholars generally agree on various analytical aspects of policy, yet they hold different views about what is best for society. Since public policy analysts come from across the political spectrum, they hold different opinions about the "best" or "right" solution to problems.

For example, in the mid-1990s, some policymakers were determined to reduce the federal deficit. Some analysts disagreed about the accuracy of the different theories regarding the impact of the deficit and the importance of balancing the budget. Analysts also disagreed on what the policy goals should be. Some believed that a full employment deficit would help create jobs, which they thought should be a major goal of public policy. Other analysts believed that the deficit would result in rising inflation, which they thought should be avoided as the primary responsibility of government. Some policymakers in Congress and in the executive branch found political advantage on either side of the question and staked out their position largely along the lines of appealing to their traditional constituents. As the deficit fell faster than most had anticipated, the disagreement shifted to the issue of whether there should be a tax cut and a further reduction in the role of government, or a reduction in the national debt. Once again, many analysts honestly disagreed on which policy should be adopted based on the theories and data available. Their disagreements were undoubtedly influenced by their individual values and which theories they believed would best address the problem.

Another perennial issue is tax policy. Are Americans taxed too much? In the long run, would individual saving and spending be a better stimulus for the economy than government spending? Public policy analysts are no better at answering this question than are physicians in determining whether the right to abortion is justifiable. Such judgments in the United States are determined by the people through the democratic process of voting into office those with specific policy goals.

Increasingly, there are cases in which policy experts agree, but the role of special interest groups obscures the consensus. For example, even though independent scholars were unanimous in their findings about the health risks of smoking, for years the tobacco companies funded research that downplayed their significance. Similarly, studies were funded as the result of the Civil Rights Act of 1964 to assess the extent to which individuals were being denied educational opportunities because of race or other attributes. The research was not politically neutral. It was limited to questions that provided information helpful to one side of the issue. Studies are vulnerable to manipulation by the choice of alternatives considered, or the interpretation of the findings.

The result is that policy analysis research is often used in the US political process to advocate opposition. Political entrepreneurs and special interest groups examine the research not for overall utility in improving policy so much as for selective findings they can use to undercut an adversary's position or to strengthen their own. Politicians and lobbyists often look for support for existing political and ideological positions rather than information to help shape and guide policy. The more ideologically motivated the administration or bureaucracy, the more policy is made on the basis of ideological inputs rather than analysis. In recent years, for example, conservatives have backed and buttressed their aims by funding policy analysis groups such as the Heritage Foundation or the American Enterprise Institute as an alternative to institutes perceived as having a more liberal orientation.[12]

The Policymaking Process

Public policy did not appear as a subfield of political science until the mid-1960s. The effort to provide an abstract framework for the entire policy process was presented by David Easton.[13] Since that time, effort has concentrated on the analysis of specific substantive areas of public policy. Research has focused on topics such as health care, education, the environment, welfare, and national security. Much of this research has provided detailed historical case studies of the development and evolution of policy. More recently, there have been greater efforts to apply theoretical models to these case studies, focusing on the factors that affect policy formulation and implementation. This evaluation research judges the formulation of the policy proposal, the process of policy adoption, and the operation of the policy program.

Public policy analysis has not progressed in developing scientifically lawlike propositions. Similarly, the current understanding of the policy process is really a heuristic model, not a theory that allows explanation and prediction. This model separates the policymaking process into five stages: problem identification, policy formulation, adoption, program operations, and evaluation. The model contains no clear and consistent postulates about what drives the process from one stage to the next. Its primary value has been that it divides the policymaking process into manageable units of analysis. Thus, the model has resulted in research projects that focus almost exclusively on a single stage without tying results into other projects. Little theoretical coherence exists from one stage to the next.[14]

Problem Identification

The first stage, shown in Figure 2.3, simply indicates that public policy begins when a problem is perceived and gets on the **policy agenda**. There are many problems in

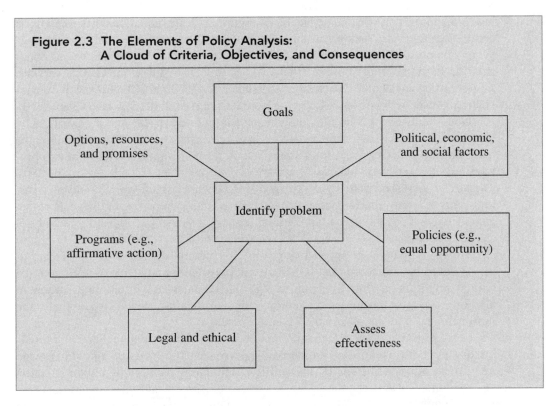

**Figure 2.3 The Elements of Policy Analysis:
A Cloud of Criteria, Objectives, and Consequences**

Goals

Options, resources,
and promises

Political, economic,
and social factors

Identify problem

Programs (e.g.,
affirmative action)

Policies (e.g.,
equal opportunity)

Legal and ethical

Assess
effectiveness

society that are not part of the policy agenda because they have not come to the attention of the authoritative actors in the government.[15] The desire for policies to provide for individual needs is insatiable while room on the agenda is scarce. This raises the question as to why some issues get on the agenda, but others do not. The dynamics of a changing political environment, new political players, policy entrepreneurs, and new windows of opportunity are major elements in new issues gaining a place on the agenda. For instance, the Great Depression provided the opportunity for legislation that ushered in various policies such as Social Security and minimum-wage laws. The conservative reaction that swept Ronald Reagan to the presidency provided a window of opportunity for the reduction of social welfare legislation and the introduction of supply-side economics on the policy agenda.[16]

Once on the policy agenda, many hurdles remain before an issue is adopted as policy. For example, health care reform languished on the policy agenda for years until President Obama proclaimed it would be a major policy initiative of his administration. While Democrats enjoy solid majorities in the House and Senate, the leadership was forced to negotiate with Republicans, conservatives within their own party, as well as assorted interest groups and lobbyists. Party leaders next faced the task of blending a health care bill approved by the Senate Finance Committee with an alternate bill approved by the Senate Health Committee. Meanwhile, three different House committees approved health care bills, which had to be reconciled into a single legislative proposal to be presented for full floor debate and passage despite solid opposition from the GOP in both the House and Senate. The House and Senate versions must then be blended in a Conference Committee and the final bill must survive a concluding vote in both houses before the president can sign it into law (see Chapter 10).

Other items may get on the policy agenda only to disappear into a black hole by the crush of other issues, then resurface later in slightly modified forms. Thus, the question as to whether the United States should develop an **industrial policy** to promote a resurgence of US business growth was placed on the agenda in the early 1980s. The idea was brushed aside by the Reagan White House, which viewed industrial policy as inappropriate interference with an unfettered free market, one of the goals of that administration. The Clinton administration quietly instituted an industrial policy designed to strengthen business and US exports as part of its overall economic program.

The first step in the policymaking process is a prerequisite for all the steps that follow. So even though getting on the policy agenda provides no assurance that an issue will go any further, failure to get on the agenda guarantees it will not go anywhere at all. For that reason, getting on the policy agenda is the most critical step, and also the most nebulous and amorphous, in the entire process.

Some researchers suggest that the policy agenda should be thought of as consisting of a systemic agenda and an institutional agenda. The **systemic agenda** is made up of those issues perceived by the political community as meriting public attention and resolution.[17] However, the systemic agendas of national and state governments are largely symbolic in nature. The issues they contain are often controversial, and some items may be on one systemic agenda, but not another. For example, some believe that the "right to bear arms" is guaranteed by the Constitution, and that it should be beyond the authority of Congress or the states to regulate in any way. Therefore, the issue of gun control has until very recently remained on the systemic agendas of the federal government and most state governments, with many gun control opponents urging its removal altogether. Another subset of items on the systemic agenda are those subject to nothing more than discussion; these are termed "pseudo-agenda items."

The **institutional agenda** consists of those items that receive the powerful and earnest attention of decisionmakers, though they are not always easily identified or agreed upon. They include those issues that are actively pursued through the various institutions of government.

Items may shift from the systemic to the institutional agenda as a result of a variety of events. For example, Congress may prefer to keep an item such as an abortion bill on the systemic agenda because it may be perceived as a no-win situation for members to take a stand on by voting. However, a decision by the Supreme Court, such as *Roe v. Wade,* may force the issue back to the national legislature and require some action. Policy issues typically move from private decisionmaking to the public agenda when they progress from the systemic to the institutional agenda.

Scope of the conflict. If policy is not made through public decisions by the government, it will be made through private decisions, primarily by businesses or financial elites. Traditionally, the principle of laissez-faire meant that government should not interfere with business. As a practical matter, it meant that government supported business decisionmaking through legislation and court decisions that legitimized and reinforced corporate interests. Thus, corporations made policy that provided pervasive control over the lives of individuals unhindered by government interference. Businesses were given a free hand to set the terms of employment, wages, hours, and working conditions for employees, and those terms were supported by government stipulations regarding the rights to private property and freedom of contract.

Under laissez-faire doctrine, business provided for individual economic needs through free enterprise, and was loosely supervised by lower levels of government. But with the rise of giant corporations in the late nineteenth century, the power of business organizations over the lives of individuals grew correspondingly. The result was an overwhelming popular demand for government action to correct the perceived abuses of power by corporate interests.

This demand for reform expanded the scope of the conflict from the private arena of management versus labor to the public arena of government versus business. For example, the national government took the lead in legislating worker compensation and child labor laws. With the Great Depression came even more pressure for the government to take an active role in managing the economy and business.

Despite this expansion of governmental regulation, businesses still have a privileged position in US politics even today. They can often make major decisions with only a minimum of government control. In arguing for corporate autonomy from government regulation, executives point out that business must submit first of all to the discipline of the marketplace if it is to be successful. When an issue affecting business does get on the public policy agenda, business organizations are well represented in the public and governmental debates. Corporate leaders are effective proponents for their companies and for the interests of capitalism in general. They also provide many people for government positions, which encourages a pro-business bias in government policymaking.

As long as decisions are made in the private sector, they are outside the realm of politics, even though those decisions may affect many people and the allocation of vast resources. Indeed, private conflicts are taken into the public arena precisely because someone or some group wants to make certain that the power ratio among the private interests shall not prevail in the final decisionmaking (see Chapter 4).[18] In fact, politics may be defined as the socialization of conflict:

The political process is a sequence: conflicts are initiated by highly motivated, high-tension groups so directly and immediately involved that it is difficult for them to see the justice of competing claims. As long as the conflicts remain *private* . . . no political process is initiated. Conflicts become political only when an attempt is made to involve the wider public. Pressure politics might be described as a stage in the socialization of conflict.[19]

Enlarging the scope. As noted earlier, democracies provide the political means for private controversies to spill over into the public arena. An issue or condition must attract sufficient attention and interest to expand the scope of the conflict into the public arena if there is to be any hope of changing its current disposition or status.

Some of those involved in the issue will prefer the status quo, and attempt to limit the scope of the conflict to keep the issue off the public policy agenda. And those with interests already on the public policy agenda will not welcome new items that threaten to displace their own. Since only a finite number of items can be considered at any given time, there is always tension when new issues erupt into public consciousness. Those items already on the agenda have a public legitimacy by virtue of having been accepted onto it. New items have not yet established their public legitimacy. For all of these reasons, the political system has a bias in favor of the status quo and will resist the addition of new issues to the policy agenda.

Who sets the public policy agenda? Determining which issues move from the systemic to the institutional agenda is an extremely important part of the entire policy-making process. The policy agenda is overburdened with a wide assortment of foreign policy issues, national security affairs, economic questions, and domestic concerns. For a problem to become a salient agenda item, it is important that it have an influential advocate, especially the president. Another route for an issue to move onto the institutional agenda is for it to be regarded as a crisis. The perception of a problem as being serious may even be more important than its actual seriousness. A triggering event, for example, the single act of a terrorist, may focus attention on an issue.

Increasingly, policy agendas are determined by tightly knit groups that dominate policymaking in particular subject areas. **Iron triangles** are the reciprocal bonds that evolve between congressional committees and their staffs, special interest groups, and bureaucratic agencies in the executive branch.[20] Members of Congress have incentives to serve on committees that deal with special interest constituencies from their districts. Senators and representatives will bargain for such appointments. And over time, committees in Congress tend to be dominated by members who are highly motivated to provide generous support for the agencies they oversee. These congressional committees make up one side of an iron triangle; they tend to be insulated from many party pressures and develop committee-member alliances that cross party lines.

The special interest groups form a second side of the triangle. These lobbyists and political action committees provide experts in the special interest area. They provide committees with resources for public relations and media coverage, and supply campaign financing to committee members. Finally, the bureaucracies of federal agencies in the executive branch are the third side of the triangle, with their own entrenched interests in particular issues or programs. Congressional hearings provide excellent opportunities for government representatives and lobbyists to build imposing cases for their positions.[21] Iron triangles exemplify disturbing problems in public policy. Policy alternatives that challenge the established interests of the triangle may never receive serious attention.

Responses to the situation created by iron triangles have been based mainly on two different approaches to understanding the nature and functioning of government: elite theory and pluralism or group theory. Those who espouse **elite theory** are critical of iron triangles, pointing to their power as proof of the victory of greedy special interest groups over the general welfare. Those who espouse **pluralism**, on the other hand, are more likely to conclude that such triangles simply reflect strategies developed to promote policies in a diverse nation whose subgroups have different interests.

Getting from the systemic to the institutional agenda. According to elite theory, elites who are powerful in their own right have relatively little trouble getting their issues before the public. Those who own the media can publish stories or air television shows.[22] A member of Congress or the president, together with their respective bureaucracies, can propose a policy. Special interest groups also frequently approach the government with their perceptions of problems and proposed solutions.

Ordinarily an individual must enlarge the scope of the conflict by mobilizing public opinion. This might be done by enlisting the aid of experts who are knowledgeable about the issue and how to publicize it. Frequently, the simplest solution is to seek out an interest group that already deals with a related topic. For example, if someone is concerned that local public school students appear to be falling below national standards in testing, he or she might approach the local parent teacher association regarding remedial steps that might be taken. Getting the local newspaper to write an article might elicit support for new school policies designed to improve the quality of education in the local schools.

The number of people affected by an issue, the intensity of the effect an issue has on the community, and the degree to which everyone's self-interest can be aroused to confront the problem are all factors to be considered when trying to get an issue on the institutional agenda. An analysis of what will happen if nothing is done about a problem, in terms of who will be affected and in what ways, can be a powerful inducement to action.

Using symbols to get an issue on the agenda. Ultimately, the need to attract broad support to get an issue on the political agenda, and to try to move it to the institutional agenda, encourages the use of symbols. A **symbol** legitimizes an issue and attracts

Case Study: The Issue-Attention Cycle

Anthony Downs contends that many issues appear on the policy agenda in a standardized process that comprises an **issue-attention cycle**. In his view, key domestic problems leap into prominence and remain the center of public attention for a short time, then fade from concern even though they remain largely unresolved. It is in part the length that public attention stays focused on any given issue that determines whether enough political pressure will be brought to bear to effect a change. This cycle is rooted in the nature of many domestic problems and the way the communications media interact with the public. The cycle has five stages, each of variable duration, which usually occur in the following sequence:

1. *The preproblem stage.* Some major problem arises, and although policy experts and special interest groups may be alarmed by the situation, the general public is generally not aware of the problem or its magnitude. The general press has given it prominent coverage. It is not unusual for some problems, such as racism or malnutrition, to be worse during the preproblem stage than they are by the time the public's interest is aroused.

2. *Alarmed discovery and euphoric enthusiasm.* Often as a result of some dramatic event (like a riot or demonstration), the public becomes aware of the problem. Authoritative decisionmakers then make speeches, which are enthusiastically received by the public, regarding the politicians' determination to resolve the problem. This optimism is embedded in US culture, which tends to view any problem as *outside* the structure of society, and naively believes that every problem can be resolved *without any basic reordering of society itself.* US optimism in the past has clung to the view that we as a nation

could accomplish anything. Since the late 1960s, a more realistic awareness that some problems may be beyond a complete "solution" has begun to develop.

3. *Realization of the cost of significant progress.* A realization that the cost of solving the problem is extremely high sets in. The solution would not only take a great deal of money, but also require that some groups give up some economic security (through taxes or some other redistribution of resources in favor of others). The public begins to realize the structural nature of the problem, and a human inconsistency regarding public policy makes itself felt: we favor collective coercion to raise our personal standard of living, and oppose it when it is used to limit our own actions and raise someone else's income.

Many social problems involve the exploitation, whether deliberately or unconsciously, of one group by another, or people being prevented from benefiting from something that others want to keep for themselves. For example, most upper-middle-income people (usually white) have a high regard for geographic separation from poor people (frequently nonwhite). Consequently, equality of access to the advantages of suburban living for the poor cannot be achieved without some sacrifice by the upper-middle class of the "benefits" of that separation. The recognition of the relationship between the problem and its "solution" is a key part of the third stage.

4. *Gradual decline of intense public interest.* As more people realize how difficult and costly to themselves a solution would be, their enthusiasm for finding a "solution" diminishes rapidly. Some come to feel that solving the problem threatens them; others merely get bored or discouraged with the perceived futility of grappling

continued

Case Study continued

---

with the issue. Also by this time, another issue has usually been discovered by the media and is entering the second stage, and it claims the public's attention.

  5. *The postproblem stage.* Having been replaced by successive issues at the center of public interest, the issue moves into a stage of reduced attention, although there may be a recurrence of interest from time to time. This stage differs from the preproblem stage in that some programs and policies have been put in place to deal with the issue. A government bureaucracy may have been given the task of administering a program and monitoring the situation. Special interest groups may have developed a symbiotic relationship with the bureaucracy and have had a successful impact even though the "action" has shifted to other issues.

  Sources: Anthony Downs, "The 'Issue-Attention Cycle,'" *Public Interest*, no. 28 (1972): 38–50; Anthony Downs, "Up and Down with Ecology: The Issue-Attention Cycle," *Public Interest*, no. 32 (1973): 39–53.

---

support for the proposed policy goals. Symbols help people to order and interpret their reality, and even create the reality to which they give their attention. A major attribute of successful symbols is ambiguity. A symbol may be a slogan, an event, a person, or anything to which people attach meaning or value. Symbols can mean different things to different people. They permit the translation of private and personal intentions into wider collective goals by appealing to people with diverse motivations and values.[23] Ambiguity permits maneuvering room to reduce opposition to a policy. For instance, in the 1980s, "welfare" came under increasing attack in a period of tight budgets and declining support for egalitarian policies. Calling the programs "workfare" rather than "welfare" reduced some of the opposition to them since the new term implied welfare recipients would not be getting a free ride. In the recent 2008 presidential election, Barack Obama's slogan "yes we can" translated to a range of economic and foreign policy issues. At the same time, others interpreted the slogan to refer to race-related or youth-related issues.

Policy Formulation

Success in getting a problem accepted onto the policy agenda may depend in part on the ability to convince others that it is amenable to some governmental solution. Policy formulation is concerned with the "what" questions associated with generating alternatives. What is the plan for dealing with the problem? What are the goals and priorities? What options are available to achieve those goals? What are the costs and benefits of each of the options? What externalities, positive or negative, are associated with each alternative?

The first option after looking at the proposed solutions may well be to do nothing. Most, but not all, public policy proposals cost money. Currently, there are severe economic constraints on new policy initiatives at the state level and particularly at the national level. The economic costs of new programs at the national level have made it extremely difficult to add any new programs.

Increasingly, programs are expected to be financed by their recipients. For example, the Medicare Catastrophic Coverage Act, which was passed with bipartisan support prior to the 1988 election, provided insurance against catastrophic illnesses for those on Medicare by imposing a ceiling on medical bills and paying 100 percent of the costs through Medicare. The goal was to relieve worry among the elderly that they would be impoverished by the high costs of medical care, especially hospitalization. This insurance was to be paid through a surtax on the income taxes of the elderly. The wealthiest elderly would pay the most, the poorest the least. The theory was that the elderly, as the program's beneficiaries, should bear the cost.[24]

Another major concern for entrepreneurs is the political costs associated with taking action. Since many policies alter the distribution of income, it can be expected that those whose incomes will be adversely affected generally oppose them while those who will be helped generally favor them. Political entrepreneurs sometimes find themselves caught between doing what they think is right and choosing the alternative that is the least costly from a political perspective.

The formulation of a policy proposal ordinarily includes not only a statement of the goals of the policy, but various alternatives (or programs) for achieving the goals. The way in which a problem is formulated will often suggest how the alternatives are proposed.

Some policy theorists promote **rational analysis** as a plan for achieving government efficiency through a comprehensive review of all the policy options and an examination of their consequences. Rational analysis selects the option that maximizes utility.

Much of the animosity surrounding the budgetary process is claimed to result from its *lack* of rationality. Everyone from the person-on-the-street, to bureaucrats, to special interest groups, to Congress, to the president believes that he or she can produce a better, more rational budget. However, rational analysis of the budgetary process implies that each option be considered, and no analyst can do this nor can any analysis of the budget be completely comprehensive.[25] Some things are inevitably left out of every analysis.

A model of all social problems that included their ranking by importance would be expensive and difficult to keep up-to-date. People's and society's concerns change constantly. For instance, until about 1980, most Americans outside the medical profession were unaware of Alzheimer's disease. Today, it is generally known to be a relatively common form of dementia that afflicts a significant percentage of the elderly population. It causes memory loss, personality disorders, and a decrease in other mental capabilities. After research helped to define Alzheimer's as a particular pathology, an organization was formed by people who had family members diagnosed with the disease. The Alzheimer's Association has since opened an office in Washington, DC, to lobby Congress to double the amount of federal funds currently dedicated to Alzheimer's research. However, a complete analysis of the appropriate amount of federal money to spend for Alzheimer's research would have to include an analysis of all other possible ways to spend the money. That is, every other item in the budget, such as aid to education, the space program, cancer research, environmental protection, even deficit reduction and lowering taxes, would have to be considered.[26]

Only the political process can do this. Budgetary decisionmaking is a political process regarding choices about values. The suggestion that this process could be replaced with an apolitical rationality is disingenuous. Several presidents have argued in favor of Congress giving the executive the power of a **line-item veto**, as though this would take politics out of the process. But nothing can take politics out of the budgetary process.[27] In 1996, Congress handed the president additional power to cut the budget by providing a limited line-item veto. The first time it was used, by President Clinton in the fall of 1997, court challenges were instituted arguing that this was an unconstitutional delegation of power to the executive.

Other policy theorists therefore contend that an incremental approach is actually much more rational. Incrementalism is an approach to decisionmaking in which policymakers change policy at the margins. That is, they begin with the current set of circumstances and consider changing things in only a small way. Particularly in budgeting, this is the typical approach. Just note that the best predictor of what next year's federal budget allocations will be is this year's allocations. Incrementalism assumes that public policy decisions will usually involve only modest changes to the status quo and not require a thorough inspection of all the available options.

Incrementalism also assumes the rational self-interest approach of individuals and groups. Since individual and group interests usually conflict, compromise will be required in which everyone will have to settle for less than they hoped for. This also results in relatively small changes in existing policy. The budgetary process is thus simplified into a task that assumes each existing program will continue to be funded at its existing level because this level is perceived as fair. If the budget is growing, each program gets approximately the same percentage increase, with those programs having unusually strong support getting a slightly larger increase and those with waning support or visibility receiving slightly less. These new funding levels become the bases for the next year's budget.

The late Aaron Wildavsky maintained that **incrementalism** is the best technique for reaching budgetary decisions, because it reduces the decisionmaking process to manageable size. It focuses only on the changes to existing programs rather than requiring a complete justification of the entire program annually. The result is also an allocation of money according to each program's political strength. Since the selection of programs is a normative decision, according to Wildavsky, it is about as good a measure as we have regarding which programs are most deserving.[28]

The result of incrementalism is **satisficing**, or adopting a policy acceptable from all viewpoints rather than seeking the best solution possible. The "best" solution might prove unacceptable to so many decisionmakers that it would be voted down if proposed. For example, many public policy experts recommended a significant tax increase on gasoline at the pump as the "best" way to reduce gas consumption and US reliance on imported oil. Fear of consumer reaction and Republican opposition forced then president Clinton to reduce a proposed gasoline tax increase from 20¢ to 5¢ a gallon. When the tax kicked in during the fall of 1993, few even noticed. In the fall of 1994, after inflation, gasoline prices were actually lower than before the tax increase. Since politics is the art of the possible, a negotiated compromise that wins some, if not all, support is preferred to defeat.

Incrementalism works, then, because it is in some ways the most rational approach to policymaking. Time and resources are too limited to permit an examination of all the alternatives. There is a legitimacy in previous policies and programs while the feasibility of new ones is less predictable. Incrementalism also permits quicker political settlements, particularly when disputes are at the margins regarding the modification of programs.

Adoption

Getting a proposed policy from the institutional agenda through the adoption process is crucial to effecting a change. In the late 1960s, many public policy scholars focused on the question of how a bill becomes a law and the many veto points in the process. The process of proposing a bill and getting it passed is straightforward in that it must follow a standardized procedure. However, the pitfalls that can befall a bill in the process are well known.

The definition of an issue and its impact on different portions of the population usually change in the debate during the policy process. Political entrepreneurs try to redraw the dimensions of the dispute so they can reconfigure political coalitions and gain a winning edge. Party leaders and senior members of the congressional committee considering the issue often bide their time, waiting for other members of the committee or of Congress to become familiar with the issue. Generally, they make their move when they sense the time is ripe for action, based on their experience in dealing with such matters.

The separation of powers in government allows each branch to judge the legitimacy, and if necessary take action to check the moves, of the other branches. The actors involved here are clearly political elites and must be persuaded not about the wisdom of the proposed policy, but of its chances of success politically. For this reason, the major concern at this point is whether the proposed policy is politically viable. The broadest support for the policy must be in evidence here to convince political entrepreneurs that it is in their own interests to promote it through their votes.

Program Operations

In the policy process, once a problem has been identified, alternatives have been examined, and a solution has been selected and legitimized through the adoption of legislation, one part of the policymaking process has been completed. But this is also the beginning of another part of the process—implementing the policy. **Implementation** means carrying out the policy or program operations. Or as Robert Lineberry asserts, implementation is "a continuation of policy making by other means."[29] Implementation has attracted a significant amount of research because policies often do not accomplish what they were designed to achieve.[30] A series of decisions and actions are necessary to put a policy into effect and, as in chess, miscalculation in the original design strategy or in implementation may bring the entire effort to naught.

Policy advocates have come to realize that the time to plan for the implementation phase is during the formulation and policy selection stage. All the earlier phases, if done well, will reach this state where the proposal is to be translated into action. Several factors in the design phase will facilitate the implementation stage. Perhaps most critical is the question of **policy design**. That is, has the problem been accurately defined? Only if the problem is accurately understood do the causal relationships become evident and allow the analyst to correctly perceive the connections between a particular policy's operation and its intent. For example, the Americans with Disabilities Act of 1990 prohibited discrimination against people with disabilities. The Equal Employment Opportunity Commission and other federal agencies held lengthy hearings to create the regulations spelling out the standards of compliance.[31]

Congress can reduce the discretion of administrators by providing very detailed legislation. For example, Social Security legislation provides precise terms for eligibility and levels of benefits and formulas for additional earnings. Even so, eligibility for benefits under Social Security Disability Insurance (SSDI) cannot be set forth with such precision. The general definition of *disability* states that an individual is unable to engage in significant gainful employment by reason of a medically diagnosable mental or physical impairment expected to last at least twelve months or result in death. This definition of necessity leaves much room for subjective judgments and interpretation.[32] Implementation of SSDI benefits has resulted in significant controversy and thousands of cases of litigation.

It is usually much easier to implement a policy if it is clearly stated and consistent with other policy objectives. Vague and ambiguous language will be received quite differently by the state officials handling the implementation than will crisp, lucid legislation. Vaguely worded laws may be subject to varying interpretations by bureaucrats or state officials tasked with implementing a program. Vagueness may even permit opponents to effectively sabotage the policy. On the other hand, there are times when vagueness may be preferred to clarity, if the alternative would be no program at all. An excellent example of this is the Constitution, which as the basic framework of the US government is also a policy statement. When the Founding Fathers were unable to agree on clear statements on several issues, they compromised on vague, broad statements and agreed to let later practice determine the outcome. The "necessary and proper" clause is an obvious instance.

Another factor that facilitates the implementation of a policy is its perceived legitimacy. For instance, a program that passes both houses of Congress with large majorities or a decision by the Supreme Court that is unanimous or nearly so will generally also have the support of those tasked with its implementation. Even those who have misgivings will be more inclined to go along with the perceived mandate.

Implementation is the most important part of the policymaking process for students of public administration. Much of the important work of implementing policy is done by the "street-level" bureaucrats, including judges, public health workers, school teachers, social workers, and other federal, state, and local government employees.

Evaluation

The last stage of the policymaking process is evaluation. Every stage involves a purposeful effort to bring about some change in the political environment. But in particular, the process of formulating a proposal and choosing among alternatives to achieve the policy's objectives suggests the need for some criteria or standard to determine if the implemented policy has achieved its objectives.

Evaluation is the assessment of how a program achieves its intended goals. All the earlier stages of the policy process look toward a future goal to be achieved; evaluation looks backward. It is a tool whose primary purpose is to appraise the operation of a program and provide feedback to those involved in the earlier stages. This feedback permits modifications in the policy to improve its efficiency and effectiveness. Evaluation also pinpoints unintended effects of a policy and allows adjustment in the implementation process to avoid those that are undesirable. In addition, it can be used to monitor the expenditure of funds to see that they were spent according to the terms of the law or grant. Thus, such assessments focus on the implementation of a program and how it has met the goals and objectives spelled out in the selection and adoption phases of the policy process.

Evaluation of public policy programs came into its own during the 1960s. Under Great Society legislation, there was a surge in government programs to deal with a variety of social ills. At the same time, critics charged that these programs resulted in many government failures, and at a significant cost to taxpayers. The media reported cases of waste and inefficiency as well as programs that were not achieving their intended goals. Congress began requiring more vigorous evaluations of programs by agencies like the General Accounting Office.

It is useful to make a distinction between policymaking and policy analysis. This book is primarily concerned with the policymaking process. Policy analysts, however, emphasize the evaluation process and use a variety of different methods to assess policy, including laboratory studies, simulations, case studies, sample surveys, and cost-benefit analyses, to name just a few. The process often also involves the use of analytical techniques, such as applied statistical analysis, to measure program effectiveness in meeting goals.

Conclusion

Public policy has developed as a subfield within the discipline of political science since the mid-1960s. As a social science, it draws on the humanities, and history in particular, for its data. It also utilizes the scientific method in an effort to explain and predict underlying causal relationships in policymaking and uses empirical methodology to test the validity of causal relationships. Existing at the confluence of the social sciences, public policy draws on theoretical developments in the various social sciences.

Policy analysts utilize the scientific method in order to understand the social world in which they work. Like other scientists, they must make assumptions and construct models to simplify a complex world to provide greater understanding. Policy analysts study all the issues that are of interest to policymakers, which is to say that policy analysis is wide ranging and interdisciplinary.

When policy analysts are engaged in positive analysis, they are concerned with understanding the world as it *is*. When policy analysts are concerned with normative issues (how the world *ought* to be), they are acting more in the role of policymaker. An objective understanding of how the world *is* will influence one's values.

Specialists in public policy issues may not always agree, because they have different scientific judgments regarding theories developed from studies. They also disagree because they have different value systems about what *ought to be* to improve society. Sometimes there may be wide agreement among policy scientists, but a public perception of a lack of consensus. That is because special interest groups often provide studies and spokespersons claiming expertise to support almost any position imaginable.

The complexity of the problems in policy analysis has made the development of public policy theory difficult. Predictions that may be valid solely in terms of the underlying assumptions of a discipline, such as economics or political science, are often based on data that is not broad enough in scope to ensure their accuracy in the larger policy scheme. Such predictions fail to take into account all the significant phenomena that influence the politico-economic variables related to a problem. This means that any effective theory development must begin at the micro level and take into account individual rational actors and their decisionmaking preferences, then move toward the macro level and take into account aspects of institutional constraints and the societal effects of policy.

Scholarship over the past two decades has resulted in a significant accumulation of knowledge regarding the policymaking process. Dividing the process into stages— getting an issue on the public agenda, formulating the policy proposal, achieving its adoption, implementing the policy as a program, and evaluating the program's effectiveness in achieving the original policy goals—has been the standard analytical approach. This has resulted in uncovering phenomena, such as "critical actors," that were previously overlooked.

The political system transfers private disagreements into public disagreements. Getting an issue on the public policy agenda is a critical procedural process. Elites in the society have far more influence than the average citizen.

Questions for Discussion

1. Discuss the role of theory in understanding phenomena from the natural sciences. Does it differ from the role of theory in the social sciences? Why?

2. Why is the development of theory in the social sciences more difficult than in the natural sciences?

3. What are the special problems in developing theory in the policy sciences?

4. Should theories and models be a completely accurate reflection of reality?

5. Why are the contributions of policy analysts often not held in high regard by policymakers?

Notes

1. From Aristotle, *Politics,* in William Ebenstein and Alan Ebenstein, *Great Political Thinkers,* 5th ed. (New York: Harcourt Brace, 1991), p. 93.

2. Bill Clinton, *My Life* (New York: Alfred A. Knopf, 2004), p. 635.

3. Hans J. Morgenthau, "The Purpose of Political Science," in James C. Charlesworth, ed., *A Design for Political Science: Scope, Objectives, and Methods,* Monograph no. 6 (Philadelphia: American Academy of Political and Social Science, 1966), pp. 67–68.

4. The concern is that humans are the makers of the tools that shape their environment, guide their vision, and help make their destiny. When people use these tools on themselves and other people, it is important to ask how these tools affect their vision of humanity. Charles Hampden-Turner, in *Radical Man: The Process of Psycho-Social Development* (New York: Anchor Books, 1971), argues that the scientific method has a very conservative bias when applied to the human environment.

5. John Maynard Keynes, *The General Theory of Employment, Interest, and Money* (New York: Harcourt Brace Jovanovich, 1966; originally published in 1936), p. 383.

6. A model is a simplified representation of how the real world works. Its usefulness is judged by how well it represents reality. Models may be depicted by mathematical equations, charts, and graphs, or may be descriptively stated.

7. Michel de Montaigne, *The Essays of Michel de Montaigne,* edited and translated by Jacob Zeitlin (New York: Alfred A. Knopf, 1936), vol. 3, p. 270 (emphasis in original).

8. See, for example, Larry Kiser and Elinor Ostrom, "The Three Worlds of Action," in Elinor Ostrom, ed., *Strategies of Political Inquiry* (Beverly Hills: Sage, 1982), pp. 179–222.

9. For further reading on the relationship between policy theory and public policy, see Michael Hill and Peter Hupe, *Implementing Public Policy: An Introduction to the Study of Operational Governance* (Beverly Hills: Sage, 2009).

10. Russell Kirk, a critic of the scientific study of politics, has argued that "human beings are the least controllable, verifiable, law-obeying and predictable of subjects." Russell Kirk, "Is Social Science Scientific?" in Nelson W. Polsby, Robert Dentler, and Paul Smith, ed., *Politics and Social Life* (Boston: Houghton Mifflin, 1963), p. 63.

11. For example, democratic society is based on the assumption that rational people acting "freely" may decide to violate the law. The cost of such action is determined by the probability of being punished. The sanction of the law makes sense in part because it presumes that most people will freely decide to obey the law. In fact, it is only because we can act freely that we can be held responsible. For example, deranged individuals are less accountable precisely because they do not freely choose their actions. These, then, are research problems, not unbeatable methodological barriers.

12. In addition to institutes funded to conduct policy research, such as the Brookings Institution, Congress employs thousands of staff members who also do such research. There are several thousand analysts who work for other government support agencies such as the General Accounting Office, the Office of Technology Assessment, the Congressional Research Service, and the Congressional Budget Office. These agencies generally respond to requests by congressional representatives and their staffs for specific studies. They also engage in studies on their own initiative. As such, they are a significant source of policy agenda items.

13. David Easton, *A Systems Analysis of Political Life* (New York: John Wiley and Sons, 1965).

14. Paul A. Sabatier, "Political Science and Public Policy," *PS: Political Science and Politics* 24 (June 1991): 145.

15. For a sophisticated and sound theoretical treatment of agenda setting, see John Kingdon, *Agendas, Alternatives, and Public Policies* (Boston: Little, Brown, 1984). See also Barbara Nelson, *Making an Issue of Child Abuse* (Chicago: University of Chicago Press, 1984).

16. See Kingdon, *Agendas,* pp. 183–184.

17. See Roger W. Cobb and Charles D. Elder, *Participation in American Politics: The Dynamics of Agenda Building,* 2nd ed. (Baltimore: Johns Hopkins University Press, 1983), p. 85.

18. E. E. Schattschneider, *The Semi-Sovereign People: A Realist's View of Democracy in America* (New York: Holt, Rinehart, and Winston, 1960), p. 38.

19. Ibid., p. 39 (emphasis in original).

20. See Jeffrey M. Berry, "Subgovernments, Issue Networks, and Political Conflict," in Richard Harris and Signey Milkis, ed., *Remaking American Politics* (Boulder: Westview, 1990), pp. 239–269.

21. The lobbying on behalf of the B-1 bomber is an excellent example of an iron triangle at work. Although various studies over thirty years recommended against its production, the US Air Force formed an alliance with various defense contractors to build the B-1. They were able to rouse political support for the program, valued in excess of $28 billion, in part because of the anticipated jobs the program would create across the country in forty-eight states. The US Air Force and defense contractors lobbied many members of Congress who were not on any of the armed services committees, emphasizing the jobs and the money that would flow into each congressperson's state. See Nick Kotz, *Wild Blue Yonder: Money, Politics, and the B-1 Bomber* (Princeton: Princeton University Press, 1988).

22. A number of works make the point that the media, popular opinion to the contrary, tend to be conservative and supportive of the conservative bias of elites. See, for example, W. Lance Bennett, *News: The Politics of Illusion,* 2nd ed. (New York: Longman, 1988).

23. Charles D. Elder and Roger W. Cobb, *The Political Uses of Symbols* (New York: Longman, 1983), pp. 28–29.

24. It may be surprising to some that an administration committed to tax reduction would propose such a program. It was put forth in part to secure the support of the elderly, whose backing of the Republicans had been weak. The pay-as-you-go plan flopped, however. Retirees who had procured insurance benefits in the private sector led an effort to repeal the bill. The wealthier elderly did not want to trade some of their economic independence to help less-well-off retirees reach an equal plane regarding health care. They resented subsidizing the less wealthy. Those leading the opposition, however, appealed to the less-wealthy retirees by arguing that the medical costs of the elderly should be the responsibility of younger Americans as well. They argued successfully that to make the elderly alone pay more, regardless of economic circumstances, was unfair, and the beginning of a reduction in benefits for all retirees was to be firmly resisted.

25. See Charles E. Lindblom, "The Science of 'Muddling Through,'" *Public Administration Review* 19, no. 2 (Spring 1959): 79–88.

26. Other supporters of the rational model agree that it is impossible to find the best of all possible courses of action. They would instead reduce the number of courses of action to a reasonable set of contenders. Then, statistical decisionmaking models might be used to decide on a final rational allocation of budgetary resources. However, critics point out that the initial selection of contenders is a political decision and arbitrary.

27. The budgeting process in the federal government is known as **line-item budgeting**. Congress presents a budget to the president, which is then broken down by organizational units, such as the Department of Energy, and then by subunits, such as renewable energy, solar energy, and so forth. Within all the subcategories, spending is broken down by accounts to include salaries, research, grants, and the like. A president using a line-item veto would merely be substituting one individual's judgment for the collective will of Congress—and a judgment presumably based just as much on ideology, special interest group pressure, partisan concerns, and personal views about the nature of the general welfare as that of any senator or congressional representative. The budget is inherently a political document.

28. Aaron Wildavsky, *The Politics of the Budgetary Process* (Boston: Little, Brown, 1964; rev. 4th ed., 1984).

29. Robert Lineberry, *American Public Policy* (New York: Harper and Row, 1977), p. 71.

30. See Paul Sabatier, "Top-Down and Bottom-Up Models of Policy Implementation: A Critical Analysis and Suggested Synthesis," *Journal of Public Policy* 6 (January 1986): 21–48. See also Laurence O'Toole, "Policy Recommendations for Multi-Actor Implementation: An Assessment of the Field," *Journal of Public Policy* 6 (April 1986): 181–210.

31. See Peter C. Bishop and Augustus J. Jones, "Implementing the Americans with Disabilities Act of 1990: Assessing the Variables of Success," *Public Administration Review* 53 (March–April 1993): 121–128.

32. See Martha Derthick, *Agency Under Stress: The Social Security Administration in American Government* (Washington, DC: Brookings Institution, 1990).

3

Rational Public Choice

This chapter is concerned with how choices are made in the political arena. **Rational choice theory** is a major tool used by political scientists in the study of the behavior of voters, politicians, and government officials as self-interested actors. A closely related and overlapping field is **public choice theory**, which focuses on economic models of political processes. **Social choice theory** is yet another related field that focuses on how voting rules and individual preferences are aggregated to produce a collective preference.

There are several differences between the economic marketplace and political markets. In most economic markets, firms compete to sell products to the consumer who makes the final choice. Theoretically at least, the consumer is sovereign. Production matches itself to the demand of consumers based on their willingness and ability to pay. Political markets are typically decided by a one-time choice at the ballot box in which a majority wins. Interested parties may continue to pressure an elected official for the duration of the term of office following the election, but all consumers get the same political goods whether it is health care, public schools, or national defense.

This chapter relays how individuals and elected policymakers make decisions. Can we develop a set of assumptions regarding individual preferences and, from these, derive principles of political behavior for individuals as well as those seeking election? Do elected officials' decisions reflect the will of the voters? Is the competition in the political marketplace as responsive to consumers' wishes as it is in the economic marketplace?

Rational Choice

Rational choice theory, sometimes called public choice, is the study of the collective decisions made by groups of individuals through the political process to maximize their own self-interest. It assumes that individuals are just as rational and self-interested in the political sector as they are in the economic marketplace.[1] According to public choice theory, when people behave differently in the political sector than in the marketplace, it is because the institutional arrangements are different and not because of a lack of self-interest.

Rational choice analysis was originally looked upon as being a value-free explanation of society as it is (positive analysis).[2] However, it is often used for normative purposes (what should be) to recommend how a system could be improved by changes in constitutional or legislative rules. Thus, it may provide an analysis of why individuals with high incomes are more likely to vote than those with low incomes, and why politicians are more attentive to voters than to nonvoters (positive analysis). But the theory may also suggest how to increase voting among low-income groups to force politicians to be more attentive to the needs of low-income constituents (normative analysis).

Personal Decisionmaking

In Chapter 2, we pointed out that human beings are multifaceted creatures. Human nature is too complex to be explained in one or two dimensions. But we do assume that people are *motivated* to engage in goal-directed actions to satisfy their needs. Each individual has a unique set of needs that are influenced by his or her own history, including gender, age, ethnic background, intellectual abilities, family situation, and financial status, to name just a few. Motivation theories tell us that we all are motivated to fulfill a variety of needs. Abraham Maslow proposed that there is a hierarchy of needs that is common to mentally healthy adults. Any of the five needs are capable of motivating behavior (see Figure 3.1).[3] He believed that these needs arranged themselves in a distinct order. According to his theory, as long as a lower-level need is unsatisfied, an individual will be highly motivated to choose actions calculated to satisfy that need.

According to this theory, once lower needs, like the physiological needs, are satisfied, a person will direct attention toward satisfying their safety needs and so on. Research on Maslow's model has resulted in several qualifications to the theory. First, a person's needs may change over time. The needs of a young adult embarking on a new career and starting a family will differ from those of a veteran employee preparing for retirement. And changes in the social environment may result in changes in the significance of different needs. For example, an economy falling into recession with rising unemployment may cause one to shift his or her attention from esteem needs to safety and physiological needs. A second criticism suggested by research is that people often work to satisfy several needs at the same time. For example, a person's employment may satisfy the physiological need to acquire money to provide for survival needs while simultaneously providing for safety needs through insurance and pension pro-

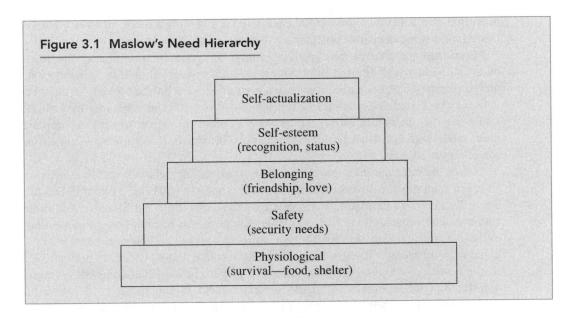

Figure 3.1 Maslow's Need Hierarchy

Self-actualization

Self-esteem
(recognition, status)

Belonging
(friendship, love)

Safety
(security needs)

Physiological
(survival—food, shelter)

grams. One's peers at work may also satisfy esteem and self-actualization needs through friendship and the mutual participation in creative work endeavors. Despite these criticisms, Maslow's theory retains a certain popularity because of its intuitive appeal and because understanding how individual needs appear is critical in understanding what motivates individual behavior.

The "public interest" may be understood as the aggregation of the individual interests or judgments into a notion of social choice expressed through voting. Society is improved when some people's preferences can be satisfied without making other people worse off. We often assume the economic market will serve best to improve society. Public policies are needed when a policy makes improvements more efficiently than does the market.[4] This is not a statement of how public policies are actually made, but how they are justified.[5]

Since the concept of rational self-interest is often a source of misunderstanding, it is important to clarify its meaning.[6] Rational self-interest means that individuals have preferences. People *intend* to act in such a way to achieve those preferences when the expected benefits exceed the costs of available choices. Since people try to make decisions by comparing costs and benefits, their behavior may change if the costs or benefits they face change. Rational choice follows the basic rule of logic that holds that behavior is rational as long as its marginal benefit is equal to its marginal cost. A rational actor is expected to choose the action that will *maximize* expected benefits. This simple rule of logic is central to rational choice thinking. The **marginal benefit** from taking certain action is the increase in total benefit from doing it once more while the

marginal cost is the increase in total costs from doing it once more. Behavior is maximized by making decisions until the net benefit equals the net cost.

Some rational choices may seem irrational. For example, a rational choice made by an individual with limited information may not appear rational to someone with more information. A consumer may pay a high price for a product when the identical item may be for sale at a much lower price elsewhere. But the consumer may not be aware that the other store carries the product, let alone at a lower price. Decisions are often made with less than perfect information. Information has a cost in time, and sometimes in money.

Often the information required for utility-maximizing behavior may not be available. For example, the government spends approximately $50 billion a year ($47.5 billion in fiscal 2008) to acquire intelligence on the capabilities and intentions of other countries and organizations like Al-Qaida. Much of the information gathered must overcome efforts to deny US intelligence collectors access to their organization or national security secrets. The government must formulate national security policy based on the best available intelligence, which will usually be less than complete information. Intelligence failures, such as the terrorist attacks of September 11, 2001, occur when there is an incorrect assessment of the intelligence information, or an inability to uncover all critical information. The terrorist attacks were a tactical surprise in that the willingness of Osama bin Laden to attack US targets had been clearly demonstrated by the 1998 US embassy bombings in Kenya and Tanzania and the bombing of the USS *Cole* in 2000. In the summer of 2001, the US intelligence community warned of the likelihood of another attack. US intelligence, however, did not uncover the means of attack or the targets.

Even if the full range of information needed to make a truly rational, self-interested choice is unavailable or too great for a person to adequately assimilate, the *process of choice* rather than the outcome of the process can still be considered rational. Behavior may be procedurally rational when it is the outcome of appropriate consideration based on incomplete information. Rational behavior does not mean that individuals never make a bad decision. Still, only a self-destructive individual will knowingly choose an inferior alternative to a more preferred one.

People may make irrational decisions, for example, by ignoring opportunity costs. An individual who squanders his money gambling and is then unable to pay his rent or mortgage has acted irresponsibly and, to a public choice theorist, irrationally. There is evidence that people learn from their experience and, when faced with a repeated situation, learn to consider opportunity costs. The concept of rational self-interest only holds that an individual would never knowingly choose a higher-cost means of achieving a given end when a lower-cost alternative is available. The notion that people will respond to incentives in predictable ways is central to rational choice and to public policy. If the cost of health care rises in real terms (adjusted for changes in inflation), less will be demanded. Drivers will buckle their seat belts if the perceived benefit (reduced risk of injury) outweighs the cost (the time spent buckling and the discomfort of the restraint). But if the cost of their use is viewed as exceeding the benefit, seat belts will remain unbuckled. People will try to reduce costs and increase their benefits.

Rational ignorance is the term used to describe ignorance about an issue that may be "rational" when the cost of acquiring all the relevant information to make an "informed" decision may be so high as to outweigh any benefit one might gain from that decision. For instance, a concern in the formation of public policy is whether people make informed choices when they vote. Anthony Downs labels the shortage of information gathered on the part of the public that votes "rational ignorance," which is the decision not to actively seek additional information. Voters often decide that it is not cost-effective to gather information. This feeling of excessive marginal cost in gathering information about political candidates can arise because information is often more ambiguous for public choices than for private choices. There are several reasons for this.

In the political market, voters must evaluate and select a package deal. This is unlike the commercial marketplace where, in buying apples or shirts, you can decide to buy one item more or one item less; that is, you can engage in making decisions at the margin. When you place an additional item in your shopping basket, you register a clear plebiscite for its production. However, when you vote in a political election, your vote is registered not for a single item supported by the political entrepreneur, but for the entire package of issues the candidate or party supports. Like many voters, you may vote for a candidate because of his or her support for a particular issue that is of intense interest to you such as defense spending. However, you also are likely to find several other items in the candidate's bundle that you really do not want.

Voting occurs infrequently and irregularly, in contrast to buying in the commercial marketplace where consumer choices are registered frequently and repetitively. In the commercial market, consumers communicate effectively when they cast millions of votes every day to producers by deciding to buy or not to buy the products offered. But the electorate does not have the opportunity, or perhaps the inclination, to vote frequently enough to send a clear signal to political entrepreneurs regarding its political desires. Voters typically get to vote for candidates only every two, four, or six years. This makes it difficult to find candidates who will reliably support public wants for their entire term and over the range of issues that often emerges after the election. It is impossible to know in advance whether a candidate will support a particular position on issues that were not foreseen at the time of the election. It also is impossible to know the final shape of future bills to be voted on by representatives.

This means political entrepreneurs are relatively free of control by the electorate.

The main control voters have is in elections in which an incumbent is running for re-election because they can retrospectively sanction or reject the candidate's record in the voting booth. With candidates running for the first time, voters can use indicators that provide clues about how the candidate might vote on unanticipated issues such as claims that he or she is "conservative" or "moderate." But picking someone based on a label is an inexact system.

The infrequency of elections also requires that many different choices be made at the same time. The many candidates and countless issues at the local, state, and national levels inevitably lead to great complexity for voters trying to make informed choices.

There also is little incentive for voters to be informed. The political realities noted above make it difficult for the best-intentioned voter to evaluate candidates and issues with confidence. The cost of acquiring useful information is very high. For example, when the financial crisis began in 2008 Alan Greenspan, the former chairman of the Federal Reserve Board, testified before Congress that he was "shocked" at the collapse of financial markets and conceded that his confidence in the ability of markets to police themselves had been a "mistake."[7] Former secretary of the treasury Henry Paulson indicated that his thinking had evolved from deregulation to regulation as a result of the financial storm.[8] Expert opinion was fluctuating and uncertain about the best way to deal with the crisis. Congressional opinion was also divided, but not clearly along party lines. Political pundits were also across the board in supporting different approaches. In such a situation, it is difficult for average citizens to obtain adequate information so that they can feel confident to make a rational assessment of how their elected officials should respond to the crisis.

Some voters will decide to remain rationally uninformed because they believe that the costs exceed the benefits of being fully informed on these issues. Others may choose to become free riders not only by refusing to gather any information, but also by not voting. If the choices of those who vote are advantageous to nonvoters, the nonvoting free riders will benefit without incurring any costs. More likely, however, the political entrepreneurs will soon discover who the nonvoters are and ignore those items in their package that would most benefit them.

Many voters reduce the cost of gathering information for themselves by relying on the "brand names" in the political marketplace: Republican and Democrat. Brand names are at least as important in the political market as in private markets. They provide information regarding general public philosophies. The packaging of a candidate as well as factors like incumbency also provide brand-name information regarding quality. An incumbent has a track record that can be evaluated and has a brand-name identification usually not found among challengers. Voters tend to support incumbent reelection bids just as consumers tend to develop brand-name loyalty to products they buy in stores.

Thus, there are important differences between the political and the private marketplaces. Communicating demands in the political marketplace through the process of infrequent voting is more problematic than communicating them on a daily basis through the process of buying and selling. Therefore, the political marketplace is less efficient than the private marketplace due in part to the design of the political marketplace.

Since any one person's vote is unlikely to affect the outcome of an election, there is less of an incentive for the average person to stay informed than if his or her vote would likely affect the outcome. This increases the power of special interest groups because unorganized voters have more diffuse interests and are less likely to become informed.

Rational self-interest may cause ambivalence because it evokes images of reason and informed decisionmaking on the one hand, but it can also suggest a sophisticated self-centered behavior. Therefore, it is important to note that rational self-interest is not the same as selfishness or greed. An individual who is injured in an accident and seeks medical attention is acting in their self-interest, but we would not accuse the individual of being selfish because of that action. By the same token, obeying the law may be in one's self-interest, but it is not selfish conduct. Selfish conduct is behavior

---

Case Study: The Irrational Voter

A more conservative view is that some activities in the public arena are the result not of rational ignorance, but of *irrationality*. This position maintains that political and religious views are sometimes held because they conform to aspects of a person's existing belief system. Many political and religious positions provide a statement of personal identification; that is, of who we are. Incorporating a new belief that does not require the reorganization of existing beliefs can be accomplished without resulting in cognitive dissonance. It can be accomplished most easily if an individual applies relaxed standards of analysis for acceptance in their belief system. However, this is not an argument that all political or religious beliefs are held for emotional reasons.

Critics claim that false beliefs about politics (and religion) are not costly to the individual, and may reinforce other already held beliefs. For example, an individual concerned about the potential of new terrorist attacks against the United States might have had a rational basis to conclude that John McCain would be a more vigorous fighter against terrorism. That individual may have accepted the charge that Barack Obama was "a Muslim" who was "not born in the United States" and who "pals around with terrorists" (even though the news media regularly debunked those claims) because the charge provided psychological support to the basic political belief that was supportive of Obama's opponent. Likewise, that individual would have been more inclined to accept the charge that Obama, as opposed to McCain, was a "socialist" because he would "redistribute the wealth," regardless of the fact that McCain also supported a progressive income tax that redistributes wealth. The irrational belief comes at no cost to the true believer, and in fact increases the comfort level of the rightness of their personal decision. However, if the average voter is irrational, the entire society may have to live with the resulting votes.

that disregards the interest of others in situations in which their interests should not be ignored. For example, to take an ample supply of food and water on a camping trip is not selfish, but to refuse to share some of the excess food with a hiker who is lost and without food would be.

Rational self-interest does not deny altruism. Individuals may act out of altruism by volunteering in soup kitchens or homeless shelters. However, rational self-interest does suggest that the altruistic behavior of individuals will be affected by changing perceptions of costs and benefits. For example, if tax deductions for charitable contributions are reduced or eliminated, contributions will decline. Conversely, increasing the tax benefit for charitable contributions will result in an increase in contributions.[9] Neither does rational self-interest mean that individuals are motivated solely by the pursuit of material goods. Individuals may be motivated by love, justice, power, and other abstract influences. It is still true, however, that economic welfare may often be the basis for achieving even many nonmaterial goals.

None of the foregoing is meant to suggest that individuals consciously calculate benefits and costs before selecting an alternative. Rational self-interest describes *behavior,* not thought processes.[10] A physicist would describe the forces involved in achieving balance in riding a bicycle quite differently than the average child who rides one. However, the child riding a bike will act as if he or she has a physicist's understanding when, in fact, he or she does not.

Rational self-interest makes an assumption about the way people actually behave, and it is not a judgment about how they *should* behave. The term *rational* does not indicate approval or disapproval of the goal itself.

The Tragedy of the Commons

Any discussion of rational self-interested behavior should point out that individual rationality and group rationality may not be identical and may even be opposed. Briefly stated, the laissez-faire doctrine of the invisible hand strongly suggests that individuals pursuing their own private interests will unintentionally, but automatically, also serve society's interest. In 1968, Garrett Hardin published an influential article "The Tragedy of the Commons," which challenges that notion.[11] He theorized that, when a resource like a meadow is held "in common" with others having equal access to the resource, a "rational" herdsman will decide to increase his exploitation of the meadow by adding additional cattle since he will receive the almost undiluted benefit of the increase while the cost will be shared by all who are entitled to access. Other herdsmen acting with the same self-interest will then also add cattle to their herds, resulting in the disintegration of the entire commons from overgrazing. In Hardin's view, humans are selfish and are unconcerned about the impact of their actions on others. Only if the meadow were privately owned would a self-interested herdsman have an incentive not to overgraze the meadow. Therefore, Hardin concluded, all publicly owned property or other "commons" should be privatized to exploit the resource more efficiently. His theory has been influential. More recently, his theory has been seriously challenged on several grounds (see Chapter 12 for criticisms).

Special Interest Groups

A basic premise of rational public choice is that "political man" (political entrepreneurs, voters, and members of special interest groups) and "economic man" (producers and consumers) are one and the same person. In both roles, people decide on their preferences based on their rational self-interest, and act purposefully to bring about desirable outcomes. This also suggests why it may be difficult to develop a broad commitment in society to transfer benefits from those who pay and those who receive the benefit. And it indicates why the haves acquire more power with which to further their self-interest than do the have-nots.

It is based on the premise that competition takes place in the political arena. Although the coercive power of government is imposing, it is nonetheless limited by several factors. It is constrained, first, by the resources that it can command. The government relies on its taxing and spending powers in many instances to conduct public policy. The function of taxes is to transfer control over capital from the private sector to the public sector. By using this purchasing power to buy goods and services for the public, the government is altering the mix of goods and services that would be demanded if everything were left to the private sector. This inevitably means a move to a different point on the production possibilities curve (see Chapter 1).

The government is also constrained by the political landscape. For example, there are only two major political parties in the United States, which constrains the selection of alternatives by the voters. In the private sector, if there were only two firms producing a good, we would define the market as a shared monopoly with no competition to give consumers a choice.

The public choice theory of government stresses that government actions result from the efforts of politicians and government workers who attempt to maximize their own interests rather than the public interest. The desire to follow policies that promote the *general welfare* is not the only motivation of government officials. There may be different philosophical views about what constitutes the general welfare, and those views may be subject to change. Dedicated officials may have conflicting goals. For example, an elected official's views may clash with the majority that elected him or her, which may create a dilemma around the desire to be reelected.

Many *pork-barrel* projects would not have the support of a well-informed general constituency. It may nevertheless make sense for politicians to support a lot of pork-barrel projects. For example, supporting a project that is of interest to a politician's local constituency will probably translate into more jobs in the district, which will increase votes for the politician as well as campaign contributions. It may even result in increased wealth for the politician by providing more job prospects as a lobbyist after retiring from politics. By spending public tax money, the politician is transferring funds from the general financial "commons" to his or her district, which pays little of the cost but receives all of the gain.

The lobbyists for the special interest groups also behave rationally in that they stand to receive government largesse worth millions or even billions in return for relatively small investments in the form of campaign contributions and public relations efforts of "selling" the project. From their perspective, lobbyists face the risk of los-

---

Case Study: The Bridge to Nowhere: When Pork Projects Are Publicized

The Bridge to Nowhere illustrates the political fallout that can occur when the public is made acutely aware of a pork-barrel project. In this case, rival politicians were alert to the potential political advantage of focusing voters' attention on the gap between a politician's words and deeds.

Ted Stevens, the senior US senator from Alaska having served since December 1968, had a reputation for being irascible when challenged by his colleagues or groups outside the Senate. A public interest group, Citizens Against Government Waste, had been a frequent critic of Senator Stevens and his many pork-barrel projects for Alaska. Stevens was unrepentant and boasted to his constituents that he had worked to "bring home the bacon" for Alaska.[a]

In 2005, Stevens pushed for federal funding of a proposed Gravina Island Bridge, which came to be known as the "Bridge to Nowhere" by critics. The proposed bridge was to replace the ferry that connects Ketchikan to Gravina Island's fifty residents and the Ketchikan International Airport, and permit the development of large tracts of land on the island.[b] The ferry makes a ten-minute run to the island every thirty minutes during the off season. From May through September, the main tourist season, the ferry runs to the island every fifteen minutes.

The cost is $5 for each adult with a free same-day return and $6 per automobile each way.

The bridge was projected to cost $398 million. It would have crossed the Tongass Narrows so it was designed to be high enough to accommodate cruise ships that travel Alaska's Inside Passage during the summer. The bridge would have been almost as long as the Golden Gate Bridge.[c]

This proposed pork-barrel spending became widely known the day after the 2006 national appropriations bill covering transportation passed in the Senate. The following day, Senator Tom Coburn of Oklahoma offered an amendment to divert the funds for the Gravina Bridge to rebuild a heavily used bridge over Lake Pontchartrain that suffered major damage by Hurricane Katrina. Senator Stevens, the senior Republican in the Senate, fiercely opposed diverting funds to be used to repair a bridge damaged by Hurricane Katrina. He angrily threatened to resign from the Senate if Congress targeted only Alaska's transportation funds to repair hurricane damage unless funds were taken proportionally from every other state. Congress passed an appropriations bill that ultimately provided the amount of money originally intended for use by Alaska, but removed the requirement that the money would

continued

Case Study continued

be spent on the bridge. The confrontation over where the money could be spent most effectively made the news, however, and became part of an ongoing controversy. Congress, reacting to the national furor over the bridge, removed the earmark designation, but granted an equivalent amount of money to be used at Alaska's discretion.

In her campaign to become governor of Alaska in 2006, Sarah Palin visited Ketchikan and supported what had already become known as the Bridge to Nowhere. In October of that year, she indicated that she would like to see the bridge built, "while our congressional delegation is in a strong position to assist."[d] As governor, in 2007 Palin put forward a budget that did not include the $185 million state share of the funding. She said that Alaska would have to live within its means, "and it's clear that Congress has little interest in spending any more money on a bridge between Ketchikan and Gravina Island. Much of the public's attitude . . . is based on inaccurate portrayals of the

project."[e] Since Alaska could use the funds at its discretion, it would not need state matching funds.

Campaigning for president in the spring of 2008, McCain used the bridge as an example of wasteful federal spending on politicians' pet projects.[f] He said that the collapse of the Minneapolis I-35 bridge could be blamed on the misappropriation of funds for projects like the Bridge to Nowhere.[g] In her speech at the Republican Convention after being introduced as McCain's vice presidential nominee, Palin said, "I told Congress, thanks but no thanks on that bridge to nowhere." Political leaders of both parties in Alaska said her claim was false as she had supported the bridge and the earmark during her run for governor and said at the time that it was insulting to use the term "bridge to nowhere."[h] Despite these challenges, Palin continued to repeat her applause line to Republican audiences that she said "thanks but no thanks to the bridge to nowhere." Democrats and Independents grew increasingly skeptical of her candor.

Notes: a. Senator Stevens Pork Tally, "Citizens Against Government Waste," available at www.cagw.org/site/PageServer?Pagename=reports_pigbook2008 (accessed November 15, 2008).

b. "Ketchikan Gravina Island Access Project," Alaska DOT, available at www.dot.state.ak.us/stwdplng/projectinfo/ser/Gravina/index1.shtml (accessed November 14, 2008).

c. Nick Jans, "Alaska Thanks You," *USA Today,* May 17, 2005, available at www.usatoday.com/news/opinion/editorials/2005-05-17-alaska-edit_x.htm (accessed November 14, 2008).

d. "Where They Stand," *Anchorage Daily News,* October 22, 2006, p. 2.

e. State of Alaska, "Gravina Access Project Redirected," September 9, 2007, press release, available at www.dot.state.ak.us/stwdplng/projectinfo/ser/Gravina/assets/scoping_summary_report.pdf (accessed November 15, 2008).

f. Yereth Rosen, "Palin, 'Bridge to Nowhere' Line Angers Many Alaskans," September 1, 2008 (Reuters).

g. David Waldman, "McCain Once Blamed Palin's Bridge for the MN Collapse," *Daily Kos,* available at www.dailykos.com/storyonly/2008/9/10/103448/087 (accessed August 17, 2009).

h. Rosen, "Palin, 'Bridge to Nowhere.'"

ing the grant of taxpayer funds to interest groups in other parts of the country if they do not win these favors.

Taxpayers likewise behave rationally. Typically, the cost of defeating any one government pork-barrel project is high, but the savings to the individual taxpayer if successful will be small. Taxpayers pay only a few dollars for any given pork-barrel project so, even if they defeat a specific project, the discretionary congressional funds may merely be transferred to another project resulting in no net savings to the taxpayer. Most taxpayers will decide that it is too costly to inform themselves about most pork and will remain rationally ignorant of projects except those that may directly benefit themselves. They reserve the right to rail against "wasteful government spending" in the abstract, however.

Politicians, taxpayers, and special interest lobbyists have rational incentives to engage in their respective behaviors, even though the goal of promoting the general welfare would be to oppose the project.

Rent Seeking

An occurrence closely related to government pork-barrel projects is known as rent seeking. **Rent seeking** involves an individual or a firm that attempts to make money by influencing the economic or legal environment rather than through a contribution to profit-seeking market transactions in which a buyer and a seller engage in mutually beneficial exchanges. Rent seeking, by contrast, is held to be detrimental because it reduces the efficiency of the market. Rent seeking is based on the premise that self-interested groups can use political power to seek legal privileges from government. We noted in Chapter 1 that government has legitimate authority to engage in numerous policies to promote the general welfare such as subsidies, contracts, and licenses. This is especially true in the face of market failure.

In practice, it may be difficult to distinguish between legitimate government intervention to remedy market failure or to prevent a market outcome that society is not willing to accept and detrimental rent seeking by a special interest group seeking the benefits of higher profit.

Taxi medallions are a classic example of the problem. Many cities attempt to encourage a viable taxi service within an urban area by requiring all legal taxies to purchase a medallion from the city. The number of medallions is limited, which limits the supply of taxi services. Presumably, the holders of medallions are required by the city to provide a required level of quality of service and training of cab drivers. But because the supply of taxies is limited, passengers are forced to pay a higher fee transferring more wealth to the medallion holder than competitive market forces would require.

Since all elected officials are subjected to their own conflicting pressures, it is not accurate to think of the government as a single entity having a well-defined set of objectives. The government acts through a distinctive assortment of institutional arrangements to develop public policy. Our representative democracy is based on majority voting, frequently focused through special interest groups, and its policies and programs are implemented by a government bureaucracy. Rational public choice theory makes it clear that government policymaking, like market allocation, may not result in the best attainable outcome. A society may be faced with the dilemma of choosing between a market solution that is imperfect and a government policy that is also not perfect. Simplistic notions demanding that we should return to basics and "let the market do it" or that we should abandon the market and "let government do it" must themselves be abandoned. Instead, the costs and benefits of market solutions to social problems, government solutions, or a combination of the two must be examined in order to select policies that will be the most effective in meeting society's needs.

Cost-Benefit Analysis

Public policy is the political decision by a state to take action. The increasing use of cost-benefit analysis to gauge the appropriateness of a policy decision typifies the application of market-based criteria to gauge the appropriateness of state action. **Cost-benefit analysis** is one of the most widely used tools of policy analysts. Cost-benefit analysis finds and compares the total costs and benefits to society of providing a public good. When several options are being considered for adoption, the one with the greatest benefit after considering the costs should be selected.

The need for public goods compels government intervention to provide a variety of goods and services that the market will not produce on its own in an optimal quantity for the society. The government must then decide what kinds of goods to provide and in what quantity. However, the government cannot easily obtain the required information since consumers of public goods have incentives not to disclose their true preferences and to downplay their willingness to pay in the hope that others will be taxed. Moreover, when government moves to use resources to alter the mix of goods and services, there will inevitably be conflicting interests between political choices. Government finds itself in the middle of the adversarial relationship between those private sector forces that stand to lose or gain as a result of government action.

In theory, determining the optimal mix of output is uncomplicated. More government sector endeavors are advisable only if the gains from those activities exceed their opportunity costs. Basically, the benefits of a proposed public project are compared to the value of the private goods given up (through taxes) to produce it. But while the notion that the benefits or utility of a project should exceed its costs is uncomplicated enough in principle, determining this ratio in practice is exceedingly complex.

In theory, all the costs and benefits of a program should be identified and converted into monetary units covering the life of the proposed project. Ideally, an attempt is made to consider the negative externalities resulting from the program such as the roadside businesses that will be lost due to the construction of a new limited-access highway. In

Case Study: The Difficulty in Applying Cost-Benefit Analysis

The most efficient use of public resources would be to rank proposed programs from highest to lowest in terms of their benefit-cost ratios, and proceed to implement those programs in priority order, beginning with those having the highest ratios. This would meet one goal of cost-benefit analysis: determining the most efficient way of using public funds. But cost-benefit analysis has a second goal: determining the merit of specific government policies such as discouraging the use of disposable containers, encouraging higher average mile-per-gallon standards for use of gasoline by automobiles, promoting transportation safety, and establishing honesty in product labeling. "Merit" is different from "efficiency," but it also has economic consequences.

In dealing with private market goods, the demand for a particular good determines the benefits of its production. But in regard to some public goods, the benefits generated by their "output" are less clear. For example, government control over air quality usually involves political tradeoffs between a healthy and aesthetic environment and the loss of production of other economic goods. Reducing air pollution from automobiles increases the price of cars, which results in the decreased production of automobiles and therefore fewer jobs. In this case, the losers from this government policy are those whose jobs are lost or who cannot afford to buy a higher-priced car. The winners are those who advocate environmental protection, and those who will suffer fewer illnesses (or perhaps will not die) because of a cleaner atmosphere. The objective of public policy is to promote the welfare of society. The welfare of society must depend on the welfare of individuals. It is people that count.

Cost-benefit analysis emphasizes measurement and tangible factors. Its insistence on quantifying measures almost invariably stresses costs over benefits. The main reason for this is that, in areas such as education, environment, and health, policies produce benefits that cannot be quantified while the costs are much more easily calculated. How does one put a value on human life, for example? To the individual or his or her spouse or child, human life is priceless in that no amount of money would be accepted for those lives. However, lives are not priceless or we would provide everyone with unlimited health care, require cars to be much safer, and require much lower speed limits. Some courts have determined the value of a life by estimating what the individual might have earned if they had had a normal life expectancy. But this leads to the absurd conclusion that a disabled or retired person's life has no value. Another method is to examine the risks people voluntarily take in their jobs and how much they must be paid to agree to take them. Citizens may be aware of the costs of programs in terms of their taxes paid, but may not be aware of noticeable benefits for a recession or flood averted, or a healthier environment. Another defect of cost-benefit analysis is that it does not consider the distributional question of who should pay the cost and who should receive the benefits. It may be that a new highway will displace residents in a low-income housing project while it will benefit affluent business investors who own commercially zoned land along the proposed highway route.

The most serious defect of cost-benefit analysis, however, is that it seeks to maximize only the value of efficiency when other values, such as equity, justice, or even the environment, might deserve inclusion in the consideration of public policy decisions. Since it is not possible to reduce moral or ethical concerns to the requirements of cost-

continued

Case Study continued

benefit analysis, this means the analysts who use this approach must go beyond it in making their policy recommendations; not to do so will have the effect of positively excluding normative concerns. In a period of tight federal budgets, government officials often defend their reliance on cost-benefit analysis by claiming that they should not be involved in controversial "ideological" debates, but instead only with the most efficient policy. They may even assert a moral obligation to apply cost-benefit analysis in order to save taxpayers money. Such analysis is useful for clarifying approaches to problems, but it is not without methodological difficulties and it is certainly not "value free."

theory also, with benefits and costs measured in the same units, the benefits and costs of alternative policies can be determined not just within a policy sector, but also across diverse sectors. For example, cost-benefit analysis could be used to determine policy alternatives in health care such as whether funds would be more efficiently spent on prenatal care for pregnant women who are indigent, on AIDS research, or on a screening and preventive medicine program to reduce mortality from cardiovascular disease.

Political Entrepreneurs

Politicians play a role similar to business entrepreneurs when they seek votes for political office and when they make collective political decisions. In markets, consumers register their opinions about the value of a product by the simple decision of whether to buy it or not. Consumers register their votes with dollar bills. In political markets, politicians demand votes supplied by citizens. Technically, votes cannot be bought and sold in electoral markets. Instead, politicians must accumulate or purchase (bribe?) votes by carefully positioning themselves on a variety of policy issues in order to appeal to more voters than can opposing candidates. All politicians appeal to voters with an argument that suggests a bribe: "You should vote for me because I will do more for your welfare than will my opponent."

Positioning includes conveying impressions of greater talent, higher moral character, and a preferred vision of the nation's future. Politicians with strong policy views on some issues may try to put them in a new context and suggest new arguments that voters may find appealing. Persuasion may be more successful with new issues about which many voters have not formed strong opinions.

An elected official also is expected to reflect the views of his or her constituents, not merely his or her own personal views. But unlike business, wherein consumers clearly "vote" on products by buying or not buying them, in politics the voting mechanism is not well suited to determining how constituents want to be represented on any given issue. Take education as an example. In theory, one votes for more education by electing the candidate committed to initiating new educational programs or putting more resources into the sector. Nonetheless, in practice it is much more complicated than this since every candidate campaigns on a whole series of issues, of which education is only one. Thus, the winning candidate may have been elected on the basis of issues other than his or her position on education or even despite it. This makes constituent views on any issue difficult to discern, and there is no reliable way to assign weights to the different views of voters.

Furthermore, fewer than half of those eligible to vote usually participate in any given election. Presidential elections draw the highest voter turnout while, for off-year congressional and state elections, the turnout rarely exceeds 40 percent of those registered to vote.[12] Presidential voter turnout peaked at 63 percent of persons over twenty-one years of age in 1960. In 2008, 131.2 million voters turned out to vote. As a percentage of the eligible voter population of 208.3 million, the 2008 turnout would be 63 percent of eligible voters, which would be the highest turnout since 1960. Another estimate calculates the eligible voter population at 212.7 million, which would put the 2008 turnout at 61.7 percent of eligible voters, the highest turnout since the election of 1968.[13] Obama won 52.9 percent of the popular vote, which was the highest percentage for a Democrat since Lyndon Johnson was elected in 1964. Voters in 2008 elected the first African American as president and the first Catholic as vice president. (See Table 3.1.)

The Voting Paradox

Majority rule does not generate such manifestly unfair results if voters act rationally in their decisions. But for rational behavior to occur, **transitivity** is necessary.[14] However, majority rule may not necessarily generate a transitive group decision, even though each individual chooses rationally.

Table 3.2 shows an example of what happens when transitivity is violated. In this example, the situation is perfectly symmetrical in that all three voters rank their preferences for three different issues. Every policy is one person's first choice, another person's second choice, and yet another's third choice. But if two policy issues are voted on at a time, it will result in an intransitive ranking. Each person presumably ranks the issues in order of importance to themselves.

We have noted that political entrepreneurs have a particular incentive to be responsive to voters rather than to nonvoters. One way to accomplish this is by identifying and paying attention to the **median voter**. The median voter is the voter whose preferences lie in the middle of an issue, with half the voters preferring more and half preferring less. The theory predicts that, under majority rule, the median voter will determine the decision.[15]

To illustrate the principle of the median voter, suppose that five people must vote

Table 3.1 A Demographic Portrait of Voters, 2008

Characteristic	All Voters (%)	Obama (%)	McCain (%)	Other/No Answer (%)
Gender				
Female	53	56	43	1
Male	47	49	48	3
Race				
White	74	43	55	2
Black	13	95	4	1
Hispanic	9	67	31	2
Other	5	64	33	5
Religion				
Protestant	54	45	54	1
Catholic	27	54	45	1
Jewish	2	78	21	1
Political party				
Democratic	39	89	10	1
Republican	32	9	90	1
Independent	29	52	44	4
Age				
18–29 years old	18	66	32	2
30–44 years old	29	52	46	2
45–64 years old	37	50	49	1
65 years or older	16	45	53	2
Education				
No high school diploma	4	63	35	2
High school graduate	20	52	46	2
Some college	31	51	47	2
College graduate	28	50	48	2
Postgraduate study	17	58	40	2
Family income				
Under $15,000	6	73	25	2
$15,000–29,999	12	60	37	3
$30,000–49,999	19	55	43	2
$50,000–74,999	21	48	49	3
$75,000–99,000	15	51	48	1
$100,000–149,999	14	48	51	1
$150,000–199,999	6	48	50	2
Over $200,000	6	52	46	2
Military background				
Yes	15	44	55	2
No	85	54	44	2
Union membership				
Member	12	59	39	3
Non–union member	88	51	47	2

Source: Election Center 2008, CNN.com, available at www.cnn.com/ELECTION/2008/results/polls/#USP00p1 (accessed May 6, 2009).

Table 3.2 The Voting Paradox

Program	Colleen	Mike	Cassie
Education	1st choice	3rd choice	2nd choice
Health care	2nd choice	1st choice	3rd choice
Housing	3rd choice	2nd choice	1st choice

on a tax increase to provide more police protection for their community, as shown in Table 3.3. Since each voter's preference has a single peak, the closer another voter's position is to one's own, the more the second voter prefers it. Christy does not perceive a need to increase expenditures for police protection at all and would prefer no tax increase for that purpose. A movement from zero expenditures to $25 would be approved by Collie, Cassie, Chip, and Jim, however. And an increase to $75 would be approved by Cassie, Chip, and Jim. A movement to $125 would be thwarted by a coalition consisting of Christy, Collie, and Cassie. A preference for either extreme will be outvoted by four votes, and a preference for the second or fourth position will be blocked by three votes. But a majority will vote for an assessment of $75, which is the median voter's preference. Notice that the median voter in this example does not prefer the average amount of the proposed expenditures, but is merely the voter in the middle.

What does the model of the median voter predict? There are several conclusions that follow:

1. *Public choices selected may not reflect individual desires.* The system will result in many frustrated voters who feel that their views are not being considered. Many, perhaps the entire minority, will not have their views accepted.

The principle of the median voter will permit, and perhaps even require, that the views of those on the extreme left or right be neglected at least to the extent that no political entrepreneurs can overtly court those views beyond listening sympathetically and pointing out that they themselves are closer to those on the far right (or left) than are their opponents, who are "dangerously out of touch"—that is, at the other end of the spectrum.

Since the median voter determines the outcome, the intensity of the views of the other voters is irrelevant. Only the intensity of the median voter's view is significant. Thus, the most dissatisfied voters will likely be those on the far right or left. This is in distinct contrast to the market in private goods, where demand counted in terms of "dollar votes" clearly records the intensity of preferences.

2. *Candidates will try to seize the middle ground first, and claim to be moderate while labeling their opponents as "out of the mainstream" on the right or left.* In their effort to command the vital middle, candidates will portray themselves as moderates.

Table 3.3 The Median Voter

Voter	Most-Preferred Annual Tax Increase for Added Police ($)
Christy	0.00
Collie	25.00
Cassie	75.00
Chip	125.00
Jim	300.00

3. *Political candidates will prefer to speak in general rather than specific terms.* Voters (and candidates for public office) are inclined to agree on the ends much more than on the means to achieve those ends or, in some cases, the feasibility of reaching the ends. For instance, voters across the political spectrum agree that an expanding economy is preferable to a contracting economy. They agree that low unemployment rates are preferable to high unemployment rates. There is also a consensus that lower taxes are preferable to higher taxes, and that a good educational system is preferable to a bad educational system. However, there are great differences between how those we might label "conservative" and those we might label "liberal" think these goals might be accomplished. Conservatives tend to prefer pursuing them through less governmental intervention and private means while liberals are more likely to perceive a positive role for government in seeking what they perceive as public goods. Candidates will therefore be more likely to talk about the ends, on which there is more of a consensus, than the means, on which there is wide disagreement.

Voting and the Political Marketplace

If politicians are the entrepreneurs of the political marketplace, voters are the consumers, looking out for their best interests by voting for the candidates who promise them the most benefits. As noted above, many people who are eligible to vote do not exercise this right. The key question is: What motivates a person to vote? There is a cost to voting, and the probability of a single voter determining the outcome of an election is extremely small. Therefore, the marginal costs of learning about the issues and the candidates' positions, registering to vote, and going to the polls may exceed the marginal benefit of voting. If, however, the candidates have staked out contrasting positions on certain issues and there are indications that the election will be close, the marginal benefit of voting increases and voter turnout also rises.[16] In essence, it appears that individuals do make a cost-benefit analysis of their interests in resolving to vote. And in addition to the benefits hoped for from a candidate's promises, voters also receive the psychological "benefit" of knowing they have performed their civic duty.

Interest Groups: Added Muscle in the Policy Market

An **interest group** is a collection of individuals with intensely held preferences who attempt to influence government policies to benefit its own members. Because their interests are strongly affected by public policies in a particular area, their members keep themselves well informed regarding legislation in that area. This contrasts with the general voter who is often uninformed on many issues because the cost of acquiring information is deemed too high relative to its benefit. And if a proposed policy will confer benefits on one group while imposing costs on another, both affected groups will probably organize—one to support and the other to oppose the policy. For example, teachers will be well informed about tax laws and programs that support public education or hurt it. Members of the teaching profession usually know much more about the laws affecting education than does the general public. Therefore, as individuals, they make informed voting decisions and, through teacher organizations, they lobby for or against specific laws.

The existence and importance of special interest groups lie in the principle of rational ignorance. Individuals, and members of groups, are more likely to have incentives to seek information concerning candidates' stands on issues that affect them personally. They are more likely to try to influence other people to adopt their positions, to take an active part in campaigning for candidates supporting their interests, and to vote. Political entrepreneurs seeking election thus try to court special interest groups at the expense of the general welfare. Consequently, special interest groups are likely to have significant effects on policy decisions in areas where they have the most to gain or lose by the outcomes.

The high costs of running modern campaigns, necessitated by television advertising and so forth, make political candidates more eager for offers of campaign contributions from special interest groups. The less the general public is informed, the more likely cost to a politician for supporting special interest group policies, related to the benefit of the campaign contribution, diminishes.

There are, however, limits on the influence of special interests. Politicians seeking election or reelection typically take money from interest groups in return for supporting positions favorable to those groups. Although they need contributions to mount successful campaigns, they may be wary of accepting money from groups whose positions may be unacceptable to **unorganized voters**. Interest groups themselves are aware that it may be best not to press legislators in causes to which the unorganized voters are hostile. Thus, legislators often vote as the unorganized, but interested, voters want, and congressional decisionmaking often takes into account the wishes of voters who are not members of interest groups. This can even diminish the possible number of special interest groups since, by not antagonizing unorganized voters, it encourages them to remain unorganized.[17]

Special interest groups propose and support legislation they perceive as important to their interests; in general, voters who are not members of such groups are not likely to oppose such legislation or to lobby politicians against it if they do not think it will affect them adversely or at all. As an example, assume that a state proposes to reduce the budget for its state-supported university system because of a shortfall of tax receipts. The state may propose a reduction in the faculty and staff, to be accompanied by an increase in tuition for the students. Since the faculty, staff, and students will bear the brunt of this decision, they may form an interest group to propose an increase in taxes within the state to be used not just to avoid layoffs, but also to maintain low tuition and even increase faculty and staff salaries. In other words, this interest group is petitioning the state to raise the wealth of its members at the expense of general taxpayers. They are demanders of a transfer of wealth from the state.

The suppliers of this wealth transfer are the taxpayers who probably will not find it worthwhile to organize to oppose having their wealth taken away by the state university system. General taxpayers probably will be less well informed about this legislation than members of the special interest group. But even if they are well informed, they will have to calculate the costs and benefits of opposing the legislation. Say that if the tax increase passed, the average taxpayer would have to pay out approximately $2. But he or she might have to spend $10 to defeat the proposal. Thus, even those who know about the legislation and are aware that its passage would cost them money probably would conclude that opposing it was not worth the cost.

The role of special interest groups in the making of public policy cannot be overemphasized. In a large and complex economy such as that of the United States, a high number of interest groups is to be expected. Many of the interest groups overlap. There are, for example, women's rights groups, minority rights groups, religious groups, physician groups, lawyer groups, and farmer groups. And special interest groups are responsible for much of the misallocation of public resources. However, legislation drafted for the benefit of special interest groups is not necessarily bad. Much of it may even benefit the general public. In the example above, education is a public good and the citizens of the state may be well served by having a good state university system for the general population. The point to be stressed is that the costs and benefits of being informed on certain issues and the marginal costs and benefits for lobbying for or against those issues are different for members of a special interest group than they are for the general public. It is this difference in the allocation of the costs and benefits of being informed and taking an active political stance that usually influences the type of legislation proposed and implemented.

James Madison denounced interest groups ("factions," he called them) as being the cause of instability, injustice, and confusion in democratic politics. He defined factions as "a number of citizens . . . who are united and actuated by some common impulse of passion, or of interest, adverse to the rights of other citizens, or to the permanent and aggregate interests of the community."[18] Since that time, every interest group has claimed to represent *the national interest* rather than a parochial interest. And each group has looked suspiciously at every other interest group as aggregations of conniving, self-seeking individuals.

The Bureaucratization of the Polity

The legislative branch of government passes laws and approves specific levels of public policy spending. The actual implementation of the laws and the actual distribution of funds are delegated to various agencies and bureaus of the executive branch. Bureaucrats, like politicians and the average voter, have a variety of interests.

In reality, bureaucrats are often attacked for being unresponsive to the public they serve. Still other critics complain that politicians make their bureaucracies too responsive to special interest groups instead of allowing them to impartially administer the programs for which they were created.

Bureaucrats are the unelected US government officials tasked with carrying out the programs approved by Congress and the president. Many laws are passed that are more symbolic than substantive insofar as they indicate the "intent" to ensure automotive safety, guarantee safe working conditions, or protect the environment, for example, without specifying exactly how to accomplish these goals. Bureaucrats must use their administrative authority to give meaning to vague platitudinous legislation and determine how the law will actually be applied.

Those working in bureaus tend to be supportive of the legislature's goals. They also prefer a growing budget, which usually correlates with opportunities for promotion and higher salaries for themselves. In public bureaucracies, there are no incentives to minimize budgets. Instead, bureaucrats try to maximize the sizes of their agencies through high salaries and the perquisites of office, power, and patronage. Within these organizations, in fact, a person's prestige and authority are measured by the number of personnel under his or her authority. (Even if bureaucrats did operate very efficiently, the general voter would be unaware of this due to the principle of rational ignorance.) Therefore, bureaucrats compete with other bureaucrats for a larger share of the available funds. Bureaus typically do not end each fiscal year with budget surpluses, but rather spend all their revenues before the end for fear of appearing not to need as much money in the future. Bureaucrats try to increase the size of their agency by influencing politicians who provide their budget. This leads them to typically exaggerate their claim of a mismatch between their responsibilities and their limited resources.

They may indeed be providing efficient services to the special interest groups that were responsible for the legislation creating the bureaus, and they may even be serving the public that is their clientele efficiently. But they must also answer to the legislature that funds and oversees them. It should be noted that, in doing this, bureaucracies have significant information advantages over the typical legislator who must be concerned with literally hundreds of different programs. And bureaucracies themselves provide the information that the legislators need to oversee the bureaus.

Those who criticize bureaucracies for being less efficient than private firms miss a fundamental point of the purpose of a bureaucracy. Typically, its existence is the result of some market failure—a situation in which market competition could not resolve some issue or issues. Consequently, a bureaucracy cannot be measured by normal market criteria. Many government bureaucracies provide services for which there is no competition. For example, there is only one place to get a driver's license or a zoning permit.

Public bureaucracies associated with high national purposes of the state, such as the military, the Central Intelligence Agency, or the Federal Bureau of Investigation, are generally held in high regard as patriotic public servants. Ironically, the members of the largest governmental bureaucracy, the military, often do not even consider themselves bureaucrats. Bureaucracies associated with domestic regulatory or redistributional programs that adversely affect the more privileged members of society are generally condemned as being wasteful and inefficient while the individual bureaucrats tasked with enforcing those policies are usually held in contempt as incompetent bumblers.

A Critique of Rational Choice

Rational choice theory began as an explanation of how a rationally self-interested person behaves in the marketplace. To the extent that individuals choose what they most prefer among potential choices in the market, they are engaging in rational behavior. The theory claims a scientific objectivity in alleging that it is descriptive of how people actually behave in markets without making any value judgment about that behavior. As a model of decisionmaking, the logic of rational choice has widespread application throughout the social sciences and has found increasing applicability in the policy sciences. Its strength is to be found in its illustration of how to make efficient choices and in the model's ability to explain individual as well as group behavior. Rational egoism, as a general rule, may be perfectly acceptable in the market. There is no reason for the individual contemplating a choice between purchases to be committed to any particular political philosophy. However, democratic forms of government require that rational individuals be concerned not only with their own personal well-being, but also with the general welfare of the community of citizens. The invasion of narrowly self-interested economic rationality into the political thought and behavior of individuals overwhelms and wreaks havoc on democratic politics.

Universal rational egoism assumes that individuals will act just as rationally, and just as self-interestedly, in political arenas as in economic markets. It is supportive of Ayn Rand's philosophy of "objectivism," which holds that unlimited greed produces unlimited good. In economic thinking, there is a strong bias in favor of free markets, and a great concern that any government intervention will reduce efficiency. This same bias against government is evident in the beliefs of many policy scientists who have adopted rational choice thinking. Supporters of the rational choice model claim the analysis describes government and political behaviors *as they are,* free from any wishful notions about how they *should be.*[19] Nevertheless, the conclusions of public choice have a clear bias in favor of free market principles and limited government. Critics point out that rational choice disregards the role that culture plays in modifying and restricting decisionmaking. Rationality can mean different things in different cultures.[20] In the fall of 2008, Alan Greenspan, former chairman of the Federal Reserve, conceded that his opposition to regulation of banks and other financial institutions had been a "mistake." Greenspan was asked by Henry Waxman, the chairman of the House Oversight and Government Committee, if he found that his "ideology was not right, it was not working?"[21] "Absolutely," Greenspan replied.

Social choice theory even interprets bureaucracy as being concerned primarily with increasing its budget and power. The conclusion is that most government agencies are not in the public interest. The obvious implication for anyone suspicious of government is that all bureaucratic organizations and budgets are too large, so budgets may be cut without fear that the affected agencies cannot continue to carry out their responsibilities. The main problem for "responsible" government, then, is little more than to rein in out-of-control agencies.

The average citizen has a modest interest in policy issues, but the costs are too high relative to the benefits for him or her to become well versed on either the specific issues or the policy positions of elected officials. Politicians have a positive incentive not to inform the voters on specific policy proposals, but only to speak in general of the goals of "peace and prosperity." Rather than speaking to the public about policy issues, they can be expected to espouse ethical principles and humbly acknowledge their own moral rectitude while castigating that of their opponent. Citizens are often rationally ignorant and not in a position to monitor public policies in a manner assumed by democratic theory. However, elites usually formulate policies in a way that maximizes their benefits in the theory.

In the rational choice model, which is descriptive of what *is,* without passing judgment, politics is little more than a game in which all participants seek to maximize their benefits while treating the cost as a negative externality to be transferred to the commons (all taxpayers). The world of politics as viewed through the lens of rational choice is almost unrecognizable to the student of liberal democratic thought. There is no doubt that the economic calculus of public choice (rational egoism) explains an important facet of the human psyche. This explanation has grown, and is accepted, to the point that it threatens to crowd out other approaches.

Rational choice theory has a difficult time explaining altruistic behavior. Why do individuals who perceive no benefit to themselves for helping others nevertheless do so? Rational choice theory would not predict that individuals would engage in "good Samaritan behavior." Nor do rational choice theorists have an easy explanation for collective action for the general welfare. For example, even though the cost of collecting information and going to the polls to vote outweighs the likelihood that the vote will have any influence on the outcome of the election, millions of people do go to the polls.

Finally, many cognitive psychologists argue that individuals usually do not have complete information and therefore cannot ascertain the "best" choice from a rational perspective. As a result, individuals are more likely to seek a minimum level of satisfaction (rather than the maximum) from their decisions. This is referred to as "satisficing."

On the positive side, a contribution of the theory has been to suggest to policymakers one avenue to develop public policies. We agree that a competitive market can allocate resources efficiently and without any guidance from government. At the same time, we recognize that the market has several weaknesses. The market is unable by itself to cope with business cycles and unemployment, income inequality, or the consequences of a concentration of market power and money. A market does not protect the commons. The market is incapable of providing public goods. Many of society's most urgent public policy issues—urban decay, pollution, the social unrest that is attributable to poverty—are to some degree the result of some market shortcoming.

Many market imperfections can be treated by policies that make use of the market's mechanisms. Policymakers increasingly attempt to take incentives of the free market into account when designing public policy. Privatizing government operations is one such effort to use the profit motive to increase efficiency. Deregulation of some industries, such as airlines and trucking, is an example. The effort to use market mechanisms to control pollution is another example. As noted earlier, many critics of this approach feel that permitting businesses to pay a fee to pollute removes the moral stigma from the act. The right to pollute is reduced to any other market good that can be bought or sold. In the case of the tragedy of the commons, each individual acts rationally in their self-interest, with the result being collective irrationality. The basic consequence of public choice is that of "rational man, irrational society."[22]

Adam Smith, writing in an earlier age, thought of economics as a part of moral philosophy. It never occurred to him that economics might be thought of as value free (see Chapter 5). On the contrary, his theory was based on the desire to improve the situation of the masses. As he wrote in *Wealth of Nations*: "Consumption is the sole end and purpose of all production; and the interest of the producer ought to be attended to, only so far as it may be necessary for promoting that of the consumer."[23]

Robert Heilbroner has pointed out that economists today claim to engage in value-free scientific thinking because the prestige associated with pursuing a science resembles the grandeur of religious pursuits in an earlier age. He holds that all "economic analysis is shot through with ideological considerations whose function is to mask the fullest possible grasp of some of the properties of a capitalist social order."[24] The social sciences cannot achieve the rigor (or objectivity) of the natural sciences as long as the worth of the individual is valued. Normative values regarding the worth of life, health, and human dignity permeate public issues. In fact, as members of a social order, it is impossible for us to describe this order without using the feelings of attachment and identification that make us a part of the fabric of society. A nonideological being could not exist as a sentient member of society.

This is as it should be, especially in public policy, since its purpose is to promote the general welfare. The next two chapters explore the relationship between the individual and society.

Conclusion

Markets fail to produce ideal outcomes in the best-attainable allocation of goods and services. Democratic governments are asked to intervene to correct the deficiencies of market outcomes, but must do so through the institutions of representative democracy with voting procedures, political entrepreneurs, and interest groups serving as intermediaries.

The process is one in which individuals in politics act, as people are assumed to do in the marketplace, on the basis of their rational self-interest. Rational public choice theory offers an explanation regarding how individuals act in the political marketplace. It should be seen as a view about how the system actually works and not how the system *should* work.

In some ways, the government is even less efficient than the private marketplace. This is particularly true in limiting voters to infrequent elections and in requiring the political "package deals."

Special interest groups are organized voters who see their self-interest bound up with a specific issue, are informed about it, and are therefore inclined to vote based on that issue. The general population of potential voters, following the principle of rational ignorance, is likely to be uninformed about and indifferent to most political issues. Special interest groups, then, have a political influence out of proportion to their numbers, although politicians are reluctant to antagonize the general voting population needlessly because they too have the potential to mobilize and retaliate through their own interest groups.

The accumulation over time of legislation for the benefit of special interest groups redirects public resources toward those groups at the expense of the unorganized and less-likely-to-vote general public, particularly the poor. This may result in further movements away from the ideal of government correction for market failures.

Rational choice thinking is a valuable tool for policy scientists. An overemphasis on the model can legitimize an approach to public policy that treats all issues and positions as of equal value. In such a scenario, the role of policy scientists is reduced to tabulating wins and losses for different groups.

Questions for Discussion

1. What is public choice theory? How does it help in analyzing public behavior and policy?

2. How can democratic voting behavior lead to undemocratic results? Can this be squared with the idea of justice?

3. Why do political candidates move to the center in a single-peaked two-party system?

4. Why do candidates prefer to campaign on general terms rather than specific issues? Conversely, why do candidates reduce an opponent's general stands into specific positions?

5. What is rational ignorance? Can this be squared with the democratic ideal of an informed citizenry?

Notes

1. The adaption of this theory from economics to political science began with William Riker at the University of Rochester in the 1950s. But it has developed most broadly in the Virginia state university system, especially at George Mason University, Virginia Tech, and the University of Virginia, and is sometimes referred to as the Virginia school. James M. Buchanan Jr., an economist from George Mason University, won a Nobel Prize for his work in this area (1986).

2. See William H. Riker, *Liberalism Against Populism: A Confrontation Between the Theory of Democracy and the Theory of Social Choice* (San Francisco: Freeman, 1982). See also William C. Mitchell, *Government as It Is* (London: Institute of Economic Affairs, 1988).

3. Abraham Maslow, "A Theory of Human Motivation," *Psychological Review* 50 (1943): 370–396.

4. As an economic term, *efficiency* is defined as maximizing output with given resources (costs). It implies the impossibility of gains in one area without losses in another.

5. Robert B. Reich, *The Resurgent Liberal and Other Unfashionable Prophecies* (New York: Vintage Books, 1989), p. 259.

6. For an excellent summary of rational self-interest, see Henry Demmert, *Economics: An Understanding of the Market Process* (New York: Harcourt Brace Jovanovich, 1991), pp. 4–6.

7. Helen Thomas, "Greenspan Hints at Humility," *New York Times,* October 29, 2008, available at www.thebostonchannel.com/news/17840602/detail.html (accessed August 14, 2009).

8. David Cho, "A Conversion in 'This Storm,'" *Washington Post,* November 18, 2008, p. 1.

9. Opinions regarding what motivates individual choices are often raised in public policy discussions. There is an often heard contention that there are no truly altruistic acts. Unselfish acts, such as volunteering to work in a soup kitchen to feed the hungry, make people feel morally correct by giving them a clear conscience. Thus, actions are altruistic only at a superficial level. On closer examination, the motivation to act "altruistically" is really a motivation to achieve the self-satisfaction of thinking of oneself as being a good person.

To derive satisfaction from helping others does not make one selfish. The unselfish person does derive satisfaction from helping others while the selfish person does not. The truly selfish person is unconcerned about the suffering of others. It is sophistry to conclude that, because an individual finds satisfaction in helping to feed the poor, he or she is selfish. If we ask *why* someone gains satisfaction from volunteering to work in a soup kitchen, the answer is that the individual cares about other people, even if they are strangers; the volunteer does not want them to go hungry and is willing to take action to help them. If the individual were not this kind of person, he or she would receive no satisfaction in helping others; this feeling of satisfaction is a mark of unselfishness, not of selfishness. See James Rachels, *The Elements of Moral Philosophy* (New York: McGraw-Hill, 1986), pp. 56–60.

10. Rachels, *The Elements of Moral Philosophy.*

11. Garrett Hardin, "The Tragedy of the Commons," *Science,* December 13, 1968, pp. 267–292.

12. Usually about two-thirds of those eligible to vote are registered in local elections. Thus, a political entrepreneur may win an election with the support of only about 20 percent of those eligible to vote, which reduces any legitimate claim to a mandate. See Norman R. Luttbeg, "Differential Voting Turnout." See also "Elections," in US Census Bureau, *Statistical Abstract 1996* (Washington, DC: US Government Printing Office, 1996), pp. 267–292.

13. "Report: '08 Turnout Same As or Only Slightly Higher Than '04," CNN, available at http://politicalticker.blogs.cnn.com/2008/11/06/report-08-turnout-same-or-only-slightly-higher—than-04 (accessed May 6, 2009).

14. The "transitivity axiom" states that, if preferences are transitive, then all the alternatives can be placed in order whenever there are more than two choices. Therefore, if *a* is preferred to *b,* and *b* is preferred to *c,* then *a* is preferred to *c.* This permits ranking alternatives from the most to the least preferred.

15. This assumes that the voters have single-peaked preferences so that, as they move away from their most preferred position in any direction, their utility of outcome consistently falls.

16. See Yoram Barzel and Eugene Silberberg, "Is the Act of Voting Rational?" *Public Choice* 16 (Fall 1973): 51–58.

17. See Arthur T. Denzau and Michael C. Munger, "Legislators and Interest Groups: How Unorganized Interests Get Represented," *American Political Science Review* 80 (March 1986): 89–106.

18. James Madison, *The Federalist* no. 10.

19. See James Buchanan, "Politics Without Romance: A Sketch of Positive Public Choice and Its Normative Implications," in Alan Hamlin and Philip Pettit, ed., *Contemporary Political Theory* (New York: Macmillan, 1991), pp. 216–228. See also Mitchell, *Government as It Is.*

20. Ellen Coughlin, "How Rational Is Rational Choice?" *Chronicle of Higher Education,* December 7, 1994, p. A16.

21. Helen Thomas, "Greenspan Hints at Humility."

22. See Brian Barry and Russell Hardin, ed., *Rational Man and Irrational Society?* (Bev-

erly Hills: Sage, 1982). See also Robert H. Frank, *Falling Behind: How Rising Inequality Harms the Middle Class* (Berkeley: University of California Press, 2007).

23. Adam Smith, *An Inquiry into the Nature and Causes of the Wealth of Nations,* edited by Edwin Cannan (New York: G. P. Putman's Sons, 1877; originally published in 1776), p. 660.

24. Robert Heilbroner, "The Embarrassment of Economics," *Challenge: The Magazine of Economic Affairs,* November–December 1996, pp. 46–49.

4

Polarized Politics, Ideology, and Public Policy

From the beginning of the American Revolution, waged against a monarch that perceived few limits to his power, until the Great Depression beginning in 1929, most Americans accepted the notion "that government is best which governs least."[1] The Founding Fathers who gathered in Philadelphia in 1787 were known at the time as "classical liberals" because they advocated the right of individuals to be free from the overwhelming, arbitrary, and often malevolent governmental power.

All the basic tenets of modern conservatism flowed from the opposition to government's power. For instance, it was widely believed that an unregulated market economy tended toward full employment of men and capital. Therefore, any economic slowdown was only temporary since the market would soon self-correct without any government intervention. Involving the government in resolving political or economic controversies should occur only as a last resort. It logically follows, then, that government should be kept small to avoid the temptation for it to meddle unnecessarily in political and economic issues. One of the highest duties of government was to protect private property. Conversely, government should not interfere in the personal lives of its citizens. Governments tend to be wasteful, and the private sector (business model) is invariably more efficient so it should be preferred over government solutions. To ensure a small and efficient government, taxes should be kept to a minimum. It was also generally believed that government spending should not exceed government expenditures. A balanced budget would force the government to live within its means. Since the status quo has a claim on legitimacy, change should come slowly when it is necessary. Those holding these beliefs would later become known as modern-day "conservatives."

By the late 1800s, many classical liberals became convinced that democratic government could increase individual freedoms through expanding voting rights, abolishing slavery, promoting education, promoting public health, and a myriad of other policies.

These individuals became modern-day liberals while the classical liberals who were primarily anxious over a powerful government became the modern-day conservatives.

The Great Depression challenged the assumptions of the classical model of economics. Franklin Roosevelt's New Deal did for public policy what John Maynard Keynes's theory did to economic notions of laissez-faire (Chapter 5 discusses the economic theory in greater detail). Although the classical theory of economics was discredited by Keynesian theory, the basic tenets of conservatism rose like a phoenix from the ashes based on the political struggle for power in public policy. Ronald Reagan embodied the antigovernment philosophy of the classical era with the slogan in his inaugural address: "Government is not a solution to our problem; government is the problem."[2]

How these ideological changes took place from the early days of the Republic and its significance today is the subject of this chapter.

Institutions and the Political Environment

The impact of the Revolutionary War, the experience with the Articles of Confederation, and the negotiations at the Constitutional Convention were determining influences on the institutions of government that were created. The institutions created have, in turn, had a profound influence on the political environment.

As noted above, the Founding Fathers were particularly concerned about protecting the citizenry from the arbitrariness of dictatorial authority, with which they were all too familiar from dealings with the British monarchy. They were determined to prevent such a concentration of power in the executive branch of government. Their concern became the Constitution's most distinguishing feature: the **institutional fragmentation** and decentralized sources of power.

It is important to remind ourselves that a major reason for frustration over the seeming inability of government to deal decisively and effectively with issues of public policy was an intentional part of the design of the Constitution. The Constitution was purposely designed to make governing difficult—not to simplify political choices, but to complicate them. Rather than entrusting political leaders with sufficient control, it hinders them with insufficient authority. The framers of the Constitution designed the institutions of government to slow the policy process, through the system of checks and balances, in the belief that this would help reason to triumph over passion.

The members of the Constitutional Convention agreed that the Continental Congress had erred in the direction of being too weak and powerless when it wrote the Articles of Confederation. Individual liberty had not been threatened, but the national government was totally dependent on the states to validate and ratify all of its actions, and could not control the competitive impulses of the states that worked against the common national interest. European powers recognized this as an opportunity and sought to exploit the competition between states regarding overlapping claims on western territories and trade and tariff policies that weakened the unity of the new nation.

The failure of government under the Articles of Confederation to meet these and other challenges was the reason for the Constitutional Convention of 1787. The delegates agreed on the need to develop a new form of national government that could avoid the problems of "excessive democracy" of the state and national government experienced under the Articles. And while there were disagreements on many features of the proposed government, there was no disagreement on the principle of **separation of powers**—the notion that the powers of government must be separated into legislative, judicial, and executive branches. They believed that this separation of powers and federalism would prevent a national government abusive of its power. James Madison also expressed concern that a legislature could not be counted on to act for the common good when competing issues were presented:

> No man is allowed to be a judge in his own cause because his interest would certainly bias his judgment, and, not improbably, corrupt his integrity. . . . Yet what are many of the most important acts of legislature but so many judicial determinations, not indeed concerning the rights of single persons, but concerning the rights of large bodies of citizens? . . . It is in vain to say that enlightened statesmen will be able to adjust these clashing interests and render them all subservient to the public good. Enlightened statesmen will not always be at the helm.[3]

Ultimately, **checks and balances** were designed to prevent any power from becoming the undisputed dominant force. Thus, governmental power was divided among the three branches, and each branch was to be given authority to prevent encroachments on its power by the others. As Madison said in his famous maxim: "Ambition must be made to counter ambition."[4]

The tendency toward excessive democracy in the House of Representatives would be checked by senators who would have staggered six-year terms (as opposed to two-year terms in the House) and were to be appointed by the state governments rather than elected directly by the people.[5] To enhance its status, the House was given exclusive power to originate revenue bills. This compromise conciliated the small states by allowing them to dominate in the Senate, and appeased the large states by allowing them to dominate in the House.

The executive branch, which was to administer and execute the laws adopted by the legislative branch, was treated in a rather cursory manner, but there were fears here too. Benjamin Franklin worried that a unified executive would have the potential to drift to monarchy because of a natural human tendency to prefer strong government. But in fact, the Constitution says little about the powers of the presidency. Chief executives have relied on the clause that declares "the executive power shall be vested in a president" to expand their authority. The Constitution does not even define "executive power," which has allowed presidents to claim that their actions fall within the realm of inherent executive powers not precisely spelled out.

In an effort to give the federal government more power, the president was given the power to appoint major department personnel and veto congressional enactments (although Congress can override a veto with a two-thirds vote). Over time, presidential power has vastly expanded relative to Congress. Congress has attempted to maintain its authority vis-à-vis a more assertive presidency by extending its own authority through more specific instructions on how public monies can be spent. The Founding Fathers wrote obscurely about the nature of the federal court system. The judiciary was expected to have a smaller role in the process of determining public policy than the other federal branches of government. The judiciary's expanded role in shaping public policy is the result of its landmark decision in *Marbury v. Madison* (1803) when it claimed for itself the right to declare a law to be unconstitutional.[6] The Supreme Court has become much more activist in overturning acts of Congress and more deferential toward the president over the past thirty years. And presidents can shape the legal environment by carefully nominating judges and justices who share the president's legal views. The judicial system has become a major player in the foreign policy process. Since it was designed to be a major factor in the framers' separation of powers design, the judicial system's deference to presidential authority has led some scholars to question whether it will continue to play an effective role in the separation of powers.[7]

The US government has expanded in ways that would have astounded the Founding Fathers. However, the survival of the key features of their design—decentralization, separation of powers, checks and balances, and limited government—affirms the permanence of their effort. This fragmentation defies the effort to bring more orderly and empirical approaches to the policy process (see Figure 4.1).

Federalism and Fragmentation

One of the greatest obstacles faced by the framers of the Constitution was the knowledge that, regardless of the design of the document, they had to obtain ratification from the state legislatures for it to go into effect. Consequently, it was understood that the states would have to retain significant autonomy regardless of other governing arrangements. The difficulty, then, was to strengthen the national government so that it could carry out its will in certain necessary areas while reassuring the states that they would retain all their essential powers. The delegates crafted a system of **federalism** because it was the most they could hope that the states would accept. It was recognized that, under the Articles of Confederation, the states had ultimate authority, leaving the national government bereft of energy for meaningful policymaking. As in other areas of constitutional debate, the framers were not able to agree on a precise relationship between the national and state governments. The result was another compromise between national government and state power.

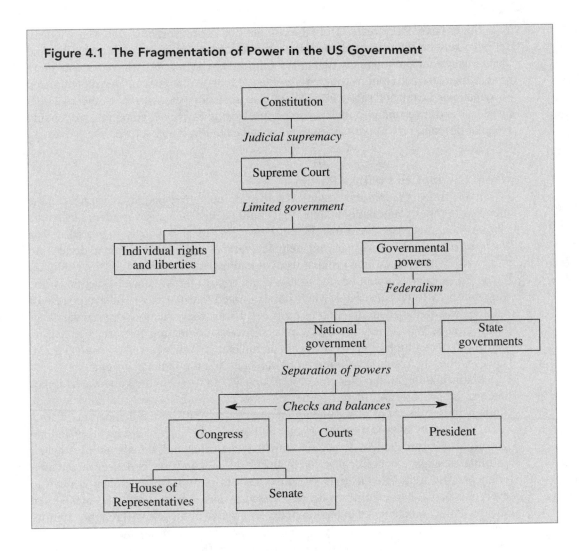

Figure 4.1 The Fragmentation of Power in the US Government

A major concern of the delegates in Philadelphia was to design a national government with enough power to protect private property and provide economic stability.[8] Since they accepted the principle that government has a responsibility to protect everyone's right to life, liberty, and property, it is clear that property held a preferred position. The delegates wanted to place the protection of property and commerce in the hands of the national government to protect them from state legislatures. They also specifically forbade the states to tax imports or exports, to coin money, to enter into treaties, or to impair obligations and contracts.

States have not retreated from the competition for power, however. Many federal policies rely on states to implement the programs. States have power through the dual banking system and the many regulations imposed by states. They have become more rather than less active in passing environmental legislation, consumer protection, and occupational health and safety laws. States also often compete with each other to attract business and investment to their jurisdictions, by offering tax exemptions, suspending regulations, and providing loan guarantees and even direct tax subsidies.

From Factions to Political Parties

While the framers feared the tyrannical rule of despots, they had also experienced the threats to property and national unity that could occur when a government lacked the ability to act because it had insufficient power. Madison famously indicated in *The Federalist* no. 10 the anxiety in Philadelphia over the tendency of people to divide into "factions" with each faction seeking its own interest without regard for the public interest. In fact, government needed to break and control the violence of factions if the Republic was to be successful. Madison also noted that the most enduring cause of factions was the unequal division of property. Today, these factions are known as interest groups. When there are many interest groups competing for influence and no one group or coalition of groups can gain dominance, they are forced to conduct themselves within the restrictions imposed by the laws and the judicial system.

Madison thought that these interest groups were a threat to the system. But today, interest groups are considered to be the essence of our modern pluralist system. **Pluralism** is a theory of government that attempts to reaffirm the democratic character of our society by asserting that public policy is the product of competition and negotiation between groups. It begins with the view that individuals acting in their self-interest engage in political action in an effort to obtain some benefit from the government. And although the right of individuals to participate in groups is open to everyone, active participation is heavily biased toward the most affluent members of society. Policy outcomes of competing interest groups, in theory, will roughly approximate the preferences of society in general. Overlapping group membership helps maintain the balance by preventing any single group from moving too far from societal norms.

Of course, groups may combine with each other to expand their power and influence with Congress through providing a combination of campaign contributions and electoral support with political parties. Groups could become powerful enough to dominate political parties.

Currently in the United States, the Democratic and Republican parties are the only two national parties that compete for elective offices and political power. In the young Republic, political parties were viewed as a threat to social order.[9] Today, it is impossible to think of a free society without competition between political parties for political power. But in fact, *political parties* are not mentioned in the Constitution, and indeed were created to override some of the features that are written into the Constitution. Political parties were developed to overcome the separation of powers and checks and balances found in the Constitution. Members of the same political party constitute an enduring coalition that encourages loyalty and cooperation between party members in all branches of government to achieve policy goals. This is despite the separation of powers and checks and balances that were designed by the Founding Fathers. Party leaders do not merely follow public opinion. As political "entrepreneurs," they try to shape the political environment by developing a public philosophy with consistent programs and policies to "sell" to the voting public. Voters, as consumers, attempt to purchase with their votes what is being offered in the political marketplace.

Political parties facilitate voter decisionmaking. Although voters often claim to vote for the best candidate, and not the party, it is clear that party labels provide a "brand-name" recognition for voters. Voters can make a decision with a reasonable amount of confidence about what position a candidate will probably take by knowing the politician's party affiliation. Voters' choices are made much simpler by determining whether a candidate's party affiliation matches their own.[10] Without the knowledge that politicians exhibit a certain loyalty to each other based on party affiliation, the voter would have to become aware of each candidate's position on a wide variety of issues to make informed decisions regarding his or her vote.

Politics in the United States is dominated by the Democratic and Republican parties, which encourage voter loyalty, provide candidates for elective office, organize campaigns and elections, and work to advance their own policy proposals. Political parties are unique among interest groups in that they try to control government by *seeking elective office*. Other interest groups *seek benefits through those holding office*. Political parties were formed primarily to develop and maintain enduring voting blocs around an interrelated set of policy issues under a given party label. The party serves to link the elites in governmental institutions and harmonize their views to the broad outlines of a public policy agenda.

Republicans and Democrats: Differing Views

From 1896 until 1932, the Republican Party was dominant. The only Democrat to win the White House in this period was Woodrow Wilson. He managed a victory when the Republican Party split in 1912 because Theodore Roosevelt failed to wrest the Republican nomination from President William Howard Taft and ran on the Bull Moose ticket. Republicans controlled the House and the Senate for all but six years of this thirty-six-year period. It was widely accepted that the business of the US government was "business." And the Republican Party accepted its role of protecting business through protective tariffs, minimal regulation, and low taxes. The Democratic Party was perceived to be antibusiness and led by radical populists.

The collapse of the US economy with the beginning of the Great Depression in 1929, and the failure of President Herbert Hoover to take sufficient action to deal with the growing problems of unemployment, poverty, and homelessness, changed those views. Economic theory at the time provided no solution. The market was expected to self-correct on its own without governmental intervention. Unemployment was also thought to be only temporary. In the meantime, everyone was supposed to tighten their belts and ride out the storm. Government intervention was unnecessary and was thought to only introduce inefficiencies into the business model that could work everything out naturally. If any action was to be taken, it would be to strengthen the financial sector so that money would flow to business and eventually "trickle down" to the workers, including the unemployed. But the economy continued to decline between 1929 and 1932, thereby setting the stage for a more liberal Democratic takeover.

President Franklin D. Roosevelt's New Deal coalition, which was cobbled together to respond to the Great Depression, developed vigorous government programs to promote social welfare, civil rights, and unions. Some New Deal legislation attempted for the first time to regulate certain business practices that threatened economic goals set by the government. Republican opponents of the New Deal who stressed laissez-faire business principles, including low taxes and little regulation, began calling themselves "conservatives." The federal government took responsibility for society's economic and social welfare to an unparalleled degree.

The New Deal coalition of farmers, union workers, Catholics, Jews, African Americans, and intellectuals provided the Democratic Party with victories in seven of the nine presidential elections from 1932 to 1964 (the exception was Dwight Eisenhower's presidency from 1952 to 1960). Democrats also controlled the House almost without interruption until 1995. In fact, many Republican voters supported popular New Deal programs like Social Security and accepted a more active role for government. Other Republicans, however, complained that the New Deal was a form of class warfare and was leading the country to socialism.

The response to the Great Depression by the New Deal was to provide public work programs to create jobs, provide unemployment insurance, and establish a bewildering variety of other government programs. As a result, unemployment came to be considered a social problem and the responsibility of the government to resolve. The Employment Act of 1946 states clearly that it is the obligation of the national government to try to create the conditions that will result in full employment. All democratic governments accept the obligation to conduct business-friendly policies to aid an expanding economy and full employment. Likewise, a government would not be considered democratic today if it did not accept responsibility for the economic well-being of its citizens.

The traditional capitalist economic system survived in the United States as a result of the alleviation of those problems that laissez-faire capitalism handles poorly by the intervention of the Keynesian welfare state. Laissez-faire capitalism cannot on its own resolve the problems of poverty, unemployment, income insecurity, and environmental pollution. Welfare state spending increased employment during periods of economic downturns. The welfare state legitimizes the capitalist system among those at the bottom of the ladder by softening the rough edges of the system.

Paul Krugman, a Nobel Prize–winning economist, wrote that by the early 1950s the United States bore little resemblance to the country it was in 1929. In the 1920s, the United States was a land of extremes between wealth and poverty as well as sharp divides between the dominant conservatives and embattled liberals. But the United States of the 1950s was one where Republicans and Democrats had a similar outlook and political thinking. In short, the United States had become a middle-class, middle-of-the-road nation.[11] Krugman wrote approvingly that there was a "sharp reduction in the gap between the rich and the working class" as well as a reduction in wage differentials among workers referred to as "the Great Compression."[12] The use of the term "the Great Compression" is meant to echo "the Great Depression" since the narrowing of income gaps was a defining event in US history "that transformed the nature of our society and politics."[13] Achieving a middle-class society, which had once seemed impossible, was taken for granted by the 1950s.

Increasing Inequality

Most Americans are unaware that the distribution of income has shifted dramatically in the past thirty years. Figure 4.2 illustrates parallel family income tabulations going back to 1966 for families at the 20th, 40th, 60th, 80th, and 95th percentiles of the income distribution. It does not reflect the incomes of the poorest or the richest Americans, but it does represent a broad range of economic circumstances. The figure shows how income increases since about 1980 have become more concentrated at the top income levels, in contrast to the pattern of widely shared progress between 1966 and 1979. After about 1980, the income of those at the top soared while those in the bottom half earned only a little more than they did in 1980.[14]

From the mid-1970s onward, income growth has been slower overall and less evenly distributed. The differences are clear in Figure 4.2. This figure compares cumulative rates of real growth in the income distribution from 1966 to 1980 and from 1980 to 2007. The growth rate before 1980 was very egalitarian. After 1980, the income growth is obviously much less evenly distributed with those at the top peeling away. The Great Depression lives on in our collective memories while the Great Compression is largely forgotten.[15]

Larry Bartels found in his work *Unequal Democracy*[16] that, in the 1960s under Presidents John F. Kennedy and Lyndon Johnson, income growth was extraordinarily strong, with lower-income families faring even better than affluent families. From 1964

Figure 4.2 The Top Takes Off: Income Distribution, 1966–2007

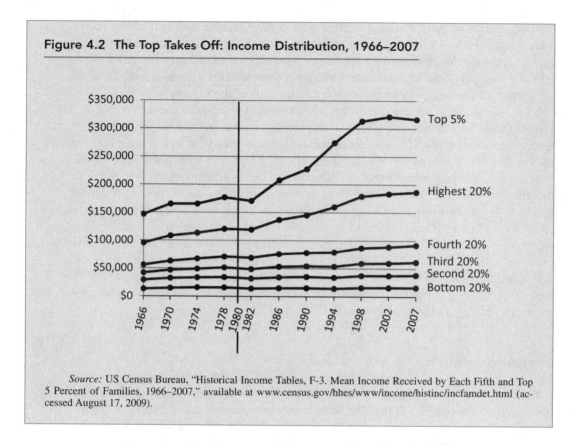

Source: US Census Bureau, "Historical Income Tables, F-3. Mean Income Received by Each Fifth and Top 5 Percent of Families, 1966–2007," available at www.census.gov/hhes/www/income/histinc/incfamdet.html (accessed August 17, 2009).

through 1969, families in 95th percentile and above had a real income growth of 4.2 percent per year while the working poor had a real income growth of 5.6 percent per year. This was at least partly attributable to Johnson's Great Society programs, including Medicare and Medicaid, Job Corps, Food Stamps, and the Community Action Program.[17] The civil rights movement destroyed the New Deal coalition since it depended on the inclusion of the South.

Bill Moyers recounted finding President Johnson disconsolate in the evening after signing the Civil Rights Act on July 2, 1964, ending segregation in public facilities. Moyers asked, "What's the matter? This was a great day. You should be jubilant." Johnson looked at Moyers and said in effect, "I think we just handed the South to the Republicans for the rest of my life and yours."[18] At first, the civil rights struggle split southern whites who supported segregation from northern Democrats who supported integration. When the civil rights movement pressed for equal access to jobs, housing, and education, northern Democrats also began to split, with lower-income workers tending to vote Republican. (Figure 4.3 illustrates the growing separation.)

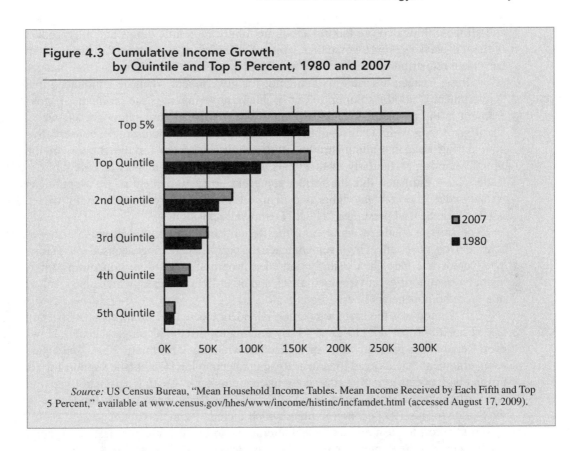

Figure 4.3 Cumulative Income Growth by Quintile and Top 5 Percent, 1980 and 2007

Source: US Census Bureau, "Mean Household Income Tables. Mean Income Received by Each Fifth and Top 5 Percent," available at www.census.gov/hhes/www/income/histinc/incfamdet.html (accessed August 17, 2009).

In 1964 the Republican presidential candidate, Barry Goldwater, linked conservatism to the American West and thereby broadened its appeal. He campaigned on a platform of significantly reduced taxes and government spending, reduction of government regulation of business, and the end of most government social programs.[19] In 1968, Goldwater's manifesto was linked to Richard Nixon's "Southern Strategy," which exploited white voters' fears of African American demands for civil rights and the riots in many cities following the assassination of Martin Luther King Jr. The New Deal coalition was completely shattered in the election of 1968.

After winning the 1980 Republican nomination, Ronald Reagan went to the Neshoba County Fair in Mississippi. There, near the site where three civil rights workers were murdered in 1964, he announced support for "states' rights," which was widely interpreted as a signal of opposition to federal enforcement of civil rights laws.[20] Lee Atwater, a Republican consultant, explained the evolution of the Republicans' Southern Strategy, which originated in opposition to the Voting Rights Act but took on a coded language: "You're getting so abstract now you're talking about cutting taxes, and all these things you're talking about are totally economic things and a byproduct of them is blacks get hurt worse than whites."[21] Therefore, government is the problem because it redistributes money from "you" and gives it to "them." In his 1981 inaugural address, Reagan asserted his contempt for government when he announced that "government is not the solution to our problem; government is the problem." If government is the problem, it raises the question of why administrators should worry about governing well. The Republicans strengthened their increasingly conservative base during Reagan's administration with his direct appeal for the support of the Moral Majority, particularly evangelicals. Christian fundamentalists and Republican leaders have estimated that the former represent up to 40 percent of the Republican primary vote. Abortion, gay rights, and stem cell research all proved to be useful wedge issues to use against presumed "elitist" Democratic positions.

The shift of southern whites into the Republican Party with a promise of lower taxes and less government involvement made the party more homogeneous ideologically. The Democratic Party increasingly defended progressive positions concerning feminism, gays, minorities, environmentalists, and other liberal causes, which also resulted in a more homogeneous liberal organization.

Bill Clinton was the first Democratic president elected to two terms (1993–2001) since Franklin Roosevelt (1933–1945) by moving toward the ideological center. However, Republicans gained control of the House, which they held until 2006. The bipartisan alignment that allowed President Reagan to gain wide Democratic support for his tax and budget cuts in 1981 suffered significant erosion by 1992. Partisan polarization was such that President Clinton failed to receive one Republican vote in the House or the Senate for his 1993 economic plan, which included some tax increases.

In an effort to push an ideological alternative to Democratic policies and to unite distant wings of the Republican Party, the new House speaker Newt Gingrich and other conservatives proposed a "Contract with America."[22] The Contract was put forward just before the midterm elections in 1994, and was signed by all but two Republican members of the House. The Contract's provisions included, some only implicitly, most of the signature issues of ideological conservatism: setting a higher moral tone, reducing the size of government, passing a balanced budget amendment, reducing federal budgets, promoting lower taxes and making it difficult to raise taxes (requiring a three-fifths majority vote), reducing the role of social welfare in the federal policy and spending, providing tort reform to make it more difficult to sue corporations, and reducing pork-barrel spending. The Contract with America remains mostly an unfulfilled list of goals since some bills died in the Senate while others were vetoed by President Clinton.

Political Turmoil from Bush to Obama

In 2000, Republicans maintained control of the House and won control of the Senate. And in a controversial decision, the Supreme Court's conservative majority overruled

Florida's Supreme Court and stopped a recount, giving G. W. Bush a majority of the electoral votes, even though he lost the popular vote to Al Gore. In 2004 Karl Rove, the Republican Party's grand strategist, said the prospects were good for a realigning election that would create a "permanent Republican majority" made up primarily of social conservatives and antitax conservatives. Much of the effort was directed not on winning a larger following, but on waging war against the Democratic Party. The plan was to use government policy to reward Republican Party supporters while crippling the financial base of the Democratic Party. Republicans in the House and Senate were to protect their majority through a combination of aggressive fundraising and a major increase in earmarks that became the major instruments for protecting incumbents against Democratic challengers and encouraging party discipline.

Conservative activist Grover Norquist, well known in Republican circles for his desire to shrink government "down to the size where we can drown it in the bathtub," was to provide the organization for such a realignment. Norquist held weekly meetings, which right-wing think tanks, Republican congressional leaders, conservative lobbyists, and White House aides attended. It was hoped that the administration could pressure members of Congress, and synchronize conservative radio talk shows, through these meetings to coordinate an effort to implement three conservative policy goals. The first goal was tort reform, which would reduce the income of "trial lawyers" so they "can't give as much money to the Democratic Party."[23] The second would be "legislative changes making it harder for unions to provide funding to political parties," which would further cut funding to the Democratic Party. And third, Republicans should support the "promotion of free trade which further weakens the influence of unions."[24] Lobbying firms would be pressured to hire only Republicans to lobby in Congress, and those firms would be expected to contribute overwhelmingly to Republican candidates. Norquist disdained a bipartisan approach to solving policy issues by indicating that "bipartisanship is another word for date rape."[25]

However, in 2001 with control of the presidency, the Senate, and the House, Republicans failed to deliver on their agenda. And it was not just the Republicans in control, but as William Rusher, a major figure in the modern conservative movement, said, the "conservative movement has come to dominate the Republican Party totally."[26] That is, the Republican Party felt it had "finally purged itself of the moderate, non-ideological" Republicans that once dominated the party. A conservative journal, *The Objective Standard,* declared: "The conservative moment—the moment when conservative Republicans [have] become America's ruling class—has arrived."[27]

A major conservative goal was to balance the budget, but instead Republicans ran up the biggest deficits in history. President G. W. Bush introduced a $1.35 trillion tax cut, one of the largest in history. When, in a cabinet meeting, Paul O'Neill cautioned that the tax cut would increase the deficit, Vice President Dick Cheney remarked, "Reagan proved deficits don't matter" and "we won the [2002] midterms. This is our due."[28] Between the time Bush entered the White House on January 20, 2001, and left eight years later, the deficit increased from $5.6 trillion to $10.6 trillion.[29] This 85 percent increase is the largest of any president in US history. And this increase occurred when the economy was not in a recession and no major war was being waged.

Regarding personal liberty, Republicans promised to downsize the government. However, the controversial USA Patriot Act[30] increased the ability of the government to search telephone, Internet, medical, financial, and other records. It eased restrictions on foreign intelligence gathering in the United States, and expanded the secretary of the treasury's authority to regulate financial transactions. When Clinton left office in 2001, federal spending equaled 18.5 percent of the gross domestic product (GDP). By the end of the first G. W. Bush term, outlays increased to 20.3 percent of GDP.

In the area of foreign policy, G. W. Bush campaigned on the notion of a "humble foreign policy."[31] In a presidential debate with Gore, Bush said the United States must be humble: "We must be proud and confident of our values, but humble in how we treat nations that are figuring out how to chart their own course."[32] He said the United States must not be arrogant or confrontational. However, US foreign policy under Bush was some of the most confrontational in modern times with claims of a right to take preemptive action and of US unilateralism (see Chapter 13 for a fuller discussion).

As already noted, Reagan declared that government is not the solution, it is the problem. If government is the problem, then why worry about governing well? The G. W. Bush administration's handling of the devastation caused by Hurricane Katrina in New Orleans reveals a fatal flaw behind conservative governing philosophy. If one believes that the government cannot solve problems, and the primary purpose of elected officials is to weaken government, it will never be there when you need it. Bill Press argued that conservatives, by their own admission, set out to reduce the size of government so it could be drowned in the bathtub. Instead, they succeeded in drowning New Orleans.[33]

At the end of his administration, G. W. Bush left office with the lowest final approval rating (of 22 percent) since Gallup began asking about presidential approval over 70 years ago. Bush also has the distinction of having had the highest approval rating for a president (90 percent right after the September 11 attacks in 2001) as well as the lowest.[34] At no time during his second term did Bush's approval ratings reach 50 percent. Shortly after Hurricane Katrina in October 2005, his approval rating dipped below 40 percent. Assessments of his handling of the war in Iraq and the economy turned decidedly negative. Many highly educated voters opposed the Republican Party's position of giving equal emphasis to teaching intelligent design as evolution in science classes, the party's opposition to stem cell research, and interference with a spouse's decision about whether to keep Terri Schiavo, a brain-dead woman, alive. The conservative legacy was a government that was "inefficient, inept, incompetent—and broke."[35] In the fall of 2008, just 16 percent approved of Bush's handling of the economy.

Many conservatives now blame the failure of the administration on G. W. Bush himself, and claim that his record as a conservative is mixed. They concede that he reduced taxes dramatically, attempted to privatize Social Security, appointed very conservative judges, placed conservatives throughout the bureaucracy and especially in the Justice Department, and reduced many government regulations on business. He also pursued other conservative goals such as strengthening the presidency, and was supportive of a more robust defense budget and a more aggressive foreign policy emphasizing the primacy of the United States. But they claim that he was a "big government" conservative in that he increased the role of government in education and in Medicare. These Republicans maintain that conservatives lost not because they were conservative, but because they were not conservative enough, and that the party failed to live up to its brand identification as the party of limited government. To be successful, they must become more disciplined conservatives. However, conservatives in Congress, including Tom DeLay, John McCain, Bill Frist, Newt Gingrich, Trent Lott, John Boehner, and Dennis Hastert, were strongly supportive of Bush during their time in Congress.

Others conclude that the conservative governing strategy was attempted, and found wanting. There is a strong suggestion that as long as conservatives believe that government is the problem, they cannot simultaneously commit to the idea of having government efficiently and effectively provide policy solutions that the electorate demands. In fact, the mainstream of US politics has never been rigidly ideological. The system is built for stalemate. Therefore, the energy and dynamism of the society ordinarily rests with the population and the economy, and the government is not thought of as an essential actor. But in times of national crisis, such as war, natural disasters, or great economic stress, citizens do look to government to solve basic problems affecting society.

Concern about a long and expensive war, an economic crisis with skyrocketing unemployment, rising numbers of uninsured Americans, and a sense of a nation in decline did not augur well for Republicans in 2008. There was also a growing opposition to the constant partisan and ideological arguments that made the electorate receptive to a candidate promising to take the country in a new direction.

Barack Obama's inaugural address signaled a sharp break from the G. W. Bush administration by promising to take up the many challenges facing the nation. He challenged Reagan's principle that government is the problem and proposed a different formulation: "The question we ask today is not whether our government is too big or too small but whether it works, whether it helps families find jobs at a decent wage, care they can afford, a retirement that is dignified. Where the answer is yes, we intend to move forward. Where the answer is no, programs will end."[36]

Obama indicated a need for greater transparency in promising that those who manage the public's dollars be held to account to spend wisely and "do our business in the light of day" because, only then, can the trust between the citizens and the government be restored. He indicated that the choice is not between the free market or government when he explained that the question is not whether "the market is a force for good or ill. Its power to generate wealth and expand freedom is unmatched. But this crisis has reminded us that without a watchful eye, the market can spin out of control. The nation cannot prosper long when it favors only the prosperous."[37] Obama said this is the surest route to our common good.

The Dynamics of Realignment

What is one to make of the election of Barack Obama as president? In some respects, Obama's electoral victory turned in part, as did Franklin Roosevelt's, on the calamitous economic conditions that the incumbent party seemed to not fully grasp. Several points should be noted, however. Democrats gained control of Congress in 2006 before the recession that began in December 2007. They again increased their majorities in Congress in 2008. Before the elections in 2006, the Democrats held forty-four Senate seats; after the 2008 elections, they presumably hold sixty. In the House, Democrats gained thirty-two seats in 2006 and twenty-one more seats in 2008; they held a 257–178 edge in 2009.[38] Obama was elected with a 365–173 electoral vote majority. Given that Gore actually won the popular vote in 2000 by about half a million votes, Democrats have won the popular vote in four of the past five presidential elections since 1992. McCain ran strongest in the South, but with Obama making significant inroads by winning both Virginia and North Carolina.

Since *ideology* is increasingly important in providing the cohesive force holding party coalitions together, it is not surprising that the 2008 campaign turned largely on ideology. Republicans attacked Obama as a liberal elitist who would raise taxes while McCain would cut them. They claimed that Obama believed in big government while McCain believed in the American people. For example, Obama would provide big government solutions for health care while McCain would make available tax cuts so individuals could shop for their own health care. Obama was also accused of being a socialist who wanted to redistribute wealth. Obama was particularly denounced for being naive in foreign policy and not being willing to support US involvement in Iraq. Obama stated that he would raise taxes, but only on the top 5 percent; that his health care solution was comprehensive and would involve government; and that redistribution of wealth is an inherent part of most tax programs. Obama insisted that, by invading Iraq, we were distracted from the real issue of Afghanistan. In the campaign, Obama tried to avoid the partisan sniping by staying on message with his issues and spent relatively less time criticizing his opponent's position.

While the election of Obama and Democratic gains in Congress in 2008 presented Republicans with a resounding defeat, it is too soon to know whether the vote signaled a realigning election or not. Republicans recognize that they are now the minority party, but those in charge of the party apparatus believe they have the basic ingredients to return to majority status. They believe that Democrats did not win the election as much as the Republicans lost it. They believe that a renewed commitment to the core party principles of lower taxes and limited government will prove successful. The Republican congressional leadership strongly and successfully discouraged members from embracing Obama's plea for a more bipartisan approach and to oppose his spending proposals. Only three Republicans (of 219 total) crossed the aisle to support the $787 billion economic stimulus package passed in February 2009. Republican Party chairman Michael Steele has indicated that withholding party funds from Republicans who voted for the stimulus or against other party positions is "absolutely on the table."[39]

Other Republicans are less confident and fear that the party is increasingly becoming identified with conservative social policies, such as opposition to abortion, same-sex marriage, gun control, immigrants, and unions, which resonate most strongly in the South, parts of the Great Plains, and the western mountain states. There is a danger for the Republican Party in being perceived as a "regional" party. To the extent that national party leaders play to the conservative southern base, they are in danger of losing their appeal and seeming unfriendly to other areas of the nation.

John Judis and Ruy Teixeira found several nongeographic demographic indicators that also demonstrate a trend toward the Democratic Party.[40] Younger voters, and especially college graduates, have been moving in a liberal direction in the past several elections. Democrats have also strengthened their support among Latinos, aided by Republican policies deemed unfriendly to immigrants. Surveys indicate increasing acceptance on racial issues as evidenced in the 2008 presidential election, and civil unions also are increasingly being accepted.[41] The percentage of Americans supportive of measures that require a major role for government ranging from Social Security to health care now consist of significant majorities.

No president has begun his term with such broad approval ratings (78 percent) as Obama.[42] Single-party control of the White House and Congress began in united loyalty to Obama. The Republican opposition was battered and demoralized. If Obama can maintain the online networks he used to win the election, he could be the first president to harness a grassroots movement as an ongoing tool of government.[43]

Obama has articulated a cohesive set of progressive public policy goals that won the election in a head-to-head contest between clashing liberal and conservative positions. While he does have momentum, whether this turns out to be a realigning election will depend on his ability to show significant progress on restoring the economy before the elections in 2010. He also must show progress in getting significant parts of his progressive program through Congress.[44] Finally, the progressive programs of his campaign, such as health care, if enacted will have to prove that they can be maintained beyond his administration. The administration's effort to reach out to gain Republican support is an essential part of a successful endeavor.

Conservative opposition is based on the argument that the United States remains a "center right" nation, and that Obama won only because of the shortcomings of the McCain campaign and the economic crisis.[45] Conservatives warn that Obama won an election, but does not have a mandate for his progressive program. They could win the argument if they convince the public that it would be a mistake for Democrats to "overplay" their hand by actually trying to change an institution like health care.[46] At the same time, the Republican Party does not want to be perceived as the party of "no," but as the party that stands for timeless principles of lower taxes and smaller government.

Does Party Ideology Influence Economic Growth and Inequality?

Stark differences surfaced between the economic policies of Obama and McCain. Obama was skewered by the Republicans for saying that he would "redistribute" the wealth. Republicans countered that Obama's proposal was "socialism" pure and simple. McCain instead proposed to cut taxes for all, including the wealthy. This debate has a long history. More recently, Presidents Reagan and G. W. Bush slashed taxes for the affluent while Clinton raised taxes on the top 2 percent. Presidents have some ideological constraints imposed by their party, but in reality they also have significant room to maneuver.

Many Americans are aware that there are economic policy differences between the Republican and Democratic parties, but are not aware of two salient facts related to which political party controls the White House and the economy. First, Larry Bartels's research findings show that *the US economy has grown faster on average with Democratic presidents than with Republican presidents.* Americans may recall the economic growth during the Clinton administration as compared to G. W. Bush's administration because it is recent. But if we go back to 1948, we find the contrast is not unusual. Table 4.1 provides this comparison. Since that time, Republicans occupied the White House for thirty-two years and the Democrats for twenty-six. The figures reflect a one-year time lag for partisan control since it is unreasonable to expect a new president to have an immediate impact on economic growth in his first year in office. So income changes in 2001 are charged to President Clinton even though Bush became president in January of that year.[47]

It is common knowledge that *income inequality* has been growing since about 1980. But Bartels has discovered a surprising statistical regularity: Over the entire fifty-seven-year period from 1948 to 2005, income inequality has trended upward under Republican presidents, but downward slightly under Democrats, which accounts for the growing income inequality overall. Growing income inequality is not limited to the poor.

Table 4.1 also shows that, when Democrats were in the White House, lower family incomes grew at slightly faster rates than upper family incomes indicating a trend toward equalization. But it also confirms a much faster income growth for the most affluent under Republican presidents, resulting in increased inequality.

Table 4.1 Real Income Growth Rates by Income Level and Presidential Partisanship, 1948–2005 (adjusted for inflation)

Percentile	Democratic Presidents 26 years	Republican Presidents 32 years	Partisan Difference
20th	+2.64%	+0.43	2.21
40th	+2.46	+0.80	1.67
60th	+2.47	+1.13	1.33
80th	+2.38	+1.39	0.99
95th	+2.12	+1.90	0.22

Source: Larry Bartels, *Unequal Democracy: The Political Economy of the New Guilded Age* (Princeton: Princeton University Press, 2008), p. 33.

Data for the entire period in which Republicans controlled the presidency for thirty-two years show an average growth of real GDP of 1.64 percent versus 2.78 percent for the twenty-six years of Democratic presidents. The 1.14 percent difference over an eight-year period would yield 9.33 percent more income per person, which is more than could be expected from a tax cut.[48]

Bartels concludes that the correlation between both higher and more equally distributed income and lower growth and greater inequality under Republican presidents is not due to chance. It is also consistent with other ideological policy positions of the two parties. Republicans have traditionally favored larger tax cuts for the affluent while Democrats often favor raising them on top-income earners. Republicans have also opposed unions and minimum-wage laws as interfering with the working of the free market economy while Democrats generally are more supportive of both. Bartels also finds that unemployment rates tend to be about 2 percentage points lower under Democrats than under Republicans while the inflation rate tends to be virtually identical despite Republicans' efforts to reduce inflation.[49]

Conclusion

The meeting of the Founding Fathers in Philadelphia in 1787 had as a backdrop the recently won hard-fought victory in a war for independence over the world's most powerful monarchy. The Founding Fathers had even more recently experienced the difficulty of maintaining national unity under the Articles of Confederation where the national government had insufficient authority to enforce its will. They were also concerned with the problem of the potential violence of factions pursuing their own self-interests. And they were aware, as Madison noted, that the most common and endur-ing cause of factions lay in the unequal distribution of property. The institutions of federalism, checks and balances, and the separation of powers were an attempt by the framers of the Constitution to impale interest groups on the machinery of gov-ernment.

The framers succeeded in their effort to fragment governmental power to prevent any faction from dominating. Political parties were formed to encourage individuals seeking political office to form alliances with other like-minded office holders to form voting coalitions and alliances across institutional divides. In this way, they overcame some of the effects of the separation of powers and federalism on behalf of interest groups seeking benefits from government. The political parties were apt, not surpris-ingly, to divide between liberal and conservative tendencies.

In the United States, the classical liberals wanted to protect individuals from the threat of an overbearing government in order to ensure individual liberty. Originally known as Jeffersonian Democratic-Republicans, they evolved into today's Democra-tic Party, the oldest political party in the United States. By the latter part of the nine-teenth century, the Democrats realized the potential for the government to enhance individual freedom through positive action to create jobs or legislate civil rights. The Republican Party was formed from the remnants of the Whig Party just prior to the Civil War. Before long, Republicans came to be known primarily as representatives of commercial and business interest groups.

The Great Depression with its accompanying economic chaos and the administration of Franklin Roosevelt made the Democrats the majority party until the 1970s. Roose-velt's policies expanded people's expectations about the responsibility of government to "promote the general welfare." Government assumed responsibility for the eco-nomic health of the nation, including regulating industry and the financial sector as well as creating the economic conditions that would result in full employment of the labor force. Roosevelt was a pragmatist in his search for policies that would get the country moving out of the depression. He borrowed policy options from across the po-litical spectrum. The Republican Party was largely swept along by the tide of the New Deal and the postwar years. Both parties followed moderate pragmatic approaches in fighting for the vital center of politics.

The Democratic coalition of labor, ethnic groups, southerners, and intellectuals was severely strained by the late 1970s. In 1980, Ronald Reagan won an important victory with a greater commitment to a "conservative" philosophy that was a return to the idea that government could not be a solution to the nation's problems because it was the problem. The Republican Party became a party that was intent on advancing a conservative ideology. Over the next several decades, the Republicans purged so many moderates from the party that, by the time of G. W. Bush's election, they boasted that there were no moderate Republicans in their leadership ranks. Throughout the term of

G. W. Bush, the conservative centers boldly stated their goal of creating a permanent conservative Republican majority.

The Republican Party ran into several problems soon after taking over all three branches of government. Huge tax cuts with the majority of the benefits going to the top 20 percent of income earners increased economic inequality while it put the nation into an immediate structural deficit. Involving the nation in a costly war that many saw as avoidable became increasingly unpopular. The lack of transparency and the opposition to US policies abroad also took their toll. The midterm election of 2006 was a warning that the realigning elections the party had so hoped for were not happening.

In 2008, the first African American was elected president along with major party victories in the House and the Senate. The strength of the rejection of the Republican Party in both 2006 and 2008 raised the very real possibility of Democratic realigning elections. President Obama made clear his intent to make a sharp break with the philosophy and policies of the G. W. Bush administration.

All of this raises the question about whether the partisan ideologies represented in the two political parties really make a difference in policy outcomes. Bartels's research shows that, since 1948, economic growth has been greater under Democratic presidents than under Republican presidents. He also shows that inequality tends to decline during Democratic administrations and to increase during Republican administrations. We agree with his convincing conclusion that the natural tendencies based on the different partisan ideologies does result in different policy selections that affect economic outcome.

Questions for Discussion

1. What are the shared values of US political culture?

2. Why are classical liberals called conservatives today?

3. Thomas Jefferson was a classical liberal and would be considered a liberal today. Why?

4. Why were decentralized parties a natural outgrowth of the impact of the framers' design?

5. Is there a natural tension between liberty and equality? Why?

Notes

1. This quote is variously attributed to Thomas Jefferson, Thomas Paine, John Adams, and Henry David Thoreau. See "Respectfully Quoted: A Dictionary of Quotations," Great Books Online, available at www.bartleby.com/73/753.html (accessed January 19, 2009).

2. Ronald Reagan, inaugural address, January 20, 1981.

3. James Madison, *The Federalist* no. 10.

4. James Madison, *The Federalist* no. 51.

5. Prior to the Seventeenth Amendment, which provided for the direct election of senators.

6. *Marbury v. Madison,* 1 Cranch 137 (1803).

7. See Theodore J. Lowi, Benjamin Ginsberg, and Kenneth A. Shepsle, *American Government: Power and Purpose,* 10th ed. (New York: W. W. Norton, 2008), p. 103.

8. The concern of the delegates to the Constitutional Convention about protecting private property has been well documented. See Calvin C. Jillson and Cecil L. Eubanks, "The Political Structure of Constitution Making: The Federal Convention of 1787," *American Journal of Political Science* 28 (August 1984): 435–458. The view that the delegates' economic self-interest was the basis for private property and economic concerns was popularized by Charles Beard, *An Economic Interpretation of the Constitution* (New York: Free Press, 1913; reprinted in 1965). On economic stability, see also John P. Roche, "The Founding Fathers: A Reform Caucus in Action," *American Political Science Review* 55 (December 1961): 799–816.

9. A famous illustration of this occurred in 1798 when the Federalist Party under John Adams controlled the national government. The opposition led by the Jeffersonian Democratic-Republicans was viewed as traitorous by the Federalists who passed the Alien and Sedition Acts, which effectively made it a violation of the law to criticize the government. This effort to suppress freedom of speech and the press failed and helped Jefferson's Democratic-Republicans win the White House in 1801.

10. See V. O. Key Jr., *The Responsible Electorate: Rationality in Presidential Voting 1936–1960* (Cambridge: Harvard University Press, 1966).

11. Paul Krugman, *The Conscience of a Liberal* (New York: W. W. Norton, 2007), pp. 38–39. Krugman points out that Michael Harrington wrote *The Other America: Poverty in the United States* in 1962 (New York: Macmillan) because he felt such a book was needed as most people were no longer poor, and the poor might disappear from view. The book was to remind Americans that not all Americans had made it to middle-class society.

12. Ibid., pp. 38–39.

13. Ibid., p. 39.

14. The Century Foundation, *The New American Economy: A Rising Tide That Lifts Only Yachts* (New York: The Century Foundation, 2004), available at www.tcf.org/Publications/EconomicsInequality/wasow_yachtrc.pdf (accessed January 25, 2009).

15. Krugman, *The Conscience of a Liberal,* p. 39.

16. Larry Bartels, *Unequal Democracy: The Political Economy of the New Gilded Age* (Princeton: Princeton University Press, 2008), p. 44.

17. Ibid.

18. Bill Moyers, *Bill Moyers Journal,* transcript, August 29, 2008, available at www.pbs.org/moyers/journal/08292008/transcript4.html (accessed January 24, 2008).

19. See Barry Goldwater, *The Conscience of a Conservative* (New York: Regnery Press, 1990).

20. Lou Cannon, *Governor Reagan: His Rise to Power* (New York: PublicAffairs, 2003), pp. 477–478. See also Michael Goldfield, *The Color of Politics: Race and the Mainspring of American Politics* (New York: The New Press, 1997), p. 314.

21. Bob Herbert, "Impossible, Ridiculous, Repugnant," *New York Times,* October 6, 2005, available at http://query.nytimes.com/gst/fullpage.html?res=9C04E6DF1E30F935A35753C1A9639C8B63 (accessed August 17, 2009).

22. The Contract used part of the text from Ronald Reagan's 1985 State of the Union address and included policy ideas from the Heritage Foundation, a conservative think tank. Larry Hunter, Newt Gingrich, Richard Armey, Bill Paxon, Tom DeLay, John Boehner, and Jim Nussle were involved in producing the final document.

23. Source Watch, "Grover Norquist," available at www.sourcewatch.org/index.php?title=Grover_Norquist (accessed January 20, 2009).

24. Ibid.

25. Jonathan Chait, *The Big Con* (New York: Houghton Mifflin, 2007), p. 220.

26. As quoted in C. Bradley Thompson, "The Decline and Fall of American Conservatism," *The Objective Standard* 1, no. 3 (Fall 2006): 2.

27. Ibid.

28. Ron Suskind, *The Price of Loyalty: George W. Bush, The White House, and the Education of Paul O'Neill* (New York: Simon and Schuster, 2004).

29. Treasury Direct, "Historical Debt Outstanding—Annual 2000–2008," available at www.treasurydirect.gov/govt/reports/pd/histdebt/histdebt_histo5.htm (accessed August 17, 2009).

30. The USA Patriot Act was signed into law on October 26, 2001. The acronym stands for Uniting and Strengthening America by Providing Appropriate Tools Required to Intercept and Obstruct Terrorism Act of 2001 (Public Law 107-56).

31. PBS, "Online News Hour: Presidential Debate—October 12, 2000," available at www.pbs.org/newshour/bb/politics/July-Dec00/for-policy_10-12.html (accessed August 17, 2009).

32. Ibid.

33. Bill Press, *Train Wreck: The End of the Conservative Revolution* (Hoboken: John Wiley and Sons, 2008), p. 14.

34. CBSNews.com, "Bush's Final Approval Rating: 22 Percent," January 16, 2009, available at www.cbsnews.com/stories/2009/01/16/opinion/polls/main4728399.shtml (accessed August 17, 2009).

35. Press, *Train Wreck,* p. 14.

36. President Barack Obama, inaugural address. January 20, 2009.

37. Ibid.

38. See *New York Times,* "Election Results 2008," available at http://elections.nytimes.com/2008/results/president/votes.html (accessed January 22, 2009). See also Federal Election Commission, "Federal Elections 2006," available at www.fec.gov/pubrec/fe2006/federalelections2006.shtml (accessed August 17, 2009). In addition, the number of Democratic governors made impressive gains in both elections. Prior to the 2006 elections, there were sixteen Democratic governors. After 2008, there were twenty-nine Democratic governors.

39. Faiz Shakir, "RNC Chair Steele Threatens Retribution Against GPO Senators Who Voted for Stimulus," February 24, 2009, available at http://thinkprogress.org/2009/02/24/steele-recession (accessed August 17, 2009).

40. John B. Judis and Ruy Teixeira, *The Emerging Democratic Majority* (New York: Scribner, 2002).

41. Ibid.

42. Barton Gellman, "Historians Say He Could Redefine the Presidency," *Washington Post,* January 20, 2009. pp. A1, A13.

43. Ibid.

44. Paul Starr, "The Realignment Opportunity," *American Prospect,* December 2008, p. 3.

45. See Center for Political Studies, University of Michigan, National Election Study Cumulative Data File, 1952–1992; 1994 National Election Study; and 1996 National Election Study. Those identifying as conservative or extremely conservative have averaged just over 20 percent of the population while those identifying as liberal or extremely liberal have averaged about 18 percent. See Patrick Frank, "America Is Not a "Center-Right Nation," January 8, 2009, available at www.opednews.com (accessed January 15, 2009). Frank argues that political identification of Americans is becoming more liberal.

46. Starr, "The Realignment Opportunity," p. 3.

47. Bartels notes that the assumption of a one-year lag in partisan policy effects is consistent with macroeconomic evidence regarding the timing of economic responses to monetary and fis-

cal policy changes. It also fits observed data better than a longer lag. Bartels, *Unequal Democracy,* pp. 32–33.

48. Alan Blinder, "Would Obama's Plan Be Faster, Fairer, Stronger?" *New York Times,* August 30, 2008, available at www.nytimes.com/2008/08/31/business/31view.html?_r=18ref= business.

49. Bartels, *Unequal Democracy,* p. 48.

5

Economic Theory as a Basis of Public Policy

Macroeconomic policy is concerned with overall levels of production, employment, and income from a national perspective. This chapter focuses on the nature of these economic forces and the competing economic theories that form the basis for contending policy recommendations. Since 1936, the free market school, now often referred to as monetarism, and Keynesian theories have dominated the policymaking level of governments worldwide.

Though not every public policy of the government involves questions of resource allocation, many do. In Chapter 1, we saw that microfailures in the economy bring about situations that force government intervention to prevent free riders and to produce certain public goods. Individuals organize to distribute the costs of public goods among those people who receive the benefits. Cost sharing is necessary through government purchases to realize an ideal supply of a public good. Other failures, such as externalities, force government intervention to influence production or to determine who pays for certain goods. Members of a society on occasion may decide that they are unhappy with the market determination of what, how, or for whom that society's goods are being produced. Government is also asked to intervene when real markets deviate from the ideal markets envisioned in classical economic theory.

The failures of the market provide specific justifications for government intervention through public policy. The trend of government growth and involvement in the public sector has increased dramatically in the United States since the 1930s. Until then, the government was limited primarily to the basic functions of providing for defense, administering the system of justice, and providing a postal service. Since the Great Depression, and largely because of it, the federal government has become involved in a whole range of new activities, including public works, environmental regulation, education, health care, and income redistribution through income-transfer programs like

Social Security and Medicare. Significant growth in government has not happened only at the federal level. State and local governments have become even more important than the federal government as sources of employment and production.

Does economic theory have anything to say about what role the government should have in policies that affect the public sector? Can economic theory suggest what effect public versus private spending will have on the economy, job creation, and social well-being? Is it supportive or negative? Can it suggest what kind of policies should be used in certain situations? This chapter will explore these questions.

Adam Smith and Classical Optimism

The year 1776 was pivotal, for the Declaration of Independence and also for the publication of Adam Smith's *Wealth of Nations*. Both were basic manifestations of the movement away from authoritarian monarchical forms of governmental control, and toward individual liberty. The American Revolution attacked not only the political control of the American colonies by England, but also the system of economic authority that made this control inevitable. The colonists—and English entrepreneurs—had already experienced what Smith argued: state domination of the economy inhibited new opportunities for increasing production and profits.

The supporters of **mercantilism**, with whom Smith took issue, advocated government regulation because they believed that the pursuit of one's own self-interest would produce chaos in society and less wealth for everyone. The mercantilists viewed competition as a zero-sum scenario in which more for one, by necessity, meant less for others. In 1776, Smith challenged that notion.

Adam Smith (1723–1790), a professor of moral philosophy, naturally saw economics as a branch of moral philosophy with a calling to improve the condition of humanity, especially that of the poor. Writing in the latter half of the eighteenth century, he recommended a system of natural liberty in which the individual would be free to pursue his or her own interests. By pursuing one's self-interest, each person maximizes benefits for himself or herself, or for other individuals and for society as a whole.

He began by challenging the notion that economic trade was a zero-sum exchange in which, if some were better off, others must necessarily be worse off. He maintained that, if Jim wants something from Kevin that Jim cannot make himself, he must produce something Kevin wants in order for them to agree on an exchange in which both "better their condition." Both benefit because they agree to give up something that has less value to themselves personally than the products they receive. Thus, the total welfare has been enhanced. Smith showed that, in free competitive markets, exchange can have positive-sum results where both parties are better off than before the exchange.

Smith, stated in a famous passage: "It is not from the benevolence of the butcher, the brewer, or the baker, that we expect our dinner, but from their regard to their own interest."[1] According to his theory, self-interest and competition will eliminate two kinds of waste: unrealized trades and inefficient production. Conversely, it will encourage mutually beneficial trades and efficient production.

Smith had none of the illusions of later classical economists that associated wealth with morality. As a moral philosopher, he intensely disliked and distrusted what he referred to as the "unsocial passions" of greed and self-interest exhibited by merchants that would try to enlist government to give them more power:

> To widen the market and to narrow the competition is always the interest of the dealers. . . . The proposal of any new law or regulation of commerce which comes from this order, ought always to be listened to with great precaution, and ought never to be adopted, till after having been long and carefully examined, not only with the most scrupulous, but with the most suspicious attention. It comes from an order of men, whose interest is never exactly the same with that of the public, who have generally an interest to deceive and even to oppress the public, and who accordingly have, upon many occasions, both deceived and oppressed it.[2]

And therein lies the problem. How could a society in which merchants driven by greed and given free rein not result in great inequalities and injustice as merchants raise prices to exact the greatest profit possible? Smith noted that people of the same trade seldom are in one another's company even on social occasions, "but the conversation ends in a conspiracy against the public, or in some contrivance to raise prices."[3] He ridiculed the concern of merchants for only their own self-interest: "Our merchants and master-manufacturers complain much of the bad effects of high wages in raising the price, and thereby lessening the sale of their goods both at home and abroad. They say nothing concerning the bad effects of high profits. They are silent with regard to the pernicious effects of their own gains. They complain only of those of other people."[4]

Smith, as a moral philosopher, was hostile to the greedy *motives* of eighteenth-century industrialists. Ironically he later came to be regarded as their greatest advocate. Today, in disregard of his actual philosophy, Smith is often mistakenly labeled as a *conservative* economist.[5] How such a misunderstanding could come about requires an explanation. Smith said that greed, self-interest, and competition are the driving forces of production. Further, all goods have two prices: a **natural price** and a **market price**. He defined the *natural price* as the price that would have to be realized to cover the costs of production, with a small amount left over for a profit. He defined the *market price* as the price the product actually brings in the marketplace. Whenever the market price deviates from the natural price, it will be driven back in the direction of the natural price as if by an invisible hand. Every entrepreneur attempting to accumulate profits in their own self-interest is held in check by other competitors who are also trying to attain profits. This competition drives down the price of goods and reduces the revenue earned by each seller. In a market unrestrained by government, the competition between entrepreneurs erases excessive profits, employers are forced to compete for the best workers, workers compete for the best jobs (usually defined in terms of wages and working conditions), and consumers compete to consume products. Consequently, producers are forced to search for the lowest-cost production methods. Finally, resources are distributed to their most highly valued use, and economic efficiency prevails.

According to Smith, the owners of business tend to reinvest their profits, thereby consuming little more than the workers. The entrepreneurs inadvertently share the produce of all their improvements with the workers, though they *intend* only "the gratification of their own vain and insatiable desires." He continued: "[Business owners] are led by an invisible hand to make nearly the same distribution of the necessaries of life which would have been made had the earth been divided into equal portions among all its inhabitants."[6] Smith expected a free market economy to result in general economic equality.

Because reality deviates from the market ideal, society experiences significant inequality and waste. Smith conceived of the idea that order, stability, and growth are intrinsic characteristics of capitalism. In the classical view, the economy is a **self-adjusting market**: it will adjust itself to any departure from its long-term growth trend. The market is self-regulating in that, if anyone's profits, prices, or wages depart from the levels set by market forces, competition will quickly force them back. Thus the market, which is the apex of economic freedom, is also an uncompromising taskmaster.[7] In a competitive economy, assumed by Smith, merchants are victims of their own greed.

Smith opposed mercantilist government intervention as a hindrance to the unfettered workings of self-interest and competition. Therefore, he has become identified with a laissez-faire economic philosophy, which is the basic philosophy of conservative-minded individuals today. His commitment to freeing individuals from the heavy hand of monarchial rule, through a commitment to liberty as benefiting the general public, was a very liberal position to take in his day. Smith is a classical liberal because he tried to free the individual from the heavy hand of monarchial oppression and mercantilist policies to control the economy. This liberalism was in contrast to the mercantilism of the day, which held that government should control the economy for the interest of the state. Liberals today see the possibility in democratic governments to provide active leadership to increase freedom in the society by solving social problems and helping the needy. By that definition, Smith would be a liberal in today's political environment because his support of laissez-faire policies was at that time not value neutral, but designed to help those who were less well off. His sympathies were clearly on the side of consumers rather than producers when he wrote: "Consumption is the sole end and purpose of all production; and the interest of the producer ought to be attended to, only so far as it may be necessary for promoting that of the consumer."[8]

Smith did see a significant, although limited, role for the state. He advocated three principal uses of government: the establishment and maintenance of national defense, the administration of justice, and the maintenance of public works and other institutions that private entrepreneurs cannot undertake profitably in a market economy.

Smith's classical economic view was optimistic. According to its principles, the economy would continue to expand through growing production based on increased investment in machinery. Machinery strengthened the division of labor that was so beneficial in expanding economic output, thereby improving the productivity of the workers. It saw the market system as an enormous power for the buildup of capital, primarily in the form of machinery and equipment, which would provide jobs and result in self-sufficiency for all. It predicted that any slowdown in the economy would be only temporary and self-correcting.

Smith was confident that the system would generate economic growth. The purpose of this growth was to improve society's welfare by extending consumption opportunities "to the lowest ranks of the people." Smith believed that free market forces would bring about an agreeable, mutually acceptable solution to the problem of individual self-interest within society as long as individuals were free to pursue their goals in a political and moral environment where everyone had equal basic rights that were acknowledged by all. This aspect of Smith's views is not usually emphasized, but in fact he was explicit in his judgment that self-interest could be destructive if it was not moderated with justice.

He condemned capitalist "rapacity," and his disdain for opulence was captured in his statement that, "with the greater part of rich people, the chief enjoyment of riches consists in the parade of riches, which in their eyes is never so complete as when they appear to possess those decisive marks of opulence which nobody can possess but themselves."[9] He was critical of civil government's lack of concern for social justice especially toward the poor when he wrote that "government is in reality instituted for the defense of the rich against the poor, or of those who have some property against those who have none at all"[10] and "all for ourselves, and nothing for other people, seems, in every age of the world, to have been the vile maxim of the masters of mankind."[11]

It should also be noted that Smith did not endorse the view that the unequal distribution of income was inherently just. He clearly indicated that coercion influences wages agreed on between capitalists and workers. Capitalists want to pay as little as possible and possess a stronger bargaining position when dealing with workers. The legal system during Smith's time also favored capitalists by permitting cooperation among manufacturers to hold wages down while prohibiting unions. Smith clearly broke with mercantilist views favoring a large working class that would be paid as little as possible to provide an incentive for hard work.

Smith also disagreed with the view that traits associated with individuals in different social classes were inherent in people's makeup, but attributed them instead to their positions in society. He held that "the very different genius which appears to distinguish men of different professions, when grown to maturity, is not upon many occasions so much the cause as the effect of the division of labor."[12] He openly sympathized with the working class over the manufacturing class and supported higher wages: "It is but equity, besides, that they who feed, cloathe and lodge the whole body of the people, should have such a share of the produce of their own labour as to be themselves tolerably well fed, cloathed and lodged."[13] In regard to raising wages of workers, he wrote: "No society can surely be flourishing and happy, of which the far greater part of the members are poor and miserable."[14] Smith argued against policies that worked against the poor. For instance, he criticized the 1662 Settlement Act, which prevented workers from moving from one parish to another to take advantage of employment opportunities.

Smith's **model** would use resources in the most efficient and economical matter while driving prices down for consumers through market forces without any government intervention. First, Smith warned that the model would not work in the face of monopoly. He was opposed to monopoly in all its forms, and all laws that restrained competition. He charged that monopolists,

> by keeping the market continually understocked, by never full supplying the effectual demand, sell their commodities much above the natural price, and raise their emoluments, whether they consist in wages or profit, greatly above their natural rate. The price of monopoly . . . is upon every occasion the highest which can be squeezed out of the buyers.[15]

Smith recognized that, when entrepreneurs became monopolists (and oligopolists), they were no longer the victim of market forces, but could control them to some degree. He realized that monopolists have an interest in understocking the market to raise the market price above the natural price without strong competitors to force the market price down to the natural price. The point was not lost on socialists of the nineteenth century. Smith's writings support the conclusion that he favored the workings of market forces and laissez-faire policies as preferable to government support of mercantilist policies that oppressed the poor. He left the door open for government policies to alleviate economic inequalities.

A second serious shortcoming of Smith's theory involves the notion of "effectual demand" and its relation to the pattern of income distribution. It was logical to argue that in a free competitive economy production will mirror *demand*. Entrepreneurs are responsive and produce for people with money. The free market, according to the theory, is a great engine that efficiently matches production with demand. Therefore, if the society has a highly unequal distribution of income and wealth, the pattern of production will also be highly unequal.[16] The market will produce a great deal for the affluent and very little for the poor. Socialists soon seized on these problems with the model to justify a different theory.

Classical Malthusian Melancholy

Thomas Malthus (1766–1834) was aware that things were not as universally rosy as Smith believed. Malthus challenged Smith's concern for the poor and suggested a resolution within a market economy framework. A minister by vocation, Malthus found the problem of poverty to be essentially *moral* in nature and, therefore, not susceptible to resolution by government policy. In his view, natural forces were at work and capitalists need not feel any pangs of conscience regarding wages that maintained their employees at subsistence levels.

Another economist, David Ricardo, argued there is a natural law of wages that tends toward the minimum necessary to sustain life. This occurs on the one hand because any increase in wages above subsistence results in workers procreating, and more mouths to feed means their wages in effect fall back to a subsistence level. On the other hand, if the price of food rises, workers then will force their wage rates up to pay for the necessities of their existence, thus maintaining the subsistence level. Either way, there is a natural wage rate that always tends toward the level of subsistence, which Ricardo termed the **iron law of wages**.

The conclusion for Malthus was inescapable: the population would grow until it was contained by "misery and vice." Assisting the poor would only transfer more resources to them and enable them to have more children, ultimately to the point of starvation. Providing the poor with assistance would divert wealth that should have been invested, slowing economic growth. Therefore, it would be futile to look for social causes and cures for poverty. According to Malthus, if the "lower classes" do not want to be poor, all they have to do is to have fewer children. The burdens associated with poverty are a natural punishment for the failure of the lower classes to restrain their urges to procreate. Their only salvation is literally dependent on their moral reform, not government assistance. The clear implication is that the causes of poverty are not to be found in the structure of society, such as the greed combined with monopoly power that had worried Smith.

On the contrary, a Malthusian view sees tragedies such as the miseries of poverty, famine, plague, and war as natural means of punishing and increasing the death rates of those who do not practice moral temperance. If it were not for these "natural" checks on population growth, the increasing numbers of poor would soon outstrip food production, which in turn would lead to their starvation. Malthus wrote that we should encourage the operations of nature in producing this mortality:

> Instead of recommending cleanliness to the poor, we should encourage contrary habits.
> In our towns we should make the streets narrower, crowd more people into the houses,

and court the return of the plague. In the country, we should build our villages near stagnant pools, and particularly encourage settlements in all marshy and unwholesome situations. But above all, we should reprobate specific remedies for ravaging diseases; and
those benevolent, but much mistaken men, who have thought they were doing a service
to mankind by projecting schemes for the total extirpation of particular disorders. If by
these and similar means the annual mortality were increased . . . we might probably
every one of us marry at the age of puberty, and yet few be absolutely starved.[17]

Thomas Carlyle, after reading Malthus's pessimistic analysis, called political economy "the dismal science." He was only partially correct since Malthus's analysis was
dismal—but only for the poor.

Malthusian analysis proved to be extraordinarily reassuring to those in search of
moral justification for selfishness. It calmed their doubts and fears by asserting that
the chase after wealth primarily served the interests of society. Perhaps more important, it claimed that the affluent, as well as business leaders, need not concern themselves with an undue sense of social responsibility for the conditions of the poor since
workers were the causes of their own miserable fates. By inference, the converse was
also true—the affluent were morally superior to the poor. The doctrine of laissez-faire
holds that the free market system has, within itself, the capacity to best resolve economic problems on the basis of justice and fairness for all participants. By reinforcing
the commitment to a doctrine of laissez-faire, Malthus devised a superb justification
for the affluent to deny any responsibility for a serious economic problem. The effects
of this reassuring and convenient theory on the affluent made Malthus one of the most
influential economic thinkers of his century. The fact that his theory was based on his
personal pondering and was not subject to empirical verification did not cause any serious objections at the time. But his harsh and arrogant analysis subsequently led to
the scathing attack on market economics by Karl Marx.

The Haunting Specter of Karl Marx

The writings of Karl Marx (1818–1883) posed a different view of market economics than those of either Smith or Malthus, and led to a radically different proposed
solution for society's problems. Marx disagreed with the capitalist assumption that
politics and economics could be separated. To the mercantilists, the state was a powerful force to direct the economy. To the classical liberals, the state was a threat to
economic freedom. To Marx, the state was not independent of the economic structure. The real purpose of the state was to serve the interests of the wealthy owners
of capital.

Marx was impressed with the ability of a capitalist economy to automatically allocate resources efficiently with no direction from the government, and to be extraordinarily efficient in producing goods and services. As Marx and his colleague
Friedrich Engels commented: "The bourgeoisie, during the rule of scarce 100 years,

has created more massive and more colossal productive forces than have all preceding generations together."[18] Capitalism transformed the world:

> The bourgeoisie, by the rapid improvement of all instruments of production, by the immensely facilitated means of communication, draws all nations . . . into civilization. . . . It compels all nations, on pain of extinction, to adopt the bourgeois mode of production; it compels them to introduce what it calls civilization into their midst, i.e., to become bourgeois themselves. In a word, it creates a world after its own image.[19]

Capitalism swept aside all former relationships and "left no other bond between man and man than naked self-interest."[20]

Marx viewed history as a continuing struggle between elites and the masses. He thought that the class struggle between capitalists and workers over profits and wages would ultimately lead to the end of capitalism. Marx, unlike Smith, saw the potential for instability and chaos in the laissez-faire market economy. His intricate analysis held that capitalists are able to increase their profits and wealth only at the expense of the workers. In his theory of **surplus value**, he argued that exploited labor generates profits, which are squeezed out through the capitalist ownership of machinery.

Marx shared Smith's distrust of entrepreneurs to seize every opportunity to use the state to enhance their power at the expense of the workers. He emphasized the importance of economic and social instability resulting from the tension between the opposing demands of capital and labor. In his view, the rapaciousness of business results in ever-larger business firms because small firms go under and their holdings are bought up by surviving firms. This trend toward a few large firms and the resulting concentration of wealth intensifies the struggle between labor and capital, and will eventually lead to a small group of wealthy capitalists and a mass of impoverished workers. In the end, the imbalance will be so great that it will cause the market system to collapse. The means of production will then be centralized; that is, taken over by the government. Great inequalities and exploitation will cease.

Critics of Marx point out that, despite difficulties in market economies, they have not collapsed. On the contrary, those systems that ostensibly have tried to model themselves on Marx's precepts have shown the most internal tension and, in most instances, have come unraveled. However, market capitalism has survived in part because it has been pragmatic and moved away from a laissez-faire model. In particular, government public policy programs have moved into many areas to ameliorate the living conditions of middle- and lower-income workers.

The Political Impact of the Great Depression

The Great Depression was a worldwide economic downturn that began in the United States. Historians usually date the beginning of the Great Depression with the collapse of the stock market on "Black Thursday" (October 24, 1929).[21] This was the deepest and longest economic catastrophe in modern history, lasting in the United States until the latter half of the 1930s.

A reminder is in order here that, when the Great Depression began, laissez-faire economics was still the accepted economic perspective and the popular culture was one of rugged individualism. Consequently, there was little expectation that government should provide assistance to individuals, but aid to business was a different matter. Herbert Hoover, two years into the depression, stated: "The sole function of government is to bring about a condition of affairs favorable to the beneficial development of private enterprise."[22]

The effects of this depression were devastating, however, and shook the very foundations of the society. It is difficult for anyone who did not live through the Great Depression to grasp the dimensions of the catastrophe. But the statistics are staggering. It wiped out half of the value of all goods and services produced in the United States. Residential construction fell by 95 percent. A quarter of the labor force lost their jobs; another quarter had their jobs reduced from full to part time or had their wages reduced. Deflation reduced prices and wages while raising the burden of debts. Over 9 million savings accounts disappeared when 5,000 banks failed, and more than 1 million mortgages were foreclosed (total US population was just 122 million). International trade fell by more than 50 percent. As jobs were lost, corporate profits and tax revenues plunged. Still, many of the more affluent who had not been seriously hurt by the depression viewed the crisis with unruffled detachment. In other countries, political upheavals resulted in dictators gaining power—including the most notorious of all, Adolf Hitler.

When Franklin Roosevelt was sworn in as president on March 4, 1933, the depression had been raging for three and one-half years. Unemployment had gone from 4 percent to over 25 percent, with all the attendant difficulties mentioned above. By 1933, the level of despair raised doubts about whether market capitalism could survive. In his speech accepting the Democratic Party's nomination for president, Roosevelt proposed a new public philosophy in his pledge for a "new deal" for the men and women "forgotten" by government:

> Throughout the nation men and women, forgotten in the political philosophy of the Government, look to us here for guidance and for more equitable opportunity to share in the distribution of national wealth. . . . I pledge myself to a *new deal* for the American people. This is more than a political campaign. It is a call to arms.[23]

Roosevelt introduced a new public philosophy that reshaped the relationship between citizens and government by proclaiming that government had a duty to intervene to promote the general welfare when capitalism failed. The federal government entered the economic life of the nation through the New Deal to assume responsibil-

Case Study: Were Franklin Roosevelt's New Deal Efforts Ineffective?

The recession that began in December 2007 is the longest since the Great Depression. President Barack Obama proposed a major package of spending to stimulate job growth and to stimulate growth of the gross domestic product (GDP). Some political opponents argued that Franklin Roosevelt's deficit spending was a failure and did not get the country out of the depression. Therefore, they were opposed to Obama's call for urgent action, and proposed a policy of spending and tax cuts instead.

With such a crucial public policy debate raging, it is important to expose the myth that the programs of the New Deal had little effect in stimulating production or reducing unemployment. Critics claim it was the major spending in preparation for war in the late 1930s that restored the nation's economic health. This myth cannot withstand the most basic economic scrutiny. Figure 5.1 illustrates the changes in the gross domestic product during the New Deal.

Department of Commerce data on the GDP indicate that it fell 28 percent from 1929 to 1932. In 1933, the nosedive was halted as it sank another 1.3 percent. It then began an ascent more rapid than its decline. Between 1934 and 1936, it climbed 32.7 percent, exceeding the previous record GDP of 1929. Real GDP never fell below the 1929 point again. Consumer spending and after-tax personal income also exceeded their 1929 summit by the end of 1936.

Having surpassed the previous high point in 1936, Roosevelt believed that the economy was over the crisis and no longer needed government support. Accordingly, he severely trimmed New Deal programs in an effort to balance the budget in 1937. At the same time, the Federal Reserve (the Fed) doubled reserve requirements for banks causing interest rates to rise. This along with Roosevelt's slashing of spending caused the nation to fall into another recession from 1937 to 1938. Roosevelt abruptly

reversed direction again and, by 1939, the GDP raced beyond the previous high of 1937. After 1939, the increased government spending in preparation for the possibility of war decisively brought the GDP to such levels that unemployment was driven to its lowest level since data have been collected.

A second major argument that Roosevelt's policies were not effective is based on the claim that unemployment shot up between 1929 and 1933 and stayed persistently high, although declining, after the enormous stimulus spending from 1933 through 1940. The monetarist argument claims that, if convergence to full employment is so slow, it should be allowed to happen without government intervention.

Interestingly, the Bureau of Labor Statistics (BLS) did not include workers as employed in the 1930s when they received their paycheck from a government program, even though they performed work for various New Deal programs. These workers were defined as "emergency workers" and excluded from the employment figures. Michael Darby discovered this "conceptual" error in that, from a Keynesian perspective, "labor voluntarily employed on contracyclical construction and other government projects should be counted as employed." A person who accepted a job with the Emergency Work-Relief Program and stopped looking for a job was clearly employed. In short, the treatment of government work-relief employees as unemployed in the BLS "data is inconsistent with both the modern BLS definition of unemployment and with the US national income accounts." The adjusted data drastically change the empirical conception of unemployment during the 1930s. As Darby states, the notion of an "extremely slow recovery from 1934 through 1941 is shown to be a fiction based on erroneous data. From 1933 to 1936 the corrected unemployment rate fell by 3.6 percentage points

continued

Case Study continued

---

per year, and there is every reason to suppose that the natural rate of about 5 percent would have been reached by 1938 had the Fed not doubled reserve requirements between August 1936 and May 1937." Figure 5.2 illustrates the significance of the uncorrected unemployment in analyzing the effectiveness of New Deal policies.

Finally, critics of Roosevelt also argue that World War II ended the depression, not his deficit spending. This misses the point, however. Roosevelt's New Deal deficits were not large enough to offset the reduction in private expenditures by business, households, and state governments to reduce unemployment to full employment levels. But massive government spending on a huge public works program, more generally known as World War II, ended the depression. This inescapable fact actually validates Roosevelt's policies and reinforces Keynes's theory of the role of government as employer of last resort and purchaser of goods to stimulate the economy.

Source: Michael R. Darby, "Three-and-a-Half Million US Employees Have Been Mislaid: Or, an Explanation of Unemployment, 1934–1941," *Journal of Political Economy* 84, no. 1 (February 1976): 1–16.

---

ity for the nation's economic well-being. Upon taking office Roosevelt proceeded, in a period now referred to as "the Hundred Days," to push several major laws through Congress, supported by new "fireside" chats and thirty press conferences.

The policies of Roosevelt made profound changes in government's attitude and responsibilities toward citizens and created the ideological conflict that animates American politics to the present day.[24] The significance of Roosevelt's policies that transformed American society was noted by the late Arthur Schlesinger Jr. who wrote:

> Who can now imagine a day when America offered no Social Security, no unemployment compensation, no food stamps, no Federal guarantee of bank deposits, no Federal supervision of the stock market, no Federal protection for collective bargaining, no Federal standards for wages and hours, no Federal support for farm prices or rural electrification, no Federal refinancing for farm and home mortgages, no Federal commitment to high employment or to equal opportunity—in short, no Federal responsibility for Americans who found themselves, through no fault of their own, in economic or social distress.[25]

Fiscal policy involves the use of government taxing and spending to stimulate or slow the economy, and the federal budget is the means by which fiscal policy is implemented. The government can increase or decrease aggregate demand by increasing or decreasing its share of taxing and spending. Tax cuts, especially when directed toward middle- and lower-income workers, will stimulate demand by putting more money in the hands of consumers and businesses. The increased spending results in increased employment to meet those demands. Conversely, increasing taxes (the least

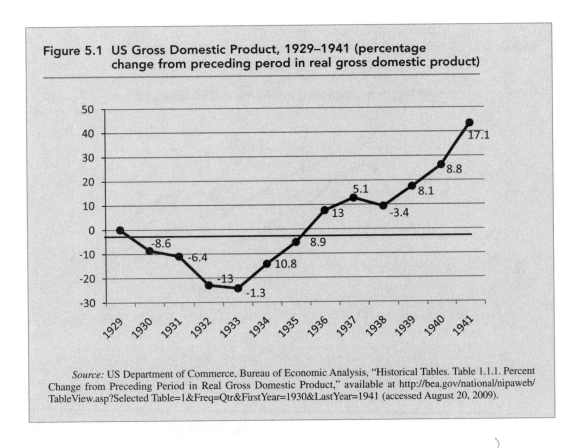

Figure 5.1 US Gross Domestic Product, 1929–1941 (percentage change from preceding perod in real gross domestic product)

Source: US Department of Commerce, Bureau of Economic Analysis, "Historical Tables. Table 1.1.1. Percent Change from Preceding Period in Real Gross Domestic Product," available at http://bea.gov/national/nipaweb/ TableView.asp?Selected Table=1&Freq=Qtr&FirstYear=1930&LastYear=1941 (accessed August 20, 2009).

popular of all fiscal policies), in addition to financing public policies, is intended to curb spending and slow an inflationary economy.

New Deal legislation built in what are referred to as **automatic stabilizers**, in which fiscal policy automatically responds countercyclically to certain economic events. For example, when the economy slows down and unemployment rises, tax revenues decline while government spending for unemployment insurance benefits, food assistance, welfare, and other transfer payments rises. The budget deficit rises as a result. Tax revenues and expenditures react automatically to changing economic conditions without requiring new policy. These automatic adjustments help stabilize the economy. On the other hand, with a reduction in unemployment, tax receipts rise at the same time that expenditures for welfare decline, reducing budget deficits. Automatic stabilizers are important because they adjust immediately to a rising or falling economy and do not require any policy debate to begin working. Therefore, the deficit will rise during a recession and shrink during a robust economy, even if there is no change in fiscal policy. So the same fiscal policy could result in a surplus, a balanced

Figure 5.2 US Unemployment Rate, 1929–1941

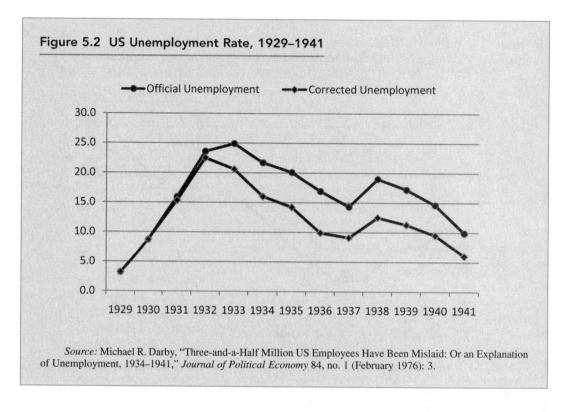

Source: Michael R. Darby, "Three-and-a-Half Million US Employees Have Been Mislaid: Or an Explanation of Unemployment, 1934–1941," *Journal of Political Economy* 84, no. 1 (February 1976): 3.

budget, or a deficit. Roosevelt's successors in the White House have stood to benefit from this legislation that works automatically to encourage economic stability.

The crisis of the Great Depression was resolved by Roosevelt's policies shifting the burden onto capital by strengthening worker rights through support for the first federal minimum wage, collective bargaining, unemployment insurance, and social security.[26] With the specter of socialism as the alternative if economic revival failed, a major portion of US business leaders grudgingly conceded the need for negotiating a compromise of higher wages for workers together with mass consumption. This led to the period of the Great Compression (see Chapter 4). The financial elite fiercely resented government regulation and opposed Roosevelt's reforms as a threat to their privileged status and longed for a return to laissez-faire capitalism.

The Realist Critique of Keynes
John Maynard Keynes (1883–1946) was most responsible for providing a new framework for macroeconomic analysis, which, not incidentally, provided a way out of the

depression. In accomplishing this feat, he directly challenged basic postulates of the classical school as well as Marx's pessimistic conclusions regarding the inevitable collapse of the market system. Keynesian theory represents his effort to explain how the chaotic conditions produced by the Great Depression of the 1930s occurred.[27]

Conservative critics of Keynes, opposing a larger role for government, charged that his views were too radical and threatened the very foundations of capitalism. Many denounced him as a socialist. Keynes, however, viewed himself as a conservative trying to defend capitalism against the growing attractions of communism. Even before the Great Depression, Keynes observed that market capitalism had imperfections that, if corrected, would strengthen it. In "The End of Laissez-Faire," he noted aspects of the unfettered market that lead to reduced efficiency and production and suggested how governments might exercise "directive intelligence" over the problem while leaving "private initiative unhindered":

> Contrariwise, devotees of Capitalism are often unduly conservative, and reject reforms in its technique, *which might really strengthen and preserve it,* for fear that they may prove to be first steps away from Capitalism itself. . . . For my part, I think that Capitalism, wisely managed, can probably be made more efficient for attaining economic ends than any alternative system yet in sight, but that in itself it is in many ways extremely objectionable. Our problem is to work out a social organisation which shall be efficient as possible without offending our notions of a satisfactory way of life.[28]

Keynes was dedicated to the preservation of the capitalist economic system and the position of those who were most favored by it. Yet his theory required some tinkering with the system by the government. The affluent were highly suspicious of any proposal that permitted government control over their interests. And they deeply resented the improved status that Keynes gave to the "working class" as an essential ingredient in the overall health of the economy (by putting their income back into the economy as demand). They found especially irritating his suggestion that their own privileges might actually contribute to economic instability (by transferring much of their income into savings).

Keynes's *The General Theory of Employment, Interest, and Money,* published in 1936, was a much more complex analysis of the market economy than Smith's. Undertaking a macroeconomic analysis, of which Smith had not concerned himself, led Keynes to conclude that laissez-faire was not the appropriate policy for a stagnant economy like that of the 1930s. Keynes stated his profound disagreement with the classical tradition in his one-paragraph first chapter:

> I have called this book the *General Theory of Employment, Interest, and Money,* placing the emphasis on the prefix *general.* The object of such a title is to contrast the character of my arguments and conclusions with those of the classical theory of the

subject . . . which dominates the economic thought, both practical and theoretical, of the governing and academic classes of this generation, as it has for a hundred years past. I shall argue that the postulates of the classical theory are applicable to a special case only and not to the *general* case. . . . Moreover, the characteristics of the special case assumed by the classical theory happen not to be those of the economic society in which we actually live, with the result that its teaching is misleading and disastrous if we attempt to apply it to the facts of experience.[29]

The classical school of economics offered no solution to the problems facing the nation during the 1930s. But obviously, the optimistic view that the economic problems were temporary, requiring only belt tightening and waiting for the economy to grow, was not acceptable to most of the population. Keynes asserted that:

The celebrated optimism of traditional economic theory [is] to be traced, I think, to their having neglected to take account of the drag on prosperity which can be exercised by an insufficiency of effective *demand*. For there would obviously be a natural tendency towards the optimum employment of resources in a Society which was functioning after the manner of the classical postulates. It may well be that *the classical theory represents the way in which we should like our Economy to behave. But to assume that it actually does so is to assume our difficulties away.*[30]

Keynes believed that the psychological and organizational conditions of the nineteenth century that permitted laissez-faire notions to work as a policy, in fact constituted a special case that was shattered by World War I. The convoluted and contrived system depended on free imports of goods and export of capital made possible by peace. It depended also on a delicate class balance between capital and labor, and a moral balance between capital and spending. In the 1920s, price instability led to the unjustified enrichment of some and the impoverishment of others, which cut the moral link between effort and reward. Worker acceptance of modest wages depended on the dominant business class producing job opportunities. There was also a psychological balance between saving and consumption in which saving was a great virtue. But increasingly, consumption and material outcomes constituted the measure of success— and failure. And increasingly, capitalism's driving force was a "vice" that Keynes called "love of money."[31]

With 25 percent of the labor force unemployed, it was also no longer possible to contend that people pushed into uncompensated unemployment were simply too lazy to get a job, or that they could find work if they would only lower their wage demands. Marxists of the day felt vindicated, believing that the depression was the death knell of the market system.

At the core of Keynes's disagreement with the classical view was his argument that a market economy is inherently unstable. The market system could reach a position of "underemployment equilibrium" in which the economy could have a high level of unemployment and idle industrial equipment. Keynes stressed the importance of **aggregate demand** as the immediate determinant of national income, output, and employment. Demand is the sum of consumption, investment, government expenditures, and net exports. Effective demand establishes the economy's equilibrium level of actual output. A **recession** occurs when the equilibrium level of actual output is less than the level necessary to maintain full employment. The basic characteristic of a recession or depression is a decline in aggregate demand or purchasing power by consumers, business, and government. The result is an economic downturn caused by a reduction in production and the consequent increase in unemployment as employers react to reduce their costs. The significance of his theory in relation to classical theory was that it claimed *there is no self-correcting property in the market system* to return a stagnant economy to growth and full employment.

If Keynes's analysis was correct, the classical nostrum of tightening your belt and riding out the storm was disastrous. It meant that, if demand was established at levels so low that unemployment would remain high and businesses would not be willing to undertake new investments, the situation would remain indefinitely in that depressed state unless some variable in the economic equation was changed. According to Keynes, political management of the economy was the solution. Government spending might well be a necessary public policy to help a depressed market economy regain its vigor. According to Keynes, to the extent that there were market failures leading to insufficient demand, government should intervene through fiscal and monetary policies to promote full employment, stable prices, and economic growth. Useful government action against recessions came down to fiscal and monetary measures designed to expand consumer and investment spending. This would simultaneously improve the general social welfare by improving the position of those who are the most vulnerable in periods of economic stagnation: the unemployed.

Keynes did not think the relationship between supply and demand was merely a mechanical relationship that could be easily manipulated by government or the market. He was aware that greed and fear have a profound psychological influence on individual economic decisionmaking. For example, he was conscious that, when people panic (perhaps in fear over a possible job loss), they stop buying and hoard their cash. Keynes referred to it as "extreme liquidity preference." This can cause markets to freeze as demand plummets. Conversely, investors are eager to invest their money when they feel a surge of what he called "animal spirits," which has the effect of making economies surge.

If Keynes was right in his analysis and prescriptions for curing the ills of capitalism, then the attraction of a planned economy as represented by communism would atrophy because people prefer to be employed and self-sufficient rather than dependent on the government for everything. His public policy solution was one in which business and government would act as partners in running the economy. The government would engage in public policies that would create a sufficient demand to maintain full employment, and profits would go to business as they had in the past. Government was the only party of this arrangement that could pull it off, however, since it alone could act in the role of a non-self-interested party. He saw government acting as a positive instrument for individual freedom by, for example, funding programs such as education that would help individuals as well as society, and for economic freedom by protecting a system whose entrepreneurs could flourish, albeit in a regulated way. Keynes maintained that economic prosperity is the only certain guarantee of a liberal political system.

Keynes's thinking was almost the opposite of Smith's. Disturbances in employment, output, or prices are likely to be magnified by the invisible hand of the marketplace. A catastrophe like the Great Depression is not a rare occurrence, but rather a disaster that will return if we depend on the market to self-adjust. Thus, when the economy stumbles, we cannot wait for an invisible hand to provide the needed adjustments. The government must intervene to safeguard jobs and income. The total number of jobs in the economy is determined by macroeconomic variables, including levels of consumption, investment, and imports and exports. Keynes's analysis also made short work of Malthusian perspectives. The poor, he made clear, were not poor because they were less moral than the affluent; they were poor because of their position in society and impersonal economic forces.

A critical factor in determining the total number of jobs in the economy, or the "employment pie," is the relationship between employment and inflation, which constrains the number of jobs that decisionmakers can or should create. Liberal Keynesians are more concerned about high rates of unemployment than inflation. They are opposed to high interest rates, and prefer fiscal—as opposed to monetary—policy to pursue broad economic goals. Conservative Keynesians are more concerned about inflation, and therefore accept higher unemployment to reduce it, and are less willing to use fiscal policy (especially deficits) to provide full employment.

Keynes's theory was a clear advancement in our understanding of market capitalism. Part of his success was also based on the fact that he addressed not only pressing problems of the moment—economic depression and unemployment—but also enduring policy concerns like growth and stability. And, like Smith before him, he developed a theory that rationalized what was already being done out of necessity. Without the Great Depression, Keynes would never have written his general theory; but already by the time of its publication, Franklin Roosevelt had been elected and was implementing his New Deal, which was Keynesian in practice.

Political leaders of both parties in the United States have long held an overwhelming presumption that, in regard to election and reelection prospects, few things are more foolhardy than a tax increase or more helpful than a tax cut. The temptation to run big deficits when the economy is not in recession was reined in by Keynesian theory, which held that large deficits would result in higher inflation, requiring high interest rates to stop rising prices and bringing about a recession, which would spell disaster in elections. The perceived close connection between short-term economic trends and politics produced an arrangement that permitted deficits, but kept them within a narrow range.

Keynes's analysis provided the rationale for governments to adopt public policies to keep inflation and unemployment low while encouraging economic growth. Governments would have a major macroeconomic role with their state, but there should be free trade between states. These policies were embodied in the Full Employment Act of 1946, which committed the government to an activist policy to stimulate enough growth to keep unemployment low. The 1946 legislation did not define precise goals so that policymakers would know what goals to shoot for to achieve "full employment," or acceptable levels of inflation or economic growth. The Full Employment and Balanced Growth Act of 1978 finally established an unemployment goal of 4 percent, an inflation rate of not more than 3 percent, and an economic growth rate of 4 percent.

Employment and Inflation

When unemployment reaches its full-employment level, we might expect wide satisfaction. Indeed, when the jobless rate declines to full employment, the most highly paid fear inflation will be touched off because it will cost more to find idle resources and bring them online. **Inflation** occurs when there is an increase in the average level of prices for goods and services (not a change in the price of any specific good or service). The conventional wisdom that says "inflation hurts us all" is simply not correct. *Inflation redistributes income and wealth. Thus, while inflation will make some worse off, it must make others better off.* Inflation acts like a tax in which money is redistributed from one group to another. For illustration, if the Organization of Petroleum-Exporting Countries (OPEC) doubles the price of oil, the price of a gallon of gas will rise, making the purchaser poorer, but the extra price will be transferred to OPEC countries, making others wealthier. Since inflation is an increase in average prices, not all prices rise at the same rate. Therefore, not everyone benefits or suffers equally from inflation.

However, the determination to wring inflation out of the economy by driving up interest rates will consistently hit some groups harder than others. Lower- and middle-income workers are much more likely to become unemployed than are the more affluent members of the labor force. Stopping inflation by creating an economic slowdown does not affect everyone equally:

> Recessions are not equal opportunity disemployers. The odds of being drafted into the fight against inflation increase steadily the lower an individual's earnings and family income are to begin with. The relative income losses suffered by the working heads

of poor families, for example, are four to five times as great as the losses for those heading high-income families.[32]

The spending side of the budget is another fiscal policy tool. An increase in government spending is also an increase in aggregate demand and raises production levels. A reduction in spending reduces aggregate demand and reduces inflationary pressures. Government spending now exceeds $2 trillion a year, so changes in the federal budget can have a significant influence on aggregate demand. The spending surge to pay the costs for the war in Iraq in 2004 significantly increased aggregate demand. Combining the surge in national government expenditures with the significant tax cuts, even when directed primarily toward the affluent, significantly increased the fiscal stimulus in 2001, 2002, and 2003.

Monetary policy refers to the use of money and credit controls to shift aggregate demand in the direction needed to attain economic growth with stable prices, such as actions taken by a central bank like the Fed in the United States, to control the money supply. These actions in turn control the volume of lending and borrowing by commercial banks and, ultimately, by investors and consumers. In a depression, the government should increase the money supply to keep interest rates down. This policy might also be matched by reducing taxes for workers to increase demand, and increasing government spending to stimulate business investments, employment, and demand.

Some policy analysts disagree over how active the Fed should be in adjusting the money supply relative to changing economic conditions. Some have argued that the Fed should be an active policymaker while others, like Milton Friedman, argue for a more passive role in which the Fed would intervene to apply fixed rules regarding the money supply. It is undoubtedly true that the Fed risks making errors in applying discretionary policy. However, in some cases, the Fed may intentionally raise interest rates to reduce inflation with the goal of increasing unemployment and reducing wages. As Paul Volcker, chairman of the Fed in 1979, said as he raised interest rates: "The standard of living of the average American has to decline. I don't think you can escape that."[33] The action had the intended effect of reducing wages and disciplining labor while finance capital flowed into the United States to take advantage of the higher rates of return.

Political Economy: The Uneasy Relationship Between Politics and Economics

From the Roosevelt administration through the administration of Jimmy Carter, Keynes's influence was dominant and at its peak in the 1950s and 1960s. Many government officials began to speak of the possibility, through Keynesian theory, of doing away with economic recessions that resulted from laissez-faire economies through skillful government management.

In the early 1960s, John Kennedy became the first president to avowedly follow the Keynesian approach to shaping public policies. For nearly eight years, this interventionist approach to policy was so successful in producing an uninterrupted expansion of the economy that economics was declared to be a science. The decision to extend the Nobel Prize to include an annual award in the area of economics capped this newfound prestige. But ironically, Keynesian economics was about to suffer an erosion in confidence at the moment of its greatest triumph.

A Monetarist Ascendancy

By the late 1970s, a variation on classical economics began to take shape that did suggest a different way for public policy to deal with inflation and economic growth. Friedman accepted Keynesian thinking in the 1930s and, from 1941 to 1943, he was an official spokesman for the New Deal before Congress. As recently as 1986, he still praised Keynes as "one of the great economists of all time."[34] But by the 1970s, Friedman argued that national prosperity would spring from markets free of government interference except in the area of a need to keep control over monetary policy (hence, the term "monetarism"). President Ronald Reagan needed an economic theory that would provide an acceptable policy doctrine as the intellectual basis for a dramatic departure from previous practice. He put together a set of policies based on Friedman's ideals that included a major reduction in taxes, especially for the most affluent; slashing government regulations of business; and selling public industries into private hands. It was promised that these policies would result in lower inflation and a dramatically expanding economy. The theory was referred to as **supply-side economics** to indicate its emphasis was not on the consumers (demand side), but on the investors, financiers, and corporate managers (supply side) who needed relief from taxes and regulations to stimulate economic activity. Their approach reopened a debate many thought had been settled by the Great Depression when they openly proclaimed their goal to widen the gap between economic "winners" and the "losers" as an incentive to work hard, save, and invest. Cynics labeled supply-side programs a return to the "trickle-down" economics of the predepression era.[35]

Despite warnings from many economists, Reagan proceeded to push supply-side policies in the fond hope that he could cut taxes, increase spending, grow the economy, and reduce inflation by tightening the money supply at the same time.[36] If correct, it would permit government to cut taxes and spend more simultaneously—the politicians' equivalent of accomplishing the medieval alchemists' quest to turn lead into gold. Not surprisingly, supply-side economics did not live up to its billing.

In 1982–1983, the economy fell into the deepest recession since the Great Depression. Productivity growth declined in the 1980s (to less than 2 percent per year from 3.2 percent in the 1970s). Finally, these policies contributed to the increase in inequality during the decade. For all of these reasons, supply-side theories never displaced Keynesian theory among academic political economists.

From 1980 through the administration of G. W. Bush, with the exception of the Bill Clinton administration, government policies have been the opposite of the 1930s solution to the economic crisis. The solution of the New Deal resolved the crisis by a downward redistribution of income. However, since the 1980s government's solution, aggressively supported by finance capital, shifted the burden to labor and the middle class by an upward redistribution of income achieved through regressive tax policies.[37]

The election of G. W. Bush in 2000 marked a sharp return to the Friedman (classical liberal) school by slashing taxes, even while the nation was entering costly military operations in Iraq and Afghanistan. Bush's mantra of cutting taxes, reducing the size of government, and reducing regulation of business offered enormous benefits to the rich and powerful. His "efforts to weaken the enforcement of securities laws or environmental regulations fit the same mold: they reflect a free market model while they also please well-organized lobbies."[38] The building pressure on labor and the middle class became increasingly intractable and finally resulted in the financial crisis beginning in 2007. Russell Baker has observed that "no Republican president since Roosevelt's death has tried harder than George W. Bush to undo what Roosevelt did."[39]

However, G. W. Bush was forced to end his presidency by asking for a $750 billion bailout package to save capitalism from its weaknesses. The most conservative administration since Hoover, which espoused the philosophy that government is the problem, was forced to adopt Roosevelt's and Keynes's solutions to the problem of the instability of capitalism. And in October 2008, Alan Greenspan was blamed for the laissez-faire economic policies that contributed to the current financial crisis. Greenspan acknowledged that he was partially wrong in opposing financial regulation. He conceded he was "shocked" to find a flaw in free-market ideology.[40]

A Keynesian Revival

The eerie parallels of swiftness and the severity of the onset of the recession beginning in 2007 suggest obvious comparisons to the Great Depression. The broad demand that government take action to stimulate the economy to save the world from a new Great Depression is a vindication for Keynes after over thirty years in Friedman's shadow. Keynesian economics was never defeated intellectually. In short, the triumph of the idea that "governments should deregulate the economy" and that "government is not the solution, government is the problem" represented a political victory for dominant financial elites, not a victory of economic ideas. The heads of the leading financial institutions were the first to approach government in deep distress demanding bailouts. While they were willing under the circumstances to accept some oversight as inevitable, they recommended that government should not reregulate business.

As Allen Sinai said, "the free market is not geared to take care of the casualties, because there's no profit motive. There's no market incentive to deal with the unemployed or those who have lost their homes."[41] Friedman is now faulted for failing to temper his admonitions with an understanding of poverty and income inequality. The monetarists, just as classical economists of an earlier era, "ignored the way elites were able to distort the policies they prescribed for their own benefit."[42] In the fall of 2008, the British chancellor of the exchequer cited Keynesian theory as he announced plans for a fiscal stimulus by the government to avoid a more serious recession.[43]

The removal of many of the key financial regulations established in the New Deal led inexorably to the return of the excesses of the 1920s. Competition is not a sufficient disciplinarian to ward off excesses, especially in financial markets. The Obama administration's effort is to try to implement both short- and long-range Keynesian policies to stimulate the economy. However, the defenders of the deregulated "free market" who are largely responsible for the current financial crisis make it clear that the policies which their failures have made necessary are still abhorrent to them. Many of the conservatives recommended that the stimulus package should lean heavily on more permanent corporate, capital gains, and individual tax cuts, which would further reduce the size of government. As a tool to stimulate the economy, tax cuts are not as effective as government spending since most individuals receiving a tax cut tend to save it or use it to pay off debts. Conversely, a government expenditure of a dollar will stimulate more demand.

The current financial crisis is a continuation of business opposition to what they considered "wage inflation" of the late 1970s when business "went on strike" against unionized labor. Reagan broke the air traffic controllers' strike in 1981 by firing 11,000 workers, signaling a sharp break in the government's support of organized labor extending from the New Deal on. Business mobilized against the pressure from labor for a higher standard of living by exporting jobs to low-wage countries and anti-union strategies that resulted in less than 10 percent of nongovernment workers unionized by the end of 2008. The effort to privatize Social Security by shifting the funds to investment firms by the G. W. Bush administration was thwarted by strong voter opposition. The effort to repeal the estate tax, which would allow the wealthy to pass fortunes from one generation to the next and avoid all federal taxes, was only partially successful. The threat of reduced consumption by middle-income workers with stagnant wages was delayed by expanding available credit to temporarily boost demand.

The current financial crisis and the reduced amount of available credit are merely the visible part of the iceberg hiding the deeper problem of diminished demand caused by the dismantling of the New Deal–Keynesian social compact and the upward redistribution of incomes at least since 1980. Henry Paulson's plan of giving money to financial institutions without any strings attached only worsened the problem. It did so because the government was taking taxpayer money and transferring it to financial institutions where it could be used for bonuses and excessive executive salaries, further increasing upward redistribution.

President Obama's reform effort in the bailout involves an attempt to encourage job-creating expenditures to encourage high wages and full employment for middle-income workers. That is the justification for large investments in repairing infrastructure and promoting renewable energy and environmentally friendly job creation. If the stimulus efforts do not result in significantly stimulating employment, the effect will be only temporary. Obama has worked tirelessly to promote bipartisan support for his policies of progressive change. He has tried to influence the corporate culture by putting executive pay limits on any company that accepts government funds. However, those who would have to accept some downward redistribution are resisting vigorously.

Is the current financial crisis proof that Keynesian policies have won the day over conservative economics? Actually, Keynesian (liberal) economics won the intellectual debate by the late 1930s. When unfettered capitalism led to the excesses of "the Gilded Age" of the 1920s and the Great Depression in the next decade, Roosevelt responded to the demand by the American public that government had to reform the system. He responded with policies to restore faith in the financial system by regulating their operation. Since that time, downward turns in the business cycle have been met with government policies to stimulate the economy through fiscal and monetary policies. The government has alternatively acted to wring inflation out of the economy by raising interest rates and tightening the money supply while, at other times, stimulating economic activity by reducing interest rates and adding demand.

The economic theory and its application are quite straightforward. Keynes thought the economics were commonsensical. The idea that short-term markets are inherently unstable and are not self-correcting is not that impenetrable a concept. Likewise, the notion that government therapies for the financial crisis are at hand is also clear. The problem is that the medicine is unpalatable to the minority who are opposed to any permanent regulation. Thus, they argue for only temporary rules until the crisis is overcome, after which the regulations should be removed so as not to inhibit the "creativity" of the market. This overlooks the fact that, especially since 1980, many financial regulations have been weakened or removed.

The difficulty in dealing with the current crisis is more political than economic. The notion from classical economics, and reinforced by Friedman, that government should not intervene and we would be better off if everyone just worked to maximize profits is based more on ideology than on positive economic theory.

Many economic failures are not failures of economic theory so much as they are failures caused by the real world of politicians. It is clear that Keynes, like Smith, was too optimistic in his economic views. He assumed that a better understanding of the relationship between economic variables would permit government to enter the market system to maximize social welfare. He implicitly accepted the notion that government would be neutral and benign and would intervene only to increase demand and provide employment, thus increasing output and improving income distribution. He assumed that an understanding of the shortcomings of market economics would lead to agreement about solutions. But he seems to have misjudged the degree to which governments are penetrated by self-interested groups who lobby for their own special interests rather than the general welfare of society.

Political actors may share the same goal of a growing economy, full employment, and price stability, but they often have different priorities. All politicians consider winning the next election their first priority. Therefore, they will be more concerned with the need to raise money and win votes than with economic theory. Politicians are notoriously reluctant to raise taxes on potential campaign contributors. They are also reluctant to cut spending to control inflation. For example, the tradeoffs relative to a political actor's main constituents will influence whether fighting inflation or fighting unemployment will receive priority. Middle- and lower-income workers, along with unions and the unemployed, would urge that achieving full employment should receive the highest priority. However, more affluent communities, along with bankers and those on fixed incomes such as retired people, prefer that controlling inflation be given the highest priority.

The politics of economic policy may actually reward politicians for behaving irresponsibly and punish responsible economic policy. For example, tax hikes rarely win votes and, despite the fact that tax increases on the wealthiest Americans had an overall effect in reducing the deficit in 1991–1992, Democrats lost control of Congress as a direct result of that policy. On the other hand, proposing tax cuts when the economy is strong because "we can afford it," as well as when the economy is weak "to stimulate growth," has a strong appeal for voters' abiding desire for a higher after-tax income.

Conclusion

The father of modern economics, Adam Smith, tried to free the capitalist market system from the inefficiencies associated with mercantilism in which government provided protection for and control over business. His theory promoted an economic model that claims full employment of workers and capital can be maintained without any government intervention as long as there are no monopolies or a highly unequal distribution of income. His sympathies were decidedly on the side of the workers and against business owners. Deviations from the ideal of full employment should self-adjust as if by an invisible hand, thus eliminating the need for government involvement. Smith's sympathies and his qualifications were largely ignored while his views in support of laissez-faire were accepted enthusiastically by entrepreneurs.

Thomas Malthus focused on the increasing economic disparity between the rich and the poor. His analysis led him to conclude that poverty is a moral problem: the poor lack moral restraints in reproduction. Any effort to improve their condition through government relief or higher wages will result in their producing more offspring until they fall back to subsistence levels again. This view of the iron law of wages, developed by David Ricardo, largely doomed any effort to improve the situation of workers through higher wages, government policy, or charity. The theory reinforced laissez-faire thinking and justified opposition to any policy proposal on behalf of the lower classes by the more affluent. Malthusian views can be directly linked to arguments that tax rates on the wealthy should be kept as low as possible, and that it is immoral and counterproductive to take wealth from the affluent and transfer it to those who are less well off.

Karl Marx seized on the problems of monopoly and the inequality exacerbated by them. Marx saw threats to the capitalist system everywhere. John Maynard Keynes's defense of capitalism against Marxism revolutionized economic theory. His analysis held that market economies are inherently unstable, and that they have no self-correcting properties. According to Keynes, government may be the only part of society capable of intervening in the economy to create the demand necessary to maintain full employment. His analysis showed the economy to be much more complex than anything suggested by the classical school. His conclusion was that there are several different areas of monetary and fiscal policy in which the government may successfully intervene. These interventions may also be geared to achieve social goals of the society other than those purely economic in nature.

It may well be that the very survival of a capitalist economy in the United States is due to the relief from some of its harshest failures (poverty, unemployment, alienation, and income insecurity) by the Keynesian welfare state. The welfare state may result less from policy choices in search of social justice than from choices to ensure the survival of a capitalist economy. Government expenditures, both national and state, now account for close to 30 percent of GDP in the United States.

The recession beginning in December 2007, often called "The Great Recession," has refocused attention on the theories of the classical school and the Keynesian school and their supporting arguments. The reaction to the crisis makes it clear that laissez-faire and self-regulation cannot be sustained economically or politically. How the crisis will be solved, has not yet been determined. If the burden of the financial crisis is shifted further from capital to the middle and working class, the economic and political problems will grow. If the president is able to shift part of the burden back to capital and Keynesianism, the prospects for greater equity and less stress will be improved.

Questions for Discussion

1. There is a generally held view that Adam Smith was an advocate of minimal government involvement in the economy. What evidence is there to support this view? Does this view need to be qualified?

2. Why and how did Karl Marx agree and disagree with Adam Smith?

3. How have the major tenets of the classical school been challenged by Keynesian theory?

4. In what ways has Keynesian theory been challenged or modified by subsequent writers?

5. How might the manner in which the financial crisis beginning in 2007 is resolved have a lasting impact on the political and economic future of the United States?

Notes

1. Adam Smith, *An Inquiry into the Nature and Causes of the Wealth of Nations,* edited by Edwin Cannan (New York: G. P. Putnam's Sons, 1877; originally published in 1776), p. 27. Smith wrote: "Every individual necessarily labours to render the annual revenue of the society as great as he can. He generally, indeed, neither intends to promote the public interest nor knows how much he is promoting it . . . he intends only his own gain and he is in this, as in many other cases, led by an invisible hand to promote an end which was no part of his intention. Nor is it always the worse for the society that it was no part of it. By pursuing his own interest he frequently promotes that of the society more effectually than when he really intends to promote it. I have never known much good done by those who affected to trade for the public good. It is an affectation, indeed, not very common among merchants, and very few words need be employed in dissuading them from it" (p. 354).

2. As quoted in Robert L. Heilbroner, *The Essential Adam Smith* (New York: W. W. Norton, 1986), p. 322.

3. Adam Smith, *The Wealth of Nations,* 6th ed. (London: Metheun, 1950), vol. 1, p. 144.

4. Ibid., p. 110.

5. Smith was against the government meddling with the market mechanism. As Robert Heilbroner has pointed out: "Smith never faced the problem . . . of whether the government is weakening or strengthening the market mechanism when it steps in with welfare legislation. . . . There was virtually no welfare legislation in Smith's day—the government was the unabashed ally of the governing classes. . . . The question of whether the working class should have a voice in the direction of economic affairs simply did not enter any respectable person's mind." Robert Heilbroner, *The Worldly Philosophers,* 3rd rev. ed. (New York: Simon and Schuster, 1967), pp. 63–64.

6. Adam Smith, *The Theory of Moral Sentiments,* edited by D. D. Raphael and A. L. Macfie (Oxford: Clarendon Press, 1976; originally published in 1759), p. 386 (emphasis added). For excellent summaries of Smith's contributions, see Robert Heilbroner and Lester Thurow, *Economics Explained: Everything You Need to Know About How the Economy Works and Where It's Going* (New York: Simon and Schuster, 1998), pp. 26–44; Robert L. Heilbroner, *The Worldly Philosophers,* 6th ed. (New York: Simon and Schuster, 1992), pp. 42–75; and Daniel R. Fusfeld, *The Age of the Economist,* 9th ed. (New York: Addison-Wesley, 2002), pp. 23–36.

7. Smith's writings in *The Wealth of Nations* were in part an effort to refute the contention of mercantilists that the economy should be regulated by the monarchy to provide support for merchants, which would ultimately increase the nation's power. The king was free to intervene in the most arbitrary and capricious ways as an exercise of "sovereign right." Smith wrote: "England, however, has never been blessed with a very parsimonious government, so parsimony has at no time been the characteristic virtue of its inhabitants. It is the highest impertinence and presumption, therefore, in kings and ministers, to pretend to watch over the economy

of private people, and to restrain their expence, either by sumptuary laws, or by prohibiting the importation of foreign luxuries. They are themselves always, and without exception, the greatest spendthrifts in the society. Let them look well after their own expence, and they may safely trust private people with theirs. If their own extravagance does not ruin the state, that of their subjects never will." Adam Smith, *An Inquiry into the Nature and Causes of the Wealth of Nations* (New York: G. P. Putnam's Sons, 1877), pp. 227–228.

8. Heilbroner, *The Essential Adam Smith,* p. 284.

9. Ibid., p. 322.

10. Adam Smith, *Wealth of Nations* (New York: The Modern Library, Random House, 1937), p. 674.

11. Ibid., p. 389.

12. Ibid., pp. 15–16.

13. Ibid., p. 79.

14. Ibid.

15. As quoted in Fusfeld, *The Age of the Economist,* pp. 32–33.

16. Ibid., p. 33.

17. Thomas Robert Malthus, *An Essay on the Principle of Population,* 6th ed., cited in E. A. Wrigley and D. Souden, ed., *The Works of Thomas Robert Malthus* (London: William Pickering, 1986), vol. 3, p. 493.

18. Robert C. Tucker, ed., *The Marx-Engels Reader,* 2nd ed. (New York: W. W. Norton, 1978), p. 477.

19. Karl Marx and Friedrich Engels, *The Communist Manifesto,* edited by Samuel Beer (New York: Appleton-Century Crofts, 1955), p. 9.

20. Ibid., p. 12.

21. The US Business Cycle Dating Committee established August 1929 as the beginning of the Great Depression, coinciding with a decline in industrial production.

22. As quoted in Russell Baker, "A Revolutionary President," *The New York Review of Books,* February 12, 2009, p. 6.

23. "The Roosevelt Week," *Time,* September 28, 1936, p. 11. The name of his program, "A New Deal," was taken from the title of a book that had caused something of a stir when it was published a few months earlier. See Stuart Chase, *A New Deal* (New York: Macmillan, 1932). The book makes reference to some of Keynes's earlier writings and generally provides an assessment of the nation's economic problems and proposes various progressive government policies to deal with the issues.

24. Baker, "A Revolutionary President," p. 6.

25. Arthur Schlesinger Jr., "The 'Hundred Days' of FDR," *New York Times,* April 10, 1983, p. 1.

26. Farshad Araghi, "Political Economy of the Financial Crisis: A World-Historical Perspective," *Economic & Political Weekly,* November 8, 2008, p. 30.

27. There is far more to Keynesian analysis than the few points made here. In addition to Keynes's own *General Theory of Employment, Interest, and Money* (New York: Harcourt, Brace, and World, 1936), recommended for further reading is G. C. Harcourt, ed., *Keynes and His Contemporaries* (New York: St. Martin's Press, 1985).

28. John Maynard Keynes, "The End of Laissez-Faire," in *Essays in Persuasion* (New York: W. W. Norton, 1963), p. 321 (emphasis added).

29. Keynes, *General Theory,* p. 3 (emphasis added).

30. Ibid., pp. 33–34 (emphasis added).

31. Robert J. Skidelsky, *Maynard Keynes: The Economist as Saviour, 1920–1937* (New

York: Viking Penguin, 1992), esp. chap 7, "Keynes' Middle Way."

32. Isabel V. Sawhill and Charles F. Stone, "The Economy: The Key to Success," in Isabel V. Sawhill and John Palmer, ed., *The Reagan Record: An Assessment of America's Changing Domestic Priorities* (Cambridge, MA: Ballinger, 1984), p. 80.

33. Steven Rattner, "Volker Asserts US Must Trim Living Standard," *New York Times,* October 18, 1979, p. 1.

34. Milton Friedman, "Keynes's Political Legacy," in John Burton, ed., *Keynes's General Theory: Fifty Years On* (London: Institute of Economic Affairs, 1986), pp. 47–48, 52.

35. See, especially, Paul Krugman, *Peddling Prosperity: Economic Sense and Nonsense in the Age of Diminished Expectations* (New York: W. W. Norton, 1994).

36. Three Nobel Prize–winning economists, James Buchanan, Milton Friedman, and George Stiegler, with impeccable conservative credentials, scorned supply-side thinking.

37. Araghi, "Political Economy of the Financial Crisis," p. 35.

38. Jonathan Chait, *The Big Con: The True Story of How Washington Got Hoodwinked by Crackpot Economics* (New York: Houghton Mifflin, 2007), p. 63.

39. Ibid., p. 6.

40. Rebecca Winters Keegan, "Greenspan 'Shocked' to Find Flaws in His Free-Market Ideology," available at www.time.com/time/specials/2008/top10/article/0,30583,1855948_1864014_1864016 (accessed February 4, 2009).

41. Peter S. Goodman, "A Fresh Look at the Apostle of Free Markets," *New York Times,* April 13, 2008, p. 3.

42. Ibid.

43. "Darling Invokes Keynes as He Eases Spending Rules to Fight Recession," *The Guardian,* available at www.guardian.co.uk/politics/2008/oct/20/economy-recession-treasury-energy-housing (accessed February 3, 2009).

6

Economic Policy: Translating Theory into Practice

The Founding Fathers wrote in the Preamble to the Constitution that they were forming a national government in order to "establish justice, insure domestic tranquility, provide for the common defense, promote the general welfare and secure the blessings of liberty to ourselves and our posterity." For most of the nation's history, the primary focus of government, as measured by spending, was to provide for the common defense. As noted in Chapter 5, prior to the 1930s most citizens accepted the economic theory that was vigorously supported by the financial elite of the time, which held that a market economy would achieve the macroeconomic goals of full employment, price stability, and productivity growth without government involvement.

The Great Depression shattered such complacent beliefs. Even so, in the 1930s, the New Deal was considered very radical. Franklin Roosevelt rallied middle- and working-class workers to his reforms as he railed against the "plutocrats" who opposed him on the eve of the 1936 election:

> They had begun to consider the Government of the United States as a mere appendage to their own affairs. We know now that Government by organized money is just as dangerous as Government by organized mob.
>
> Never before in all our history have these forces been so united against one candidate as they stand today. They are unanimous in their hate for me—and I welcome their hatred.[1]

In truth, the plutocrats had good reason for their hatred of Roosevelt. He had raised taxes on the wealthy and their corporations, encouraged the growth of unions, and reduced income inequality from the 1920s.

After World War II, it was clear that raising taxes on the wealthy, providing unemployment insurance, providing Social Security, and supporting worker unionization had not been disastrous for the economy as Roosevelt's critics had predicted.[2] The success of the federal government in organizing the huge mobilization of national resources to wage a global war also made it difficult for critics to argue that government could not do anything well. Republicans regained control of Congress in 1946, and opposed institutions of the New Deal as "socialistic." Emboldened by passing the Taft-Hartley Act, which significantly weakened the protections for labor in the National Labor Relations Act of 1935, conservatives ridiculed President Harry Truman and predicted a Republican victory in the 1948 presidential election. Truman won by campaigning against the "do-nothing" Republican Congress while defending the New Deal. Conservatives were forced to accept the notion that an active role for government had become respectable for a majority of voters.[3] When Republicans did regain the White House with Dwight Eisenhower in 1952, most party leaders accepted the general contours of the New Deal as an enduring part of the political landscape.

The crisis of the Great Depression made the New Deal possible. And it was the success of the New Deal that challenged the accepted wisdom that government cannot do anything successfully and should remain on the sidelines. The New Deal began to shift national priorities away from "common defense" and toward promoting "the general welfare." This profound change in the public philosophy regarding the nature and purpose of government spending is the most basic transformation in public policy in the past century.

These governmental programs started in the 1930s are labeled collectively **social welfare** (see Chapter 2), in which governments and frequently nongovernmental organizations (NGOs) provide a minimum level of income for marginalized groups such as the poor or elderly. Social welfare payments are usually provided at taxpayer expense, or by private charitable organizations.

In practice, the distinction between social welfare and social insurance is often blurred. **Social insurance** refers to government programs with several common characteristics. The government transfers risks to a program in which the government becomes legally required to provide relief for individuals or groups against adverse situations or events. Individuals may be required to participate by paying into an insurance program such as Social Security, Medicare, unemployment insurance, or workers' compensation. Eligibility requirements are usually defined by statute. Eligibility for benefits is typically not **means-tested**; that is, it is not dependent on the level of a person's income or assets. Such programs are usually a response to market failures, but may also occur when the market provides an outcome that is deemed unacceptable to societal values.

This chapter and the ones that follow focus on a variety of social welfare programs designed to provide regulation or greater equity between groups such as labor regulation.

Promoting the General Welfare in Practice

Nations with well-developed social welfare and social insurance programs are often referred to as welfare states. In many of these countries, access to such government programs is considered a basic right based on *social justice* for those in need. This view is supported by the International Covenant on Economic, Social and Cultural Rights which has been ratified by 156 countries, but not by the United States.[4] This is significant when one considers that health care is thought of as a natural right of the individual based on principles of social justice throughout Europe, Canada, and other developed countries of the world. In the United States, it is a "privilege" for those able to afford it, not a "right."

The point is that the obligation of democratic government to "promote the general welfare" was embedded in the United States Constitution long before democratic revolutions spread throughout Europe. However, the idea of the welfare state has evolved throughout most of the developed world to indicate a greater responsibility of the state to provide comprehensive and universal welfare for its citizens than it has in the United States.

Government and Workers' Right to Unionize

US government policies toward labor and labor unions present a sharp contrast with the espoused position of the signatories of the International Covenant on Economic, Social and Cultural Rights on the right of workers to form unions. Throughout Europe trade union membership, which is protected by the treaty, varies from country to country.[5] But on average, membership is much higher than in the United States. It should also be noted though that there has been some erosion of union membership throughout most of the European Union (EU) countries in recent years. The policies of the US government toward labor that were put in place in the 1930s to fit a more industrial economy and work force are woefully out of date. Even many on the business side agree that, since the last major reform was the antiunion Taft-Hartley Act of 1947, the laws need to be updated. The issue of labor unions in US policy is complicated politically because unions have, at least since the New Deal, generally supported Democrats. The Republican Party has long resented the voter organization and campaign finance support labor traditionally gives to Democrats, and has sought to weaken labor's power. Adam Smith noted a bias in favor of management over labor based on a lack of understanding of management's universal struggle to keep wages as low as possible:

> We rarely hear, it has been said, of the combinations of masters; though frequently of those of workmen. But whoever imagines, upon this account, that masters rarely combine, is as ignorant of the world as of the subject. Masters are always and everywhere

in a sort of tacit, but constant and uniform combination, not to raise the wages of labour above its natural rate.[6]

In 1935 as part of the New Deal, Congress passed the National Labor Relations Act (NLRA) or Wagner Act, which placed the federal government squarely on the side of the right of workers to organize and bargain collectively. Over the next fifteen years, the percentage of US workers in unions rose from 11 percent to over 35 percent. During this time, unions played an active role in helping to create standards such as a minimum wage that equaled about 50 percent of the average wage, paid pensions, wage and hour laws, and health and safety rules.[7]

Even nonunion workers benefited because the threat of union activity encouraged nonunionized employers to offer their workers approximately what their unionized counterparts received. The period from the end of World War II until the 1970s was characterized by "pattern wages," in which the wage and benefit agreements of major unions and corporations established norms for the nonunionized counterparts as well. Powerful unions also acted as a restraint on the incomes of management since senior executives were aware that, if they paid themselves exorbitant salaries and bonuses, they would be inviting increased wage demands from labor. And companies that made high profits and rewarded management while failing to raise wages were putting management relations with labor at risk.[8]

The federal government also intervened generally to support labor while restraining perceived overreach at the top. For example, when adjusted for inflation, the minimum wage was considerably higher in the 1960s and 1970s than it is today. The government could generally be counted on to interpret and enforce labor laws that were supportive of labor unions. And there were notable instances where government might apply direct pressure on large companies when top executives were perceived to have overstepped implicit lines. President John F. Kennedy, in an effort to contain inflation, persuaded steel unions to accept a wage settlement that was actually less than their increase in productivity since the last union contract. Within a few days, steel companies raised the price of steel by an average of 18 percent, citing the new union contract. Kennedy criticized the price hikes as inflationary and demanded that the steel companies rescind their price increases. Yet John Weeks maintains that the increased income inequality in the United States reflects a "growing imbalance in the economic and political power of capital and labor."[9] The declining strength of labor is blamed for workers' wages lagging behind productivity and a less-progressive tax structure.

Seventy-five years after the passage of the NLRA, union membership in the private sector has fallen to 7.4 percent, a level not seen since the 1920s. When government workers are included, the numbers rise only to 12 percent.[10] The dramatic decline in private sector unions has resulted from a more hostile political environment, unfavorable legislation and court decisions, and the changing character of the domestic economy toward globalization.

Nevertheless, unions are still an important factor in politics because not only do they mobilize their own members to get out and vote, but they also join coalitions with like-minded organizations on issues like immigration, health care, and the minimum wage. Unions encourage their members to be politically involved and to vote. As a result they raise the voter turnout, not only of their members but of other people in their general income level by encouraging non–union members to vote, thereby increasing the influence of middle- and lower-income workers. Unions have had the effect of lowering the upper-income bias of the electorate.

The less-friendly political environment is illustrated in President Ronald Reagan's response to the nation's air traffic controllers' union strike in 1981. The union went on strike for higher pay and shorter hours in defiance of a prohibition against work stoppages by federal employees. Reagan fired all 11,345 union members who had defied the legal ban, which sent a strong message to business that it could actively oppose unions without fear of government enforcement of regulations supporting workers. Reagan's willingness to take such strong action against the union strengthened the hand of company managers who began warning workers that, if they went on strike, they might lose their jobs.[11]

Critics blame unions for driving up the cost of labor, making US companies unable to compete with foreign labor. This theory does not stand up to empirical research, however. Various studies challenge the notion and, in fact, conclude that "unions have no net effect on a firm's closure."[12] Josh Bivens of the Economic Policy Institute found that blue collar workers in manufacturing provide a competitive edge over many trading partners since they typically earn lower wages than many US trading partners while posting higher productivity levels. Instead, the US advantage has been squandered in several other ways:

1. US manufacturing workers are not overpaid. Of the twenty richest countries tracked by the Bureau of Labor Statistics, the United States ranks seventeenth in hourly pay.

2. US workers are highly productive. Of the sixteen nations with higher compensation for production workers in manufacturing, the United States ranks only behind Ireland in terms of "value-added per employee."

3. This competitive advantage has been largely offset by exchange rates that have given US trading partners a 10 percent to 16 percent cost advantage.

4. If US health care costs were the same as those of its comparable trading partners, workers would reap a 4.6 percent cost advantage. High health care costs hurt US manufacturers.

5. US managers are overpaid. If wages of managerial and nonsupervisory labor in the United States were the same as the median of comparable trading partners, US manufacturing would have a 6.4 percent cost advantage over trading partners.[13]

Union officials, and other observers, claim that the bargaining power in labor markets has been heavily weighted toward employers who engage in "union-busting" practices through "antiunion" campaigns. Under current federal law, at least 30 percent of employees are required to sign cards indicating support for a union. Subsequently, a federal official will conduct a secret ballot between forty-five and ninety days after the requisite number of cards are received. The union must receive 50 percent plus one of the votes to form a union with collective bargaining rights. Many employers use the forty-five- to ninety-day period to hire union-busting consultants to derail the pro-union vote. Employers hold lunchtime meetings to discuss the pros and cons of union organizing. Managers often threaten to shut the company down or move jobs overseas and, as a last resort, they may fire those known to be pro-union. Firing an employee for indicating a desire to form a union is against the law, but the penalties are so minor as to not be a deterrent. Unions insist that a secret ballot in the context of the ability of the employer to intimidate is no guarantee of a democracy.

In the spring of 2009, legislation designed to strengthen the right of workers to organize was introduced in both houses of Congress with the support of the president. The legislation, known as the Employee Free Choice Act (EFCA), would impose significant penalties on employers who harass, fire, or otherwise try to intimidate workers away from a union. Even when unions are voted in, many employers drag out negotiations with the new union for years. About half of all new unions do not actually sign a contract with the employers since the current law requires only that employers bargain in "good faith," but has no way to enforce it. Under the proposed law, if both sides are not able to reach an agreement within a specified time (three months), the dispute would be turned over to binding arbitration. The proposed law would retain the method of a secret ballot as described above, but it would also allow workers to form a union by an alternative method if the workers so choose. It would permit workers to choose a union by signing a card and submitting it to a union representative, thereby short-circuiting the waiting period in which employer-dominated campaigns against unions are conducted. Conversely, employers complain that, under the proposed law, workers would be exposed to union intimidation.

An alternative proposal designed to reduce Democratic support for the EFCA and avoid a threatened filibuster would strengthen penalties for employers that illegally fire workers who appear pro-union. This alternative would also require elections to be held within three weeks after organizers request one to reduce time available to employers to exert pressure on workers while improving unions' access to workers and acquire binding arbitration if a contract agreement could not be reached.

Both political parties have promised a major effort to support their opposing constituencies' position; that is, Republicans (business) and Democrats (labor). This issue will probably still be roiling in 2010 and 2012.

Evolution of Political-Economic Thinking

Several economic policy goals generally accepted by all governments include: full employment, price stability (low inflation), and economic growth. The insights provided by John Maynard Keynes held that, left alone, the economy might not reach equilibrium at full employment. However, if policymakers were to use monetary and fiscal policies wisely, these policies could increase economic activity and reduce unemployment. According to Keynes's theory, monetary and fiscal policy could be employed throughout the business cycle to maintain low inflation and high employment. For example, the **full-employment budget**, based on calculations of what government tax revenues would be if the economy were operating at full employment, is one fiscal policy that could be used to maintain high employment. Government expenditures would be based on the projected level of revenues at full employment. The additional spending at the level as if there were full employment would provide additional demand to the economy and stimulate job creation. Keynesian theory provided some hope that economic policy could insulate society from the wildly fluctuating business cycles of the past. More important, the theory provided an intellectual justification for active involvement by the state and social spending.

It would be difficult to overstate the importance that Keynes's economic theory has had as a political doctrine. Keynesian theory provided an intellectual framework that justified state activism and social spending for policymakers. Previously, policymakers who increased spending during economic downturns were charged with being fiscally irresponsible and threatening to bankrupt the nation. Now, measured deficit spending in that situation could help stabilize the economy. Programs, such as unemployment compensation, could be designed to automatically inject spending into the economy, thereby offsetting an economic slowdown caused by rising unemployment. When the economy begins to expand, unemployment payments decline as more people return to work, reducing the potential for inflationary pressures.

Policy Instruments

If unregulated markets generated full employment, price stability, economic growth, and an equitable distribution of income as classical economic theory suggests, there would be no need for government intervention. However, markets do fail and governments are called on to intervene. Does government intervention accomplish its goal of economic growth and reduced unemployment and inflation? If not, government intervention also fails. In the real world, of course, nothing is perfect, so the real choice is between imperfect markets and imperfect policy interventions.

The separation of powers fragments the responsibility for economic policy and weakens the government's ability to control the economy. While the president is by far the single most important player in economic policy, the executive branch's ability to control events or policy is often overestimated. Taxing and spending is largely determined by the performance of the economy at the time that the budget is introduced to Congress, and the forecast during the period the budget moves through Congress. Much of the budget includes programs over which a president has little control such as debt refinancing and various entitlement programs.

Policymakers do not prefer high unemployment to full employment, inflation to price stability, or economic recessions to economic growth. But political entrepreneurs have short time horizons and may not find it in their interest to take the action required to reduce inflation, or to get a vigorous economic expansion under way. They may agree with the notion that there is no free lunch, but they are also aware that the price of lunch may be deferred. Elected officials prefer policies that provide short-term benefits before election day, and bills that will not come due until after voters have cast their retrospective ballots. Thus, in the US political process, there is a bias in favor of policies with short-term benefits and long-term costs. This fact has profound implications for the conduct of long-term economic growth and stabilization policies as opposed to near-term policies.

The collapse of the housing bubble in 2008 and the resulting financial meltdown has required the spending of more money by the government, but the string of massive federal deficits in recent years has alarmed many politicians. A conspicuous solution to increased spending needs and huge deficits is large tax increases. But such increases would cause pain to taxpayers and threaten a further reduction in consumer demand that could lead to greater unemployment long before a reduction in the deficit would reduce inflation or free up new government monies. In this case, the political "bads" arrive rather promptly while the "goods" would likely arrive much later and be felt only gradually.

For example, G. W. Bush campaigned in 2000 and 2004 on the platform of cutting taxes. However, with Republicans in control of both houses of Congress and the presidency, there was considerable reluctance to directly cut expenditures also desired by other constituents.

Political entrepreneurs thus have a bias toward expansionary fiscal and monetary policies since lower taxes and increased expenditures for special interest groups provide strong support for an incumbent's bid for reelection. Policies to reduce spending and increase taxes cause unrest among voters. Even though the optimal policy often requires long-term strategies, the political incentives for incumbents may not reflect the long-term economic interests of the nation. Political entrepreneurs find it extremely difficult to continue unpleasant policies since the exigencies of elections threaten their futures.

Taxes as an Instrument of Policy

Through its ability to adjust taxes, especially income taxes, the government can guide the economy and pay for goods and services. The idea of monetary policy was not entirely new in the 1930s, but the idea regarding the use of taxes and national budgets as management tools of economic policy to counter economic cycles of boom and bust *was* new. Although the government borrows money to finance its operations, taxes collected from a variety of sources are the main reservoir of government expenditures.

But the question of who pays is inextricably linked to several other questions regarding tax policy. What is a fair distribution of income? What are the major issues involved in deciding who should bear the burden of taxes? What do political scientists and policy analysts take into consideration when they talk about a fair tax system? Does the US tax system meet the criteria for fairness while promoting the general welfare?

Government intervention is a conscious decision not to leave the provision of certain goods or services to the marketplace. It is a determination that political, not economic, considerations will prescribe which services the government will provide. Taxes are required to finance these goods and services. Therefore, the main purpose of taxation is to move purchasing power from the private to the public sector. Awareness of the distributional consequences of shifting purchasing power to the public sector is essential in judging the consequences of the policies. Antitax sentiment has always run high in the United States. Recall that the American Revolution began as a tax revolt with the dumping of tea into the Boston Harbor because the colonists objected to the taxes levied on the tea. After the adoption of the Constitution, the government relied primarily on customs duties to fund the limited national budget. Congress enacted an income tax during the Civil War, but it expired at the war's end. In 1894, Congress passed another income tax bill that was declared unconstitutional by the Supreme Court in 1895. As a result, the Sixteenth Amendment to the Constitution was ratified in 1916, which gave Congress the power "to lay and collect taxes on incomes *from whatever source derived.*"

Even though Americans are among the least-taxed people in the industrialized world, aversion to taxes runs high and politicians are usually rewarded for a vigorous and righteous defense of constituents against rapacious tax collectors. The data in Figure 6.1 support the evidence that the United States raises significantly lower tax revenues as a percentage of gross domestic product (GDP) than do most countries in the Organisation for Economic Co-operation and Development (OECD). The data in the figure support the evidence that Americans are not overtaxed compared to OECD countries. Taxes from all levels of government are expressed as a percentage of each country's GDP, or output. This is the best measure of relative taxation because it includes not only the tax burden, but also an indication of the ability to pay the taxes levied.

The OECD found that, of thirty countries examined (mostly Western, industrialized nations), only Mexico and Turkey collected a smaller share of revenues as a percentage of GDP than the United States.[14] The reality is that, when compared to most industrialized nations, the United States is a tax haven.

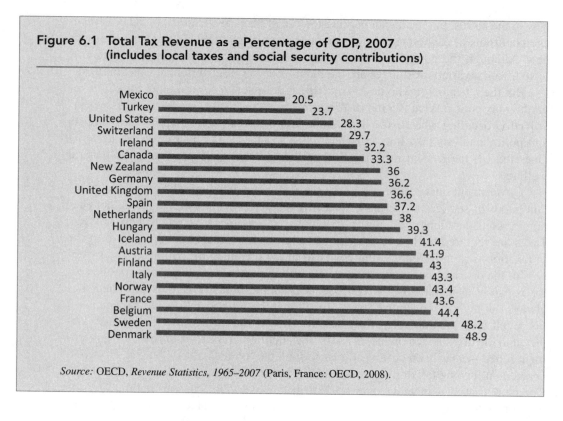

Figure 6.1 Total Tax Revenue as a Percentage of GDP, 2007
(includes local taxes and social security contributions)

Country	%
Mexico	20.5
Turkey	23.7
United States	28.3
Switzerland	29.7
Ireland	32.2
Canada	33.3
New Zealand	36
Germany	36.2
United Kingdom	36.6
Spain	37.2
Netherlands	38
Hungary	39.3
Iceland	41.4
Austria	41.9
Finland	43
Italy	43.3
Norway	43.4
France	43.6
Belgium	44.4
Sweden	48.2
Denmark	48.9

Source: OECD, *Revenue Statistics, 1965–2007* (Paris, France: OECD, 2008).

Federal Taxes Paid
Versus Spending Received by States

The federal government depends primarily on the individual income taxes sent by tax-payers to Washington each year, and the states receive federal spending by the national government in return. However, some states receive a greater benefit from the government's taxing and spending policies than others. Some states receive less back from the federal government than they send in, making them net donors or "givers" (see Figure 6.2). Other states receive more from the government than they send to Washington in the form of taxes, making them net beneficiaries or "takers." The most important indicator regarding whether a state is a net giver or taker is per capita income. Because of the progressive structure of the federal income tax, states with higher per capita incomes pay higher taxes to the national government. Other categories of federal taxes, including business, social insurance, excise, estate, and gift taxes as well as customs duties, are all tabulated to determine the total tax burden for each state. That figure is compared to the flow of federal funds back to the state. Other factors include

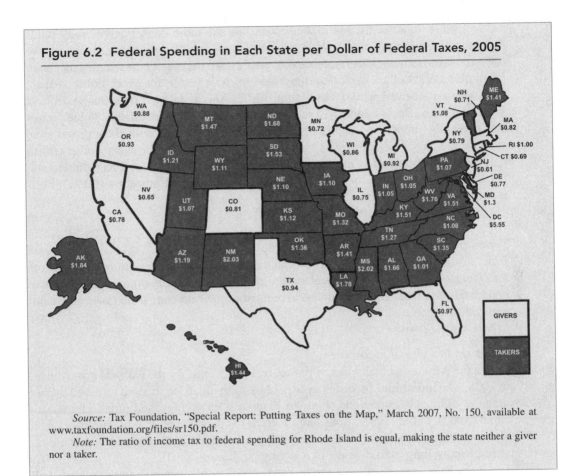

Figure 6.2 Federal Spending in Each State per Dollar of Federal Taxes, 2005

Source: Tax Foundation, "Special Report: Putting Taxes on the Map," March 2007, No. 150, available at www.taxfoundation.org/files/sr150.pdf.

Note: The ratio of income tax to federal spending for Rhode Island is equal, making the state neither a giver nor a taker.

the influence of the state's congressional delegation, the number of federal employees within the state, and the percentage of residents receiving Social Security, Medicare, or other federal entitlements.

In fiscal year 2005, just seventeen out of the fifty states were net givers (indicated in the nonshaded areas in Figure 6.2), thirty-two states plus the District of Columbia were net takers (shaded areas), while Rhode Island broke even receiving back one dollar for each dollar sent to the federal government. Several states were closely balanced between their donations and their benefit received. Michigan, Oregon, Texas, and Florida were mild donor states while Georgia, Ohio, Indiana, Utah, Pennsylvania, North Carolina, and Vermont were modest takers.

Ironically, most of the low-paying states are the more conservative "red" states that usually support policies such as lower taxes and smaller government and oppose using the tax system to redistribute wealth, yet they are the major beneficiaries receiving far more federal dollars back than they send in. As a result, for every dollar sent in, New Mexico received $2.03, Mississippi $2.02, Alaska $1.84, Louisiana $1.78, and West Virginia $1.76. By comparison, most donor states are more affluent "blue" states that generally support more progressive policies. Consistent with their progressive support, the largest net giver was California (receiving $0.78 for every dollar sent to the federal government) while New Jersey received only $0.61 for every dollar sent. Other major donor states include Connecticut ($0.69), New Hampshire ($0.71), Minnesota ($0.72), and Illinois ($0.75).

Types of Taxation in the United States

Federal, state, and local governments obtain revenue to finance programs through various mechanisms. While the federal government relies primarily on individual income taxes, state and local governments receive most of their revenue from taxes on wealth and consumption.

Taxes on Individual Income

Figure 6.3 presents a breakdown of the sources of revenue for the national government in 2008. The **individual income tax** is paid by individuals on income received during the year. This includes income from work, interest on savings, and often refers to income from an entire family (household income) not just from an individual worker. It also includes income taxation from **capital gains**, which is the tax on the income realized from selling capital assets like stocks and houses.

A tax levied specifically on the income earned from a person's job(s) is a **payroll tax**. In addition to income taxes, wages are subject to a payroll tax, which is levied on a company's payroll (half of which is deducted from an employee's paycheck) to finance the Social Security and Medicare programs. Payroll taxes are now the second major source of revenue. Workers transfer part of their earnings to retired workers through mandatory payroll deductions that, in 2009, amounted to 6.2 percent of wages on income up to $106,800. Employers contribute an equal amount.

Taxes on Corporate Income

The earnings of corporations are taxed through taxes levied on the profits of the corporation. States as well as the federal government may levy taxes on corporations, but a state tax is deductible by the corporation in calculating the federal corporate tax.

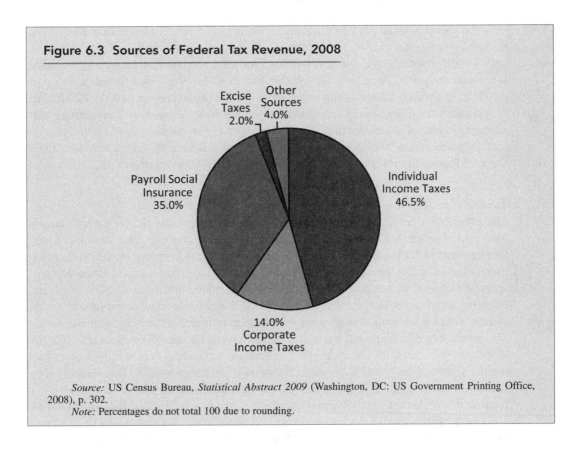

Figure 6.3 Sources of Federal Tax Revenue, 2008

Excise Taxes 2.0%
Other Sources 4.0%
Payroll Social Insurance 35.0%
Individual Income Taxes 46.5%
14.0% Corporate Income Taxes

Source: US Census Bureau, *Statistical Abstract 2009* (Washington, DC: US Government Printing Office, 2008), p. 302.
Note: Percentages do not total 100 due to rounding.

Taxes on Consumption

The most common form of taxation in the EU and most states within the United States is a **consumption tax**, which is paid on the consumption of goods (and oftentimes services). Consumption taxes usually come in the form of **sales taxes** or **excise taxes** paid by the consumer to a vendor at the time of purchase of a good or service. Excise taxes are applied to specific goods such as gasoline, alcohol, cigarettes, airline tickets, and firearms. A tax levied on the sale of tobacco products or alcohol is often referred to as a "sin tax," based on the idea that use of these products imposes externalities on nonusers in the form of air pollution, litter, or health hazards.

Some excise taxes are targeted at purchasers of certain goods who will eventually benefit when the money is spent by the government. Gasoline taxes, for example, are used to finance highway construction. An excise tax that is levied on buyers of expensive nonessential items, such as yachts or expensive jewelry, is referred to as a **luxury tax** since the incomes of these people are assumed to be high enough to absorb the costs.

Many excise taxes are levied on goods with a relatively **inelastic demand**. If the demand were highly elastic, the tax would push sales down significantly, resulting in only small government revenues.[15] Politicians find that raising taxes usually costs some voter support. Therefore, they prefer that taxes be borne by as small a group as possible, or by such a large group that it is a minimal burden on each payer. Politicians find it easier to impose excise taxes than any other form because they can raise a significant amount of revenue while affecting a relatively small number of voters. Nevertheless, excise taxes have declined in importance as a source of federal revenue. Their share of federal tax revenues fell from 13 percent in 1960 to 2 percent in 2008.

Taxes on Property and Wealth

The **property tax** typically is a direct tax paid not on income as it is earned, but on the value of assets held such as real estate, stocks, bank deposits, and art work. Many local governments tax private homes, land, and business property based on their assessed market value. Some states and local governments impose taxes on the value of specific types of personal property such as cars, boats, and occasionally livestock. Property taxes account for over 75 percent of the revenue raised through taxes on wealth. Other taxes imposed on wealth include inheritance, estate, and gift taxes.

A measure of income known as the **Haig-Simons income** defines taxable income as the change in an individual's power to purchase (consume) goods and services during the year to include any increase in the person's stock of wealth. The Haig-Simons definition focuses on the taxpayer's *ability to pay,* based on the resources a person has regardless of whether the individual decides to spend (consume) or save (add to their stock of wealth). The US tax code diverges from the Haig-Simons model by allowing **tax deductions**, which are expenses that are subtracted from the gross amount on which tax is assessed, and **tax exemptions**, which are a part of a person's income on which no tax is imposed. For example, an employer's contribution to an employee's health insurance is *exempted* from inclusion as taxable employee income. But the employer's contribution relieves the employee from paying for that portion of the health insurance, allowing the worker to have more discretionary income to save or spend. Taxpayers who are paying on a home mortgage may *deduct* the interest paid on that mortgage from their tax bill.

Principles of Taxation: Fairness and Efficiency

Although no one likes to transfer control over part of their income to the government, most people grudgingly comply. But as Margaret Thatcher learned, compliance is by no means guaranteed when people feel a tax system is unfair. "Maggie" Thatcher was a popular British prime minister when her government proposed a Community Charge, commonly referred to as a poll tax to replace a system of property taxes that took into account the value of the property on which the householder was taxed. The poll tax was a flat tax to be levied equally on all individuals regardless of whether they were rich or poor. Various Anti–Poll Tax Unions called for a demonstration on the Saturday before the tax was to be implemented. On March 31, 1990, demonstrators began gathering in London and, by evening, the crowds had grown and became mixed with commuters and the general public. Soon scuffles with police broke out. Rioters began looting some upscale shops, Barclays Bank, and the National Westminster Bank, and set Porsches and Jaguars on fire. But they left older cars and small shops unscathed. Thatcher defiantly continued to support the implementation of the tax, even though public opinion polls showed that only 2 percent of the population supported the tax (presumably the most affluent 2 percent of the population). John Major replaced Thatcher in November of that year and, in his first speech as prime minister announced that the Community Charge would be replaced by a return to the Council Tax, which took into account the value of the property held and so was less harsh on lower-income earners than the poll tax.

The point is that it is important for the tax system to be perceived as being *fair* and *just.* Yet the perceptions of justice and fairness often depend on how a tax affects the individual. Voluntary compliance is related to the perceived **tax efficiency** (or neutrality) and **tax fairness** of the system.

If the system is perceived as unfair, people are more likely to evade taxes if possible, or pressure political entrepreneurs more aggressively to reduce their tax burden. Since the 1980s, the US federal income tax has become less and less progressive due to several tax cuts that have been directed primarily to those in the top tax brackets. The reduced progressivity is widely seen as having contributed to the increasing inequality in the distribution of income and wealth (see Chapter 7). Repeated tax cuts favoring the wealthy began to arouse greater opposition by the beginning of the administration of G. W. Bush who signed several tax cuts that reduced the income tax rates and expanded deductions and tax breaks for corporations.

Democratic critics opposed the 2003 tax cuts on the grounds of "fairness." They pointed out that 44 percent of the tax deductions would go to the top 1 percent of taxpayers. Defenders of the tax cut did not dispute that point, but argued that, since the top 1 percent paid about 38 percent of the taxes, it was only "fair" that they should get the largest reduction and a more proportional tax would be more fair. Democratic critics responded by pointing out that the top 1 percent may pay 38 percent of *income taxes,* but they pay just 30 percent of *all* taxes since payroll taxes are flat (and Social Security is regressive after the current maximum is reached). Therefore, they argued that giving 44 percent of the tax reductions to the top 1 percent was out of proportion to the 30 percent of the taxes they paid and "unfair."

The White House responded with a statement claiming that, even if high-income taxpayers received the largest gains from the tax cuts, taxpayers across the income spectrum benefited. Critics countered saying the claim that all taxpayers are winners from the tax cuts rests on the false assumption that the government can provide trillions of dollars in tax cuts without anyone ever footing the bill. But in the long run, funds that are borrowed must eventually be paid back. Data from the Tax Policy Center show that, on average, the bottom four-fifths of households will lose more than they will gain from the combination of tax cuts and the financing for them. That is, if we include the need to pay for the tax cuts, they are best seen as *net tax cuts* for the top 20 percent of households as a group, financed by *net increases or benefit reductions* for the remaining 80 percent of households.[16]

The tax cuts including reductions in capital gains and dividend taxes contributed more to the budget deficits during the G. W. Bush administration than did the increase in spending due to military action in the Middle East. Faced with the faltering economy upon entering the White House, the administration of Barack Obama has indicated his intention to raise the top tax rates out of "fairness."

Average and Marginal Tax Rates

The **marginal tax rate** refers to the percentage of the next dollar of income that is paid in taxes. In the United States, the marginal tax rate rises with income. The 2009 tax rate for married couples filing jointly is for taxable income: not over $16,700 (10 percent), $16,700–$67,900 (15 percent), $67,900–$137,050 (25 percent), $137,050–$208,850 (28 percent), $208,850–$372,950 (33 percent), and taxable income over $373,950 is taxed at 35 percent.[17]

Because the marginal tax rate is graduated among six brackets, the **average tax rate** is also an important concept. The average tax rate is the percentage of the total income that is paid in taxes. We can calculate a married couple's tax bill by progressing through the marginal rate schedule until we reach their income level. Let us assume that Bonnie and Clyde have an income of $150,000. Their total tax bill is

$$(\$16,700 \times 0.1) + (\$51,200 \times 0.15) + (\$69,150 \times 0.25) +$$
$$(\$13,950 \times 0.28) = \$30,543.50$$

Bonnie and Clyde's *marginal tax rate* is 28 percent because that is the rate they pay on their next dollar of income. Their *average tax rate* is 20.3 percent, which is the tax they owe ($30,543.50) divided by their income ($150,000). This is, in fact, the weighted average of the marginal rates reflecting their share of income in each bracket.

Another factor that adds to the complexity of the tax code is the distinction between the **statutory tax rate**, which is the rate specified in the tax brackets, and the **effective tax rate**, which is the rate actually paid. Because of a variety of exemptions and deductions from taxable income, the actual taxable income is lower than total income. That is why when we divide the total taxes paid by the total income, the *effective tax rate* is lower than we would expect by looking at the income tax brackets and **gross income**, which is the total income from all sources. A tax filer subtracts *deductions,* such as contributions to Individual Retirement Accounts (IRAs), which result in the taxpayer's **adjusted gross income** (AGI). It is the *effective tax rate,* which is invariably lower than the *statutory tax rate,* that will influence how individuals perceive their tax situation.

Tax Efficiency

Efficiency, or neutrality, suggests that unless there is adequate justification, we should try to interfere as little as possible with the market allocation. The freest movement of goods and services maximizes economic efficiency and, therefore, overall economic well-being. Unfortunately, every tax invites concerted efforts to avoid it and influences economic activity and the allocation of resources, even in cases where the market process works well and needs no outside regulation. For example, the preferential treatment that allows individuals to deduct from income taxes the cost of mortgage interest and property taxes on their homes, distorts the market by increasing the demand for homeownership over rental units. Similarly, tax laws allow child care payments to be deducted from taxes owed. Such preferential treatment, referred to as a **tax expenditure**, or "loophole," represents a loss in government revenue just as though the government wrote a check for the amount of the deduction. Likewise, the mortgage interest deduction provides a financial advantage to buying over renting. But the subsidy is a significant cost to the government. The tax revenues forgone by permitting mortgage interest deductions are $85.9 billion per year. If the deduction were stopped, federal tax revenues would rise by roughly $86 billion per year.

Special interest groups that receive preferential treatment are vigorous defenders of their tax subsidies, and thus subsidies are very difficult to eliminate.

Benefit Principle

The **benefit principle** holds that people should pay taxes in proportion to the benefits they receive. This principle tries to make public goods similar to private goods in that payment for services is commensurate with the amount of goods or services received. If the purpose of taxes is to pay for government services, then those who gain from those services should pay. A toll bridge is justified using the benefit principle. Tolls collected are used to pay the bonds used for bridge construction and to maintain the bridge. Since those who pay the toll are the same people who use the bridge, the toll is viewed as a fair way to pay for the government service. The more people use the bridge, the more they will pay. Those who do not pay can be excluded. The major disadvantage of this principle is that it will not work for public goods from which nonpayers cannot be

Case Study: Tax Expenditures

A *tax expenditure* is defined as the reduction in tax revenue that results when government programs or benefits are provided through the tax system rather than reported as budgetary expenditures. The reductions are usually made by offering special tax rates, exemptions, or tax credits to programs' beneficiaries. Governments introduce tax expenditures primarily to achieve social policy objectives such as wealth transfers to lower-income families or to promote economic development and job creation.

The federal government "spends" hundreds of billions of dollars on tax expenditures each year. The largest tax expenditure—the exclusion for employer pension plan contributions and earnings (see Table 6.1)—is also the fastest growing. The main reason that the government reports tax expenditures is to improve account-ability by providing a more complete picture of its spending.

Governments use the tax system to deliver programs to reduce their own administrative costs and reduce compliance costs for recipients. There are several negative aspects to tax expenditures. Their overall cost receives less public scrutiny than is the case for spending programs because it does not need to be formally approved every year. The benefits of the major tax expenditures tend to go to high-income earners to an even greater degree than do entitlements. This can run counter to the objective of incorporating progressiveness into the tax system. Tax expenditures are big and automatic, and costs are often hard to control since many of the benefits tend to be more open ended and enforcement is often more difficult than for spending programs.

Table 6.1 Largest Tax Expenditures, 2009

Rank	Tax Expenditure	Cost to Treasury (in $ billions)
1	Exclusion for employer pension plan contributions and earnings	120.8
2	Exclusion of employer contributions for medical insurance	114.5
3	Reduced rates of tax on dividends and long-term capital gains	99.6
4	Deduction for mortgage interest on owner-occupied residences	85.9
5	Exclusion of capital gains at death	69.7
6	Tax credit for children under age seventeen	46.0
7	Earned Income Credit	44.5
8	Exclusion of Medicare benefits (Part A & B)	41.2
9	Deduction for charitable contributions other than for education and health	36.8
10	Deduction of state and local government income and personal property taxes	28.1
11	Deferral of capital gains on sales of principal residences	26.3
12	Exclusion of Social Security benefits for retired workers	25.9

Source: Estimates of Federal Tax Expenditures for Fiscal Years 2006–2010, prepared for the Committee on Ways and Means by the Staff of the Joint Committee on Taxation (Washington, DC: US Government Printing Office, 2006).

excluded, or where it is difficult to determine who benefits or by what amount. For example, who benefits most from law enforcement and the judicial system, the rich or the poor? Figure 6.4 indicates where the federal dollar is spent.

The benefit principle is often used to argue that the more affluent citizens should have a higher tax burden than poorer citizens because they benefit more from public services. For example, the wealthy receive more benefit from a police force than do poor citizens because they have more wealth to protect and their losses would be much greater in the event of theft. Therefore, since police protection is more beneficial to the affluent, they should contribute more.

The welfare of the wealthy is best served by the Securities and Exchange Commission, the Federal Reserve system, national security, and by the judicial system. If

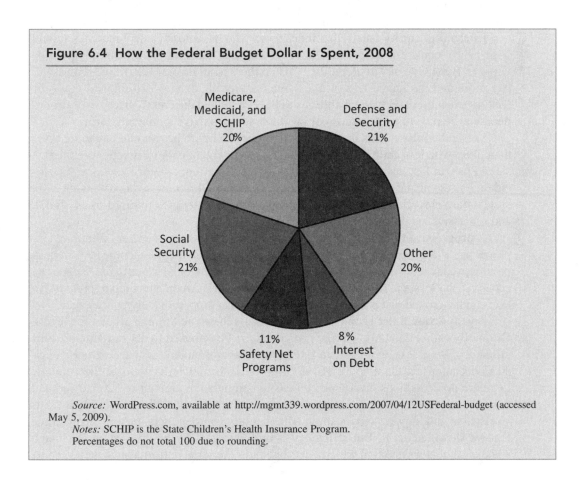

Figure 6.4 How the Federal Budget Dollar Is Spent, 2008

Medicare, Medicaid, and SCHIP 20%

Defense and Security 21%

Social Security 21%

Other 20%

11% Safety Net Programs

8% Interest on Debt

Source: WordPress.com, available at http://mgmt339.wordpress.com/2007/04/12USFederal-budget (accessed May 5, 2009).
Notes: SCHIP is the State Children's Health Insurance Program.
Percentages do not total 100 due to rounding.

there was agreement on who benefits and by how much, then taxes could be allocated accordingly. Allocating taxes by this principle provides an incentive to insist that someone else is the main beneficiary. If these taxes could be allocated accurately, there would be no income redistribution.

Ability-to-Pay Principle

The **ability-to-pay principle** claims that fairness requires that taxes be allocated according to the incomes and/or wealth of taxpayers, regardless of how much or how little they benefit. According to this principle, the wealthy may benefit more than the poor from some government expenditures and less than the poor from others. But since they are better able to pay than the poor, they should pay more in taxes. This principle is justified by the argument that all citizens should make an "equal sacrifice." Fairness in this system requires both horizontal and vertical equity.

Horizontal equity means that individuals who have nearly equal incomes should have nearly equal tax burdens. This is the concept that Plato had in mind when he wrote in Book One of *The Republic:* "When there is an income tax, the just man will pay more and the unjust less on the same amount of income." Horizontal equity is lacking when those with equal abilities to pay are treated differently because of tax deductions, credits, or preferences not available to all taxpayers on equal terms.

Vertical equity means that those with higher ability to pay should pay more taxes than those with less ability to pay. There is less agreement on how much more the rich should pay. In fact, taxes are generally classified according to their incidence. **Tax incidence** is the actual distribution of the tax burden on different levels of income. Tax systems are classified as progressive, proportional (sometimes referred to as "flat"), and regressive, as illustrated in Figure 6.5.

A **progressive tax** is one in which the tax rate rises as income rises. Wealthier taxpayers pay a larger percentage of their income in taxes than do low-income taxpayers. A progressive tax redistributes wealth from the more affluent to the less affluent. Keynesian economic theory supports a progressive income tax. Most Americans support progressive taxes on the ground that ability to pay rises more than proportionately with income.

A **proportional tax** is one in which the tax is the same through all income levels. Ordinarily called a flat tax, a proportional tax is often praised by its supporters for its efficiency. By assessing a tax as a fixed percentage of income, a wage earner's decisions do not affect the amount of tax owed or distort incentives. Since theoretically there are no deductions, everyone can easily compute the amount of taxes owed and there is little need to hire accountants or tax lawyers. Because the proportional tax is so efficient and imposes only a slight administrative burden on taxpayers, many argue that we should adopt it. But efficiency is only one goal of the tax system. Although some think that a system in which everyone pays the same percentage of their income

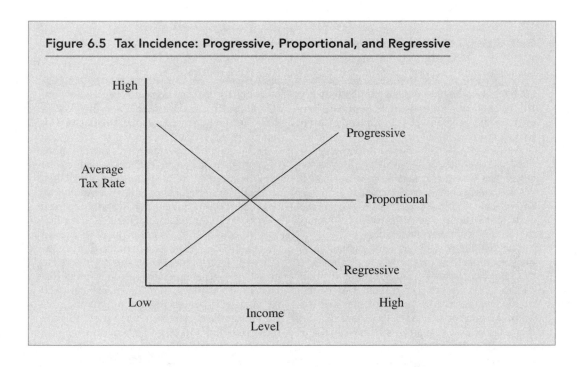

Figure 6.5 Tax Incidence: Progressive, Proportional, and Regressive

is fair, others argue that is not equitable. A proportional tax is neutral in regard to income distribution.

Under a **regressive tax**, the average rate declines as income rises. It is called "regressive" because high-income taxpayers pay a smaller percentage of their income than do low-income taxpayers, even though they may still pay a higher amount in absolute dollars. A regressive tax redistributes income from the poor to the wealthy. Regressive tax systems are so manifestly unfair that few openly advocate them. A notable exception is George Gilder, a conservative writer with refreshing frankness but doubtful logic who wrote that "regressive taxes help the poor."[18] Gilder, whose work was widely and approvingly read by supply-siders of the early 1980s, also declared that "to help the poor and middle classes, one must cut the taxes on the rich."[19]

Because state and local governments often rely on sales and property taxes, these tend to be regressive. State and local sales taxes increased during the 1980s along with local property taxes. A sales tax is often confused with a flat tax because two individuals with vastly different incomes will pay the same sales tax on the purchase of ten gallons of gas. Sales and property taxes are regressive because poorer people must spend a higher percentage of their income for goods and services, as well as housing costs, than do the affluent.

Case Study: Lotteries as a Regressive Tax

Gambling generates enormous amounts of revenue for governments and the gaming industry. But its enchanting promises of significant benefits for the general welfare frequently do not live up to expectations.

A study by Alicia Hansen found that, in 2002, the average American spent more on lotteries than on reading materials or movies. In 2003, total spending on lotteries was almost $45 billion, or $155 for every man, woman, and child in the United States. About $14 billion of that money went into state coffers.

The fact that playing the lottery is voluntary does not make the "profit" any less of a tax. It is analogous to states raising revenue from an excise tax on alcohol. The purchaser of alcohol does so voluntarily, but no one denies that it is a tax. Some then concede that it is a tax, but that a tax of choice is preferable to a tax that is paid reluctantly and, presumably, the purchaser of alcohol or a lottery ticket is willing to pay the tax.

Political entrepreneurs have discovered that the average voter does not think of the lottery as a tax, which removes a major barrier to taxation. The transfer of lottery revenues to state treasuries is an implicit tax on lottery bettors. There is a consensus among researchers that state lotteries are a decidedly regressive form of taxation in that average lottery sales are highest in low-income areas and lower in areas of higher economic and educational levels.

Sponsored gambling allows many state governments to use lotteries to minimize taxes that would otherwise have to be paid by middle- and upper-income groups. The result is that states have increasingly resorted to lotteries to increase revenues as a way of sidestepping opposition to tax increases. New Hampshire started the first modern state lottery in 1964. In 2005, forty-one states and the District of Columbia sponsored lotteries.

Per capita lottery ticket sales were three times higher in inner city Detroit than in the suburbs in 1988. Of $104 million contributed to Michigan's school aid fund by Detroit lottery ticket purchasers, inner city schools received only $80 million. The remaining $24 million was transferred to more affluent suburban school districts. A 1988 study of the Florida lottery, which also earmarks profits from sales to go into the general education fund, found that when one includes the tax incidence (who pays) and the benefit incidence (who receives the funds), the tax was regressive for those with incomes below $40,000. The benefits of the net tax are proportionally distributed at incomes between $40,000 and $70,000 and become progressive at incomes above $70,000. Congress commissioned a National Impact Study, which found that gambling had not improved Florida's education or health services. Prior to the introduction of the state lottery, Florida allocated 60 percent of its budget for school improvement. Five years after the introduction of gambling, only 51 percent of its budget was allocated to education. The study noted that "the problem with a lottery is that lottery profits are used as a substitute for tax dollars, not as a supplement to them."

Lotteries violate the tax principles of both neutrality and equity. There is also the ethical question of exploiting human desire to extract a regressive tax on the poor.

Sources: Alicia Hansen, "Lotteries and State Fiscal Policy," Tax Foundation Background Paper no. 46 (Washington, DC: Tax Foundation, October 2004); Mary Borg, Paul Mason, and Stephen Shapiro, *The Economic Consequences of State Lotteries* (New York: Praeger, 1991).

In theory, the federal income tax supports the principle of vertical equity by being mildly progressive. The tax cuts in 2001, 2002, and 2003 have significantly reduced the progressivity of the federal income tax. The election of Reagan gave a boost to an alteration of the revenue structures that continued through the administrations of G. H. W. Bush and Bill Clinton. The restructuring accelerated under the leadership of G. W. Bush and the Republican-dominated Congress at the dawn of the twenty-first century.

Federal tax progressivity has been declining for almost three decades. Although both political parties bear some responsibility for these changes, Republicans have been more forceful in pushing the discredited ideas of supply-side economics, which claims that tax reductions for the affluent will "trickle down" to the middle and lower classes.

President Obama has indicated that he wants to reduce the charitable tax deduction for those with incomes above $250,000 from 35 cents for each dollar donated to 28 cents to match the level of deductions for people making less than $250,000. His argument is that deductions under the current system are unfair. In a press conference in March 2009, he said there is little evidence that reducing the tax deduction would have a significant impact on charitable giving. Rather, he argued "what has a significant impact on charitable giving, is a financial crisis and an economy that's contracting. And so the most important thing that I can do for charitable giving is to fix the economy . . . [and] to get people back to work again."[20] Why should a high-income household save 35 cents on a dollar of mortgage interest while a low-income household saves 15 cents? Why should homeowners with large mortgages be able to use a tax-deductible home equity loan to buy a car when renters with similar incomes cannot?

Many who support the neutrality of the tax system argue that efforts to redistribute wealth through tax transfers are not very effective. They maintain that a progressive income tax reduces the incentives for the more affluent to work and save. By encouraging the affluent to invest their wealth, the size of the total economic pie will be increased so that the benefits that trickle down to the poor will exceed any benefits from redistribution through tax transfers. They insist that the fact that some entrepreneurs become extraordinarily wealthy is irrelevant because their actions have improved society.

Social Security tax (the payroll tax) is an example of a tax that is proportional in the lower ranges, but regressive for those receiving income in excess of the maximum wage for which taxes are withheld. As mentioned above, this payroll tax requires individuals and employers to pay the same rate on wages up to $106,800 (in 2009). Above $106,800, the marginal tax rate is zero (recall that the marginal tax rate is defined as the tax on additional income). Rather than exempting low incomes, it exempts high incomes. Once the ceiling is reached, no more payments are made for the year. Also, since only salaries are subject to the payroll tax while income from interest is untouched, it is ultimately regressive. There is an additional Medicare payroll tax of 1.45 percent with a matching 1.45 percent paid by employers with no upper salary limit.

Broad Uses of Tax Policy

Tax policy may be used to pursue various goals simultaneously. For example, its most basic use is to achieve macroeconomic goals of expanding the economy and employment. Taxes may be used as an economic policy to provide income security, to increase investment spending, and to stimulate aggregate spending.

President Kennedy announced his intention to provide a tax cut aimed primarily at middle- and low-income families in order to stimulate a lethargic economy. Lyndon Johnson, who succeeded to the presidency when Kennedy was assassinated, agreed with Kennedy's logic and shifted the emphasis from expanding federal spending to boosting private consumer demand and business investment. He cut personal and corporate taxes by $11 billion, and economic activity increased exactly as the model had predicted.

Much larger tax cuts were implemented by President Reagan in 1981. These cuts were directed primarily at reducing the tax burden of the affluent rather than that of middle- and lower-income workers. The top tax rate was cut from 70 percent to 28 percent. All told, personal taxes were cut by $250 billion over a three-year period and corporate taxes were cut by $70 billion. The deficit spending and increased consumer demand that resulted did help get the economy out of the deep recession of 1981–1982. Reagan, alarmed at the huge looming deficits, raised taxes a grand total of four times between 1982 and 1984. By 1988, the combined burden of income and payroll taxes meant that "middle-income families with children" were paying 18.4 percent of income, up from 17.7 percent in 1980. Taxes were reduced overall for corporations and affluent citizens, but were higher for middle-income families.

President Clinton was elected by campaigning against policies that kept the economy lagging behind its potential, using the slogan "it's the economy, stupid." He cited the need for more fiscal stimulus during the campaign and suggested the need for middle-income tax cuts. Upon his election, however, Clinton recognized that the economy had hit the bottom of the recession and was starting to expand. He was aware of the Keynesian multiplier at work, and decided that an additional stimulus might create the problem of inflation. Instead, he chose to take the difficult and politically risky strategy of dealing with the long-term problem of the deficit and its drag on the economy. He raised taxes on the top 2 percent of income earners over the unanimous opposition of Republicans who predicted economic catastrophe. He also cut government spending while providing tax credits for investments to stimulate economic expansion. Budget deficits declined each year of the Clinton administration and turned a surplus in 1998.[21] The longest uninterrupted economic expansion since World War II resulted.[22] (See Figure 6.6.)

When G. W. Bush took office, unemployment rates and inflation were at record lows; however, economic growth had slowed markedly in the last year of the Clinton administration. During the first three years of his administration (2001, 2002, and 2003), Bush proposed and obtained through a Republican-led Congress the largest tax cuts in history. He argued that, with the government surpluses from 1998 through 2001, the

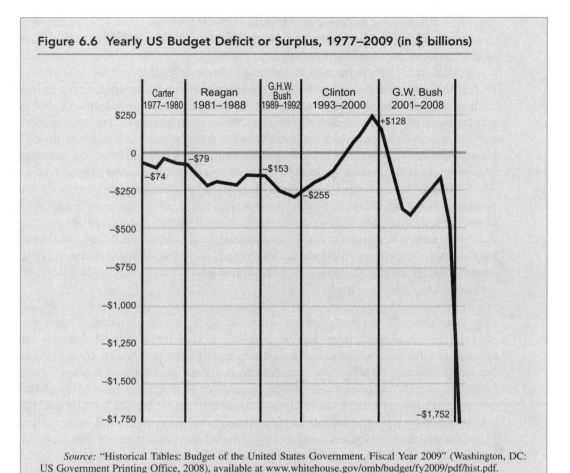

Figure 6.6 Yearly US Budget Deficit or Surplus, 1977–2009 (in $ billions)

Source: "Historical Tables: Budget of the United States Government. Fiscal Year 2009" (Washington, DC: US Government Printing Office, 2008), available at www.whitehouse.gov/omb/budget/fy2009/pdf/hist.pdf. *Note:* Does not include military appropriations for Middle East, between 2003 and 2009.

nation could afford the tax cuts. He also argued that, because the economy was slowing even though the nation was essentially at full employment (4 percent unemployment), *tax relief* was needed to stimulate the economy and create jobs. Political strategists found that "tax cuts" attracted little support among voters but, if the issue was framed as "tax relief," it gained much more traction. Tax relief implies that people were "oppressed," and those offering relief were the people's champions (even if most of the relief went to the most affluent).

By the end of G. W. Bush's second term, the economy was in a recession that began in December 2007.[23] Real GDP decreased at an annual rate of 6.3 percent in the fourth quarter of 2008.[24] Bush left office in January 2009 with unemployment at 7.6

percent. a fifteen-year high. He had increased the federal budget by 104 percent in eight years, and raised the national debt by the largest percentage and real dollar value of any president in the nation's history.

Since the G. W. Bush tax cuts that almost exclusively benefit affluent households, such as the elimination of the estate tax and the removal of the limitation on itemized deductions, will be phased in over the next several years, the ultimate effect will be greater inequality. Some defenders of the tax cuts have argued that everyone is a "winner" since everyone received a tax cut. However, the tax cuts were financed through growing deficits. The tax cuts must eventually be financed through either tax increases or spending cuts because the economy cannot sustain such large and persistent deficits.

While advocates of the G. W. Bush tax cuts routinely describe them as being designed to favor families and small businesses, a study by William Gale and Peter Orszag at the Brookings Institution shows in a distributional analysis of the tax cuts that "most families (that is, tax units with children) and most tax units with small business income will be worse off once the financing is included."[25] Since the tax cuts disproportionately benefit the wealthy, middle- and low-income households will suffer corresponding benefit losses.

The tax cuts of the G. W. Bush administration were poorly designed to achieve their stated goal of stimulating economic growth. Those with the highest incomes benefit most, but they are the most likely to save than to spend their tax cuts. Tax cuts that targeted middle- and low-income households would have resulted in an increase in consumer demand, creating the stimulus sought by the Bush administration. Lower taxes can stimulate growth by improving incentives to work and invest. The policy provided windfall gains to asset holders, and undermined incentives for new activity; and, by raising the budget deficit, it reduced national savings and raised interest rates. Jobs created following the tax cuts fell 2.67 million below the administration's predictions made in 2003.[26] In fact, Mark Zandi, chief economist at Economy.com, points out that most Americans experienced a decline in real household income between 2001 and 2004. He noted that "no other President since World War II has suffered outright job declines during their term."[27]

Data by the G. W. Bush administration's 2004 Mid-Session Budget Review indicated that the tax cuts played a larger role than all other legislation or policies in raising the budget deficit. In fact, until mid-2004, the tax cuts accounted for 57 percent of the worsening fiscal picture, more than all other policies combined.[28]

Some defenders have argued that the G. W. Bush administration's tax cuts actually made the tax system more progressive. They posited that high-income taxpayers generally paid a greater percentage of federal income taxes because of the 2001–2003 tax cuts. In their view, high-income taxpayers had only a "comparable reduction" in their tax burden relative to middle-income taxpayers. This ignores taxes other than the income tax. Unlike the income tax, which is mildly progressive, other federal taxes like the payroll tax are regressive, with middle- and low-income households paying a greater share of their income to these taxes than the wealthiest taxpayers. Congressional Budget Office (CBO) data show that 75 percent of all taxpayers pay more in payroll taxes than they do in income taxes. Analyzing tax burdens by focusing solely on the *income tax* and ignoring other taxes produces misleading results. That upper-income groups pay a higher share of taxes tells us only that the upper-income group is paying a larger share of the *smaller amount of federal income taxes* being collected after the tax cuts. It is possible to increase the share of taxes paid by the affluent at the same time that the law makes after-tax income less equal. Focusing on changes in the share of taxes paid misses the more meaningful after-tax income, which determines households' *ability to pay.*[29]

Some tax cut supporters justified the tax policy as an effort to reduce government spending.[30] In this view, the cuts were justified in an effort to "starve the beast" of excessive social welfare spending. But the effort to reduce social welfare spending does not justify regressive tax cuts. It could be argued that, since most spending cuts would be regressive (hurting the least well off the most), a tax cut aimed at reducing spending should on fairness grounds be progressive (i.e., give greater tax cuts to households with relatively lower income). The tax cuts did not reduce spending; in fact, spending increased in all budget categories.

As baby boomers begin retiring in 2010, strains on health care and other social welfare costs will grow. Because the G. W. Bush administration ruled out any tax increase to reduce the deficit, the only remaining options are to cut spending and to expand the economy. Since the deep recession that began in the last year of the Bush administration caused the GDP to decline, deficits must inevitably rise, which will further complicate the choices available for President Obama to reform the social welfare system.

President Obama's Fiscal Policies

The history of US fiscal policy since World War II can be divided into the period known as "the Great Compression" from roughly 1945 to 1980 when government policy reduced economic inequality, and the period from 1980 to the present when the twin forces of government policy and economic globalization caused inequality to skyrocket. And just as Franklin Roosevelt's tax increases on the affluent following the stock market crash, which had already depressed their wealth, ushered in the Great Compression, President Obama's proposals if ultimately enacted will once again reverse growing inequality.

President Obama's agenda is a sharp departure from the policy trends since 1980. His administration won key victories in April 2009 when the House and Senate passed companion budget resolutions, which are nonbinding blueprints that set goals for future legislation, broadly supporting his agenda. Obama's proposals would raise taxes on the wealthy while reducing taxes for everyone else. The budget attempts to alleviate some major causes of middle-class income stagnation such as soaring medical and educational costs. The details of the tax code promise to become more progressive with relatively higher rates on the affluent and lower rates on the middle- and lower-income groups.

Social Security and Reducing Poverty Among the Elderly

Until the twentieth century, few Americans could look forward to a retirement period at the end of their working lives. In 1900, the life expectancy for men was about forty-four years. Nevertheless, about two-thirds of men age sixty-five and older were still in the labor force.[31] With insufficient savings and without a pension program, most were forced to work as long as they were physically able. Because of changing trends in employment, retirement, and life expectancy, the average age at which individuals retire dropped (i.e., in the United States from seventy-four years in 1910 to sixty-two in 2002), but at present the retirement age is trending upward. By 2008, with a life expectancy of about 78.1 years, the average age of retirement for men rose to just under sixty-five.[32] Americans tend to stay in the labor force longer than the citizens of many OECD countries.[33] Advances in life expectancy and an extended retirement are clear advances in the general welfare of society. They also present challenging public policy issues.

Since the administration of Franklin Roosevelt, the government has developed programs and legislation to make sure that the elderly have sufficient income to provide for their needs during retirement. Social Security began in 1935 at the depths of the Great Depression, which wiped out the lifetime savings of many elderly citizens, The basic motivation for Social Security—technically, Old Age, Survivors, and Disability Insurance (OASDI)—was to ensure that most elderly would have sufficient savings and income to adequately provide for themselves in retirement. Thus, the program was designed to compel workers to save for their retirement years by paying taxes during their working careers that would entitle them to receive benefits upon retirement. The program was intended to provide a basic safety net, but was never intended to meet all retirement needs. Nevertheless, this New Deal system has become the nation's largest social insurance program.

The Federal Insurance Contributions Act (FICA) requires employers to withhold 6.2 percent of a worker's wages through a payroll tax. The employer (or the worker if self-employed) also pays 6.2 percent on the same earnings for a total tax burden of 12.4 percent up to $106,800 of earnings in 2009. Actually, the worker is considered to be making the entire contribution since the employer could raise the worker's salary by the amount of the tax if he or she was not sending it to the Social Security Administration.

To be eligible to receive Social Security benefits upon retirement, persons must have worked and paid the payroll tax for forty quarters (ten years), and must be age sixty-two or older. When eligible, the recipient receives an annuity payment paid out monthly until his or her death. The amount of the payment is determined by the average lifetime earnings expressed in today's dollars by inflating their value since the earnings were received. The government averages the worker's earnings over his or her thirty-five highest earning years. If a person has worked for less than thirty-five years, the missing years are averaged in as years of zero earnings. Conversely, if a person has worked more than thirty-five years, the lowest earning years are not counted when calculating the average. The thirty-five-year average of monthly earnings is called the Average Indexed Monthly Earnings (AIME).

For most families, the primary savings for their retirement years consist of pensions and savings plans encouraged by tax incentives. Legislation providing tax incentives for employer-based pensions was passed in 1921. Legislation establishing Keogh accounts in 1962 and IRAs in 1974 expanded the eligibility for workers to participate in tax-sheltered savings plans. Nevertheless, only about half of all workers are covered by any form of a pension plan, with higher-income workers much more likely to be covered than low-income workers. The result is that, for the average worker, Social Security makes up a larger part of their retirement income than private pensions, as indicated in Figure 6.7. By requiring workers to contribute to the program through payroll taxes, the Social Security program does crowd out private savings for retirement to some degree. But the value of the program in providing income to the elderly is shown by the great reduction in poverty rates among the elderly over the past fifty years.

Currently, about 95 percent of married couples, one of whom is age sixty-five or older, receive Social Security benefits. Social Security is the only form of pension income for about half of these households. Many financial planners suggest that most families need about 70 percent of their preretirement income in order to maintain their standard of living. Currently, Social Security accounts for about 41 percent of the preretirement earnings of an average wage earner who retires at age sixty-five.[34] This percentage is expected to decline to 36 percent until 2027, when the "normal retirement age" will reach age sixty-seven. It is expected to remain at 36 percent after that.

Social Security is a critical resource, especially for low-income retirees. As Figure 6.7 indicates, many retirees can add significant income to their Social Security benefits with pensions and continued earnings. Many low-income individuals do not have that option. Social Security constitutes about 90 percent or more of income for adults age sixty-five or older in the bottom quintile, compared to 28 percent for the middle quintile and 5 percent for the highest quintile.[35]

In 1961, a White House conference on aging found that over half of elderly couples could not afford decent housing, proper nutrition, or adequate medical care. Presidents Kennedy and Johnson subsequently pushed to expand Social Security and establish Medicare. Since 1959, poverty rates among the elderly have declined from 35 percent to 9.4 percent in 2006, compared to the national poverty rate of 12.3 percent. The major

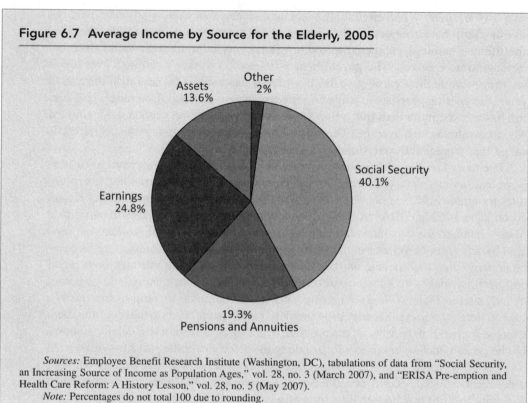

Figure 6.7 Average Income by Source for the Elderly, 2005

Other 2%

Assets 13.6%

Social Security 40.1%

Earnings 24.8%

19.3% Pensions and Annuities

Sources: Employee Benefit Research Institute (Washington, DC), tabulations of data from "Social Security, an Increasing Source of Income as Population Ages," vol. 28, no. 3 (March 2007), and "ERISA Pre-emption and Health Care Reform: A History Lesson," vol. 28, no. 5 (May 2007).
Note: Percentages do not total 100 due to rounding.

events that have contributed to this change in the lives of the elderly in the United States are the significant increases in Social Security benefits enacted in the 1960s and 1970s, and the indexing of those benefits to average wage increases. Without Social Security, about half of the elderly would fall below the poverty line. Conversely, the existence of Social Security does affect retirement decisions. There is a spike of increased retirements when individuals reach age sixty-two, the **early entitlement age** (EEA), and again when the **full benefits age** (FBA) is reached, which has risen from age sixty-five to age sixty-six.

The system has a deliberate redistributive slant to reduce poverty. Retirees who earn lower wages during their working careers get higher returns. The Social Security benefit schedule is progressive and, although some benefits are subject to partial taxation, the benefits are not means-tested. This allows many people to add other sources of income, such as pension benefits, to their Social Security benefits to achieve a level of income in retirement close to the level achieved during their working years. Social

Security lifts more elderly people out of poverty—nine out of ten—than all other transfer programs combined.

Social Security also works as a national group insurance plan to provide payments to roughly 5 million disabled adults and 3 million children every month. About half the children who receive benefits have lost one or both parents. In short, Social Security is a valuable program that replaces income in the event of retirement, disability, or death, serving to reduce the income inequality across certain groups.

In order to improve the system in 1983, a commission headed by Alan Greenspan recommended several legislative changes to strengthen the program. For example, the commission recommended taxing some Social Security benefits, providing coverage of federal employees under Social Security, and increasing the retirement age for full coverage from age sixty-five to age sixty-seven to offset increased life expectancy, which will be fully implemented in 2027.

The most important recommendation in the commission's final draft report was to change Social Security from an **unfunded** plan, usually referred to as a "pay-as-you-go" system in which taxes collected from workers today were "transferred" to today's retirees. An unfunded plan differs from private pension plans, which are **funded** plans in which corporate savings are invested in financial markets and the funds with accumulated capital gains pay the future benefits promised by the pension plan. As a result of the 1983 revisions, which raised payroll taxes to take in more money than it paid out while baby boomers were still in the work force, Social Security is now a *partially funded* system. The surplus payroll tax receipts are placed in the Social Security Trust Fund to pay out a higher amount when baby boomers begin retiring. In essence, those who have paid Social Security payroll taxes from 1983 onward have been funding their own retirement.

The Social Security Trust Fund and how it works is crucial to understanding the current debate about Social Security. Basically, Social Security is supported by a payroll tax dedicated to providing checks to current retirees in a pay-as-you-go system in which most taxes received are paid out to current retirees in a "defined benefit" plan. The Social Security surplus (i.e., taxes collected in excess of that needed to pay retirees) is used to buy government bonds. Accounting entries indicate the amount of "assets" deposited in the Social Security Trust Fund. However, the government "borrows" these funds from the Treasury Department to pay for current government operations. From the perspective of the government, once the money is used for government operations, which reduces the annual deficit, the bonds are "unfunded liabilities" in that the government is liable to pay back the funds it has borrowed. The money, and the bonds, do not belong to the government or to the general public. They belong to the Social Security Trust Fund and to the workers whose payroll tax contributions created the Social Security surplus.[36] Without the Social Security surplus, the government would have been forced to cut other programs, raise taxes, or increase the deficit. The government must pay the interest on the bonds and redeem them because the alternative of defaulting on them would be catastrophic to its ability to sell bonds to finance its deficit. As of March 2009, the government has borrowed $2.2 trillion from the Social Security Trust Fund.[37]

It was projected that, in 2019, retiree benefits would begin to exceed payroll tax receipts. At that time, Social Security tax receipts were to be supplemented by redeeming money held in the interest-bearing trust fund accounts. Money from the trust funds was not projected to be exhausted until about 2042. However, in 2009, the CBO reported that rising unemployment had resulted in a sharp decline in the *payroll* tax revenue that finances Social Security benefits for nearly 51 million retirees.[38] As a result, the trust fund is projected to run only a mild surplus until 2016. Thus, the government will be forced to find sources other than the Social Security Trust Fund to borrow to balance the nation's books.

Critics argue that "there is no trust fund," and the idea of a separate pot of money for Social Security is meaningless in a unified budget. But the government does have dedicated taxes for things like pollution control and highway maintenance. Paul Krugman has pointed out that, if Social Security is just part of a unified federal budget with no trust fund of its own, there cannot be a Social Security crisis. All one can have then is a general budget crisis. Rising Social Security payments may be an element of the crisis, which then must be dealt with along with other parts of the budget.[39] Other studies point out that, even when the money from the bonds is exhausted, projected benefits would exceed revenue by just 19 percent.[40]

President G. W. Bush proposed to restructure Social Security as the centerpiece of his second term. He appointed a Social Security Commission, which put forward a plan to dramatically shrink Social Security benefits, replacing a much smaller share of preretirement wages for workers who retire in the future. This "privatization" plan would allow workers to divert up to 4 percent of the 12.4 percent payroll tax (roughly a third), up to $1,000, into a personal investment account. The Bush administration claimed this would bring more Americans into the "ownership" society since they would own part of their retirement. Guaranteed benefits would be cut by the amount contributed to personal accounts.

Another problem with this plan is that, since the stock market goes down as well as up, the stock market cannot offer the security of the current Social Security system. Moreover, the less wage earners make, the less they have to invest and the smaller their return will be. It would be especially shortsighted to make retirement benefits more risky for those who earn low wages. In contrast, under the current system, Social Security deliberately distributes benefits to provide a slightly more generous annuity to those recipients whose incomes were low during their wage-earning years.

The problem of achieving retirement security is compounded by the fact that the proposed shift to the stock market for Social Security corresponds to a shift in employer-provided retirement plans. In 1980, almost two out of five households (39 percent) had defined-benefit pension plans; in 2005, only about one in five (21 percent) did. Increasingly, workers in 401(k) investment plans are dependent on the vagaries of the stock market in their primary pension plan. A counterproposal would permit wage earners to add to the basic Social Security contribution with tax-deferred investment contributions, not reduce it.

The Bush administration's proposals to reform Social Security were greeted with such general opposition that it dropped Social Security from its agenda for reform. Nevertheless, Social Security is facing a major imbalance in funding. The ratio of the elderly to the working-age population will change dramatically in the next several years due to the aging of the baby boom generation that was born after World War II. This will result in the projected obligations exceeding the value of the taxes it will collect by several trillion dollars. A number of proposals for reform that stay within the existing structure are available to the Obama administration, which has indicated that it intends to tackle the issue.

1. *Raise the retirement age.* The age at which individuals can receive their full Social Security benefit, or the FBA, is scheduled to rise to sixty-seven by 2027. The problem is that life expectancy has been rising more quickly than the FBA. For example, a man who reached age sixty-five in 1980 could expect to live another 12.7 years on average. By 2005, a man at age sixty-five could expect to live another 17.1 years on average.[41] For women, the figure went from 16.3 years to 20.0 years.[42] It seems reasonable that, as individual life expectancy increases, people could work longer so they do not stretch out the retirement period that must be financed at the full benefit level. It is possible to receive benefits as early as age sixty-two (the EEA) at a reduced rate of 80 percent of the FBA when benefits can be taken without reduction. In 2025, a worker will receive only 70 percent if he or she retires at age sixty-two. There are many proposals to change the EEA to age sixty-seven as early as 2015 as well as raising the FBA to age sixty-eight.

2. *Raise the Social Security payroll tax.* The problems of financing Social Security are serious, but not insurmountable. The 2008 Trustees' Report states that, when the trust fund is exhausted around 2041, the Social Security program will still be able to pay 78 percent of full benefits and, by 2082, it will still be able to pay 75 percent of benefits. The report held that, if no other reform was taken except to raise payroll taxes by 3.2 percent (to a total of 15.6 percent of payroll), the plan would have an "infinite horizon."[43]

3. *Raise the upper limit on the Social Security payroll tax.* Milton Friedman has criticized Social Security for redistributing wealth from the poor to the rich.[44] Workers and their employers pay a total of 12.4 percent of their wages below the wage base ($106,800 in 2009), but no tax on income over that amount. The tax rate for Social

Security above that base is zero, making the tax regressive above that level. Also, the proportion of earnings that goes untaxed has accelerated in the past two decades since income for the already affluent has increased rapidly while that for middle- and low-income workers has stagnated. As if to add insult to injury, poor people have shorter life expectancies than more affluent people (see Chapter 10) so wealthier recipients of Social Security can expect on average to collect benefits for a longer time than poorer recipients.

An obvious solution is to raise the wage base for Social Security taxes. While higher contributors would get a higher annuity, part of the increased taxes could make up the shortfall.

4. *Broaden the base of workers contributing to Social Security.* Many state and local workers are exempted from Social Security payroll taxes if they are enrolled in state or local pension plans. Bringing more workers into the system would provide an infusion of funds into the system.

5. *Lower benefits.* Some have argued that it would be less burdensome to simply change the benefit structure to lower the benefit amounts paid by Social Security. The annual cost of living adjustment is pegged to the Consumer Price Index (CPI). One suggestion is to have the adjustment lag behind the CPI by about 1 percent. Its supporters say it would curb the excessive growth of Social Security benefits.

Conclusion

It took the Great Depression and the presidency of Franklin Roosevelt to redefine the social compact of the Constitution "to promote the general welfare" and give the idea of responsive government in the United States new meaning. Through the New Deal, Roosevelt tried to correct the weaknesses in the economy and to build up its workings by promoting the countervailing power of labor vis-à-vis big business through strengthening labor unions. The result was the Great Compression in which the inequality of the second gilded age of the 1920s was replaced by a greater equality in the distribution of income and wealth. Since the 1980s, changing government policies turned decidedly against unions. A decline in labor unions reflected a decline in government support of a variety of social welfare goals supporting a progressive income tax, a meaningful minimum wage, and laws supportive of workers. This was accompanied by a resurgence of laissez-faire as an appropriate government philosophy. President Obama has sent clear signals of his intention to reverse these general trends of the past thirty years. This promises to be very contentious.

The increasingly ideological dimension of partisanship in politics is a major hurdle in achieving these goals. The economic theory is fairly settled, even if coordinating monetary and fiscal policies to achieve the basic goals is far from foolproof. Ideology not only provides different perspectives regarding sound social welfare policy, but it also elevates ideological commitment over pragmatic problem solving in public policy. Ideology frequently trumps practical politics. Years of conservative marketing have convinced many Americans that government programs always create inefficient, bloated bureaucracies while private markets are always more efficient, despite evidence to the contrary as in the case of Social Security.

However, President Obama was elected after promising to take action to reverse the policies that had led to greater inequalities. There is considerable disagreement over the proper role of government in using fiscal policy to redistribute income.

Social Security has become the nation's greatest retirement program and is of particular importance to lower-income workers. The program has been very successful in improving the standard of living of the elderly. Social Security does face a long-run financing problem that must be dealt with in the near future. There are many proposed reforms that can help alleviate the coming shortfall. The reform proposals will include some combination of the policy tools available. Partisan differences can be expected to make the resolution of the problem one of the Obama administration's most contentious issues.

Questions for Discussion

1. In what way has history provided a test for Keynesian economics and a theory of government spending? Was it conclusive?

2. What kinds of problems do large budget deficits pose for the nation's economy? What are the different problems in the short run as opposed to the long run?

3. Why are investments critical in determining the level of prosperity?

4. What alternative tax policies are available to the government? What are the positives and negatives associated with each?

5. What are the characteristics of a "good" tax system? Why are vertical and horizontal equity important?

6. Consider the reforms available to resolve Social Security's funding problems. Explain how each would benefit or penalize younger versus older workers. Is there a combination that you think would be the most fair? Explain.

Useful Websites

American Enterprise Institute, www.aei.org.
Brookings Institution, www.brookings.edu.
Center on Budget and Policy Priorities, www.cbpp.org.
Congressional Budget Office, www.cbo.gov.
Economic Policy Institute, www.epinet.org.
Heritage Foundation, www.heritage.org.
National Bureau of Economic Research, www.nber.org.
Office of Management and Budget, www.access.gpo.gov/usbudget.

Office of Tax Policy, US Treasury, www.ustreas.gov/taxpolicy.
Organisation for Economic Co-operation and Development (OECD), www.oecd.org.
Social Security Administration, www.sss.gov.

Notes

1. Franklin D. Roosevelt's campaign address at Madison Square Garden (1936), available at www.milestonedocuments.com_FDR (accessed March 26, 2009).

2. Paul Krugman, *The Conscience of a Liberal* (New York: W. W. Norton, 2007), p. 62.

3. Ibid., p. 58.

4. Adopted by the UN General Assembly at New York on December 16, 1966. Annex to GA Res. 2200. Entered into force on January 3, 1976. The United States has not ratified the covenant to date.

5. Article 8 of the treaty reads in part: "1. The States Parties to the present Covenant undertake to ensure: (a) the right of everyone to form trade unions and join the trade union of his choice, subject only to the rules of the organization concerned, for the promotion and protection of his economic and social interests. No restrictions may be placed on the exercise of this right other than those prescribed by law and which are necessary in a democratic society in the interests of national security or public order or for the protection of the rights and freedoms of others."

6. As quoted in Robert L. Heilbroner and Laurence J. Malone, ed., *The Essential Adam Smith* (New York: W. W. Norton, 1986), p. 321.

7. Thomas Kochan and Beth Shulman, "A New Social Contract: Restoring Dignity and Balance to the Economy" (Washington, DC: Economic Policy Institute, February 2007), p. 2.

8. Krugman, *The Conscience of a Liberal,* p. 138.

9. John Weeks, "Inequality Trends in Some Developed OECD Countries," in Jomo K. S., ed., with J. Baudot, *Flat World, Big Gaps: Economic Liberalization, Globalization, Poverty and Inequality* (New York: Zed Books, 2007), pp. 159–175.

10. Harley Shaiken, "Unions, the Economy, and Employee Free Choice," EPI Briefing Paper (Washington, DC: Economic Policy Institute, February 2009), p. 1.

11. Steven Greenhouse, *The Big Squeeze: Tough Times for the American Worker* (New York: Random House, 2009), p. 82. At almost the same time (January 1982), Reagan spoke movingly of the essential role of unions in democratic societies in their battle to "sustain fundamental human and economic rights" including "the right to work and reap the fruits of one's labor, the right to assemble, the right to strike, and the right to freedom of expression." However, Reagan was speaking of the Solidarity union movement in Poland. It is easier to see virtue in foreign rather than national unions. Ronald Reagan, Proclamation 4891—Solidarity Day, January 20, 1982, available at www.presidency.ucsb.edu/ws/?pid=42487 (accessed March 29, 2009).

12. John Dinardo, "Still Open for Business: Unionization Has No Causal Effect on Firm Closures," EPI Briefing Paper (Washington, DC: Economic Policy Institute, March 20, 2009), pp. 2–3.

13. Josh Bivens, "Squandering the Blue-Collar Advantage: Why Almost Everything Except Unions and the Blue-Collar Workforce Are Hurting US Manufacturing" (Washington: Economic Policy Institute, February 2009). pp. 1–2.

14. Organisation for Economic Co-operation and Development, *Revenue Statistics 1965–2007* (Paris, France: OECD, 2008).

15. The decline in sales resulting from the tax that is not offset by the tax revenue generated is referred to as a "deadweight loss," in that no one gets the money. Since a relatively small number of voters buy cigarettes and alcohol, the price increase will not significantly affect

sales. A much larger number of voters buy gas, but the political cost to an elected official of a tax on petroleum is acceptable because the deadweight losses are minimal and because the tax burden on each voter is relatively small.

16. Center on Budget and Policy Priorities, "Tax Cuts: Myths and Realities," updated May 9, 2008, available at www.cbpp.org/cms/index.cfm?f (accessed April 2, 2009).

17. These numbers were projected by George Jones of CCH, a Walters Kluwer business; William Massey of the tax and accounting business of Thomson Reuters; and Northern Illinois University professor James C. Young. Their numbers are based on inflation data released on March 30, 2009, available at www.bargaineering.com/articles/2009-federal-income-tax-brackets-projected.html (accessed April 2, 2009).

18. George Gilder, *Wealth and Poverty* (New York: Basic Books, 1981), p. 188.

19. Ibid.

20. Michelle Levi, "Obama Says Charitable Giving Not Affected by Tax Increases," *CBS News,* March 25, 2009, available at www.cbsnews.com/blogs/2009/03/24/politicsalhotsheet/entry4890928.shtml (accessed April 2, 2009).

21. In 1998, 1999, 2000, and 2001, tax revenues as a percentage of GDP were 20 percent, 20 percent, 20.9 percent, and 19.8 percent, respectively. Outlays as a percentage of GDP for the same years were 19.2 percent, 18.6 percent, 18.4 percent, and 18.6 percent, respectively. See *The Budget and Economic Outlook: Fiscal Years 2005–2014* (Washington, DC: US Government Printing Office, January 26, 2004), Historic Budget Data, app. F, tab. 2.

22. According to the National Bureau of Economic Research, the expansion of the 1990s lasted 120 months. "What Is a Recession?" available at http://nber.org/cycles/dec2008.html (accessed April 6, 2009).

23. The National Bureau of Economic Research provides the official dates marking the beginning and ending of recessions. It dates the recession beginning toward the end of G. W. Bush's second term as having begun in December 2007 after an expansion of seventy-three months; the previous expansion in the 1990s lasted 120 months. "What Is a Recession?" available at www.nber.org/cycles/dec2008.html (accessed April 6, 2009).

24. Bureau of Economic Analysis, "Real GDP in Chained 2007 Dollars," available at www.bea.gov/national/index.htm#gdp (accessed April 4, 2009).

25. William G. Gale and Peter R. Orszag, "Tax Notes," in William G. Gale and Peter R. Orszag, ed., *Bush Administration Tax Policy: Summary and Outlook* (Washington, DC: Brookings Institution, November 29, 2004), p. 1280.

26. See Economic Policy Institute, "Job Watch: Tracking Jobs and Wages," available at http://web.archive.org/web/20080127072044/www.jobwatch.org, (accessed August 17, 2009).

27. Mark M. Zandi, "Assessing President Bush's Fiscal Policies," July 2004, available at www.economy.com/dismal/economycom_bushfiscalpolicy.pdf (accessed April 6, 2009).

28. David Kamin and Isaac Shapiro, *Studies Shed New Light on Effects of Administration's Tax Cuts* (Washington, DC: Center on Budget and Policy Priorities, 2004), p. 2.

29. Ibid., p. 11.

30. Gale and Orszag, "Tax Notes," p. 1282.

31. Dan McGill, Kyle Brown, John Haley, and Sylvester Schieber, *Fundamentals of Private Pensions,* 7th ed. (Philadelphia: University of Pennsylvania Press, 1996), p. 5.

32. US Census Bureau, *Statistical Abstract 2009,* tab. 1295 (Washington, DC: US Government Printing Office).

33. US Census Bureau, *Statistical Abstract 2003* (Washington, DC: US Government Printing Office), p. 857.

34. *OASDI Trustee's Report 2004,* tab.VI.F (Washington, DC: US Government Printing Office).

35. Melissa Favreault and Gordon Mermin, "Are There Opportunities to Increase Social Security Progressivity Despite Underfunding?" Discussion Paper No. 30 (Washington, DC: Urban Institute, 2008), p. 1.

36. On this point, see Allen W. Smith, *The Looting of Social Security* (New York: Carroll and Graf, 2003).

37. Michael Hodges, "Government Trust Fund and Deficit/Surplus Report," available at http://mwhodges.home.att.net/deficit-trusts.htm (accessed April 8, 2009).

38. Lori Montgomery, "Recession Puts a Major Strain on Social Security Trust Fund: As Payroll Tax Revenue Falls, So Does Surplus," *Washington Post,* March 31, 2009, available at www.washingtonpost.com/wp-dyn/content/article/2009/03/30/AR2009033003291.html?hpid=topnews.

39. Paul Krugman, "About the Social Security Trust Fund," *New York Times,* March 28, 2008, available at http://krugman.blogs.nytimes.com/2008/03/28/about-the-social-security-trust-fund.

40. Congressional Budget Office, *The Outlook for Social Security* (Washington, DC: US Government Printing Office, June 2004).

41. US Census Bureau, *Statistical Abstract, 2009,* tab. 1296 (Washington, DC: US Government Printing Office).

42. Ibid.

43. See "Social Security Trustees' Report, 2008" (Washington, DC: US Government Printing Office, 2008). See also Robert Greenstein and Chad Stone, "What the 2008 Trustees' Report Shows About Social Security," Center on Budget and Policy Priorities, March 27, 2008, available at www.cbpp.org/cms/index.cfm?f (accessed April 9, 2009).

44. Milton Friedman and Rose Friedman, *Free to Choose* (New York: Harcourt, Brace, Jovanovich, 1980), pp. 102–106.

7

The Politics and Economics of Inequality

This chapter focuses on the oldest story in every society: the tension between the haves and the have-nots. As Plutarch observed early in the first millennium: "An imbalance between rich and poor is the oldest and most fatal ailment of all republics." Throughout history, elites have boldly justified their special claim to wealth, power, and privilege through the development of national myths that legitimize their position at the expense of the masses. Democracy in its most narrow formal requirement of individual freedom of expression, by means of regular elections with full citizen participation and a responsive government, was not possible where an aristocracy not only controlled all political power, but also had tight control over land, labor, and capital. Democracy, based on the fundamental principle of equality, sweeps aside all claims of privilege. As Supreme Court Justice Louis Brandeis said: "We can have democracy in this country or we can have great wealth concentrated in the hands of a few, but we cannot have both."[1] When great wealth is concentrated in relatively few hands that also control the institutions of governmental power, government will serve the interests of those elites first. Democratic government's stated primary purpose of serving "we the people" to "promote the general welfare" can become an illusion manipulated by the powerful to gain approval of the nonelites. Democracy is always threatened by the possible collusion between the rich to take control of government for their own benefit. When that effort succeeds, the institutions of democracy will continue to exist long after the political system has degenerated into an oligarchy.

The study of income and wealth distribution is concerned with an analysis of the way the national income is divided among persons. A basic question of public policy is: Why should the government be involved in attempts to redistribute income? In Chapter 1, we pointed out that the distribution of resources by the market does not necessarily result in a socially optimal (or even socially acceptable) outcome. We also mentioned that oftentimes market failures necessitate government intervention (such as in health care or the severe economic crisis that began in December 2007). The Rawlsian philosophy, also discussed in Chapter 1, provides arguments for redistribution particularly to help low-income members of society. For economists such as Adam Smith, Thomas Malthus, Karl Marx, and John Maynard Keynes (Chapter 5), distribution was a central issue.

The private sector however, as economic theory makes clear, is not likely to help redistribute income because of the self-interest observed in all free rider problems when providing public goods. "I would like the poor to have the ability to buy more education, health care, housing, and so forth. But I will be better off if others provide the poor with the means of increasing their consumption while I do not bear any of the costs." The problem is that everyone else's self-interest is the same as mine. Other major questions regarding the distribution of wealth and income include whether or not inequality is inevitable. If so, how much inequality is optimal? Is there a threshold beyond which inequality in wealth or income undermines political democracy? What kinds of public policies regarding inequalities would improve the quality of life for most citizens? Should there be a coordination of policies by democratic governments to reduce the variability of inequality in various nations?

The Promise of Equality in the First New Nation

Politics is often defined as the ongoing struggle over who gets what, when, and how. Throughout history much of the struggle was determined by the ability of a powerful actor, whether a warlord, a monarch, or an oligarch, to maintain his life of wealth and privilege at the expense of others. The eighteenth-century Enlightenment thinkers challenged the domination of society by a hereditary and tyrannical aristocracy. They believed that human reason was the indispensable weapon needed to battle ignorance, superstition, and tyranny and build a better world. Thinkers of the Enlightenment stressed individualism over community, and freedom replaced authority as a core value. Many Enlightenment thinkers were merchants who resented paying taxes to support a privileged aristocracy who contributed little of value to society. It was particularly galling that the aristocrats were unwilling to share power with the merchants and manufacturers who actually created the national wealth.

The intellectual leaders of the American Revolution were captivated by the Enlightenment's opposition to unchecked privilege since they hoped to build a democracy that would require tolerance, respect for evidence, and informed public opinion. Their notion of democracy was one in which government would make decisions on behalf of the "general welfare," not for the advantage of the privileged few. The concept of equality written into the Declaration of Independence, together with the concept of "human rights" which has become an essential part of US culture, is our "civil religion."

These notions from the Enlightenment were not seen by early Americans as naive optimism, but as the promise of the **American Dream**—the widespread belief in an open, vigorous, and progressive community committed to equal opportunities for all in which life would improve for each generation. It includes the belief that the income and wealth that the economy generated would become more evenly distributed.

The leaders of the American Revolution intended to do more than free themselves from forced obedience to a monarch; they wanted to create a government that would offer greater freedom and dignity to the average citizen. Some went so far as to propose that all free white males be allowed to vote. Other influential delegates to the Constitutional Convention in Philadelphia in 1787 were more dubious and proposed a government administered by gentlemen of property to maintain their life of privilege at the expense of others. The Constitution that resulted from all the compromises provided a system of separation of powers between the president, Congress, and the judiciary. It specifically provided for the House of Representatives to represent interests of "the people." Congress, aware of the unprecedented grant of power to the people, used the words of the Roman poet Virgil in the Great Seal of the United States—"a new age now begins."[2] The principle of checks and balances resulted from the inability of the framers of the Constitution to agree on precisely how power should be distributed among the branches. Although the commitment to hold all men as being created equal and endowed by their creator with inalienable rights to life, liberty, and the pursuit of happiness was not enforced, a war on inequality began immediately to force the government to live up to the promise. Property rights for voting were abolished, but it took a civil war to free slaves and another century passed before civil rights legislation gave substance to that freedom.

Equity and Equality

To the leaders of the American Revolution, democracy was looked upon as the completion of the human struggle for freedom. The constitutional framers were well aware of the difficulty of reconciling individuality and liberty with democratic equality. James Madison expressed his concern over the inherent conflicts a democratic society would have to address when he wrote in *The Federalist* no. 10 that the "most common and durable source of factions" in society is "the various and unequal distribution of property."

Thomas Jefferson's bias in favor of equality is also well known. He believed that the innate differences between men were small.[3]

I am conscious that an equal division of property is impracticable. But the consequences of this enormous inequality producing so much misery to the bulk of mankind, legislators cannot invent too many devices for subdividing property. . . . Another means of silently lessening the inequality of property is to exempt all from taxation below a certain point, and to tax the higher portions of property in geometrical progression as they rise.[4]

Jefferson went on to say that the government should provide "that as few as possible shall be without a little portion of land" as the "small landholders are the most precious part of a state."[5]

Opponents of the trend toward equality used the vocabulary of the Enlightenment and Jeffersonian liberalism, but provided their own definitions to words like "individualism" and "progress." For example, Charles Darwin expressed concern for the poor when he wrote: "If the misery of the poor be caused not by the laws of nature, but by our institutions, great is our sin."[6] Nevertheless, his theory of natural selection, which led to the theory of evolution, was revised by Herbert Spencer into "social Darwinism" and endorsed as a scientific finding that the destruction of the weak and the "survival of the fittest" constituted the essence of progress.

Americans have often boastfully quoted Alexis de Tocqueville's observation of "the equality of conditions" in the United States in the 1830s. US culture has always emphasized equality rather than deference. Politicians, especially wealthy politicians, claim that they share the same social and cultural *values* of the average American, even if they do not share the same tax bracket. Indeed, de Tocqueville believed that the Americanization of the world in terms of the ever-increasing equality of conditions was inevitable. He realized that the creation of democratic forms of government was not the end of the struggle, but that it was a continuous process. And he believed that inevitably the rest of humanity would finally arrive at an almost complete equality of conditions. He noted, however, a growing "aristocracy of manufacturers" who had no sense of public responsibility and whose aim was to use the workers and then abandon them to public charity. He believed that the manufacturing aristocracy "is one of the harshest which ever existed in the world. . . . [T]he friends of democracy should keep their eyes anxiously fixed in this direction; for if ever a permanent inequality of conditions and aristocracy again penetrate into the world, it may be predicted that this is the channel by which they will enter."[7]

Writing a century later, Keynes pointed out that we could hardly expect business to act on behalf of the well-being of the workers, let alone the entire society. He noted that, in democracies, the government has the responsibility to protect the economic well-being of the nation. The main failure of capitalism, according to Keynes, is its "failure to provide for full employment and its arbitrary and inequitable distribution of wealth and incomes."[8] Keynes was not opposed to economic inequality. What was required, he said, was a collective management of the system that would be as efficient as possible without offending our notions of a satisfactory way of life. The problem is to determine what is a socially optimal amount of economic inequality.

US political institutions declare the equality of citizens. However, capitalism creates economic and social inequalities. The disparity between presumed equal rights and economic inequality creates tension between capitalism and the principles of democracy. Owners of capital may use money or their position of power in imperfect markets to deny others a minimum standard of living. Beginning in the Progressive era and reaching its high points during the administrations of Franklin Roosevelt and Lyndon Johnson, democratic institutions were used to keep market excesses within acceptable limits. During the 1930s, President Roosevelt inaugurated the New Deal. The Great Depression caused a national crisis that resulted in a third of the nation being ill-fed, ill-housed, and ill-clothed. The minimum wage, the eight-hour day, Social Security, trade union legislation, civil rights, women's rights, a progressive federal income tax, and civil service reform based on merit rather than a spoils system were all achieved over the vigorous opposition of business interests, which were concerned that such benefits to workers would reduce profits. The American Dream was reinforced by the notion that business prospers when workers are paid wages sufficient to allow them to buy what they produce. We prosper as "one nation, indivisible" when workers are paid wages that allow a "middle-class" income. A broad middle class contributes to prosperity for all. Government responsibility to narrow the gap between rich and poor was largely accepted by liberals and conservatives alike after the New Deal. Others sought to preserve equality of opportunity by opposing any alliance between government and business elites. That effort, and the unsteady progress by reformers in advancing the American Dream of equality, was seriously challenged in the 1980s by a resurgence of conservatism under President Ronald Reagan. Supply-side economic thinking defended economic inequality as a source of productivity and economic growth.

Many of those most adversely affected by the economic changes did not respond with anger toward those primarily responsible for their economic decline. Rather than focusing their anger on the corporate and financial elite derided by Roosevelt as "economic royalists" and "malefactors of great wealth," they identified their antagonists as "liberals." Conservative strategists successfully cast the problem as "cultural" rather than "economic." Activists, with the support of conservative think tanks, pundits, lobbyists, ministers, and right-wing radio talk-show hosts, provided a smoke screen that shielded the dismantling of middle- and working-class protections while they added fuel to their anger against liberals.

A recent study by Thomas Frank titled *What's the Matter with Kansas?* analyzes how many vulnerable Americans have been persuaded that cultural issues override economic issues, and influenced to vote against their economic and social interests.[9] Political liberals are portrayed as waging cultural warfare against a fundamentally Protestant Christian culture that is perceived as the basis of US society. Conservatives argue that this is a battle to determine whether US culture as we have known it can be saved. On issue after issue, they feel threatened: gay marriage, abortion rights, the Pledge of Allegiance, prayer in schools, the promiscuity portrayed in movies and television programming, to name just a few.

The economically disadvantaged segment of the US population provided critical electoral support in the 2004 elections to politicians who acted against their economic interest by implementing policies that increased the gap between themselves and the affluent. Political campaigns increasingly rely on professional managers, constant polling, focus groups to test appeals to voters, and expensive television advertising. The wealthy are inclined to contribute money to politicians and organizations that endorse reductions in many government programs, including social welfare programs, taxes, and government regulation of business. They are very aware of the benefits of economic inequality for themselves and focus clearly on the goal of protecting their economic status when they contribute to political candidates. It is estimated that the richest 3 percent of the voting population accounts for 35 percent of all private campaign contributions during presidential elections.[10]

The nonelites are aware of the downside of economic inequality, but often vote on the basis of noneconomic issues like crime, abortion, or immigration.[11] The poor are more cynical regarding government and are less likely to register and vote.[12] The federal government is responsive to the pressure and acts to advance the economic interests of the wealthy and the noneconomic interests of the less affluent.

As labor organizer Oscar Ameringer observed, in such a scenario, politics becomes the art of winning votes from the poor and campaign contributions from the rich through promises "to defend each from the other."[13]

Elites' contributions give them greater political influence than less-affluent voters. The process results in economic policies that add to elites' share of total wealth and income, which is at variance with theories of democracy. The alliance between government and the rich (the US equivalent of the aristocrats' relationship to King George III), so long feared by the reformers, has been realized.

Income Distribution

There is no established theory of income distribution to guide us to an optimal amount of inequality. **Income** is defined as the total monetary return to a household over a set period, usually a year, from all sources of wages, rent, interest, and gifts. Income refers to the flow of dollars within a year. Labor earnings (wages) constitute an ever-larger component of total income as one moves down the income ladder. Income tends not to be as unequally distributed as wealth. Income inequality threatens the political stability of many developing countries. Even in a wealthy country like the United States, great inequality in income and wealth is a social problem and, therefore, an issue for the policy agenda. A society that cares about maximizing the welfare of all its members may consider that social welfare for low-income individuals (for whom the marginal utility of an extra dollar is high) would be improved by transferring a dollar from a high-income person (for whom the marginal utility of having one less dollar is low).

Whether government *should* reduce great inequality between the rich and poor is the focus of debate.

The concept of liberty and egalitarianism has been a cornerstone of US social and political culture. Liberty, protected by government as the pursuit of one's own self-interest, permits each person to acquire material goods according to their circumstances and abilities. The result has been a vast disparity in income and wealth. We hear a great deal about political equality, which typically means that individuals are equal before the law, and that regardless of ability or income, each has the right to vote. There appears to be an assumption that this narrow technical political equality is *the* significant equality in the United States, and we disregard or minimize the broader implications of economic inequality. Most countries of the Western world have policies designed to *reduce* the differences between rich and poor based on a consensus that the role of government should not be to widen the gap between rich and poor, but rather to reduce it.

How has income distribution changed? Between 1935 and 1975, a period known as the Great Compression, there was a clear trend toward a more equal distribution of income in the United States, primarily because of four factors:

1. Policies to end the Great Depression and a wartime economy provided full employment, significantly raising the wages of labor.
2. During World War II, a more progressive income tax and excess-profits taxes reduced the after-tax income of the rich more than that of the poor.
3. Labor scarcity during the war reduced discrimination against minorities and increased economic opportunities for them.
4. Union membership quadrupled and increased the relative income of labor.

In the decade between 1945 and 1955, the trend toward greater equality continued at a much slower pace as unions began meeting more resistance after the war such as the passage of the Taft-Hartley Act. From 1955 through about 1975, the distribution of income remained relatively constant. Since then, inequality in income has increased. After 1980, the gap between pay for higher- and lower-paid workers accelerated, particularly among men.[14]

Income Distribution and Poverty

One way to begin thinking about what income distribution would be optimal is to examine how income is distributed throughout society at present. We begin by examining **relative income inequality** in which we measure the share of total income that is received by various segments of the community, especially how much the poor receive relative to the rich.

Similarly, **relative poverty** is usually defined as having significantly less access to income and wealth than most members of society. There consequently is a direct link between income inequality and relative poverty. Conservatives in the United States have been particularly opposed to the use of relative definitions of poverty because it would be extremely difficult to demonstrate progress. For example, suppose the poverty level was defined as including all those with incomes in the bottom fifth of the country. Then, even if everyone's income increased by 20 percent, there would still be a bottom 20 percent remaining in poverty by definition.

The Census Bureau takes a survey each year regarding the income received throughout society. For the purposes of the survey, society is divided into fifths (quintiles) with the goal of determining how much income is allocated to each quintile from the lowest to the highest. The survey is concerned with money received before payment of taxes. Notably, the data do not include the monetary value of nonwage fringe benefits like employer contributions to health care packages or pension programs.

Table 7.1 displays the share of total income that is received by each quintile over time. For example, in 1980, the bottom 20 percent received 4.3 percent of the aggregate income while the top quintile received 44.1 percent. But by 2006, the bottom quintile's small share declined to 3.4 percent (a 21 percent decline) while the top quintile received half of all income (a 13 percent increase). The collective share of the bottom four quintiles fell from 56 percent of total income to 49.4 percent while the top quintile's share rose an equivalent amount from 44.1 to 50.5 percent. That is, just over half of all income in the United States goes to the richest 20 percent of the population. If income were equally distributed, each quintile would receive an equal share of income (20 percent). The table shows that income in the United States was distributed

Table 7.1 Share of Aggregate Income Received by Each Fifth and Top 5 Percent of Households, 1980–2006 (percentages)

Income Quintile	1980	1985	1990	1995	2000	2005	2006
Lowest 20%	4.3	3.9	3.8	3.7	3.6	3.4	3.4
Second 20%	10.2	9.8	9.6	9.1	8.9	8.6	8.6
Third 20%	16.8	16.2	15.9	15.2	14.8	14.6	14.5
Fourth 20%	24.7	24.4	24.0	23.3	23.0	23.0	22.9
Highest 20%	44.1	45.6	46.6	48.7	49.8	50.4	50.5
Top 5%	16.5	17.6	18.5	21.0	22.1	22.2	22.3

Source: Data compiled from US Census Bureau, Historical Income Tables—Households, Current Population Survey, tab. H-2, available at www.census.gov/hhes/www/income/histinc/h02A.html (accessed August 16, 2009).

very unequally in 1980, and it became more unequally distributed in 2006. The top 5 percent increased its share by almost 28 percent (from 16.5 to 22.3 percent).

The inequality in the distribution of income is greater in the United States than it is in any other Organisation for Economic Co-operation and Development (OECD) country except Mexico, as is indicated in Table 7.2. The share of income received by the lowest quintile is smaller than in any other OECD nation and is less than half of the average for OECD nations (7.7 percent). At the highest quintile, the share of income in the United States is higher at 50.4 percent than any other OECD nation except Mexico, and is 25 percent higher than the average top quintile in other OECD countries (40.5 percent). The second quintile in the United States at 8.6 percent is only

Table 7.2   Distribution of Income by Quintile for OECD Countries

Country	Survey Year	Gini Index	Income Quintile				
			Lowest	Second	Third	Fourth	Highest
Austria	2000	29.1	8.6	13.3	17.4	22.9	37.8
Belgium	2000	33.0	8.5	13.0	16.3	20.8	41.4
Canada	2000	32.6	7.2	12.7	17.2	23.0	39.9
Czech Republic	1996	25.4	10.3	14.5	17.7	21.7	35.9
Denmark	1997	24.7	8.3	14.7	18.2	22.9	35.8
Finland	2000	26.9	9.6	14.1	17.5	22.1	36.7
France	1995	32.7	7.2	12.6	17.2	22.8	40.2
Germany	2000	28.3	8.5	13.7	17.8	23.1	36.9
Greece	2000	34.3	6.7	11.9	16.8	23.0	41.5
Hungary	2002	26.9	9.5	13.9	17.6	22.4	36.5
Italy	2000	36.0	6.5	12.0	16.8	22.8	42.0
Korea, Republic	1998	31.6	7.9	13.6	18.0	23.1	37.5
Mexico	2002	49.5	4.3	8.3	12.6	19.7	55.1
New Zealand	1997	36.2	6.4	11.4	15.8	22.6	43.8
Norway	2000	25.8	9.6	14.0	17.2	22.0	37.2
Poland	2002	34.5	7.5	11.9	16.1	22.2	42.2
Portugal	1997	38.5	5.8	11.0	15.5	21.9	45.9
Slovak Republic	1996	25.8	8.8	14.9	18.7	22.8	34.8
Sweden	2000	25.0	9.1	14.0	17.6	22.7	36.6
Turkey	2003	43.6	5.3	9.7	14.2	21.0	49.7
United Kingdom	1999	36.0	6.1	11.4	16.0	22.5	44.0
Unweighted Average			7.7	12.7	16.7	22.2	40.5
United States	2006	46.6	3.4	8.6	14.5	22.9	50.4

Sources: World Bank, *2006 World Development Indicators* (Washington, DC: World Bank, 2006), pp. 76–79; US Census Bureau, Historical Income Tables—Households, Current Population Survey, tab. H-2, available at www .census.gov/hhes/www/income/histinc/h02A.html (accessed August 16, 2009).

70 percent of the average OECD share of 12.7 percent, and is lower than any other country except Mexico. The third quintile in the United States also receives less than any other country except Turkey and Mexico. In fact, the lowest three quintiles in the United States receive a smaller share than in any other OECD nation except Mexico, and the difference is reallocated to the top 20 percent of US households. Not surprisingly, the United States has some of the highest relative poverty rates among industrialized countries, reflecting in part the high degree of inequality.[15]

The distribution of relative shares of income in the United States more closely resembles the distribution of less-developed countries like Iran, Venezuela, Nicaragua, or Nigeria than advanced OECD countries.[16]

Table 7.3 illustrates what the shares going to each quintile mean in terms of constant 2006 dollars. It also shows that, as income increases, income rises at a faster rate. Note that in 1980, the average for the highest fifth was over ten times that of the lowest, but by 2006 the average for the highest fifth was almost fifteen times that of the lowest fifth. Also in 1980, the top 5 percent had an income average that was sixteen times the bottom fifth, which grew to twenty-six times the average of the bottom fifth by 2006.

Tables 7.2 and 7.3 actually understate the chasm between those at the top and the bottom. A study by G. Ross Stephens analyzed public policy and income distribution focusing on the adjusted gross income (AGI).[17] He found that only the top 10 percent of AGI tax returns increased their shares of income since 1980. The share losses increase as people descend the income scale.[18] Although the federal income tax has been mildly progressive, changes in tax rates and in the mix of taxes, such as payroll taxes

Table 7.3 Mean Household Income Received by Each Fifth and Top 5 Percent of Households, 1980–2006 (in constant 2006 dollars)

Year	Bottom Fifth	Second Fifth	Third Fifth	Fourth Fifth	Highest Fifth	Top 5 Percent
1980	10,041	24,990	41,234	60,753	108,322	161,874
1985	10,032	25,423	42,199	63,477	118,570	182,903
1990	10,716	26,963	44,536	67,147	130,309	207,503
1995	10,963	26,795	44,804	68,874	143,729	248,057
2000	11,892	29,693	49,447	76,868	166,571	295,515
2005	11,004	28,254	47,819	75,213	164,815	290,373
2006	11,352	28,777	48,223	76,329	168,170	297,405

Source: US Census Bureau, Historical Income Tables—Households, Current Population Survey, tab. H-3, available at www.census.gov/hhes/www/income/histinc/h03A.html (accessed August 13, 2009).

Note: The upper limit for each fifth: lowest, 20,035; second, 37,774; third, 60,000; fourth, 97,032.

and especially when including state and local taxes, have downgraded the federal income tax as the most importance source of government income. Specific types of income not included in AGI, such as 85 percent of dividends and capital gains, obviously reduce the progressivity of the income tax.

Another way to consider income distribution and poverty is to analyze the amount of money necessary to provide an individual or a family with a minimally adequate level of income. When President Johnson declared the "War on Poverty" in 1964, he adopted an **absolute standard of poverty** based on a standard put forward by Mollie Orshansky, an economist working for the Social Security Administration. She based her definition on a finding by the Department of Agriculture that most families spent about one-third of their income after taxes on food. Four budgets were provided for a diet for families adjusted for by family size, gender of the family head, the number of children under eighteen years of age, and whether the residence was farm or nonfarm. The government chose the least costly "minimum but adequate diet" and multiplied the diet by three to determine the threshold below which families were considered to lack the resources to provide for the basic needs of food, clothing, and shelter to maintain health. The guidelines have been used by the federal government ever since, and have simply been updated to account for inflation since as noted in Table 7.4.

According to the federal poverty guidelines shown in Table 7.4, a family of three with an annual income $18,500 is officially above the federal poverty line, even though that family would feel poor. Additionally, a worker employed at the minimum wage of $7.25 an hour who works fifty weeks a year with two weeks off at no pay would earn $14,500, which would be insufficient to support anyone but

Table 7.4 Federal Poverty Guidelines by Family Size, 2009

Size of Family Unit	100% Federal Poverty Level Yearly
1	$10,830
2	$14,570
3	$18,310
4	$22,050
5	$25,790
6	$29,530
7	$33,270
8	$37,020
For each additional person, add $3,740	

Source: Health and Human Services, "Federal Poverty Guidelines by Family Size, 2009," available at http://aspe.hhs.gov/poverty/09poverty.shtml (accessed August 15, 2009).

the worker and his family would not officially be in "poverty." The most recent figures available indicate that, as of December 2008, 45 million Americans (15 percent of the population) were below the federal poverty level.[19] That number is certain to grow.

Criticism of the absolute standard of poverty has grown over the years. One major criticism is that the price of food has declined from a third of the average family budget to just over 20 percent. Thus, the formula could understate poverty since food is a smaller portion of the average budget. Some have suggested that the cost of an "average" market basket of goods might provide a more accurate measure. Second, the federal definition does not take regional differences in the cost of living into account. Food and housing, for example, would both cost more in Massachusetts than in Mississippi. Third, the absolute definition excludes noncash transfers such as Medicaid or food stamps. Adding the value of government assistance through food stamps or health care would raise the income level of many and result in a reduced defined level of poverty in the country.

Relative Versus Absolute Poverty

Some critics claim that poverty in the United States is only relative. They indicate that some of the poor in Bangladesh would find their standard of living high if they could be poor in the United States. Therefore, the argument goes, the poor in the United States are only relatively poor, not absolutely poor when compared to the poor in some countries. But as Table 7.2 shows, the poor in many OECD countries actually enjoy a higher level of income in those states.

Second, people usually measure their living standards by what others in their country have. There are also studies that suggest that higher mortality rates in a country are associated with greater economic inequality rather than merely a given standard of living (see Chapter 9).

Factors Contributing to Economic Inequality

Why did wage inequality expand so rapidly in the United States during the past quarter century? Several policies contributed to the reversal of relative equality, discussed earlier in this chapter, the so-called Great Compression. Since the Reagan administration, enforcement of antitrust laws has been given a low priority. Mergers of large corporations have become a method for concentrating wealth, undertaken because of the huge payouts received by chief executive officers (CEOs) and senior executives when two companies merge. Historically, an increase in worker productivity resulted in a similar increase in income for the average worker. The pay gap between more highly educated workers and workers with less education has indeed increased. Those with more human capital can demand more for their more highly skilled labor, which pushes up pay levels. Highly educated (or skilled) workers are often in a more inelastic supply position, and rising demand forces up their wage rate.

For most Americans, successive federal tax cuts were actually tax shifts that redistributed after-tax income from the bottom to the top quintile, exacerbating the inequality between the rich and everyone else. The federal government has concentrated on eliminating estate taxes and reducing taxes for the wealthy while ignoring social safety net policies for the poor like raising the minimum wage, providing health care for the uninsured, or providing more funds for housing the poor.

Several factors besides government policies have contributed to the rise in inequality in income. Demand for more highly educated workers in a more technical age has also fueled an increase in the demand for college graduates. Technological innovations now allow machines to perform many tasks that were previously performed by less-educated workers. Machines, robots, and computers have reduced the demand for workers ranging from bank clerks, workers on automobile assembly lines, and retail clerks. More products and services can be produced using fewer low-skill workers while those with the technical skills to manage the robots and machinery receive much larger rewards. Others point to the winner-take-all nature of society made possible by technical advances that allow individuals to listen to or see the best artists, athletes, and entertainers perform while destroying the market for those with only slightly less talent.[20]

Perhaps **globalization** and international trade are a partial explanation for growing income inequality. International trade has made it easier for producers to outsource the manufacture of goods to countries where the wage rates are much lower. But others posit that there is an offsetting rise in the demand for services that cannot be outsourced. So undoubtedly, free trade does exert a downward pressure on US wages, but some scholars are skeptical that it is a major cause of rising inequality.[21] Paul Krugman observes that, if technology and globalization are the driving forces behind inequality, "then Europe should be experiencing the same rise in inequality as the United States."[22] However, the European experience is very different, in that unions remain strong and the tendency to condemn excessive pay for management is still strong. The rising inequality that is especially notable in the United Kingdom and the United States, Krugman concludes, is not based on technology or globalization, but on changing institutions and norms. In particular, Krugman cites the collapse of the US union movement.[23]

The norm that has changed in the United States is the gradual acceptance of excessive pay at the top of the pay pyramid, which reflects social and political change rather than the invisible hand of the market. There is a built-in conflict of interest in determining pay at the top of the scale. How is the determination made regarding the amount CEOs must be paid to keep competitors from enticing them to bring their talent to a rival firm? Corporate boards, largely selected by CEOs, hire compensation "experts" also chosen by CEOs to determine how much they and senior board members are worth. Those evaluating a CEO's worth to the firm can be counted on to be duly impressed with the extraordinary capabilities of the entire board if they entertain any hope of being hired for future evaluations.

The Federal Minimum Wage

At the other end of the wage spectrum is the **federal minimum wage**, which is the lowest hourly wage that employers may legally pay to workers. It is, conversely, the lowest wage at which workers may legally sell their labor. The minimum wage was first proposed as a way to prevent employers from paying substandard wages to workers due to the fact that employers may often have an unfair advantage when negotiating the terms of employment, particularly with low-skilled workers. A federal minimum-wage law was first passed in the United States in 1938 when it was set at $0.25 per hour ($3.75 in 2007 dollars). The minimum wage has varied from a maximum of 90 percent of the poverty level in 1968, but since 1980 it has tended to hover between 55 percent and 60 percent of the poverty level. The lowest percentage that the minimum wage has been below the poverty level was in 2006, just before Congress raised it for the first time in a decade. The period from 1997 to 2007 was the longest period since 1938 during which the minimum wage was not raised. The minimum wage was increased from $5.15 per hour in three increments of 70 cents each to $7.25 in mid-2009.

Many critics of a mandated minimum wage point out that classical economic theory concludes that mandating a minimum wage above the equilibrium wage will cause unemployment to rise. This is because a greater number of workers will be supplied at the higher wage while employers will reduce their demand for labor at the higher cost. Those workers who are hired at the higher wage will be helped, but the lowest-skilled workers who lose their jobs as employers reduce employment will be hurt.

The theory that raising the minimum wage will cause an increase in unemployment is challenged by the existence of monopsony in labor markets. A **monopsony** exists when there are several sellers in a market with only one buyer. In that situation, a single buyer has advantages over competing sellers. The situation is rarely so stark as the "company town." Yet firms hold a considerable degree of wage-setting power because of the likelihood that there will be more potential workers than jobs available, the limited mobility of labor, and the information advantage of the employer regarding employment needs and the labor supply. Wages, particularly at the low end of the scale where the labor supply (and therefore competition) is greatest, allow an employer to set wages below the workers' marginal value to the firm. This is exactly what happens when the unemployment rate falls below about 4 percent. At full employment, workers' bargaining power is increased because the firm has a smaller supply of available workers to choose from, which forces employers to raise wages closer to the marginal value of the workers' contribution. It is no accident that firms support "guest worker" programs or turn to "undocumented workers" to increase the available supply of workers to provide downward pressure on wages.

Empirical studies have found that raising the minimum wage did not raise unemployment as the theory predicted.[24] There are various explanations ranging from the obvious, like raising wages may reduce worker turnover and training costs, to the claim that the minimum wage is set so low that it represents such a small part of business costs that the increase is too small to make a significant difference. Paul Krugman, a Nobel Prize winner, states that studies which have found no evidence that raising the minimum wage results in job losses have been attacked "because it seems to contradict Econ 101 and because it was ideologically disturbing to many. Yet it has stood up very well to repeated challenges, and new cases confirming its results keep coming in."[25]

A Living Wage

The concept of a **living wage** refers to a minimum hourly wage necessary for a person working full time to afford a specified standard of living that would include adequate shelter, food, utilities, health care, and transportation. It differs from a minimum wage, which is not expected to equal a specific standard of consumption.

The living-wage concept was put forward by Pope Leo XIII in an 1891 document titled *Rerum Novarum* (literally, "Of New Things") in which he attempted to navigate a middle course between the harshness of laissez-faire capitalism and the suffocating aspects of state-run communism.[26] *Rerum Novarum* was an open letter to all Catholic bishops in which Pope Leo criticized the "greedy excesses of capitalism" in which many saw the Darwinian struggle for the "survival of the fittest" playing out in the clash between the owners of wealth against the masses. The struggle would lead logically and inevitably to the domination and repression of the laboring classes by the financiers.

In his letter, Pope Leo reaffirmed the right of private property and its protection by the state while also affirming the right of the state through regulation to require a living wage in the interest of the common good. He criticized such evils as excessive hours of labor, including labor on Sundays, child labor, low wages, and unhealthy and dangerous working conditions. The letter supported the right of workers to form unions and bargain collectively to improve their condition. At the same time Pope Leo considered Karl Marx's goal of the abolition of private property as an immoral injustice to the working class that would deprive them of the ability to improve their economic condition. Depriving workers of the freedom to use their wages to acquire property, a house, or to save or spend without interference was opposed to the natural law. *Rerum Novarum* resulted in many reform movements throughout the world to eliminate child labor, reduce the work week, improve worker conditions, and establish minimum, if not living, wages.

In 1994, an alliance between a labor union and religious leaders conducted a successful campaign in which the Baltimore city council passed a bill requiring companies that had service contracts with the city to pay workers $6.10 per hour, though the federal minimum wage was $5.15 per hour.[27] The living wage usually requires a wage significantly above the national minimum wage, which applies to only certain businesses such as those that have a contract to provide goods or services to a local jurisdiction. Since the Baltimore agreement, over 150 have been signed in different municipalities throughout the United States. Living-wage agreements vary according to the distinct conditions of the particular community.

The criticisms of the living wage are similar to the criticisms of the minimum wage—that it will increase unemployment. Since the wage rate is higher than the minimum wage, this criticism may have more validity.

There are several appealing attributes of the minimum wage and a living wage as public policy. Primarily, they raise the standard of living for the lowest-wage workers while motivating employees to work harder. In this regard, they are also held to improve the work ethic of those with low earnings. Second, they do not have any budgetary consequences for the government since the government does not need to use tax revenue to pay for them. By putting more money in the hands of low-income workers, they stimulate demand. By increasing the income of the lowest-paid employees, they work to reduce income inequality.

Immigration Policy and Inequality

Immigration is one demographic factor that has certainly contributed to income inequality by increasing the supply of less-educated workers. In the early 1970s, about 5 percent of the labor force was comprised of around 5 million foreign workers. Increased immigration, particularly from Latin America, resulted in immigrants making up about 16 percent (approximately 25 million workers) of the labor force in 2007. Although many immigrants are highly educated and highly skilled workers, most come from less-developed countries and are likely to be less educated than the average US worker. Roughly a third of the immigrant workers are high school dropouts and, therefore, compete primarily against other low-income workers in the US labor pool. Overall, foreign workers earn less than most low-wage US workers and may depress those wages by up to 10 percent. For immigrants, low wages by US standards are preferable to unemployment or even lower wages in their native countries. While they are a labor safety valve in their native countries, they increase income inequality in the United States.

Krugman has argued that the downward pressure on wages for low-income US workers may be overstated, and the real immediate political effect of immigration is political.[28] Many native-born whites perceive many of the immigrants to be nonwhite, which makes immigration a potentially divisive issue for political conservatism in the United States. Conservative business leaders are mainly pro-immigration because they favor a large supply of low-cost and docile labor. Wages can be kept low by threatening to hire from the abundant supply of cheap immigrant labor if US workers press their demands too aggressively. But many white working-class voters who left the Democratic Party after the enactment of civil rights legislation during the Johnson administration are still influenced by appeals to race and suspicious of foreign nationals. The result is a split within the conservative coalition over immigration policy. The anti-immigrant wing of the Republican Party has driven many Hispanics into the Democratic Party.

How Much Inequality?

It is largely a matter of public choice as to how much inequality a society will permit. Growing inequality has become a politically charged topic in recent years, which raises the question of what public policy should do, if anything, to reduce growing inequalities. Some conservatives have argued that significant differences in economic inequalities do not necessarily have policy implications. They argue that the wealthy are inclined to invest their money, creating jobs and contributing to faster economic growth. Conservatives accuse liberals of fomenting class warfare when they point to the growing inequality of income and wealth in society.

Others see the growing inequality as a serious threat to society's political, social, and economic well-being. They argue that income inequality causes spillover effects into the quality of life, even for those not necessarily in poverty. Wide economic disparities result in frustration, stress, and family discord, rising crime rates, violence, and homicide. Robert Putnam has suggested that the breakdown of social cohesion brought about by income inequality threatens the functioning of democracy. He found that low levels of civic trust spill over into a lack of confidence in government and low voter turnout at elections.[29] There is a serious concern that too much inequality could lead to a cycle in which lack of trust and civic engagement reinforce a public policy that does not result from the collective deliberation about the public interest, but merely reflects the success of campaign strategies. In a democracy, voters elect their representatives. However, members of Congress increasingly choose who can vote for them through gerrymandering. In the 2004 election, fewer than 3 percent of the seats in the House of Representatives were competitive.[30]

Americans' Bias in Favor of Equality

While Americans may declare sympathy for policies favoring equality, most would support inequality if it resulted from certain conditions.

1. *People would agree that inequality is justified if everyone has a fair (not necessarily equal) chance to get ahead.*[31] Not only would most people not object to inequality in the distribution of wealth or income if the race was run under fair conditions with

no one handicapped at the start, but they would actively support it as well. However, the situation quickly becomes murky. Many people do try to compete for scarce highly paid jobs by attending college so their future incomes will be higher. Some may choose not to attend college while others may have grown up in families who could not afford to send them to college or provide a background conducive to preparation for it. For those people, the resulting lower income is not voluntary.

What parameters make conditions fair? Of particular concern is the fairness of inheritances. What of the genetic inheritance of talent? Much of our most important human capital is carried in our genes, with the ownership of productive resources just an accident of birth. Is it fair that some individuals through their genetic endowment, a factor beyond the control of the person so equipped, have high innate intelligence, physical abilities that allow them to become professional athletes, or physical attributes that allow them to become highly paid models while the genetic inheritance of others determines that they will be mentally or physically limited, or even both? We usually do not worry too much over this kind of inheritance, but its effects are very real.

What about the inheritance of gender? Studies make it plain that women born in the United States doing the same job as men receive approximately 75 percent of the pay received by a man. Is that fair? What about the inheritance of those who grow up as an ethnic minority in a culturally deprived family in a ghetto neighborhood, as opposed to a child born to a white privileged family who can afford the most stimulating environment and best schools available for their children?

Then, there is the income differential resulting from inherited wealth. Many of the super-rich in the United States got that way through merely inheriting large sums of money. That it should be possible to pass some wealth on from one generation to another is generally conceded, but the passing on of large fortunes virtually intact is frequently challenged. Classical conservatives tend to be most supportive of the theory of social Darwinism, which holds that society is a place of competition based on the principle of "survival of the fittest" in which those who are most fit win the competition for material goods. Social Darwinists are opposed to the passing on of large inheritances from one generation to the next because it nullifies the fairness of the competition. Someone who inherits a fortune may have mediocre talent, but does not have to "compete" with others and prove their ability through competition. As Barry Switzer famously said, "some people are born on third base and go through life thinking they hit a triple."[32] The wealthy who truly believe in the theory maintain their consistency by opposing the repeal of estate taxes. They are not a large group.

Any discussion of inheritances suggests the role of chance in income distribution. Chance operates not only in inheritances, but also in the wider region of income differentials. One individual hits a lottery jackpot, another finds a superhighway built adjacent to their farm which increases its value several times, another unexpectedly finds oil on their land. On the other hand, workers may find themselves out of work for a prolonged period due to a recession beyond their control, or expensive debilitating illnesses, or because the highly paid positions they were trained for disappear.

2. *No one objects to inequality if it reflects individual choice.* If an individual decides to turn his or her back on the secular world to become a Franciscan and take a vow of poverty, no one would object. If someone decides to take a job that offers financial incentives because of unpleasant or inconvenient working conditions, or because it is more dangerous, no one will object to their higher wages. The problem is that frequently these decisions do not result from free choices, but are brought about by circumstances. A person raised in a ghetto, with no opportunity to sacrifice *current* income to improve skills through education so that a *future* income will be higher, may not have the option of choosing to work in a highly paid profession.

3. *People accept inequality when it reflects merit.* Nearly everyone believes in the correctness of higher pay when we can show that it is justified by a different contribution to output.[33] Some people work longer hours than others, or work harder when on the job. This may result in income differences that are largely voluntary. Other workers acquire experience and technical skills over time that may result in their earning a higher wage. This is part of the justification for a wage differential based on seniority.

4. *People accept and even support inequality when we are persuaded that the inequality will benefit everyone.* Often the common good is thought to include an increase in the gross domestic product (GDP) since greater productivity typically means a brisk demand for labor, higher wages, and greater economic activity. Therefore, the argument is often made by some politicians and economists that policies encouraging inequalities that benefit those with higher incomes are justified because they will lead to higher savings for the wealthy, which in turn will ultimately be translated into investments that will create the jobs to enrich the prospects of everyone else. That argument really states that the economic problem with the country is that the rich do not have enough money. So to help the poor we must cut the taxes of the rich. The proposal for a lower capital gains tax is just such a suggestion. This is the **trickle-down theory**, which suggests that, if the wealthy only had more money, they would be more highly motivated to invest more of it in the hope of making a profit and these investments would then create more jobs, thus helping society in general.[34]

These four general principles describe how the unequal distribution of income and wealth *is* defended. But there is no suggestion that this is the way we *should* think about inequality.

The Functional Theory of Inequality
The **functional theory of inequality** maintains that inequality in society is necessary because no society could remain stable or long survive without it.[35] According to the

functional theory of inequality, society must first distribute its members into the various jobs or roles defined by the society and then motivate them to perform their tasks efficiently. Some jobs are more important than others in the sense that successful performance of them is crucial to the welfare of the whole society.[36] Additionally, some tasks require skills that are either difficult or scarce because they require special training. To ensure that the most important jobs are performed competently, every society provides a system of unequal rewards to produce incentives to channel the most competent people into the most important and difficult jobs. This ensures the greatest efficiency in the performance of these jobs.

It should be emphasized that, according to this theory, "a position does not bring power and prestige because it draws a high income. Rather it draws a high income because it is functionally important and the available personnel is for one reason or another scarce."[37] So the population comes to understand that inequality is functional. The system of unequal rewards works to the advantage of the whole system by guaranteeing that jobs essential to society's welfare are performed efficiently and competently.

Milton Friedman believes that the market is the most efficient way of filling the most important positions with the most capable people. Equality of opportunity is the principle that allows the market to select the most competent individuals: "No society can be stable unless there is a basic core of value judgments that are unthinkingly accepted by the great bulk of its members. I believe that payment in accordance with product has been, and in large measure still is, one of these accepted value judgments or institutions."[38] The functional theory of inequality is intuitively appealing, but it immediately raises several problems.

Tradeoffs Between Equality, Equity, and Efficiency

The main argument against an equal distribution of income is based on efficiency. An unequal distribution does provide incentives. To illustrate the point, imagine the consequences if the society decided to achieve equality by taxing away all individual income and then dividing the taxes collected equally among the entire population. Realizing that harder work would no longer lead to a higher income would eliminate an important incentive. Any incentive to forgo current consumption to purchase capital goods would also be abolished because there would be no chance of additional income. Since all rewards for harder work, investing, entrepreneurship, and taking risks by developing capital and acquiring land would disappear, the GDP would decline dramatically. This suggests that policies that increase the amount of economic equality (or reduce inequality) may reduce economic efficiency: that is, lower the incentive to produce (thus lowering the GDP).

A second argument against an equal distribution of income or wealth is based on the concept of equity. As noted earlier, people with different natural abilities and who make unequal contributions to output should not receive the same income. An equal distribution is not equitable if individual contributions are unequal. US society has been based on the idea of equality of opportunity rather than equality of results.

The case in favor of an equal distribution of income must include the argument that an unequal distribution leads to unequal opportunities. Some income differences arise because of differences in wealth. Many with income-producing assets such as stocks and bonds may receive sizable incomes from them. Not only are these individuals able to acquire additional income-producing assets such as land or capital investments (i.e., more stocks and bonds), but they are also more able to invest in human capital through training and education to increase even further the amount of income they can earn in the future. Recent research indicates that a member of one generation will probably experience an economic status close to his or her parents. A child born to parents in the top 20 percent of households by income is five times as likely to remain in the top 20 percent than is a child born to parents in the bottom 20 percent. The research implies that income differences based on family background are likely to persist for many generations.[39] Such a concentration of wealth can turn a meritocracy into an aristocracy and stifle economic growth by putting much of the nation's capital in the hands of inheritors rather than innovators.

Another argument made by those in favor of a more equal income distribution is that a highly unequal distribution that provided a great deal for the few and little or nothing for the many creates political unrest and threatens the stability of the society. When 25 percent of the population lives at the subsistence level and the top 10 percent who receive most of the income also dominate the political and economic levers of power, the poor may be driven to rebel against the economic and political elites.

Qualifications to the Theory

The functional theory of inequality is open to some criticisms that do not demolish it, but significantly narrow the range of inequalities that can be justified as functionally imperative.

1. *It is relatively easy to determine which skills are in scarce supply, but difficult to tell which jobs are the most important to the welfare of a particular society.* Questions of comparable worth, for example, are notoriously complex problems. After agreement is reached regarding the extremes (e.g., the importance of the cardiovascular surgeon compared to the street-sweeper), it becomes very difficult to determine the relative importance of jobs more at the "center" (e.g., managing a corporation versus teaching young children, or working as an accountant versus being a dentist). How does one decide? Those supporting the functionalist approach usually shift from an

assessment of the relative importance of any particular position to assessing its relative skill level and the scarcity of that skill in the society.

2. Contrived scarcity can affect the supply of skilled personnel. Once we shift attention from the importance of the job to the scarcity of talent, we must confront the reality that a critically located profession can control the supply of talent. Any profession tries to promote the economic interest of its members by increasing their income. Competitive conditions would attract more members, potentially developing a surplus and driving incomes down. So the profession will typically try to limit its membership through occupational licensing, creating a contrived scarcity. Many occupations require a state license. Frequently, the licensing process is strongly influenced by the profession, whose members claim that they alone are competent to judge the criteria necessary for training and certification. Members justify their control by citing the need to exclude "quacks." But the certification, whether for architects, accountants, lawyers, or physicians, has substantial economic value. Frequently, the license is fundamentally a way to raise wages in a particular profession by limiting competition. Typically, licenses are granted by a panel of practitioners in the field who determine how many are to be granted and to whom. The potential for conflicts of interest is apparent.[40] Restricting competition raises the income of the rent seekers. But if those who benefit can then buy more political influence, which further increases their share of income, it undermines the democratic notion of equality of competition.

The point is that once the first criterion of the functionalists (the importance of a particular kind of job) recedes into the background, the functionalist interpretation of the second criterion (the scarcity of needed skills) becomes doubtful.

3. Functionalists emphasize the positive side of their theory and ignore its negative aspects. The theory does identify the value of talent and shows how rewarding various talents motivates those who possess them to work efficiently. However, it ignores the demotivating effects for those with fewer talents. Those at the higher end of the income stream can be motivated with the aspiration to bonuses, higher wages, life and health insurance benefits, promotions, and pension programs. But workers at the lower end of the income stream cannot be motivated by higher pay, for at least two main reasons. First, low income at this end of the pay scale must provide the differential to fill the higher positions with competent and conscientious workers. Second, the money needed to pay some people more must be taken from those who will be paid less. Thus, in functionalist theory, the workers on garbage trucks who are quick and efficient cannot be rewarded by higher pay or bonuses, although they may be valued employees. As these individuals get older and slower, they must continue to work because of the need to provide for their families, even under the most adverse conditions. Consequently, low income, unemployment, and the threat of unemployment are concentrated among those jobs where the skill levels are the lowest and the supply of people having the skills is the greatest. In sum, the carrot motivating those at the upper-income levels requires the stick to motivate those at the lower levels of income. Functionalist theory rarely mentions this.

4. *For the functionalist system of inequality to operate smoothly, the society as a whole must see it as working to benefit the entire population.* Most of the population must also believe that their tasks and income levels reflect their skills and relative contributions to the society. The stratified system will then rest on a consensus in which even those at the lower end of the income stream understand that their low wages and the threat of unemployment are necessary motivators to keep them working. Not surprisingly, those who wholeheartedly believe in the system tend to be found at the upper end of the income stream. Those at the lower levels cannot both believe in the system *and* have a sense of self-esteem.

Trends in Wealth Inequality

Wealth refers to the monetary value of the assets of a household minus its liabilities (or debt), which is its net worth. Wealth includes the accumulation of unspent past income and is a source from which capital income is realized. An examination of wealth provides a more complete picture of family economic well-being than does an examination of income. Power also flows from wealth. Fortunes can be a source of political and social influence that goes beyond having a high income. There is a correlation, although not a strong one, between wealth and age since older individuals typically have worked more years and have accumulated more assets. There is also a correlation between income and wealth in that we expect those with high incomes to have more wealth.[41] Since about 1980, both poverty and wealth have been increasing together, indicating that the distance between the rich and poor is widening.

A recent study completed by the Federal Reserve Board used data from a triennial Survey of Consumer Finances (SCF) that were compiled from 1989 through 2007. The study found that wealth is highly concentrated, with the top 1 percent of the wealthiest households owning one-third (33.8 percent) of all household net worth in 2007, up from 30.1 percent in 1989 (see Figure 7.1). Note that the share of assets for those in the bottom 94 percent of the population declined while only the top 6 percent (95th to 100th percentile inclusive) saw their share of ownership increase. And the largest gains went to those in the top 1 percent. As Figure 7.1 indicates, according to the Federal Reserve Board's data, the bottom half of families in the country have seen their meager share of 3 percent of the nation's wealth in 1989 decline by 16.6 percent to just 2.5 percent of the nation's wealth in 2007. The next 40 percent (50th to 89th percentile) saw their share drop almost 4 percentage points from 29.9 percent to 26 percent of the total wealth. Those in the top 1 percent have more wealth to divide between them (33.8 percent) than does the bottom 90 percent of the people. The bottom 90 percent of the population has just over 28 percent of the nation's total wealth. Also

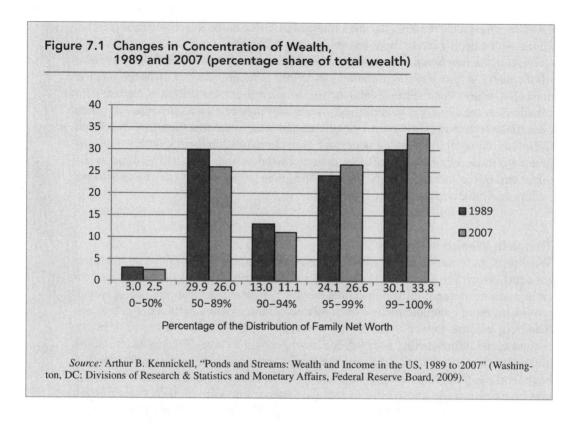

Figure 7.1 Changes in Concentration of Wealth, 1989 and 2007 (percentage share of total wealth)

Percentage of the Distribution of Family Net Worth

Source: Arthur B. Kennickell, "Ponds and Streams: Wealth and Income in the US, 1989 to 2007" (Washington, DC: Divisions of Research & Statistics and Monetary Affairs, Federal Reserve Board, 2009).

surprisingly, those in the top 6 percent have half again as much wealth (60.4 percent) than the bottom 94 percent of the population at 39.6 percent.

The top 1 percent significantly increased their share of holdings in stocks, bonds, and business investments, including equity in commercial real estate holdings. The wealthiest 1 percent owned approximately 52 percent of all stocks in 2007, and over 62 percent of all bonds. Interestingly, the top 1 percent owned 9.4 percent of the total worth of houses while the bottom half of the population owned a total of 12.6 percent. At the same time, the bottom half of the population held just 5.8 percent of the housing debt while the top 1 percent held 13.6 percent, indicating the value of mortgage deductions for wealthier Americans. The bottom half of the population held 53 percent of all installment debt and 43 percent of credit card debt while the top 1 percent held 4 percent of installment debt and 1 percent of credit card debt.[42] For the bottom 90 percent of the households, homes (their largest investment) and automobiles were the most important assets. Mortgages were by far their major liability.

Since the data preceded the current recession that began in 2007, the income of the most affluent is likely to be significantly reduced, which may even shrink the income gap between the rich and the poor. As wealth is concentrated among a relatively small number at the top of the pyramid, they will likely lose more in absolute terms in the short run due to the recession, largely because they own more stocks and bonds than most Americans. Only about 40 percent of households own stock, and most of those own relatively small amounts in retirement accounts. The smaller losses among those at the bottom that lose lower-wage jobs would prove more devastating in terms of their inability to make mortgage payments and provide the necessities for their families. To the point, even after Bill Gates lost a reported $19 billion, he still was worth $40 billion.[43]

The Lorenz Curve and Income and Wealth Inequality

A **Lorenz curve** can be used to measure the degree of inequality in a given population by plotting a cumulative percentage of income against a cumulative percentage of population (see Figure 7.2). If every household had the same income and wealth, the distribution would follow the 45 degree line of complete equality. Any variance from equality will result in the graph falling below the line of equality. The shaded area shows the amount of income inequality. The larger this area, the more unequal is the distribution of income. If there were no government policies to transfer income from the rich to the poor, income inequality would be even greater.

Those OECD countries that have more corporatist institutions, such as Belgium, Sweden, and Denmark, together with a greater tendency to intervene with social welfare programs, have experienced much smaller increases in inequality. The resurgence of income inequality in US society is abrupt enough to be called the "great U-turn" by Bennett Harrison and Barry Bluestone who place the beginning of the increased inequality in the early 1970s.[44]

Child poverty is a particular concern of all governments because children are not responsible for their life situation. There is also an abundance of evidence that strongly indicates that living in relative poverty and experiencing income inequality, especially in childhood, may have a detrimental influence on health and well-being throughout one's lifetime.[45] Childhood poverty has also been associated with higher rates of infant mortality, low birth weight, child mortality due to unintentional injuries, low educational attainment, dropping out of school, being bullied, teenage birth rate, childhood obesity, and mental health problems.[46] It is also generally accepted that deprivation may limit cognitive and social development of children, limiting their life chances.

Having a low socioeconomic position as a child is also positively correlated with increased adult mortality from stomach, liver, and lung cancer; diabetes; coronary

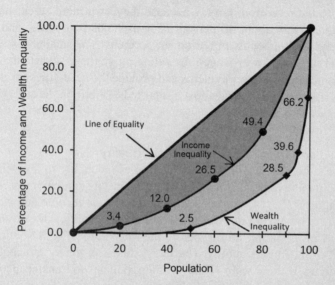

Figure 7.2 Lorenz Curve Showing Cumulative Percentage of Income and Wealth Inequality, 2007

Sources: US Census Bureau, "Historical Income Tables—Households," *Current Population Survey,* Table no. 2, available at www.census.gov/hhes/www/income/histinc/h02A.html (accessed August 16, 2009); Arthur B. Kinneckell, "Ponds and Streams: Wealth and Income in the US, 1989 to 2007" (Washington, DC: Divisions of Research & Statistics and Monetary Affairs, Federal Reserve Board, 2009).

Note: If everyone had the same income and wealth, the distribution would follow the 45 percent degree complete equality line. The darker shaded area shows the amount of income inequality. The lighter shaded area shows the inequality in the distribution of wealth. The larger the shaded area, the greater the inequality.

heart disease; stroke; respiratory diseases; and diseases of the digestive system, among others.

The OECD conducted a study in which children (younger than age eighteen) were considered as sharing the income earned by other household members. To facilitate comparisons across households, disposable household income in cash was adjusted for household size. Household income includes earnings, transfers, and income from capital, and after direct taxes and social security contributions were paid by households. The indicator of poverty used in the study was the *child poverty rate,* or the share of all households with children with an income of less than 50 percent of the median income. The results are displayed in Table 7.5.

The highest child poverty rates are found in the United States, Turkey, Italy, and

Table 7.5 Variation in OECD Child Poverty Rates (percentage), 2005

Country	Child Poverty	Single Parent Working	Two Parents	
			One Worker	Two Workers
Austria	6	11	4	3
Belgium	10	10	11	3
Canada	15	32	22	4
Czech Republic	10	10	9	1
Denmark	3	4	5	0
Finland	4	6	9	1
France	8	12	12	2
Germany	16	26	6	1
Greece	13	18	22	4
Hungary	9	16	6	3
Italy	16	16	24	1
Korea	10	26	10	4
Mexico	22	34	27	11
New Zealand	15	30	21	3
Norway	5	5	4	0
Poland	22	26	28	6
Portugal	17	26	34	5
Slovak Republic	11	24	18	2
Spain	17	32	23	5
Sweden	4	6	14	1
Turkey	25	32	19	20
United Kingdom	10	7	9	1
OECD	12	21	16	1
United States	21	36	27	6

Source: OECD Family Database, "CO8: Child Poverty," available at www.oecd.org/els/social/family/database (accessed August 16, 2009).

the United Kingdom, and the lowest are found in the Nordic countries. Table 7.5 reveals the vulnerability of single-parent households, 36 percent of which are in poverty in the United States.

Single-parent families are an important demographic change contributing to economic inequality. Suppose the combined income of a husband and wife is around the median of about $49,000 per year. Since men's wages tend to be higher than women's, let's assume that he earns $30,000 and she earns $19,000. If they separate or divorce, their combined median income is now separated into two households. If the husband pays child support of $5,500 per year, we would now have two families with incomes of approximately $24,500 each, which will increase economic inequality.

Note that two-parent households in which both are working drastically reduce the likelihood of poverty. Most often, a one-parent household is headed by a mother with one or more children. About half the countries have taken steps to prevent a significant increase in inequality. Actions taken in the United States and the United Kingdom have, as a whole, actually reduced the equalizing effects of taxes and transfers.[47]

What Is the Relationship Between Inequality and Economic Growth?

Simon Kuznets received the Nobel Prize in 1971 for research on economic growth and income distribution. He found that economic growth in poor countries increased the income gap between rich and poor people. However, once a threshold level of maturity was crossed in its transition from a rural to an industrial and urbanized society, economic growth reduced income disparity. Kuznets argued that income distribution follows a U-curve in which economic expansion makes poor people relatively poorer during the initial stage of a country's development. However, the concentration of workers in urban areas encourages both unions and political organizations to press for worker rights, the regulation of business, progressive taxes, and public social expenditures, all of which reduce inequality. Kuznets's data showed, for example, that income inequality in the United States peaked in the 1890s, and did not begin to decline until after World War I.[48]

However, the United States is an anomaly since it is the richest OECD country and has the most inequality. But as Gary Burtless and Christopher Jencks point out: "If we eliminate the United States and look at the sixteen remaining big OECD countries, the richer ones have *less* inequality than the poorer ones, as the Kuznets model predicts."[49]

Some investigators have found evidence of a cycle in which wealthy power elites wage a counteroffensive to reestablish their dominant control.[50] Noted economist John Galbraith suggests that there is a struggle in which the elites, in defense of their social and economic advantage, must now persuade the majority of voters in a democracy that government must accommodate the needs of the haves.[51]

The late Arthur Okun noted that political institutions proclaim the equality of individuals while economic institutions inevitably create inequalities in material welfare.[52] Whenever the market denies a worker a minimum standard of living or when the wealthy use their power and privilege to obtain more of the rights that are supposedly equally distributed, then "dollars transgress on rights," in Okun's expression. According to Okun, the US system of mixed capitalism is a workable compromise in which the market has its place as long as democratic institutions are able to keep it within acceptable boundaries.

Does Economic Inequality Threaten Democratic Equality?

As noted previously, there is considerable research indicating that social mobility has declined in recent decades.[53] Corporate strategies to control labor costs, such as hiring temporary employees, fighting unions, dismantling internal career ladders, reducing benefits, and outsourcing, are successful in restraining consumer prices. Unfortunately, these tactics trap about 35 million workers, over a quarter of the labor force, in low-wage and usually dead-end jobs. Many middle-income employees face fewer opportunities as work is shifted to temporary agencies and jobs are outsourced overseas. The result has been an erosion of one of the most cherished values in the United States: the ability to move up the economic ladder over one's lifetime.

The myth of income mobility has always exceeded the reality. But it is true that there has been considerable intergenerational mobility. One study cited by Aaron Bernstein shows, for example, that only 10 percent of men from families in the bottom 25 percent of the economic ladder make it into the top 25 percent by the end of their working careers.[54] Fewer children of lower-class families are making it to even moderate affluence.

For mobility to increase in relative terms, someone has to move down the pecking order to make room for another to move up. The new reality has a greater impact on those at the bottom who tend to stay poor because of the creation of millions of jobs that pay at around the poverty line wage of $8.70 an hour. Business strategy is putting a lid on the intergenerational progress that has been a part of the American Dream, but public policy also plays a role.

Krugman speculates about what policies someone who controlled government and wanted to entrench the advantages of the haves over the have-nots might engage in.[55] One policy initiative would definitely be to get rid of the estate tax, to allow fortunes to be passed on to the next generation untouched. Other policies would include a reduction in tax rates on corporate profits and on unearned income such as dividends and capital gains. Tax rates would be reduced on people with high incomes, shifting the burden to the payroll tax and other revenue sources that bear most heavily on people with lower incomes. On the spending side, Krugman suggests that one should cut back on health care for the poor and on federal aid for higher education, which would result in rising tuitions and make it more difficult for people with low incomes to acquire the education essential to upward mobility.

The election of Barack Obama was based on a populist promise to reverse these policies. The effort is complicated by the financial crisis that he inherited, but his eventual success or failure will be measured by his ability to change these trends.

How Inequality Harms the Middle Class

Robert Frank has written extensively on how inequality encourages the middle class to engage in excessive spending that ultimately becomes self-defeating.[56] Frank focuses on **positional goods**, which are goods whose value to an individual is largely determined by how much of the good you have in comparison with others. These are typically goods in which differences in quality and size are readily apparent. In modern cultures, people care about the *relative consumption* of some goods more than others. When asked whether they would rather own a 4,000-square-foot home in a community where others lived in 6,000-square-foot homes, or a 3,000-square-foot home in a town where everyone else had 2,000 square feet, most people would choose the 3,000-square-foot home. Frank points out that the desire to avoid "relative deprivation" drives consumption in a range of positional goods in which differences in quality and size are readily visible. The purchase of goods like large homes, expensive cars, and the most up-to-date computers are driven by a desire to keep up with the Joneses. The value of positional goods appears to be relative.

Other goods are more absolute in their valuation. Vacation time is such a good. When asked whether they would rather have four weeks of vacation per year when other people have six weeks, or instead have two weeks when other people have only one, most people opt for four weeks.[57] Vacation time seems to be absolute.

Excessive concern over positional goods may in part reflect Adam Smith's observation regarding greed and self-interest being the driving force of so many human activities. But Frank also points out that comparing the possession of certain positional goods may reflect a more "rational" judgment. For instance, when parents move to a new community, they are concerned about the quality of schools in a district. Since better-funded schools are usually found in more affluent communities, and individual student achievement levels tend to be higher when other students come from a high socioeconomic level, many middle-income parents typically move to the wealthiest community they can afford. Buying the most expensive house that one can afford is not irrational since the school district is part of the purchase.

The problem for positional goods is that, since others are making the same decision you are based on the same rationale, the individual decision is nullified by others making the simultaneous effort to move to a more affluent community to enroll their children in the same superior school. The result is that the neighborhood is made up of families who have collectively bid up the price of housing while those who move out are vying to buy homes in an even more expensive neighborhood. The reverse is also true, in that if everyone is trying to move up the socioeconomic ladder, you may feel that you need to strive to get ahead to avoid being left behind. But once everyone has tried to move up, their position relative to other families striving to improve their circumstances is that no one is better off relative to their neighbors than before the move. Now, they are all poorer since they are burdened with larger mortgages.

Likewise, since the relative weight of cars is a significant factor in injuries and death, a buyer may be persuaded to buy a bigger and heavier family car than if everyone drove small cars. There is also the problem that a small car in a ritzy neighborhood may be a visible sign of relative poverty. The buyer may now be saddled with a higher mortgage and car payment, like most neighbors in the community who are all trying to keep up with the Joneses. What is "smart for one," is "dumb for all."

Frank claims that the value we place on positional goods is based on our contextual situation. Generally, it is the position of households just above or below our economic level that forms the basis for our contextual comparisons. We may not be directly affected by the decisions of the super-rich in their choices of houses or cars, but other rich people are influenced. Their choices influence the merely wealthy and, in this way, comparisons ripple down through the income distribution.

Frank claims that societal competition for the "best" positional goods has exacerbated the increasingly futile efforts to gain status by spending more. During the period of the Great Compression, the incomes of the bottom 80 percent grew faster than the incomes of the top 1 percent, and those in the bottom 20 percent grew the fastest. Since 1979, incomes of the top earners have grown most rapidly. In a society in which the wealthiest set the norms for consumption, people at every step on the income ladder strain to maintain the consumption level of those just above them. As the wealthy grow ever more affluent faster, those further down are pulled along and the middle class is pressured to buy more expensive houses and other positional goods. Between 1980 and 2001, the median size of new homes in the United States increased from 1,600 to 2,100 square feet, even though the family's median real income remained stagnant in the intervening years. According to the data, the end result is that the average American now works more hours, saves less, and has shorter vacations, longer commutes, and greater debt.

At the same time, beleaguered voters are more supportive of candidates proposing to cut taxes and costly public services. Voters are less likely to support goods that are insensitive to context and position, such as more leisure, because they cannot afford them.

Frank's recommended policy solution is to institute a progressive consumption tax. The tax would encourage saving by taxing households at a higher rate as their consumption went up. He argues that a greater reliance on a consumption tax, as is generally applied in Europe, would ratchet down the consumption race by making it progressively more expensive to consume the higher one is on the income ladder. This would reduce the pressure to compete by buying positional goods.

Conclusion

The American Revolution ushered in a new age of democracy. The democratic ideal, based on the fundamental principle of equality, sweeps aside all claims of special power and privilege. Democracy as a form of government is an ideal to be pursued rather than a goal to be fully achieved merely through recognition of the rights to free speech or the right to vote. The framers of the Constitution dedicated themselves to the proposition that all men are created equal, even though some were slaves and others without property were denied the right to vote. The United States became more democratic when it abolished ownership of property as a requirement to be a voting member of society. Democracy, as the Constitution attests, is based on compromise between society's elites and nonelites. The elites, not surprisingly, resist with every means at their disposal any movement toward greater equality that challenges their interests. Control over the political institutions is always central to the struggle since the elites can use the political institutions to influence the perceptions, values, and political preferences of the nonelites by their dominant position as opinion-makers in mass communication. Through money and organization, the elites more than make up for their small numbers while the poor, lacking both resources and organization, are not as powerful a political group as their numbers might suggest.

The Great Depression encouraged a rethinking of economic theory and the role of government. Keynesian theory showed that excessive economic inequality could not only hinder economic growth and stability, but also threaten the very survival of democratic systems.

It is now widely accepted that a major role of government in the United States and the rest of the world is to provide for a distribution of resources that comports with our ideas concerning justice and fairness. President Kennedy lamented the practical problem for public policy when he said, "If a free society cannot help the many who are poor, it cannot save the few who are rich."[58]

Redistribution may be concerned with relative inequality or absolute deprivation. Since about 1980, inequality in both income and wealth distribution has increased markedly. The increase, which has been greater in the United States than in other OECD countries, is due to a variety of factors, including globalization, oligopolistic power, and changes in tax and social welfare legislation designed to redistribute income toward those already at the top.

The functional theory of inequality holds that economic inequality has a beneficial effect in a capitalist society. The theory has several drawbacks, however, that justify government involvement to redress the power imbalance of dominant economic groups. Economic theory makes no claim that capitalism distributes income and wealth in a just fashion.

To the extent that the political apparatus becomes dependent on a financial elite, democracy is undermined. In the extreme case, the old hereditary aristocracy is merely traded for a financial aristocracy. An economic elite with inordinate political power moves the democratic ideal of meaningful political equality further from our grasp.

Some inequality is not only inevitable, but also necessary. However, many scholars think a healthier democracy would result from less inequality than now exists. Policies that would reduce inequality include raising the minimum wage, strengthening antipoverty programs such as the Earned Income Tax Credit, strengthening the social safety net to include health care, and increasing rather than decreasing progressiveness in the tax code.

Questions for Discussion

1. Democracy is based on the principle of equality while capitalism as an economic system inevitably leads to inequality. Are the two systems incompatible and destined to produce frustration, or even cynicism? Will either capitalism or democracy dominate?

2. What are the strengths and weaknesses of the functional theory of inequality? Do the qualifications destroy the value of the theory? Why or why not?

3. Can you explain what public policy decisions were made throughout Europe and the OECD countries that have resulted in greater equality than is present in the United States?

4. If you were to recommend public policies to reduce inequality in the United States, what would you recommend? What are the negative consequences of your proposals?

5. Is there such a thing as an optimal amount of inequality? What criteria would you use to determine it?

Useful Websites

Bureau of Labor Statistics, Consumer Expenditure Survey, http://stats.bls.gov/cex/home.htm.
Census Bureau, www.census.gov/population/socdemo.
US Office of Management and Budget, www.whitehouse.gove/omb/budget.
World Trade Organization (WTO), www.wto.org.

Notes

1. Cited in Irving Dilliard, *Mr. Justice Brandeis, Great American* (St. Louis: Modern View, 1941), p. 42.
2. See Page Smith, *A New Age Now Begins* (New York: McGraw-Hill, 1976), for a detailed discussion of the importance of this idea.
3. Garry Wills develops the thesis that the idea of all men being created equal was more than just rhetoric. See Garry Wills, *Inventing America: Jefferson's Declaration of Independence* (New York: Doubleday, 1978).
4. Thomas Jefferson, *The Papers of Thomas Jefferson*, edited by Julian P. Boyd (Princeton: Princeton University Press, 1953), vol. 8, p. 682.
5. Ibid.
6. The Quote Garden, "Quotations on Poverty," available at www.quotegarden.com/poverty.html (accessed April 14, 2009).
7. Alexis de Tocqueville, *Democracy in America,* cited in William Ebenstein and Alan Ebenstein, *Great Political Thinkers* (New York: Harcourt Brace, 1991), p. 641.
8. John Maynard Keynes, *The General Theory of Employment, Interest, and Money* (London: Macmillan, 1936), p. 372.

9. Thomas Frank, *What's the Matter with Kansas? How Conservatives Won the Heart of America* (New York: Metropolitan Books, 2004).

10. Robert Putnam, "The Strange Disappearance of Civic America," *American Prospect,* Winter 1996, pp. 34–48. See also Sidney Verba, Kay Schlozman, and Henry Brady, *Voice and Equality: Participation in American Politics* (Cambridge: Harvard University Press, 1996).

11. Gary Burtless and Christopher Jencks, "American Inequality and Its Consequences," in Henry J. Aaron, James M. Lindsay, and Pietro S. Nivola, ed., *Agenda for the Nation* (Washington, DC: Brookings Institution, 2003), p. 62.

12. The Pew Research Center for the People and the Press reports that 84 percent of those making $75,000 or more are registered to vote, compared to just 66 percent of those earning $20,000–$29,000, and only 60 percent of those earning less than $20,000. See Pew Research Center for the People and the Press, *Evenly Divided and Increasingly Polarized: 2004 Political Landscape* (Washington, DC: Pew Research Center for the People and the Press, November 5, 2003), pt. 6, "Cynicism, Trust, and Participation," p. 5.

13. The Quote Garden, "Quotations About Politics," available at www.quotegarden.com/politics.html (accessed April 14, 2009).

14. Martin Dooley and Peter Gottschalk, "Earnings Inequality Among Males in the United States: Trends and the Effects of Labor Force Growth," *Journal of Political Economy* 92, no. 1 (1984): 59–89. The gap between high- and low-wage women is increasing as well, just not as rapidly as for men.

15. S. Moller, E. Huber, J. D. Stephens, and D. Bradley, "Determinants of Relative Poverty in Advanced Capitalist Democracies," *American Sociological Review* 68, no. 3 (February 2003): 22–51.

16. World Bank, *2006 World Development Indicators: Japan* (Tokyo: Shufusha, November 2007); see also "Table 2.8 Distribution of Income or Consumption," available at http://dev data.worldbank.org/wdi2006/contents/section2htm (accessed August 16, 2009). In Japan (not a member of the OECD), going from the lowest to the highest quintile reveals the following (percentages): 10.6, 14.2, 17.6, 22.0, and 35.0. On the other hand, Iran, a less-developed state, reported the following shares (percentages): 5.1, 9.4, 14.1, 21.5, and 49.9.

17. G. Ross Stephens, "Public Policy, Income Distribution, and Class Warfare," *Poverty and Public Policy* 1, no. 1 (2009), art. 3, available at www.bepress.com/pso_poverty/vol1/iss1/art3 (accessed August 16, 2009).

18. Ibid.

19. US Department of Health and Human Services, *The 2008 HHS Poverty Guidelines,* available at http://aspe.hhs.gov/poverty/08poverty.shtml (accessed August 16, 2009).

20. Robert H. Frank and Philip J. Cook, *The Winner-Take-All Society: Why the Few at the Top Get So Much More Than the Rest of Us* (New York: Penguin, 1996).

21. See Gary Burtless, "International Trade and the Rise in Earnings Inequality." *Journal of Economic Literature* 33 (June 1995): 800–816.

22. Paul Krugman, *The Conscience of a Liberal* (New York: W. W. Norton, 2007), p. 140.

23. Ibid., p. 141.

24. See, in particular, David Card and Alan B. Krueger, "Minimum Wages and Employment: A Case Study of the Fast-Food Industry in New Jersey and Pennsylvania," *American Economic Review* 84 (September 1994): 772–793.

25. Paul Krugman, *The Conscience of a Liberal,* p. 261.

26. Pope Leo XIII, *Rerum Novarum,* May 15, 1891. The text of *Rerum Novarum* may be found at www.osjspm.org/majordoc_rerum_novarum_official.aspx (accessed April 16, 2009).

27. Living Wage Resource Center, "The National Movement," available at http://livingwage campaign.org (accessed April 16, 2009).

28. Krugman, *The Conscience of a Liberal,* pp. 207–298.

29. Robert Putnam, "Bowling Alone: America's Declining Social Capital," *Journal of Democracy* (January 1995): 65–78.

30. See *The Cook Political Report,* October 8, 2004, "Competitive House Races 2004," available at www.cookpolitical.com/races/report_pdfs/2004_house_competitive_oct8.pdf (accessed August 17, 2009).

31. See, especially, Robert Heilbroner and Lester Thurow, *Economics Explained,* rev. ed. (Englewood Cliffs, NJ: Prentice-Hall, 1994), pp. 216–218. This discussion on the bias in favor of equality relies heavily on this source.

32. The Quote Garden, "Quotations About Humility," www.quotegarden.com/humility .html (accessed August 17, 2009).

33. Economic discrimination occurs when duplicate factors of production receive different payments for equivalent contributions to output. This definition is hard to test because of the difficulty of measuring all the relevant market characteristics. For example, it might not be discrimination if a woman with a high school diploma receives a lower salary than a man with a college degree (although discrimination might help in explaining their educational achievements). It is too simplistic to try to measure discrimination by merely comparing the typical incomes of different groups. The question is not, Do women earn less than men? Rather it is, Do women earn less than men *with like market characteristics* (work experience, age, education, etc.)?

34. We could achieve the same goal without yielding to inequality by financing the investment through taxation and government purchases (public investment) rather than through private investment through savings.

35. The functional theory of inequality is a variation on the **marginal productivity theory** (MPT) of distribution, which holds that the income of any factor will be determined by the contribution that each factor makes to the revenue of the endeavor. The functional theory challenges the assumption of the MPT that a perfect market exists. If it does not, then the earnings of each factor may not reflect their contribution to output. The MPT cannot explain the variation of incomes due to nonmarket factors such as discrimination, imperfect markets, and other factors.

36. Kingsley Davis and Wilbert Moore, *Some Principles of Stratification,* Reprint Series in Social Science (New York: Columbia University Press, 1993).

37. Ibid., p. 37.

38. Milton Friedman, *Capitalism and Freedom* (Chicago: University of Chicago Press, 1962), p. 167.

39. The Century Foundation of New York and Washington, DC, "Class Warfare: Fact and Fiction" (New York: Century Foundation, 2007), available at www.tcf.org/asp (accessed August 16, 2009).

40. See Doug Bandow, "Doctors Operate to Cut Out Competition," *Business and Society Review* 58 (Summer 1986): 4–10. Bandow illustrates that entry into the medical profession is essentially controlled through the use of licensing arrangements, which increase health care costs and decrease the options available to patients.

41. Edward N. Wolff, *Top Heavy: A Study of the Increasing Inequality of Wealth in America* (New York: Twentieth Century Fund, 1995), p. 6.

42. Arthur B. Kennickell, "Ponds and Streams: Wealth and Income in the US, 1989–2007"

(Washington, DC: Divisions of Research and Statistics and Monetary Affairs, Federal Reserve Board, 2009), p. 63.

43. Wealth Inside Story, "Bill Gates New Worth $40 Billion: 2009," available at www .billgatesmicrosoft.com/networth.htm (accessed April 20, 2009).

44. Bennett Harrison and Barry Bluestone, *The Great U-Turn: Corporate Restructuring and the Polarizing of America* (New York: Basic Books, 1988).

45. Eric Emerson, "Relative Child Poverty, Income Inequality, Wealth, and Health," *Journal of the American Medical Association* 301 (January 28, 2009): 425.

46. Ibid.

47. Burtless and Jencks, "American Inequality and Its Consequences," p. 62.

48. Simon Kuznets, "Economic Growth and Income Inequality," *American Economic Review* 45 (March 1955): 1–28.

49. Burtless and Jencks, "American Inequality and Its Consequences," pp. 80–81.

50. Kevin Phillips, *Arrogant Capital: Washington, Wall Street, and the Frustration of American Politics* (Boston: Little, Brown, 1994). Phillips continued the theme in *American Dynasty: Aristocracy, Fortune, and the Politics of Deceit in the House of Bush* (New York: Viking, 2004). William Simon's *A Time for Truth* (New York: Reader's Digest Press, 1978) was frequently cited as a call to arms for US business to recover the privileges it lost after 1929.

51. John Kenneth Galbraith, *The Culture of Contentment* (New York: Houghton Mifflin, 1992).

52. Arthur M. Okun, *Equality and Efficiency: The Big Tradeoff* (Washington, DC: Brookings Institution, 1975).

53. Aaron Bernstein, "Waking Up from the American Dream," *Business Week,* December 1, 2003, available at www.bearcave.com/misl/misl_other/businessweek.html (accessed August 16, 2009).

54. Ibid.

55. Paul Krugman, "The Death of Horatio Alger," *The Nation,* January 5, 2004, p. 16.

56. Robert H. Frank, *Falling Behind: How Rising Inequality Harms the Middle Class* (Berkeley: University of California Press, 2007).

57. Ibid., p. 2.

58. John F. Kennedy, inaugural address, January 21, 1961.

8

Crime: Changing Issues, New Concerns

As the twenty-first century opened, fear of violent crime fell, decidedly reflecting new policies and attitudes about ways to control crime. The policies appear successful, as data since the mid-1990s show that the United States has experienced the longest sustained drop in crime rates since the end of World War II. Nowhere was this more evident than in New York City (NYC). Directed by the city's celebrated police commissioner, William J. Bratton, the NYPD aggressively targeted petty criminal acts like turnstile jumping, shoplifting, and drinking in public. Bratton worked with then NYC mayor Rudy Giuliani to implement the "broken windows theory" proposed by criminologists George L. Kelling and James Q. Wilson.

In their *Atlantic Monthly* article, Kelling and Wilson argued:

> Consider a building with a few broken windows. If the windows are not repaired, the tendency is for vandals to break a few more windows. Eventually, they may even break into the building, and if it's unoccupied, perhaps become squatters or light fires inside. Or consider a sidewalk. Some litter accumulates. Soon, more litter accumulates. Eventually, people even start leaving bags of trash from take-out restaurants there or breaking into cars.[1]

Broken windows proponents urge communities to fix problems caused by social deviance before they drain and overwhelm resources. Often controversial, the policy encourages the police to "stop and frisk" anyone suspected of carrying a gun. Critics complain that the policy targets minority men and violates their civil rights. Nonetheless, Bratton's success in NYC led to his subsequent selection as the Los Angeles police commissioner in 2002. Again, crime dropped. Commissioner Bratton combined this zero-tolerance approach, now copied in major US cities, with technology. Computerized Statistics (Comp Stat), a real-time police intelligence system that is a spreadsheet program introduced in NYC, requires police officers to gather data on criminal incidents daily. Tracking and analysis of the data identifies pockets of criminal activity that are followed up immediately. Police are challenged to come up with new preventative practices in these crime prevalent areas.

As encouraging as this evidence suggests, crime still remains a chronic social problem. New criminal activity, typically drug related, combined with a sustained vigilance for domestic terrorism keeps crime control on the public policy agenda. In this chapter, we explore the crime problem by asking how much crime is out there, what its causes are, and how to create policies that prevent crime, punish criminals, and protect the innocent from becoming victims.

New Fears: Changing Attitudes

Despite growing urban gang action, Midwest methamphetamine labs, shootings on college campuses, and corporate scandal, crime control was not an agenda item during the 2008 presidential campaign. Republican candidates Rudy Giuliani and Mitt Romney attempted to exploit the topic, but to little avail. The Iraq War and the engulfing economic crisis diminished their attempts to make a political statement out of being "hard" or "soft" on crime. Candidates, Republican John McCain and now president Democrat Barack Obama, resorted to party lines. McCain favored the hard-line positions of orthodox conservatives: stricter sentencing, broader use of the death penalty, and prosecuting youths accused of felonies as adults. Obama countered with a conventional populist position complaining about the large number of imprisoned African American men and the disparity in criminal sentencing. Neither candidate supported unequivocal gun control; Obama noted that "I have no intention of taking away folks' guns," though he did support community-based local gun bans.[2]

Americans expressed great fear of violent crime during the years of the Bill Clinton administration and crime control initiatives peaked. In 1994, Congress passed the Violent Crime and Law Enforcement Act. The omnibus crime bill channeled $30 billion into various federal programs. The most prominent of those were the Brady Bill, a ban on assault weapons, and the Department of Justice's **Community-Oriented Policing Services** (COPS) program, designed to improve relations between law enforcement and communities and to put thousands of local police officers on a street beat. Nearly two decades later, US attitudes about crime have changed. With governments floundering under the high cost of incarceration, Americans are beginning to question prevailing practices to combat crime. The United States has almost one-fourth of the world's prisoners, but less than 5 percent of the world's population. As the US economy declines, reevaluating this cost seems urgent. The following brief review of US crime policy puts current practice into perspective.

In the mid-1960s, US concern for "law and order" propelled President Lyndon Johnson to initiate federal legislation to combat crime. Public Law 89-197, the Law

Enforcement and Assistance Act, was passed in 1965. It set up a special office within the Department of Justice to fund local projects to experiment with new methods of crime control and law enforcement. In 1968, the federal government's role in local jurisdiction grew again with the passage of Public Law 90-351, the Omnibus Crime Control and Safe Streets Act. This act lived up to its name by granting funds to state and local jurisdictions for recruitment and training of law enforcement personnel and crime prevention education. Eventually, the grants were phased out, though they left Americans with expectations for a larger federal role in local crime control and prevention. No longer were Americans satisfied with the Federal Bureau of Investigation (FBI) Ten Most Wanted Fugitives list as a way to combat crime and build public awareness. It is interesting to note, however, that today's list includes Osama bin Laden and offers a reward of up to $25 million for information leading to his apprehension.

Federal activity renewed in the 1980s. Over the next ten years, Congress passed three comprehensive crime bills dealing with different aspects of what Americans then perceived as a terrible crime problem. In 1984, Public Law 98-473, the Comprehensive Crime Control Bill, overhauled federal sentencing procedures and created a new grant administrative agency, the Office of Justice Programs. In 1990, Congress passed Public Law 101-647, the Crime Control Act, which authorized $900 million for local law enforcement assistance and included a "victim's bill of rights." Four years later, President Clinton added his solutions to the crime problem with passage of the omnibus bill described earlier. From then until September 11, 2001, Americans thought about and fought crime locally and asked the federal government to help pay the bill.

The September 11 attacks altered perceptions about the federal government's role in combating a different violent crime: terrorism. The attacks invigorated the Department of Justice, whose authority and direction were expanded and refocused. But as circumstances changed, Gallup polls began to show a decline in Americans' tendency to cite violent crime as a top government priority. In January 2007, fewer than 1 percent of respondents to a national Gallup poll noted violent crime as an important problem facing the country, compared to 37 percent in January 1993.[3] More Americans now view the Iraq War, the economy, and health care as far greater priorities.

More recently, the G. W. Bush administration denounced the popular COPS program mentioned earlier and the related Edward Byrne Memorial Justice Assistance Grant program. These programs, designed to provide federal assistance and boost manpower to fight crime at the local level, were rolled into Bush's Justice Assistance Grant (JAG) program under the Department of Justice. Members of the Bush administration argued that crime fighting was "overfederalized" so they restricted federal funding to just those local programs designed to fight terrorism. After his election, President Obama reversed this and announced $2 billion in Recovery Act 2009 funding allocations to the JAG program. The formula for allocating JAGs will combine local population figures with violent crimes figures, adjusted for a minimum allocation, to assure that all states receive some share of federal funding.

Since 1929, the FBI has published an annual report on crime titled the *Uniform Crime Report* (*UCR*). This statistical summary, compiled from data supplied by state and local agencies, presents a detailed breakdown of criminal activity in the United States. For years, the most commonly cited *UCR* statistic was the **crime index**, a highly aggregated measure of the volume and rate of reported crime, but in June 2004 the FBI decided to stop publishing the crime index because it was inaccurate. Instead, the agency broke the crime statistics into two measures: total violent crime and total property crime. The FBI yearly snapshots reveal that violent crime and property crime actually have declined in the United States.

How Much Crime?

The 2007 *UCR* (see www.fbi.gov/ucr) and a preliminary 2008 report proudly announced that the level of US crime, particularly violent crime, is down overall. Though over 1.4 million violent crimes occurred in 2007, the *UCR* reported that violent crime is down about 1 percent from 2006 and 8 percent from 1998.[4] Most violent crime, which includes murder, forcible rape, robbery, and aggravated assault, occurs during the heat of July and August. Aggravated assault is the most common category of violent crime (61 percent of violent crime); murder is the least often committed (10 percent of violent crime). In 2007, 44 percent of those arrested for violent crimes were under twenty-five years of age; most were men (82 percent) and, by race, more were white (69 percent) than black (28 percent). Firearms were used in 21 percent of violent crimes reported, down 3 percent from 2006. Knives were used in 15 percent of cases. According to the *UCR,* crime is highest in metropolitan areas and lowest in rural counties; it is highest in the southern United States, the nation's most populous region, and lowest in the Midwest.

Murder nationwide reached a high in 1991, with 24,703 incidents reported.[5] By 2007, the number of criminal homicides was down nearly 8 percent to 16,929. Most murder victims, like offenders, were male (78 percent) adults (88 percent). Altogether, the murder rate for US cities was 6.8 per 100,000 residents; the murder rate increased for larger cities (over 250,000 residents) by nearly double (11.9 percent).[6] Seven out of ten murders involved the use of firearms. Most murder victims knew or were related to their assailants; most were family affairs. Nearly one-third of the murders resulted from arguments; typically, over money. Juvenile gangs, brawls involving alcohol or drugs, and sniper activity counted for about 20 percent of homicides.[7]

Nearly one-third (32 percent) of violent crimes were robberies, with most occurring during the December holidays. Robberies differ from burglaries because they involve the use of force. The 2007 *UCR* found that over $588 million was lost to robberies, and the average monetary value of property taken was about $1,321. According to *UCR* data, robberies declined slightly (1.2 percent) from 2006, but five-year robbery trends increased 7.5 percent; most were residential crimes. Research by David T. Lykken reports that those at highest risk of violent crime are the young, between fifteen and twenty-four years old. Youths are ten to fifteen times more likely than those over age sixty-five to be assaulted, robbed, or murdered.[8]

Loss from nonviolent, property crime, which includes larceny theft, burglary, and motor vehicle theft, equaled $17 million in 2007, a decline of 10 percent since 1998.[9] Over $7 billion was estimated to have been lost to motor vehicle theft; the FBI estimates 363 motor vehicle thefts per 100,000 people.[10] Table 8.1 displays a regional breakdown of the US crime categories.

As part of these *UCR* summary statistics, the FBI also reports **clearance rates**. These are offenses cleared by arrest or "other exceptional means."[11] The 2007 clearance rate for violent crimes was not quite half (44.5 percent), though 61 percent of murders were cleared. Typically, property crime has a lower clearance rate. In 1994, the FBI began collecting hate crime statistics. Hate crimes are not distinct crimes, but are motivated by prejudice based on race, religion, ethnicity, sexual orientation, or disabilities both mental and physical, and are committed against persons, property, and society. The *UCR* reported in 2007 that racial bias represented the largest proportion of hate-motivated offenses. Most hate crimes take the form of intimidation against persons and vandalism against property.

While the overall *UCR* data present an encouraging summary of crime in the United States, the puzzle for analysts is finding the reason for the decline. International comparisons offer some clarification and perspective. Cross-national comparisons of crime rates indicate that "lethally violent crime is much higher in the United States than in other nations . . . in contrast, the United States has lower rates of serious property crime than other similar nations."[12]

Though tempting to conclude that the drop in overall crime statistics indicates progress in the "war on crime," data alone fail to give the full picture. Much data underreport the extent of particular crimes. For example, the *UCR* reports that rape has dropped to its lowest level since 1989. Yet two studies conducted in the 1990s found a significantly higher incidence of rape victimization than *UCR* data reflect.[13] Looking at existing data, criminologist Elliott Currie commented: "While guarded optimism may be in order, complacency is not. And there is no guarantee that the respite that we are now enjoying will last."[14]

Crime: A Definition

In their book *Crime and Human Nature,* Harvard University scholars James Wilson and Richard Herrnstein explore the meaning of **crime**.[15] Wilson and Herrnstein tell us that crime is not easily measured, categorized, or defined. For example, categories like property crime, crime against persons, white collar crime, victimless crime, or public corruption fall short because they are not mutually exclusive. Crimes have different social costs. Most people fear property loss from street crime, yet the financial loss

Table 8.1 US Offense and Population Percentage Distribution by Region

Region	Population	Violent Crime[a]	Murder	Forcible Rape	Robbery	Aggravated Assault	Property Crime[b]	Burglary	Larceny Theft	Motor Vehicle Theft
NE	18.1	14.5	13.4	12.0	16.9	13.5	12.2	10.5	13.2	9.8
MW	22.0	19.4	19.1	25.3	19.0	19.0	21.3	20.6	22.1	18.2
S	36.6	43.1	45.8	38.8	40.4	44.9	42.7	46.7	42.4	36.4
W	23.2	23.1	21.8	24.0	23.7	22.7	23.8	22.2	22.4	35.7

Source: Federal Bureau of Investigation, *Uniform Crime Report 2007* (Washington, DC: US Government Printing Office, 2007).

Notes: a. Violent crimes are offenses of murder, forcible rape, robbery, and aggravated assault.

b. Property crimes are offenses of burglary, larceny theft, and motor vehicle theft. Data are not included for the property crime of arson.

NE = Connecticut, Maine, Massachusetts, New Hampshire, New Jersey, New York, Pennsylvania, Rhode Island, Vermont.

MW = Illinois, Indiana, Iowa, Kansas, Michigan, Minnesota, Missouri, Nebraska, North Dakota, Ohio, South Dakota, Wisconsin.

S = Alabama, Arkansas, Delaware, District of Columbia, Florida, Georgia, Kentucky, Louisiana, Maryland, North Carolina, Oklahoma, South Carolina, Tennessee, Texas, Virginia, West Virginia.

W = Arizona, Alaska, California, Colorado, Hawaii, Idaho, Montana, New Mexico, Oregon, Utah, Washington, Wyoming.

Due to rounding, column percentages may not sum to 100.

Case Study: How Accurate Are the Numbers?

Conventional wisdom says that no data are better than bad data. How accurate are crime statistics? The most commonly reported numbers are those collected by the FBI in its *Uniform Crime Report* (*UCR*) and the Census Bureau in its *National Crime Victimization Survey* (*NCV*). Both data collections are compiled annually. Both report on similar crimes, though the *NCV* surveys do not include arson and homicide. Both collections also suffer from errors of measurement and bias, and both underreport crime.

The *UCR* data are based on police reports. Underreporting is largely due to citizen unwillingness to call the police. Not surprisingly, much petty theft (like someone stealing your wallet) goes unreported. Most people wager the police cannot do much about the loss, so why bother? A second source of inaccuracy comes from the reporting methods used. Some police departments do a better job reporting crime than others. Perhaps, their collection techniques are better. Sometimes it is in a department's best interest to report crime; it reflects a job well done. It might even help the department's budget allocation. On the other hand, sometimes a police department would rather not report as much crime. It raises questions about the competence of the police force. If the FBI discovers intentional underreporting, it refuses to publish the statistics of the offending agency until the discrepancies are corrected. Further, when the *UCR* data are collected, the police report all crimes committed in a given locality. Consequently, big cities, like New York, which experience lots of commuters and visitors, report high crime rates. Police reports also emphasize certain types of crimes and not others. Selling drugs, for example, is not included. And if several crimes are committed by a criminal at once, only the most serious is counted.

Victimization studies are equally flawed. The Census Bureau randomly selects households for inclusion in the study and it too underreports crime, but for different reasons. *NCV* studies count only personal and household crimes, not crimes against business. Consequently, the studies are not as sensitive to crime rates overall, nor are the rates they report as volatile as *UCR* statistics. On the other hand, *NCV* studies report up to three times the number of crime victims that police reports do. It makes sense that, if five people are robbed at gunpoint, the victim study presents a different tally than the police report.

Other factors also skew the data collected in each report. Victims are likely to report some kinds of crime to the police, and others, like rape (possibly by a relative), to interviewers. Over time, people also forget or grow confused about when a crime occurred. Human error tends to creep into *NCV* data since these studies collect information longer after a crime than do most police reports. Further, *NCV* interviews include data from the previous year. All of this makes data from the two sources difficult to compare. Comparisons between the two sources are difficult as *UCR* data report perpetrators while NCV data report victims.

So are no data better than bad data? It depends. Certainly, if crime statistics are used for political convenience, the public is not well served. But if policymakers use the data with an awareness of their inaccuracies and a sense of appropriateness to the crime issue, then they serve a valuable purpose. Slight yearly data shifts probably indicate little while large differences

continued

Case Study   continued

---

probably tell something. As noted by James Wilson, statistical summaries do not specify what proportion of a given population consists of criminals or the number of crimes committed per year by the average criminal. These indicators would give a more valid measure of crime in the United States. Wilson warns that the best statements about crime are those supported by as many different measures as possible.

Sources: James Q. Wilson, ed., *Crime and Public Policy* (San Francisco: ICS Press, 1983); US Department of Justice, *Criminal Victimization in the United States 1992* (Rockville, MD: Bureau of Justice Statistics, March 1994), p. 9.

---

from white collar crime is far greater. Obviously, some crimes are more abhorrent and more destructive to the social fabric than others.

Wilson and Herrnstein use a legalistic definition of crime: "any act committed in violation of the law that prohibits it and authorizes punishment for its commission."[16] A serious crime is aggressive, violent behavior categorized as murder, rape, assault, and theft. The legalistic definition of crime is the least ambiguous, though not all scholars are happy with it. Critics complain that criminal law reflects the values of society's most powerful. What is a crime and who is criminal can vary over time and differ between societies. Clive Coleman and Clive Norris illustrate this point by recounting the US experience with Prohibition during the 1920s, noting that it "represented a political victory for the moral code of one segment of American society at the expense of another." They emphasize that "the more complex society [is], the more likely that norms [will] come into conflict."[17] Criminal law and crime are social constructions and thus problematic.

One way to gain an understanding about crime is to look at the **causes of criminal behavior**. This approach focuses attention on the criminal and his or her relationship with the rest of society. A second approach explores the processes and characteristics of the **criminal justice system**, established to deal with crime. Here, one asks how effectively the system protects the innocent, punishes offenders, and reduces the level of crime.

Causes of Crime: What Do We Know?

Considering the amount of crime reported, many observers maintain very little is known about causes of criminal behavior. Wilson and Herrnstein argue overall that "crime is as broad a category as disease, and perhaps as useless. To explain why one person has ever committed a crime and another has not may be as pointless as explaining why one person has ever gotten sick and another has not."[18] But in fact, scholars who study the determinants of criminal behavior know quite a bit about its etiology or origin. This scholarly endeavor forms the field of **criminology**. Social scientists have learned more about why some people commit crimes than they have about how to lower the overall crime rate.

Criminologists have proposed many scientific, empirically testable theories of criminal behavior, often based on multidisciplinary research. Recently, research has drawn on fields like economics and biology. The field has a long history. Since the eighteenth-century Enlightenment period, scholars have focused attention on the nature of crime, criminal behavior, and the criminal justice system. As recounted by Coleman and Norris, early researchers

> opposed the unpredictable, discriminatory, inhumane and ineffective criminal justice systems that were to be found in their day, systems that often left much to the discretion of judges (including the frequent use of "mercy" and "pardons"), employing barbaric, cruel methods of punishment (and torture for extracting confessions) and seemed to any intelligent observer to be very ineffective in preventing crime.[19]

In the eighteenth century, Catherine the Great of Russia invited a young Italian named Cesare Beccaria to help reform Russia's criminal laws. His treatise *On Crimes and Punishment* advocated criminal laws "severe enough to offset the advantage gained by the crime."[20] Facilitated by publication of national crime statistics, first in France during the early 1900s, moral statisticians looked for patterns in criminal behavior and attempted to design models comparing their work to that of the natural sciences. Later in the nineteenth century, Italian Cesare Lombroso claimed to have discovered actual physical differences in the anatomical makeup of criminals. Though thoroughly discredited, Lombroso's work helped to further establish the academic and scientific nature of criminology.[21]

George Vold and Thomas Bernard, in their book *Theoretical Criminology*, designate three essentially different ways of thinking about crime: "Two frames of reference focus on the behavior of criminals. The first argues that behavior is freely chosen, while the second argues that it is caused by forces beyond the control of the individual. The third frame of reference views crime primarily as a function of the way criminal law is written and enforced."[22]

Given these different points of departure, it is no wonder there is a great deal of scholarly disagreement among criminologists over the causes of crime. Those who see a **criminal behavior as freely chosen** describe people as rational. A criminal act is considered like any other act—as a rational purposeful choice whose aim is to promote one's best self-interest, much as a choice is described by public choice theory.[23] This "classical" deterrence view is highly legalistic and emphasizes ways society can maximize the cost and minimize the benefits of criminal behavior. More recent analysis of crime by economists like Gary Becker has integrated key economic concepts into research on criminal behavior. Economic ideas like **expected utility** represent an offender's expected reward compared to the likelihood of punishment.

The second perspective, **criminal behavior as caused**, is deterministic. It dominated the early field of criminology proposing that people behave as they have been determined to behave, biologically. Contemporary positivists argue that social scientists will never be able to say what causes a person to commit a crime, but research can determine what factors predispose or increase the risk of a life of crime. These theories explore the relationship between socioeconomic settings and emotional, psychological, and physical factors. Some of these criminologists even question the efficacy of punishment in dealing with criminal behavior. They emphasize the value of psychological therapy and counseling.

The last perspective, the **behavior of criminal law**, emerged in the 1960s when, as Vold and Bernard explain: "some criminologists [began] to address a very different question: why some individuals and behaviors are officially defined as criminal and others not."[24] These scholars ask why, given a place and time, certain people and behaviors are defined as criminal. Those who focus on crime as an opportunity emphasize crime incidents rather than offenders, along with victims' lifestyles, which might expose them to offenders.

Thus, the field of criminology offers compelling theoretical arguments and divergent explanations. Some criminologists argue that crime relates to intelligence, hyperactivity, or chromosomal characteristics. Others assert that poverty and economic inequality lead people to criminal behavior. A traditional view, associated with sociologist Emile Durkheim (1858–1917), argued that, in the process of social change and modernization, societies became highly differentiated. A consequence of differentiation was **anomie**, or a breakdown in social norms and rules. Crime is one normal consequence of anomic society. It is a price society pays for progress. Many criminologists and sociologists in the tradition of Durkheim look to society as a whole to explain criminal behavior.

More recent explanations, like **strain theory**, offer the intuitive appeal of a causal relationship between social inequality, lack of economic opportunity, and crime.[25] Some see crime as learned behavior. Others offer a Marxist or feminist interpretation. All theories of criminal behavior have been extensively criticized. They are afflicted with a large number of theoretical and empirical problems, and many offer limited guidance to the policymaking community.

In the introductory chapter to their book on crime, Wilson and Herrnstein summarize the facts we do know:

> Predatory street crimes are most commonly committed by young males. Violent crimes are more common in big cities than in small ones. High rates of criminality tend to run in families. The persons who frequently commit the most serious crimes typically

begin their criminal careers at a quite young age. Persons who turn out to be criminals usually do not do very well in school. Young men who drive recklessly and have many accidents tend to be similar to those who commit crimes. Programs designed to rehabilitate high rate offenders have not been shown to have much success, and those programs that do manage to reduce criminality among certain kinds of offenders often increase it among others.[26]

For the policymaker, individual indicators of crime like age, gender, personality, or intelligence do not translate easily into practical policy. Even policies emphasizing the deterrence of **criminogenic factors**, like drugs, alcohol, and guns, are hotly debated (see later sections of this chapter).[27] As a result, policy attention shifts to an area more easily identified and controlled, the criminal justice system. Here, consideration is given to the relative costs of legal protection and punishment and the efficient delivery of criminal justice services.

Characteristics of the Criminal Justice System

There is no single criminal justice system. What exists is a jumble of legal avenues that, when mapped out, look more like a poorly designed interstate road system than a carefully constructed legal structure. The US criminal justice system is **decentralized**. It consists of local, state, and federal jurisdictions. Again, this reflects the US historical experience; when drafting the Constitution, the Founding Fathers left most criminal law to the states. They wanted criminal law to reflect community standards and enforcement to be localized. The consequence is variability in laws and consequences throughout the fifty US states, resulting in challenges to equity and justice.

The Courts

Generally, state and local criminal jurisdictions follow similar organizational patterns, although they often use different names to describe similar functions. The design and size of jurisdictions vary. To fully explain all the systems of each jurisdiction would require a separate look. Nevertheless, they all share basic similarities in organization and process. Generally, at the bottom of each state system are courts of **limited jurisdiction** (or "special" jurisdiction). They hear civil cases and criminal misdemeanors.[28] The next level of courts has **general jurisdiction**. Here, the state prosecutes individuals accused of serious felonies and certain types of important civil cases. The **appeals courts** review and rule on the legality of decisions made by the lower courts. State **supreme courts** are the top appellate courts.

Organizationally, the federal court system is divided into ninety-seven district courts and ten courts of appeal. Again, cases originate in federal district court and move upward in the appeals process to the US Supreme Court. The Supreme Court hears only those cases with far-reaching policy implications.

Case Study: Youth Gangs

Two weeks before the Christmas holiday in 2004, residents of Charles County, Maryland, woke to a $10 million fire burning homes in a new subdivision, named Hunters Brooke. The fire destroyed ten large houses and damaged sixteen others. Police investigators quickly seized on arson as the motive and found their culprits, members of a local youth gang named the Unseen Cavaliers. Members of the gang held grudges against the builder and, during meetings in the parking lot of a fast food restaurant, purportedly planned to set the blaze.[a]

Youth gangs are on the rise in the United States, according to the Justice Department's National Youth Gang Center. The center reported over 24,000 youth gangs nationwide, with 760,000 gang members.[b] The extremely violent gang, MS-13 or La Mara Salvatrucha, operates in forty-two states with some 10,000 members. MS-13 originated among Salvadoran immigrants and includes drug distribution, robbery, carjacking, and vandalism among its activities. Different from the "teddy boys and the mods" of the 1960s, with their curious combination of pop culture and high art, youth gangs today bear a stronger resemblance to gangs in the 1920s. Historically, gangs originated in the United States after the Revolutionary War. By the 1920s, they consisted mainly of Irish, Jewish, and Italian groups. From the 1960s to 1990s, the demographics changed, with African American and Hispanic gangs gaining prominence. Gangs today are more dangerous because of access to lethal weapons. The old tactics of hit-and-run have given way to frightening "drive-by shootings." Gang members today are both older and younger (average age of seventeen years), more likely to have prison records, and more likely to use drugs and alcohol. Significantly, a rise in female gangs has accompanied the trend in gang activity, with many female gang members acting as auxiliaries to male gangs.

Categorizing gangs is troubling to sociologists who represent them by their degree of organization, from the loosely formed teenage groups "hanging out" in shopping malls, to street gangs, to semistructured criminal organizations that often feed into organized crime groups. Gangs are not isolated to the inner city, though Los Angeles's Hispanic gangs and Chicago's African American gangs record the highest memberships. Recent data indicate that gang formation has cascaded to the suburbs and rural areas, where members participate frequently in property crime that is often marked by gang graffiti. The most established mega-gangs and specialty gangs deal drugs and fight over their geographic control of territory.

While African Americans, Hispanics, and Asians disproportionately join gangs, studies show that they are not predisposed to rebellious or illegal activity. Rather, groups like Chicago's Black Gangster Disciples Nation are often carriers of community traditions and offer their members an identity they crave. Studies point to the roots of gang formation in low neighborhood integration, faulty parental supervision, lack of stable work opportunity, poverty, and, for many, the excitement and prestige of gang membership. Contemporary sociologists point to gangs as symptomatic of problems in the wider social context. The Department of Justice funds its National Youth Gang Center to demonstrate its commitment to a community-wide approach to gang prevention and suppression. In September 2007, Senators Diane Feinstein (D-CA) and Orrin Hatch (R-UT) cosponsored the Gang Abatement and Prevention Act to appropriate $1 billion over a five-year period for antigang enforcement. The FBI's Central

continued

Case Study continued

American Fingerprint Exploitation (CAFÉ) initiative denies entry to gang members based on fingerprints collected in Central America and Mexico. Gangs today cross borders and often lack national leadership. Members use tattoos to signify their affiliation and status.

Notes: a. Rick Lyman and Gary Gately, "Behind the Maryland Fires: A County in Transition," *New York Times,* January 7, 2005, p. A11.
   b. National Youth Gang Center, "National Youth Gang Survey Analysis," 2006, available at www.iir.com /nygc/nygsa.

Many people take part in the administration of justice. Key participants include police officers, prosecutors, public defenders, judges, wardens, psychiatrists, and parole officers. Often, they have competing goals. Some seek to protect citizens' rights under the law; others see that punishment is effectively carried out. Ultimately, there is a struggle between speed and due process of law, between protection and punishment.

Our criminal justice system seeks to investigate and arrest, prosecute, determine guilt or innocence, and punish and/or rehabilitate. The process from arrest to sentencing has changed little from colonial times. A crime is investigated and an arrest is made by the police. The prosecutor seeks an indictment and an arraignment follows. A trial consists of the admission of evidence and questioning of witnesses until a verdict is reached. If guilt is determined, a judge or jury establishes the appropriate sentencing. From there, the penal system takes over.

Understand too that most criminal cases never follow this process; rather, a **plea bargain** is forged. Here, a defendant pleads guilty to a certain charge in exchange for the court dropping more serious charges or in exchange for the promise of a lighter sentence. In the United States, if a defendant pleads guilty, there is no trial. By reducing court loads and avoiding long and costly trials, plea bargaining expedites the judicial process. Critics argue that the plea bargain works against those who insist on the constitutional right to trial by jury. But trials too can work against defendants. As noted by one author: "If defendants exercise this right, they risk a harsher sentence."[29]

The Role of the Police

Because the police are the most visible part of the criminal justice system, much attention focuses on their effectiveness. One author writes that the police represent "that 'thin blue line' between order and anarchy."[30] The United States has no national police force, and state and local police agencies operate autonomously. Local autonomy has its roots in historical opposition to any type of standing army in the United States. Today, the FBI catalogs 14,676 police agencies, or 3.6 law enforcement officers per 1,000 inhabitants.

The chief function of the police is keeping the peace, not enforcing the law. Police officers share a subculture not unlike the military subculture. Police departments are organized to follow a chain of command, and regulations and discipline govern police behavior. As peacekeepers, the police use patrolling techniques to protect public safety and enforce the law.

Many argue that the police have been restricted in their ability to exercise their **investigative and arrest powers**. These powers, to stop, question, detain, use force, and search, have been constrained by Supreme Court decisions. Much public policy debate about the criminal justice system centers on legal decisions that critics claim have tied the hands of law enforcement agencies.

During the tenure of Supreme Court Justice Earl Warren (1953–1969), a revolution in **procedural rights** occurred. Because the rights of the accused are the same as the rights of the innocent, constitutional protections against unjustified searches, admission of hearsay as evidence, and inadequate legal defense apply. Since the 1960s, the rights of the accused have been expanded. This expansion may have been stopped by the appointment of more conservative justices to the Supreme Court during the Reagan-Bush years.

The exclusionary rule. Once such expansion involved the **exclusionary rule**, which prohibits illegally obtained evidence from being introduced in a court of law. Despite the arguments by critics that the rule protects only the guilty, the Supreme Court fully extended the principle to the state justice systems in *Mapp v. Ohio* (1961).[31] *Mapp* produced immediate reactions from enraged police departments throughout the country, which felt it seriously diminished their legal investigative powers. Conservatives feared that criminals would now be able to walk away due to mere legal technicalities.

The exclusionary rule was eventually set back by the **good faith exception**, enunciated in *US v. Leon* (1984). Here, the Supreme Court ruled that, even if a search was determined to have been technically illegal, if the police acted in good faith the evidence obtained could be introduced in court. The USA Patriot Act signed into law in October 2001 changed Fourth Amendment protections considerably. Federal law enforcement now can track Internet communications to intercept the content of electronic communications. "Sneak and peak" warrants allow searches of a person's home or a business to seize property without disclosure for months. These enlarged practices conducted to combat terrorism are done in the name of national security.

Custodial interrogation. The Supreme Court extended the right to counsel at state expense to all felony cases with *Gideon v. Wainwright* (1963). Shortly afterward, the

Court moved even further to protect defendants by addressing police conduct during arrest and interrogation in *Escobedo v. Illinois* (1964), when it decided suspects have the right to counsel back to the point of arrest. And two years later, in *Miranda v. Arizona* (1966), it required police to inform every suspect of their constitutional rights upon arrest. These cases and others represented the belief that convictions often resulted from confessions obtained through inappropriate interrogations by the police; in other words, from defendants who were unaware of their constitutional rights in regard to criminal matters. Since most convictions result from confessions, once again bitter reactions followed. NYC's police commissioner argued that "if suspects are told of their rights they will not confess."[32]

Many argue that the *Miranda* decision has reduced the effectiveness of confessions as a crime-fighting tool and symbolizes an obsessive concern for the rights of the accused. However, the original strength of the *Miranda* rule has been diluted through decisions reached in cases beginning with the 1970 Burger Court.[33] Chief Justice Warren Burger, a Nixon appointee, espoused a "law and order" position. More recently, concern with custodial rights has centered on the use of plea bargaining, as discussed earlier. Today, the number of defendants deciding to "cop a plea" far exceeds those opting for jury trials. Some critics maintain that the practice subverts justice by violating constitutional protection against self-incrimination and the guarantee of a fair jury trial. But its widespread use also lessens pressure on the criminal justice system.

Often manipulated, blamed, or even hated, police departments are caught in the crossfire of criminal justice policy debates. The police find it difficult to balance the demands for more aggressive anticrime measures, which require more expenditures and greater intrusiveness on people's lives, with demands that they adhere to constitutional protections that ensure proper investigative and arrest procedures. Increasingly, the police are forced to use discretion, or **selective enforcement of the law**, in doing their job.

Police Theory

In September 1994, President Clinton signed a $30 million crime bill into law. Critics of the law denounced its lack of coherence and proposed benefits while its proponents argued that the law represented a fundamental change in the role the federal government played in fighting crime. The centerpiece of the law was the COPS program mentioned earlier, which proposed hiring 100,000 new police officers. Community-oriented policing represents a change in police strategy. The first large, organized police force was set up in London in 1830; New York and other large cities followed.[34] Before that, policing was a voluntary, citizen-based effort. To these early police departments, a policy of high visibility and low response time was very effective. According to criminologist Lawrence Sherman: "There is substantial evidence that serious violent crime and public disorder declined in response to the 'invention' of visible police patrol."[35]

Over the past twenty-five years, research has shown that police visibility really does not matter anymore. An influential experiment was done by the Kansas City, Missouri, police department that compared crime rates in three groups of patrol beats. One group was given two to three times as much coverage as the others, another group no coverage, and a third group normal police coverage. Results showed no difference in crime across the groups.[36] Researchers speculate that changes in population density resulting from the growth of suburbs in the 1950s and 1960s have reduced the effectiveness and practicality of police visibility and quick response time. As Carl Klockers explains: "It makes about as much sense to have police patrol routinely in cars to fight crime as it does to have firemen patrol routinely in fire trucks to fight fire."[37]

Yet police visibility does make a difference if it is concentrated and directed at "hot spots"—areas and times of high crime. For example, police crackdowns—sudden and massive increases in police presence or enforcement activity—are very effective, especially if they are short in duration and unpredictable.[38]

Today, the police are adopting strategies that emphasize "security guard" and "public health" activity. Community-based policing treats a neighborhood the same way a security guard treats a client's property, by looking for risk factors for crime. Security guards, however, protect private property while the police protect public space. The police cannot use trespassing laws to protect public space. They rely on programs that address risk factors such as traffic stops to control handguns, repeat offender programs to track parolees, and curfews and truancy regulations to monitor juveniles. Using public health strategies, police departments consider long-term trends and "situational factors" that contribute to crime. They use this analysis, for example, to make recommendations to communities for siting automatic teller machines or determining business closing hours. Both of these approaches represent a new philosophy of policing, one that emphasizes prevention, problem solving, and peacekeeping alongside traditional law enforcement. Gradually, police strategy is moving toward a balance between the taxpayer demand for "fair share" approaches to policing, and focused, risk-reduction strategies.

Prisons: Perspectives on Punishment and Correction

By the 1960s, not only had the orientation of the courts changed, but so had public attitudes toward crime. The decade was in many ways a turning point in criminal justice policy. Citizens had come to fear crime as never before, in part due to increasing street crime, drug use, and civil rights protests. Consequently, President Johnson declared a war on crime, and established a presidential commission to study the psychology and sociology of crime in the United States, and appropriate policy responses to it. Commission recommendations led to passage of the Omnibus Crime Control and Safe Streets Act in 1968. This act was viewed by some as a way to offset criticism that the country had gone soft on crime.

The emphasis on law and order continued through the 1970s. President Richard Nixon supported increased funding to local governments via the Law Enforcement Assistance Administration for researching and conducting programs directed at crime abatement.[39] By the 1980s, both Presidents Ronald Reagan and G. H. W. Bush fought hard for strict law enforcement policies along with protection for victim rights and stricter drug laws. And the emphasis has not been just at the federal level. A landmark study reported in the 1990s that: "Criminal justice is the fastest growing area of state and local spending, expenditures grew 232% between 1970 and 1990. In comparison, public expenditures on hospitals and health care increased 71%; public welfare, 79%; and education, 32%."[40] Associate Justice Anthony M. Kennedy reported in a 2003 speech to the American Bar Association that "the cost of housing, feeding and caring for the inmate population in the United States is over 40 billion dollars per year."[41] In 1984, Congress created the US Sentencing Commission (USSC) to launch federal sentencing guidelines. The USSC's purpose was to make sentences more uniform by providing judges a "grid with the offense for which the defendant has been convicted on one axis and the offender's history and other details on the other. The grid gives the judges a range of possible sentences and the system instructs them [judges] to go above that range if they make certain factual findings."[42]

In January 2005, the US Supreme Court decided that federal sentencing guidelines were unconstitutional because they violated a defendant's Sixth Amendment right to trial by jury. Essentially, sentencing guidelines empowered judges to increase sentences beyond those set by a jury. The Supreme Court justices opposing the decision argued that Congress's original intent when passing the Sentencing Reform Act in 1984 was to ensure that similar sentences were given to those committing similar crimes. Now, they argued, allowing juries to set the sentences shifted "too much power to prosecutors."[43] Ironically, many judges also have complained about the USSC guidelines, particularly when they want to show more leniency. As a result of the Supreme Court decision, the USSC will continue to exist, but its guidelines will be advisory. Members of Congress reacted by promising to respond with hearings as they continue to compete with the judiciary for control over the criminal punishment process.

In 1994, President Clinton launched passage of a crime bill that represented a shift in philosophy for his administration. Frustrating his Republican counterparts, Clinton took up the crime issue and campaigned on it as a central pillar of his presidency. Among the "new Clinton" proposals were a "one strike, you're out" rule for violent criminals and drug offenders living in public housing, proposals for school uniforms and curfews, statements inveighing against the entertainment industry's showcasing of drugs and violence, and allocation of nearly $8.7 billion spread over six years to help states build more prisons.[44] Policies like one strike, you're out have had costly consequences. As illustrated in Table 8.2, incarceration rates in the United States are many times higher than those in other countries in the world. According to data collected in 2003 from the International Centre for Prison Studies (www.pris-

Table 8.2 International Comparison of Prison Populations, 2007

	Prisoners per 100,000 Population
United States	738
Russia	607
Cuba	487
Ukraine	360
Singapore	350
Botswana	339
South Africa	335
Taiwan	259
United Arab Emirates	250
Poland	228
France	95
Sweden	75
Japan	58
India	29

Source: International Centre for Prison Studies, "World Prison Population List," available at www.prisonstudies.org.
Note: Canada's rate of incarceration is 107 per 100,000, and Mexico's is 196.

onstudies.org), US incarceration rates are comparable to those of countries like Cuba, Belarus, and Belize. Research from the National Council on Crime and Delinquency (NCCD) in 2007 claims that the US incarceration rate is four times the world average.

According to Marc Mauer, assistant director of "the Sentencing Project," criminal justice policies in the United States continue to become more punitive.[45] The higher incarceration rate can be tied directly to the shift to mandatory and determinate sentencing. Crowded prisons, housing in excess of 2 million inmates in 2007 (1 in 100 adults), have placed a tremendous financial burden on the states and the federal government. Fully two-thirds of those in prison are ethnic and racial minorities. Most of those newly incarcerated are there for nonviolent, drug-related charges, often associated with crack cocaine. The federal prison system has grown to the third largest in the United States, after the state systems of Texas and California. To offset the expense of the massive federalization of crime, a shift to private prisons has been considered. Claiming more efficiency and cost savings, proponents maintain that the private market should take on the prison problem. Philosophically, though, a private prison system can lead to serious conflicts of interest. Any private claim to incarceration would have a vested interest in sentencing policies that encourage longer sentences and a large prison population. The cost of public oversight of private prisons would likely offset any savings.

To counteract soaring prison populations, some states began experimenting with "reentry" programs designed to reintegrate prisoners back into society. The Justice Department established a national Reentry Resource Center to highlight successful approaches and offer training.

Despite recent trends, no explicit philosophy serves as an underlying rationale for US criminal justice policy. Traditionally, such policy has been based on one of four competing philosophical attitudes about punishment—retribution, incapacitation, rehabilitation, and deterrence. Emphasis on which particular attitude prevails depends on shifting national values and growing or waning fears about crime.

Retribution is the age-old philosophy of "an eye for an eye." Now often referred to as a policy of "just deserts," it emphasizes punitive sanctions: criminals must pay their debts to society through punishment that "fits" the crime. Somewhat related is the philosophy of **incapacitation**, which postulates that, through restraint or incapacitation, criminals are removed from society so that they can no longer endanger others. Incapacitation emphasizes citizen protection and crime prevention.

Rehabilitation seeks to reintegrate criminals into society through corrections programs and services. More humanitarian in its outlook, this philosophy looks to social causes to explain crime. As noted earlier, rehabilitation dominated most twentieth-century thinking and policymaking about crime.

In recent years **deterrence** philosophy has come to the fore. Here, some argue that the effective use of sentencing will function as an example to deter would-be offenders (general deterrence) or to convince criminals not to commit another crime (specific deterrence).

Often the appeal of a particular philosophy is tied to our assumptions about human nature. In an effort to sort through competing policy approaches, David Gordon has laid out the logical flow of conventional criminal justice policy.[46] He notes that liberal and conservative philosophies about crime correspond to liberal and conservative positions on other social issues. Both liberals and conservatives share the assumption that criminal behavior is irrational. To a conservative, the problem and the solution are for the most part straightforward. Social order, as reflected in the law, is rational. Because criminal behavior is irrational, it must be met with a response that protects public safety. Policies to combat crime must emphasize forces that deter crime. This translates into more police, more equipment, and more prisons.

On the other hand, although liberals agree that criminal behavior is irrational, they also see imperfections in the social order. And because the system is imperfect, they note, some people are more likely to be driven toward a life of crime. As Gordon states: "Criminality should be regarded as irrationality, but we should nonetheless avoid blaming criminals for irrational acts."[47] Liberals postulate relationships between poverty and racism and crime. Consequently, their answer to crime is found in more research, more technology, and more professional counseling for criminals. Liberals argue that societies will never rid themselves of crime until the root causes are discovered and eliminated.

The conservative emphasis on law and order and protection leads to policies promoting incapacitation and deterrence. The liberal emphasis on justice and equality has a stronger connection to rehabilitative techniques.

Sometimes laws contradict ideological integrity. For example, all states enacted a version of **Megan's Law**, which requires convicted sex offenders to register with their local police after their release from prison and allows officials to publicize names of some offenders. Despite a string of court challenges that argued the registration represented an additional punishment, appeals courts have determined that the law is an administrative action and not a criminal penalty. Some, including members of the various state civil liberties unions, oppose the registration, arguing that the decision about how to characterize an offender (one of three groups ranging from low to high risk; all information on high-risk offenders, including name, address, physical description, and detailed criminal history, is published) can lead to prejudice and mistakes. Liberals and conservatives alike are torn between offender and victim rights.

More recent economic analysis of crime began to question traditional liberal and conservative assumptions in another way.[48] These scholars challenge the assumption that criminal behavior is irrational. Building on nineteenth-century utilitarian thinking, they argue that criminal behavior is a rational choice, as follows: "A person commits an offense if the expected utility to him exceeds the utility he could not get by using his time and other resources at other activities. Some persons become 'criminals,' therefore, not because their basic motivation differs from that of other persons, but because their benefits and costs differ."[49]

The rational choice model of crime claims that criminals rationally calculate the cost-benefit ratio of an act. In doing this, they consider the likelihood of being caught, the probability of punishment, and the length and nature of their possible punishment. Solutions to crime from this perspective can be found in an analysis of why criminals make the choice they do and in the development of cost- or punishment-optimizing policies to deter people from making that choice. Public policy should thus aim at raising the cost of crime disproportionately to its potential benefits.

Still, notions of deterrence pervade current policy for combating crime as evidenced by the continued enthusiasm for definite and determinate sentencing policies. A **definite sentence** sets a fixed period of confinement that allows no reduction by parole while a **determinate sentence** is a fixed confinement, set by the legislature, with parole eligibility. The more customary **indeterminate sentence** offers more court discretion and is based on a correctional (not deterrent) model of punishment. Recent **truth-in-sentencing** rules mandate that a prisoner must serve at least 85 percent of his or her sentence. As noted above, all of these practices have led to large-scale crowding and considerable expense.

The Implications of Punishment and Reform

Many find fault with the increased emphasis on deterrence and especially question the assumption of criminal rationality. They argue that, even if individuals know that the risk of being caught for committing a crime is low, most would not commit a crime, particularly a violent crime. Further, critics point out that the assumption that criminals understand and weigh the possible costs and punishments for their criminal acts lacks empirical support. Analysts argue that it takes more than the threat of punishment to keep people in line.[50] Those who defend deterrence argue that, while **particular deterrence**, or the effect of deterrence on criminals, may be hard to prove, it is likely to have a great effect of **general deterrence**. They claim that the average citizen is less likely to commit a criminal act because of the "demonstration effect" of punishment.

Some assert a relationship between the **certainty, severity, and swiftness of punishment** and crime levels.[51] This proposition helped build arguments against the more traditional rehabilitative policies. Research has found that traditional rehabilitation has achieved only limited success. Alfred Blumstein explains that, by the mid-1970s, studies showed that rehabilitation programs had a "null effect."[52] In other words, corrections programs broke even on reducing **recidivism**.[53] Recidivism seems more closely associated with personal characteristics of the criminal and the outside environment to which the prisoner returns upon release. As Robert Blecker explained, this is what led policymakers to pass laws like the Sentencing Reform Act of 1984, in which Congress rejected rehabilitation as an outmoded philosophy.[54]

But tougher sentencing has not had the desired deterrent effect either. Data since 1975 show that longer sentences have not reduced the level of crime. As noted in a National Research Council study: "If tripling the average length of incarceration per crime had a strong deterrent effect, then violent crime rates should have declined in the absence of other relevant changes. While rates declined during the early 1980s, they generally rose after 1985, suggesting that changes in other factors . . . may have been causing an increase in potential [violent] crimes."[55]

Some even argue that longer sentences may have aggravated the crime problem. A number of experts fear that jail houses and prisons have become "schools for crime." Blumstein points out how some critics argue that "prison is harmful because it socializes prisoners, especially younger ones, into a hardened criminal culture."[56] Table 8.3 describes the current prison population.[57]

Recent findings from the Bureau of Justice Statistics note that "at midyear 2008, there were 4,777 black male inmates per 100,000 black males held in state and federal prisons and local jails, compared to 1,760 Hispanic male inmates per 100,000 Hispanic males and 727 white male inmates per 100,000 white males."[58]

How society finds a suitable mix of retribution, incapacitation, rehabilitation, and deterrence to fight crime is a practical issue, but it also has important moral dimensions. Blecker makes the following trenchant critique: "What actually happens to prisoners—

Table 8.3 US Prison Population

Demographics

- Women were 12 percent of the local jail inmates in 2002, up from 10 percent in 1996.
- Jail inmates were older on average in 2002 than 1996: 38 percent were age thirty-five or older, up from 32 percent in 1996.
- More than six in ten persons in local jails in 2002 were racial or ethnic minorities, unchanged from 1996.
- An estimated 40 percent were black, 19 percent Hispanic, 1 percent American Indian; 1 percent Asian; and 3 percent of more than one race/ethnicity.

Conviction offense

- Half of jail inmates in 2002 were held for a violent or drug offense, almost unchanged from 1996.
- Drug offenders, up 37 percent, represented the largest source of jail population growth between 1996 and 2002.
- More than two-thirds of the growth in inmates held in local jails for drug law violations was due to an increase in persons charged with drug trafficking.
- Thirty-seven percent of jail inmates were convicted on a new charge, 18 percent were convicted on prior charges following revocation of probation or parole, 16 percent were both convicted of a prior charge and awaiting trial on a new charge, and 28 percent were unconvicted.

Source: US Department of Justice, Office of Justice Programs, "Criminal Offenders Statistics," revised October 1, 2009, available at www.ojp.usdoj.gov/bjs/crimoff.htm.

their daily pain and suffering inside prison—is the only true measure of whether the traditional concepts have meaning, the traditional goals are fulfilled, the traditional definitions apply."[59] Equally important are the ethical questions associated with incarceration rates that disproportionately represent ethnic and minority populations. For example, as a result of highly publicized crack cocaine use in the 1980s, two federal laws were passed that have resulted in more serious consequences for crack users than for users of regular powder cocaine. Crack is cheaper and sold in the streets, and thus is more likely to involve inner city residents. It is no coincidence that the increased incarceration of nonviolent drug offenders, especially for crack use, involves low-income minorities.

Ingredients of Violence: Drugs, Guns, and Poverty

Crime abatement has been linked with policies aimed at low levels of drug and gun use, along with policies designed to lift people out of poverty. The relationship between these factors and crime is controversial. Politicians often proclaim such policies because they appeal to voters. But prudent analysis shows that the connection between drugs, guns, poverty, and crime is not obviously direct or causal.

The War on Drugs

The shattering effects of drug dependency lead citizens to endorse just about any program directed at eliminating illegal drug use. Public drug policies are based on medical, commercial, and moral concerns, and, increasingly, they are connected with crime policy. Most Americans support the "war on drugs," and believe that any efforts to decriminalize drug use are morally bankrupt. But the links between drugs and crime are unclear, and the empirical evidence demonstrating their relationship is weak.

Supply and demand considerations govern current drug policies. Reducing drug supplies through interdiction and the punishment of drug traffickers, and reducing demand through the education, incarceration, and rehabilitation of drug users, form the basis of the government's antidrug strategy. This strategy relies heavily on the criminal justice system, particularly the Department of Justice's Drug Enforcement Agency, for its effective implementation. Most Americans buy into the argument that drugs and crime are closely related. Consequently, they support employing the resources of the criminal justice system to fight the war on drugs. But is doing so justified?

Illegal drugs today include a wide range of psychoactive products such as opiates, cocaine (and its derivative crack), amphetamines, PCP, and hallucinogens. Medical research reveals that the behavioral response to these various drugs differs significantly from one person to the next, and from one drug to another. But setting up good scientific research on drug use and behavior is difficult. Reactions to drugs are highly individualistic and depend on factors like how much and how often a drug is taken.

Scientists do know that different drugs elicit different reactions.[60] For example, heroine and opiates tend to inhibit behavior, though it is not at all clear what happens during periods of withdrawal. The chronic use of these drugs may affect the central nervous system and lead to aberrant social behavior. Drugs like cocaine, LSD, and PCP, and amphetamines like methamphetamine (meth) produce effects not unlike alcohol. In small doses, individuals tend to act out in a disruptive fashion while higher doses lead to more disorganized, clumsy behavior that may have an inhibiting effect on social interaction. Crack cocaine may lead to a psychotic state, though no direct relationship has been established. Essentially, the analysis of individual drug use and crime levels shows no consistent relationship. Research conducted by James Inciardi noted that: "New York, with the highest cocaine prevalence of the five cities [Detroit, Los Angeles, New York, Miami, Washington, DC], and Los Angeles, with the second lowest, have the lowest homicide rates. The New York, Miami, and DC data resemble, if anything, an inverse relationship between homicide rates and arrestees' cocaine use."[61]

While the physiological connection between drugs and crime is not verifiable, economic arguments are persuasive. Do drug addicts steal or kill to feed a drug habit? Again, good data to confirm this proposition are hard to come by. One study found the empirical support for economic violence to be very inconclusive. But the report's first author, P. J. Goldstein, further concluded from a study done on the NYPD that drug-related violence can be categorized as **systemic violence** rather than just **economic violence**.[62] That is, it can be understood as the result of factors concerned with the overall drug "marketplace," in line with the following analysis: current public policy aims at minimizing the supply of drugs. An artificial drug scarcity results, which drives up the price of drugs. Dealers capture these excess profits, and drug users are forced to find ways to pay the contrived high prices. Among the reactions to this systemic condition is violence resulting from territorial disputes, gang warfare, battles with police and informers, the creation of black markets, and the lure of corruption. Prostitution increases, and drug dealers enter the school yards. In the case of meth, small toxic mom and pop labs compete with super meth labs, often creating serious environmental cleanup costs. Meth is synthesized from chemicals, which until recently were readily available in household products. In 2000, the US Congress passed the Methamphetamine Antiproliferation Act, making access to meth-derivative household chemicals much more difficult.

A logical extension of this discussion is the **iron law of prohibition**. If all drugs are prohibited, dealers have a greater incentive to traffic in the more profitable and more dangerous drugs. In other words, if the punishment for dealing marijuana is the same as that for dealing cocaine, then logically it is preferable to deal cocaine, which is more profitable.[63] Analysts point to the rising use of expensive "designer drugs" as an indication of this trend.

One public policy direction consistent with this reasoning is **decriminalization** of drugs. Not surprisingly, some elected officials have concluded that, given the costs of combating drug use, decriminalizing them makes the most sense. Proponents of this position argue that studies fail to confirm that drug use causes crime, and that maybe coincidentally criminals just use drugs. In addition, some worry that effective drug programs will infringe on civil liberties.

Decriminalization has only a small following. Most Americans simply will not accept the risk. It is estimated that as many as 6 million people already use drugs, and that legalizing them could lead to even greater numbers. Yet the costs of treating drug use as a crime are also great. Prison overcrowding, caseload pressure, and ballooning police and military budgets raise practical questions about the policy. Some argue that de-emphasizing the crime connection and re-emphasizing the public health aspects of drug use is a more viable and appropriate course.[64] This approach would target education and rehabilitation rather than interdiction and prosecution as its main goals. The growing use of anabolic steroids, particularly among professional athletes, is an interesting example of a public health problem that has become a crime problem. These performance-enhancing drugs can promote uncontrolled bursts of violence known as "roid rage," thus daring new responses from the war on drugs.

Gun Control

Like drugs, guns represent something tangible that policymakers can control in the fight against crime. Policymakers point to the experience of other countries, like the United Kingdom, which have tough gun control policies and far lower crime rates. But the relationship between guns and crime is complex. While analysts concede that tough gun laws could mitigate crime, they argue that those laws would not work unless all states agreed to the same standards.

Gun control policies affecting the availability, use, distribution, and deadliness of guns are already in place in the United States. Legislation dating to the 1930s regulated the use of machine guns and required gun sellers to be licensed. In 1968, Congress passed the Federal Gun Control Act in reaction to public outcries over the assassinations of Senator Robert Kennedy and Reverend Martin Luther King. The act emphasized restrictions on the availability and distribution of guns. It banned mail order sales of guns and outlawed sales to convicted felons, fugitives, and individuals with certain mental illnesses. It restricted private ownership of automatic and military weapons. The law

---

Case Study: Capital Punishment—The Enduring Debate

In March 2009, Maryland governor Martin O'Malley agreed to sign legislation sent from the state General Assembly severely restricting the death penalty. Governor O'Malley announced that state money spent on death penalty prosecutions ($3 million versus $1.1. million on non–death penalty prosecutions) could better be used on crime prevention. The new law—a compromise—permits the death penalty only with corroborating DNA evidence and a videotape of the crime or confession. Support for the death penalty ebbs and flows because it raises problems of proportionality of punishment, consistency of state statutes, and the vagaries of sentencing.

When the Bill of Rights was added to the Constitution, few intended the Eighth Amendment's "cruel and unusual punishment" to preclude capital punishment. The concern was to ensure that punishment be proportional to the offense. Fla-

grant acts of punishment, like burning at the stake, were outlawed. The use of capital punishment continued historically. It peaked in the 1930s, and began to decline precipitously in the 1960s. Critics denounced the variability in state statutes and pointed out that the poor, blacks, and underrepresented groups were more likely to be executed. By the 1960s, the National Association for the Advancement of Colored People and the American Civil Liberties Union had mounted a campaign against the use of capital punishment, making the issue one of public policy debate.

Beyond the question of arbitrary use, others raised the larger question of "evolving standards of decency." They argued that, though our colonial ancestors found no moral distaste in imposing the death penalty, perhaps contemporary standards of decency had changed. These two concerns, combined with growing worry that juries lacked sufficient directions in imposing

continued

Case Study continued

the death penalty, led to a virtual moratorium on its use by the late 1960s.

Perhaps inevitably, the question came before the Supreme Court. The first challenge to the death penalty addressed questions like the legality of "death-qualified juries," that is, jurists selected for their willingness to impose the death penalty. The Court ruled such juries unconstitutional. The Court also invalidated the death penalty as mandated under the Federal Kidnapping Act.

The major challenge to the death penalty occurred in *Furman v. Georgia* (1972). The Supreme Court temporarily struck down the death penalty because of the "arbitrary, capricious, and racist manner" in which it had been applied. Essentially, the Court reacted to how the death penalty had been used, not to the death penalty per se. Though the decision was complex, it did leave two legal avenues open to the states. They could pass laws that established a bifurcated procedure for the death penalty. Here, defendants would face a trial to establish culpability. If found guilty, then a second proceeding would follow to establish grounds for the death penalty. The other legal avenue available to states was to make the death penalty mandatory for certain crimes.

The Supreme Court ruled on the legality of the two-step procedure in *Gregg v. Georgia* (1976). In this case, the Court ruled that the death penalty for murder did not necessarily constitute cruel and unusual punishment. Further, it declared the bifurcated system constitutional. However, the Court ruled in *Woodson v. North Carolina* (1976) that the death penalty may not be made mandatory.

Despite the fact that the *Gregg* case upheld the constitutionality of the death penalty, a series of rulings has eroded the jury discretion in applying the statutory guidelines. In addition to these fundamental legal questions, other objections have been voiced regarding the cost and effectiveness of the death penalty. While some are persuaded that it is a cost-effective form of punishment, others point out that, given the need to guarantee procedural safeguards, its costs are much higher than are those of other forms of punishment. In other words, the studies show that the deterrent effect of the death penalty is far from proven. Comparisons show few differences in crime rates for those states with the death penalty and those without it. And in states with the death penalty, comparisons of the crime rate before and after an execution show no differences. The most compelling arguments against the death penalty result from wrongful convictions. DNA fingerprinting revolutionized criminal laboratories beginning in the late 1980s. Because of DNA findings, exonerated convicts have walked off death row creating a stirring indictment of the prosecutorial system. DNA results, though expensive, present a staggering blow to death penalty arguments.

Many conclude, however, that the death penalty is popularly supported by many Americans and politically useful. Some elected officials—among them the former governor of New York, Mario Cuomo—have argued forcefully for life in prison without parole as a preferable sentence. As noted by Cuomo in a *New York Times* editorial: "That alternative is just as permanent, at least as great a deterrent and—for those who are so inclined—far less expensive than the exhaustive legal appeals required in capital cases."

Sources: Mario M. Cuomo, "New York State Shouldn't Kill People," *New York Times,* June 17, 1989, p. 23; Donald D. Hook and Lothar Kahn, *Death in the Balance: The Debate over Capital Punishment* (Lexington, MA: D. C. Heath, 1989); Bonnie Szumski, Lynn Hall, and Susan Bursell, ed., *The Death Penalty: Opposing Viewpoints* (St. Paul, MN: Greenhaven Press, 1986).

required that gun dealers be licensed by the Bureau of Alcohol, Tobacco, and Firearms (ATF) and that the serial numbers on all guns sold by licensed dealers be recorded. Finally, it required that individuals buying guns from licensed dealers must show proof of identification and residency, and certify their eligibility to own guns. In 1986, Congress set mandatory penalties for those convicted of using guns in a federal crime and prohibited the use of bullets that could penetrate bulletproof clothing: "cop-killer" bullets. The import and manufacture of semiautomatic assault weapons was banned in 1990.

Despite this effort to control the distribution and availability of guns, gun ownership today is widespread. The ATF estimates that 150 million to 200 million firearms are privately owned, mostly used for hunting, sport, or self-protection. Twenty-four percent of privately owned guns are easily concealed handguns, which are used disproportionately in homicides. Estimates provided by the FBI indicate that, in 2007, about 72 percent of all homicides resulted from the use of firearms. A study published in the *Journal of the American Medical Association* estimates the treatment cost of gun injuries at $17,000 per person.[65] These frightening statistics led to a ground swell of support for more effective gun control. Many states tightened their gun ordinances by insisting on waiting periods before purchase, licensing of purchasers, and laws against carrying concealed weapons. But these stricter requirements were often undercut by the less-demanding regulations of neighboring states. Such frustration mounted until Congress finally passed the popular **Brady Bill**. The bill, named after presidential press secretary, James Brady, who was seriously wounded in the 1981 assassination attempt on President Reagan, required a background check and a five-day "cooling off" period prior to purchasing a gun.

Despite widespread popular support, particularly among law enforcement, the Brady Bill met with ongoing congressional opposition. Its original passage came only after a threatened filibuster attempt by Senate members and an aggressive advertising campaign mounted by the National Rifle Association (NRA). Both failed to sway public sentiment. In an emotional ceremony, President Clinton signed the Brady Bill shortly after Thanksgiving 1993. Despite this, the Brady Bill initiatives have been rolled back. The five-day waiting period and required background checks were found unconstitutional, as the Supreme Court argued in *Printz v. United States* (1997) that they infringed on states' rights. A national computer system (the National Instant Criminal Background Check System) now provides background checks, so the need for a waiting period no longer exists. The ban on assault weapons expired in 2004, despite considerable political pressure to extend its duration.

Gun enthusiasts complain that legislation like the Brady Bill misses the point. Their common refrain, "Guns don't kill people, people kill people," reflects their belief that gun control will not solve the crime problem. Further, they argue that gun control violates individual rights. Supported by the aggressive lobbying of the NRA, gun control opponents challenge any attempt to curtail their right to own and use weapons. They base their opposition on the right to bear arms as protected by the Constitution's

Second Amendment, and on what they perceive as a commonsense judgment that ownership of guns is uncontrollable. They find efforts to control certain types of guns (e.g., the ban on imported assault rifles imposed by President G. W. Bush) to be illogical, particularly when no such ban was placed on similar domestic-made weapons. Opponents also point to studies that show no difference in crime patterns between jurisdictions with strict gun laws and those without.[66]

Despite this opposition, US public opinion still insists that policymakers do something to counteract gun availability. Children with access to firepower, perhaps spurred by the indiscriminate violence absorbed from television, movies, and video games, alarm even die-hard opponents of gun control. Horrifying school violence like the 2007 Virginia Tech massacre, where troubled student perpetrator Seung-Hui Cho killed thirty-two people, drew worldwide criticism of US gun laws.[67]

Scholars point out that gun use tends to be an instrumental act much more than an intentional act. They point out that firearms are rarely used by serial killers. Tragically, gun availability has changed victimization patterns. Empirical evidence supports the conclusion that, while guns do not increase the overall levels of crime, they seem to increase the seriousness of criminal attacks. One study concludes:

> Where guns are available, commercial targets are robbed more than individual citizens, and young men more frequently than elderly women. Similarly, in domestic assaults husbands are more frequently the victims. Thus the most important effects of guns on crime are that they increase the seriousness of criminal attacks and affect the distribution of victimization; they do not seem to markedly increase the overall levels of criminal attack.[68]

Poverty and Crime

Does poverty cause crime? The connection between these two societal illnesses is far from simple. Yet many propose that the antidote to crime is the elimination of poverty. Unfortunately, what research tells us about the relationship between poverty and crime is inconclusive and sometimes misleading.

Much of the research about crime and poverty takes, as its starting point, assumptions about criminal behavior. In this model, individuals choose crime over employment when crime seems a more expedient course of action. They do this particularly if the risk of being caught is low and the utility (money) to be gained is high. It follows, then, that the appropriate reaction to this rational choice is to increase the deterrent (punishment) for prospective criminals. A further implication is that poor people are more likely to make this rational calculus than are members of other segments of society. They have less to lose than those who have sufficient income sources.

Empirical research advanced to confirm this rationale is common, but methodologically weak. Many studies use unemployment statistics to measure poverty, but these have proven to be very unrefined measures, neither reliable nor valid. Time-series studies comparing crime rates and unemployment statistics fail to explain mounting crime rates, nor do they show that unemployment causes crime. Cross-sectional studies comparing crime rates and unemployment trends across different geographic areas are even more difficult to interpret. States and cities differ widely in the nature and extent of the crimes committed within their jurisdictions. Fluctuations in differing labor markets make unemployment figures difficult to compare. Nonetheless, the intuitive sense that, if individuals have jobs, they are less likely to commit crimes has resulted in politicians promoting job programs as an antidote to crime. The consequences of these policies have been unclear, leading some to wonder if the causes of unemployment and crime are the same, if some people simply cannot succeed economically no matter what help they receive, or if the problem is simply that criminals choose a life of crime (a return to rational choice notions). Analysts continue to struggle with these questions. Though unable to explain how crime factors relate, researchers continue to point to correlations between delinquency, homicides, and the socioeconomic characteristics of communities.

Indicators like population density of households, residential mobility, family disruption, the presence of gangs, gun density, and drug distribution typically characterize low-income communities. All correlate with high crime rates. Studies point out that population density of households, residential mobility, and disrupted family structures, in particular, are significant indicators of crime.[69] They are typical of communities with high numbers of teenagers and single-parent households.

Research concludes that poverty today goes hand in hand with significant social disorganization. In his study *The Truly Disadvantaged: The Inner City, the Underclass, and Public Policy,* William Julius Wilson writes of the social isolation of the inner city.[70] Beyond the extreme racial segregation of inner cities in relation to other parts of the social fabric, there is a further breakdown within these communities themselves. People live side by side, but do not know one another. Great mistrust exists among neighbors. In these communities, unlike poor communities of the past, parenting becomes highly individualistic. Everyone is a stranger. Intergenerational relationships fall apart. There are no positive identifications with a neighborhood, no explicit community norms, and no sanctions against delinquent behavior. A street culture develops with its own set of norms and symbols. Embedded in this culture is a deep distrust for established institutions such as the police, schools, and businesses. Furthermore, given the current ongoing structural economic change toward service production and away from traditional industrial production, little opportunity exists in these communities to find good jobs and move out of the inner city culture. Crime is convenient, pervasive, and attractive.

The crisis for policymakers is where and how to break into this cycle. In the 1970s, theories proposing the concept of "defensible space" took hold.[71] Here, the objective was to create a more livable and more easily protected environment. City planners embraced these ideas and experimented with better architectural design, improved lighting, and more green space. Thirty years later, these experiments have met with mixed success. While still aware of the need to make communities more hospitable, studies now recommend the use of more informal social controls. Community watch programs, beat police patrols, and exact-change requirements for public transportation are all examples of the changing emphasis. Increasingly, policymakers have come to consider crime and poverty as social illnesses that need not just deterrence, but also improvements in areas such as public health. The complex relationship between crime and poverty defies any simple solution. Better studies, improved social and anticrime programs, and better economic opportunities may help shed light on the issue.

White Collar Crime

White collar crime is defined as illegal activity conducted in the course of one's occupation. It differs from **organized crime**, which is economic gain through illegal business practices like gambling, loan sharking, prostitution, and narcotics. Organized crime *is* one's occupation; white collar crime is perhaps more insidious. The activities of white collar criminals cut across business and politics, the professions, and labor organizations. The scope of white collar crime is broad, including financial, environmental, safety, and consumer affairs misconduct. The current wave of white color crime has been blamed on dubious financial arrangements, lax regulations, the increasing importance of stock options, and, to some, a pro-business Washington attitude. While the Justice Department reports on murders and robberies, there is no comparable data collection reporting corporate and white collar crime.

Study of white collar crime dates to 1939. Criminologist Edwin Sutherland studied these crimes not "ordinarily included within the scope of criminology." He defined white collar crimes as those "committed by a person of respectability and high social status in the course of his occupation."[72] Sutherland's definition and research were controversial at the time, but are less so today. The financial corruption and scandal associated with the economic boom of the 1990s affected many unsuspecting Americans. They found themselves caught up in the misdeeds of corporate white collar executives who exploited their privileged positions at the expense of many. As the current economic recession erodes personal savings, jobs, retirement incomes, and homeownership, outraged Americans blame Wall Street "irregularities" for undermining the US economy.

Too often white collar offenders hide behind corporate or professional sanctuaries, leading to claims that white collar criminals experience more lenient penalties. Critics say that white collar crime is just a "better racket." Unfortunately, the criminal justice system reacts differently to white collar crime than to street crime. Some criminologists theorize that judges and criminal justice personnel are often reluctant to view white collar crime as seriously because they identify with the socioeconomic standing of these offenders. To illustrate this, consider the savings and loan (S&L) crisis of the 1980s. After the Reagan administration deregulated the S&L industry, some S&L owners and executives violated laws and regulations by engaging in fraudulent, unsafe business practices that resulted in billions of dollars of losses.[73] Table 8.4 compares prison sentences for S&L offenders with those of selected federal offenders. The authors of this study concluded that the latter offenders often received longer sentences, "despite the fact that these crimes almost never approached $500,000, the average S&L offense."[74] White collar offenders typically have the resources to mount a good defense and, as argued by Richard Posner, because the "social stigma" associated with white collar crime is so great and the civil law procedure so costly, white collar criminals are best punished by "monetary penalties—by fines . . . rather than by imprisonment or other 'afflictive' punishments (save as they may be necessary to coerce payment of the monetary penalty)."[75]

In part, the legal system's historical reaction to white collar crime reflects the difficulty in conceptualizing and measuring it. These crimes do not fit easily into wider definitions of crime. On the sidelines of criminology, they are often complex and easily concealed, and present measurement problems. Responsibility for these crimes is easily diffused and sadly, victims are often unaware of what actually has happened to

Table 8.4 Prison Sentences for Savings and Loan Offenders and Selected Federal Offenders

	Mean Prison Sentence (months)
Savings and loan offenders	36.4
All federal offenders, convicted of:	
Burglary	55.6
Larceny	27.5
Motor vehicle theft	38.0
Counterfeiting	29.1
Federal offenders, with no prior convictions, convicted of:	
Property offenses (nonfraudulent)	25.5
Public order offenses (regulatory)	32.3
Drug offenses	64.9

Sources: Federal Criminal Case Processing, 1980–90 (Washington, DC: US Department of Justice, Bureau of Justice Statistics, 1992), p. 17; *Compendium of Federal Justice Statistics, 1988* (Washington, DC: US Department of Justice, Bureau of Justice Statistics, 1991), p. 43.

them. A recent *New York Times* article by journalist Floyd Norris derides the chief executive officer (CEO) of a large international corporation who claimed he "didn't know" about the company's wildly inflated revenues and hidden expenses. The CEO's defense was that "he worked on the strategy vision part, talking to key clients, being on the outside of the company." As Norris concludes about bosses walking away while their subordinates go to jail: "It's good to be the king."[76]

Classifications of white collar crime include financial manipulations known as "theft after trust," fraud (including tax fraud), corruption such as acceptance of bribes, and "restraint of trade" such as phony limited partnerships and pyramid schemes. Embezzlement is crime by an individual in a subordinate position against a strong corporation. Corporate crime includes price fixing and "collective embezzlement," or crime *by* a corporation *against* a corporation. Some occupations are more easily susceptible to crime, especially those in frequent contact with money or those that require specialized, technical information. Some industries, like the automobile or pharmaceutical industries, are more vulnerable. A car dealer wants to sell that used car for as much as possible; a pharmaceutical company can so easily falsify a research result.

In their study of the savings and loan crisis of the 1980s, *Big Money Crime,* researchers Kitty Calavita, Henry Pontell, and Robert Tillman explain that "'collective embezzlers' were not lone, lower-level employees," but thrift owners and managers, acting within networks of co-conspirators inside and outside the institution. Indeed, "this embezzlement was company policy."[77]

Corporate crime is distinctive because its primary objective is to advance corporate interests and, thus, Calavita and colleagues find many similar characteristics between corporate and organized crime. Both are premeditated, organized, and continuous, and they develop connections to public officials to avoid prosecution. These types of crimes reflect the dark side of the business subculture of competition and profit maximization. Crimes like false advertising, misuse of campaign funds, and occupational and environmental violations are further examples of betrayals of the public trust by business and political leaders. Ironically, most citizens worry little about or are unaware of the effects of this activity. In fact, the systematic, empirical study of white collar crime did not take hold until recently.[78] Yet while the average bank heist nets a robber $10,000, the average computer crime has reached a figure of $430,000.[79] Another study reports that "about 30 percent of business failures were the result of employee dishonesty . . . [and] about 15 percent of the price paid for goods and services goes to cover the costs of dishonesty."[80]

Of similar interest are recent theories about white collar crime. Some economists apply rational choice theory to the white collar criminal, claiming that self-interest in the absence of control best explains why it occurs. Others disagree, arguing that the wider social context must be explored. Financial performance, the search for profitability, the values of individualism, and the pursuit of wealth—all features of US capitalism—give rise to white collar crime, a notion first identified by sociologist C. Wright Mills in his work *The Power Elite* in the 1950s.[81] Author D. Quinn Mills argued that psychological traits like obsession with power lead to large-scale misuse and abuse are evident in recent white collar crimes.[82]

The general lack of documentation and prosecutorial activity regarding white collar crime is not surprising. Its nearly invisible and very diffuse nature complicates investigation. One investigator complained that it was like "doing someone else's checkbook."[83] Paper trails are papered over, increasingly with the help of computers and other sophisticated forms of technology. Nevertheless, the FBI has established a special branch of forensic accountants and lawyers to investigate and prosecute white collar criminals. In 1987, Congress enacted the Computer Fraud and Abuse Act, which has been supplemented by various state laws to counteract computer fraud and abuse. Computer specialists are now routine members of law enforcement agency staffs. This, combined with new tougher sentencing guidelines, means the criminal justice system is starting to focus on these illegal operations.

Nothing prepared the American public for the white collar crime spree of the 1990s. An array of prominent corporations confronted charges of large-scale financial abuse, stock price manipulation, and theft. Beginning with the inflated sales and profits of Sunbeam Corporation's CEO Alfred J. Dunlap, and continuing to Enron's notorious creative accounting schemes, the result has been millions of dollars lost to small investors. Enron began as a gas pipeline company and grew into an Internet company involved in energy trading. Company officials, with the help of the Arthur Andersen company's accounting wizardry, concealed losses from investors and made a fortune by running off balance-sheet partnerships. Andersen, which ceased to exist after the Enron fiasco, pioneered an accounting procedure called the "integrated audit." Essentially, the practice allowed Andersen accountants to work a company's books both on the inside and on the outside. In the absence of auditor independence, the accounting industry was compromised so seriously that Congress passed legislation to regulate the profession. Historically, the industry had relied on peer review but, as of 2002, with the creation of the Public Company Accounting Oversight Board established under the Sarbanes-Oxley Act, auditing guidelines and professional discipline have been imposed on the accounting profession. Corporations including WorldCom, Tyco, Adelphia, and ImClone (which ensnared Martha Stewart) have been charged with egregious white collar crimes—egregious in the sense that the leaders of these large corporations stood to profit whether stockholders prospered or not. In a summary study conducted for the American Bar Association, John Cassidy states: "From the beginning of 1999 to the end of 2001, senior executives and directors of these doomed companies walked away with some $3.3 billion in salary, bonuses, and the proceeds from sales of stock and stock options."[84]

CEO compensation skyrocketed by the end of the twentieth century. Peter Drucker once suggested that the ratio of CEO earnings to average employee compensation

Case Study: A Ponzi Scheme

The housing market collapse signaled the beginning of the most serious economic recession since the Great Depression. Beyond significant losses of jobs, homes, savings, and retirement accounts, a devastating stock market tumble blackened financial markets. In the midst of the crisis, Americans reeled from reports of financial agents profiting from the questionable and risky transactions charged as a leading cause of the economic collapse. No one better represented the excesses of Wall Street than one-time financial elder statesman, Bernard L. Madoff. Madoff pled guilty to an eleven-felony-count criminal complaint of defrauding thousands of investors in a Ponzi scheme of enormous proportions. Prosecutors claim that Madoff owes $170 billion in restitution to clients, making the former chair of the NASDAQ stock exchange the perpetrator of the largest single investment fraud in US financial history.

A Ponzi scheme involves fraudulent investment activities built on a house of cards. Madoff found it impossible to continue paying the high returns that he had promised his clients. By the early 1990s, he resorted to a Ponzi operation where he paid clients returns from his personal account at Chase Manhattan Bank, and lured other investors with a fraudulent promise of high returns. Investors received monthly payouts, never suspecting that Madoff had never actually invested their savings and that eventually the scheme would collapse.

By late 2008, Madoff confessed his activity to his two sons; the sons notified the Securities and Exchange Commission (SEC). Madoff faces spending the remainder of his life in prison, but his many clients now confront the loss of life savings. The Madoff debacle drew questions about the vigilance of the SEC in monitoring investment activity, especially because some years earlier financial analyst Harry Markopolis had informed the SEC that Madoff's operations did not add up. Markopolis argued that the returns Madoff offered were legally and mathematically impossible. Despite his whistleblowing, the SEC failed to intervene.

should be no higher than twenty times. As Drucker argues, when the salary gap goes beyond this amount, it makes a mockery of the contribution of the ordinary employee.[85] Today's CEOs and chief financial officers (CFOs) prosper by way of stock options, which they can exercise to vastly increase their salaries. Historically, CEO salaries were tied to the size of a company but, in the late 1970s, this switched to stock profitability. Based on models developed by two University of Chicago graduates, Michael Jensen and William Meckling, the use of the stock option was promoted as a way to better tie the CEO incentive structure to the company's profitability. Whereas in the past the CEO worried about employees and customers, this concern was refocused to shareholder value. A **stock option** is a legal contract that grants the owner the right to buy stock in the future at a certain price. These largely unregulated stock options marked the course for corporate irregularity since they led to creative accounting that overvalued corporate stock.

The betrayal by corporate leaders of many trusting employees and investors has alerted the policymaking community to the need for different regulatory devices in the areas of finance and securities. Regrettably, the role of lawyers and accountants is too easily compromised when part of their job is determining just how much a company can get away with.

With the white collar crime price tag estimated by the FBI at approximately $300 billion per year, society can no longer afford to allow professional and business standards alone to regulate the workplace. The heavy artillery of criminal law is increasingly being used. Many Americans have yet to learn that there is a much greater property loss associated with white collar criminal activities than with street crime. Paradoxically, crime prevention funds are allocated in just the opposite way.

Conclusion

While Americans are united, often passionately, over the need to fight crime, no public policy problem is more elusive. Science offers advances in medical treatment and environmental protection, but tells us little about how to keep peace in our streets.

How much crime is there? Newspaper accounts give the impression that crime-free, safe neighborhoods no longer exist. The days of unlocked cars and houses are of another era. Systematic studies of crime like FBI and police reports, along with academic studies, confirm this impression and tell us that violent crime in particular has reached record levels. The associated physical, emotional, and financial costs have forced policymakers at all levels to put crime at the top of their agendas.

What are the causes of crime? Efforts to answer this question have so far offered minimal direction to policymakers. Diverse theories point to a range of possible origins, but none explain conclusively why some individuals commit criminal acts and others do not. More is known about specific conditions associated with crime like the use of drugs, the availability of guns, and poverty. Unfortunately, policy recommendations based on this knowledge are controversial and too often aimed at achieving political aims rather than true solutions.

How can the US criminal justice system create effective policies to control crime, punish offenders, and protect the innocent? The criminal justice system is the crossroads for testing our resolve to protect the rights of the victims and of the accused before conviction, yet to punish offenders. Often bogged down by its own size and complexity, the system is characterized by the right to legal appeals, pervasive plea bargaining, and complex sentencing requirements. The police, the front line in fighting crime, typically suffer "whiplash" from the need to observe procedural safeguards, protect victims, and respond to society's demand that they catch the criminals.

Consequently, crime abatement creates a policy quagmire. There is no consensus and there are no viable remedies. A rough starting point is the healthy uneasiness about current crime control practices voiced by individuals like former attorney general Janet Reno. Reno called for redirection in fighting crime to emphasize prevention and the welfare of children, rather than tougher punishment. Despite this, President Clinton's

$30.2 billion crime bill passed after an aggressive partisan battle over what some representatives saw as "social pork." The resulting crime bill, the biggest in history, suggested few links between public health and education. It called for $13.4 billion in grants to localities to hire more police, $9.9 billion to build more prisons, and just $5.5 billion for crime prevention programs—the pork. The bill also banned nineteen more types of assault weapons, increased to sixty the number of federal crimes punishable by death, and introduced the so-called three strikes penalty for repeat offenders. The future portended stronger gun control laws, more prisons, new antidrug campaigns, and increased police visibility as the plan of action.

The current economic slump lays bare the very real tradeoffs between effectively financed public policy and economic growth. President Obama's measured take on social problems, like crime, remains firm only as long as bills are paid. Crime rates, crime fighting, and crime prevention are encircled by the wider issue of economic recovery facing the Obama administration.

This chapter's discussion calls for a warning: finding the answer to crime has proven as intractable as eradicating any of humanity's most deadly diseases. Like disease, crime rots the social system. Analysts know that, until the true root causes of this social illness are determined, money spent and prisons built will treat only the symptoms.

Questions for Discussion

1. Is there a relationship between public expenditure and crime abatement?

2. How accurate are crime statistics? Why is crime underreported?

3. Compare and contrast leading theories of criminal behavior. What policy guidance have they offered?

4. Describe the competing philosophies of criminal justice. How does deterrence differ from other philosophies?

5. Discuss contemporary police theory. What policies reflect these new approaches?

6. Why are Americans less concerned about white collar crime? How important is the "fear factor" in our criminal justice policy?

Useful Websites

Criminology Web Site's An Annotated "Webliography,"
    www.infotoday.Com/searcher/sep03/fink.shtml.
Federal Bureau of Investigation, Uniform Crime reports, www.fbi.gov/ucr/ucr.htm.
Federal Bureau of Investigation, White Collar Crime, www.fbi.gov/whitecollarcrime.htm.
Financial Crimes Enforcement Network, www.fincen.gov.
National Crime Prevention Council, www.ncpc.org.
Organized Crime Research, www.organized-crime.del.

US Department of Justice, Computer Crime & Intellectual Property Section,
www.usdoj.gov/criminal/cybercrime/index.html.
US Department of Justice, Crime Analysis in America,
www.iaca.net/Articles/CAinAmerica.pdf.

Notes

1. George L. Kelling and James Q. Wilson, "Broken Windows," *Atlantic Monthly,* March 1982, available at www.theatlantic.com/doc/198203/broken-windows.

2. On the Issues, "Barack Obama on Gun Control," available at www.ontheissues.org/domestic/Barack_Obama_Gun_Control.htm (accessed April 3, 2009).

3. Lydia Saad, "Perceptions of Crime Problem Remain Curiously Negative," *Gallup,* October 22, 2007, available at www.gallup.com/poll/102262/Perceptions-Crime-Problem-Remain-Curiously-Negative.aspx (accessed April 5, 2009).

4. Federal Bureau of Investigation (FBI), *Uniform Crime Report 2007* (Washington, DC: US Government Printing Office, 2008), p. 11.

5. US Department of Justice, "Crime in the US 2007," available at www.fbi.gov/ucr/cius2007/offesnse/violent_crime/murder_homicide.html (accessed May 3, 2009).

6. Ibid.

7. Ibid.

8. US Department of Justice, "Crime in the US 2007," available at www.fbi.gov/ucr/cius2007/offenses/property_crime/index.html (accessed May 3, 2009).

9. Ibid.

10. US Department of Justice, "Crime in the US 2007," available at www.fbi.gov/ucr/cius2007/offenses/property_crime/motor_vehicle_theft_html (accessed May 3, 2009).

11. US Department of Justice, "Crime in the US 2007," available at www.fbi.gov/ucr/cius2007/offenses/clearances/index.html (accessed May 3, 2009).

12. James Lynch, "Crime in International Perspective," in James Q. Wilson and Joan Petersilia, ed., *Crime: Public Policies for Crime Control* (Oakland, CA: ICS Press, 2002), p. 17.

13. A 1992 study titled *Rape in America,* conducted by the National Crime Victim Center and the Crime Victims Research and Treatment Center at the Medical Center of South Carolina, found that every year in the United States, 683,000 women are forcibly raped. Partly in response to this finding, the Bureau of Justice Statistics completed a redesign of its National Crime Victimization Survey and documented in *Violence Against Women: Estimates from the Redesigned Survey* (August 1995; NJC-154348) that women report about 500,000 rapes and sexual assaults to interviewers every year.

14. Elliott Currie, *Crime and Punishment in America* (New York: Henry Holt, 1998), p. 4.

15. James Q. Wilson and Richard J. Herrnstein, *Crime and Human Nature* (New York: Simon and Schuster, 1986).

16. Ibid., p. 22.

17. Clive Coleman and Clive Norris, *Introducing Criminology* (Portland, OR: Willan, 2000), p. 7.

18. Wilson and Herrnstein, *Crime and Human Nature,* p. 21.

19. Coleman and Norris, *Introducing Criminology,* pp. 18–19.

20. Marquis of Beccaria Bonesana, *On Crimes and Punishment 1763–1764,* as reported in

Criminiology Encyclopedia, available at www.statemaster.com/encyclopedia/criminology (accessed August 21, 2009).

21. Cesare Lombrosco, *L'Uomo Delinquente* (Milan: Hoepli, 1876).

22. George B. Vold and Thomas J. Bernard, *Theoretical Criminology* (New York: Oxford University Press, 1986), p. 9.

23. Gary Becker, "Crime and Punishment: An Economic Approach," *Journal of Political Economy* 76, no. 2 (March–April 1968): 9.

24. Vold and Bernard, *Theoretical Criminology,* p. 13.

25. For an excellent discussion of strain theories, see ibid., pp. 185–204.

26. Wilson and Herrnstein, *Crime and Human Nature,* p. 19.

27. Mark H. Moore, "Controlling Criminogenic Commodities: Drugs, Guns, and Alcohol," in James Q. Wilson, ed., *Crime and Public Policy* (San Francisco: Institute for Contemporary Problems, 1983), pp. 125–143.

28. In a civil case, individuals bring action against one another in the hopes of recovering financial damages. A misdemeanor is a crime that is less serious than a felony and punishable by less than a year in jail.

29. Marianne LeVert, *Crime in America* (New York: Facts on File, 1991), p. 116.

30. James A. Inciardi, *Criminal Justice,* 3rd ed. (New York: Harcourt Brace Jovanovich, 1990) p. 168.

31. In 1957, Cleveland police officers sought entrance to the home of Dollree Mapp in search of a man suspected of an earlier bombing and of possessing gambling paraphernalia. The police forced their way into Mapp's home, forcibly arrested her, and conducted what was later established to be an illegal search. The US Supreme Court ruled that evidence seized from Mapp's home was illegally obtained and, therefore, not admissible in any courtroom in the country.

32. Robert F. Cushman, *Cases in Constitutional Law* (Englewood Cliffs, NJ: Prentice-Hall, 1979), p. 400.

33. For example, in 1975 the US Supreme Court ruled that, even if a suspect asserts the right to remain silent during interrogation, the police can commence questioning him or her about another crime (*Michigan v. Mosely*). Beginning in the 1980s, a series of cases were heard that dealt with the issue of public safety. In *Berkemer v. McCarthy* (1984), the Court held that roadside questioning of suspected drunken drivers does not require *Miranda* warnings.

34. Lawrence Sherman, "The Police," in James Q. Wilson and Joan Petersilia, ed., *Crime* (San Francisco: ICS Press, 1995), p. 330.

35. Ibid.

36. George L. Kelling, Tony Pate, Duane Dieckman, and Charles Brown, *The Kansas City Preventive Patrol Experiment* (Washington, DC: Police Foundation, 1974).

37. Carl Klockers, ed., *Thinking About Police* (New York: McGraw-Hill, 1983).

38. Sherman, "The Police," p. 332.

39. The Law Enforcement Assistance Administration (LEAA), now defunct, grew out of the earlier Office of Law Enforcement set up within the Department of Justice. The LEAA was designed to financially assist local governments in fighting crime.

40. US Advisory Commission on Intergovernmental Relations, *Guide to the Criminal Justice System for General Government Elected Officials* (Washington, DC: US Government Printing Office, 1993), p. 11.

41. Speech at the American Bar Association Annual Meeting, an address by Anthony M. Kennedy, Associate Justice, Supreme Court of the United States, August 9, 2003.

42. Linda Greenhouse, "Supreme Court Changes Use of Sentence Guides," *New York Times,* January 13, 2005, p. A27.

43. Ibid.

44. David Johnstone with Steven Holmes, "Experts Doubt Effectiveness of Crime Bill," *New York Times,* September 14, 1994, p. 16.

45. Marc Mauer, "Thinking About Prison and Its Impact in the Twenty-First Century," fifteenth annual Walter C. Reckless Memorial Lecture, Ohio State University, April 14, 2004.

46. David M. Gordon, "Capitalism, Class and Crime in America," in Ralph Andreano and John J. Siegfried, ed., *The Economics of Crime* (New York: John Wiley and Sons, 1980), pp. 163–187.

47. Ibid.

48. See, in particular, Gary S. Becker, "Crime and Punishment: An Economic Approach," *Journal of Political Economy* 76, no. 2 (April 1968): 169–217; and Gordon Tullock, "An Economic Approach to Crime," *Social Science Quarterly* 50, no. 2 (June 1969): 59–71.

49. Quoted from Gordon, "Capitalism," in Andreano and Siegfried, *Economics of Crime,* p. 169.

50. See James Q. Wilson, *The Moral Sense* (New York: Free Press, 1993), which argues that to combat crime, societies need to nurture more private virtue.

51. See studies noted in Albert J. Reiss Jr. and Jeffry A. Roth, ed. (of the National Research Council), *Understanding and Preventing Violence* (Washington, DC: National Academy Press, 1993), pp. 291–294.

52. Alfred Blumstein, "Prisons: Populations, Capacity and Alternatives," in James Q. Wilson, ed., *Crime and Public Policy* (San Francisco: ICS Press, 1983), p. 232.

53. Recidivism refers to recurring criminal behavior.

54. Robert Blecker, "Haven or Hell? Inside Lorton Central Prison: Experiences of Prison Justified," *Stanford Law Review* 42, no. 3 (1990): 1149–1249.

55. Reiss and Roth, *Understanding and Preventing Violence,* p. 292.

56. Blumstein, "Prisons," p. 232.

57. See US Advisory Commission on Intergovernmental Relations, *Guide to the Criminal Justice System,* p. 30.

58. US Department of Justice, Bureau of Justice Statistics, "Prisoner Statistics," available at http://ojp.usdog.gov/bjs/prisons.htm (accessed May 2009).

59. Blecker, "Haven or Hell?" p. 1152.

60. For a detailed summary of the leading scientific research on drugs and their effects, see Reiss and Roth, *Understanding and Preventing Violence.*

61. Quoted in ibid., p. 188.

62. P. J. Goldstein et al. (of the National Institute on Drug Abuse), *Drug Related Involvement in Violent Episodes: Final Report* (New York: Narcotic and Drug Research, 1987). See also P. J. Goldstein, "Drugs and Violent Crime," in N. A. Weinder and M. E. Wolfgangs, ed., *Pathways to Violent Crime* (Newbury Park, CA: Sage, 1989), pp. 16–48.

63. This argument is presented by David Boaz, "The Case of Legalizing Drugs," in Herbert Levine, ed., *Point Counter Point Readings in American Government,* 4th ed. (New York: St. Martin's, 1992).

64. In October 1993, then attorney general Janet Reno agreed to a new approach to fighting the war on drugs. Drug offenders arrested in Washington, DC, would come before a "drug court" rather than the DC Superior Court. The drug court would supervise intensive treatment for nonviolent offenders. The goal, as expressed by Reno, was to deal with the underlying prob-

lems of drugs, rather than adjudicate for criminal charges. A 2005 Government Accounting Office (GAO) report concluded that adult drug courts substantially reduced crime. See "GAO-05-219 Adult Drug Counts: Evidence Indicates Recidivism, Reductions, and Mixed Results for Other Outcomes" (Washington, DC: US Government Printing Office, 2005), p. 86.

65. Phillip Cook et al., "The Medical Cost of Gunshot Injuries in the United States," *Journal of the American Medical Association* 282 (August 1999): 447; Dorothy P. Rice et al., *Cost of Injury in the United States: A Report to Congress 1989* (San Francisco and Baltimore: Institute for Health and Aging, University of California and the Injury Prevention Center, Johns Hopkins University, 1989).

66. The National Research Council reports estimates showing that only one out of six firearms used in crimes is legally obtained. Charles F. Wellford, John V. Pepper, and Carol V. Petrie, ed., *Firearms and Violence* (Washington, DC: National Research Council, 2004).

67. Christine Hauser and Anahad O'Connor, "Virginia Tech Shooting Leaves 33 Dead," *New York Times,* April 15, 2007, available at www.nytimes.com/2007/04/16/us/16cnd-shooting .html (accessed August 21, 2009).

68. A study of children's hospitals, reported in the *Washington Post* (November 26, 1993), estimated the average cost of treating a child for a gunshot wound at more than $14,000. Another study reports that gunshot wounds cost the nation $2.3 billion a year in medical treatment, and almost half of that is paid by taxpayer dollars. Philip Hilts, "Annual Cost of Treating Gunshot Wounds Is Put at $2.3 Billion," *New York Times,* August 4, 1999, available at www .nytimes.com/1999/08/04/US/annual-cost-of-treating-gunshot-wounds-is-put-at-2.3-billion.html (accessed August 21, 2009).

69. Mark H. Moore, "Controlling Criminogenic Commodities: Drugs, Guns and Alcohol," in Wilson, *Crime and Public Policy,* p. 130.

70. William Julius Wilson, *The Truly Disadvantaged: The Inner City, the Underclass, and Public Policy* (Chicago: University of Chicago Press, 1987).

71. Oscar Newman, *Defensible Space: Crime Prevention Through Urban Design* (New York: Macmillan, 1973).

72. Edwin H. Sutherland, *White Collar Crime* (New York: Holt, Rinehart, and Winston, 1949), p. 9.

73. Charles Keating, Don Dixon, and Erwin Hansen were the three best known of the thrift defendants.

74. Kitty Calavita, Henry N. Pontell, and Robert H. Tillman, *Big Money Crime* (Berkeley: University of California Press, 1997), p. 164.

75. Richard Posner, "Optimal Sentences for White Collar Criminals," *American Criminal Law Review* 17 (Winter 1980): 410.

76. Floyd Norris, "Chief Executive Was Paid Millions and He Never Noticed the Fraud," *New York Times,* January 7, 2005, p. C1.

77. Calavita, Pontell, and Tillman, *Big Money Crime,* p. 63.

78. "White collar crime" as a term was first used by Edward Sutherland in an address to the American Sociological Society in 1939.

79. Paul W. Keve, *Crime Control and Justice in America* (Chicago: American Library Association, 1995), p. 33.

80. Charles R. Wagner, *The CPA and Computer Fraud* (Lexington, MA: Lexington Books, 1979).

81. C. Wright Mills, *The Power Elite* (New York: Oxford University Press, 1956).

82. D. Quinn Mills, *Wheel, Deal and Steal: Deceptive Accounting, Deceitful CEOs, and Ineffective Reforms* (New York: Prentice Hall, 2003).

83. Comment quoted by a reporter for "Sheriff's Investigation Follows More Paper Trails," *St. Petersburg Times,* August 30, 1993, p. 1.

84. John Cassidy, "The Greed Cycle: How the Financial System Encouraged Corporations to Go Crazy," *New Yorker,* September 23, 2002, p. 64.

85. As cited by Peter Schwartz, "The Relentless Contrarian," *Wired Magazine,* August 1996, p. 119.

9

Education: A Larger Role for National Government

In the United States, state and local governments are primarily responsible for providing education for their residents. In fact, education is the single largest expenditure item for state and local governments, averaging just over one-third of their budgets. When the federal government's contribution to spending on education from kindergarten through twelfth grade (K–12) is included, the United States spends more money per pupil than nearly every other nation. However, in the most recent data available, US students performed only slightly above average on the 2007 Trends in International Mathematics and Science Study (TIMSS).[1] Unfortunately, in the eighth grade US students scored below their cohorts in nine countries in science and math, and fell further behind in the percentage of students scoring in the top 10 percent.[2] There is reason for concern since, once students from Boston graduate and enter the work force, they do not just compete with workers from Pittsburgh; instead, their competitors now include well-educated workers from Tokyo and Taipei. As globalization is pressing in on US workers more every day, the nation's once-vaunted educational system appears to be languishing while other nations are charging ahead. Today, the United States' national dropout rate is near the top of the developed nations of the Organisation for Economic Co-operation and Development (OECD). Since human capital is an absolute prerequisite for success in the global economy, the United States cannot maintain economic competitiveness without major policy changes to improve the quality of education of graduates joining the work force.

President Barack Obama proposes a sweeping policy change in the US education system. To accomplish this, despite the budgetary issues the nation faces, he first aims to significantly increase the role of the federal government in the educational system. As he stated during the 2008 presidential campaign:

This agenda starts with education. Whether you're conservative or liberal, Republican or Democrat, practically every economist agrees that in this digital age, a highly educated and skilled workforce will be the key not only to individual opportunity, but to the overall success of our economy as well. We cannot be satisfied until every child in America—and I mean every child—has the same chances for a good education that we want for our own children.[3]

Education is a distinct departure from other services provided by the government. Unlike social welfare or health care, which are concerned with the maintenance of human capital, education seeks to *develop* it. Americans agree that providing a quality education is one of the most important items on the public policy agenda. Policies that remove obstacles to achieving a quality education, such as reducing school violence or discouraging disruptive behavior, receive widespread support. Beyond these areas of obvious agreement, the unity quickly dissolves when more fundamental questions are raised. Education policy provokes debate because no policy issue is more important to the nation's future. For example, what should be the purpose of the educational endeavor? Is it primarily to help individuals succeed to their full potential? Or is its main ideal to contribute to the public good by creating a more skilled labor force? Perhaps, it is some combination of both propositions. These two separate ideas are the basis for conflicting educational goals and policies. The first view suggests that parents have a right to give their children the best education possible, one that will give them access to the most important jobs available (or allow them to pass on their privileged position in society to their children by giving them education advantages). The second proposition leads to the view that education should promote the public good, which is best achieved by a dedication to educational equality. Many hold both views simultaneously. The result is widespread dissatisfaction with the US educational system. Unfortunately, little consensus exists about *what* should be done to resolve the problems and *who* has the primary responsibility for taking corrective action.

Education: Why Governments Intervene

In Chapter 1, we pointed out that competitive markets are efficient mechanisms for meeting consumer demand. Why, then, should government be involved in providing education when a competitive market is such an efficient mechanism? Nevertheless, in the United States, 90 percent of all elementary and secondary students are in publicly financed schools rather than privately funded institutions.

Education is a **quasi-public good** in that important positive externalities result from an educated society. A more highly educated and skilled work force is more productive and produces more wealth than a poorly educated one. But education is not a pure **public good** since it does not meet the conditions of *nonrivalry* or *nonexcludability*. That is, the consumption of education by one individual (one person's education) does not reduce the availability of education for others, or prevent another from using educational skills. In the real world, there may be no such thing as an absolutely nonrivaled and nonexcludable good. For example, an overcrowded classroom may reduce the efficiency and quality of the educational process. But some goods approximate the concept closely enough for useful analysis.

Productivity

Education provides a potential positive externality of productivity. The person who most benefits from an education is the person who is educated. After all, education has some elements of a private market; for example, education raises a worker's productivity and brings private rewards to individuals through higher income, more satisfying work, and more pleasant working conditions.

The positive externality comes in the form of "spillover effects" to other workers. The educated worker's productivity may also result in more workers being hired in the company. The society will also receive a benefit reflected through higher pay for the educated worker as well as added income for additional workers that will result in the government collecting more revenue through tax receipts that can be used to improve the "general welfare."

However, individuals demand education based on their expectations of personal benefit without regard to the larger benefits to society. Since the individual will not be compensated for all the positive spillover effects from their education, they may decide to consume less education than is optimal for society. The external benefits justify that government provide education for everyone through subsidies.

Citizenship

Public support of education has long been touted because of its positive impact on society. **Functionalism** holds the view that society can exist in harmony because its institutions spring from a shared culture. Consequently the family, the educational system, and the economy, among other institutions, perform specific "functions" necessary for the survival of society. The function of education is to (1) transfer societal values; (2) produce a more informed citizenry; (3) produce workers with more productive skills; and (4) provide for "equal opportunity" by providing everyone, regardless of circumstance, with basic education skills. School serves as a halfway house to assist a child's passage between the familiar world of the family and the impersonal world of adult careers and community life.[4] The belief that formal education correlates with good citizenship has assimilated into US culture.

To Level the Playing Field: Redistribution

Functionalism also supports the notion that all members of society should have an equal chance for educational and economic success. This meritocratic ideal strongly supports equality of *opportunity*. Education is a *normal good,* a good for which demand increases when income rises and demand falls as income declines while the price of the good (education) remains constant. If education was provided through a privately financed model, affluent families would provide more education for their children than would lower-income families. More education should result in greater productivity and higher income for children of high-income families, especially later in life. The result is that income and social mobility would be limited because children of high-income parents would have better opportunities than low-income families. Supporters of functionalism and public education contend that a public education system fosters greater equality because it provides the knowledge and skills necessary to perform those jobs that society rewards highly. Thus, wealthier members of society are not able to monopolize access to highly paid jobs. By broadening the equality of opportunity, education encourages social mobility. We will return to the critics of this view after discussing the implications of human capital theory.

Human Capital Theory

To most people, the notion of **capital** means a factory, shares of stock, or a bank account. They are forms of capital in that they are assets that provide income in the future, as opposed to **consumption**, which provides immediate benefits but does not increase one's ability to earn future income. **Human capital theory** holds that expenditures on education, medical care, and training make individuals inherently more productive and, therefore, more highly valued workers. Adam Smith was the first to point out that education is an investment that will improve the future productive capacity of workers and their future earnings, just as an investment in machinery or a factory will generate future income. He said that the capital stock of a nation includes the

> useful abilities of all the inhabitants or members of the society. The acquisition of such talents, by the maintenance of the acquirer during his education, study, or apprentice-ship, always costing a real expense, which is a capital fixed and realized, as it were, in his person. Those talents, as they make a part of his fortune, so do they likewise of that of the society to which he belongs. The improved dexterity of a workman may be considered in the same light as a machine or instrument of trade which facilitates and abridges labour, and which, though it costs a certain expense, repays that expense with a profit.[5]

During preindustrial periods, the value of an individual to society was measured primarily in physical productivity rather than mental ability. The size of a nation's population was a strong indicator of its power. With the advent of the industrial and commercial revolutions, it became apparent that a nation's power was less dependent on physical labor and more dependent on skills. A country with the largest population was not necessarily the most productive or powerful. The ability of colonial England and France to control far more populous territories illustrated this.[6]

Education can be thought of as human capital because individuals cannot be separated from their knowledge or skills in the same way as they can be separated from material assets. Just as a corporation commits some of its profits to buying new equipment to generate more profits at a later date, the individual may reduce current income (and consumption) by investing in education in the hope of increasing future income. By obtaining a college degree, an individual anticipates that they will acquire useful knowledge and skills that will improve their employment opportunities and lifetime earnings, resulting in a more pleasant job than a high school friend who did not continue his or her education would have.

The Rate of Return to Human Capital

The theory holds that those with more human capital should be more productive than those with less. The productivity and quality of labor will be largely determined by the education and skill of the work force. The educational process replicates many of the skills the job market rewards generously in the form of wages. Most efforts to measure the rate of return to investment in education concentrate on direct monetary benefits and ignore the spillover benefits that accrue to society because of the difficulty in measuring them. The fact that private rates of return to educational investment are higher and more easily measured than the social rates of return, especially for higher education, has been used to justify adding tuition fees and student loans at the university level.

There is a positive relationship between education and lifetime earnings. High school graduates ordinarily have higher lifetime earnings than those without a high school degree, and college graduates earn more during their lifetime than high school graduates (see Table 9.1). This leads to the conclusion that one is better off with more rather than less education. That more education *correlates* with higher lifetime earnings does not prove that higher education *causes* the higher earnings.

Costs and Benefits of Human Capital Investment

Further, estimates of educational benefits may be too low because of the difficulty of distinguishing between consumption and investment benefits.[7] Education is not only an investment, but also a consumption good in that many enjoy learning during the process. The financial benefit of the investment is plainly evident as Table 9.1 illustrates.

Who pays for the costs of education? In regard to the public school system, government at the federal, state, and local levels underwrites the costs of education through tax **subsidies**, especially at the elementary and high school levels where compulsory attendance is required at least through age sixteen. Individuals during the years of their elementary and high school education forgo minimal income since the law precludes

Table 9.1 Average Income by Highest Degree Earned, 2006 (in dollars)

	Not a High School Graduate	High School Graduate Only	Associate's	Bachelor's	Master's	Professional	Doctorate
All	20,873	31,071	39,724	56,788	70,358	116,514	103,944
Age 25–34	21,153	28,448	35,180	48,724	55,069	78,119	62,158
Age 35–44	24,333	35,083	45,018	63,335	75,724	133,151	116,721
Age 45–54	25,436	37,173	45,600	66,061	85,166	131,011	121,238
Age 55–64	25,688	34,845	40,497	60,393	67,911	123,759	103,112
Age 65 and over	18,740	24,072	28,184	43,805	45,271	88,361	82,623

Source: US Census Bureau, *Statistical Abstract 2009* (Washington, DC: US Government Printing Office, 2009), p. 146.

significant employment below the age of sixteen. All taxpayers, including parents and those without children in the affected age groups, absorb the cost of the educational subsidy.

A college education is far more expensive since the government does not fully subsidize its costs. The student, or his or her parents, must pay directly for room, board, tuition, books, and other assorted fees. In addition, the individual receiving the education can forgo significant income during the typical four- to five-year period that it increasingly takes to complete a college degree. And after the college education is completed, it may take time before the college graduate will surpass high school graduates in income levels since the latter have already acquired four years of seniority and experience on the job. The variation in income as related to gender and education, as shown in Table 9.2, is striking.

Human capital theory maintains that education provides skills and technologies, such as reading, writing, mathematical calculation, and problem solving, that are directly related to the production process. Education therefore raises productivity and the earning capacity of the individual worker. This is called the **marginal productivity theory**, which states that an employer will be willing to pay a worker only for what he or she adds to the firm's utility.

Higher educational attainment provides the individual not only with higher income, but also with greater job security. One way to measure job security is to compare unemployment rates and educational attainment, as shown in Table 9.3.

As less-developed countries have dramatically increased their own supply of college graduates, businesses have found that even many highly skilled jobs can be sent

Table 9.2 Average Income by Highest Degree Earned and Factors of Gender and Racial/Ethnic Background, 2006 (in dollars)

	Not a High School Graduate	High School Graduate Only	Associate's	Bachelor's	Master's	Professional	Doctorate
Sex							
Male	24,072	37,356	47,575	69,818	87,981	132,991	116,473
Female	15,352	23,236	33,052	43,302	53,209	86,010	77,968
White	21,464	32,083	40,465	57,932	71,063	117,787	105,541
Male	24,579	38,833	49,061	71,735	89,837	133,988	118,003
Female	15,483	23,334	32,889	43,142	53,062	85,112	78,389
Black	17,823	26,368	35,817	47,903	55,654	101,374	85,237
Male	21,294	30,122	36,534	52,569	62,396	(B)	(B)
Female	14,277	22,643	35,328	44,326	50,916	80,038	(B)
Hispanic[a]	20,581	27,508	36,106	45,371	65,240	82,627	(B)
Male	23,060	32,148	41,445	51,336	81,885	97,035	(B)
Female	15,072	20,608	31,675	38,825	51,344	(B)	(B)

Source: US Census Bureau, *Statistical Abstract 2009* (Washington, DC: US Government Printing Office, 2009), p. 146.
Notes: a. Persons of Hispanic origin may be of any race.
B = Base figure too small to meet statistical standards for reliability of a derived figure.

Table 9.3 Unemployment Rates by Educational Attainment, 1992–2007

	Total	Not a High School Graduate	High School Graduate Only	Some College or Associate's Degree	Bachelor's Degree or More
1992	6.1	11.5	6.8	5.6	3.2
1995	4.3	9.0	4.8	4.0	2.4
2000	3.0	6.3	3.4	2.7	1.7
2003	4.8	8.8	5.5	4.8	3.1
2007	3.6	7.1	4.4	3.6	2.0

Sources: US Census Bureau, *Statistical Abstract 2007* (Washington, DC: US Government Printing Office, 2007), p. 376; US Census Bureau, *Statistical Abstract 2009* (Washington, DC: US Government Printing Office, 2009).

overseas. For example, India is now producing over four times as many engineers annually as is the United States. Many jobs that rely on highly skilled and educated Americans can now be contracted out at far lower costs. The result is that higher education is less able to provide the safeguard against economic shocks that it once did. As pressure to cut costs rises, US businesses are replacing high-quality, high-wage workers in the United States with high-quality, low-wage workers abroad.

Qualifications to Human Capital Theories

Early theories of human capital that claimed precise relationships between education and economic growth, both at the individual level and at the national level, have been forced to acknowledge that supportive empirical evidence is weak.

One social science theory that broadly supports the human capital theory maintains that education functions to distribute workers into the jobs for which they are best suited based on their educational skills. Critics of functionalism accuse human capital theory of disregarding the social class divisions in society perpetuated by the educational system. They charge that students are separated into vocational, general education, and college preparatory programs along the general class lines of their families. One researcher suggested a similar sorting mechanism takes place in the way curriculums are presented in different communities.[8] Many hoped that, as education became more available and equally distributed, children from disadvantaged families would get as much education as those from advantaged families. That has not happened. Therefore, the critics claim, while education can provide social mobility, it tends to "transmit inequality from one generation to another."[9] One study shows that high school graduates who are in the top quarter in socioeconomic status are almost twice as likely to go on to college as those in the bottom quarter.[10] The gaps in educational achievement are a major factor in the transmission of inequality. Another study, by Christopher Jencks and his colleagues, found that about 40 percent of the association between male childhood family background and adult occupational status was due to students' educational attainments, after controlling for the effects of IQ test scores. In other words, upper-class graduates receive higher-status jobs than do working-class graduates because the former receive more education and not because of greater innate ability.[11]

Pierre Bourdieu, a French sociologist and leading critic of higher education, has focused on the glaring inequalities in the distribution of wealth and status that persist despite the expansion of educational opportunities for everyone.[12] He is concerned with how inequalities of position endure over generations. Bourdieu argues that individuals use education to maintain their positions of privilege. The educational system has displaced the family, church, and workplace as determinant variables for the transmission of **social stratification**. Since democratic societies originated in a rebellion against privilege, and therefore affirm a belief in the essential equality of individuals, privileged groups cannot openly claim a right to dominating positions. Modern democracies rely on indirect and symbolic forms of power rather than physical coercion to maintain authority. Dominant groups have found that higher education can transmit social inequalities by converting them into academic hierarchies.[13] Several points are stressed in Bourdieu's research. His investigation supports other findings that academic performance of students is highly correlated with parents' cultural background. This further relates to degree of success in the labor market, which hinges on both the *amount* of education received and the academic *prestige* of the institution attended. Ultimately, educational institutions frequently develop their own academic interests and agendas that may differ significantly from those put forth by the existing social order.

Class Conflict Model

Another explanation for the expansion of education in the United States argues that education grows to meet the rising technical skill requirements of jobs. Given this premise, the **class conflict model** claims that employers use education to *screen* workers, although no demonstrable connection exists in most cases between education and job performance. According to this model, formal education developed to meet the growing problems created by industrialization and urbanization in the United States. Rather than meeting objectives like supplying workers with more complex technical skills or reducing social inequality, public education has provided social control by instilling behavior attributes like obedience, discipline, and respect for and compliance with authority.[14] Thus, employers are willing to give a preference to more educated workers in hiring and salary because those workers are more willing to accept traditional corporate values.[15] Thus, education serves to legitimize inequalities rooted in the economic structure of society.

Research by Gregory Squires concluded that the upgrading of the educational requirements related to work cannot be explained in terms of the increasing technical skill requirements of jobs.[16] He points out that the Census Bureau reports that the increasing educational achievements of workers show that educational accomplishments have risen faster than technical skill requirements. He states that there is a misconception that a change from farm laborer to assembly line worker, or from blue collar worker to white collar worker, necessarily represents an increase in skill requirements. Although an assembly line worker may use more sophisticated machinery than the farmer, the assembly line worker is not necessarily a more highly skilled worker.[17] Employers frequently raise the educational specifications of jobs in reaction to an increase in the supply of better-educated workers. And better-educated workers receive the preferred positions within the job structure. With the expansion of schooling, both employers and occupational groups increasingly require formal education as an entry requirement.[18] One result is that individuals have responded by acquiring higher levels of educational achievement to improve their competitive position within the job market, thereby continuing the ever-higher spiral of educational credentials and requirements.

As the gap between the supply and the demand for college graduates continues to increase, competition between them extends further down in the labor market, leaving those with less education with even fewer job opportunities. Thus, the wage gap between those with high school degrees and those with college degrees increases while both groups experience underemployment. More highly educated workers receive higher pay, but it is based on the amount of education rather than the content of learning or the skills required for the job.

Human Capital Theory and Its Limits

Supporters of human capital theory believe that there is a clear relationship between formal education and economic growth at the individual (micro) level and national (macro) level. It also suggests a solution—more education—as a key component to resolving US economic problems. Education is viewed increasingly as a form of economic policy rather than social policy, although the two are not mutually exclusive. Supporters of human capital theory justify an emphasis on education policy to produce the economic drive needed to reverse the declining fortunes of the national economy.

The commitment of the United States to the principles of free trade also means a commitment to competition in the global economy. Jared Bernstein of the Economic Policy Institute agrees that highly educated workers are far more likely to be employed and to be well compensated than those with less education. However, there is little evidence of a shortage of highly skilled US workers; the problem is a lack of jobs. Highly skilled jobs are moving overseas, including jobs for computer software engineers, architects, radiologists, and financial analysts. Such workers are among the most highly educated in our country. Many less-developed countries have been producing a greater number of skilled workers, which results in the exportation of jobs and an erosion of our comparative advantage. This increased supply of skilled workers abroad brings a downward pressure on the earnings of skilled workers at home who have a significant wage advantage over workers with similar skills abroad. Human capital investment theory assumes that, by further educating our most skilled workers, we will justify once again the wage differential in our favor in the global labor market with even more workers with still higher skills than were previously available.[19] But since these workers are already among the most skilled workers in the country, they would require education beyond anything now contemplated. Bernstein concludes that, although the educational system has problems, the "problems do not stem from a national lack of quality, but rather from inequities in the distribution of that quality."[20]

Case Study: Education as Market Signaling

Human capital theory suggests that college graduates should receive an increased income that at least compensates them for their extra investment in education. It assumes that students acquire skills as they successfully complete high school, and gain even more skills improving their productivity as they invest in a college education.

Other social scientists challenge this view of how education raises income. One view claims that the educational process teaches students little in the way of relevant knowledge or skills for subsequent job performance. Rather, the educational system *sorts* people according to ability. Supporters of this view claim that competencies like perseverance, intelligence, and self-discipline are needed to succeed in college and also correlate with success in the labor force. A college degree indicates to employers that the individual is a high-quality worker who can be trained easily, thus lowering productivity costs. Employers are therefore willing to pay a differential to more highly educated workers because they will be more productive on average.

Academic credentials thus provide a mechanism by which better-educated workers may separate themselves from those with less education. Suppose the labor force is divided equally between low- and high-skilled workers: a low-skilled worker has a marginal revenue product (MRP) (the additional revenue when the firm uses an additional unit of input) of $300 per week, and a high-skilled worker has an MRP of $500 per week.

If an employer cannot be sure whether a new worker has the qualities of a high- or low-quality worker when first hired, the wage will be based on the *anticipated* MRP. Thus, the firm will calculate that a new hire has a 50 percent chance of being a high-quality worker and a 50 percent chance of being a low-quality worker, and pay a wage based on the expected MRP of $400 ([0.50 × $300] + [0.50 × $500] = $400).

Because firms pay the average MRP, low-quality workers are better off, since they receive $400 rather than $300, while high-quality workers are worse off, since they receive $400 rather than $500. High-quality workers would like to signal to the firm that they possess the characteristics associated with high productivity in the labor force. The educational system provides the means for them to signal the firm in a way that low-quality workers would be unable to do. Employers are aware of the correlation and screen workers based on their education. Although education by itself does not increase a worker's productivity, it signals to the employer the probable possession of other qualities that improve productivity. Signaling does not change the *average* wage, but only its distribution. It has a positive effect on the income of the more highly educated workers, and a negative effect on the incomes of those less educated.

A more radical view holds that the wealthy are able to buy the best education regardless of ability. Education thus sorts people according to social class, not ability. In this way, education is a device by which the privileged members of society are able to pass on their favored position to their already privileged successors while providing the appearance of legitimacy for higher wages. In this model, education does not enhance ability, but does cultivate noncognitive traits like discipline, respect, obedience, and acceptance that are valued in the business culture.

Source: A. Michael Spence, "Market Signaling: Informational Transfer in Hiring and Related Screening Processes," in *Harvard Economic Studies,* vol. 143 (Cambridge: Harvard University Press, 1974).

Current Administration Goals

President Obama has made clear that he intends to expand the role of the federal government in providing direction in education policy. He places more of an emphasis on education policy as a national priority than has any previous president. He has indicated that he intends to pressure states to raise their educational standards, and will embarrass those states that fail to make improvements. He plans to use a $100 billion education stimulus fund to bring about the changes he envisions.

Obama has made his belief clear that education was underfunded at all levels during the years of the G. W. Bush presidency, and that he intends to use his political clout to increase funding for education. He has also indicated a willingness to make his case for reform before the voters and not be limited to working only with interest groups inside the Washington beltway. The president is very critical of the variation of standards between states, for example, standardized tests that show fourth-grade readers in Mississippi score 70 points lower than students in Wyoming, but the students receive the same grade. He has pointed out that several states have standards so low that students are on par with the bottom 40 percent of students around the globe. President Obama and Arne Duncan, secretary of education, have made it clear that states accepting money will have to create data collection systems and monitor how students are performing over time. Obama expects Congress to incorporate these reforms in the upcoming reauthorization of the No Child Left Behind (NCLB) Act of 2001.

Obama is the first president to suggest major government involvement in early childhood (e.g., prekindergarten) education. Research shows that learning begins in infancy, long before formal education begins. Early experiences and accomplishments can lay the foundation for developing skills for future learning, behavior, and success. Recent analysis of an ongoing Chicago early childhood education program for disadvantaged families, now over twenty years old, found that every dollar invested resulted in a $7 to $10 return to society or to the participant.[21] Savings resulted from a decreased need for remediation services in school, higher graduation and employment rates, less crime, and less use of the public welfare system as well as improved health. This is the only study of a sustained public school program that goes into adulthood. It is doubtful that, if the program was expanded to middle-class families in universal preschool programs, such a high return on investment would be expected.

Over 1 million three- and four-year-olds currently attend public preschool (i.e., prekindergarten) programs in the United States, but twelve states still do not have publicly financed programs while twenty-five states devote no funding whatsoever for children younger than age four.[22] Most of the children who do not attend government-financed preschool are from middle-class families that cannot afford expensive private preschools. In those states that do have preschool programs, they tend to be welfare programs for the poor. Obama's Zero to Five Plan will provide critical support to *all* young children and their parents by emphasizing early care and education for infants to prepare them for kindergarten. It will help states move toward voluntary, universal preschool. The plan includes an increase in Early Head Start and Head Start funding.

Providing universal access to programs for four-year-olds is intended to level the playing field for all children in the year before they enter kindergarten. Considerable research has explored the differences that make some prekindergarten programs highly effective in producing significant benefits to participants while others do not. The program is most critical to low-income families, but should be open to all children, which will broaden political support. Qualified teachers are critical to the success of developing validated interactive curriculums and classroom strategies that contribute most to child development. Successful programs have also stressed that teachers should spend a substantial amount of time with parents, educating them about their child's development and how they can extend the learning experiences into their homes.[23]

The Elementary and Secondary Education Act (ESEA) was first enacted in 1965 as a component of the War on Poverty. The original ESEA program was designed to offset the inequality of per pupil spending within states, even though there is a greater inequality in the per pupil expenditures between rich and poor states. It was the first program to provide significant federal funds targeted toward the educationally disadvantaged children from kindergarten through twelfth grade. The act was originally authorized through 1970, but it has been reauthorized a total of eight times as of 2009. The basic purpose of the law—to assist disadvantaged students—remains. The act, which is the central federal law in precollegiate education, has funded: Head Start, Native American education, bilingual education, class-size reduction, and education technology.

President G. W. Bush reauthorized the ESEA, now renamed NCLB, in January 2002. The NCLB law expanded the federal role in education by requiring states to demonstrate achievement by putting accountability systems in place to cover all public schools and students. These systems basically require states to administer standardized tests in reading and mathematics for all students in grades three through eight. Students in high school must be ranked as either: advanced, proficient, basic, or below basic. Under the law, all students must be "proficient" in reading and math by the 2013–2014 academic year. Schools that fail to make adequate annual progress toward statewide proficiency goals will be subject to corrective action and restructuring. There are penalties for failing schools (including being closed), and teachers whose students fail to achieve the standards. NCLB contains only sticks, no carrots. The problem is that some schools that are deemed to be failing in one state would get passing grades in another.

Another widespread criticism of NCLB points out that teachers often feel pressure to spend the academic year preparing students to take the standardized tests. The result is that schools achieve inflated test scores at the expense of classroom curriculums. Or as Harvard researcher Daniel M. Koretz noted, the nation's K–12 students seem to be attending Lake Wobegon schools where all the children are above average.[24]

The centerpiece of the NCLB law is that it gives children who are attending failing schools the opportunity to attend public schools, within the local area, that have attained acceptable standards, which may include charter schools.

While national standards would allow teachers to know how the achievement of their students compares with the rest of the country, some question the fairness of requiring all students to meet national standards if some attend underfunded schools. As Secretary Duncan points out, applying national standards will "force the conversation about funding inequities that we skirt now."[25] NCLB does appear to stimulate achievement gains by low-performing students, but many teachers feel that too often getting underachieving students to "proficiency" has become so central to classroom activity that the needs of advanced students have been neglected. They point out that there is also an obvious connection between the needs of advanced students and national competitiveness.[26]

The Obama administration supports the goal of NCLB to ensure that all high school graduates can meet high standards. One goal is to establish clear and well-defined standards at the national level if possible. The president and his secretary of education maintain that the law tries to force teachers and schools to accomplish those goals without providing the necessary resources.

School-Centered Analysis:
Choice and Innovative Schools Programs

There are few ideas that provoke more controversy in US education than school choice. Choice became a controversial topic in 1990 when John Chubb and Terry Moe of the Brookings Institution published their research titled *Politics, Markets, and America's Schools*.[27] Their research challenged the premise that a major reason disadvantaged students receive less education is because they go to inferior schools. In contrast, middle- and upper-income students attend schools having substantially more resources and more experienced teachers and, therefore, receive a better education. This explanation has an appealing inherent logic.

Researchers began in the 1960s to investigate schools commonly considered effective and compared them, where possible, with schools commonly regarded as ineffective. This approach provided insight into the critical performance factors within the larger population of schools. By the late 1970s and early 1980s, a number of studies reached the inescapable conclusion that school organization does have an important impact on learning.

Interestingly, one of the major arguments in favor of the significance of school organization on the learning process came from the late James Coleman. In their study, Coleman and his colleagues at the University of Chicago used the High School and

Beyond data set to conduct a comparative study of public, parochial, and private schools.[28] They concluded that parochial school students generally received the highest scores on achievement tests, followed by private school students and then public school students. This finding remained constant even when background characteristics of students, such as family income or parental education, were controlled. The study also found that parochial schools, primarily those serving inner city racial minorities, were more integrated than public schools.[29] Parochial and private schools on average did a better job of educating the typical student than public schools. The superior performance seems clearest in inner city settings, where lower-income students have fewer options. Coleman recognized the difficulty of separating the performance of these schools from the selection decision. That is, attending public school is an option but, because parents of some students invest additional resources for a private or parochial school, students who attend the latter schools are different from public school students with otherwise identical characteristics. When the selection issue is taken into account, various studies conclude that there is still an advantage from attending parochial schools, but not for attending elite private schools.[30] Coleman and his colleagues established an important theoretical point that schools matter.

"Effective schools research," as studies of school organization came to be called, generated considerable debate for its indictment of the public school system in general and for its policy recommendations. The recommendations included providing children with vouchers that would permit them to attend the school of their choice—public, private, or parochial. The educational establishment, led by teachers' unions, warned that vouchers would result in the destruction of public education since, if given an alternative, most parents would not choose to send their children to a public school. Some critics warned of the skimming effect in which better students would use vouchers to attend private or parochial schools, leaving the poor to remain in underfunded public schools. Other critics charged that it would violate a constitutional argument requiring the separation of church and state.

These policy debates continue to be heard today, but they are no longer central. The Supreme Court has defined standards that permit government to provide vouchers for parents to send their children to parochial schools. Public school choice programs in a variety of possibilities, usually based on economic need, now exist in a majority of states.

The new alternatives are based on the implication from the research that suggests that it should be possible to generalize those structural features of mainly parochial and private schools, but also many public schools as well, that influence teacher behavior and expectations and affect student success. Researchers then isolated those factors that differentiate such atypically effective schools. Comparing "effective schools" with those commonly regarded as "ineffective" also provides insight into the general elements of effectiveness within the educational system.

Effective schools, these studies have concluded, are characterized by several ingredients that conventional wisdom has all along suggested to be important:

- *Clear school goals.* Effective schools have clear goals and a strong principal or school-based leadership. In other words, schools should have a mission rather than operate from force of habit.
- *School autonomy.* Effective schools are free from extensive outside bureaucratic controls.
- *High expectations.* Effective schools have high expectations for student performance, from teachers as well as principals.
- *Vigorous leadership and involvement.* In effective schools, the principal plays a leading role in the instructional program.
- *Rigorous academic standards.* Effective schools employ teachers with high expectations for students—that they become good readers, graduate from high school, go to college, and become good citizens.
- *Professionalism among the teachers.* In effective schools, teachers spend their time actually teaching and monitoring their students, and providing feedback to them. Teachers rely on tests they have developed in judging student achievement.
- *Experimentation and adaptation.* In effective schools, principals and teachers are able to experiment and adapt techniques and procedures in response to the circumstances encountered.

The research on effective schools came at a time when dissatisfaction with the educational system reached a critical level. It is consistent with the views of those who suggest a "back-to-basics" approach that accentuates order and discipline, emphasizing basic skills, more testing to measure progress, and higher educational standards. Coleman and others found in their research that Catholic parochial schools tend to be more effective and provide a significantly better education than public schools, due to their focus on just such aspects of education.[31]

Effective schools research revealed several unexpected aspects of parochial and private school education. In the private education sector, the formal right to control a school is vested with a church, a corporation, or a nonprofit agency that has the legal right to make all the educational decisions. In the public education sector, different interests struggle over educational decisions. Ironically though, a basic market or "choice" principle gives parents and students a more influential role in private sector schools than in the public educational system. Those who run private or parochial schools have a strong motivation to please their clientele because they know that, if parents do not like the educational services their children receive, they can switch. This is invariably a strong possibility, since the low-cost public school system is always an alternative. Moreover, private sector schools that cannot attract a clientele of sufficient size must be able to pass along the higher per pupil charges to the families of the students they are able to attract or to their sponsoring organizations. Otherwise, they will go out of business.[32] This provides a strong financial motivator to be responsive to parents and provide a good education.

Chubb and Moe concluded that the low cost of public schools permits them to attract students without being particularly good at teaching them. The major disincentive to leaving is that public education has a very low out-of-pocket cost. Therefore, private or parochial schools must be far superior to public schools to attract students.

Public school systems will be directed to

> pursue academic excellence, but without making courses too difficult; they will be directed to teach history, but without making any value judgments; they will be directed to teach sex education, but without taking a stand on contraception or abortion. They must make everyone happy by being all things to all people—just as politicians try to do.[33]

The winning coalition inevitably sets up a bureaucratic arrangement to force compliance on the losers and to ensure against the risks of future defeat by opponents who would like to impose their own rules. Bureaucratic control means that teacher behavior will be regulated in minute detail, and through enforcement procedures set up by the winners that permit verification of teacher compliance with rules and standards.

Blaming the public education bureaucracy for educational problems is to misunderstand the nature of the problem. It is true that bureaucrats are rewarded for devising rules and regulations and setting standards based on policies and programs defined in the past. But the bureaucrats are put in place by the victors of the political struggle to enforce compliance with their vision of what education should be. Not to put bureaucrats in place would result in an uncertain political victory and an inability by the victors to enforce their terms.

Neither are teachers to blame for problems in public education. Good teaching consists of skilled operations that are extremely difficult to measure in formal bureaucratic assessments. Educational output results from the interaction between a teacher and a student. This is the primary relationship in education. Professionalism requires that teachers have the freedom to exercise their judgment in applying their knowledge and teaching skills to the specific students and circumstances they encounter. When the system is bureaucratized, the most important relationship for the teacher is with the supervisor, not the student. Increasing bureaucratic regulations and reporting standards guarantee that teacher discretion will be reduced and initiative stifled.[34]

Chubb and Moe's conclusions have been supported and reinforced by the more recent research findings of Anthony Bryk and his colleagues, as reported in their work *Catholic Schools for the Common Good*.[35] Their most significant finding is that Catholic schools have been particularly effective in educating inner city minority students with profiles very similar to those associated with failing public schools. These parochial schools are typically more racially integrated and operate at a per capita cost of between 50 percent and 60 percent of public schools.

School Choice and Vouchers

Chubb and Moe's research resulted in a national movement in support of vouchers. The implication of the effective schools research is that policy alternatives need to be implemented that will move the educational system in the direction of decentralized educational "markets." Public schools would be forced to compete with other private and parochial schools. Advocates argue that this would give parents more choice in selecting schools for their children and force schools to compete for financial support that would come through parental choice. As a necessary component of choice, proponents point out, schools must be given greater autonomy in deciding their academic programs, principal, and staff, and how to compete for students. Thus, they would resemble private and parochial schools more closely. The projected benefits would be a public education guided more by markets and, therefore, it would be less prone to the debilitating effects of excessive bureaucratic controls. More competition would reward clear goals and efficiency. Finally, proponents argue, the choice exercised by the consumers of education—parents and students—should foster more positive and cooperative affiliations between parents, students, and the school.[36]

The firestorm of controversy generated by these studies demonstrates that education is not an issue that neatly divides liberals and conservatives. Much of the subsequent literature is subordinate to ideological considerations and has not been particularly scientific.[37]

Chubb and Moe's research led them to conclude that Americans think that having good public education is worthwhile, and they are reasonably satisfied that their local school system is performing well. However, many Americans, especially supporters of vouchers, also think that private and parochial schools are better than public schools in terms of relative performance. Further, they think that the education system tends to be inequitable and that parents do not have enough influence. They also believe that many schools are too big and that, generally, they do poorly in teaching moral values.

On the other hand, some critics of vouchers are fearful that they have the greatest appeal to the affluent and that, if adopted, there would be an exodus of advantaged students from the public system, which would exacerbate the existing social biases of the schools. There is a legitimate fear that "elitists" want to separate themselves from lower classes. Chubb and Moe's research found evidence that parents think primarily about finding a good school for their children, and not about race or elitism. In fact, choice has the greatest appeal to parents who are low-income and minority (especially blacks and Hispanics), and who reside in disadvantaged school districts.

Supporters argue that vouchers would be a better system, especially for poor children most in need of choice. As they see it, this would give the disadvantaged more of the choices that the affluent already have, which appears inherently democratic. With affluence comes the ability to buy homes in the preferred public school district or to opt for private school alternatives. The affluent have also been able to press for the best principals, teachers, and facilities. It is only equitable to provide an open enrollment plan (market oriented) to give disadvantaged families the same market power to choose that the affluent have always had. Currently, the poor have little choice.

Another concern frequently expressed is how to prevent the affluent from using the recommendations for vouchers to divert more resources to the affluent. The contention is that the NCLB law applies *testing* not only to students, but also to schools. Schools can "fail" just as students can. Failing schools are overwhelmingly in poor districts with the attendant funding and student problems. Failing schools would be "punished" by cuts to their funding, which would make it more difficult for them to improve, and many would face elimination. The failing public schools would be replaced by a voucher system that would be insufficient to provide payment to good private schools. But the wealthy could convert a voucher to be used as a portion of the tuition payment in a private school, reducing the cost of the private school by the monetary value of the voucher.

Low-income families would not be able to pay the difference between the value of their voucher and the tuition costs of elite academies. Legislators in Wisconsin provided one solution to the problem by limiting eligibility for state vouchers to families whose income did not exceed 175 percent of the federal poverty level. Means-testing the program does eliminate a concern over the wealthy taking advantage of the system to subsidize their leaving the public educational system. Another proposal to thwart the affluent using the voucher as a tax deduction would be to require the receiving school to accept the voucher as "payment in full," which would eliminate affluent private schools while still permitting some parochial schools to take part.

Charter Schools

Another option chosen by some states to avoid the public-private debate was the creation of charter schools. **Charter schools** may be elementary or secondary schools that receive public funding, but are exempted from some of the rules and regulations that apply to other public schools. In exchange for their regulatory autonomy, the schools provide a "charter" with their mission statement, academic goals, and an accountability statement regarding meeting their goals. Charter schools may not charge tuition since they are part of the public education system. With their greater autonomy, charter schools are seen as a way to provide the choice and innovation found in the effective schools research pioneered by Chubb and Moe. Many charter schools are, in fact, run by private companies in a clear salute to the notion of a more responsive market model.

The first charter school law was passed by Minnesota in 1991. By 2009, forty states and the District of Columbia had charter school laws. Many charter schools were launched with much fanfare and commitments that their students would soon outperform regular public schools. But the data collected over several years show decidedly mixed results. A number of studies have found that charter students were on average no better off than their public school cohorts.[38] Several charter schools went bankrupt during the academic year, leaving many students temporarily stranded.[39] Other charter schools performed at a lower level than the local public schools.[40] Still other studies have found that charter schools actually increase racial segregation.[41] Nevertheless, some charter schools have been successful in raising the rate of college enrollment above that of traditional high schools.

President Obama has called for an expansion of funding only for states that improve accountability for charter schools and are willing to close down underperforming charter schools. The administration has indicated a readiness to help the successful charter schools expand and serve more students. Secretary Duncan has said that the federal government will use the stimulus funding to target the local school systems and nonprofit organizations willing to adopt policies that have proven to work. Thus, the stimulus funds would be directed at regular public as well as charter schools to prevent teacher layoffs, overhaul aging schools, and educate lower-income children. Duncan pointed specifically to "longer school days" instituted by some schools as essential to help struggling students make up lost ground.[42]

Leaving Children Behind: The Dropout Crisis

Policy concern over high school dropouts stems primarily from the importance of having an educated work force. Throughout most of the twentieth century, there was a clear trend of each new cohort of individuals being more likely to graduate from high school than the preceding one. Higher graduation rates were reflected in increased worker productivity and healthy national economic growth. Thus, it is surprising that the high school dropout rate is rising while proportionately more high school graduates are attending college and graduating than ever before.[43] This is contributing to the increasing polarization of the US society.

Technological advances have increased the demand for skilled labor to the point that a high school education is increasingly a minimum requirement to enter the work force. Students who drop out of school before completing their high school education exact a high cost on themselves and US society. Higher rates of unemployment and growing income differentials between high school dropouts and graduates have increased the economic incentives to graduate from high school. The real wages of high school dropouts have declined over the past thirty years while those of more skilled workers have risen.

The average annual income of male dropouts is approximately 65 percent of the income of male high school graduates ($24,072 vs. $37,356 in 2009).[44] Women who drop out of high school are more likely to become pregnant at an early age, and to become a single parent.[45] They are also more likely to receive public assistance. Half of all families on welfare are headed by high school dropouts.[46] The stress and frustration associated with dropping out mean an increased risk of turning to crime for financial support; dropouts account for about half the prison population and over half of death row inmates.[47]

For all these reasons, graduation rates are an important indicator of the performance of the school system. For years, it was known that different states used different criteria for defining a "dropout." For example, New Mexico defined its dropout rate as the percentage of twelfth graders who did not received a diploma, which grossly undercounted dropouts by ignoring all students who left before the twelfth grade.[48] Many school districts have an interest in underreporting dropout rates in order to receive matching funds from the state. For instance, since many states match the local funds raised for a school district, school districts may keep students who drop out because of a pregnancy or incarceration on the school rolls if they do not formally withdraw. In this way, they are eligible to receive matching state grant money for each student "enrolled" in the district's schools.

The most significant source of bias in the official statistics of graduation rates comes from including General Educational Development (GED) recipients as high school graduates. GEDs are dropouts who pass an exam to certify as the equivalent of an ordinary graduate. Several studies summarized in Heckman and LaFontaine[49] show that the GED certificate does not benefit most recipients, and that GEDs perform at the level of dropouts in the US labor market. The inclusion of GEDs as high school graduates results in an upward bias of 7 percent to 8 percent in high school graduation rates.

Some states used an inflated graduation rate for federal reporting requirements under NCLB and a different one within the state. Also, states routinely reported graduation rates of 88 percent to 90 percent to avoid the embarrassment of reporting how far their state educational system lagged behind others.

The National Governors Association made a concerted effort to persuade states to voluntarily agree to use common measures of dropping out in 2005. Graduation was defined as on-time with a regular diploma. Its findings are discouraging. Nationally, only about 70 percent of students entering the ninth grade graduate with a diploma in four years.[50] African American and Latino students are significantly more likely to drop out than white students.

The Obama plan announced in 2009 is consistent with his proposals during the campaign. He proposes to provide funding to school districts to invest in intervention strategies in middle school. The strategies include teaching teams, mentoring, intensive reading and math instruction, requiring parental involvement, extending learning time at school each day, and lengthening the academic year. The plan also proposes funding for students in need of extra instruction after regular school hours. He has noted that the typical school day is a throwback to an earlier agricultural era, and is not on par with most other developed countries around the world.

Some policymakers note that the difficulty of keeping more students in school until they graduate while also raising school standards may constitute a "mission impossible."[51] Higher standards usually do not come with funding for remedial programs. Increasing the number of required courses and upgrading course content may result in teachers adding units to a course, but allowing less time to aid students who are falling behind. There are many programs with substantial funding to promote "excellence" in education, but few that take "equity" into account, which may be essential in helping potential dropouts to remain in school.

Students drop out of school for reasons that are largely unchanged over several decades. In the High School and Beyond study, researchers found that the most often cited reason for leaving school was poor academic performance. High-risk students frequently find school to be a hostile environment where they are confirmed as failures daily. School agendas prize uniformity, harmony, regulation, and intellectual competition. These behaviors are often especially difficult for high-risk students. Their rebellion against those behaviors leads to truancy or other forms of misconduct within school that can lead to suspension. They are more likely to report that they are not popular with their classmates, are less likely to take part in extracurricular activities, and feel estranged from school life. Boys who are older than average for their grade (who tend to have repeated a grade at least once) and racial and ethnic minorities (other than Asian Americans) are more likely to experience disciplinary problems and become dropouts. Dropouts by and large are capable of doing the academic work; however, though they are inclined to be underachievers, the High School and Beyond survey found that their tested achievement levels were seven to twelve percentiles higher than their grades.

A variety of programs have been developed to increase pupil retention. First, programs should address those school practices that discourage high-risk students and substitute practices and arrangements that encourage them to remain in school until graduation. Recommendations of several studies include the following.

1. *Higher requirements should be accompanied with support for low-achieving students.* Higher standards without additional assistance for those with lower aptitudes and achievement will reinforce their sense of failure and negative views of school.

2. *Promotion policies.* The dropout rate among students who have repeated a grade is more than double that of those who have not been held back. This connection begins as early as the first grade. Research shows that holding a child back a grade in elemen-

tary school is less cost effective than providing the special services that the student needs to perform at the grade level. Several states are instituting standardized tests to determine competence for promotion and graduation. If such programs are implemented without remedial programs, they may simply divide "winners" and "losers" without identifying where help is needed. Retaining a student without remedial help is a form of punishment.

3. *School and class size.* The larger the school and its classes, the more problems are reported by both teachers and students with the quality of teaching. Teacher workloads are increased with overcrowded classrooms, making it difficult to provide individual attention or remedial help with learning difficulties. Students experiencing problems in overcrowded classrooms find teachers less accessible, increasing their feelings of frustration and alienation. The greatest overcrowding occurs in poorer school districts where there is insufficient funding to provide extra classroom space or hire the additional teachers needed. Obama's plan specifically supports transitional bilingual education.

4. *Lack of support for minorities.* Many ethnic minority students, primarily Hispanics, underachieve because they attend schools that do not provide sufficient bilingual education. Few Hispanic children with limited English proficiency, even in areas where they make up the majority of the class, are placed in a bilingual program. Obama's plan specifically supports transitional bilingual education.

5. *Work-study programs.* Schools should develop programs to provide relevant work experiences for students who are faced with the necessity of helping to provide a family income.

Growing up in poverty does not determine school failure. But when the difficulties of deprivation are not alleviated by the dedication of substantial resources and the commitment of concerned adults, it is extremely difficult to succeed. There is little help in many poor rural communities and inner city schools.

Expand College Enrollment and Affordability

In a speech during his campaign for the White House, President Obama said: "Every American has the right to pursue their dreams. But we also have the responsibility to make sure that our children can reach a little further and rise a little higher than we did."[52] To exceed the level of their parents suggests that today's students will have to be more educated than their parents. Secretary Duncan said: "Just having students graduate from high school can't be our goal. We're working to change the culture of expectations."[53] This policy also supports the goal of having a more productive and innovative work force than our competitors in the global economy of the twenty-first century.

One specific educational goal of the administration is to restore US leadership in higher education. Our competitiveness in a global work force depends on expanding the opportunity of higher education for more US students. The United States ranks seventh in terms of the percentage of eighteen- to twenty-four-year-olds enrolled in college, but only fifteenth in terms of the number of certificates and degrees awarded.[54]

To improve on the numbers of high school graduates going to college, several things have to happen. Public high school graduation rates vary between states from New Jersey that graduates about 90 percent of its students to a low of South Carolina that graduates less than 55 percent. Nevertheless across the nation, public high school graduation rates have remained fairly flat at about 65 percent to 68 percent over the past few decades. Nationally, the percentage of all high school graduates who graduated with the skills and qualifications necessary to attend a minimally selective college has risen about 10 percent in the past fifteen years to around 35 percent. Relatively flat graduation rates and improving college readiness rates probably reflects higher standards over the past fifteen years, which forced students to take more courses required for college admission without more marginal students dropping out. In fact, there is not a large gap between the number of high school graduates who are college ready and the number that enroll for the first time. Many states have requirements for receiving a high school diploma that are below the minimum standards required to attend the state's public colleges. Further improvement in the college attendance rate must include a continued emphasis on providing more support for students needing remedial help to improve high school graduation rates. Standards for graduation must be simultaneously raised to make the diploma more meaningful and raise the percentage of high school graduates who are eligible for admission into college.

Another obvious barrier to college for many high school graduates is the soaring cost of college. Nationally, college tuition and fees have gone up over 400 percent in the past twenty-five years, almost double the increase in medical costs over the same period.[55] The affordability problem is exacerbated by the failure of federal grants to keep up with inflation. The president proposes restoring the buying power of the Pell Grant for the country's neediest students and guaranteeing an annual increase tied to inflation.

In economic downturns, state governments cut back on aid to colleges, forcing colleges to raise tuition. As a result, many students have savings and assistance that may get them through one or perhaps two years of college before they are financially exhausted and drop out. The percentage of students at four-year colleges has actually declined so that less than half typically graduate. Just 54 percent of students entering four-year colleges in 1997 had a degree six years later, and that figure is lower for minorities.[56] The percentage of students graduating from more elite private institutions is actually much higher, suggesting that money is less of an issue for those attending more expensive private colleges from more affluent families.

President Obama has proposed creating a national Make College a Reality initiative with a goal of increasing students taking Advanced Placement (AP) or college-level classes nationwide by 50 percent by 2016. He also has proposed providing federal grants for students seeking college-level credit at community colleges if their school does not provide those resources. His plan will invest in community colleges to conduct an analysis of high-demand skills and technical education, and shape new degree programs for emerging industries.

The administration also supports outreach programs, like Upward Bound to encourage more young people from low-income families to consider and prepare for college. Upward Bound aids high school students from low-income families and students from families in which neither parent holds a bachelor's degree. The goal is to increase the rate at which participants complete high school. and enroll in and graduate from postsecondary institutions. Upward Bound projects must provide instruction in math, laboratory sciences, composition, literature, and languages. The program may also provide assistance in preparing for college entrance exams, help in completing financial aid applications, and personal counseling.

Also in this regard, the administration wants to make college more affordable for all Americans by creating a new American Opportunity Tax Credit, which will ensure that the first $4,000 of a college education is free. Recipients of the credit would be required to conduct community service to receive the credit. Finally, in his effort to make college more affordable, the president has proposed a major change in the way that the federal government provides student loans. He has proposed that all federal loans should revert to the original method of the government lending directly to students, cutting out the middlemen banks. That is the way the program began with the Higher Education Act of 1965. In the Republican effort to "privatize" federal loans, the government guaranteed that banks would not lose money on student defaults. Banks then made money by simply putting their name on the loan. This amounted to a welfare handout to the banks that the government was already subsidizing in various other ways. Under President Bill Clinton, the direct lending program was reinstituted on a small basis compared to the privatized program. The 1994 Republican Contract with America targeted the direct loan program for elimination. Universities complained that direct loans were more efficient at getting money where it was needed than the more cumbersome, middleman-operated loan apparatus. President Obama is proposing to restructure the loan program by ending wasteful subsidies to banks under the Federal Family Education Loan (FFEL) program and redirecting billions in savings toward student aid. There will be opposition to this proposal in Congress as many Republicans are ideologically committed to "privatization," and many Blue Dog Democrats have been courted by financial institutions interested in maintaining their profitable risk-free middleman status.[57]

Fairer Pay for Teachers

The president has also raised the central issue of the importance of recruiting, retaining, and rewarding teachers. He said: "We know that from the moment our children step into a classroom, the single most important factor in determining their achievement is not the color of their skin or where they come from; it's not who their parents are or how much money they have. It's who their teacher is."[58]

The point is that teachers play a crucial role in student achievement, but the teaching profession is beset with many problems. Teachers often have rather different levels of preparation. Most teachers receive low pay, and have demanding working conditions. This leads to high turnover and difficulties in hiring highly qualified teachers in some schools and subjects. Since teachers are the single most important resource in a child's learning, we must attract and keep competent and effective teachers.

Obama plans to create new Teacher Service Scholarships that will cover four years of undergraduate or two years of graduate teacher education. In addition, he proposes alternative programs for midcareer recruits in exchange for teaching at least four years in a high-need field (primarily, science and math) or in a location with a high need. He would upgrade the preparation of teacher training by requiring all schools of education to be accredited. He has called for incentive pay for teachers who work in shortage areas like math and science, and merit pay for teachers who are shown to produce significant achievement gains over time. Conversely, he has called for developing processes for removing ineffective teachers from the class.

One of Obama's more interesting and controversial proposals is to reward teachers "with more money for improved student achievement."[59] He proposes a method to give successful teachers a salary increase and also have those teachers serve as mentors to new teachers. Teachers' salaries in general should be raised as he proposes lengthening the school day and the school year. Incentive pay for teachers who work in shortage areas like science and math or inner city schools would be in addition to an enhanced pay schedule. So would the incentive pay for those who consistently raise student achievement scores.

These may prove to be contentious issues to get through state legislatures as teachers' unions generally oppose linking pay to specific measures of performance like raising test scores. And teacher unions hold considerable sway with Democrats at the state level.

Conclusion

Most modern societies spell out the right to education in their constitutions. However, education is not mentioned in the US Constitution, which was drafted in 1787 when formal education was a rarity and not perceived as critical to society or its citizens. This was because, in an economy based on tradition, production techniques changed at a glacial pace, and the needed knowledge and skills were passed from one generation to the next through apprenticeships and work experience. Thomas Jefferson, however, believed that a democratic form of government (as opposed to monarchies) required an educated citizenry. He famously wrote that, "if a nation expects to be ignorant and free, in a state of civilization, it expects what never was and never will be."[60]

Jefferson was so concerned about the political necessity of an educated electorate that he submitted an amendment to the Constitution in 1806 to provide federal support for education. Jefferson believed that education would equalize the differences in wealth and circumstances so that individuals could progress according to their abilities. His proposed amendment was never seriously considered. As a result, states and local governments took primary responsibility for public education in the nineteenth century.

Education is a quasi-public good, however, and the development of human capital has made it increasingly important for the federal government to be involved. It has only been in the post–World War II period that the federal government has become involved in public education at the precollegiate level. For many years, the federal government's involvement was limited to influencing state policy through the carrot of financial assistance. The result was that education policy was never a major aspect of national policy. The Department of Education as a cabinet-level department was signed into law by President Jimmy Carter in October 1979 and began operating in May 1980. Ronald Reagan campaigned in 1980 on the platform of abolishing the Department of Education since he maintained that education was not a question for national policy. Education policy has frequently been limited to matters of symbolic politics.

More recent studies in education have focused on the factors that affect learning. School-centered approaches are the primary focus of effective schools research, which suggests that decentralized systems that encourage market competition are strongly correlated with effectiveness in educational achievement.

The US model is decidedly unlike the systems in many other countries, where education is a function of national governments based on more recently drafted constitutions. Students from many OECD and Asian countries with more national dominance in public education have outperformed US students on standardized international tests. President Obama has seized on lagging US test scores and a weakening economy to increase the federal government's role in education policy as necessary to compete in a global society. His policy goals, if enacted, will revolutionize the federal government's role in education policy. He proposes sweeping changes from prekindergarten through college.

Questions for Discussion

1. Does the economy grow because of its investment in human resources, or does it invest in education because it is growing and can afford it?

2. Acquiring high levels of education was assumed to guarantee job security. What evidence is there that this may no longer be as valid as in the past? Does that mean that investment in education is no longer as valuable as in previous years?

3. What is the concept of human capital investment? In what ways can education and training be considered investment? In what ways can they be considered consumption?

4. Should parents be able to apply school vouchers to public schools only, or should they be able to use them for private or parochial schools as well? What are the arguments for and against their use in public schools, let alone private or parochial schools?

5. How could we provide for equality in public education? Is there a realistic chance of resolving the issue?

Useful Websites

American Association for Higher Education, www.aahe.org.
American Federation of Teachers, www.aft.org.
Center for Education Reform, www.edreform.com.
Children's Defense Fund, www.childrensdefense.org.
Democratic Committee on Education and the Workforce,
    http://edworkforce.house.gov/democrats.
Education Policy Analysis Archives, http://epaa.asu.edu.
Educational Resources Information Center, www.ericsp.org.
Educause, www.educause.edu.
House Committee on Education and the Workforce, http://edworkforce.house.gov.
National Center for Education Statistics, www.nces.ed.gov.
National Center for Public Policy and Higher Education, www.highereducation.org.
National Education Association, www.nea.org.
US Department of Education, www.ed.gov.

Notes

1. See Patrick Gonzales et al., "Highlights from TIMSS 2007: Mathematics and Science Achievement of US Fourth- and Eighth-Grade Students in an International Context," no. 2009-001 (Washington, DC: US Department of Education, National Center for Education Statistics, December 2008).

2. Eighth graders from Singapore, Taiwan, Japan, Korea, the United Kingdom, Hungary, the Czech Republic, and the Russian Federation generally scored significantly above US eighth graders.

3. President Barack Obama, speech at Flint, Michigan, June 16, 2008. Quoted in *The Obama Education Plan: An Education Week Guide* (San Francisco: Jossey-Bass, 2009), p. 1.

4. Kevin J. Dougherty and Floyd M. Hammack, *Education and Society* (New York: Harcourt Brace Jovanovich, 1990), pp. 13–14.

5. Adam Smith, *The Wealth of Nations,* edited by Edward Cannon (New York: G. P. Putnam's Sons, 1877), bk. 2, chap. 1, p. 377. Smith did not develop this idea beyond the statement quoted. Theodore Schultz and Gary Becker are usually given credit for developing human capital theory. See Theodore W. Schultz, "Investment in Human Capital," *American Economic Review* 51 (March 1961): 1–17; and Gary Becker, *Human Capital* (New York: National Bureau of Economic Research, 1964).

6. Roe J. Johns, Edgar L. Morphet, and Kern Alexander, "Human Capital and the Economic Benefits of Education," in Dougherty and Hammack, *Education and Society,* pp. 534–535.

7. Many look on their school days, especially college, as the most rewarding years of their lives. Therefore, if half the cost of education is assigned to consumption, then the benefits derived, compared to investment, would be doubled. The share assigned to consumption and investment might vary with the focus of the education. Vocational training, on-the-job apprenticeships, work-study and other programs, and training for a particular job may have less consumption and more investment aspects. On the other hand, the study of art, drama, music, and the humanities may have a higher consumption portion than the study of some of the sciences. In any case, the difficulty of assigning portions of educational cost to consumption and investment has resulted in most studies attributing all cost to investment, thus underestimating the rate of return to education.

8. For example, one study of three communities—an affluent community with politically active adults, a lower-middle-class community with reduced levels of involvement, and a working-class neighborhood with primarily apolitical adults—concluded that the students in each community were being taught to play "different" political roles. Only in the affluent community were students taught the subtleties and nuances of decisionmaking and given the expectation that they should be a part of the process. The lower-middle-class neighborhood covered mechanics and procedures without stressing the utility of participation. See Edgar Litt, "Civic Education, Community Norms, and Political Indoctrination," in Richard Flacks, ed., *Conformity, Resistance, and Self-Determination* (Boston: Little, Brown, 1973), pp. 136–141.

9. Dougherty and Hammack, *Education and Society,* p. 248.

10. Ibid.

11. Christopher S. Jencks et al., *Who Gets Ahead?* (New York: Basic Books, 1979), pp. 224–227. For more recent confirming research, see Sanders Korenman and Christopher Winship, "A Reanalysis of the Bell Curve: Intelligence, Family Background, and Schooling," in Kenneth Arrow, Samuel Bowles, and Steven Durlauf, ed., *Meritocracy and Economic Inequality* (Princeton: Princeton University Press, 2000), pp. 136–178. See also Samuel Bowles and Herbert Gintis, "Does Schooling Raise Earnings by Making People Smarter?" in Arrow, Bowles, and Durlauf, *Meritocracy,* pp. 118–136.

12. Pierre Bourdieu and Jean-Claude Passeron, "The School as a Conservative Force: Scholastic and Cultural Inequalities," in John Eggleston, ed., *Contemporary Research in the Sociology of Education* (London: Methuen, 1974), pp. 32–46.

13. Pierre Bourdieu and Jean-Claude Passeron, *The Inheritors: French Students and Their Relation to Culture* (Chicago: University of Chicago Press, 1979), p. 153.

14. Gregory Squires, "Education, Jobs, and Inequality: Functional and Conflict Models of Social Stratification in the United States," *Social Problems* 24 (April 1977).

15. Ibid.

16. Ibid., p. 445.

17. Ibid., p. 551.

18. Hammack, "The Changing Relationship Between Education and Occupation: The Case of Nursing," in Dougherty and Hammack, *Education and Society,* pp. 561–573. Requiring greater educational achievement and "credentials" increases the prestige of a profession while encouraging higher pay and control over access to the profession.

19. Jared Bernstein and Amy Chasanov, *Viewpoints* (Washington, DC: Economic Policy Institute, April 2, 2004).

20. Jared Bernstein, "School's Out," *American Prospect Online,* March 18, 2004, available at www.prospect.org (accessed April 8, 2009).

21. Linda Jacobson, "Long-Term Payoff Seen from Early-Childhood Education," in *The Obama Education Plan,* pp. 3–5.

22. Samuel J. Meisels, "Universal Pre-K: What About the Babies," in *The Obama Education Plan,* p. 18.

23. Lawrence J. Schweinhart, "Creating the Best Prekindergartens," in *The Obama Education Plan,* pp. 22–23.

24. In Scott J. Cech, "NCLB Testing Said to Give 'Illusions of Progress,'" in *The Obama Education Plan,* p. 32.

25. David J. Hoff, "City Leaders Back Stronger Accountability," in *The Obama Education Plan,* p. 31.

26. Debra Viadero, "Top Students Said to Stagnate Under NCLB," in *The Obama Education Plan,* pp. 37–38.

27. John E. Chubb and Terry M. Moe, *Politics, Markets, and America's Schools* (Washington, DC: Brookings Institution, 1990).

28. James S. Coleman, Thomas Hoffer, and Sally Kilgore, *High School and Beyond* (Pittsburgh: National Center for Educational Statistics, November 1981).

29. A RAND Corporation study in 1990 concluded that parochial schools had particular success with disadvantaged and minority students. Although minority students scored lower than their white classmates in Catholic and public schools, the gap decreases significantly by the eleventh grade. However, in Catholic schools, children in single-parent homes drop out only at the same rate as those in two-parent homes.

Although the educational level of parents of parochial school students exceeded that of parents of public school students, Catholic schools' achievement advantage over public schools was the greatest for children whose parents have the least education. Reported in Tim Baker, "Successful Schools Are Right Under Our Noses," *Baltimore Sun,* June 3, 1991, p. A5.

30. J. T. Grogger and D. Neal, "Further Evidence on the Effects of Catholic Secondary Schooling," in W. G. Gale and Pack J. Rothenberg, ed., *Brookings-Wharton Papers on Urban Affairs* (Washington, DC: Brookings Institution, 2000), pp. 151–193.

31. See, for example, James S. Coleman, "Families and Schools," *Educational Researcher* 16 (August–September 1987): 32–38. For research comparing public and private schools, see Coleman, Hoffer, and Kilgore, *High School and Beyond;* and James Coleman and Thomas Hoffer, *Public and Private High Schools* (New York: Basic Books, 1987).

Coleman's research has been challenged. For example, see *Sociology of Education* 55 (April–July 1982); and *Harvard Educational Review* 51 (November 1981): 481–545, which were devoted to a critique of Coleman, Hoffer, and Kilgore, *High School Achievement* (New York: Basic Books, 1982).

32. Chubb and Moe, *Politics, Markets, and America's Schools,* pp. 32–33.

33. Ibid., p. 54.

34. The problem of greater bureaucratic control has increased as responsibility for funding has moved from localities to the states, and with the growth of federal regulation with such initiatives as NCLB. Court decisions on funding equity and racial integration have also contributed to the trend. Increased regulation contributes to instruction taking a smaller portion of educational expenditures.

35. Anthony Bryk, Valerie Lee, and Peter Holland, *Catholic Schools for the Common Good* (Cambridge: Harvard University Press 1993).

36. See John Chubb and Eric A. Hanushik, "Reforming Educational Reform," in Henry J. Aaron, ed., *Setting National Priorities: Policy for the Nineties* (Washington, DC: Brookings Institution, 1990), pp. 223–224.

37. See "Schools, Vouchers, and the American Public," a discussion by Terry Moe at the

Brookings Institution's Brown Center on Education Policy, available at www.brookings.edu/comm/transcripts/2001 (accessed May 3, 2009).

38. See Eric W. Robelen, "NAEP Gap Continuing for Charters: Sector's Scores Lag in Three Out of Four Main Categories," in *The Obama Education Plan,* pp. 60–61.

39. Center for Education Reform, "Charter School Closures: An Opportunity for Accountability," February 2006, available at www.edreform.com/_upload/closures.pdf (accessed March 10, 2009).

40. Gary Miron, "Strong Charter School Laws Are Those That Result in Positive Outcomes" (pdf file), Western Michigan University, paper presented at the American Educational Research Association (AERA) annual meeting, Montreal, Canada, April 2005, available at www.wmich.edu/evalctr/charter/aera_2005_paper_charter_school_laws.pdf.

41. Linda Renzulli and Vincent Roscigno, "Charter Schools and the Public Good," in *Contexts,* available at http://caliber.ucpress.net/doi/abs/10.1525/ctx.2007.6.1.31 (accessed March 10, 2009).

42. Bill Turque and Maria Glod, "Stimulus to Help Retool Education, Duncan Says," *Washington Post,* March 5, 2009, available at www.washingtonpost.com/wp-dyn/content/article/2009/03/04/AR2009030403523.html (accessed August 18, 2009).

43. James J. Heckman and Paul A. LaFontaine, "The Declining American High School Graduation Rate: Evidence, Sources, and Consequences," February 13, 2008, available at www.voxeu.org/index.php?q=n (accessed February 28, 2009).

44. US Census Bureau, *Statistical Abstract of the United States, 2009,* tab. 224 (Washington, DC: US Government Printing Office, 2008), p. 146.

45. Paige Johnson, "Reduce Teen Pregnancies to Reduce the Dropout Rate," available at www.carrborocitizen.com/main/2008/05/08/reduce-teen-pregnancies-to-reduce-the-dropout-rate (accessed March 11, 2009).

46. Karl L. Alexander, Doris R. Entwisle, and Carrie S. Horsey, "From First Grade Forward: Early Foundations of High School Dropouts," *Sociology of Education* 70, no. 2 (1998): 87.

47. US Census Bureau, *Statistical Abstract of the United States 2009,* tab. 337 (Washington, DC: US Government Printing Office, 2008), p. 208.

48. Sam Dillon, "States' Data Obscure How Few Finish High School," *New York Times,* March 20, 2008, available at www.nytimes.com/2008/03/20/education/20graduation.html (accessed August 18, 2009).

49. James J. Heckman and Paul LaFontaine, *The GED and the Problem of Noncognitive Skills in America* (Chicago: University of Chicago Press, 2008).

50. See Cheryl Almeida and Adria Steinberg, "Raising Graduation Rates in an Era of High Standards," in *The Obama Education Plan,* p. 116.

51. Ibid., p. 117.

52. Barack Obama, speech in Bettendorf, Iowa, November 7, 2007, as quoted in *The Obama Education Plan,* p. 169.

53. Christina A. Samuels, "District Focuses on Pathways to College," in *The Obama Education Plan,* p. 172.

54. White House, Office of the Press Secretary, "Statements from the Press Secretary," March 10, 2009.

55. See, for example, estimates by Scott J. Cech, "College-Cost 'Emergency' Jeopardizes Access," in *The Obama Education Plan,* p. 175.

56. Associated Press, "US College Drop-out Rate Sparks Concern," September 27, 2006.

57. The Blue Dog Democratic Coalition is a group of approximately fifty conservative-leaning Democrats in the House of Representatives.

58. Barack Obama, speech at Manchester, New Hampshire, November 20, 2007, as quoted in *The Obama Education Plan,* p. 138.

59. David Stout, "Obama Outlines Plan for Education Overhaul," *New York Times,* March 10, 2009, available at www.nytimes.com/2009/03/11/us/politics/11web-educ.html (accessed August 18, 2009).

60. Quoted in Saul K. Padover, *Thomas Jefferson on Democracy* (New York: Appleton-Century, 1939), p. 89.

10

Health Care: Diagnosing a Chronic Problem

Health care reform is consistently a high priority in public opinion polls[1] and in US politics. Success at building a national consensus on providing a universal health care system for all Americans has been stymied for decades. President Lyndon Johnson provided a significant step toward universal health care when he signed Medicare into law in 1965. He hoped the Medicare legislation would be the model for incremental additions that would ultimately result in universal health care in the United States.

Health care reform is rather unique in public policy in that the issues are unusually complicated and often not well understood. In addition, although public opinion polls still show clear majorities in favor of health care reform, support for specific changes is divided.[2] Many interest groups favor change, but all interest groups prefer the status quo as their second choice if the proposed change is not completely to their liking. The political system provides them with many opportunities to thwart change.

Voter frustration over the US health care system made it a major campaign issue in the campaign of 2008 in which both candidates promised to find a solution to deal with the 48 million Americans who had no insurance. The polarization of attitudes made it difficult to agree on many basic issues to lead to a compromise. Even the issue of looking at the wide variety of experiences and solutions tried by other nations in their effort to resolve health care problems became a matter of controversy. Some feel that learning from the experience of other nations diminishes US "exceptionalism" to the wisdom and values of other countries. Much of the objection to adapting foreign models to the US experience stems from opposition to national health insurance, which has been adopted by almost every other advanced nation in the world. "European style socialism" is frequently used as an epithet to oppose any policy ranging from the 2009 stimulus package to health care policy.

A poll released by the Harvard School of Public Health (HSPH) and Harris Interactive in late spring of 2008 found that 56 percent of Democrats said they would be more likely to support a presidential candidate who was supportive of making US health care more like that of other countries; 37 percent of Independents and 19 percent of Republicans agreed.[3] However, 45 percent of the Republicans as well as 17 percent of Independents and 7 percent of the Democrats indicated that they would be less likely to support such a candidate. The health care debate involves very different views of the US health care system. "One party sees it as lagging other countries across a broad range of problem areas while the other party sees the system as the best in the world with a more limited range of problems."[4]

The differences were clear during the 2008 presidential campaign. John McCain's proposals focused largely on open market competition to make insurance more affordable. Barack Obama called for universal health care. His plan would create a National Health Insurance Exchange that would include both private insurance plans and a government-run option modeled after Medicare.

A poll released in November 2008, found that voters supporting Barack Obama listed health care as their second priority while voters voting for McCain listed health care as fourth, tied with Iraq.[5] A survey of Republican and Democratic delegates to their respective conventions found starkly contrasting views. A random sample of attendees was asked what was more important: to provide health care coverage for all Americans or to hold down taxes. As compared with 94 percent of the Democratic delegates who selected expanding coverage, only 7 percent of Republican delegates agreed. However, 77 percent of Republican delegates and 3 percent of Democratic delegates agreed that holding down taxes was more important.[6]

The election of Obama raised expectations that he would make good on a pledge made during the campaign when he said: "The time has come for universal health care in America. . . . I am absolutely determined that by the end of the first term of the next president, we should have universal health care in this country."[7] There will be many obstacles to overcome before achieving this goal, however. Many in Congress will oppose Obama's health care proposals for ideological and partisan reasons. There are also many powerful health care interest groups ranging from medical practitioners, to the pharmaceutical industry, to insurance carriers, all of whom have more than a passing interest in how the issues are resolved. Finding the resources to pay for expanded coverage will be very difficult, especially in light of the current economic climate. A global recession that began in 2007 and is expected to be the most severe downturn since the 1930s is sure to affect the prospects for health care reform. Some maintain that large budget deficits projected for several years will make the increased government spending necessary for national health care all but impossible. Others believe that, since employer-sponsored insurance declined from 65 percent in 1999 to less than 63 percent in 2007, the conditions are ripe for bold and imaginative new approaches to expanding coverage.

In this chapter, we will examine the state of health care in the United States with a view toward determining what the optimal health care plan would be expected to accomplish. We must not lose sight of several factors in health care reform. First, if it were easy, it would have been done already. It involves a complex set of issues for which there are no quick fixes. The administration must proceed cautiously and deliberately to clarify public understanding and put together a coalition that can command the support necessary for legislative success. Second, and in many ways more difficult than the first factor, the problems are interrelated in that cost is a major reason for the lack of coverage for many while the low quality of health care for the uninsured is an obvious confounding factor. Therefore, health care reforms must buttress each other. Notably, Obama's proposals will (1) clearly increase coverage; (2) bring down premiums by $2,500 for the average family through cost savings in Medicare, electronic record keeping, and other savings; and (3) improve the quality of health care for newly covered individuals. Some skeptics, as we will note, question his ability to accomplish all three. In this regard, we might note that any bold plan is bound to be contentious. Relatively minor reforms at the periphery, such as G. W. Bush's support of health savings accounts that had no effect on the contours of the US health care system, aroused no opposition. Perhaps, the most important argument that is increasingly recognized by US industry is that universal health care would act as a subsidy to business to level the playing field with foreign auto manufacturers who already have it. The Big Three US auto manufacturers cite the private health care provisions as a major reason for their financial difficulties. Universal coverage could play an important role in stimulating economic growth while permitting us to shift our attention to controlling escalating health care costs.

Quality of Health Care in the United States

Health care in the United States is characterized by great inequalities in access and delivery. Some Americans have access to the most sophisticated health care in the world while the infant mortality rate in many inner city areas is closer to that of a third world country. A child born to a mother living in poverty and without prenatal care will be more likely to develop asthma or another disease that may be a largely left untreated chronic condition. Such a child will probably have poorer dietary habits and a lower level of education. He or she will be more likely to marry at an earlier age and have inadequate health insurance. If chronic diseases develop later in life, he or she is much less likely to have access to adequate treatment. These health problems will lead to a shorter life span, on average, than that of the affluent child.

The Institute of Medicine of the National Academy of Sciences points out a second problematic feature of health care noting that the United States "is the *only* wealthy, industrialized nation that does not ensure that all citizens have coverage."[8] Over 48 million Americans, about one-sixth of the nonelderly population, are uninsured. The Institute of Medicine found that lack of health insurance causes roughly 18,000 unnecessary deaths every year in the United States.[9] The lack of universal health coverage drives up medical costs because of uneven access to health care. Conditions that could be treated at early stages are often deferred until they become major health crises that are more expensive to treat. The number of the uninsured is expected to climb rapidly with rising unemployment and many employers deciding they can no longer provide health insurance for employees and their families.

A third problem with the US health care system is its fragmented nature. Americans acquire health insurance on their own, through an employer (roughly 58 percent), or, if they qualify, through a government program.[10] A dazzling variety of private plans are available ranging from health maintenance organizations (HMOs), **preferred provider organizations** (PPOs), managed care, and medical underwriting, to name a few. Private employer-sponsored health insurance costs have increased rapidly as premiums for family coverage have increased by 78 percent, wages have risen by 19 percent, and inflation has risen by 17 percent.[11] Annual premiums for family coverage averaged $12,106 in 2007, with workers paying $3,281.[12] The number of options for low-wage earners is more limited, and the greatest burden of health care costs falls on this segment of the population.

Government programs are also fragmented. Several publicly funded programs provide health care to the elderly, the disabled, active duty military families, veterans, children, or the poor. Different government bureaucracies administer programs such as Medicare, Medicaid, the Military Health System, TRICARE, the Department of Veterans Affairs (VA), the Indian Health Service, the State Children's Health Insurance Program (SCHIP), and the Federal Employees Health Benefits Program.

The fragmented delivery of coverage drives up costs for health care in the United States. There are thousands of health insurance companies, which require costly and redundant administrative structures. Significant insurance costs are spent in marketing and underwriting costs. Underwriting involves analyzing a particular market and determining what benefits can be offered at what premium levels while negotiating deductibles and copayments. Marketing and underwriting account for about two-thirds of private insurance overhead, which is almost completely avoided in public programs.[13] A widely cited study in the New England Journal of Medicine found that administrative costs accounted for 31 percent of US health care expenditures ($1,059 per person) and 16.7 percent of health care expenditures in Canada.[14] The study concluded that the gap between US and Canadian spending on health care administration grew to $752 per capita. Considerable savings would result in administrative costs in the United States if the Canadian-style health care system were implemented.

Improvement in medical technologies is another factor that has driven up the cost of health care. New and more expensive drugs permit the treatment of a number of conditions, such as asthma, that previously were essentially untreatable. Technology that permits heart bypass surgery, kidney dialysis, and chemotherapy and radiation for cancer may not cure or even arrest chronic diseases, but may permit a much longer and higher quality of life. Other expensive technologies are used with increasing frequency such as magnetic resonance imaging (MRI) for diagnostic purposes.

The demand for and financing of health care is greatly influenced by the demographic structure of a nation and how it changes. The percentage of the population that is age sixty-five or older has risen in all Organisation for Economic Co-operation and Development (OECD) countries and is expected to continue to do so for the next two decades. In the United States, those age sixty-five and older constitute about 12.4 percent of the population. For OECD countries, this population is just under 15 percent; several countries, like Japan (20 percent), Italy (19.3 percent) and Germany (19.2 percent), have significantly older populations.[15] The baby boomers (those born between 1946 and 1964) will begin turning sixty-five in 2011. Those age sixty-five and older will grow from the current 12.4 percent to about 20 percent of the population in 2030. From 2030 on, the proportion of the population age sixty-five and older will be relatively stable at around 20 percent. On average, the elderly tend to be in poorer health and in greater need of health care than either working-age adults or children. Thirty percent of Medicare's annual costs are spent on the 5 percent of the patients who will die in a given year. And about one-third of those dollars spent in the last year of a patient's life are paid out in the last month.[16] An aging population can be expected to lead to increased public spending on health care. As a larger share of the population will be retirees, the decline in the labor supply will reduce the growth of per capita gross domestic product (GDP) in those countries.[17]

Health care spending has been growing faster than the economy. The Congressional Budget Office concluded that, although many factors contributed to that growth, "the bulk of the long-term rise resulted from the health care system's use of new medical services that were made possible by technological advances, or what some analysts term the "increased capabilities of medicine."[18] Rising real incomes and advances in medical technology have resulted in many people deciding that they no longer have to endure the pain, discomfort, or lack of mobility associated with conditions like osteoarthritis. Patients now demand a hip or knee replacement operation rather than accept the reduced mobility that used to be accepted as inevitable.

Why has the demand for health care grown so much? Obviously, the desire to remain healthy has led to a continuous growth in the demand for health care but, more specifically, there has been a shift from a focus on infectious diseases to often more costly chronic diseases.[19] With the development of vaccines and antibiotics, the incidence of infectious diseases has decreased and concern shifted to chronic ailments, such as heart disease, diabetes, and cancer, for which cures are not available. Patients with chronic diseases often undergo lifelong treatment, driving up costs.

Another reason for the high cost of health care in the United States is the fact that, by encouraging private sector mechanisms, the government has little price influence over the pharmaceutical industry to keep prices down. Other countries with universal health care negotiate prices with pharmaceutical firms to keep costs down. As a result, pharmaceutical expenditures are almost 92 percent higher in the United States than in other OECD countries.

Similarly, critics charge that other medical technologies are often overused in the United States, thereby contributing to the high expenditures for health care. The ironic result is that many who defend the US health care system precisely because it utilizes the free market system are startled to find that private insurance and markets are the reason for higher health care costs.[20]

A comparison of US health care spending with other OECD countries reveals that other countries now enjoy certain cost advantages over the United States. All OECD countries except the United States as the wealthiest, and Mexico and Turkey as the two poorest, have national health care. The United States spends more money on health care than any other country in the OECD in both relative and absolute terms (see Table 10.1). The data indicate that 15.3 percent of the US GDP goes to health care, which is almost double the GDP average of 8.6 percent among the other OECD countries. In fact, the most recent data available indicate that in 2008 US health care spending reached 16.6 percent of GDP and in 2009 it is expected to reach 17.6 percent of GDP, the largest one-year increase to date.[21] By 2018, health care spending in the United States is projected to climb to $4.4 trillion and account for 20.3 percent of GDP. Since 2000, health care costs in the United States have risen more rapidly than throughout the OECD countries. But what is remarkable is that nations with universal coverage spend only about 50 percent of what the United States spends on health care while there are still 48 million Americans with no health care coverage. Table 10.1 also indicates that over 45 percent of US health care is funded by federal, state, or local government sources, signifying a significant public component.

Comparing health care costs in the United States to OECD countries reveals additional reasons for higher expenditures when measured against nations in similar socioeconomic conditions. A recent study done for Congress comparing health care costs found that there were "far fewer doctor visits per person compared with the OECD average; for hospitalizations, the US ranks well below the OECD and is roughly comparable in terms of length of hospital stays."[22] On the other hand, it was noted that the *intensity* of care was generally higher, although the United States does not have the *highest* levels in the OECD. It also found that the level of intensity is not nationwide or consistently high for all services or for all similarly situated individuals within the United States.

In assessing what drives the difference between US health care spending and the rest of the world, some leading health economists responded with: "It's the prices, stupid."[23] Simply put, their conclusion is that health care labor prices for treatment and physician and nursing care are higher in the United States than in other countries. US health care professionals (including specialists, general practitioners, and nurses) are among the world's highest paid professionals. In the United States, medical school

Table 10.1 Health Care Spending in OECD Countries, 2006

Country	Health Care Spending per Capita US$ Purchasing Power Parities	Health Care Spending as Percentage of GDP	GDP per Capita US$ (2007)	Percentage of Health Care Publicly Financed
Australia	3,141	8.7	37,577	67.7
Austria	3,606	10.1	37,119	76.2
Belgium	3,462	10.3	35,382	n/a
Canada	3,678	10.0	38,500	70.4
Czech Republic	1,509	6.8	24,027	88.0
Denmark	3,362	9.5	35,961	84.1
Finland	2,668	8.2	34,718	76.0
France	3,449	11.0	32,686	79.7
Germany	3,371	10.6	34,391	76.9
Greece	2,483	9.1	28,423	61.6
Hungary	1,504	8.3	18,754	70.9
Iceland	3,340	9.1	35,697	82.0
Ireland	3,082	7.5	45,027	78.3
Italy	2,614	9.0	30,381	77.2
Japan	2,578	8.1	33,626	81.3
Korea	1,464	6.4	24,801	55.7
Luxembourg	4,303[b]	7.3[b]	79,793	90.9[b]
Mexico	794	6.6	14,004	44.2
Norway	4,520	8.7	53,477	83.6
Poland	910	6.2	15,989	69.9
Portugal	2,120	10.2	22,815	70.6
Slovak Republic	1,308	7.4	20,079	68.3
Spain	2,458	8.4	31,586	71.2
Sweden	3,202	9.2	36,603	81.7
Switzerland	4,311[b]	11.3[b]	41,101	60.3
Turkey[a]	580	7.7	12,993	72.1
United Kingdom	2,760	8.4	35,669	87.3[c]
United States	6,714	15.3	45,489	45.8

Sources: OECD, "OECD Health Data 2008—Version: December 2008," available at www.oecd.org/document /16/0,3343,en and http://stats.oecd.org/WBOS/Index.aspx?DataSetCode=DCOMP (accessed April 17, 2009).
Notes: a. Turkey's data from 2004.
b. Estimate.
c. Differences in methodology.
n/a indicates data not available.

enrollment has been essentially level since 1980. Much of the increase in the number of physicians has come primarily from physicians who immigrate to the United States after having received their medical education.[24] General practitioners and nurses are the highest paid within their profession among reporting OECD countries in Table 10.2.

Table 10.2 Average Compensation in Certain Health Professions, 2004 (dollars in US purchasing power parities)

Country	Specialists $1,000s	Specialists Ratio in Per Capita GDP	General Practitioners $1,000s	General Practitioners Ratio in Per Capita GDP	Nurses $1,000s	Nurses Ratio in Per Capita GDP
Australia	247	7.6	91	2.8	48	1.5
Belgium	188	6.0	61	2.0	n/a	n/a
Canada	161	5.1	107	3.4	n/a	n/a
Czech Republic	35	1.7	32	1.7	14	0.8
Denmark	91	2.9	109	3.4	42	1.3
Finland	74	2.5	68	2.3	29	1.0
France	149	5.0	92	3.1	n/a	n/a
Germany	77	2.7	n/a	n/a	n/a	n/a
Greece	67	3.1	n/a	n/a	33	1.5
Hungary	27	1.7	26	1.6	14	0.9
Ireland	143	4.0	n/a	n/a	41	1.1
Mexico	25	2.4	21	2.1	13	1.3
Netherlands	253	6.0	117	3.6	n/a	n/a
New Zealand	89	3.6	n/a	n/a	34	1.4
Norway	77	1.9	n/a	n/a	35	0.9
Poland	20	1.6	n/a	n/a	n/a	n/a
Portugal	64	3.5	64	3.5	34	1.9
Sweden	76	2.5	66	2.2	n/a	n/a
Switzerland	130	3.8	116	3.4	n/a	n/a
United Kingdom	150	4.9	118	3.9	42	1.4
Average excluding United States	107	3.6	78	2.8	32	1.3
United States	230	5.7	161	4.1	56	1.4

Source: Congressional Research Service (CRS), *US Health Care Spending: Comparison with Other OECD Countries* (Washington, DC: US Government Printing Office, September 17, 2007), p. 18.
Note: n/a indicates data not available.

It is important to point out that higher education in most OECD countries is much less expensive, or often even free, when compared to that of the United States. Thus, health care professionals in most OECD nations begin their careers with significantly smaller student loan payments than is the case in the United States. In 2008, 87 percent of new medical school graduates had average educational loan debts of $154,607.[25]

The OECD data provide some insight regarding why health care spending is higher in the United States than in other countries. The data also suggest that any system adopted requires its own tradeoffs. Americans spend more money on health care than do citizens of any other nation in the world, yet there is widespread dissatisfaction with the result. Who gets health care and how much they receive is an ethical and a practical problem in society. Why is it that, despite spending huge sums of money, we never seem to have the health care we want? It is so costly that almost 48 million Americans are without health insurance and do not have access to high-quality care. Whatever the amount we spend on health care, how can we spend it efficiently so that we get the most effective health care for a given commitment of resources? Efforts to control rising costs are held in check by new treatment technologies, which drive up costs.

What the United States Receives for Its Health Care Spending

Since we pay more for health care than any other country both per capita and as a percentage of GDP, one might expect that our society would lead the world in indices of what constitutes health. We are also the *only* developed democratic capitalist state that leaves most of health care up to market forces and the *only* country without national health insurance. The fact that Americans spend over 17 percent of GDP on health care while citizens of other developed countries spend approximately 8 percent would suggest that, by paying so much more, we would have more services available than do other countries. Unfortunately, the United States lags behind most countries in several leading health indicators. Table 10.3 illustrates the problem.

Table 10.3 Health Indicators for Selected OECD Countries

Country	Infant Mortality Rate per 1,000 Live Births	Life Expectancy at Birth (years) (2008)	Life Expectancy at Age 65 (2005) Women	Men	Percentage of Adult Population Considered Obese (2005)
Australia	4.8	81.5	21.4	18.1	21.7
Canada	5.1	81.2	21.0	17.7	18.0
France	3.4	80.9	21.4	17.1	9.5
Germany	4.0	79.1	19.6	16.1	13.6
Italy	5.6	80.1	20.7	16.7	9.9
Japan	2.8	82.1	23.2	18.1	3.0
Netherlands	4.8	79.3	20.0	16.4	n/a
Spain	4.3	79.9	20.7	16.8	13.1
United Kingdom	4.9	78.9	19.1	16.1	23.0
United States	6.3	78.1	20.0	17.1	32.2

Source: US Census Bureau, *Statistical Abstract, 2009* (Washington, DC: US Government Printing Office, 2008).
Note: n/a indicates data not available.

Since the United States spends more than any other country on health care, do we get a reciprocal value for the money we spend? The data in Table 10.3 raise questions even though they do not provide clear answers. For example, the United States has a significantly higher infant mortality rate and a shorter life expectancy than similar OECD nations. If a nation has more obese people, one might expect them to have to spend more on health care. But the data also raise the question as to whether health care can compensate for lifestyle differences between countries. For example, one reason for a shorter life expectancy at birth is because more individuals will be victims of homicide or car accidents than in most other OECD countries. Others have noted methodological problems with comparative data.[26]

Health Insurance in the United States

Individuals usually pay for most of their medical expenditures by purchasing health insurance. Private health insurance provided through an employer purchasing on a group basis to cover company employees is the most important source of coverage. The percentage of Americans covered by private health insurance, according to the most recent figures available, is 67.5 percent, of which 59.3 percent were covered by employer-provided health insurance (covering 177.4 million people).[27] Only 8.2 percent of those with private insurance purchased insurance on their own through the nongroup insurance market. The number of employees with work-sponsored health insurance is declining as employers respond to growing cost pressures. However, the percentage of those covered by government health programs went up slightly to 27.8 percent.

Corporate-sponsored health care is usually offered to full-time employees after some probationary period (such as six months). Workers in employer-sponsored programs are expected to contribute to their own coverage. Workers usually contribute about 28 percent of the total premium for family coverage. In addition to premium contributions, patients are responsible for **deductibles**, in which they must pay the full cost of their health care up to some limit. For example, a $500 deductible means the patient must pay the first $500 of his or her medical costs for the year and the insurance company will pay all or part of the subsequent medical costs incurred. Patients may also be responsible for **copayments**, a fixed payment that they pay when they receive a medical service; a $15 copayment for an office visit with a doctor is rather typical. Some insurance policies require a patient to pay **coinsurance**, a set percentage of each medical good or service received (such as 18 percent, rather than a flat copayment). In an effort to reduce health care costs, many employers are responding to the current economic downturn by shifting more health care costs to employees through requiring larger deductibles and copays by the patient at the time health care services are received. Other increased costs to employees include requiring workers to pay a larger share of the premium for family coverage. As a result of the rising costs of premiums, deductibles, copays, and reduced coverage, more employees are choosing not to take the insurance offered by their employers. Approximately 18 percent, or 14 million private sector employees, decline insurance coverage from their employers.[28]

How Employer-Sponsored Insurance Became the Norm

The first reason **employer-sponsored insurance** evolved as it has in the United States is based on the political evolution of health care in the nation's history. Theodore Roosevelt proposed a publicly financed universal health care system when he ran for president on the Bull Moose Party ticket in 1912, but it garnered little support. Before the development of medical expense insurance, patients were expected to pay all health care costs under the fee-for-service model. Although private health insurance was introduced in the early part of the twentieth century, it was not until 1929 when Blue Cross offered hospital insurance, followed a few years later by Blue Shield's offering of prepaid physician care, that health insurance began to grow. Before then, few Americans had prepaid health insurance that covered hospital or doctor bills. In the 1930s and 1940s, labor unions, strengthened by New Deal legislation, pressed for higher wages *and* fringe benefits. President Franklin Roosevelt considered adding medical care to the Social Security legislation in 1935 because so many poor and unemployed individuals during the Great Depression had no secure access to health care. Blue Cross developed a vigorous campaign to persuade the middle class that the availability of private insurance made national health insurance unnecessary and even illegitimate in that private, not public, programs were the American way. Roosevelt decided that adding health care to legislation already deemed radical by opponents would destroy the chance for passage of Social Security by Congress.

The situation changed rapidly during World War II, when unemployment virtually disappeared. Companies were not allowed to raid rival corporations' workers by offering higher pay because strict wage controls to fight inflation were in effect. However, the tax code, after energetic lobbying efforts by a growing insurance industry and labor unions, allowed employers to claim the cost of health insurance as a tax-deductible business expense. Insurance premiums were not counted as wages, or taxable income, to workers. This policy continued after the war.

The employee actually pays for the health insurance fringe benefit since it is part of overall compensation. If he or she did not receive it as insurance coverage, it would be paid in higher wages. But an employee would rather receive $100 as an untaxed health care benefit than $100 in wages, which would be subject to federal, state, and payroll taxes (Social Security and Medicare). As a result, almost every major company provided health benefits to its employees as a standard fringe benefit by the end of the 1950s. Since employees receive a subsidized (i.e., untaxed) benefit, they have an incentive to buy more insurance coverage than if they had to pay the premium out-of-pocket as well as a tax on the income.

After World War II, the recipient of health care services usually had to pay only a minor deductible or copayment, and the insurance company became the major payer for care itself. Under this **third-party-payer** system, both consumers and physicians had little incentive to consider costs when seeking or providing medical care. And the more medical services the physician performed, even questionable procedures, the more his or her total personal income increased.

Employment-sponsored, prepaid private health insurance became the standard so that, shortly after the war, lack of medical insurance coverage was seen as a problem primarily of the poor and the elderly. In 1945 and again in 1948, President Harry Truman proposed national health insurance to cover those without employment-related insurance. His program was defeated, largely because the American Medical Association (AMA) launched a well-financed and harsh attack to defeat Truman and his congressional sponsors of "socialized medicine."[29] Truman, even in filing his bid for national health insurance, helped solidify the legitimacy of employer-sponsored insurance.

Predictable Risk Pools

The second reason employer-sponsored insurance has come to dominate private insurance has to do with large employers and **risk pools**. Insurance companies try to manage the risk they accept in providing insurance to the employees of a corporation, known as the *risk pool*. Keep in mind that health insurance companies are in business to make money. They really do not want to sell insurance to people who are most likely to make claims against the policy. The bottom line is that an insurance company must take in more money in premium dollars than they pay out in administrative costs and benefits. What is important from the insurance underwriter's view is that, when it sells a health insurance policy to a company, it gets all the company's employees, the healthy as well as the sick. A company with a large number of employees constitutes a risk pool that allows actuaries to calculate a predictable distribution of medical risk. The insurance carrier can predict fairly accurately the claims that it will have to pay out and calculate a premium structure to cover the expected claims along with the insurance company's overhead. The statistical *law of large numbers* means that, as the size of the risk pool grows, the odds greatly improve that the insurer will be able to predict the average cost outcome of the members of the pool. Another factor is the reduction of adverse claim selection. The larger the group of employees, the less the risk of a larger than average number of individuals with costly medical risks. There is less reason to suspect that particularly high- or low-medical-risk individuals have decided to seek employment at a large firm. For these reasons, companies (particularly, large firms) are an attractive market for insurance companies.

Conversely, the law of large numbers also explains why an individual policy purchased directly from an insurance company is so expensive. An insurer cannot rule out adverse selection on the part of the individual seeking insurance or average out the probability of whether a single individual may be badly injured in an accident and need prolonged expensive medical care. It also explains why large companies can offer their employees health insurance at significantly lower rates than a smaller company employing only seventy-five workers. The smaller firm will be forced to charge higher premiums for less coverage.

This largely explains why the percentage of large employers (companies employing over 200 workers) offering coverage has remained at around 98 percent or 99 percent while the percentage of small employers (3–199 workers) offering coverage has declined steadily since 1999 from 68 percent to 59 percent by 2007. The claim by small firms that cost is the main reason for not offering health benefits is supported by a RAND Corporation study that concluded the cost of employer-sponsored insurance places a greater burden on small firms, as a percentage of payroll, than on large firms.[30] The study concluded that the economic burden of providing health insurance was particularly acute for small businesses, which have difficulty containing costs due to their limited bargaining power. That study concluded that, if health insurance costs continue to rise, all employers—large and small—will experience increasing difficulty in providing health insurance.

Case Study: Insurance and Adverse Selection

A successful health insurance company must estimate the level of risk accurately. The adverse-selection problem occurs because information on the health status of a company's employees may be incomplete. The insurance company may set the premium at an average risk level. But employees who are low-risk (very young and in excellent health) may decide that the "average" risk policy is too expensive and do not buy the insurance. When the best risks select themselves out, it is called **adverse selection**.

Those who buy the premium will tend to be higher-risk people and will prove to be too costly for an insurance company that does not receive enough premiums from low-risk people. Insurance companies may respond by offering different premiums related to the level of risk, for example, nonsmokers may be offered a lower premium than smokers. This practice of offering low cost to low-risk groups is known as **cherry picking**. Conversely, it means that high-risk groups, such as the elderly, must be charged high premiums. The result is that health insurance is often too expensive, especially for those most in need of health care.

The Tax Subsidy Advantage

A third reason why employers provide most private insurance is because there is a tax subsidy for employer-sponsored insurance. Under the current US tax code, all wages are subject to taxation, but compensation in the form of health care is not taxed. This creates a subsidy for health care provided by employers. Suppose an employer pays an employee $50,000 in wages. The worker gets to keep $50,000, less the taxes owed. If the tax rate is 20 percent, the worker keeps $40,000, or only $0.80 of every $1.00 earned. If the employer provides the worker with health care worth $5,000, the worker keeps the entire $5,000, which reduces the worker's *effective tax rate*. This tax expenditure is only available for employer-sponsored insurance. It is not available for individually purchased insurance.

This is a benefit to the *employee,* not the *employer.* The employer would be indifferent regarding paying $1,000 more in wages or employer-sponsored insurance benefits since either compensation is deductible from corporate taxes. It does make a difference to the employee's tax burden, however, since the $1,000 received in employer-sponsored insurance is not taxed while an additional $1,000 in wages would equal only $750 in a 25 percent tax bracket. Therefore, a government decision to end the tax subsidy would include employer-sponsored insurance as part of an employee's taxable income.

Individually Purchased Insurance

There is a rather small and declining group, 8.9 percent in 2007, of Americans who are covered under individually purchased health insurance.[31] As noted above, the individual policy purchaser pays the entire premium without the benefit of employer contributions. Self-employed individuals may receive a tax deduction for their health insurance, but most purchasers in the individual market receive no tax benefit. Although the range of coverage is theoretically the same as those provided by employer-sponsored insurance, the reality is that out-of-pocket spending is much higher because of higher deductibles, copayments, and coinsurance provisions. Insurance premiums will vary widely by age, occupation, and health status, among other things. Nongroup insurance is often simply not available for those who are deemed to be in a high-risk category. Nongroup policies, in an effort to guard against adverse selection, generally exclude any "preexisting condition." Thus, the issuer of the policy will refuse to pay for costs associated with any condition (e.g., arthritis, diabetes, cancer, hypertension, being twenty pounds over- or underweight, or any chronic disease) that existed prior to the policy coming into force. Because of the high cost, many individually purchased policies are limited to major medical coverage.

Medicare

The second major source of health insurance, and the largest public health insurance program in the United States, is Medicare, which is a federal health insurance program for those age sixty-five or older, and for disabled persons under age sixty-five. Medicare, which operates as a single-payer health care system administered by the federal government, was signed into law by President Johnson as an amendment (Title XVIII) to the Social Security Act of 1965.

Johnson's policy goal was to have the federal government accept responsibility for paying the health care costs of the poor and the elderly—through Medicaid and Medicare at the top of the Great Society agenda. The poor could not afford health insurance and, frequently, their physical condition precluded their coverage in any event. Since most insurance was employment based, retirees found that advancing age made them ineligible for private insurance coverage or that it was prohibitively expensive.

Johnson, with an overwhelmingly Democratic Congress in 1965, enacted the legislation over the opposition of the medical profession and the insurance industry. John Kingdon writes that issues move to the top of the policy agenda when two conditions are met.[32] First, an abrupt shift in how a problem is perceived or a change in who controls the levers of power in government may open a "window of opportunity" for policy innovation. Second, three "streams" in the policy process—problems, policies, and politics—must come together. For example, the election of a new president and a new Congress, especially if all are controlled by the same party, may influence how a problem like health care is perceived and defined by public opinion. Both of these conditions were met when Johnson became president after the assassination of John F. Kennedy and both houses of Congress were controlled by a Democratic majority.

Medicare, in contrast to Medicaid, is strictly a federal program, not related to income level. It is the largest federal health program, serving all those who have reached the age of sixty-five and have worked for ten years in employment covered by Social Security or railroad retirement. It was designed to relieve the threat of financial ruin due to medical expenses among the elderly, although there are significant gaps in its coverage.

Opposition by the AMA did result in a compromise that created two separate programs: Parts A and B. Part A, officially known as the Hospital Insurance (HI) program, pays all covered costs of hospital care, except for a deductible approximately equal to the first day of hospitalization, for up to sixty days per illness. Medicare will pay for an additional thirty days, less a coinsurance payment. Part A helps pay for a semiprivate room, meals, regular nursing services, rehabilitation services, drugs, medical supplies, laboratory tests and x-rays, and most other medically necessary services and supplies. Part A also pays for hospice care for a patient certified by a physician as terminally ill (i.e., not likely to live more than six months).

Medicare, like private insurance, contains premiums, deductibles, and copayments, which the beneficiary must pay out-of-pocket. In fact, the deductibles and copayments are higher than for most employer-sponsored insurance programs, and significantly higher than those for Medicaid patients. Part A is compulsory and is financed by the HI portion of the Social Security payroll tax: that is, 1.45 percent of an employee's

Case Study: Medicare and Prescription Drugs

The original Medicare program covered hospital and doctor visits, but did not include payments for prescription drugs. This is not surprising since as recently as the mid-1960s there were few, and in some cases no outpatient drugs for treating high cholesterol, hypertension, stomach ulcers, diabetes, mental disorders, and many other health problems that were responsive to prescription drugs by the mid-1990s. By the late 1990s, however, Medicare recipients were spending over $2,000 a year on prescription drugs, which was more than the average American spent on all health care in 1965. And since almost all private insurance plans for working Americans covered prescription drugs, Medicare's lack of coverage became a glaring deficiency in a program to assist the nation's retirees. The pressure to add a prescription drug benefit to plug a gap in Medicare became a political agenda issue in the congressional campaigns of 1998, 2000, and 2002 as well as an issue in the presidential campaign of 2000.

Democrats and Republicans supported two different plans. Democrats proposed adding a drug benefit to Medicare with the government having the responsibility to negotiate directly with drug companies for the lowest drug price. Republicans proposed that governments subsidize private insurance companies to offer prescription drug benefits to the elderly, either combined with HMOs or as a stand-alone prescription drug plan. Many private insurers were reluctant to offer stand-alone drug policies for fear of adverse selection by retirees. Part D insurance plans establish their own list of drugs they cover. They preferred that the Medicare beneficiary agree to join an HMO and agree to more limited Medicare benefits, but ones including prescription drug benefits.

G. W. Bush with a Republican-led Congress signed the Medicare Modernization Act of 2003 into law, better known to most Americans as the Medicare prescription drug law, that generally followed the Republican proposal. The bill went into effect in January 2006. A White House "fact sheet" declared the law provided the biggest "improvements in senior health care in nearly 40 years" and would provide seniors with drug benefits and more choices in which "health plans will compete for seniors' business by providing better coverage at affordable prices and helping to control the costs of Medicare by using market-place competition, not government price-setting."[a] Medicare beneficiaries must enroll in the Part D Prescription Drug Plan (PDP) to participate. The average monthly premium in 2008 for stand-alone PDPs was $30.14. In 2007, a lower than expected 8 percent of Medicare enrollees signed up for Part D.

The law prohibits the federal government from negotiating the price of drugs on behalf of the 22 million Americans who signed up for the additional insurance program under Medicare. Another federal agency, the VA, is allowed to negotiate on behalf of veterans, with the result that one study found that the average cost of drugs for Medicare recipients was 58 percent higher than for veterans.[b] For example, for the cholesterol-lowering drug Zocor, the cost of a year's supply of 20-milligram tablets would be $1,485.96 under the "cheapest" Medicare PDP, compared to $127.44 under the VA. And for a year's supply of 200-milligram caplets of the anti-inflammatory drug Celebrex, the lowest Medicare PDP price was $946.44, but $632.09 under the VA.[c]

Just before the prescription bill was ready for a vote, the G. W. Bush administration estimated the cost to taxpayers would be $395 billion over ten years. But when Richard Foster, an auditor for the US Health and Human Services Administration, analyzed the bill, he concluded its cost would be $551 billion. The higher projection, if

continued

Case Study continued

known to legislators, would have jeopardized the bill's passage. Thomas Scully, the chief administrator and Foster's superior, threatened to fire Foster if he disclosed the results of his analysis. It was not known until after the bill was signed that Scully was negotiating for two new jobs, one with a lobbying firm and the other with a law firm representing drug manufacturers. Scully's action to prevent accurate communication to Congress appears to be in violation of express prohibitions of federal law. After the bill became law, the administration

changed its estimate of the cost of the drug bill to $534 billion.

Congressman Billy Tauzin (R–LA), as chair of the House Energy and Commerce Committee, played a key role in crafting and steering the bill through Congress. He retired soon after the bill's passage and took a job for $2 million a year as chief of the Pharmaceutical Researchers and Manufacturers of America, an industry trade group that includes among others the Pfizer, Johnson & Johnson, and Bristol-Meyers Squibb companies.

Notes: a. Ceci Connolly and Mike Allen, "Medicare Drug Benefit May Cost $1.2 Trillion: Estimate Dwarfs Bush's Original Price Tag," *Washington Post,* February 9, 2005, p. A1.

b. "Medicare Part D Patients Pay More for Drugs Than Veterans," January 10, 2007, available at www .azstarnet.com/news/163911 (accessed May 3, 2009).

c. Ibid.

---

wage paid by both the employer and the employee (2.90 percent total). The government contracts with private companies to act as "fiscal intermediaries," which administer bills received by hospitals and write checks. They are then reimbursed from the Medicare trust fund. Part B, unlike Part A, is voluntary, and those electing coverage have the premium withheld from their Social Security benefit checks. Most Americans age sixty-five or older do enroll in Part B (about 93 percent), technically known as Supplemental Medical Insurance (SMI). Neither Part A nor Part B pays for all of a covered person's medical costs, which has created a marketing niche for Medigap insurance. **Medigap** refers to private health insurance policies specifically designed to provide coverage for health care needs not covered by Medicare. Most policies require the policy holder to be enrolled in Medicare Parts A and B to be eligible to purchase a Medigap policy.

The Medicare payment system is, like Social Security, one in which taxes deducted from current workers pay the claims of today's retirees, which has serious policy implications because of changing demographic patterns. The approaching wave of retirements from baby boomers means that spending is projected to grow dramatically. Total Medicare spending takes up more of the federal budget than any other category except Social Security and defense. The Board of Trustees for Medicare and Social Security reported that Medicare expenditures exceeded its receipts in 2008 and that, without changes, the Medicare hospital insurance trust fund will become insolvent by 2019.[33]

On a positive note, Medicare has been a model system for efficient administration of a large government program. The typical measure of efficiency in health care is the percentage of all costs that goes to administration rather than patient care. Most employer-based insurance administration and other costs unrelated to patient care (e.g., corporate profit) range between 10 percent and 30 percent. Medicare Part A spends about 1 percent on administrative costs and Part B spends about 2.6 percent.[34] It is the most efficient medical payment system in the nation. On the downside, Medicare is vulnerable to fraud since less than 5 percent of the claims are audited.

Medicaid

Medicaid, unlike Medicare, was designed to be strictly an insurance program financed jointly by the federal government and the states. It is financed from general revenues rather than a payroll tax to provide basic medical care for the poor. Medicaid is federally mandated, but administered by states subject to federal guidelines. To qualify for Medicaid assistance, one must first become eligible for welfare support in their state of residence. Eligibility requirements, benefit levels, and costs vary widely between states. Medicaid does not cover all of the poor because, in addition to being poor, one has to meet other criteria such as receipt of Supplemental Security Income (SSI) benefits, eligibility for public assistance, or membership in particular demographic groups (e.g., low-income children or pregnant women). Since states administer Medicaid, they determine who is eligible to participate in this national program.

Participating states are obligated to provide a federally mandated minimum package of services to recipients. Other options are provided only at state discretion. Within the federal mandates, states have a good deal of flexibility to establish their own income levels for eligibility and benefit packages. And within states, Medicaid spending can vary significantly by beneficiary group. States that meet federal eligibility requirements receive matching payments based on their per capita income. The federal government's contribution to the state programs ranges from an 80 percent subsidy for the poorest states to only 50 percent for the most affluent states. Accordingly, there are large variations in coverage and expenditures between states. The program originally targeted low-income single-parent families. In recent years, many states have expanded Medicaid coverage to groups, such as poor children and pregnant women, who do not otherwise qualify for cash assistance even though they have low incomes. In 1997, the program was expanded by the **Children's Health Insurance Program** (CHIP). The goal of the CHIP program is to expand the eligibility of children by including two-parent families and raising the income limits to participate. To encourage states to expand their coverage, the federal government pays a higher percentage of each state's CHIP expenditures than to its Medicaid expenses.

Efforts to expand health coverage of low-income children were vetoed twice by G. W. Bush in 2007, and attempts to override failed. With the election of President

Obama, congressional Democrats prepared a bill to increase spending on CHIP programs by almost $33 billion over the next five years, enough to add well over 5 million children to the program. The new administration referred to the program as a "down payment" on health care reform.

Federal rules require states to cover major expenses, such as physician and hospital care, but do not require payment for prescription drugs, dental care, or optometrist services. All states do cover prescription and optometrist services, and all but one covers dental services. Generally, the services are provided with only a small copayment or in many cases none required. However, since most states reimburse physicians at such a low rate (often about half the private sector payment rates), many physicians refuse to serve Medicaid patients. The poor who are covered by Medicaid often have difficulty finding physicians who will accept them or their children as patients.

Some, predominantly conservatives, worry that if Medicaid were made more generous, low-wage workers who have private insurance might decide to leave their plans for public insurance, which would be more generous since there would be no wage contributions, deductibles, or copays. Their concern is that employers of even low-wage earners deduct roughly $2,500 from a worker's wages in addition to deductibles, but there are no Medicaid fees for workers whose income is so low that they are eligible for Medicaid. At current Medicaid benefits, there is no evidence of "crowding out" by workers moving from private to public health care.

The Uninsured

An increasing number of Americans work for an employer that does not provide for health insurance, and either they cannot afford insurance, underwriters will not qualify them, or they choose not to purchase private health insurance. And these individuals may not qualify for government-sponsored public health care such as Medicare, Medicaid, or VA benefits.

Seventeen percent of the nonelderly population (under age sixty-five and not eligible for Medicare) in the United States is uninsured as of mid-2009. The uninsured have lower than average incomes, with nearly 67 percent having incomes that put them in the bottom 40 percent in income. However, about one-fifth of the uninsured are in the top half of the population in terms of income ($50,000 or above) and could afford private insurance. It is estimated that about 10 percent of the unemployed fall into the "uninsurable" category because of preexisting conditions. About 20 percent of the uninsured are children.

A major concern in US health care today is the growing number of uninsured Americans. An insurmountable hurdle for most of the uninsured is that they work for an employer that does not offer health insurance. Thus, they have no ability to form a large risk pool to drive down the price of insurance. The result is that many low-wage workers lack access to affordable private insurance. Conversely, small businesses are very opposed to a government **mandate** that would require employers to offer insurance or to pay into a fund that would provide insurance. Small businesses united to fiercely oppose the Bill Clinton administration's attempt to insure low-wage workers.

When other socioeconomic factors, such as income or family status, are controlled, uninsured Americans receive about 60 percent of the health services as do insured Americans. When they are hospitalized, uninsured Americans (adults as well as children) die from the same illness at almost three times the rate observed for equally situated insured patients.[35] Over the long run, uninsured Americans die at an earlier age than similarly situated insured Americans.

Why the Uninsured Are a Public Policy Concern

A major reason for concern about the uninsured is negative health externalities associated with communicable diseases. The uninsured are less likely to receive medical treatment for communicable diseases such as the swine flu virus. They are also less likely to receive vaccinations that might stop the spread of communicable diseases.

A second externality is financial. When the cost of treating the uninsured is **uncompensated**, health care providers try to pass the cost on to the insured or to taxpayers through the practice of **cost-shifting**. Cost-shifting results in higher insurance premiums or it may be paid through higher taxes.

Another aspect of the negative financial externality is that the uninsured may not receive appropriate treatment, which further distorts the price of health care. For example, the uninsured are more likely to delay seeking medical treatment, hoping that their medical condition will be transitory and heal by itself as is often the case. However, if the condition worsens while they are delaying, the end result is to seek emergency room treatment, which is a very expensive way to treat what might have started out as a minor illness.

Another reason for providing universal insurance is because of **job lock**, or the fear that millions of workers will experience losing their health insurance. Many are very reluctant to search for a job in which they might be more productive because they might lose their health insurance coverage. New employers must undergo a waiting period before becoming eligible for health insurance. Insurance carriers may limit coverage for preexisting conditions such as hypertension or diabetes. A situation where workers who would like to move to a new job because of a better match between skills and talent, but remain in jobs in which they are not challenged, leads to lower productivity. The immobility of labor due to job lock lowers national productivity.

A final reason for caring about the uninsured is because it is widely felt throughout the industrialized world that health care is a basic right that should be available to all citizens such as the right to a public education or freedom of speech. Note that all the industrialized nations of the OECD provide universal health coverage. Uwe Reinhardt, a well-known health care researcher, has written that, in the United States, we seem to be interminably involved in debating whether as a matter of national policy the child of a poor family should have the same chance of avoiding preventable illness or of being cured from a given illness as does the child of a rich family.[36] Reinhardt points out that the yeas in all other industrialized nations won this debate decades ago by providing universal health care systems in place to carry out that decision. He deplores that, only in the United States, have the nays so far won:

> As a matter of conscious national policy, the United States always has and still does openly countenance the practice of rationing health care for millions of American children by their parents' ability to procure health insurance for the family or, if the family is uninsured, by their parents' willingness and ability to pay for health care out of their own pocket or, if the family is unable to pay, by the parents' willingness and ability to procure charity care in their role as health care beggars.[37]

Deficiencies of Health Insurance in the United States

The insurance industry defends high premiums, waiting periods, condition-specific payment denials, and denial of coverage to people with preexisting conditions as necessary to protect companies from the moral hazard of people who want to pay for insurance only when they need it. The practices are actuarially sound, they contend, and permit more affordable rates for other employers and employees. Many workers agree, and argue that they cannot afford to subsidize others. However, this approach, by definition, is at variance with the idea of insurance as a way to spread risk. Competition in the insurance market now means insurance companies search for ways to avoid risks rather than for ways to share them. Employer-based coverage has become insecure and insured workers face the threat that their coverage will dissolve when they need it most.

Insurance companies prefer to insure those who are the least likely to have health care claims. Many insurance companies have resorted to occupational blacklisting to avoid high-risk employees. Among blacklisted occupations, for example, are gas station attendants, taxi drivers, security guards, and those who work for liquor and grocery stores, because of the increased likelihood of injuries due to robberies. Florists and hair dressers are often blacklisted because insurers insist that the higher proportion of gays working in these job categories means an increased likelihood of AIDS. Other occupations, such as logging, commercial fishing, and construction, are sometimes excluded because of the high risk of injury associated with them.

In response to the rising costs of health insurance or its unavailability, many companies decided to pay for their employees' health care rather than pay an insurance company. They have become **self-insured**, which also relieves them of state insurance regulations. Under the Federal Employee Retirement Income Security Act of 1974, passed to encourage the development of employer pension programs, companies may structure their own health plans if they act as their own insurers rather than using an insurance company. The law permits companies to hold the funds needed for medical claims in company accounts, thereby permitting them to realize investment income from those funds and pay out benefits themselves rather than using an insurance company—they are exempt from all state taxes and regulations governing health insurance. The original purpose of the exemption was to allow companies with employees in several states to offer uniform health care coverage throughout those states. But companies soon discovered that self-insurance was a way to avoid state laws mandating certain minimal coverage, and that it allowed them to restructure health plans to reduce costs.

A study appearing in *Health Affairs* found that medical problems are cited in about half of all bankruptcies.[38] In fact, the study found that the medical debtors, like most bankruptcy filers, were primarily middle class (by education and occupation). The chronically poor are less likely to build up debt, and have fewer assets like homeownership to protect. Those declaring bankruptcy for medical reasons each year (about 1 million people) differed from others filing for bankruptcy in an important respect: they were more likely to have experienced a lapse in health care coverage. Many (75 percent) had coverage at the beginning of their medical problems, but lost it (38 percent lose coverage) by the time they filed for bankruptcy.[39] In 2005, bankruptcy regulations were reformed to make it more difficult to file for personal bankruptcy. Despite that, bankruptcies rose by 80 percent in just two years.

In many other cases, even continuous coverage left families with ruinous medical bills. Many of the debtors in the study blamed high copayments and deductibles for their financial collapse.[40] The fact that the deductibles and copayments are so high leads many with what are generally thought of as "good" insurance policies to put off seeing a physician until a minor problem has become more serious and more expensive to treat than it might have been otherwise. Many insurance companies also employ physicians and researchers to develop justifications for denying claims. Thus, in many cases, bureaucrats rather than the physician providing the care make major decisions regarding health care access, even though they may have no medical training.

The Managed Care Revolution

From the early 1900s, the AMA endorsed a **fee-for-service** model for reimbursement of physician services. In this model, physicians and other health care providers receive a fee for each service rendered. An insurance plan based on a fee-for-service standard would allow a patient to seek care from doctors or hospitals of their choosing. If a patient was responsible for a small deductible or copayment and the health care provider billed a third party payer (the insurance company), neither the patient nor the doctor had an incentive to restrain spending. This standard model has been criticized as driving up the cost of health care since the insured patient and the physician utilize more health care services than would be supported in a normal demand-driven market because of the third party payer. (See Figure 10.1.)

Managed care evolved as an alternative to a fee-for-service system beginning in the early 1930s and flourished despite strong opposition from the AMA. Managed care organizations were attractive mainly because they seemed to avoid the moral hazard of the fee-for-service system. Enrolled patients are restricted to those physicians who were members of the organization. HMOs hire their own doctors, who are paid a salary that is not dependent on the amount of care delivered. In theory, putting physicians on salary should remove any incentive for excess care as in a fee-for-service system. Money saved by reducing unnecessary surgery or other care could be directed toward preventive care. There was a fixed annual budget from which all necessary services were paid. Since an HMO contracts to provide all necessary care to its members, it must monitor costs carefully. If physicians provide more care than is absolutely necessary, the HMO could run out of funds by the end of the year and be unable to pay physician salaries.

The AMA vigorously opposed HMOs because it objected to physicians being paid a salary, which made them employees of the organization and undermined the fee-for-service independent practitioner model. In fact, the AMA actually succeeded in outlawing

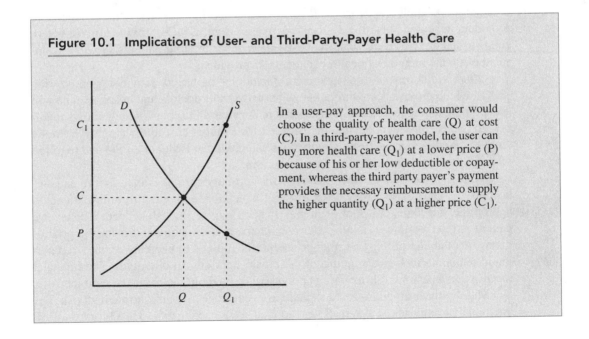

Figure 10.1   Implications of User- and Third-Party-Payer Health Care

In a user-pay approach, the consumer would choose the quality of health care (Q) at cost (C). In a third-party-payer model, the user can buy more health care (Q_1) at a lower price (P) because of his or her low deductible or copayment, whereas the third party payer's payment provides the necessay reimbursement to supply the higher quantity (Q_1) at a higher price (C_1).

such consumer-controlled cooperatives in several states. Nevertheless, several HMOs survived and even flourished. Kaiser-Permanente became the largest and most well known, but there were several others.

A conversation between President Richard Nixon and John Ehrlichman recorded on the White House taping system in the Oval Office is a good introduction indicating of how Nixon was convinced to go forward with the Health Maintenance Organization Act of 1973. Nixon and Ehrlichman were discussing various policy issues when the topic of health care arose. Nixon said: "You know I'm not too keen on any of these damn medical programs." Ehrlichman replied: "Edgar Kaiser is running his Permanente deal for profit. And the reason that he can do it. . . . All the incentives are toward less medical care, because . . . the less care they give them, the more money they make." Nixon responded: "Fine."[41] Richard Nixon saw HMOs as an appealing alternative to liberal-backed national health insurance plans. The Nixon administration repackaged prepaid group health care plans as HMOs, with federal legislation providing for endorsement, certification, and subsidies.[42] More important, the administration pushed the HMO law through Congress, which provided start-up grants and loans for HMOs, and required businesses with more than twenty-five employees to offer at least one HMO as an alternative to conventional insurance if one was available in the area. The act nullified state laws restricting HMOs. It required that a "federally qualified HMO" be organized on a nonprofit basis. In a concession to the AMA, the law broadened the definition of an HMO to include a fee-for-service option, known as an independent practice association (IPA). In an IPA model, the HMO contracts with independent providers to provide health care to its members. Here, HMOs provide a **prospective reimbursement** based on what the HMO determines treating patients *should* cost instead of on the amount of health care actually provided.

Other variations of managed care include a preferred provider organization (PPO), which provides care through a wider network of doctors and hospitals who will accept a lower negotiated fee, and a **point of service** (POS) plan, which allows members to choose providers outside the network for a higher cost to the employee. Many large corporations in the 1990s simply contracted with an HMO or a PPO and required all employees who wanted to be insured to join.

Almost 90 percent of HMOs require that primary care physicians serve as gatekeepers. As gatekeepers, they often have a financial incentive not to refer patients to appropriate specialists. A pool of money is set aside for the gatekeeper. Whenever a patient is referred to a specialist, the cost of the care is subtracted from the pool of money. At the end of the year, the gatekeeper is allowed to keep any money remaining in the pool. Such financial incentives create stark ethical dilemmas. The financial incentive to withhold or limit care is pervasive throughout the managed care industry.

Many of these programs try to exclude from coverage patients who are high risk. The traditional group plans accepted all who applied, to spread the risks. HMOs practice risk avoidance in the interest of profits. In so doing, they deny care to those most in need. This shifts the cost of caring for the sickest patients to other plans, which are then viewed (incorrectly) as high cost and therefore less efficient.

Managed care has few supporters among either physicians or patients. Physicians find the system less generous than the fee-for-service model. They often feel constrained by the need to hold down costs, which hinders them from providing some health care options permitted under the traditional system. There is a widespread negative reaction among patients who feel that the savings have come at the expense of quality care.

Managed care and prospective reimbursement reversed the problems in a fee-for-service business model. In the fee-for-service model, where physicians bill for each service rendered, they have an incentive to render more services to increase their income. Under prospective reimbursement, physicians are paid a retainer for the number of patients enrolled. Now, the fewer services delivered, the more money they will make. So fee-for-service offers financial rewards for excessive care while prospective reimbursement rewards insufficient care.

Proposals for Reform

Those who oppose a universal health care system for Americans usually acknowledge problems in US health care. Opposition most frequently takes the form of criticizing perceived flaws in the national health care systems in OECD countries.[43] For example, opponents often argue that there are inevitable shortcomings in all bureaucratized public systems resulting in delays for treatment and a lack of availability of the latest medical technology and drugs. In contrast, it may be argued that market efficiencies and competition lead to shorter wait times and the latest drugs and technology available in the mixed public and private system of the United States.

Recent polling data does show that over half of US residents say that they or a member of their household has either delayed or gone without health care in the past year.[44] It found that about 67 percent of US residents support a public health insurance option "similar to Medicare," with about 80 percent of Democrats, 60 percent of Independents, and 49 percent of Republicans in favor of such a plan. Support declined significantly when questions about cost were included. Therefore, some conservatives suggest supporting incremental reforms to control costs and make insurance more affordable for the uninsured. These are less-controversial reforms because liberals agree that a comprehensive reform must include many incremental adjustments.

Everyone agrees that a greater effort should be made to reduce fraud, waste, and abuse. President Obama, in an address to a joint session of Congress, committed his administration to rooting out waste, fraud, and abuse in Medicare that does not make seniors any healthier.[45] Some estimates place waste, fraud, and abuse at about 10 percent of the cost of the Medicare program. However, even if the cost of Medicare was reduced by 10 percent, it would not provide an adequate long-term strategy.

Another approach has been to incorporate more prospective reimbursement in Medicare and Medicaid spending. This approach also promises very little over the long term. If physician reimbursements were lowered significantly, Medicare patients could run into the same problem that Medicaid patients have experienced with doctors refusing to accept them.

One incremental reform that Obama used to expand coverage of the uninsured was to expand the eligibility of children to the CHIP program. Even those opposed to public health care find it difficult to deny health care to children of poor families. Variations on this approach are to offer families tax subsidies, or vouchers, to purchase health insurance.

More major reforms that would build on the mixed public and private system in existence in the United States would consist largely of extending government subsidies for the uninsured with a variety of choices in deductibles and copayments. Those who support this position point out that most Americans do have health coverage based on their employment. The status quo has legitimacy because the market, even if imperfect, has provided many Americans with access to some of the highest-quality health care in the world. They claim that the current system's shortcomings can be resolved by mandating that all employers provide health insurance.

Existing structures would remain, although it is not clear if the existence of government-subsidized programs might not lead to a crowding out of many employer-sponsored insurance programs. A major advantage of this approach is that it would not require as much new public financing as an entirely new single-payer system. Consumer choice would permit individuals to seek out health care policies more tailored to their needs.

Others maintain that building on the existing structure will inevitably end up with the same inefficiencies, such as high administrative costs, and inequities in the delivery of health care between those who can afford more expensive high-end insurance and the less-affluent who will have access to only more limited policies. Those holding this view believe that the only way to resolve these issues is to provide national health care with a single-payer system. This would require a higher initial outlay, but would result in the administrative savings inherent in a single-payer system. The cost of the program would be offset by reduced spending on many existing public health programs. There would also be a reduction in spending on private health insurance. It would completely resolve the problem of the uninsured in America.

Those who support a fundamental restructuring of health care generally think it should be a right and not a privilege. If it is a right, it should not be based on one's ability to pay. If health care becomes a right in the United States, people would be more likely to seek treatment earlier and thus have better long-term health, as is the case in most OECD nations. The 48 million uninsured would be expected to receive the most immediate benefit of access to quality health care.

Still, as Reinhardt observes, many of the elite in the United States believe that rationing by price and ability to pay serves a high national purpose. He points out that virtually everyone who shares that view

> tends to be rather comfortably ensconced in the upper tiers of the nation's income distribution. Their prescriptions do not emanate from behind a Rawlsian veil of ignorance concerning their own families' station in life. Furthermore, most . . . who see the need for rationing health care by price and ability to pay enjoy the full protection of government-subsidized, employer-provided, private health insurance that affords their families comprehensive coverage with out-of-pocket payments that are trivial relative to their own incomes and therefore spare their own families the pain of rationing altogether.[46]

Conclusion

The quality of health care in the United States has made great strides since the 1960s. For most Americans with adequate health insurance, the health care market seems to be working well. For the growing number of Americans with inadequate health insurance or who are uninsured, there is market failure. Health care costs are much higher in the United States than in any other country in the world, yet we have at least 48 million Americans with no health care coverage. Although we spend more of our national treasure on health care than any other nation, we cannot show that US health care is superior.

All other economically advanced countries in the world, except the United States, have universal health care. The cost, unequal access, and unequal quality of health care have placed it on the US policy agenda as both political parties promise to solve the health care "crisis." The decline of a bipartisan approach within the government to providing health care has shattered the old coalitions and reduced them to two warring camps, making it difficult to reach a solution. The conservatives are committed to trying to enlarge the role of markets and reduce the role of government in providing health care. The liberals are not opposed to trying to harness the efficiencies of the marketplace, but claim that government must become involved because the market has failed.

At the center of the current debate is whether we as a nation should recognize health care as a right, as do all other industrialized nations, and not merely a privilege for those who can afford it. The United States is only incrementally moving in the direction of providing universal health care for the elderly through Medicare, the poor through Medicaid and CHIP programs, and the military through the VA and Military Health System.

The current economic problems highlight the need to address the growing numbers of the uninsured even while the problem of how to pay for it grows.

Questions for Discussion

1. Should health care be a right or a privilege? Why?

2. Why are health care costs rising faster than growth in GDP, despite various attempts to contain costs?

3. Why have insurance companies shifted from risk sharing to risk avoidance? What, if anything, can be done about this phenomenon?

4. Explain how health care is rationed in the US system of health care delivery. How does this differ from rationing in a system of universal health care? Which is fairer? Why?

5. How is it possible for the United States to spend almost twice as much on health care as do many countries that provide their citizens with universal coverage (and have better health indicators) while still having millions of citizens without regular access to it? Is this a demonstrated case of market failure? Could this be tied in to unequal distribution of income? How?

Useful Websites

American Medical Association, www.ama-assn.org.
Centers for Medicare and Medicaid Services, www.cms.hhs.gov.
Families USA, www.familiesusa.org.
Journal of the American Medical Association, http://jama.ama-assn.org.
Physicians for a National Health Program, www.pnhp.org.

Notes

1. Kaiser Daily Health Policy Report, "Tracking Poll Examines Public Opinion About Health Care Reform," April 23, 2009, available at kaisernetwork.org (accessed April 28, 2009).

2. Victor R. Fuchs, "Reforming US Health Care: Key Considerations for the New Administration," *Journal of the American Medical Association* 301, no. 9 (March 4, 2009): 963.

3. Harvard School of Public Health (HSPH), "Most Republicans Think the US Health Care System Is the Best in the World. Democrats Disagree," press release, March 20, 2008. See also HSPH, "Americans Views on the US Health Care System Compared to Other Countries," press release, March 20, 2008.

4. HSPH, "Most Republicans Think the US Health Care System Is the Best in the World. Democrats Disagree," p. 2.

5. Robert J. Blendon et al., "Voters and Health Reform in the 2008 Presidential Election," *New England Journal of Medicine* 359, no. 19 (November 6, 2008): 2050–2061.

Obama supporters put health care as their second priority behind "economy/jobs" and just ahead of "Iraq." McCain supporters ranked "economy/jobs" as their number one priority, "energy/gas prices" second, and "terrorism" third while "health care" and "Iraq" were tied for fourth.

6. Ibid., p. 2050.

7. Nedra Pickler, "Obama Calls for Universal Health Care," *Washington Post,* January 25, 2007, available at www.washingtonpost.com/wp-dyn/content/article/2007/01/25/AR2007 012500764.html (accessed April 28, 2009).

8. Institute of Medicine at the National Academies of Science, "Insuring America's Health: Principles and Recommendations," January 14, 2004, available at www.iom.edu/?id= 17848 (accessed April 29, 2009).

9. Ibid.

10. Kristin Wikelius et al., *National Health Insurance: Lessons from Abroad* (New York: Century Foundation Press, 2008), p. 6.

11. Kaiser Family Foundation, "Health Industry Premiums Rise 6.1 Percent in 2007, Less Rapidly Than in Recent Years but Still Faster Than Wages and Inflation," September 11, 2007, available at www.kff.org/insurance/ehbs091107nr.cfm (accessed on April 29, 2009).

12. Ibid.

13. Wikelius et al., *National Health Insurance,* p. 8.

14. Steffie Woolhandler, Terry Campbell, and David Himmelstein, "Costs of Health Care Administration in the United States and Canada," *New England Journal of Medicine* 349 (August 2003): 768–775.

15. OECD, *Health Data 2007,* p. 12, available at http://dxdoi.org/10.1787/113121435865 (accessed August 15, 2009).

16. Reuters, "Discussions About End-of-Life Care Reduce Healthcare Costs in Last Week of Life," March 19, 2009.

17. OECD, *Health Data 2007,* p. 12.

18. US Congressional Budget Office, "Technological Change and the Growth of Health Care Spending," January 2008, p. 1, available at www.cbo.gov/ftpdocs/89xx/doc8947/01-31-techHealth.pdf (accessed May 1, 2009).

19. Approximately 40 percent of all deaths in 1900 were caused by eleven major infectious diseases (typhoid, smallpox, scarlet fever, measles, whooping cough, diphtheria, influenza, tuberculosis, pneumonia, diseases of the digestive system, and poliomyelitis). Only about 16 percent of all deaths were caused by three major chronic conditions (heart disease, cancer, and stroke). See Jay M. Shafritz, ed., "Health Policy," in *The International Encyclopedia of Public Policy and Administration* (Boulder: Westview Press, 1998), vol. 2, p. 1053.

20. Wikelius et al., *National Health Insurance,* p. 8.

21. Steven Reinberg, "Recession Scrambling Health Spending in US," February 24, 2009, available at www.medicinenet.com/script/main/art.asp?articlekey=98009 (accessed August 18, 2009).

22. Chris Peterson and Rachel Burton, *US Health Care Spending: Comparison with Other OECD Countries,* Congressional Research Service Report for Congress, September 17, 2007, p. 1.

23. Gerard Anderson, Uwe E. Reinhardt, Peter S. Hussey, and Varduhi Petrosyan, "It's the Prices, Stupid: Why the United States Is So Different from Other Countries," *Health Affairs* 22 (March 2003): 89–105. Also available at http://content.healthaffairs.org/cgi/reprint/22/3/89.pdf.

24. Ibid., p. 96.

25. Association of American Medical Colleges, *Medical Student Education: Costs, Debt, and Loan Repayment Facts,* October 2008, available at www.aamc.org/programs/first/debtfact card.pdf (accessed August 18, 2009).

26. For example, although the OECD provides estimates of the percentage of the population that is overweight and obese, only the United Kingdom and the United States used actual measurements of people. The other OECD countries used results from survey questions that yielded lower rates. However, corroborating evidence was obtained. The United States ranked first in daily calorie consumption and annual sugar consumption per person among OECD countries. The US sugar consumption was 156 pounds per person per year, compared with the OECD average of 99 pounds per year.

27. US Census Bureau, "Income, Poverty, and Health Insurance Coverage in the United States 2007," *Current Population,* August 2008, p. 19.

28. Mark W. Stanton, "Employer-Sponsored Health Insurance: Trends in Cost and Access," US Department of Health and Human Services, Agency for Healthcare Research and Quality, available at www.ahrq.gov/research/empspria/empspria.htm (accessed May 1, 2009).

29. T. R. Marmor, *The Politics of Medicare,* 2nd ed. (New York: Aldine de Gruyter, 2000), pp. 6–14.

30. Research Brief, "Is the Economic Burden of Providing Health Insurance Greater for Small Firms Than for Large Firms?" Kauffman-RAND Institute for Entrepreneurship Public Policy, available at http://rand.org/pubs/research_briefs//2008/RAND_RB9340.pdf (accessed May 2, 2009).

31. US Census Bureau, "Income, Poverty, and Health Insurance Coverage," p. 21.

32. John W. Kingdon, *Agendas, Alternatives, and Public Policies,* 2nd ed. (New York: HarperCollins, 1995), pp. 127–128.

33. US Department of Health and Human Services, "2008 Annual Report of the Boards of Trustees of the Federal Hospital Insurance and Federal Supplementary Medical Insurance Trust Funds," available at www.cms.hhs.gov/ReportsTrustFunds/downloads/tr2008.pdf (accessed May 2, 2009).

34. Donald Barr, *Introduction to US Health Policy: The Organization, Financing, and Delivery of Health Care in Ameica,* 2nd ed. (Baltimore: Johns Hopkins University Press, 2007), pp. 103–104.

35. David M. Cutler, *Your Money or Your Life: Strong Medicine for America's Health Care System* (New York: Oxford University Press, 2004), pp. 64–65.

36. Uwe Reinhardt, "Wanted: A Clearly Articulated Social Ethic for American Health Care," *Journal of the American Medical Association* 278, no. 17 (November 5, 1997): 1446–1447.

37. Ibid.

38. David Himmelstein, Elizabeth Warren, Deborah Thorne, and Steffie Woolhandler, "MarketWatch: Illness and Injury as Contributors to Bankruptcy," *Health Affairs: The Policy Journal of the Health Sphere,* February 2, 2005, available at http://content.healthaffairs.org/cgi/content/full/hlthaff.w5.63/DC1 (accessed May 4, 2009).

39. Ibid., p. 9.

40. Ibid.

41. "Nixon Launches the HMOs: What a Sicko," available at www.youtube.com/watch?v=9QkgUKM0o6Q (accessed May 4, 2009).

42. Robert Kuttner, "Must Good HMOs Go Bad?" *New England Journal of Medicine* 338 (May 1998): 1558.

43. See "The Myths of Single-Payer Health Care," available at http://freemarketcure.com/singlepayermyths.php (accessed May 4, 2009). Freemarketcure.com is a website dedicated to extolling the virtues of private health care and deploring all national health care systems.

44. Kaiser Daily Health Policy Report, "Tracking Poll Examines Public Opinion About Health Care Reform," April 23, 2009, available at www.medicalnewstoday.com/articles/147455.php (accessed May 5, 2009).

45. "President Obama Pledges to Root Out Medicare Fraud, Waste and Abuse," *Medicare Update: Medicare Compliance, Reimbursement and Enforcement Resource,* available at http://medicareupdate.typepad.com/medicare_update/2009/02/medicarereform.html (accessed May 5, 2009).

46. Uwe Reinhardt, "Wanted: A Clearly Articulated Social Ethic for American Health Care," *Journal of the American Medical Association* 278 (March 1997): 1446–1447.

11

Housing: Mortgage Meltdowns and Reregulation

The financial crisis that began in 2007 was caused by collapse of an $8 trillion bubble in the housing industry. The financial system was vulnerable because US monetary policy maintained unusually low rates of interest, which encouraged highly leveraged processes throughout an industry with little federal regulatory oversight. In 2002, warnings were raised by Dean Baker that a bubble was forming in the housing market.[1] Baker showed that for over forty years housing prices closely followed the rate of inflation but, from 1995 on, housing prices rose much more rapidly than inflation. He predicted that the housing bubble would burst and create a crisis that would inevitability test the survival of several financial institutions, including Fannie Mae and Freddie Mac.[2] Nevertheless, Alan Greenspan and the Board of Governors were not convinced. They continued to maintain low interest rates, which helped feed the speculative bubble.

Housing is unique in that it is the primary form of savings, the largest asset of most households as well as the largest single form of investment in the nation. Housing also fulfills a basic human need for shelter.

The basic US public policy toward housing was established seventy-five years ago. Prior to the Great Depression, only a minority of Americans owned a home. Between 1900 and 1930, homeownership remained steady at around 46 percent.[3] This was despite the fact that the federal income tax system, created in 1913, provided for a tax deduction on mortgage-interest loans. Nevertheless, during the Great Depression (with only 30 million households in 1930), millions of Americans lost their homes to bank foreclosures.[4] At that time, almost all home mortgages were short-term (three to five years), with no amortization. The banking crisis of the depression forced banks to take back mortgages when the three- or five-year period was up. Refinancing was not available and many unemployed borrowers who were not able to make mortgage payments saw their homes foreclosed. Housing starts came to a virtual halt, putting a majority of those in the home-building industry out of work.

The response of the Franklin Roosevelt administration was the National Housing Act (NHA) of 1934, which created the Federal Housing Authority (FHA) and the Federal Savings and Loan Insurance Corporation (FSLIC).[5] The FHA made it easier for people to borrow money to buy a house by regulating interest rates and helped bring about longer-term mortgages. The effect was lowered monthly payments and an increased size of the market for single-family homes. Monthly payments also provided for a reduction of the debt with each payment.

The NHA was intended to stop the rising number of bank foreclosures on family homes. Some unintended consequences of the act were that it contributed to urban blight and promoted suburban sprawl. The FHA targeted its funding to middle-class, mostly white, citizens building homes in the suburbs while declining loans to lower-income workers in urban areas. This played a part in segregation and resulted in directing investment toward more expensive single-family detached homes, away from urban housing. Conversely, the deduction encouraged people to buy larger, single-family detached homes out of the city.

The surge in homeownership after World War II was astonishing. Between 1940 and 1960, the homeownership rate rose from 43.6 percent to 61.9 percent. President Harry Truman made housing the focus of his Fair Deal and his campaign against the "do-nothing Congress." Truman's underdog presidential victory provided the thrust necessary to pass the Housing Act of 1949. It emphasized the goal of "a decent home and suitable living environment for every American family." This dramatic change was facilitated by a booming economy, favorable tax laws, and easier financing along with a high percentage of households being in the prime home-buying age groups.

The post–World War II economy contained several factors that supported increased homeownership. The increased demand for houses was assisted by federal highway and infrastructure construction and the availability of newly affordable cars, which enabled more people than ever to consider moving to the suburbs to escape the unpleasantness of crowded city life. The absence of land for constructing new homes in cities and an increase in real incomes beginning in the 1950s also exacerbated the decline of central cities by expediting the exodus to the suburbs. Suburban development patterns promoted greater segregation by income. The realities of the housing market ultimately determined that the less affluent would live in the older, deteriorated housing inventory in the central cities.

Housing Policy and the "American Dream"

The cultural importance of homeownership has deep roots in Western society. The anguish of those with no fixed abode has a special place in Judeo-Christian thought. The Old Testament admonishes the faithful to be kind to the stranger and to remember that they were once "strangers" wandering in the land of Egypt. And the New Testament recounts that Christ was born in a cave, as there was "no room in the inn." Christ spoke of his own sense of homelessness when he said: "The foxes have their lairs and the birds in the sky have their nests, but the Son of Man has nowhere to lay his head" (Matthew 8:20). Today's nonprofit Christian organization, Habitat for Humanity, was founded on the conviction that "every man, woman and child should have a simple, decent, affordable place to live in dignity and safety."[6]

In many societies, homeownership signifies belonging and status as a full member of the community. Nevertheless, the United States is unusual in the significance attached to owning a home. Homeownership represents more than shelter; it has come to represent a means to financial independence. Generous tax breaks have increased the enthusiasm for purchasing the most expensive home possible. The cultural attachment and tax subsidy together make housing of special importance in the US economy and in public policy. With over 67 percent of American families owning a home, homeownership has become a more central part than ever of the American Dream.

These factors provide the ingredients for powerful bipartisan, political constituencies in housing. The leaderships of both political parties have encouraged homeownership and pledged to work for a decent home for every citizen.

Policymakers encourage homeownership in the belief that it fosters positive social behaviors, social stability, and civic engagement. According to the theory, widespread homeownership benefits the nation because those who have literally invested in their communities are more responsible citizens. Edward Glaeser and Jesse Shapiro looked at the evidence for the social benefits of homeownership.[7] They found evidence for three positive externalities resulting from ownership. First, ownership encourages individuals to take better care of their property than renters. Second, homeowners have greater commitment to the community because individuals accumulate wealth through the equity in their homes, giving them a stake in the system. Therefore, they might work harder to make their community more pleasant. And third, homeowners face higher mobility costs and so they might invest more in their community. Homeowners should favor more policies that increase property values through longer-term local investments and through the political process than renters. Recall that voting was originally limited to male *property* holders, on the theory that they would vote more responsibly than those without property.

Studies confirm that homeowners are more likely to vote in local and federal elections than are renters, although this may reflect the economic status of owners relative to the average renter rather than homeownership per se.[8] Consequently, government at all levels has provided assistance for households of various incomes.[9]

To achieve the goal of decent housing and a suitable living environment for every American family, the government established Fannie Mae and Freddie Mac to guarantee mortgages against nonpayment by mortgage holders. The government also provides a major subsidy to mortgage holders in the form of the home mortgage federal income tax interest deduction, which cost the federal government approximately $74 billion in federal tax expenditures in 2007 alone. This homeowner tax subsidy benefits those with the largest mortgages the most since the higher the mortgage, the more that can be deducted from federal taxes. (See Figure 11.1.) Thus, homeownership is encouraged through subsidized mortgages, mortgage interest deductibility through the income tax, tax benefits for first-time homeownership, and even subsidies for home improvements.

Figure 11.1 Estimated Distribution of Housing Subsidies, by Income Quintile, 2004 (constant 2004 US$ billions)

Quintile	Tax Expenditures	Housing Outlays	Total	Percent	Quintile Income Limit	Quintile Average Income
Bottom	1.4	30.4	31.8	20.3	18,464	10,295
Second	6.6	4.5	11.2	7.1	34,397	26,177
Third	16.8	1.7	18.5	11.8	54,787	44,111
Fourth	37.2	0.6	37.8	24.1	86,585	69,384
Top	57.2	0.1	57.4	36.6	n/a	148,138
Total	119.3	37.3	156.7	100.0	n/a	59,988

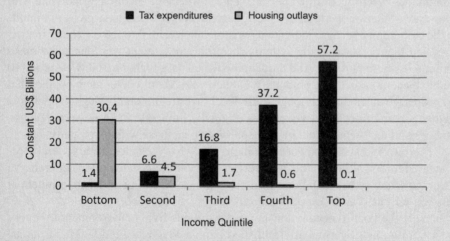

Source: Cushing Dolbeare, Irene Saraf, and Sheila Crowley, *Changing Priorities: The Federal Budget and Housing Assistance, 1976–2005* (Washington, DC: National Low-Income Housing Coalition, 2004), p. 7.
Note: n/a indicates data not available.

The mortgage interest deduction is the second largest tax expenditure in the federal budget at $67 billion. Only the exclusion of employer contributions for medical insurance premiums and medical care is larger.[10] The top income quintile households in 2004 received approximately 48 percent of housing-related tax expenditures, amounting to $57.2 billion in 2004. Also in 2004, the average income of households in the bottom quintile was $10,295, less than the equivalent of a full-time job at the federal minimum wage ($5.15 per hour in 2004). The bottom quintile received $1.4 billion in housing tax expenditures and $30.4 billion in housing assistance outlays.[11] Only 13 percent of the households in the bottom income quintile (all of whom had annual incomes less than $18,500) received federal housing assistance. The deduction is extremely regressive. The tax savings for households earning more than $250,000 is ten times the tax savings for households earning between $40,000 and $75,000 a year, according to research by James Poterba and Todd Sinai.[12]

It should be noted that those in lower income brackets must often pay a larger share of their income than the more affluent to obtain housing. In 2006, the latest period for which data is available, 39 million households were "moderately cost burdened" (paying over 30 percent of income on housing) and 18 million were "severely cost burdened" (paying over 50 percent of income on housing).[13] Because of the increased cost of housing and anemic real income growth between 2001 and 2006, the number of severely burdened households increased by 23 percent, surging from 14 million to 18 million. The data for 2006 also reveal that 47 percent of households in the bottom quartile were severely cost burdened.[14]

Not only was the housing market attractive for potential homebuyers, but it also attracted the financial industry's interest as a huge lending market. In the 1940s and 1950s, the tax subsidy encouraged homebuyers to invest in homes that included indoor plumbing and other amenities. During that same time period, it was probably worthwhile to encourage Americans to house themselves and their children in larger homes. But by 2000, the average family size had declined to just 3.15 per household while the average square feet of housing increased.[15]

Housing trends indicate increases in square footage, the number of bathrooms, the percentage of new units with central air conditioning, and the number of units having parking facilities. Every category of amenity has grown. The number of single-person households increased from 18 percent to 28 percent between 1980 and 2005 while the number of two-person households increased from 25 percent to 37 percent.[16] The trend toward larger houses is expected to be reversed, based on the skyrocketing cost of housing, the trend toward smaller households (including the surge of retired baby boomer couples), and concern for a smaller carbon footprint.

One response to housing trends is Smart Growth, which promotes better planning at the local level. To improve land use and avoid sprawl, planners recommend "infilling" older neighborhoods with housing closer to jobs, shopping, and entertainment. Proponents of New Urbanism, the design part of Smart Growth, construct communities like Kentlands, Maryland, which mix housing, retail, and business with sidewalks, bike paths, and easy access to public transportation. The large parking lot fronting buildings is replaced with multiuse buildings hugging the street. The trend for families to invest an ever-increasing share of their income in more sumptuous housing is indicated in Table 11.1.

Many also point to broader societal gains related to homeownership. For example, homeowners are able to save at a higher rate than are renters. This occurs through home equity, or the portion of their mortgage payments paid directly on the principal, the appreciation of the worth of their homes over time, and the tax advantages homeowners enjoy. These savings make funds available for national investment, which stimulates greater economic growth.

Table 11.1 Characteristics of New Privately Owned Single-Family Houses Completed, 1970–2007

	Percentage of Units		
	1970	1990	2007
Floor area (sq. ft.)			
Under 1,200	36	11	4
1,200–1,599	28	22	14
1,600–1,999	16	22	20
2,000–2,399	21	17	17
2,400+	—	29	45
Median square feet	1,385	1,905	2,227
Bedrooms			
2 or fewer	13	15	12
3	63	57	50
4 or more	24	29	38
Bathrooms			
1.5 or less	20	13	5
2	32	42	36
2.5 or more	16	45	59
Central air conditioning	34	76	90
Fireplaces, 1 or more	35	66	51
Garage	58	82	89

Source: US Census Bureau, *Statistical Abstracts 1993, 2008* (Washington, DC: US Government Printing Office, 1993, 2009).

The Housing Bubble and the Financial Crisis of 2007–2009

The housing bubble began to follow the stock market bubble in the mid-1990s. Higher home prices beginning in the middle of the decade resulted in housing starts climbing to almost 25 percent above the average rate of the early 1990s. Simultaneously, low interest rates encouraged stock market investors to borrow to invest. An extraordinary run-up of stock prices encouraged many investors to increase consumer spending based on their newfound wealth in the stock market by the late 1990s. Stock prices crested and began to decline with the recession of 2001–2002 and a very weak recovery. Meanwhile, Greenspan cut interest rates to 1 percent in 2003, driving mortgage interest rates to fifty-year lows. The bursting of the stock market bubble actually fed the housing bubble as many people shifted their investments from the stock market to the housing market in search of a safer alternative. The transfer of funds from stocks to housing further stimulated the housing market as people spent some of their new wealth from the stock market on more expensive houses.

This transfer of large sums from stocks to the housing market drove prices up because, at least in the short run, the supply of housing is relatively fixed.[17] From the fourth quarter of 2002 to the fourth quarter of 2006, real house prices rose by 31.6 percent, or an annual rate of over 7 percent. Not surprisingly, the result was more home construction with housing starts peaking at 2.07 million in 2005, over 50 percent above the prebubble years.[18] Spiraling house prices encouraged many to take out home equity loans and transfer equity in their homes to the economy in the form of demand for more goods and services. The resulting boom in personal consumption in the years 2005–2007 did not result in the development of productive industries or services. It was driven by the housing market and facilitated by foreign purchases of US bonds.

The housing boom years gained momentum after the turn of the century, even though the economic recovery from the recession of 2001–2002 was weak as wages began lagging behind inflation. During the boom years, the financial industry developed new products to attract more borrowers who previously would have been unable to qualify for loans. In the desire for higher returns, lenders offered buyers "teaser rates" on **adjustable rate mortgages** (ARM) that would adjust upward in two years even if market interest rates remained the same. Fixed rate mortgages had been standard through most of the 1990s because they offered buyers the security that the house payment would take a smaller percentage of income since salaries generally rise over time while the mortgage payment would not.

Subprime mortgages refer to loans that were often aggressively sold to homeowners with modest incomes and poor credit or employment histories. These loans usually were not to finance a new home, but for homeowners who wanted to borrow on the equity in their home to pay bills, remodel their home, or make some other major purchase. The interest rates on subprime loans were often three, or even four, percentage points higher than interest rates available at the prime rate. The subprime market went from less than 9 percent in 2002 to 25 percent in 2005.[19] Many families who had been relatively secure in their homes were suddenly faced with foreclosure from the twin problem of higher interest rates and a weaker labor market.

Another instrument was known as **Alt-A loans**. These loans were made to home-buyers and those purchasing investment properties. They were often made without full documentation of the buyer's creditworthiness. In many cases, the buyers were borrowing close to the total value of the property, sometimes as interest-only loans until a reset date (usually five years after issuance). This occurred because appraisers who are generally hired by banks to give an "appraisal" verifying that the collateral on the house is sufficient, and that the individual is creditworthy, were under pressure to recommend in favor of the loan. Banks were increasingly intent on "selling" the mortgage in the secondary market. If the appraiser gave low appraisals, he or she would not be hired by the bank for subsequent appraisals. Therefore, appraisers had an incentive to recommend the loan without fully documenting a borrower's income or job history. Much of the lending was predatory since loans were approved even when it was known that the borrower likely would default, but it was expected that the bank would resell bundled **mortgage-backed securities** (MBS) in the secondary market before the default occurred. Banks made money on the fees associated with selling rather than holding MBS themselves.

The ability of banks to sell their MBS, with an increasing number of questionable quality mortgages, depended on the "appraisal" of the bonds. The banks hired a rating agency, such as Moody's, to rate the quality of their bonds. The agency, like the bank's loan appraiser, also had a strong incentive to issue high ratings on the bank's securities or the bank would hire a competitor to rate them in the future. These major incentive structures placed an enormous premium on short-term profits at the expense of longer-term profits. The pay structure for executives in much of the financial sector is based largely in bonuses from hitting profit targets, which means it is responsive to short-term profits.

It should be pointed out that many senior executives became fabulously wealthy while their companies were casualties of the mortgage meltdown. For example, Angelo Mozila of Countrywide Financial, one of the largest originators of subprime mortgages, received several hundred million dollars in compensation over the past decade. Countrywide was taken over by Bank of America at a fraction of the price of its worth at the peak of the bubble. James Cayne, the chief executive officer of Bear Stearns, also made hundreds of millions of dollars while leading the company into bankruptcy. Many hedge fund managers of real estate received 20 percent of the munificent gains during the good years, but then watched from the sidelines as their clients lost most of their investments after the bubble burst. The incentive structure, with a weak regulatory system, gave executives a powerful incentive to use financial engineering to gain quick profits regardless of the long-term costs.

Subprime and Alt-A loans made up over 40 percent of the loans issued by 2006.[20] Such an increase in subprime lending should have been a clear signal of problems in the housing market. By 2006 ARMs, rather than fixed rate mortgages, accounted for about 35 percent of all new mortgages. Rather than being alerted by the warning signs, the Federal Reserve Board continued to make money available to fuel the demand by maintaining low interest rates. President G. W. Bush celebrated the low interest rates and boasted of record rates of homeownership.[21]

The building boom led to such an oversupply of housing that prices began falling by mid-2006, with the decline in prices gaining speed through 2007 and into 2008.[22] The national median single-family home price fell in nominal terms for the first time since recordkeeping began.

There are 52 million US homeowners with a mortgage and, of those, almost 14 million (27 percent) are underwater. They owe more on their mortgage than their home is worth. By December 2007, with the economy sinking into a recession, and the value of many homes sinking below the value of the mortgage and mortgages resetting to higher rates, owners began falling behind in their payments. To be clear, when housing prices are below the value of the mortgage (underwater), these home-owners are essentially renters. They are "owners" in name only. Like renters, when they sell their home and move, they would have no equity to help them buy a new home. Since the median period of homeownership is seven years (four years for low-income families), many homeowners who are underwater today, having purchased their homes a few years ago at the height of the housing bubble, will face this problem in the near future.

As prices plummet, an increasing number of homeowners face foreclosure. In many cases, the owner is unable to borrow against the equity of the house to stave off foreclosure if the value of the house falls to less than the value of the mortgage. In other cases, individuals may decide foreclosure is preferable if the value of the house is less than what is owed on the mortgage. They may decide to pocket the difference (which may be worth hundreds of thousands of dollars) by simply walking away from their mortgage.[23] In either case, foreclosure (whether voluntary or not) increased the supply of housing on the market and drove home prices down.

As the economy weakened and mortgage interest rates reset upward, delinquencies on mortgage payments climbed. Falling home prices meant that many who fell behind in their payments could not resell their houses to avoid foreclosure. Banks responded by tightening loan requirements to make certain the collateral in the house would cover the value of the mortgage, and demanding a higher down payment that further depressed the sale of existing houses and new housing starts. Investors in mortgage securities were caught by surprise at the swift decline in the performance of their securities. Many investors were also forced to sell at a loss. Some investment firms and mortgage companies had borrowed heavily to buy mortgage securities and were unable to borrow more. The sheer size of the outstanding mortgage debt and the danger to the banking system soon spread to a freeze in credit markets and the full-blown financial crisis of the fall of 2008.

As a public policy matter, it is important to be aware that the media frequently report that the collapse of the housing market began to spill over into nonhousing credit and to financial institutions not connected with mortgage lending. While that is true, the implication is often inaccurate. Baker insists that we not lose sight of the real issue:

> Why do reporters keep telling us that the economy's problem is a credit crisis? Yes, consumers and businesses can't get credit as easily as they could a year ago. There is a really good reason for tighter credit. Tens of millions of homeowners who had substantial equity in their homes two years ago have little or nothing today. Businesses are facing the worst downturn since the Great Depression. This matters for credit decisions. A homeowner with equity in her home is very unlikely to default on a car loan or credit card debt. They will draw on this equity rather than lose their car and/or have a default placed on their credit record. . . . A homeowner who has no equity is a serious default risk. In the case of businesses, their creditworthiness depends on their future profits. Profit prospects look much worse in November 2008 than they did in November 2007. . . . While many banks are obviously at the brink, consumers and businesses would be facing a much harder time getting credit right now even if the financial system were rock solid. *The problem with the economy is the loss of close to $6 trillion in housing wealth and an even larger amount of stock wealth.*[24]

A homeowner who finds that their house is worthless reacts very much like someone in the stock market who finds their stock has fallen in value. They may not be able to get a home equity loan to buy a car or remodel the house, and they generally will reduce their spending. The crisis has made undeniable what we have been hearing for a long time, but hoped to finesse: we have been living beyond our means based on the housing bubble's inflated housing prices and large amounts of foreign purchases of bonds to consume more than we have produced. The national adjustment is both painful and inevitable.

The dark side of the tax subsidy is that it encouraged borrowers to get the maximum loans allowable to invest in the most expensive homes possible. This investment in housing fueled by the tax subsidy increased the demand and price of housing. Homeowners paid more for a house than they would have without the tax subsidy, and they have larger mortgages. The larger flow of funds into housing than would have been the case means that less money is available for capital investment, which reduces economic growth. The result is a housing bubble amplified by risky loans and assets that is subject to wide gyrations.

The most dramatic increase of homes in foreclosure occurred among the riskier subprime loans. Foreclosure rates on adjustable subprime mortgages were about five times higher than those on adjustable prime loans. The existence of hundreds of thousands of foreclosed homes has forced home prices sharply downward in many communities, reducing home equity of nearby homeowners. Local jurisdictions also experienced a significant drop in real estate tax receipts. The regions at greatest risk are those with troubled economies, such as Detroit and Cleveland, with a high percentage of low-income communities and subprime and Alt-A loans, and an excess supply of housing.

The housing industry and the G. W. Bush administration had encouraged the notion that the market without government intervention developed "creative" financial instruments that would increase the rate of homeownership. The administration touted the resulting "ownership" society in which more people would be able to own a home while government would simply encourage low interest rates to empower the market. In fact, the greatest homeownership gains occurred between 1994 and 2001 as homeownership rates grew from 64.2 percent of the population to 68 percent, when the subprime share was small and price appreciation was more modest. According to the Joint Center for Housing Studies at Harvard University, after 1994 the economy entered a period of unusually vigorous and broad-based growth with strong increases in incomes across the board.[25] Therefore, the expansion of mortgage credit in the 1990s was accomplished with traditional products and without adding much to risk.[26]

The growth in mortgage credit after 2003 came largely from riskier subprime, interest-only, and payment option loans that provided only a temporary lift to homeownership. From 2001 to 2004, homeownership increased from 68 percent to 69.2 percent, and has since retreated to its level in 2000 of 67.5 percent.[27] Given the rate of foreclosures, it is entirely possible that the homeownership rate could decline to the level of 1996. Homeowner vacancy rates in 2008 averaged 2.85 percent, which is the highest level over the past fifteen years.[28]

The mortgage meltdown and the high number of foreclosures ensures that, on the supply side, a large number of houses will be for sale at least through 2011 as banks will be anxious to sell the properties from their ledger. On the demand side, the sales of existing homes continued to fall through the summer of 2009, even as plummeting prices made houses less expensive. The deteriorating economy restrained potential buyers as job losses continued to climb and consumer confidence dropped. Added to those concerns were more rigorous lending requirements and larger down payment requirements than previously. These requirements had the effect of reducing the pool of potential buyers over the past several years. The ongoing stream of foreclosed houses being placed on the market also raised the fear that home values would continue their descent.

The Obama Administration's Housing Stabilization Policy

The new administration was presented with a difficult policy problem. The collapse of the housing market had catastrophic effects in the financial industry that resulted in higher unemployment, forcing the administration to deal with the crises in all three areas simultaneously. The key issue going forward is the underlying general weakness in the economy. Recovery in the housing market is dependent on people feeling more secure in their jobs. Policy must address stabilizing the financial industry by bailing out stressed institutions while, at the same time, helping financially stressed workers stay in their homes to improve worker confidence and stabilizing the housing market.

President Barack Obama's plan provided $75 billion to help families refinance their mortgages or avoid foreclosure. The plan was a decisive turn away from the G. W. Bush administration's policy, which provided support for financial institutions, but not for homeowners. During the final two years of his administration, G. W. Bush did not give the mortgage industry any incentive to restructure the subprime and Alt-A mortgages that had been so recklessly marketed. In that period, approximately 2 million families lost their homes to foreclosure. The Obama policy's goal was help as many as 9 million homeowners avoid foreclosure. The policy was designed to aid homeowners in financial jeopardy who took out prudent mortgages and had a substantial down payment, and who had been keeping up with their monthly payment. These homeowners wanted to refinance into a lower-rate mortgage, but could not qualify because banks would not refinance when equity evaporated.

The president's plan was also intended to help homeowners whose home price was no more than 5 percent below the value of the mortgage (the loan could not exceed 105 percent of the current value of the property). This would permit only borrowers with loans owned or backed by Fannie Mae and Freddie Mac (almost 50 percent of all mortgages) to refinance their loans to lower rates. Fannie and Freddie will receive an additional $200 billion for this refinancing. Consequently, a homeowner's ability to refinance depends on who holds the mortgage.

The president's plan will not help homeowners where prices have fallen almost 50 percent in Arizona, California, parts of Florida, and cities like Cleveland, Las Vegas, and Detroit where most homes are much more than 5 percent underwater.[29] Some estimates are that less than 1 million of the nearly 14 million underwater homeowners will be helped by this part of the plan. Those that are helped by the plan will see their mortgage payment decline due to lower interest payments, but it will not reduce the amount they owe on their mortgage. And since these homeowners are still underwater or close to it, they will not be able to build up equity in their home in the short run.

The second group to receive help are homeowners who can no longer afford their mortgage payments, either because the family income has fallen or because their ARM has reset at a higher level. The plan will take $75 billion from the taxpayer bailout funds for financial institutions to help some homeowners stay in their homes. If the mortgage payment is more than 38 percent, but less than 43 percent of income, the homeowner may be able to get help. The lender would have to agree to temporarily reduce the interest rate to bring the monthly payment down to 38 percent of family income. The government would then subsidize the lender to further reduce the payment to 31 percent of the homeowner's income. After five years, lenders will be able to raise the interest rates back to the market rate. In this way, it is like an ARM. Banks receive a subsidy to encourage them to go along with the plan.

The bottom line is that the plan will make mortgage payments more affordable for some, at least temporarily. It should slow the rate of foreclosure and it may slow the decline in house prices in some neighborhoods. But the plan will not prop up home prices in areas mentioned above where homes are overvalued and prices will continue to fall. That is as it should be. If the government could keep the price above the equilibrium level, it would have the effect of putting homeownership out of the reach of many potential buyers.

The administration's plan makes a serious effort to help homeowners, but it still leans heavily toward bailing out banks. The effort was to develop a bailout plan that would not rescue the "unscrupulous or the irresponsible." As President Obama said: "It will not reward folks who bought homes they knew from the beginning they would never be able to afford."[30] Critics complain that the program creates a "moral hazard" when it bails out institutions that never should have extended mortgages to people likely unable to afford the mortgage payments over the long term. In normal circumstances with the economy at or near full employment, a Keynesian would agree. But the financial crisis is eerily reminiscent of the onset of the Great Depression. Keynesian theory provides a remedy of government intervention to reverse the downward spiral by putting millions of distressed homeowners on a firmer footing and stopping the blight of empty homes and shattered neighborhoods.

Baker proposed a policy to help homeowners that does not help banks. He proposed that judges or court officers handling a foreclosure be required to ask the homeowner if they want to stay in their houses as a renter. If they say yes, there would be an appraisal of the market rent of the home. The homeowner would then have the option to remain in the house for a substantial period of time (perhaps up to ten years), paying the fair market rent. For most homeowners, these rents would be far lower than their mortgage payments even after they were restructured. The proposal is a simple no-cost and no-bureaucracy alternative to paying banks about $20,000 to keep a homeowner in a home in which they have no equity. It does not require taxpayer dollars and could have gone into effect the moment that the bill was signed into law. It would not bail out lenders who made predatory mortgages, and there are no windfalls for homeowners facing foreclosure. These individuals could stay in the home for a period of time, but they would no longer be homeowners.[31]

Long-Term Housing Policy Considerations

There is a growing body of analysis that maintains the current crisis provides an opportunity to rethink our long-term housing policy. Specifically, Edward Glaeser and Joseph Gyourko, at Harvard and the University of Pennsylvania respectively, say that federal housing policy "should ensure that our poorest citizens are able to live in decent housing, and should address the high housing costs facing many middle-income Americans."[32] They maintain that the diverse US housing markets are poorly served by their one-size-fits-all policies that placed too much faith in the immense subsidized borrowing of the home mortgage interest deduction. The more an individual borrowed, the greater was the homebuyer's tax advantage. But housing policies contained contradictory objectives such as higher homeownership rates, more affordable housing units, and, most recently, higher prices.[33] In this regard, Fannie Mae and Freddie Mac's policies, the guaranteeing of mortgages against default, and the mortgage interest tax deduction applied the same policy prescription to every housing market despite wide variations of whether housing was abundant and inexpensive or scarce and highly priced.

Glaeser and Gyourko divide the nation into three distinct types of housing markets that policymakers must recognize to provide policies to reflect these differences. The first housing market involves the shortage of housing for the poor. These regions have low consumer demand for housing because their incomes are so low. Prices in these areas are low, but few new homes are being built because construction costs are higher than most potential buyers are able to pay. Here, the problem is best solved by providing direct income transfers to the poor through housing vouchers, not through a tax program focused on providing affordable housing. They maintain that "subsidizing developers to build new housing for the poor makes no more sense than paying auto companies to provide a special line of poor people's cars."[34] The current system in which the poor generally buy used cars is a much more efficient way of providing lower-priced transportation.

Glaeser and Gyourko recommend eliminating all federal subsidies for the production of low-income housing, which often tie impoverished workers to areas where they have limited job opportunities. Instead, they propose using the funds to increase the scope of the Housing Choice Voucher Program (often referred to as the "Section 8 voucher program" after the section of the US Housing Act that authorizes it). Vouchers are provided to particular tenants to rent where they choose. The vouchers can also be used to help families buy homes. They propose making the Section 8 program national in scope to be administered nationally by the Department of Housing and Urban Development (as opposed to being administered by local authorities at present). Their proposal would also eliminate supply-side barriers to building modest-priced housing.

A second problem is related to middle- and upper-income homebuyers. The value of the tax deduction increases as income goes up. The benefits go primarily to richer homeowners who itemize deductions on their tax returns and own more expensive homes. The current tax code allows homeowners to deduct the interest on loans used to buy a home up to $1 million. And the ability to deduct the interest on home-equity loans up to $100,000 allows mortgagees, but not renters, to use tax-sheltered borrowing to buy new cars and major appliances. The home mortgage deduction benefits go primarily to more affluent Americans who are likely to own homes in any event.

For these reasons, Glaeser and Gyourko recommend the reduction or elimination of the home mortgage interest deduction. Most of those who are on the margin between renting and buying have relatively lower incomes. But the interest deduction targets its benefits on the most affluent who buy the most expensive homes. A small targeted subsidy for first-time buyers could encourage homeownership just as effectively without encouraging people to borrow vast amounts or buy larger, more expensive homes. It is unlikely that the home mortgage deduction would reduce levels of homeownership. It was phased out in the United Kingdom where homeownership rates are the same as in the United States. Canada also has a 67 percent homeownership rate.[35]

The most dramatic increases in home prices occurred in places like Boston, New York City, and San Francisco where housing supply is limited. These areas have restrictive zoning laws to keep home prices up. It would be counterproductive, where the housing bubble has not fully deflated, to try to sustain prices at bubble-inflated levels. In contrast, in areas like Nevada and Arizona where there are fewer housing restrictions, the building boom responded dramatically to demand. And the collapse in the demand resulted in housing prices responding by adjusting dramatically downward.

There is a strong case to be made that the government should not try to make housing less affordable to average citizens by raising the price. There is no reason why middle-income citizens should pay more for any basic commodity, whether it is oil or housing. Government should encourage lower prices in housing, and not try to artificially inflate housing prices. Note that, if the cost of constructing a building in an unrestricted market is $175,000, then credit and bailout policies are not going to keep prices above that equilibrium point.

Rental Housing

Roughly a third of US households lived in rented housing even at the peak of the homeownership boom. That percent has held fairly steady for the past twenty-five years. Many renters prefer the convenience of renting and the relative straightforwardness of moving that renting gives. Others view rent as the most prudent financial option. However, most households rent because they cannot qualify for a mortgage at their low income level. Not surprisingly, many are young, foreign born, and divorced individuals.[36] Between 2004 and 2007, economic stress produced an increase of over 2 million more renter households. The increase in renters was driven by how unaffordable homeownership had become.

By 2008, the meltdown in housing and credit markets made renting more attractive for a growing number of households. Many former homeowners lost their homes to foreclosure and moved into rental units. Over the long term, those who defaulted on their loans will remain in rental units for at least five to ten years because they will need years to overcome the damage to their credit rating. But it is primarily the effect of tighter credit requirements and the insecurity of declining home prices that is driving increased demand for rental units.[37] In fact, about a third of applicants with mortgage delinquencies were rejected by large rental properties.[38]

For the next several years, rental markets will play a more central role as the housing market adjusts to excess supplies and rising foreclosures. Many homeowners discouraged by their inability to get an "acceptable" price will decide to rent their property rather than have it remain vacant.

The Homeless

Recent data indicate that, due to the financial crisis, the number of homeless is rising. But a precise determination of the number of homeless in the United States is very difficult due to the lifestyle and habits of the homeless. There are several national estimates of homelessness, although none are definitive. The best approximation appears to be from a study done by the National Law Center on Homelessness and Poverty, which states that approximately 3.5 million people, 1.35 million of them children, are likely to experience homelessness in a given year.[39] This translates to approximately 1 percent of the US population. The US Conference of Mayors says that 840,000 people are homeless on any given night.[40] The number of precariously housed families who are only one rent payment away from eviction or forced to double up with others also continues to increase. Especially vulnerable are low-income families who pay over half of their income for housing.

To be homeless is to be at the very bottom of the socioeconomic ladder in the United States. In his work *Down and Out in America,* Peter Rossi, a professor of sociology, defines literal **homelessness** as not having customary and regular access to a conventional dwelling.[41] Homelessness is not an absolute condition, but a matter of degree.

In the United States, the official federal definition of homelessness provides the criteria to determine who is able to receive shelter from social service providers. The federal definition is an individual who lacks a fixed, regular, and adequate nighttime residence; and an individual who has a primary nighttime residence that is:

1. a supervised publicly or privately operated shelter designed to provide temporary living accommodations (including welfare hotels, congregate shelters, and transitional housing for the mentally ill);
2. an institution that provides a temporary residence for individuals intended to be institutionalized; or
3. a public or private place not designed for, or ordinarily used as, a regular sleeping accommodation for human beings.[42]

Homelessness has been a facet of US society since colonialism, but was not considered a public policy issue until the Great Depression overwhelmed the private charities and local governments that provided almost all of the aid to the poor and homeless at the time. World War II marked a change, and the demand for labor remained high enough after the war to ensure that homeless rates stayed low throughout the 1950s. In the 1960s, Lyndon Johnson's War on Poverty aimed, with some success, at reducing poverty and homelessness. In the 1980s, concern about homelessness was confounded by moral distinctions between the "deserving" and the "undeserving" poor. In 1981, the government restructured many programs for the poor by reducing both funding and federal oversight while providing block grants to states to administer most welfare funds.

The increasing number of homeless families with children is a foreboding indicator of future challenges to society. Children in lower-income families change residences twice as often as nonpoor children because of their parents' tenuous hold on jobs and rental units. Research indicates that it takes a child four to six months to recover academically after changing schools.[43] Not surprisingly, such children are significantly less likely to finish high school on time. The infant mortality rate among the homeless is roughly 30 percent higher than for infants born into families living in homes. Young children who are homeless often show signs of emotional distress. Unstable housing can put them far behind their peers in physical and cognitive development. They are diagnosed with learning disabilities at twice the rate of other children, and often suffer from emotional or behavioral problems. About 21 percent of these children must repeat a grade (compared to 5 percent of other children) because of frequent absences from school, a key predictor of becoming a school dropout. About 37 percent of homeless children do drop out of school.[44]

Studies vary, but generally agree that up to half of the adult homeless have or have had a substance abuse problem, and that up to one-third suffer from some form of mental illness. The homeless also have a higher incidence of physical illness, such as tuberculosis and HIV/AIDS, than does the general population.

The homeless are a subset of the very poorest in society. Such grinding poverty has always been problematic in the United States both for humanitarian reasons and because it clashes with the ideal of a decent standard of living for everyone. The White House website (whitehouse.gov) describes several housing and poverty issues. The website promises to restore cuts to public housing operating subsidies. As a senator, President Obama supported the creation of the National Affordable Housing Trust Fund to increase the supply of affordable housing. He indicates that he will also support increasing the minimum wage and expanding the Earned Income Tax Credit. Obama also indicates that he is committed to establishing a "zero-tolerance" policy toward homelessness among veterans.

There is little doubt that the financial crisis of 2007–2009 will cause a significant increase in homelessness, particularly as families face foreclosure on their mortgages. The harm and stress caused to families, particularly children, is substantial. Therefore, Barbara Sard of the Center on Budget and Policy Priorities proposes that Congress include a one-time funding for 200,000 new housing vouchers to prevent an additional several hundred thousand families from becoming homeless.[45] The **housing voucher** program, usually referred to as Section 8 after the section of the US Housing Act that authorized it, was created in the 1970s and has become the largest federal housing assistance program. The federal funds are distributed to low-income families. The cost would be only one-half of 1 percent of the overall package and would substantially diminish the increase in homelessness during the recession while providing a short-term stimulus.

Homelessness is a problem that can be reduced with appropriate policy intervention. As Christopher Jencks wrote:

> If no one drank, took drugs, lost touch with reality or had trouble holding a job, homelessness would be rare. But if America had a system of social welfare comparable to that of Sweden or Germany, homelessness would also be rare. In those countries job training is far better, unskilled jobs pay better, benefits for the unemployed are almost universally available and the mental health system does much more to provide housing for the mentally ill. It is the combination of widespread individual vulnerability and collective indifference that leaves so many Americans in the streets.[46]

Conclusion

Homeownership occupies a central place in our culture and in the American Dream. It has been a goal of most citizens throughout the nation's history. Government support of homeownership became more direct during the Great Depression. Policies created during the depression had the effect of encouraging the growth of the suburban United States while contributing to housing segregation and the decline of many cities. After World War II, the Housing Act of 1949 reflected the renewed goal during the Truman administration that the United States could raise living standards and provide for urban renewal in cities that had been neglected since the 1930s. The act concentrated on building more housing units, but did not address the social and economic problems of an increasingly stratified society. By the late 1950s, policymakers began to back away from urban renewal projects that threatened not only middle-income, but also low-income, urban dwellers. As government retreated in its commitment to rebuild inner cities, Section 8 became the focal point of low-income housing policy. Funds for vouchers became the main policy for low-income individuals seeking to purchase or rent housing. More Americans are spending an ever-increasing percentage of their incomes on housing, leaving them with insufficient means to purchase other necessities such as food, clothing, and health care.

Policies like the mortgage interest deduction, or real estate property deduction, provide a much greater subsidy to more affluent homeowners than to lower-income homeowners. The greater value of the subsidy for the affluent encourages them to view a home as an investment while middle- and lower-income workers view a home as "shelter."

The housing bubble is at the center of housing policy today. The Obama administration's efforts to stabilize the housing market is part of the broader effort to stabilize the economy.

Questions for Discussion

1. How is the bursting of the housing bubble and the plummeting price of houses at the center of the broader financial crisis?

2. Is there any evidence that the mortgage interest deduction is a regressive form of taxation?

3. Is housing in the United States becoming less racially segregated? Is it becoming more segregated by income? Explain how this works.

4. How does the fragmentation of power between federal, state, and local authorities complicate housing policy?

Useful Websites

American Bar Association Commission on Homelessness and Poverty,
    www.abanet.org.
Beyond Shelter, www.beyondshelter.org.
National Association of Housing and Redevelopment Officials, www.nahro.org.
National Coalition for the Homeless, www.nationalhomeless.org.
National Low-Income Housing Coalition, www.nlihc.org.
Urban Institute, www.urban.org.
US Department of Housing and Urban Development, www.hud.gov/homeless/index.cfm.

Notes

1. See Dean Baker, "The Run-Up in Home Prices: Is It Real or Is It Another Bubble?" Center for Economic Policy Research (CEPR), August 2002, available at www.cepr.net/index.php/publications/reports/the-run-up-in-home-prices-is-it-real-or-is-it-another-bubble (accessed February 12, 2009). See also Dean Baker, "The Housing Bubble Starts to Burst," CEPR, March 6, 2007, available at www.cepr.net/index.php/op-eds-&-columns (accessed February 12, 2009).

2. Baker, "The Run-Up in Home Prices." Baker's analysis was reinforced with the construction of a data set from 1895 to 1995 by Robert Shiller, which showed that real house prices had been essentially unchanged for that 100-year period. See Robert Shiller, *Irrational Exuberance* (Princeton: Princeton University Press, 2006).

3. Homeownership was (in percentages) 46.5 in 1900, 45.9 in 1910, 45.6 in 1920, and 47.8 in 1930 at the beginning of the Great Depression. See US Census Bureau, Census of Housing, "Historical Census of Housing Tables," available at www.census.gov/hhes/www/housing/census/historic/owner.html (accessed February 23, 2009).

4. See US Census Bureau, *Statistical Abstract of the United States 2003,* Mini-Historical Series (Washington, DC: US Government Printing Office, 2003), p. 19. It reports a total population of 122 million people in the United States, 30 million households, and 23 million married couples.

5. In 1965, the FHA became part of the Department of Housing and Urban Development (HUD).

6. Habitat for Humanity, available at www.habitat.org/how/christian.html (accessed August 19, 2009).

7. Edward Glaeser and Jesse Shapiro, "The Benefits of the Home Mortgage Interest Deduction," NBER Working Paper Series, Working Paper 9284 (Cambridge, MA: National Bureau of Economic Research, October 2002).

8. See Raymond J. Struyk, *Should Government Encourage Home Ownership?* (Washington, DC: Urban Institute, 1977).

9. The government has supported homeownership beginning with the Homestead Act of 1860, extending through the federal income tax in 1913, up to tax policies currently in effect. However, it is debatable whether homeowners are more responsible than renters in all respects: there is some evidence that free rider behavior leaving neighborhood improvements to others extends across both groups.

10. *Estimates of Federal Tax Expenditures for Fiscal Years 2008–2012,* prepared by the Joint Committee on Taxation (Washington, DC: US Government Printing Office, October 31, 2008), pp. 51, 56.

11. Cushing N. Dolbeare, Irene Basloe Saraf, and Sheila Crowley, "Changing Priorities: The Federal Budget and Housing Assistance 1976–2005," in *The National Low-Income Housing Coalition* (Washington, DC: National Low-Income Housing Coalition, October 2004), p. 8.

12. James Poterba and Todd Sinai, "Tax Expenditures for Owner-Occupied Housing Deductions for Property Taxes and Mortgage Interest and the Exclusion of Imputed Rental Income," paper presented January 5, 2008, at the Wharton School, University of Pennsylvania, available at http://real.wharton.upenn.edu/~Sinai/papers/Poterba-Sinai-2008-ASSA-fin (accessed February 24, 2009).

13. Joint Center for Housing Studies, Harvard University, *The State of the Nation's Housing 2008* (Cambridge: Joint Center for Housing Studies, Harvard University, 2008), p. 4.

14. Ibid.

15. American Fact Finder, American Housing Survey, "Nation's Housing Stock Reaches 128 Million," October 6, 2008, available at http://factfinder.census.gov/servlet/SAFFFacts (accessed February 13, 2009).

16. US Census Bureau, *Statistical Abstract 2003* (Washington, DC: US Government Printing Office, 2003), p. 61, and *Statistical Abstract 2009* (Washington, DC: US Government Printing Office, 2009), p. 53.

17. Dean Baker, "The Housing Bubble and the Financial Crisis," *Real-World Economics Review* 46 (May 20, 2008): 73–81, available at www.paecon.net/PAEReview/issue46/Baker46.pdf (accessed August 19, 2009). This section relies heavily on Baker's noncopyrighted, freely available article.

18. Ibid., p. 74.

19. Ibid., p. 76.

20. Joint Center for Housing Studies, *The State of the Nation's Housing 2008,* p. 2.

21. Edwin Chen, "Bush, in Pennsylvania, Hails Record Homeownership," *Los Angeles Times,* March 16, 2004, available at http://articles.latimes.com/2004/mar/16/nation/na-bush16 (accessed August 19, 2009). See also "HUD Secretary Jackson Announces $161.5 Million in Downpayment Assistance for First-Time Home Buyers," HUD news release no. 04-050, June 2, 2004, in which the administration announced the "American Dream Downpayment Initiative," to provide for up to $10,000 or 6 percent toward a down payment in grants to those making less than 80 percent of the median income to put toward the purchase of a house.

22. Joint Center for Housing Studies, *The State of the Nation's Housing 2008,* p. 1.

23. Baker, "The Housing Bubble and the Financial Crisis," p. 75.

24. Dean Baker, "It's Not the Credit Crisis, Damn It!" Beat the Press Archive, November 29, 2008, available at http://prospect.org/csnc/blogs/beat_the_press_archive?month=11&year=2008 (accessed February 18, 2009).

25. Joint Center for Housing Studies, *The State of the Nation's Housing 2008,* p. 4.

26. Ibid.

27. Robert R. Callis and Linda B. Cavanaugh, "Census Bureau Reports on Residential Vacancies and Homeownership," *US Census Bureau News* newsletter, February 3, 2009, p. 4. The homeownership rate is the proportion of households that are owner-occupied.

28. Ibid., p. 1. The homeowner vacancy rate is the proportion of the homeowner inventory that is vacant and for sale.

29. David Leonhardt, "Obama's Housing Plan: Who Will Benefit?" Economix, *New York Times,* February 18, 2009, available at http://economix.blogs.nytimes.com/2009/02/18/obamas-housing-plan-who-will-benefit (accessed February 19, 2009).

30. Ibid.

31. Huffington Post, "Right to Rent: Helping Homeowners Without Throwing Money at Banks," available at www.huffingtonpost.com/dean-baker/right-to-rent-helping-homeowners-without-throwing-Money-at-Banks/156913.html (accessed February 27, 2009).

32. Edward L. Glaeser and Joseph Gyourko, "Two Ways to Revamp US Housing Policy," Economix, *New York Times,* December 16, 2008, available at http://economix.blogs.nytimes.com/2008/12/16/two-ways-to-revamp-us-housing-policy (accessed February 7, 2009).

33. Ibid.

34. Ibid.

35. "EU Homeownership Rates, 2002," paper presented at a conference on housing in Europe 2007, available at www.sigov.si/umar/conference/2005/papers/Doling.pdf (accessed February 25, 2009).

36. Joint Center for Housing Studies, *The State of the Nation's Housing 2008,* p. 22.

37. Ibid.

38. Ibid., p. 23.

39. National Law Center on Homelessness & Poverty, "Homelessness and Poverty in America," 2008, available at www.nlchp.org/hapia.cfm (accessed February 25, 2009).

40. US Conference of Mayors, Task Force on Hunger and Homelessness, "Homelessness and Hunger Survey" (US Conference of Mayors, December 2003), available at http://usmayors.org (accessed August 19, 2009).

41. Peter Rossi, *Down and Out in America: The Origins of Homelessness* (Chicago: University of Chicago Press, 1989), p. 11.

42. US Department of Housing and Urban Development, United States Code, Title 42, chap. 119, subchap. I, available at www.hud/gov/homeless/definition.cfm (accessed April 30, 2007).

43. Children's Defense Fund, *The Bush Administration: Set to Exacerbate Growing Housing Crisis for Families with Children* (Washington, DC: US Government Printing Office, January 2005), p. 3.

44. Ralph S. Hambrick and Debra J. Rog, "Homelessness: United States," in Neil J. Smelser and Paul B. Baltes, ed., *International Encyclopedia of the Social and Behavioral Sciences* (New York: Elsevier, 2001), pp. 35–65.

45. Barbara Sard, "Number of Homeless Families Climbing Due to Recession: Recovery Package Should Include New Housing Vouchers and Other Measures to Prevent Homelessness" (Washington, DC: Center on Budget Policy and Priorities, January 8, 2009), pp. 1, 14.

46. Christopher Jencks, "The Homeless," *New York Review of Books,* April 21, 1994, p. 22.

12

Environment:
Issues on a Global Scale

Environmentalism is a relatively new social movement that challenges institutional-ized politics. The purpose of environmental policy as a field of study is to inform pol-icy choices regarding the relationship between human society and the environment. The more specific purpose of environmental policy is to protect the natural environ-ment from overexploitation and degradation. It recognizes that Earth's resources are finite and that excessive exploitation through overpopulation, pollution, or resource extraction imposes costs on society and should be recognized as an inefficiency. The environment has been altered by industrial waste, reckless use of technology, and gov-ernment indifference. Until recently, many environmentalists had directed their efforts to persuading the public that there was in fact an environmental crisis. The public awakening to environmental issues has fostered an urgency in certain quarters to the need for environmental policies. Measurable degradation of air and water quality, oil and sewage spills, and contaminated beaches and drinking water have served to dra-matically focus attention on the environment. Public opinion polls now regularly reveal that overwhelming majorities of Americans place a high priority on environmental policies. Environmental policies are not designed to preserve the environment in its un-altered state as much as they are designed to protect the environment while promoting the social and economic welfare of the nation's inhabitants.

Environmental policy is distinctive because of the scientific nature of the funda-mental questions raised. Environmental issues are complicated and multifaceted, and environmental choices are often intertwined with consequences for energy policy. Moreover, the technical nature of scientific debates may discourage some from trying to inform themselves on the issues. Nevertheless, energy and environmental issues have a very real impact on the average person's daily life. Those who support major initiatives typically want ensured energy resources at reasonable prices with accept-able environmental consequences. This is difficult to accomplish in fact.

Despite increased awareness and growing efforts to protect the environment, disruptions have surfaced with increasing frequency. Environmental issues have emerged in different forms, including projected scarcities of energy resources, damage from releasing harmful substances and pollution into the environment, deforestation and soil erosion, water shortages, depletion of the ozone layer, the greenhouse effect, and global warming.

Evolving Environmental Themes

Most approaches to environmental problems can be categorized as protection or regulation. The first is based on the notion that there are finite limits to Earth's resources. This approach springs from **conservationist** and **preservationist** beliefs. The conservationist stance began in the early to middle 1800s, when various writers such as Thomas Malthus and Henry David Thoreau viewed Earth's resources as existing for the benefit of mankind, but also recognized the limits to natural resources and believed in an ethical obligation to use them wisely and efficiently rather than squandering them.

In contrast, preservationists, as the name indicates, want to preserve rather than conserve the natural environment. Concerned about the well-being of all nature, both living and nonliving, they view the world as containing many species, not just humans, that have an equal right to live on the planet. Saving various species, whether whales or the great apes, as well as protecting them from hunting, is supportive of this view. For this reason, preservationists support biodiversity among plants as well as animals. The natural environment in its pristine state, encompassing such features as mountain ranges, rivers, and wetlands, has a value that is not reducible to the people or the wildlife that live within its confines. John Muir, the founder of the Sierra Club in 1892, is often looked upon as the founder of the preservationist movement.

The Sierra Club and the Audubon Society were organized to call attention to the environmental destruction caused by unrestricted and destructive exploitation of the nation's resources. The preservationist movement had an interest in protecting natural areas from the encroachment of industrialization. Few political elites got involved, nor did most Americans seem to take seriously the damage that unregulated growth and development were inflicting on the environment.

President Theodore Roosevelt, a leader of the conservationist movement, prevailed over the preservationists of the time. He and a few politicians and scientists were largely motivated by a concern for resource conservation and management. The movement was driven by a fear of resource exhaustion and a need to manage natural resources before they were destroyed. This approach tried to make rational choices based on utilitarian principles of the greatest good for the greatest number, from an economic perspective. Such mid-twentieth-century projects of the Franklin D. Roosevelt administration as the Tennessee Valley Authority and the Civilian Conservation Corps reflect this desire to use nature for society's benefit.

Although the conservationist movement emphasized the efficient consumption of resources while the preservationists emphasized the long-term protection of animal and plant life, they shared a goal of protecting and managing the environment to achieve maximum **sustainable development**. The essential idea of sustainable development, while difficult to define precisely, emphasizes the need for policymakers to include a consideration of environmental, social, and economic factors in policy decisions. Policymakers will further take into account the interest of current and future generations and attempt to provide intergenerational equity. Policies should give a preference to strategies that provide the maximum sustainable yield of benefits. An application of this principle is the setting of maximum levels for fish catches. While no one owns the ocean and the fish and other animals that live within it, everyone has an incentive to exploit these resources, but no incentive to manage or conserve them. The problem of the "commons" may be dealt with by setting up regulations and incentives to encourage the management of the common stock in question to its maximum sustainable yield. This principle is consistent with the goal of protecting those most vulnerable to the spillover effects of policy choices as well. Since later generations are vulnerable to present-day choices, setting maximum sustainable yields guarantees that succeeding generations are provided with benefits roughly equal to those enjoyed today. This principle also encourages renewable energy sources such as solar, wind, and wave over the use of scarce nonrenewable forms of energy.

The concept of sustainable development has been included in several environmental treaties and is now viewed as an essential principle of international environmental and development policy. However, both industrialized and developing states are not in complete agreement on the obligations the concept imposes.

Environmental policy is also concerned about **environmental justice**. Lower-income groups are much more likely to face the hazards associated with pollution than are more affluent groups. Poor communities far more often have a chemical plant, incinerator, sewage treatment plant, landfill, or other polluting or unhealthy industry located nearby than do affluent communities. Many environmentalists believe that the unequal distribution of financial resources is a crucial cause of environmental degradation. Society must first alleviate the vastly unequal distribution of wealth in order to provide a more equitable distribution of polluting industries. The environmental justice movement includes the notion that all communities are entitled to equal protection and enforcement of laws that affect the environmental quality of life. Environmental justice means that policies should give special consideration to those most vulnerable to the consequences of policy choices. Too often, the poor may find themselves at the mercy of decisions made by the more economically powerful members of society. But no socioeconomic or racial group should bear a disproportionate share of environmental degradation resulting from industrial or municipal operations or decisions. Protesters, particularly minorities, rail against what they claim is "environmental racism," and organize "not in my backyard" (NIMBY) demonstrations against the placing of environmentally polluting factories or other waste sites in their neighborhoods and against locally unwanted land uses (LULUs) that could locate environmentally noxious waste sites in their communities.

Many environmental problems extend beyond national boundaries and require international responses. International problems of environmental degradation frequently mirror domestic problems writ large. This is especially the case concerning the unequal distribution of wealth. Many, if not most, threats to the global environment can be traced to the wealthy nations' demand for goods while much of the actual pollution occurs in poorer countries attempting to supply the goods demanded. Activists in many developing nations organize to protect their natural resource base of forests, minerals, and rivers, as well as their culture, from the pressures of globalization. These movements parallel the movement for environmental justice in the United States. These groups often see themselves at odds with their political elites who are perceived as being in the pockets of multinational corporations. These environmental groups oppose globalization and hold that environmental justice goes beyond the calculation of the marketplace.

Market Failure and the Environment

Government has a function of providing the legal framework within which economic activity takes place. Public policy scholars often debate the extent to which governments need to intervene in the market. Those who prefer free market solutions contend that government intervention should be kept to a minimum while more centrist scholars believe that there are many examples of a need for intervention.

Until recently, this debate relied heavily on Garrett Hardin's notion of the tragedy of the commons (see Chapter 3), which illustrates the conflict between individual and communal interests. Hardin's parable suggests that communal ownership of resources (rather than private ownership) will lead to depletion. Each individual will treat communal property as free goods and maximize their advantage by using as much of a resource as possible. Individual self-interest will lead to behavior to maximize private gain and prove suboptimal for the community in the long run. Therefore, if communal property were turned over to private owners with property rights over the resource, they would have an intrinsic interest to preserve the resource over a longer period of time. Over a century ago, large landowners made the argument for their taking control of the commons that remained, for a modest fee, to bring order to an unregulated and chaotic situation. In the current environmental debate, the pollution of air and water, global warming, and the exhaustion of ocean fisheries seem to reinforce the notion that private property rights rather than community ownership will guarantee efficient management of resources. Ironically, people may worry about the need to save the whales that are not privately owned but, because cattle and chickens are privately owned, no one worries that they will become extinct.

The tragedy of the commons is an example of market failure, which can occur for several reasons. First, the environment may be thought of as a public good. Communal property where there are no established property rights, such as the oceans beyond national jurisdiction, provides little incentive to manage the resources of the sea. Or farmers who cut down trees to gain more arable land in Brazil may not incur a business cost, though the new farmland can no longer be used for preserving wildlife.

Second, the production and consumption of goods may involve external costs or negative externalities that affect people other than those producing or consuming the good. One of government's primary policy roles is to provide remedies for the inefficiencies resulting from externalities. We noted in Chapter 1 that externalities exist when a producer or a consumer does not bear the full cost (negative externality) or receive the full benefit (positive externality) of economic activity. Since externalities do not pass through the market system, the market cannot allocate them. The fact that externalities, whether positive or negative, do not pass through the market system results in some of our most intractable problems.

Pollution is the classic example of an externality problem. Pollution is the production of wastes that we do not want such as industrial wastes, smoke, congestion, or noise. These externalities exist for various reasons. The first is technical: we do not know how to produce some goods without creating waste products. Second, even if we do know how to produce goods without creating waste, their production or consumption may be very expensive without those externalities. For example, an automobile manufacturer may find it cheaper to drain industrial waste into a nearby river than to ship it to a waste dump. Neither the factory owners nor the customers pay for this use of the river. The river is a scarce resource, however, and degrading it does not take into account the rights of those downstream to fish or swim in it, or enjoy it for other forms of recreation or natural beauty. Consequently, the cost of the pollution is borne by the public at large. If these external costs could be taken into account and charged to the producer or consumer, it would result in a higher price and a necessarily lower output equal to the socially efficient level of output. This is an external cost—a cost not reflected in market prices. That cost, moreover, is imposed on the public without its consent. In the example of the automobile, since the cost of such pollution is not reflected in the price of the car, the factory will tend to produce more cars (and pollution) than is socially desirable.

Third, as in the case of health care, markets fail when lack of information results in decisions that do not meet the criteria of rationality. For example, scientists conducting the first nuclear tests were unaware of the devastating effects that radiation had on human health. If they had been, different decisions might have been made.

And finally, self-interest, a major principle of the free market, fails to take into account the future interests of the community. There should be a preference for policies that are not irreversible. A fisherman catching an endangered species may not worry about the impact of the extinction of the species on future generations. Many individual choices will make it difficult to go back and choose an alternative that was rejected. But policy choices should not be of the sort that irrevocably close out other options. For example, many conservationists feel that policies aimed at preserving endangered species from extinction should rank above those aimed at maintaining jobs since new jobs can be created but, once a species is extinct, its loss is irreversible.

Thus, there arise demands for the government to intervene and change the market outcome through laws and regulations. Those who argue against government intervention to control externalities emphasize that business is, or can be, socialized to be responsible through voluntarism. But there are many instances where feelings of social responsibility and voluntarism are not sufficient. In the early 1960s, despite mounting public pressure to reduce automobile pollution, car manufacturers lobbied against legislation to mandate pollution control devices. The auto makers in a public relations campaign gave assurances that they were conducting research, but solving the problem was extremely difficult. In 1963, California passed a law requiring pollution control devices on all new cars sold within one year after a state board had certified that at least two systems were available at reasonable cost. California certified four devices, made by independent parts manufacturers, and mandated their requirement on 1966-model cars. Although automobile manufacturers had insisted that they would not be able to produce such devices before 1967 at the earliest, they announced that they would be able to install emission control devices on their 1996-model cars.[1]

In Chapter 9 we discussed how positive externalities, such as those resulting from education, will tend to be undersupplied in the market. In such cases, government may respond to raise output to a socially optimal level by subsidizing their cost through student loans or research programs. Likewise, government must oversee solutions to negative environmental externalities. As Figure 12.1 suggests, economic efficiency requires greater expenditures on environmental protection than would occur in a free market. The equilibrium price (E) does not include the positive benefits received by others. If a firm installs pollution control equipment in its smokestacks, it will have a social marginal benefit higher (E') than its private marginal benefit. A firm that takes only its private interests into account will operate at point E, and not voluntarily install equipment to provide a situation where marginal social benefits equal the marginal costs for society, at point E'. A major public policy role for the government, then, is to correct for market inefficiencies that result from externalities.

Environmental Politics in the United States

Growing affluence after World War II resulted in ever-increasing numbers of people spending leisure time traveling, hiking, and camping outdoors, which increased their commitment to preserving wildlife and areas of natural beauty. Scholars also began documenting scientific evidence of environmental degradation. The publication of Rachel

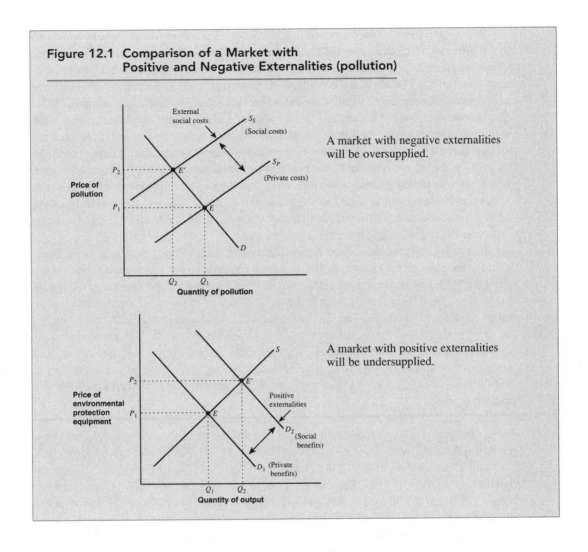

Figure 12.1 Comparison of a Market with Positive and Negative Externalities (pollution)

A market with negative externalities will be oversupplied.

A market with positive externalities will be undersupplied.

Carson's book *Silent Spring* in 1962 was an important contribution to the modern environmental movement. She warned of the effects of toxins as they move up the food chain, and argued that a fragile balance in nature was being upset by the excessive use of DDT on bird reproduction. As a result of her book, DDT was banned as an insecticide in the United States and throughout most of the world. The disastrous effect of pesticides on birds was a warning of the risk of chemical pollution to humans as well. Carson's work suggested the interconnectedness of all life, which has become a central theme of environmentalists.

Reacting to the increased environmental concern, President John Kennedy convened the White House Conference on Conservation in 1962. Kennedy and a Democratic Congress passed the Clean Air Act of 1963, despite fierce opposition led by the business community. The act had a complicated enforcement procedure that relied on state action to initiate lawsuits against polluters. In 1965, the Lyndon Johnson administration passed the Water Quality Act. Federal grants were made available to states for sewage treatment plants to improve water quality. But again, conservatives wrote provisions into the law allowing states to formulate plans to meet the federal standards. In 1969, a major oil spill in Santa Barbara received significant television coverage, which increased the visibility of pollution disasters. The increased public concern about the environment resulted in the passage of several pieces of legislation in the early 1970s. Both Republicans and Democrats vied with each other to prove themselves as the real champions of the environment.

In 1969, Congress passed the National Environmental Policy Act (signed by President Richard Nixon on January 1, 1970), which requires an environmental impact statement (EIS) for any major federal construction. The EIS must show either that government projects will not significantly impair the environment or that satisfactory steps can be taken to mitigate damage. The Environmental Protection Agency (EPA) was created in 1970; prior to that, many different agencies in several federal departments, such as the Departments of Interior and Agriculture, had responsibility for monitoring and regulating air and water pollution. The EPA was given the responsibility to enforce environmental laws regulating toxic waste, air and water pollutants as well as solid waste and pesticides.

In 1970, Congress renewed the Clean Air Act and set national standards for ambient air quality. Congress also set a timetable for the reduction of auto hydrocarbon, carbon monoxide, and nitrogen oxide emissions. The 1970 act was intended "to protect and enhance the quality of the Nation's air resources so as to promote the public health and welfare."[2] The EPA was directed to promulgate the National Ambient Air Quality Standards (NAAQS) in an effort to limit the amount of certain pollutants in the atmosphere that adversely affect public health—sulfur oxides, particulates, carbon monoxide, hydrocarbons, nitrous oxides, and photochemical oxidants. The act required states to adopt plans to meet NAAQS requirements. After approval by the EPA, each state was required to enforce its plan. The EPA was given the authority to prepare and enforce a state plan if it did not meet federal requirements. The EPA was also to set exhaust emission standards for the auto industry and require the use of catalytic converters and the use of fuels with reduced lead.

The Water Pollution Control Act amendments of 1972, passed over President Nixon's veto, attempted to limit the discharge of pollutants into navigable waters by 1985. It provided $25 billion in grants for local governments to build waste treatment plants and to install the best-available technologies by 1983. The Clean Water Act of

1977 allowed for more flexibility in meeting compliance deadlines and effluent limitation requirements.

Industrial expansion after World War II resulted in the disposal of enormous amounts of solid and hazardous wastes into the atmosphere, into the water, and onto the land. The potentially dangerous impact on the atmosphere and groundwater of hazardous waste dumping was apparent. Since the states controlled waste disposal, some industries were encouraged to shop for states with the weakest regulatory controls. Congress finally responded with the Resource Conservation and Recovery Act of 1976, which required that hazardous waste storage and disposal be regulated so as to minimize the threat to public health and the environment. The EPA was authorized to establish standards for the disposal of hazardous waste.

A serious weakness in several pieces of environmental legislation in the 1970s was that the EPA had to negotiate with states and local governments to obtain compliance. The agency simply did not have the personnel or the budget to force compliance in an efficient manner.

Nonetheless, many states began to complain that they were overburdened by these environmental laws. By the late 1970s, critics began complaining that environmental legislation was causing inflation and slowing down economic growth. Business and conservation groups began mounting a counterattack against environmentalists. They ultimately argued that, while the excesses of the past could not continue, "reasonable" future controls would allow the environment to purify itself. They pointed out how a certain amount of pollution is inevitable in a growing economy. Therefore, they claimed, the benefits of any environmental regulation must be balanced against the economic costs to business. There was general acceptance of the view that little additional legislation to protect the environment was necessary. Ronald Reagan wove these views into his campaign for president in 1980; he was not opposed to "reasonable" environmentalism, he said, but the government had gone too far.

Reagan interpreted his victory as clear support for a reversal of the federal government's role in environmental protection. His administration moved immediately to repeal several regulations approved by the Jimmy Carter administration. He appointed individuals who were openly hostile to the federal government's role in environmental policy such as Ann Gorsuch Burford to head the EPA and James Watt as secretary of interior.[3] Several thousand EPA employees were fired, including many attorneys experienced in environmental law. The entire staff of the President's Council on Environmental Quality, whose views were unapologetically environmentalist, was fired.

The Reagan administration required that any new EPA regulation clear a cost-benefit analysis hurdle, one with a built-in bias against regulation. The administration claimed that it was using cost-benefit analysis as a neutral tool to make sure that the dollar benefits of any proposed regulation exceeded the dollar costs. The problem was that no uncontested dollar value could be assigned to the value of a human life, let alone to the value of an endangered species like the spotted owl or the beauty of a natural setting, while the costs incurred by industry were more precisely quantifiable. As a result, most new regulations were predestined to fail the test of cost-benefit analysis. The Reagan administration was less interested in protecting the environment than in encouraging industrial growth through reduced regulation. Reagan's antagonism toward environmental policy galvanized renewed support for environmental organizations and policy.

In 1988, George H. W. Bush campaigned for vigorous action to improve the environment. He indicated that he wanted to be known as "the environmental president." Indeed, one of his more famous charges against his opponent, Michael Dukakis, was that he had not cleaned up the pollution of Boston Harbor. During the first two years of his term, President Bush supported amendments to the Clean Air Act, put areas of the US coastline off-limits for oil exploration, approved an increase in the EPA budget, and was generally supportive of other environmental issues. In 1990, Congress approved Clean Air Act amendments that provided far stricter regulations than those Bush had proposed. He reluctantly signed the amendments, but indicated his reluctance to enforce them.

Environmentalists became disenchanted during the last two years of G. H. W. Bush's term. They charged that his administration had undermined the most dynamic provisions of the Clean Air Act by waiving rules that would have restricted pollutants from automobile, chemical, and pharmaceutical industries. Bush also refused to support an environmental treaty at the 1992 Earth Summit, held in Rio de Janeiro, until its provisions designed to slow global warming were watered down. Additionally, he refused to sign a second treaty at the same summit designed to protect endangered species. In the 1992 presidential campaign, Bush dismissed his Democratic opponents, Bill Clinton and Al Gore, as dangerous "environmental crazies." Clinton campaigned on a pledge to take an activist stance on the environment and reverse his Republican predecessors' weak record.

The new administration did install forceful administrators committed to environmentalism, such as Secretary of Interior Bruce Babbitt, in critical agencies. But for most of Clinton's two terms, he was confronted with an aggressive congressional majority controlled by Republicans intent on frustrating most of the president's policy initiatives. Clinton was forced to back down and was defeated by Congress in several of his environmental efforts. For example, administration proposals to elevate the EPA administrator to the cabinet, to overhaul the Clean Water Act of 1972, and to strengthen the "superfund" effort to clean up hazardous waste sites were all defeated by Congress. After the Republican takeover of both houses in 1994, the Republican majority set out to implement its "Contract with America," proposing legislation to reduce the federal government's ability to enact regulations. President Clinton was thrown on the defensive and took a policy stance designed to neutralize the Republican momentum of environmental deregulation. Clinton took up international environmental policy-making negotiations, the most notable being a commitment to the Kyoto Protocol to control global warming. However, the Senate refused to give its consent to the treaty, thereby preventing its ratification.

Antienvironmental Politics of the George W. Bush Administration

The environmental movement was united in opposition to the election of George W. Bush and his vice presidential candidate, Dick Cheney, who had a record, as a congressman and as the chief executive officer of Halliburton, of opposition to government regulation. The new president insisted he was a moderate on environmental issues and would support reasonable reforms. However, the worst fears of many environmentalists seemed to be validated from the beginning of Bush's presidency, when the administration filled critical policymaking jobs in the EPA and the Departments of Energy, Justice, Interior, and Agriculture with individuals from the very industries they were to regulate. By the end of Bush's first term in 2004, the environmental community was unanimous in its criticism of the administration's environmental record.

Response of the Obama Administration to Antienvironmental Politics

The eight-year G. W. Bush administration oversaw the dismantling of much environmental regulation. President Barack Obama's environmental team—secretary of the interior, Ken Salazar; EPA administrator, Lisa Jackson; and secretary of energy, Stephen Chu—represents a "green" administration that faces environmental commitments compromised by an economic downturn and industries easily drowned by soaring energy costs. They travel a long road back from earlier environmental legacies. In 2002, the Natural Resources Defense Council (NRDC), an environmentalist organization, began publishing an annual report documenting the antienvironmental actions of the Bush-Cheney administration.[4] The report was a devastating indictment of troubling policy decisions.

Failure to enforce. Criminal penalties against polluting industries dropped during the first two years of the G. W. Bush administration by more than one-third while new referrals dropped by over 40 percent and civil penalties dropped by almost half.[5] Budget requests to Congress called for cuts in hundreds of enforcement personnel positions. Bush's EPA administrator meanwhile lauded the agency's "smart enforcement approach," which emphasized voluntary compliance.[6] Current plans announced by Administrator Jackson will terminate the "Performance Track Program" supported by the Bush administration, which rewarded voluntary pollution controls. Critics denounced the program as being largely public relations with little bite.

Sewage in waterways and drinking water. During the Clinton administration, the EPA proposed to address the problem of the contamination of beaches and rivers by bacteria, fecal matter, and other wastes from sewage releases through new Clean Water Act rule-making. A consensus agreement was reached after exhaustive hearings and negotiations that included environmentalists and federal, state, and local authorities. The G. W. Bush administration, upon taking office in January 2001, shelved the proposal for three years of "internal review." The administration ultimately proposed to legalize the release of inadequately treated sewage into waterways, as long as it was diluted with treated sewage, a process the EPA delicately labeled "blending."

Updated guidance from the Obama administration recapitalizes programs for clean water and drinking water through the American Recovery and Reinvestment Act of 2009. The administration supports new legislative initiatives like the Senator Paul Simon Water for the World Act of 2009, which calls for safe, affordable sanitary water worldwide.[7]

Mercury pollution. Power plants and other industries discharge over 150 tons of mercury into the air each year. Because methylmercury accumulates in the blood, it is particularly dangerous for pregnant women since it disrupts the brain development of fetuses, causing attention disorders, learning disabilities, and mental retardation. This hazardous air pollutant is deposited in lakes and streams and enters the food chain through a buildup in fish. In 2003, forty-four states issued warnings about eating mercury-tainted fish. California grocery chains began posting warnings at fish counters advising consumers about shark and swordfish. Internal electric utility documents made public in 2004 disclosed that the utility industry knew for more than a decade that enormous increases in mercury pollution violated the Clean Air Act.

The G. W. Bush administration refused to regulate mercury through the same standards applied to other hazardous air pollutants under the Clean Air Act, and proposed weaker regulations for mercury emissions. As the Bush administration came to an end, the Food and Drug Administration (FDA) battled with EPA scientists about the tradeoff between fish dietary value and mercury risk. The FDA claimed that increased fish consumption could increase a child's IQ by three points.[8] The Obama platform announced the president's pledge to protect children from health hazards caused by environmental toxins like mercury. After taking office, the administration announced first-time regulatory standards for cement plants, which are the fourth largest source of airborne mercury.

Wilderness preservation program. The federal policy at the heart of the wilderness preservation program protects public lands while federal land managers assess them for possible inclusion as officially designated wilderness areas. In 2003, the EPA settled a suit with the state of Utah in which the administration "renounced the government's authority to conduct wilderness inventories on public lands or to protect more areas for their wilderness values."[9] The settlement was made without public comment or input and jeopardizes millions of acres of public lands as it allows industry to apply for drilling, mining, road-building, and other development rights. While in the US Senate, President Obama fought efforts to drill in the Arctic National Wildlife Refuge and supported the Roadless Area Conservation Rule to protect millions of acres of national forests. He supported land acquisition and park maintenance, and fought illegal logging. Early in his presidency, Obama signed the Omnibus Public Land Management Act of 2009 to conserve over 2 million of acres of wilderness in nine states, establishing new national trails, parks, and legal status for the National Landscape Conservation system.

Lobbyists, scientists, and administration policy choices. Environmentalists were particularly exasperated that the G. W. Bush administration made a public pretense of support for environmentally friendly policies while secretly allowing major polluters to help draft policy. In an unprecedented event in 2004, over 4,000 scientists, including 48 Nobel Prize winners and 127 members of the National Academy of Sciences, accused the administration of suppressing, distorting, or manipulating scientific fact and misleading the public to suit its own partisan political objectives.[10]

These criticisms are not unique to past administrations. Current EPA administrator Jackson ran afoul of similar criticism for her mixed record in regulating toxic waste sites in New Jersey. As chief of staff for the New Jersey governor, Jackson drew criticism for her "close" relationship with industry, in particular policy proposals to outsource toxic waste cleanup. A historic choice, as the first African American woman to head the EPA, Jackson was assailed by critics for her failure to aggressively scrub New Jersey's 115 superfund sites.[11] The Comprehensive Environmental Response, Compensation, and Liability Act (CERCLA), or superfund policy, protects communities from heavily contaminated toxic waste sites. New Jersey leads the nation in superfund sites at 116.

President Obama assumed office committed to broad policy reversals from the G. W. Bush administration. The Obama-Biden campaign proclaimed: "We cannot afford more of the same timid politics when the future of our planet is at stake." Along with a new direction in energy policy, the Obama administration directed $8 billion in stimulus funds for high-speed passenger rail. His 2010 budget designates state grants of $5 billion over five years.[12] Improving the railroad tracks currently shared with freight trains will begin the initiative. The US infrastructure is a long way from supporting a Japanese-style Shinkansen bullet train, but a high-speed rail program could create jobs, ease auto congestion, cut travel costs, and induce people to go places, thereby fostering commercial ties. Advocates claim that the time is right for government policymakers to shift focus from the Interstate Highway System, gas-guzzling cars, and flagging airlines to twenty-first-century train travel.

Policy Debates on Environmental Issues

A well-known environmental slogan is "Think globally, act locally." And in fact, many of the successes of the environmentalist movement have been at the local or national rather than the international level, although international efforts have been growing. Much environmental action occurs in the form of protest politics, the main action of which often takes the form of street marches and demonstrations. But protest politics are often associated with human rights movements, such as those for feminist, gay, and lesbian rights, that pursue their goals outside the ordinary channels of political parties and legislative assemblies. This may reduce their political influence.

As with other public policy issues examined in this book, there is spirited debate regarding what role, if any, the government should play in environmental policy. Most people admit to being concerned about environmental degradation at some level. But individual views differ markedly about the perceived level of threat to the environment from different sources such as global warming, ozone depletion, or deforestation. Experts often differ regarding the nature of the threats as well as the most effective responses to them. Frequently, there is sufficient scientific uncertainty to allow people to reach different conclusions based on the same evidence.

Global Warming: Clear Facts and Hazy Conclusions

Over a century ago, Swedish chemist Svante Arrhenius theorized that all the carbon dioxide and other gases released from burning vast amounts of coal were trapping solar heat in Earth's atmosphere, similar to the way the glass roof and walls of a greenhouse trap solar energy. He predicted that **global warming** would occur: industrialization would release more gases into the atmosphere, trapping increasing amounts of solar heat and causing global temperatures to rise several degrees. Only in recent years, however, has scientific study proven that Earth is getting warmer due to the environmental effects of **greenhouse gas** (GHG) concentrations. GHGs are atmospheric gases that are almost transparent to incoming solar energy, but trap infrared energy reflected from Earth's surface. There are about twenty such gases, but scientists primarily focus on carbon dioxide (CO_2), the predominant GHG, which occurs naturally, as do other GHGs such as methane, nitrous oxide, and water vapor. Each GHG differs in its ability to absorb heat in the atmosphere. For instance, methane traps over 21 times more heat per molecule than does carbon dioxide, and nitrous oxide absorbs 270 times more heat per molecule than carbon dioxide.[13] The primary GHGs are considered **stock pollutants**, which means that they have a long lifetime in the atmosphere and therefore can build up over time. Carbon dioxide, for example, has an atmospheric lifetime of between 100 and 200 years.[14] Given the long lifetime of GHGs, they tend to be well mixed in the atmosphere, independent of where they were emitted. Thus, the problems associated with GHGs must ultimately be addressed on an international scale.

As solar radiation, or heat from the sun, approaches Earth, about 30 percent is absorbed by the atmosphere and by the planet's surface; the rest is reflected back into space. GHGs permit solar radiation to pass relatively freely to Earth's surface, but then trap significant amounts in the atmosphere that would otherwise be reflected back into space. Without the **greenhouse effect** to prevent some radiation from escaping, life on Earth would be impossible. Earth's temperature would be about sixty degrees Fahrenheit colder. At the other extreme, a runaway greenhouse effect, extremely unlikely, could change long-term weather patterns and make Earth unbearably hot.

In 1995, the United Nations Intergovernmental Panel on Climate Change, a worldwide network of 2,500 leading scientists, announced that the evidence of global warming was "undeniable." There is little doubt that the buildup of GHGs is largely the result of human activities. According to the EPA, the United States emits more GHGs per person (approximately 6.6 tons, or about one-fifth of all global GHGs) than does any other country.[15] About 82 percent of the emissions result from burning fossil fuels to generate electricity and to fuel cars. The remaining emissions are methane from landfill waste, livestock, natural gas pipelines, coal, industrial chemicals, and other sources.

According to the National Academy of Sciences, average global temperatures have risen about one degree Fahrenheit in the past century. Accelerated warming has occurred during the past two decades, along with an unexplained jump in carbon dioxide levels since 2002.[16] The ten warmest years of the twentieth century all occurred after 1985, with 1998 being the warmest year since records have been maintained. Global warming is greatest in the polar regions, where average temperatures are rising more than twice as fast as they are elsewhere. Snow cover, glaciers, and ice in the polar regions have retreated. Melting glaciers contribute to rising sea levels and threaten low-lying areas with erosion and coastal flooding. Over the past century, the sea level has risen about six inches. Scientists project as much as a three-foot sea-level rise by 2100, which would flood over 22,400 square miles of land along the Atlantic and Gulf coasts in the United States alone. For example, a three-foot rise would extensively flood New York City, Houston, Charleston, South Florida, and many coastal towns along the East Coast. Many other countries, such as the Netherlands, Egypt, Bangladesh, and China, would face even more extreme problems.

A warmer world could lead to more frequent and intense storms such as hurricanes. If the oceans are warmer, evidence indicates that hurricanes would be stronger. Projections also suggest that the temperature in some areas will rise between three and ten degrees Fahrenheit causing severe problems and disruptions for human society.

Now that global warming has moved from an abstract threat to an urgent reality, the policy debate concerns what to do about it. We do not know precisely how much and how fast global warming will occur. Nor is it clear what the beneficial and adverse effects will be. We do not know if we can determine the cost of reducing GHGs, or if the computer-generated models of global warming are accurate.

Most political leaders around the world have been reluctant to act on the early warnings, for fear that reducing emissions of carbon dioxide would require actions undercutting economic growth. International pressure to take action has begun to build, however. For example, deforestation in Brazil increases the amount of carbon dioxide in the atmosphere by destroying the trees necessary to absorb it. When the trees are burned, even more carbon dioxide is added to the atmosphere.

Since most GHGs come from power plants and vehicles, the most effective way to reduce heat-trapping gases in the atmosphere is to burn fewer fossil fuels. The technology already exists to make cars that run cleaner and get better gas mileage. Power plants can be modernized to reduce pollution. Buildings and appliances like refrigerators and air conditioners can be designed to use less power.

In *Massachusetts v. EPA 549 US 497* (2007), the US Supreme Court ruled that the EPA must assess the environmental consequences of global warming.[17] The Commonwealth of Massachusetts along with eleven other states, three cities, and environmental groups sued the EPA over the question of global warming. In 2003, the EPA reinterpreted its authority, reasoning that global warming pollution does not constitute air pollution under the federal Clean Air Act. The Supreme Court issued a historic 5–4 decision contradicting that claim. Justice John Paul Stevens wrote that, under the Clean Air Act, the EPA must take action to control global warming pollutants. To avoid action, the EPA must determine scientifically that GHGs do not contribute to climate change. In the majority decision, the justices noted that the harms associated with climate change are serious and well recognized. The decision presented a stunning rebuke to the G. W. Bush administration, which had refused to regulate carbon dioxide emissions despite earlier campaign pledges.

During his campaign, Obama pledged to reduce carbon emissions by 80 percent by 2050. He supports a market-based cap-and-trade system to reach that goal. Using marketplace incentives, the government would auction emission allowances to industry. Because the allowances have "value," industries can buy and sell them. Allowances would decline over time and revenue earned from the auctions would fund further research and development.[18]

Greenhouse Gases and the Climate Treaty

In 1992, the Conference on Environment and Development, better known as the Earth Summit, was held in Rio de Janeiro. The resulting Rio Declaration on the Environment and Development set forth twenty-eight guiding principles to reinforce global environmental authority. The United States was severely criticized for refusing to take part in subsequent efforts to reduce GHG emissions. President Obama, speaking before the United Nations summit on climate change in September 2009, indicated that he was determined to act on the threat of climate change despite domestic political opposition. He indicated that he was supportive of the effort to produce a treaty on climate change in Copenhagen, scheduled for December 2009.

Case Study: Acid Rain

Acid rain is any precipitation, whether rain, snow, sleet, hail, or fog, that is acidic. Acidic water has a pH lower than the 5.6 average of rainwater. The term **pH** refers to the free hydrogen ions (electrically charged atoms) in water and is measured on a scale from 0 to 14. On this scale, 7 is considered neutral; measurements below 7 indicate acidity, and those above indicate alkalinity. Each point on the scale represents a tenfold increase over the previous number. For example, a pH of 3 is ten times more acidic than a pH of 4, and a pH of 9 is ten times more alkaline than a pH of 8.

Actually, rain is naturally acidic because carbon dioxide, which is found normally in Earth's atmosphere, combines with water to form carbonic acid. "Pure" rainwater's acidity is about 5.7, but actual pH readings vary depending primarily on the sulfur dioxide (SO_2) and nitrogen oxides (NO_x) present in the air. Rainfall with a pH below 5.6 is considered acidic. Some acid rain falling in the eastern United States has been in the range of pH 3.5. Sulfur dioxide and nitrogen oxides are pumped into the atmosphere by coal-fired electric utilities, smelter smokestacks, and motor vehicle exhausts. About half of the acidity in the atmosphere falls back to Earth's surface as dry deposition of acidic particles and gases. These dry deposits can be washed from trees and other surfaces by rainstorms. When this happens, the runoff water adds to the acid in the rain. These pollutants combine with water vapor, forming either sulfuric or nitric acid, and then return to Earth's surface as acid rain. In the United States, electric utilities are responsible for over two-thirds of all sulfur oxides, and motor vehicles are responsible for over 40 percent of all nitrogen oxides. Sulfur dioxide is about twice as acidic as nitrogen oxides. Predictably, NO_x emissions are more evenly dispersed around the nation than sulfur oxides, which are concentrated in the Ohio Valley. However, high smokestacks, electric utilities, and industries in the valley have reduced local sulfur dioxide concentrations. Typically, these oxides are then carried by the prevailing winds for hundreds of miles in a northeasterly direction before returning to Earth's surface as precipitation.

Acid rain contributes to the deterioration of metal and stone in buildings and statues. It has also been linked to health problems like asthma, emphysema, and chronic bronchitis. The New England states and Canada have linked the acidity of rivers and lakes, and the resultant destruction of aquatic life and forest, to emissions originating in the Ohio Valley. Aquatic plants grow best in water that has a pH of 7 to 9. But as acidity increases, aquatic plants begin to die, depriving waterfowl of their food source. At a pH of about 5.5, the bottom-dwelling bacteria that decompose leaf and organic debris begin to die. As undecomposed organic leaf-litter increases, toxic metals such as aluminum and mercury accumulate, harming people who drink the water or eat its tainted fish. Most frogs, insects, and fish die when the water reaches a pH of 4.5.

The amendments to the Clean Air Act of 1990 did establish goals and deadlines for a two-phase reduction in sulfur and nitrous dioxide emissions, and caps on future sulfur dioxide emissions; they also created a system of marketable "allowances" for allocating reductions from different emissions sources. Since 1995, electrical utilities must obtain a permit for each ton of sulfur dioxide they emit. These permits are distributed in limited supply to utilities each

continued

Case Study continued

year by the government, and can be resold among the utilities. They roughly reflect the per ton costs of pollution control. It was expected in the early 1990s, when the permits were being designed, that the per ton cost would be about $1,100. By 1997, they were selling for around $100. Compliance costs have been less expensive than either industry or the EPA had predicted. G. W. Bush alarmed environmentalists when he proposed the construction of 1,800 new electric power plants while relaxing regulatory controls on new fossil fuel–burning electric utilities. During the recent presidential election, Obama was quoted as saying electricity bills would "skyrocket" under his plan to fight global warming.

Sources: Adapted from Sharon M. Friedman and Kenneth A. Friedman, *Reporting on the Environment: A Handbook for Journalists* (Bangkok: Asian Forum of Environmental Journalists, 1988); Thomas H. Moore, *Acid Rain: New Approach to Old Problem,* Editorial Research Report No. 9 (Washington, DC: Congressional Quarterly Press, March 9, 1991); Obama interview, "Energy Prices Will Skyrocket Under My Cap and Trade Plan," *San Francisco Chronicle,* January 2008, available at http://newsbusters.org/blogs/kerry-picket/2008/11/02/obama-energy-prices-will-skyrocket.

The United Nations Framework Convention on Climate Change was adopted in Kyoto in 1997. It was to enter into force only after at least fifty-five parties to the convention, the sum of whose CO_2 emissions accounted for at least 55 percent of the world total, had ratified it. Many industries in the United States were adamantly opposed to bound targets and timetables, and aggressively sought help in Congress to defeat any agreement that would require mandatory cuts in GHG emissions. Although President Clinton had signed the protocol, G. W. Bush, shortly after his inauguration in January 2001, announced that his administration had no interest in implementing it. The announcement infuriated US environmentalists and European nations. The Bush administration, forced to respond to both domestic and international environmental opposition, defended its actions by pointing out that restrictions in the United States would be greater than in developing countries. Many complained that the US refusal would slow the ratification process, which it did. The United States emits more CO_2 than any other country, with 22 percent of global CO_2 emissions (almost all from fossil fuel combustion). In the fall of 2004, the convention finally came into effect when Russia ratified it, bringing the number of signatories to over 100 and the sum of their CO_2 emissions to over 55 percent of the world total. Commitment was popular in Western Europe, which had become frustrated with a series of foreign policy decisions by the Bush administration that reflected disinterest for that part of the world.

Environmental policy is often caught between the competing concepts of sovereignty over domestic resources (e.g., domestic business and financial sectors that want to lower the cost of production by reducing environmental controls), and the international legal obligation not to damage the environment of other states. Many environmental problems, such as acid rain, are transboundary; for example, a downstream nation may bear the major brunt of the pollution produced by an upstream nation. International environmental diplomacy is just beginning to emerge as a power to mitigate the force of unbridled sovereignty and encourage the development of a global environmental consciousness. There is growing pressure to consider environmental issues within international diplomacy, rather than after issues of national security and economics have been resolved.

Ozone Depletion

Stratospheric ozone depletion is undoubtedly the best example of the international community accepting the scientific characterization of an environmental problem and successfully mobilizing a global response.

Ozone (O_3), a molecule that comprises three oxygen atoms, is the most frequent chemical implicated in depletion of the stratosphere. Ninety percent of all atmospheric ozone is found in the stratosphere, which ranges from approximately twelve to thirty-five miles above Earth's surface. Most of the upper-level ozone is concentrated about fifteen miles above Earth's surface in what is known as the "ozone layer." Ozone occupies only a small fraction of Earth's atmosphere, but its existence is extremely important to all forms of life since it is the only gas that absorbs most lethal ultraviolet-B (UV-B) radiation from the sun and reduces it to reasonably safe levels. Depletion of the ozone shield allows more UV-B to reach Earth's surface, producing increased rates of skin cancer, eye cataracts, and weakened immune systems in humans. It also damages ecosystems, resulting in decreased photosynthesis in plants, and reduces crop and fish yields. While ultraviolet radiation is necessary to synthesize vitamin D, it also damages DNA, which is the protein code necessary for cell reproduction. Animal and plant life on Earth has adapted to "natural" levels of UV-B. Without such UV protection, most life forms experience cell damage. Without the ozone layer, much higher levels of UV-B would reach Earth's surface, wiping out most life on the planet.

Chlorofluorocarbons (CFCs), first created in 1928, are a family of nonreactive, nontoxic, and nonflammable gases and liquids. Their properties soon made them valuable for use as refrigerants, in urethane and polyurethane foam for insulation, and in fast food wrappings, aerosol sprays, and other convenience items. Because CFCs are nonreactive, unlike ozone, they have expected lifetimes of twenty-five to thirty years per molecule and may drift in the environment for years until they reach the stratosphere. They are insoluble and, therefore, unaffected by rainfall. Scientists estimate that it takes six to ten years for the average CFC molecule to reach the stratosphere through convection and diffusion. Once there, UV radiation decomposes the CFCs, producing chlorine, which acts as a catalyst—a compound that can be used repeatedly in a reaction without being consumed—in breaking down ozone. Consequently, the resulting chlorine atom is not used up in the process. One chlorine atom can break down well over 100,000 molecules of ozone before it becomes part of a less-reactive compound and is precipitated out of the stratosphere in water. The level of chlorine in the atmosphere is estimated to be about six times higher now than it was at the turn of the century. Other CFCs, like halons, which are primarily used in fire extinguishers, have far more ozone-depleting capabilities than does chlorine.

Ozone, an unstable atom, is primarily produced over the tropics, where solar radiation is strongest, and then diffused through air circulation toward the polar regions. Therefore, ozone tends to be spread thinner at the poles. Although we often refer to an "ozone layer," what actually exists is a diffusion of O_3 throughout the upper reaches of the stratosphere, not a "layer" of pure ozone. If the ozone in the stratosphere were compressed to surface pressures, the layer would be less than two inches thick.

By the mid-1970s, laboratory studies demonstrated the ability of CFCs to break down ozone in the presence of UV light, and projected that CFCs would deplete the ozone layer by about 7 percent within sixty years. In 1985, a team of British and US scientists confirmed the existence of a "hole" in the ozone layer, covering an area greater than the United States, that lasted for several weeks of the Antarctic spring. Subsequent discoveries of ozone depletion over other areas, especially over the Arctic, led to considerable research to determine the specific forces behind ozone destruction. Studies by the National Aeronautics and Space Administration found, by 1988, that the ozone layer around the entire globe was decreasing by 8 percent, a rate much faster than had been previously suspected. In 2000, the area of the ozone hole reached a record 18 million square miles. While no hole has appeared elsewhere, the ozone layer over the North Pole has thinned by up to 30 percent while the depletion over Europe and other high latitudes varies from 5 percent to 30 percent.[19]

In 1985, the Vienna Convention for the Protection of the Ozone Layer encouraged international cooperation on research, systematic observation of the ozone layer, and monitoring of CFC production. A stronger agreement, to limit CFCs, could not be reached because some members of the United Nations wanted a phaseout of CFCs while others wanted production caps. In 1987, a compromise was reached and the Montreal Protocol, signed by 184 countries, placed quantitative limits on the production and consumption of CFCs and halons. The protocol was designed so that the phaseout schedules could be revised on the basis of periodic scientific assessments. Funds were also provided to pay the incremental costs incurred by developing countries in phasing out their production of ozone-depleting substances. The protocol was amended on five different occasions to introduce new control measures and to add new controlled substances to the list; ninety-six chemicals are now controlled for. Governments are not legally bound until they ratify the protocol as well as each successive amendment.

The results of the protocol have been most gratifying. Without it, ozone depletion by 2050 had been projected to double the amount of UV-B radiation reaching Earth's surface in the northern middle latitudes, and to quadruple the amount of radiation in the southern latitudes. Without the protocol, the ozone-depleting chemicals in the atmosphere would be five times greater by 2050, resulting in a staggering 19 million more cases of nonmelanoma cancer, 1.5 million more cases of melanoma cancer, and 130 million more cases of cataracts.[20] Instead, the total consumption of CFCs worldwide dropped from about 1.1 million tons in 1987 to about 110,000 tons in 2001.

The Montreal Protocol has been hailed as an extraordinary success. Scientists now predict that ozone depletion will reach its worst point during the next few years, and then decline until the ozone layer returns to normal around 2050. The success of the international community's intervention was possible because science and industry were able to develop alternatives to ozone-depleting chemicals, allowing countries to end the use of CFCs more quickly and with less cost than originally anticipated. However, there is no room for complacency since some countries have not yet ratified various amendments, and the global economic slowdown has made it difficult for others to comply. At the same time, illegal trade in CFCs has increased. Although all new CFCs are banned in developed countries, millions of CFC-dependent refrigerators and other equipment are still in service. Although there are alternatives to this equipment, they are often more expensive. Also, many chlorofluorocarbon-based refrigerators are being exported to the developing world by countries that have phased out the use of CFCs.

Additionally, CFCs are being replaced by hydrofluorocarbons (HFCs), such as ammonia and hydrocarbons, which have no ozone-depleting properties. However, HFCs have a high global-warming potential and are included in a basket of six GHGs that are to be reduced by the industrialized states.

There are several lessons to be learned from the Montreal Protocol that can be applied to other environmental issues. First, a precautionary principle was applied. It was agreed that, to avoid potentially irreversible damage, the world had to take immediate action despite lacking complete scientific proof. Second, the negotiators sent consistent signals by adopting legally binding phaseout schedules so that industry had an incentive to develop efficient alternative technologies. The negotiators also took pains to ensure that improved scientific understanding could be easily incorporated in the treaty provisions. The negotiators encouraged broad participation by recognizing that, while all had a common interest in the protocol, developed countries had a responsibility to provide the financial and technological support to developing countries to ease their cost of phasing out CFCs.

Hazardous Wastes

Most toxic and hazardous wastes are the direct result of the chemical revolution during and after World War II. Today, literally a ton of hazardous waste is produced for every person in the United States per year. Although most chemical wastes are harmless to humans and the ecosystem, many chemicals have not been thoroughly tested to determine their toxicity. However, cancer is probably the most widely dreaded impact of toxic wastes, and over 300 chemicals have been shown to be carcinogenic. Hundreds of other chemicals have been linked to other debilitating and even fatal diseases. Widely used pesticides have been identified as highly toxic, with many types having ingredients containing carcinogens.

Awareness of the dangers from toxic waste dumps was symbolized by public reaction to the discovery that a subdivision of Niagara Falls, New York, known as Love Canal had been built directly over a 20,000-ton highly toxic chemical waste dump. Many of the residents of Love Canal suffered a wide range of serious illnesses, from birth defects to cancers, as a result of the toxic contamination of the area. Their struggle motivated Congress to pass a law to clean up hazardous waste in 1980 known as the superfund legislation, which provided $1.6 billion to clean up the worst of the abandoned and hazardous waste sites. The legislation also provided a superfund corporate tax. The legislation required the EPA to prioritize a list of the nation's most dangerous hazardous waste sites, and begin cleaning up sites based on their ranking. By 1995, the year the superfund corporate tax expired, polluters were paying 85 percent of cleanup costs. In 2004, 79 percent of the superfund cleanup costs were paid by US taxpayers while corporate polluters picked up the remainder. In February 2009, the US Supreme Court heard arguments about the Shell Oil case in an effort to determine who pays for cleaning up polluted sites.[21] Of the 1,596 sites on the National Priorities List, 1,060 of them have been cleaned up. Unfortunately, new sites are added as others are removed. The EPA announced, in April 2009, that $600 million will be directed to fifty of the most polluted waste sites.

Because of the high costs involved, the debate over who should pay has been contentious from the start. Many in industry claim that, since all Americans have profited from cheaper consumer goods that resulted from the improper disposal, taxpayers should pay for the cleanup. Environmentalists argue that, since polluters have most directly profited from imposing negative externalities on the general public, they should be liable for the cleanup. The CERCLA of 1980, however, is based on the "polluter pays" principle by holding anyone who produces or handles hazardous wastes strictly, jointly, and severally liable for cleanup and damages caused. When the federal regulations were enacted, however, no one understood the tremendous expense that would be involved in hazardous waste cleanup. Industry critics claim that many regulations impose unacceptable costs for the strict control of substances based on fragmentary evidence of risk. In their view, Congress and the EPA are overly risk-averse, preferring to err in the direction of stringent control and accepting the most pessimistic projection based on tenuous scientific evidence.

In the 1990s, the scientific community began focusing on a long list of human-made synthetic chemicals known as endocrine disruptors, which can interfere with the endocrine system with catastrophic consequences. The endocrine system is composed of glands that secrete hormones that, together with the nervous system, integrate many different processes that allow the human body to function. Endocrine disruptors, if they are present in the right concentrations, can adversely affect hormone balance. According to the EPA's working definition, endocrine disruptors "interfere with the synthesis, secretion, transport, binding, action, or elimination of natural hormones in the body that are responsible for the maintenance of homeostasis (normal cell metabolism), reproduction, development, and/or behavior."[22] Many of the disruptors appear to accumulate in human tissue over long periods of time. The various health problems may include cancer of the reproductive system, reduced sperm counts in men, abnormalities of fetal development leading to learning and behavioral disorders, and other pathologies associated with hormonal malfunctions.[23] The chemical industry argues that risk aversion too often results in a regulatory intolerance for minimal health risks and excessive regulatory costs. The political chemistry, environmentalists claim, is one in which negatively inclined administrations combined with industry have slowed progress on the regulation of toxic and hazardous wastes beyond any justification.

Population Growth

The sheer numbers concerning the world's population growth raise the specter of a collision between the expanding needs of human beings and the limits on human ability to increase production. Understanding the relationship between population, pollution, and poverty is necessary before one can consider policies to deal with these issues.

Throughout most of human history, the population has grown very slowly, with the net death rate nearly equal to the net birth rate, both of which have been high. The crude birth rate minus the crude death rate equals the increase in population for a given year. Mortality started to decline just as life expectancy started to increase, beginning in the late seventeenth century in Europe. Improving infant survival rates led to potentially much larger populations to produce the next generation of children.

The world's population reached 1 billion around 1830. By 1900, Earth had a population of about 1.6 billion people. The global population quadrupled between 1900 and 2000. The population increase between 1990 and 2000 was equal to all those who lived in the seventeenth century. Significantly, 80 percent of the growth had taken place in the world's developing nations. It took several million years of human history to reach the first billion, about 130 years to reach the second, and today a new billion is added in less than ten years. World population now stands at 6.5 billion, and is growing by about three people every second, or more than a quarter of a million people every day. As an illustration, the world is adding a city the size of New York every month. Between 90 and 100 million people—roughly equivalent to the population of Mexico—will be added each year of this decade. A billion people, almost the population of China, will be added over the decade. About 97 percent of the world's population growth now takes place in poorer and developing countries. In some countries, the rate of increase is over 3 percent per year, which means the population will double within twenty years. The result is that social dislocations caused by population growth are more severe in the poorer countries, which also tend to have the fewest natural resources. Several million will migrate to more industrialized countries, but most will remain in the country of their birth, taxing natural resources and adding to the burden of the local society.

Global Projections

The recent population growth has resulted not from increased birth rates, but from worldwide decreases in the death rate. In the preceding millennia, plagues, famines, and epidemics kept normal death rates high and population growth rates very low. Although all living beings eventually die, it is mortality at an early age that keeps population growth rates low. With the decline of famines and epidemics with improvements in hygiene, death rates were significantly reduced in the industrialized states by the beginning of the twentieth century.

Throughout most of history, a large and growing population was invariably regarded as a sign of a robust and prospering society while a small or declining population indicated decay. In the colonial eras of the eighteenth and nineteenth centuries, many believed that population size and national power were closely related. Even in the twentieth century, Nazi Germany initiated a pronatalist policy urging German women to produce more children. At the same time, Germany invaded neighboring states to appropriate additional living space for its growing population. To be sure, skeptics began pointing out that, in the modern world, economic and technological superiority contributed more to national power than did population. It was on that basis that a small country like Great Britain could dominate the much larger populations of India and the Middle East. Since World War II, improved water and sewage treatment and the availability of antibiotics removed the major checks to population expansion, resulting in unprecedented growth.

Poor countries have traditionally sustained high levels of population growth to support agricultural production. But the modernization of agricultural production in those countries has displaced labor-intensive sharecropping systems in favor of mechanized farms using seasonal wage labor. As a result, urban areas have grown rapidly as unemployed farm workers search for jobs in cities. Continued population growth in many poorer countries has led to overcultivation and the destruction of rainforests in a search for new arable land. Desperately poor people are often driven to further ravage the environment in their struggle to survive. In many cases, the consequence is an actual decline in per capita agricultural production and a further increase in poverty. The gap between rich and poor widens. Hence, all too often, agricultural development has not only failed to eliminate poverty but also increased it, with unfortunate consequences for population growth and the environment.

Almost one-third of Earth's 6.5 billion people are age fourteen or younger. Population growth will continue because of the momentum of large numbers of young people just reaching their reproductive years. An international environmental disaster characterized by starvation, unemployment, poverty, and civil unrest is not idle speculation. The basic concern regarding population growth has been put forward by the US National Academy of Sciences and the UK Royal Society: "If current predictions of population growth prove accurate and patterns of human activity on the planet remain unchanged, science and technology may not be able to prevent either irreversible degradation of the environment or continued poverty for much of the world."[24] Because population growth rates are not evenly distributed around the world, there will be significantly altered population densities. For example, Europe and North America made up about 22 percent of the world population in 1950, but by 2025 they will make up less than 9 percent. By contrast Africa, which made up 9 percent of the world's population in 1950, will make up approximately 20 percent in 2025. Over 90 percent of the global population growth over the next thirty-five years will occur in the developing countries of Africa, Asia, and Latin America. The sheer numbers indicate that there will be an increasing impact on the environment.

Migration from one country to another is also at an all-time high. In the mid-1990s about 125 million people, mostly in developing countries, lived outside the country in which they were born. At the same time, there is a systematic shift from rural to urban living. Problems arise when cities grow so rapidly that governments cannot provide the necessary public services, such as adequate housing and sanitation, and when the job market is unable to absorb all those who move to the cities.

There was a fear that continued population growth would lead to mass starvation, internal conflict, and perpetual poverty. In the late 1960s, fear of impending famine and environmental degradation encouraged the development of the first population policies. The idea that the state would provide family planning services to reduce the rate of population growth was a novel idea. Prior to this time, most contraceptives were awkward or illegal. The contraceptive pill in 1960 resulted in a revolution in sexual behavior and the idea of family planning in the United States.

In 1973, in *Roe v. Wade,* the Supreme Court struck down the laws outlawing abortion as a violation of the right to privacy inferred from the Fourth, Fifth, and Ninth Amendments to the Constitution and applied to the states through the due process clause of the Fourteenth Amendment. The Court held that states had no "compelling interest" to ban abortions during the first trimester, when abortions performed by qualified medical personnel are safer for the mother than is childbirth. During the second trimester, states may regulate abortions, as they become more dangerous as pregnancy progresses. During the third trimester, a fetus may survive outside the womb and therefore becomes a new "compelling interest" for the state.

By the 1990s, the revival of the religious right challenged both the Court decision and the abortion providers. The Republican Party backed away from most family planning

---

Case Study: US Population Trends

The United States is the most populous of the developed countries and also has one of the highest population growth rates of the industrialized nations: about 1 percent annually. The Census Bureau reported that the US population grew by 32.7 million people between 1990 and 2000, the largest single-decade population increase in the nation's history. In fact, between 1980 and 2000, population growth in the United States equaled the entire population of France (55 million people). This adds 2.75 million people to the population each year. The annual growth is equal to a city about the size of Chicago. The United States is almost the only advanced industrialized state with such a high rate of population increase.

There is a new birth in the United States about every seven seconds, a death about every thirteen seconds, and one net migrant gain every twenty-four seconds, which produces a net gain of one person every ten seconds.

The United States is undergoing a significant change in its geographic distribution. The stream of immigrants into the country is highly directed toward six states—California, New York, Texas, Florida, New Jersey, and Illinois. And within these states the flow is primarily to a few metropolitan areas. The population within the United States is also shifting to the south and the west.

The nation is also undergoing significant changes in ethnic composition. Forty percent of the present population of the United States is now comprised of African American, Asian, and Hispanic minorities. Hispanics are now the largest minority, at 13.7 percent of the population, or 39.9 million (not counting 3.9 million in Puerto Rico). The Hispanic population is projected by the Census Bureau to rise from 13.7 percent of the population in 2004 to 24 percent by 2050 due to a combination of immigration and higher fertility.

Sources: US Census Bureau, Public Information Office, available at www.census.gov/press-release/ www/releases/archives/population/index.html (accessed August 19, 2009); Carl Haub, "Global and US National Population Trends," *Consequences* 1, no. 2 (Summer 1995), available at www.gcrio.org/ CONSEQUENCES/summer95/population.html.

---

programs. The leaders of the Republican Party began to appeal explicitly to religious fundamentalists and to conservative Catholics on an antiabortion agenda that opposes all forms of family planning. The Democratic Party has consistently supported family planning and the right of women to make choices in this area.

International Population and Environmental Policies

There are two views of the ability of developing countries to adjust to changes in the environment and population growth to avoid economic decline. One is the **Cornucopian** position of Julian Simon, who opposes all attempts to restrain population growth. He believes that people are the highest resource, so it is unbelievable that a society can have too many people. According to Simon, people will use their creativity to develop technologies to provide for ever-growing population. Cornucopians historically have been right in that technological progress has allowed most Western economies to avoid the dire warnings of Malthus, because output has grown faster than population. Food production has increased faster than expected because of technological improvements, and populations have grown more slowly than anticipated. Higher standards of living and improved health care have increased life expectancy and reduced infant mortality. These factors have contributed to population growth. They have been offset, however, by the fact that children become an economic liability in developed societies. This has encouraged family planning and has contributed to the stabilization of populations in developed countries. Developed countries have also benefited from improved health care. There are fewer incentives for family planning in developing societies, where children are an economic asset as a source of labor. In countries without pension programs or social security, children may also be a source of support for parents in their old age. Unfortunately, many less-developed agrarian countries have not been able to avoid Malthusian predictions because of diminishing marginal productivity. As more people live on a fixed amount of land, the output per worker declines. Even though the economies are growing, per capita growth is negligible or even declining.

The other view is known as **neo-Malthusian**, and as its name implies, its proponents believe that in the long run population will exceed the means of subsistence. Populations will increase to the limit that natural resources can support.

Paul Ehrlich is a leading exponent of the neo-Malthusian view. He developed an "impact equation" to explain the relationship between human beings and their environment: $I = P \times F(P)$, in which I is the total impact, P is the population, and F is a function that measures the per capita impact.[25] The larger the population, the greater the impact on the environment. A world population of less than 1 billion people in the 1600s had less of an environmental impact than did a population of 6 billion people at the end of the twentieth century. A larger population puts more stress on clean water and air than does a smaller population.

In addition to the size of the population, lifestyles have an impact on the environment. The lifestyle of an individual in an affluent country like the United States creates more of an environmental burden than the lifestyle of the typical Ethiopian. Americans make up about 6 percent of the world's population, but are responsible for producing over two-thirds of the world's atmospheric carbon monoxide and almost one-half of its nitrogen oxide emissions.

Many charge that there are ethical implications for such affluence. They argue that, if Americans ate less meat, more land could be used to raise grain to feed hungry people abroad. Currently, about one-quarter of world cropland, and 38 percent of grain production, are devoted to feeding livestock. In the United States, this amounts to about 135 million tons of grain annually out of a total production of 312 million tons, sufficient to feed a population of 400 million people on a vegetarian diet.[26] A move away from diets high in animal protein toward diets higher in vegetable protein would result in more grain being available for populations in poorer countries.

"Overpopulation" provided a rationale for advanced as well as developing nations to explain poverty's hold on much of the third world. It was easier to ascribe the lack of development to excessive population than to confront economic inequality, female subjugation, or other social, religious, or governmental factors that contribute to poverty and underdevelopment. When population issues did come to the fore, population control caught the attention of many Western nations since it required few changes in the international social and economic structure. Many elites in developing countries also embraced overpopulation as an explanation for their societies' underdevelopment, and population control as the solution, since it provided them with a justification for their elite status and relieved them of responsibility for society's failures.

During the 1970s, the United States encouraged developing countries to voluntarily limit population growth before it began to seriously erode living standards. In 1974, the United Nations held an intergovernmental conference on population. The United States lent its strong endorsement to the program and actively encouraged nations to adopt education programs for family planning; it was a major donor to the United Nations Population Fund, the International Planned Parenthood Federation, and other family planning programs in developing countries. At the conference, many developing countries criticized the US position, arguing that poorer countries needed more economic assistance, not contraceptives. At a similar conference a decade later in Mexico City, the positions were reversed. Most developing countries were now in favor of family planning programs and actively sought assistance for that purpose. However, in the 1980s, Presidents Reagan and G. H. W. Bush stopped all financial assistance for family planning and refused to cooperate with multilateral efforts to reduce population growth. Some nations that usually were closely allied with the United States, such as Canada, the United Kingdom, Japan, and Germany, increased their donations to the United Nations Population Fund to try to fill the void.

There are several reasons why the threat of population growth fails to attract our attention as a critical problem. The world's population grows by over 250,000 people a day, every day. What networks report as news usually involves climactic occurrence rather than daily happenings. Nevertheless, many of the consequences of overpopulation, such as deforestation, malnutrition and starvation, and toxic waste, do make the news on a daily basis.

Another reason overpopulation does not seem a serious threat is that Malthus's dire warnings of economic collapse resulting from growing populations have so far failed to materialize. While many aspects of the Malthusian analysis have proven wrong, Malthus did focus on at least two important points: (1) that growing populations could be a problem, and (2) that there is a relationship between population size and poverty. A growing population within a nation means that the national economy must grow by at least the same rate just to maintain the same standard of living. A country with a population growth rate of 2.7 percent a year must maintain economic growth of 2.7 percent just to maintain the status quo. Continual economic growth rates above that level are difficult to maintain. It is rather like running up a down-moving escalator. Since much of the population growth rate is occurring in underdeveloped countries, it means that their industrial revolutions can be undone by a Malthusian revolution. Another factor that militates against the perception that population growth is a problem is that many individuals and businesses benefit from population increases. Landlords, banks, manufacturers, and merchants all stand to benefit by providing a growing population with goods and services.[27]

Population Policy Choices

Population, poverty, and pollution are related in complicated ways. World population has grown beyond an optimal level of "carrying capacity" at the present stage of technological development. At least 1.8 billion people today, over one in five, live in absolute poverty.

People do create wealth and earn incomes, and without people there would be neither. But the more people there are, the greater the impact on the environment. And larger populations often reduce the income per person and the output of economic goods produced per worker. A country can reduce poverty by increasing income while holding its population constant, or by holding income steady while decreasing its population.

Reduction of poverty is seen by many policymakers as a moral obligation. It is also necessary for the preservation of the environment and the health of the world economy. A healthy environment can more easily support the present or growing population than can a devastated one, so policies to protect the environment are necessary to reduce poverty. Because pollution and poverty are twin problems, economic development programs to reduce poverty must take into account the necessity of environmental protection. But it is not easy to work toward the seemingly antithetical goals of reducing pollution while promoting economic development. Poorer countries have few incentives to limit GHGs. They do have an incentive to transfer the added costs of pollution to the global environment as an externality, giving themselves a cost advantage in the process.

Although threats to the environment are global and thus require international cooperation, political power often lies with the wealthier members of society who have much at stake in accommodating the current economic interests of business leaders. Political leaders in most countries tend to remain fixated on narrow aspects of sovereignty and feel they are accountable solely to their domestic constituents. Moreover, nations differ in their contributions to environmental degradation. The wealthier nations of the North make a greater per capita contribution to environmental degradation by emissions of GHGs through the burning of fossil fuels. In poorer countries, over-population contributes to environmentally unsound deforestation. The destruction of watersheds by bringing less arable land under cultivation threatens many ecologically fragile areas, along with the economic viability of the countries in question.

To reduce world poverty, per capita income in poor countries must be raised. However, there is no realistic way poor countries can achieve the economic development needed for them to significantly raise their standards of living unless their population growth rates are decreased. Population control is an important first step in reducing poverty levels, but other steps are needed also. One possibility would be to encourage technology transfers of low-population, energy-efficient production procedures to poorer countries. In addition, subsidizing the investment costs of installing the equipment needed to implement those procedures would be beneficial.

Environmental Policy Responses

Politics is said to be the art of the possible. The task of the political scientist engaged in policy analysis, then, is to devise solutions derived from principles that different interests share. Policy responses that result in non-zero-sum solutions are generally to be preferred. For example, many businesses view environmentalists' concerns with alarm, fearing that any regulatory measures will drive costs up to intolerable levels. Business leaders tend to dismiss negative externalities as inevitable by-products of market forces. Environmentalists, for their part, tend to view businesses as callous for pursuing profits without sufficiently considering the needs of the environment. The ideal solution would accommodate the needs of both sides, not sacrifice one set of needs to the other.

Command and Control

Diametrically opposed views such as those just described lead to bitter struggles and political polarization. Simply put, government finds itself pressured to outlaw a negative externality, even though many oppose any regulation. Thus, the government may adopt direct regulation in which it determines permissible levels of pollution, and may fine or shut down firms that exceed them while allowing pollution by other firms that remains within the defined limit.

This regulatory technique is usually referred to as the **command and control** approach because it requires such heavy government involvement. It requires the government to determine the maximum safe level of emissions and then set uniform standards for every smokestack or waste pipe. Policy analysts are uncomfortable with it because the standards promulgated are usually "all or nothing" in nature and do not necessarily reach their stated goals as efficiently or as fairly as possible. The standards require every company to meet the same target regardless of differing costs. This is inefficient because some businesses may have to use more expensive technologies to control pollution than others. Perhaps more important, businesses have no incentives to reduce pollution below the standards set by the government. They have no incentives to develop or utilize technologies to exceed the regulated targets. Money that might be used to develop technologies to further reduce pollution is often diverted to fighting the standards or getting an exemption based on the threat of eliminating jobs if the standard is imposed.

Market Incentive Programs

Huge budget deficits, anemic economic growth, and sharp foreign competition have inspired searches for policies that reduce bureaucratic intrusion into business decisions. At the same time, policymakers wish to be sensitive to the need for cost-effective solutions to get a high rate of return for the regulatory effort.

Political scientists recognize that pollution externalities represent a failure of the market in which the production of a good exceeds the optimal level. Business and consumers tacitly agree to pass some costs on to the public. Since firms can pass the costs of pollution on to society, they have little incentive to consider them in business decisions. To the contrary, any firm that unilaterally tried to reduce external costs would be less competitive in the market. However, rather than rejecting market mechanisms as a source of help in favor of direct regulation, or forsaking pollution control by returning to laissez-faire economic policies, policy analysts recognize that **market incentives**—trying to make the market price of a good include the cost of any negative externality—might suggest creative solutions. There are several ways to ensure that environmental costs are included in choices made by firms and individuals.

Tax incentives. A **tax incentive** uses taxes to provide incentives for individuals to pattern their behavior in a way that achieves the desired goals. This tactic charges a fee (tax) on the amount of good consumed that generates pollution, or imposes effluent charges. The threat of taxes is a stick to encourage the desired behavior to protect the environment.

For example, suppose that 100 gallons of gasoline are consumed each month in a society consisting of just three people. And suppose they mutually agree that total gas consumption should be reduced by 15 percent. Let us assume Mrs. A uses 50 gallons per month, Mr. B uses 35 gallons, and Ms. C uses 15. Direct regulation would require that each decrease their consumption by an equal percentage (15 percent each) to achieve the reduction. The difficulty with this approach is that it does not reward anyone for saving more than he or she is required to save. It may be that Mrs. A could easily reduce her consumption by 10 gallons with little inconvenience, and Mr. B can easily reduce his by 15 gallons, while Ms. C has always been frugal and would find it difficult to reduce her consumption by more than 1.5 gallons (10 percent) per month.

On the other hand, if they agree to levy a tax of $0.25 per gallon on the gasoline they consume, each will have an incentive to reduce consumption. Mrs. A will likely reduce her consumption by 10 gallons (20 percent) and pay $10.00 in taxes, Mr. B will reduce his consumption by 15 gallons (42 percent) and pay $5.00 in taxes, while Ms. C will reduce her consumption by 1.5 gallons (10 percent) and pay $3.38 in taxes each month.

In this illustration, the tax achieves the goal more efficiently than does direct regulation. Since the incentive to conserve is included in the price, each person has to choose how much to reduce their consumption. Each is influenced by the marginal utility of consuming an additional gallon. Those who consume less, pay less in taxes. The tax gives individuals an incentive to reduce their consumption as much as possible, and to find new ways of reducing consumption. For example, they may buy more fuel-efficient cars, use carpools, consider public transportation alternatives, or consider walking short distances instead of driving.

A variation on this market-based incentive is to provide a subsidy (a carrot rather than a stick). For example, a business could receive a tax credit for installing pollution abatement equipment, such as a scrubber, in a smokestack. Society is still better off, with less pollution, since the gap between the market price and the social costs is reduced. Businesses almost invariably prefer subsidies to taxes. Policy analysts typically prefer tax incentives because they encourage companies to seek greater efficiency in reducing consumption or reducing pollution rather than just achieving a defined standard.

Marketable permits. Through a **marketable permit**, the government establishes an upper limit of allowable pollution and allows businesses to emit some fraction of that total. If companies reduce their pollution (or consumption) below the level allocated to them, they receive a permit, which they can then sell to another firm that has chosen not to reduce its emissions to less than its allowable amount. For example, a utilities firm may want to expand production, but under an emissions cap may be unable to do so unless it can purchase permits to increase its emission of pollutants.

This method is aimed at encouraging firms to significantly reduce their pollution in order to generate marketable permits for other firms that, for one reason or another, do not find such a reduction worthwhile. The 1990 Clean Air Act explicitly used this market incentive to deal with pollution. The act provided for a 10-million-ton reduction in sulfur dioxide emissions from the 1980 level by the year 2000. Nitrogen oxide emissions were to be reduced by 2 million tons in that time frame. The law also provided a cap that limited emissions to about 50 percent of 1990 levels by 2000. To meet these goals by the year 2000, the EPA issued permits designed to reduce the amount of pollution allowed each year. Utilities were forced to take a number of actions to reduce the levels of emissions: install scrubbers, switch to low-sulfur coal, implement conservation measures, close down obsolete plants, use renewable energy sources such as hydroelectric power where feasible, and build new, more efficient utilities and transfer the emission allowances to the new plant. The act also contained a system of pollution allowances that encouraged utilities to exceed their required reduction of pollutants and recover their costs by selling their marketable certificates to other companies.

Assessing Policy Approaches

Market incentive policies like taxes, subsidies, and marketable permits are attractive to policy analysts for many reasons. They reduce the market inefficiency of pollution by discouraging undesirable activities that produce externalities. Charges levied for pollution require that businesses share the cost burden of externalities, and therefore include consideration of externalities in their daily business decisions. Firms for which pollution reduction is cheapest will reduce pollution more while those for which reduction is expensive will reduce it less. Such policies also make the price that consumers pay for an externality more closely reflect its cost.

Since pollution cannot be reduced to zero, many see market-based incentives as a pragmatic approach to achieve the optimal level of pollution. The optimal level of anything produced from a purely economic perspective is the point at which its price reflects the marginal costs of its production. The difficulty is in accurately determining the marginal social cost of pollution and setting the incentives appropriately. If properly set, firms will pursue pollution abatement to the point that its marginal cost equals its marginal benefit to society. If the tax is too low, firms will commit to insufficient environmental protection while, if it is too high, production of the good will be excessively cut back.

Market approaches to controlling pollution are rapidly gaining acceptance among many policymakers. For example, many states have instituted market-based incentives known as "bottle-bills": a deposit must be made on the purchase of beverages in aluminum or plastic bottles, which is refunded when empty containers are returned. The effect has been to reduce litter and promote recycling.

Nevertheless, there is still significant skepticism regarding market-based incentives, for several reasons. Many environmentalists oppose them because it seems that selling permits to pollute legitimizes pollution. Many business firms oppose market approaches because they involve taxes, which are associated negatively with government interference. Also, businesses and their lobbyists often prefer direct-market regulation because they have become very effective at countering this approach. For example, they can appeal for a delay in the implementation of regulatory rules by citing economic hardship and the possibility of layoffs due to increased costs, and they often get what they want.

Ethics and Environmentalism

The appeal of market approaches to encourage environmentally sound policies is their efficiency. The market provides a framework in which trade takes place based on the choices of individuals between a given supply and demand for goods. Through cost-benefit analysis the government can try to set policy while relying on the efficiency of the market, even as decisions aimed at protecting the environment are incorporated into the market process. This is built on the assumption that the policy goals embody an ethical consensus that can be promoted better by market mechanisms than by any other means.

There are problems with this utilitarian approach. Cost-benefit analyses are carried out by individuals, and individual preferences may provide a weak foundation for policymaking. Individual preferences are the result of personal experiences, which are necessarily limited and based on incomplete information. Even if we were willing to accept individual preferences, we may have a problem in translating the aggregate conflicting preferences into a single policy decision. Another major objection to this form of utilitarianism is that it may result in decisions that are an affront to our sense of justice. Cost-benefit analysis would permit the loss of income of thirty families at $30,000 per year each, rather than the loss of one person's income at $1 million. That is, cost-benefit analysis does not require (or preclude) us from taxing distribution. Cost-benefit analysis, then, cannot be the sole guide to decisionmaking on environmental matters.

Policies should also give special consideration to those most vulnerable to their consequences. For example, the poor may find themselves at the mercy of decisions made by the more economically powerful members of society. Dolphins, whales, or spotted owls are affected by human choices. And later generations will have to live with results of decisions made today regarding the use of fossil fuels versus nuclear energy.

The poor have always suffered more than the affluent because of the deleterious effects of inferior living conditions, and industrialization has only added to their burden. We have noted how housing policy generally stratifies society, with the poor living in deteriorating urban areas close to factories and pollution while the wealthy move to the suburbs. Discrimination against minorities can compound the problem, making the poor even more likely to live in areas where hazardous waste and other toxins make for unhealthy living conditions. Poor nonwhite Americans are disproportionately impacted by environmental degradation.

When the environmental movement began in the 1970s, it largely reflected the views of some of the more prosperous upper-income people in the United States. However, since the mid-1980s, minorities and the poor have increasingly assumed a leadership role.[28] President Clinton assumed office in 1993, promising to restore the role of the government in environmental protection. The following year, he issued Executive Order 12898, requiring all federal agencies to include the achievement of "environmental justice" as part of their mission.

Conclusion

Environmental issues have taken center stage in public policy debates in only the past three or four decades. Almost every environmental issue is related to the impact of humanity on the environment. Nature everywhere tends to be treated as a mine or a dump. As we make more and more demands on the environment, we use up natural resources, destroy habitats for wildlife, increase biological extinction, and increase environmental pollution. Earth's natural systems, such as climate and temperature, the ozone layer, and water supply, have all been affected by human demands that outrun its capacity.

Although many other countries initially lagged behind the United States in environmental regulation, many have now overtaken us. "Green parties" have emerged in Europe to push standards beyond those of the United States.

It is increasingly recognized that global environmental degradation requires global solutions. Meaningful actions are difficult to achieve, however, when populations resist any increase in cost as a threat to material affluence. Markets do not provide an efficient outcome when negative externalities exist because business firms have a market incentive not to take the marginal social costs into account in their business decisions. To do so would put them at a competitive disadvantage.

Business interests usually react negatively to any government regulation that they fear will drive up prices. Politically, the Republican Party has emerged as the standard bearer of those who would dismantle the environmental regulation that is in place as damaging to US competitiveness.

The world faces tradeoffs regarding the environment. Eliminating all pollution would be impossible. However, the planet does appear to be nearing a real environmental crisis. When private people cannot solve externalities such as pollution, the government has a responsibility to step in. The problem is that special interest groups resist any regulation that would limit their negative externalities. The crucial problem in devising market-based programs is to determine the level of incentives needed to achieve the optimal policy outcome, which is where the marginal cost of the program equals its marginal benefit.

Questions for Discussion

1. Distinguish between environmental protection and environmental regulation. How are these practices informed by moral principles, particularly utilitarian principles?

2. What is meant by sustainable development and what environmental problems threaten this goal?

3. Compare the concept of a public good with the NIMBY attitude. What incentives can government offer to protect public goods and avoid NIMBY?

4. When and why did environmentalism become part of the political agenda? Did any specific events help to "politicize" the environment?

5. Discuss the plight of public interest groups devoted to the environment. What sources of funding do they have and how do they compete with private sector interests?

6. Much criticism is leveled about the "greenhouse" effect. What criteria do scientists rely on to evaluate scientific findings regarding the environment? Is science always objective?

Useful Websites

Audubon Society, www.audubon.org.
Clean Air Task Force, www.catf.us.
Environmental Integrity Project, www.environmentalintegrity.org.
Institute for European Environmental Policy, www.ieep.org.uk.
US Department of Energy, www.energy.gov.
US Department of the Interior, www.doi.gov.
US Energy Information Administration, www.eia.doe.gov.
US Environmental Protection Agency (EPA), www.epa.gov.
US Environmental Protection Agency, Global Warming site, www.epa.gov/globalwarming.

Notes

1. Lawrence White, *The Regulation of Air Pollutant Emissions from Motor Vehicles* (Washington DC: American Enterprise Institute, 1982), p. 14.

2. Public Law 91-604, 84 Stat. 1713 (1970).

3. Ann Burford had been a vocal critic of all environmental regulation from Colorado before going to the EPA. She was forced to resign in 1983 after evidence was made public that strongly suggested secret collusion between the EPA and the industry it was to regulate. For example, amendments to the Clean Air Act of 1977 were based on public health concerns. Agency records showed that there were thirty high-level meetings between officials of the EPA and the oil industry before leaded gasoline standards were set, but that no meetings were held with public health officials about leaded gasoline standards. James Watt was a leader of the "Sagebrush Rebellion," which was an effort by businesspeople, lobbyists, and state officials to persuade the federal government to ease its regulation and thereby the costs of public land used by cattle, mining, and real estate interests. As secretary of the interior, Watt antagonized environmentalists when he sold and leased federal lands to mining and timber interests at a fraction of their commercial market value.

4. Robert Perks, *Rewriting the Rules: The Bush Administration's Assault on the Environment,* 3rd annual ed. (Washington, DC: Natural Resources Defense Council, April 2004), p. 101.

5. Ibid., p. 1.

6. Ibid.

7. "S. 624: Senator Paul Simon Water for the World Act of 2009," available at www
.govtrack.us/congress/bill.xpd?bill=s111-624 (accessed May 3, 2009).

8. Michael Hawthorne, "Mercury Tainted Fish on FDA Menu," *Chicago Tribune,* December 14, 2008, available at www.ewg.org/node/27453 (accessed May 3, 2009).

9. Perks, *Rewriting the Rules,* p. iv.

10. Elizabeth Shogren, "Researchers Accuse Bush of Manipulating Science," *Los Angeles Times,* July 9, 2004, available at www.commondreams.org/headlines04/0709-03.htm.

11. "Critics Say EPA Pick Failed to Clean Up New Jersey's Toxic Sites," December 15, 2008, available at www.grist.org/article/Jeers-for-Jackson (accessed May 1, 2009).

12. Thomas J. Billitteri, "High Speed Trains," *CQ Researcher* 19 (May 2009): 18.

13. US Environmental Protection Agency, *Global Warming: Emissions,* available at www
.yosemite.epa.gov/oar/globalwarming.nsf/content/emissions.html (accessed April 30, 2009).

14. Ross Gelbspan, "A Global Warming," *American Prospect,* March–April 1997, p. 37.

15. US Environmental Protection Agency, *Global Warming.*

16. Alister Doyle, "Greenhouse Gas Jump Spurs Global Warming Fears," Reuters, October 11, 2004.

17. US Supreme Court, "Slip Opinion of *Massachusetts v. EPA,*" April 4, 2007, available at www.supremecourtus.gov/opinions/06pdf/05-1120.pdf (accessed May 3, 2009).

18. Juliet Eilperin and Steven Mufson, "Budget Expects Revenue from Limits on Emissions," *Washington Post,* February 26, 2009, p. A4.

19. United Nations Environment Programme (UNEP), "Basic Facts and Data on the Science and Politics of Ozone Protection" (Paris: United Nations, August 2003), p. 1. See also www.unep.org/ozone.

20. UNEP, "Basic Facts," p. 4.

21. "Merit Briefs for February Supreme Court Cases," February 9, 2009, available at www.abanet.org/publiced/preview/briefs/feb09.shtml (accessed May 3, 2009).

22. "Questions About Endocrine Disruptors," January 1998, available at http://extoxnet
.orst.edu/faqs/pesticide/endocrine.htm (accessed August 19, 2009).

23. Walter A. Rosenbaum, *Environmental Politics and Policy* (Washington, DC: Congressional Quarterly Press, 2005), p. 228.

24. US National Academy of Sciences and Royal Society of London, "Population Growth, Resource Consumption, and a Sustainable World," joint statement, February 27, 1992.

25. Paul R. Ehrlich and John Holden, "Impact of Population Growth, *Science,* March 26, 1971, pp. 1212–1217.

26. Henry W. Kindall and David Pimentel, "Constraints on the Expansion of the Global Food Supply," *Ambio* 23, no. 3 (May 1994): 198–205.

27. Garrett Hardin, "Population Policy," *E: The Environment Magazine,* November–December 1990. p. 5.

28. Mary H. Cooper, "Environmental Justice," *CQ Researcher* 8 (June 1998): 537.

13

US Foreign Policy:
A Time for Reassessment

There was a pervasive sense of decline in US global power and prestige as the eight years of the G. W. Bush administration came to an end. The administration was widely held to have distorted information to persuade the public and Congress to acquiesce in the invasion of Iraq in response to the attacks of September 11, 2001, despite Iraq's having had nothing to do with those attacks. The public's fears that Saddam Hussein had weapons of mass destruction (WMD) and was planning an attack were exploited by the president who said: "We cannot wait for the final proof—the smoking gun that could come in the form of a mushroom cloud." The news that the United States tortured prisoners at Guantánamo, and engaged in the secret rendition of individuals to prison camps outside this country shocked the conscience of many. The loss of US standing in the world was accompanied by spiraling budget deficits. Those deficits were caused by the largest tax cuts in history that coincided with embarking on wars in two countries that have lasted longer than World War II and proven costlier than any war, except World War II, in US history. The result has been a growing dependence on China and Japan to finance US borrowing and a steep recession causing severe strains in the economy.

The Obama administration has made it clear that it intends to revise US national security and defense policy. Polls, not surprisingly, indicate wide support for change in defense policy. By the end of 2008, national defense expenditures were close to $700 billion, or about 46 percent of all military spending worldwide.[1] The United States has approximately 440,000 troops deployed overseas, which is about the same number overseas as during the end of the Cold War. And although over 5,000 US servicepeople have been killed and almost 35,000 wounded since 2001 in Iraq and Afghanistan, terrorist activity throughout the world has increased. Despite this costly effort, the lesson to the rest of the world is that the United States, unhindered by its Cold War nemesis the Soviet Union, has not been able to stabilize two less-developed countries possessing just 1 percent of the world's population. The recent US inclination to rely on military force to achieve foreign policy goals despite the opposition of general world opinion has resulted in a threat of repolarization. Thus, the overreliance on military power beyond the limit of its utility has resulted in not just diminishing, but negative, returns. The unfortunate result is that the United States is paying more for less and less security.[2]

During the presidential campaign of 2008, both candidates presented sharp contrasts in their views on foreign policy. Senator John McCain welcomed the opportunity to make the campaign primarily about foreign policy. He campaigned as the candidate in favor of a more forceful foreign policy based on his military experience, and attempted to portray his opponent as weak and naive. However, global and domestic opinion had turned decidedly against the war in Iraq. By 2007, over two-thirds (67 percent) of public opinion around the world thought that US-led forces should leave Iraq, including a majority of public opinion in the coalition countries.[3] By December of 2008, even domestic opinion within the United States thought that, although there was "significant progress toward restoring civil order in Iraq" (56 percent), the war in Iraq was "not worth it" (64 percent to 34 percent).[4] McCain was in the unenviable position of trying to revive support for a policy that had already been decided in the negative by US public opinion.

The Obama campaign made clear that a reassessment of US foreign policy was in order. Concern that US foreign policy had overreached and relied too heavily on a proactive military policy rather than negotiation became a major issue in the campaign. This has resulted in a reorientation toward greater reliance on diplomacy, guided by a reinvigorated Department of State under Secretary Hillary Clinton and a de-emphasis on military solutions. We will briefly look at the evolution of foreign policy that highlights the need to rebalance the US foreign policy posture.

The Evolution of US Foreign Policy

Following the Japanese attack on Pearl Harbor and the subsequent declaration of war against the United States by Nazi Germany, this country entered the war on the Allied side. As the "arsenal of democracy," the nation's industries surged with the production of war materials. By the end of the war, the United States had changed from a regional to a global power as had the Soviet Union. The United States did not return to its prewar isolationism, but became a major influence in creating the United Nations to encourage broad international cooperation and the preeminence of the rule of law in the international community. The United States became one of the five permanent members of the Security Council to emphasize its commitment to international negotiation and cooperation.

From 1946 until 1991, US foreign policy was characterized by the Cold War. Britain's wartime leader Winston Churchill delivered a speech in Fulton, Missouri, using the term "iron curtain" to describe a line between the nations of the West and those in Eastern Europe under Soviet control. This speech is often cited as a recognition that Russia and the West were engaged in a prolonged struggle.[5] Churchill proposed that the West should work for the grand pacification of Europe within the Charter of the United Nations.

One year later, President Harry Truman announced his foreign policy of **containment** by committing the United States to support free peoples who were resisting the expansionist goals of the Soviet Union. This became known as the Truman Doctrine. Political leaders, regardless of party, accepted the general rubrics of the policy. The Cold War, while it avoided global war, was a period of many regional wars fought between client states of the United States and the Soviet Union.[6] The Soviet Union collapsed in 1991 and, for most of the last decade of the twentieth century, the United States under President Bill Clinton was primarily focused on shoring up the nation's domestic prosperity.[7] Despite considerable opposition in Congress, President Clinton did, however, intervene to stop the "ethnic cleansing" in the former Yugoslavia. His national security policy of **engagement and enlargement** was designed to forge closer relations between countries, particularly on economic matters, in the hope that, by providing collective benefits, it would discourage smaller countries from challenging the primacy of the United States.

An early sign that not all US leaders were willing to rely on international institutions, with their implied constraints on unilateral US decisionmaking, occurred when Republicans won control of both houses of Congress for the first time since the Dwight Eisenhower administration. Many in the new Republican majority were *neo-conservatives* who criticized the post–Cold War policies of Bill Clinton for reducing military expenditures and lacking an idealistic aggressiveness in promoting US interests.[8] In 1998, a Republican-led Congress defied President Clinton and refused to appropriate funds to pay a backlog of US dues owed to the United Nations in excess of $1 billion. At the same time, reductions in US foreign aid programs left the United States, the world's largest economy, with the lowest aid contributions as a percentage of gross domestic product.

Then, in 1999, a Republican-led Senate denied President Clinton's request for consent to ratify the Comprehensive Nuclear Test Ban Treaty. Although Clinton pledged that the United States would maintain its policy of not conducting nuclear tests, the Senate's unwillingness was a clear indication that there was a growing strength among politicians in the United States who were increasingly at odds with the more than 150 nations that supported the treaty.

At the turn of the twenty-first century, the United States was in its longest period of economic expansion in history. The stock markets reached record highs while unemployment and inflation fell to negligible levels. There was a brief period of optimism that democracy would now be dominant in the world. Francis Fukuyama wrote that the world was entering a new age, and that we may be witnessing "not just the end of the cold war, or the passing of a particular period of history, but the end of history as such, that is, the end point of mankind's ideological evolution and the universalization of Western liberal democracy as the final form of government."[9] US prestige was at its zenith, as many foreign governments tried to fashion their democratic reforms on the US model. US culture, from capitalism to music and language, was admired and copied throughout the world. The sheer predominance of the United States was without historical precedent.

Thus, as the twenty-first century began, it seemed to be the best of times for US foreign policy. The unprecedented power of the United States has been noted by many observers. Joseph Nye observed: "Not since Rome has one nation loomed so large above the others. . . . The United States bestrides the globe like a colossus. It dominates business, commerce, and communications; its economy is the world's most successful, its military might second to none."[10] The end of the Cold War left the United States with a margin of military power greater than any other nation in the history of the world. Indicative of the growing power of the United States was its growing share of world military spending. US military spending rose from 28 percent of the world total in 1986 to approximately 46 percent of total world military spending in 2008.[11] Even more indicative was the changed balance of power between the United States and potential adversaries. In 1986, Russia, China, and their allies together spent about 50 percent *more* on defense than the United States but, by 2008, US defense expenditures—*not* including expenditures in Iraq and Afghanistan—were more than twice as great as those of Russia and China combined, in terms of purchasing power.[12] This seemed to provide the power the nation might use to preserve its military preeminence while enhancing its military security.

The dissolution of the Soviet bloc resulted not only in a smaller Russia, but it provoked a significant strategic realignment as former satellite nations gained their independence and turned toward the West. Russian support for client states was effectively terminated. States in the Middle East, Africa, Asia, and Latin America were essentially cast adrift.

The Soviet challenge to Western power since the end of World War II suddenly seemed to evaporate. The competition of ideologies between communism and capitalism that helped fuel the logic of the bipolar model, and defined the relations between the Soviet Union and the United States, was also gone. US goals of advancing democracy and market economies over communism were apparently accomplished, and even China's economic system submitted to market forces. The United States was now unchallenged as the world's dominant military and economic power.

The new dominance of the United States with the end of the Cold War revealed another set of problems that proved to be more complex than anticipated. Many in the US foreign policy establishment were captivated by imagining the possibilities of how such excessive military and economic power could be used to our best advantage. The relatively enhanced power of the United States might even permit a vision of a "new world order" led by the United States. On the other hand, to the consternation of many in the US foreign policy elite, allies are more dismissive of US power as simply being less relevant with the implosion of the Soviet threat. The military unity required in a bipolar world is no longer a pressing issue. Many US allies have been simply unwilling to accept US global leadership.[13] The leaders of the former rival bloc including Russia and China may no longer be adversaries engaged in a Cold War with the West, but they are certainly military and economic competitors. A major problem is that, in the area of military policy, the world can be thought of as unipolar. But military power is viewed by many as amounting to nothing more than a costly surplus unless it can be effectively used. Unfortunately, the use of the US military in Iraq and Afghanistan has shown significant limits on the effectiveness of military power in certain situations.

George W. Bush and Force as an Instrument of Policy

As a candidate in 2000, G. W. Bush suggested he would not emphasize foreign policy. He came into office with the intention of pulling back from what he and many Republican politicians regarded as excessive engagement and **nation building**. In fact, the election of Bush spelled the end of engagement and enlargement and advanced **unilateralism**. The new president surprised most observers by aggressively rejecting US policy goals, pursued since World War II, of encouraging the progressive development of an interdependent world community. He made clear that he would pursue a narrower view of the "national interest" and be more selective in overseas involvement.

The foreign policy process often involves only a small elite group who provide input based on their supposed expertise. This is in contrast to the formulation of most domestic policy issues, where the emphasis is on a broad democratic participation in the process. Most problems involving crisis management issues typically require quick responses and are dealt with by presumed military and political experts at the top of the executive branch's foreign policy bureaucracy. The secretary of defense typically is the primary adviser on military affairs while political leaders typically have a broader array of policy concerns. The secretary of state is the president's primary foreign policy adviser. The Department of State is the oldest of all the cabinet departments, which makes the secretary of state (Thomas Jefferson being the first) the ranking cabinet member. Secretaries of state, as with all presidential advisers, have only as much policymaking authority as the president chooses to delegate. However, the Bush administration was unique in the latitude Vice President Dick Cheney was given in policy decisions.

Ideally, there should be cooperation and a sharing of information and open discussion regarding the formulation and coordination of foreign policy. The general balance of power between the leaders representing the State Department and Department of Defense (DOD) affect how and what ultimate decisions are made. G. W. Bush was clearly more attuned to foreign policy advice from the neoconservatives, including Vice President Cheney, Deputy Secretary of Defense Paul Wolfowitz, adviser Richard Perle, and Secretary of Defense Donald Rumsfeld. This group operating under the particular worldview espoused by the neoconservative ideology was much more narrowly focused on military solutions. Their zeal and intensity led them to try to control debate within the administration regarding Middle East policy. Their effort was to get others to accept their view rather than to seriously assess the strategic assessment of the relative capabilities and strategies between the United States and Iraq.

Bush's secretary of state and former chairman of the Joint Chiefs of Staff, Colin Powell, was marginalized as the odd man out in giving foreign policy advice to the president, Thus, the State Department lost its role as the president's primary foreign policy adviser. For example, regarding the proposed preemptive attack on Iraq, Powell urged the administration to return to the UN Security Council to get its endorsement to use force against Iraq, as it had before launching an attack against Afghanistan. President Bush challenged the UN to authorize force against Iraq or risk becoming "irrelevant." The Security Council refused to pass a resolution authorizing the use of force against Iraq and instead called for a new round of UN inspections for WMD in Iraq. This was a clear illustration of the attempt of other nations, including many major US allies, to form a counterbalance to provocative US actions. Nevertheless Bush, armed with a congressional resolution endorsing his authority to use military force, became impatient with the failure of UN weapons inspectors to find WMD.

As a new president, G. W. Bush ultimately adopted the views of the neoconservatives after the attacks of September 11. The following January, in his State of the Union speech (which was largely written by a neoconservative, David Frum), Bush named Iraq, Iran, and North Korea as constituting an "axis of evil" that "pose a growing danger." He then signaled the potential of the United States to launch an attack on such states and "preemptive war" when he said: "I will not wait on events, while dangers gather. I will not stand by, as peril draws closer and closer. The United States of America will not permit the world's most dangerous regimes to threaten us with the world's most destructive weapons."[14]

Bush elaborated on the implications of a more aggressive foreign policy in a commencement address at West Point in June 2002. He stated:

> Containment is not possible when unbalanced dictators with weapons of mass destruction can deliver those weapons on missiles or secretly provide them to terrorist allies. . . . If we wait for threats to materialize, we will have waited too long. The war on terror will not be won on the defensive. We must take the battle to the enemy . . . and confront the worst threats before they emerge. . . .
>
> America has, and intends to keep, military strengths beyond challenge—thereby making the destabilizing arms races of other eras pointless, and limiting rivalries to trade and other pursuits of peace.[15]

With this address, "the Bush Doctrine" replaced "the Truman Doctrine." It claimed US primacy around the world. Rather than trying to deter and contain foreign involvement, getting involved at the earliest perceived threat was now deemed preferable.

The attacks of September 11 and the resulting war on terrorism led the president and his advisers back to global involvement. The Bush administration also came to believe that the war against Islamic terrorism required democratic reform and even nation building in the Middle East. The desire to promote democracy grew out of the conviction that US security interests are aided by democratic forms of government and represented a return to principles that go back to Jefferson. The notion of using military force to "install democracies" as a gift of "freedom" that the United States will share goes far beyond earlier principles of encouraging democratic forms of government.

The restraint against the use of force was significantly lowered by the Bush administration. The Bush Doctrine of preemptive war was explicitly stated in the National Security Council's (NSC) statement of National Security Strategy of the United States in 2002: "We must deter and defend against the threat before it is unleashed . . . even if uncertainty remains as to the time and place of the enemy's attack. . . . The United States will, if necessary, act preemptively."[16] The NSC's statement asserted: "For centuries, international law recognized that nations need not suffer an attack before they can lawfully take action to defend themselves against forces that present an imminent danger of attack."[17] The statement claimed, without supporting evidence, that there was an evolving right under international law for the United States to use force preemptively (in a clear reference to Iraq) against threats posed by "rogue states" possessing WMD.

Reducing the threshold for the use of force while claiming the right of the Bush administration to determine when that decision is justified implies an increased readiness to take unilateral action. It also suggests that the president, acting as "the decider," is freer to use more coercive techniques in negotiating with a "rogue state." Without Soviet countervailing power, the likelihood of small states receiving aid and escalating a small war into a large war is reduced.

Vice President Cheney, who drove much of US foreign policy after September 11, described terrorist activities as often "low-probability, high-impact events." He announced the "one percent doctrine" as meaning that, "if there's a one percent chance" of a terrorist event occurring, "we have to treat it as a certainty in terms of our response."[18] The doctrine certainly lowers the threshold in deciding to resort to the use of force. Ron Suskind, in his book *The One Percent Doctrine,* points out a less-obvious implication of the doctrine. The Bush administration did not react to every one percent threat as if it were a certainty. The doctrine does more than just rationalize a hawkish posture, it actually justifies *ignoring unwanted, time-consuming analysis.* Since any perceived threat has at least a one percent chance of happening, it meets the required threshold allowing the United States to take action if the administration so decides.

Therefore, under the one percent doctrine, there was no reason to waste time with deliberation or policy analysis.

Suskind pointed out that a defining characteristic of President G. W. Bush's personality is his confidence in his own instinct and his disdain for policy analysis. The one percent doctrine was a perfect fit for Bush's hostility to policy discussions and provided a justification for avoiding them.[19]

International Law and the Use of Force

One consequence of the wars of the nineteenth and twentieth centuries was the emergence of a general prohibition of the legitimacy of the use of force to resolve international disputes. War should be the instrument of last resort restricted to the legitimate right of self-defense. In fact, the UN Charter was brought into being to emphasize the requirement in international law requiring member states to "settle their international disputes by peaceful means in such a manner that international peace and security, and justice, are not endangered."[20] Article 33 of the Charter obligates states to attempt to settle their disputes through negotiation, mediation, conciliation, arbitration, or judicial settlement. The general prohibition on the use of force by states is found in Article 2(4), which states:

> All Members shall refrain in their international relations from the threat or use of force against the territorial integrity or political independence of any State, or in any other manner inconsistent with the Purposes of the United Nations.

Almost all international legal scholars agree that Article 2(4) was intended to be a very strong prohibition on the use of force by states since allowing exceptions would provide states with too much discretion in deciding in their own case when they could resort to war.

Nevertheless, the UN Charter does note exceptions to the prohibition on the use of force found in Article 2(4). Article 51 recognizes the *inherent* right of self-defense possessed by all states. Article 51 makes this right unequivocal:

> Nothing in the present Charter shall impair the inherent right of individual or collective self-defence if an armed attack occurs against a Member of the United Nations, until the Security Council has taken measures necessary to maintain international peace and security. Measures taken by Members in the exercise of this right of self-defence shall be immediately reported to the Security Council.

The Charter thus preserves an inherent right that states had under customary international law predating the UN. Note that the use of force in self-defense in the Charter requires a previous "armed attack" to have occurred.[21] It was on this basis that US defense policy throughout the Cold War was based on "deterrence." That is, the US defense posture was based on the premise that it would not launch a first strike against the Soviet Union. But any decision by an adversary to launch an attack against the United States would be irrational because the United States would retain sufficient counterstrike capability to annihilate the aggressor state.

Allowing a state to decide for itself to engage in anticipatory or preemptive self-defense prior to an armed attack would replace the clear standard of Article 51 with a vague standard allowing each state to arbitrarily determine if a threat justified its preemptive military action. Such a view would effectively destroy the rule explicitly enunciated in Article 51.[22]

Torture, the Law, and World Reaction

Few people challenge the right of nations to hold prisoners of war (POWs) or even suspected enemies during war. However, there is widespread objection when suspects are held indefinitely without being charged with a criminal act. And when information was reported in reliable sources that the G. W. Bush administration was holding POWs and suspects in "secret" prisons and routinely subjecting them to torture, public opinion around the world was united in its condemnation. The release of images of torture at Abu Ghraib prison in Baghdad and reports of torture at the prison at Guantánamo Bay in Cuba focused international attention on one of the most controversial aspects of the "war against terror."

World reaction highlighted the obvious hypocrisy of G. W. Bush administration claims of fighting a war on terror to bring freedom, democracy, and the rule of law to others while violating its own laws as well as international law. The European Parliament voted overwhelmingly for a resolution urging the United States to close Guantánamo and to give the inmates a fair trial. World opinion generally opposed the idea that torture is a useful tool for combating terrorism. Neither Abu Ghraib, nor Guantánamo, or other secret Central Intelligence Agency (CIA) prisons helped capture the perpetrators of September 11 or avoid future attacks against civilians.[23] In fact, torture often was cited as creating martyrs and recruiting additional fighters for Al-Qaida.

Arguments about whether torture is effective or not miss the more salient point that torture is a violation of US law. It is prohibited by the Eighth Amendment of the Constitution. The US federal antitorture statute defines the crime of torture and provides harsh punishment for anyone who commits an act of torture outside the United States.[24] The law was passed in 1994 to bring the United States into compliance with the UN Convention Against Torture (CAT).[25] The CAT requires all parties to the treaty to "take effective legislative, administrative, judicial, or other measures to prevent acts of torture in any territory under their jurisdiction." Article 1 of the CAT prohibits "*any* act by which severe pain or suffering, whether physical or mental, is intentionally inflicted on a person for such purposes as obtaining from him or a third person information or confession." The UN Committee Against Torture demanded that the United States rescind any interrogation technique that constitutes torture or cruel, inhuman, or degrading treatment in all places of detention under its control.

Many of the counterterrorism measures that were adopted in the wake of September 11 that inevitably led to torture were based on legal opinions that were sloppily reasoned and claimed extraordinary constitutional authorities on behalf of the president. Jack Goldsmith, a legal scholar with excellent conservative credentials and now a Harvard law professor, was hired to head the Justice Department's Office of Legal Counsel (OLC), which advises the president about the legality of presidential actions. Goldsmith reported in a book recounting his time in the OLC that President G. W. Bush and Vice President Cheney made clear that a central priority was to maintain and expand the president's formal legal powers. He noted that lawyers quickly realized that they could get a favorable hearing for a particular course of action by arguing that alternative proposals would diminish the president's power.[26]

In 2002, a memo from the OLC at the request of White House counsel Alberto Gonzales was sent to the CIA redefining US torture policy. That memo began by redefining torture so narrowly that it included only those methods that result in pain associated with "death, organ failure or the permanent impairment of a significant body function."[27] After largely redefining torture out of existence, the memo went on to explain that, even if someone died during torture, the torturer would not be guilty if he or she felt the torture was necessary to prevent some worse evil. The memo concluded by claiming that the president has the right to order torture because he is above the law during wartime, even if Congress has not declared war.[28]

In 2003 John Yoo, then a deputy in the OLC, sent a memo classified "secret" to DOD. This memo made a similar claim of the right to take action by redefining torture. Then, it went even further by asserting without qualification that during wartime, the president's commander-in-chief power overrides the Constitution's prohibition against torture in the Eighth Amendment as well as the due process guarantee of the Fifth and Fourteenth Amendments.[29]

The legal views expressed in the memos cited above found little support beyond the Offices of the President and Vice President, Secretary of Defense, and those in the OLC. The American Civil Liberties Union (ACLU) and others[30] filed a suit under the Freedom of Information Act against the government for release of documents that provided evidence that prisoner abuse in US detention facilities was systematic. The storm of criticism that resulted led the G. W. Bush administration to deny that they engaged in torture. While they admitted to water boarding, a practice cited as a war crime at Nuremberg, in the past, they claimed it was no longer being used. The claim that the president is not bound by statutes, treaties, and the constitutional prohibitions against torture during war does mark a major reversal of US policy extending back for over a century. In 2006, then senator Obama said that torture "is not how a serious Administration would approach the problem of terrorism. And the sad part about all of this is that this betrayal of American values is unnecessary."[31]

The Iraq War as a Threat Prevention Strategy

Events in Iraq have made most Americans painfully aware that US military dominance is far more limited than many G. W. Bush administration policymakers imagined. In fact, excessive reliance on the military to achieve political results more to our liking has become counterproductive. Critics pointed out the arrogance in the belief that US policymakers could increase national security by selectively reacting to threats having a slight chance of occurring and treating them as threats that will certainly occur. The case of Iraq makes the point. The neoconservatives in the administration overestimated US military power and believed that the country could achieve complete security by preemptively removing threats. Further, they believed they could take action to prevent the development of adversarial situations several years down the road. The cost in lives and national treasure were wildly underestimated.

March 19, 2009, marked the six-year anniversary of the US-led invasion of Iraq supposedly to find and eliminate WMD that Saddam Hussein was using to threaten the United States. Over 5,000 Americans have been killed and approximately 35,000 wounded since 2001 in Iraq and Afghanistan. Joseph Stiglitz, a winner of the 2001 Nobel Prize in economics, and coauthor Linda Bilmes calculate the Iraq War will ultimately cost the United States $3 trillion, about the same as World War II.[32] In early 2009, expenses in Iraq were averaging over $12.5 billion a month and, with Afghanistan, the total is $16 billion per month. One month's expenses on these military operations is equal to the annual budget of the United Nations. As of 2009, the wars in Iraq and Afghanistan have cost over $800 billion.

The cost of the Iraq War is far more than the G. W. Bush administration projected at its outset. In 2002 Mitchell Daniels, then head of the Office of Management and Budget, estimated the war could cost as much as $60 billion. Lawrence Lindsey, director of the National Economic Council in 2002, gave an unofficial estimate that the costs could reach as much as $200 billion.[33] Lindsey was fired shortly after giving his estimate. That estimate was dismissed as "baloney" by Rumsfeld, then secretary of defense.[34] Rumsfeld's deputy, Wolfowitz, suggested that postwar reconstruction could be paid for through Iraq's expected increased oil revenues. Rumsfeld and Daniels projected costs of between $57 billion and $69 billion (in 2007 dollars), some portion of which would be paid by other countries.

Operational costs have been driven up by the use of private contractors to perform jobs previously carried out by the military. Over 100,000 private contractors in Iraq and Afghanistan perform tasks from cooking and cleaning to servicing weapons systems, providing logistical support, and protecting US diplomats. By 2007, Blackwater employed 845 private security contractors in Iraq who earned up to $1,222 a day, or up to $445,000 per year. By comparison, an Army sergeant earned between $140 and $190 a day in pay and benefits, between $51,100 to $69,350 a year.[35] The high pay for contractors is one factor that has forced the Army to offer higher bonuses for reenlisting since soldiers can work as contractors for much higher wages when their tour of duty is over. Reliance on contractors has been criticized, not just for the higher costs, but also because they are not subject to military discipline. The use of contractors amounts to a partial *privatization* of the military.

The wide use of contractors brings a potential for profiteering and corruption. Good government policy usually tries to encourage competition by awarding contracts through competitive bidding. However, the G. W. Bush administration primarily relied on "sole source bidding," claiming that in the emergency situation there was no time to allow the competitive process to work. There may be some justification for sole sourcing at the beginning of a war that is unexpected. However, it was clear for several months that the United States intended to invade Iraq. Giving multiyear contracts to such companies as Halliburton, formerly headed by Vice President Cheney, should have been avoided. To make matters worse, many of the sole source contracts were "cost-plus" contracts in which a contractor is reimbursed for all expenses and is provided a profit margin over costs incurred. This provides a contractor with an incentive to increase spending to increase profits. As a result, with insufficient personnel to provide adequate oversight, there have been many reports of financial irregularities. The Defense Contract Audit Agency reported $10 billion in questionable bills, and $8.8 billion disappeared from the Development Fund for Iraq.[36] And payoffs may take the form of campaign contributions. So, for example, in a five-year period, Halliburton contributed $1.1 million to the Republican Party and $55,650 to the Democratic Party. Meanwhile, Halliburton received over $19.3 billion in sole source contracts.[37]

Instability created by US military involvement in the Middle East has also contributed to the run-up in the price of oil, which is also a factor in the current economic crisis. Stiglitz links the run-up in the price of oil and the $800 billion spent in Iraq that could not be spent elsewhere in the economy as also contributing to US economic woes.[38]

War spending is not an efficient way to encourage jobs and growth. The US infrastructure, such as roads, bridges, and education, would have benefited greatly by the expenditure of such funds. Spending on the Iraq War suppressed spending on such goods and services in the United States. Finally, the G. W. administration relied entirely on borrowing to finance the war for the first time in US history. Not only were taxes not raised, but those for the wealthy were cut. Forty percent of the money to purchase bonds to finance the deficit now come from abroad. But from an economic perspective, borrowing today equals an equivalent tax increase in the future. Thus, a future generation will have to foot the entire bill for the cost of the war.

Reassessing Defense Policy in the Obama Administration

A recognition of the failures in US defense policy over at least the past decade provide the obvious agenda for change in the new administration's foreign policy. President Obama has the task of forging a consensus among foreign policy elites to support a defense policy that will reverse the erosion of US prestige and standing in the world community. It will require a consistency of decisionmaking over the whole range of foreign policy issues in which security interests are consistent with military force size, training readiness, and missions. The defense budget should also be consistent with national security planning based on broader economic considerations and the willingness of taxpayers to actually provide the given level of defense spending necessary rather than relying on deficit financing (borrowing).[39]

Three fundamental concerns over the conduct of policy over the past decade, when taken together, capture the dilemmas of current policy.[40] One concern is the use of perceptual frames that influence our assessment of security policy and strategy employed for achieving them. The use of the shorthand term "war on terror" has provided the major organizing theme of US security policy.[41] Slogans like that are carefully crafted to produce support for policies. It suggests that the nation is under a military attack that can only be defended militarily. This war frame was used to justify special war powers for President G. W. Bush. A nation at war evokes a duty of patriotism, and the idea that a lack of support for the war is treasonous. It was used to pressure Congress to give unlimited powers to the president, lest members of Congress be charged with a lack of patriotism. The war on terror frame was used to justify torture and restrictions on due process.[42]

The obvious criticism of such a slogan is that "terror" is a strategy. So a war against a strategy makes no sense. A war on terror does not name a nation or a group, but an emotion and as such it cannot be defeated by weapons or the signing of a peace treaty. And since a war on terror does not have an end, it puts the United States on a permanent war footing.

Secretary Powell, among others, suggested "crime" as the proper frame to use since it justifies an international hunt for the criminals, and would allow "police actions" when military involvement was required. But it would have maintained the focus on the need for intelligence, diplomacy, and economics.[43] Use of the term "war on terror" degrades conceptual clarity since the Israeli-Palestinian conflict and tensions with Iran and North Korea have also been framed as "fronts" in the war on terror, making clear analysis of policy more difficult.

Although a broad cross-section of the news media still uses the term, the Obama administration consistently refers to the war in Iraq, not the war on terror. This allows a greater focus on broad international cooperation in reducing stress and sources of instability in the international system. De-emphasizing fronts on the nebulous war on terror, it permits the administration to work to win the confidence of people in troubled areas and address concerns such as food, water, energy and economic development.

In this regard, the Obama administration has clearly signaled its intent to place a much greater emphasis than its predecessor on the "soft power" of the United States, and that it will seek to lead by diplomacy and negotiations rather than by coercive pressure.[44] A major part of this effort has been signaled by naming a high-profile secretary of state in former rival Hillary Clinton. Secretary Clinton has also indicated that the United States will be very engaged in global policy and will work both with individual nations and through international organizations, not around them.

A second issue of concern in US defense policy and the global environment is the evolving use of force in foreign policy. The social changes that have occurred inside advanced democracies since World War II have raised the costs of using hard military power. However, the United States has been more, rather than less, inclined to consider force as an instrument of policy in the post–Cold War period. Postindustrial democracies tend to be more focused on social welfare than on military glory. In most advanced democracies, the use of force now requires a convincing moral justification to attract popular support.

The military can serve many functions besides serving in combat. Increasingly, in addition to the security function, they may be used to provide humanitarian assistance, to provide civil construction projects such as building electric grids and providing potable water, as well as conducting diplomacy. Changes to current defense policy must also provide guidance regarding the use of force and the role of the military.[45]

The third issue is a posture that is designed to meet the new world circumstances. A realistic defense policy that integrates US security needs with the global environment should provide more security at a lower cost. A greater reliance on planning and soft power whenever possible, rather than treating each event as new and unexpected with resulting emergency funding requests, should result in more security at lower costs.

An Agenda for Policy Reassessment

With so many items on the public policy agenda, we will note only major items that are essential to reverse the recent unfortunate trends in US defense policy.

Iraq and US Defense Policy

Obama opposed the war in Iraq from the beginning, claiming that it would lead to "an occupation of undetermined length, with undetermined costs and undetermined consequences."[46] He has consistently stated that "we must be as careful getting out of Iraq as we were careless getting in."[47] Iraq has diverted resources from the war in Afghanistan, making it harder to capture Osama bin Laden and others involved in the September 11 attacks. The continued occupation of Iraq contributes to tensions in the region, and feeds the divisions that continue to divide Iraq.

The problem for the Obama administration is the threat of a resurgence in sectarian violence that might accompany the withdrawal of US troops. To reduce the threat, the United States will need to continue and even increase efforts to train and support Iraqi security forces.

The G. W. Bush administration concluded two major agreements, which were approved by Iraq's parliament in late November 2008. The administration agreed to a total withdrawal of US troops from Iraq by the end of 2011. The final version also required US combat troops to coordinate missions with the Iraqi government and hand over prisoners to Iraqi authorities as well as a pullout from Iraqi urban areas by July 2009.[48] The agreement also allowed for nonmilitary contractors to be subject to Iraqi law, a change resisted by the Bush administration.

President Obama retained Robert Gates, the secretary of defense in the G. W. Bush administration, to stay on in his administration. In announcing the appointment, President Obama restated his belief that US combat troops could be withdrawn in sixteen months, but that he was "prepared to listen to his commanders."[49]

The clear intent is to redouble efforts to train Iraqi security forces to take over the security requirements for Iraq. While there will be no "permanent" US bases in Iraq, it is possible that over 20,000 US troops might remain for some time to provide "training."

Israel-Palestine: A Never-Ending Conflict

The confrontation between Hamas and Israel left in tatters the peace plan put forward by President G. W. Bush in Annapolis. As usual in the Middle East, there is plenty of blame to go around. Bush did not press the Israeli government to stop building settlements in Palestine. Ehud Olmert's government in Israel continued building settlements and failed to give the Palestinian president Mahmoud Abbas support he needed to oppose the radical Palestinian Hamas organization. Arab leaders did not ask Hamas to cut its ties with Iran and take part in efforts to work out a peace settlement.

When Hamas ended a six-month cease-fire by launching rocket attacks into Israel, the response of Israel was predictable. Israel launched devastating air strikes against the Gaza Strip. Both candidates to succeed Olmert in elections in February 2009 wanted to be seen as more in favor of a muscular response. In Gaza, where most people feel the restrictions put them in a virtual prison, there is even greater support for Hamas.

This conflict is responsible for much of the instability throughout the Middle East. In 2006, the US House of Representatives passed slightly different resolutions that, among other things, condemned the governments of Iran and Syria for their support of Hamas and Hezbollah (a Lebanese Shiite Muslim group) and urged the president to bring sanctions against the governments of Syria and Iran for their support of these groups.[50] Both Hamas and Hezbollah have successfully resisted all attempts to isolate and weaken them.

It is not clear that the United States or Israel is willing to try to engage these groups in the effort to achieve peace. Other countries in the region, such as Iran and Syria, might be influential, but thus far have not been given much incentive for cooperation. Israel, with justification, is extremely wary of any agreement that might compromise its security. Many presidents have placed a settlement of the Israeli-Palestinian issue as high on their agenda, but to date none have been successful. Obama delivered a major address in Cairo in June 2009 to the Muslim world. In this address, he emphasized his effort to recast the role of the United States as a positive force for peace in the region.

To Reassert US Support for International Law

The world consists of over 190 states that make up the world community. Even though the political elites in the state system emphasize their primary loyalty to the nation-state system, there is an explosion of transnational activity. The international political system is increasingly committed to the rule of international law as a means to depoliticize and bring predictability to the conduct of much of international affairs. Not surprisingly, the most powerful states tend to have the most influence in determining what aspects of international politics are codified into law.

The United States was most successful in influencing the progressive development of international law when it shared the world arena with the Soviet Union from 1945 to 1991. Since then it has enjoyed the status of the world's hegemonic power. But even for the world's dominant state, unrivaled power should not be confused with omnipotence. In fact, since 1991, US efforts to shape the environment through negotiating multilateral treaties have met failure time after time. The United States has been embarrassed on several occasions when even its close allies have joined with other nations and have brought multilateral treaties into force without US participation. Some of the treaties receiving the support of most of the world powers, but not the United States, include: the Rome Statute, which brought the International Criminal Court (ICC) into being; the Kyoto Protocol on Climate Change; the Convention on the Rights of the Child; and the Ottawa Anti-Personnel Landmine Treaty.

Not only has the United States lost its reputation as a leader of the progressive development of international law through treaty making, but many of its policies appear to range from at minimum a heavy-handed use of power to a flouting of international legal obligations. The result has been that the United States was cast as an international pariah.

For example, President G. W. Bush provoked widespread criticism for his address at West Point in which he indicated that the United States would "impose preemptive, unilateral, military force when and where it chooses."[51] These recent justifications of preemptive war are in conflict with the UN Charter's provisions on the use of force. Only the Security Council may authorize the use of force to deal with any threat or breach of the peace. This is the reason why the Security Council refused to authorize the use of force against Iraq, despite significant pressure by the United States for an authorizing resolution.

Bush also claimed the right to try foreigners charged with terrorism. He signed an order authorizing detainees to be held by the military in Guantánamo Bay, Cuba, without the right to any legal review by any US or international court. Protection under the Geneva Conventions was not to be extended to the detainees who could be held without trial for the duration of the war on terror. Responding to diplomatic pressure and criticism from major allies such as the United Kingdom and Australia on behalf of citizens of theirs who were being detained, Secretary Powell advised the administration to release or transfer those detainees whose offenses were uncertain or minor.[52] But Powell's plea was ignored. The administration's claim that it had the exclusive right to determine the legal status of the detainees was later rejected by the Supreme Court in a 6–3 ruling that federal courts do have jurisdiction to hear prisoners' legal challenges.[53] These and other controversial decisions—the result of what Pope John Paul II called an "arrogance of power"—damaged US ties to European allies and tarnished the image of the United States throughout the world.[54] President Obama has indicated his intention to close down Guantánamo and bring to an end what is widely seen as an example of the United States ignoring its treaty obligations.

In his inaugural address, President Obama signaled to the world that our foreign policy approach would change from the G. W. Bush emphasis on US supremacy. He referred to the Cold War when he reminded his listeners that "earlier generations" won it "not just with missiles and tanks," but by leaders with "sturdy alliances and enduring convictions." These leaders "understood that our power alone cannot protect us, nor does it entitle us to do as we please. Instead, they knew that our power grows through its prudent use."[55] Understanding that our security "emanates from the justness of our cause" and the tempering qualities of "restraint," we will meet new threats that demand "even greater cooperation and understanding between nations."[56] The new president indicated his concern for the decline in the United States' reputation abroad and his determination to emphasize soft power, and leading through the force of ideas and one's example. The president and Secretary of State Clinton have both indicated their intent to be particularly careful to operate within the perceived boundaries of international law. The administration intends to strike a new balance in remaining faithful to its ideals while working through international rules, and not seek to weaken accepted norms of international conduct or claim special exemptions.[57]

To Rein in the Pentagon Relative to the State Department

The increased readiness of the G. W. Bush administration to use or threaten to use military options to maintain US dominance overreached and became counterproductive.

The reminder to other nations of our willingness to consider military options to attain national goals actually encouraged them to engage in behavior that counterbalances US military power in favor of economic issues. The extent to which that military coercion was ignored or rejected by others suggests that the United States was overinvested in a less-relevant option.

The Pentagon, for example, moved into what had been traditional CIA functions in the area of intelligence. Secretary Rumsfeld argued successfully with President G. W. Bush that CIA operations in Iraq should be under the control of DOD. In this regard, Rumsfeld created the new Office of the Undersecretary of Defense for Intelligence to be the secretary's troubleshooter. Rumsfeld and his undersecretary for intelligence took "aggressive" steps to diminish the director of national intelligence's power.[58] Bush's decision to accept the resignation of Secretary Rumsfeld brought the dream of Pentagon control over intelligence to an end.[59] Secretary Gates, in a direct slap at Rumsfeld, dismantled some of Rumsfeld's pet programs, including the Talon database used to spy on US citizens. He also agreed that future undersecretaries for intelligence would also report to the Office of the Director of National Intelligence (ODNI). There have been other proposals to take the National Security Agency (NSA), the National Geospatial Intelligence Agency (NGA), and the National Reconnaissance Office (NRO) out of DOD's hands and put them under the direct control of the ODNI and the White House, to ensure that they are under true civilian control. Removing them from DOD would give future presidents greater control and allow them to be used for broad national goals, including protecting human rights and monitoring the environment, that would never be a high priority of the military.[60]

In this regard, the Pentagon had expanded its activities in several areas that were thought of as more properly belonging to the Department of State. For example, DOD increasingly came to consider public information both in foreign countries and in the United States as something that must be managed. Thus, a campaign to control perceptions was conducted not only in countries like Iraq, Afghanistan, or Iran, but also in the United States. The *New York Times* successfully sued the DOD to gain access to 8,000 pages of records describing years in which individuals belonging to the fraternity of television and radio "military analysts" were used by the Pentagon information apparatus to generate favorable news coverage of the G. W. Bush administration's wartime performance.[61] Analysts were wooed in hundreds of private briefings with senior military leaders, including officials with significant influence over private military contracts as well as people from the White House. Members of the groups echoed administration talking points, even when they suspected the information was false or inflated, because they feared jeopardizing their access. Internal Pentagon documents frequently referred to the military analysts as "message force multipliers" or "surrogates" who would deliver "themes and messages" on behalf of the administration.[62]

As planning for an Iraq invasion got under way in early 2002, many polls showed a national uneasiness about invading a country with no clear connection to the attacks of September 11. Secretary Rumsfeld's assistant secretary of defense for public affairs Torie Clarke was given the task of achieving "information dominance" to sway opinion by voices "perceived as authoritative and utterly independent."[63] Since it was noticed that the military analysts were getting more airtime than network reporters, they were identified as "key influentials" who could frame how viewers ought to interpret events. In 2002, the decision was made to make the analysts the main focus of the DOD public relations effort to construct a case for the war. Journalists actually became secondary. This was not a case of a complaint regarding the "media filter," but a case of co-opting the filter into an administration amplifier. While one might expect the Pentagon to make covert payments to Iraqi journalists and television broadcasters to publish coalition propaganda, many were not aware that taxpayer dollars designated for the Pentagon were being used to propagandize citizens in the United States.[64]

Conclusion

Since the collapse of the Soviet Union in 1991, and especially since the terrorist attacks of September 11, there has been a greater tendency to rely on military solutions for foreign policy issues. Initial military successes in Iraq and Afghanistan did not provide a lasting political solution. Removal of troops too quickly can revert to a status quo ante. The result has led to the United States being militarily involved in Afghanistan and Iraq for a longer period than we had been involved in either World War I or World War II, at a cost exceeding all wars except World War II. In human terms, the cost, just to the United States, includes well over 5,000 troops killed and 35,000 wounded as of July 2009. This effort has not reduced terrorism. In fact, terrorist acts around the world are increasing, not decreasing. Neither has this activity made the Middle East any more stable. On the contrary, in 2009, there are military operations under way in Iraq and Afghanistan, with strikes into Pakistan by the United States. And Israel was involved in an incursion into the Gaza Strip. Instability is bleeding into other countries as US military operations spread.

The result is unchallenged even by its historical rival the Soviet Union, and the United States has found it far more difficult and costly to impose its will on much smaller and weaker states than expected. The increased use of military force has resulted in a rise in demonstrations of anti-Americanism as US prestige has declined. Many states, including close allies, have registered their disapproval of its use of hard power by being less supportive of the United States in the UN and in alliance organizations.

The collapse of the Soviet Union reduced the constraint against the selection of a military option as a primary policy alternative. The bureaucracy responsible for foreign policy in the G. W. Bush administration (i.e., the Department of State and the Pentagon) brought a pronounced shift in the power balance toward the neoconservatives who dominated the Pentagon and away from the Department of State with its emphasis on the soft power of negotiation and diplomacy. The alliance of Secretary of

Defense Rumsfeld, and Vice President Cheney who took an unusually active role in translating national security objectives into national military objectives, outmaneuvered Secretary of State Powell.

Deterrence strategy was discarded in favor of a much more aggressive and proactive military strategy summed up in Cheney's one percent doctrine and the Bush Doctrine, both of which included a statement of the willingness to use preemptive force against a threat to US interests. Claiming a right to boldly stake out US interests was intended to discourage other states from actions that challenged our power. However, when US attempts to persuade other nations to accept its hegemony were perceived as constraining the sovereign rights of other states to act in their own perceived self-interest, those nations tended to form weak alliances opposing the United States by again engaging in balancing behavior.

The lesson to the Obama administration is that a proactive military policy represented by the one percent doctrine or the Bush Doctrine is too expensive and counterproductive. An effective national security policy requires a more realistic and pragmatic assessment of the potential military and political power to achieve US objectives. A one percent doctrine results in a lack of focus on more likely threats. And the Bush Doctrine of a willingness to act unilaterally should be discarded in favor of a much greater emphasis on negotiation and multilateral actions to defend global peace. This also implies the use of intelligence for broad international concerns that go beyond pure military interests. For example, intelligence satellites can also be useful to encourage cooperation regarding global warming, environmental issues, water, and energy. The emphasis will surely be less on divisive military confrontations and more on diplomacy to bring nations closer together.

The Obama administration has sent a clear signal of its rejection of expansive claims of unlimited presidential authority in time of war. The damage done by torture conducted as a matter of policy against prisoners in US detention has been incalculable. President Obama has indicated his intention to close Guantánamo Bay and require that detainees be charged and tried in the United States, or before an international tribunal, or held in accordance with the law of armed conflict. Obama has rescinded the previous administration's policy of enhanced interrogation techniques that had led to charges of torture.

Questions for Discussion

1. What lessons can be drawn from foreign policy over the past twenty years regarding the collapse of the bipolar model of world politics and a world hegemon?

2. Does the term "superpower" have any meaning after analyzing the limits of US power?

3. What role does international law play in the twenty-first century?

4. What are the implications of US and European soft power?

5. What are the goals of intelligence policy? What should they be?

6. Is much of US military power a superfluous expense? How should military power be best configured to meet the nation's needs in the twenty-first century?

7. Discuss how the Bush Doctrine contributes to global instability.

Useful Websites

Center for the Study of Islam and Democracy, www.islam-democracy.org.

Centre for Foreign Policy Studies, www.dal.ca/~centre.

Foreign Policy Research Institute, www.fpri.org.

Institute for Foreign Policy Analysis, www.ifpa.org.

International Studies Association, www.isanet.org.

National Center for Policy Analysis, www.ncpa.org.

Notes

1. Project on Defense Alternatives, "Re-Envisioning Defense: An Agenda for US Policy Debate and Transition" (Cambridge, MA: Commonwealth Institute, December 2008), p. 1, available at www.comw.org/pda/newparadigm2009.htm (accessed December 8, 2008). See also pda @comw.org.

2. Carl Conetta, "Forceful Engagement: Rethinking the Role of Military Power in US Global Policy," Project on Defense Alternatives (Cambridge, MA: Commonwealth Institute, December 2008), p. 2.

3. BBC World Service Poll, "Global Poll: Majority Wants Troops Out of Iraq Within a Year," September 7, 2007, available at www.WorldPublicOpinion.org (accessed January 5, 2009). The BBC World Service Poll of 23,000 people was taken across twenty-two countries. Less than one in four (23 percent) thought foreign troops should remain in Iraq until security improved. Sixty-three percent of South Koreans and 63 percent of Australians wanted troops out within a year.

4. Polling Report, Inc., December 15, 2008, available at www.PollingReport.com/iraq.htm (accessed January 5, 2009).

5. Winston Churchill delivered this speech at Westminster College in Fulton, Missouri, where he received an honorary degree.

6. During the Cold War, the United States sought to "contain" Soviet expansionism by involvement in the Korean War, the Vietnam War, the Six Day War, and the Yom Kippur War as well as aiding the mujahidin forces against the Soviet Union in Afghanistan and various covert operations to influence policy in a number of countries.

7. Nevertheless, in 1991, the United States did use military force against Iraq in response to that country's invasion of Kuwait. Later in the decade, under President Clinton, the United States participated in UN peacekeeping efforts in the former nation of Yugoslavia (primarily in Kosovo and Serbia).

8. The neoconservatives were also critical of the Republican leadership of G. H. W. Bush and General Colin Powell's decision to leave Saddam Hussein in power after the first Gulf War.

9. Francis Fukuyama, "The End of History?" *National Interest* 16 (Summer 1989): 3–18.

10. Joseph S. Nye, *The Paradox of American Power* (New York: Oxford University Press, 2002), p. 1.

11. Conetta, "Forceful Engagement," p. 2.

12. Ibid., pp. 2–5.

13. Ibid., p. 5.

14. "The President's State of the Union Speech," White House press release, January 29, 2002.

15. President G. W. Bush's speech at West Point, June 1, 2002.

16. White House, "National Security Strategy of the United States" (Washington, DC: National Security Council, September 17, 2002). The Bush Doctrine, as stated in this NSC strategy document, has a strong resemblance to a Defense Planning Guidance written by neoconservative Paul Wolfowitz in 1992 during the G. H. W. Bush administration. See, for example, "The War Behind Closed Doors," *Frontline,* PBS, February 20, 2003.

17. Ibid.

18. Ron Suskind, *The One Percent Doctrine* (New York: Simon and Schuster, 2006).

19. Ibid. See also Ron Suskind, *The Price of Loyalty* (New York: Simon and Schuster, 2004). In *The Price of Loyalty,* Suskind analyzes how G. W. Bush made policy on war, taxes, and other matters. Based on his interviews, he claims that the overthrow of Saddam Hussein and the US occupation of Iraq was planned as early as the first NSC meeting in January 2001.

20. UN Charter, Article 2, para. 3. The Charter is a treaty ratified by President Truman and, as such, is binding on the United States under international law. Article VI, para. 2, of the US Constitution states: "This Constitution, and the Laws of the United States which shall be made in Pursuance thereof; and all Treaties made, or which shall be made, under the Authority of the United States, shall be the supreme Law of the Land; and the Judges in every State shall be bound thereby, any Thing in the Constitution or Laws of any State to the Contrary notwithstanding."

21. International law accepts the right of a state to respond in self-defense to blatant armed attacks (e.g., Pearl Harbor). Disagreements have arisen over whether self-defense can be legitimately used in response by a state that engages in humanitarian intervention such as intervening in a second country to rescue its nationals whose lives are being threatened.

22. One might consider the consequences if President Truman had accepted the advice of some of his advisers who suggested, at the end of World War II, that the United States should attack Russia, rather than wait for the Soviet Union to grow stronger and decide to launch an attack on the United States that many saw as inevitable.

In 1836, then secretary of state Daniel Webster challenged England's claim of "self-defense" in what became known as the *Caroline* incident. The *Caroline* was a small boat that was used to transport supplies to Irish rebels in Canada. The British sent troops into the United States and cut the *Caroline* adrift, sending it over Niagara Falls to its destruction. The British justified their action based on self-defense. Webster rejected the British claim, and famously stated that self-defense is limited to "cases in which the necessity of that self-defence is instant, overwhelming, and leaving no choice of means, and no moment for deliberation." Letter from Daniel Webster to Lord Ashburton, August 6, 1842, as quoted in John Bassett Moore, *A Digest of International Law* (Washington, DC: US Government Printing Office, 1906), p. 412. Since that time, Webster's formulation is usually quoted as the standard application of the principle.

23. John Burke, "Disgust over Abu Ghraib, Disbelief over Guantanamo," commentary, February 20, 2006, Nieman Watchdog: Questions the Press Should Ask, available at www.niemanwatchdog.org/index.cfm?fuseaction=background.view&backgroundid=0 (accessed January 7, 2009).

24. The federal antitorture statute is, technically, Title 18, Part I, Chapter 113C, of the US Code.

25. The technical name is the United Nations Convention Against Torture and Other Cruel, Inhuman or Degrading Treatment or Punishment. It was adopted by the UN in 1984, but formally adopted by the United States in 1994.

26. See Jack Goldsmith, *The Terror Presidency: Law and Judgment Inside the Bush Administration* (New York: W. W. Norton, 2007).

27. The memo was titled "Standards of Conduct for Interrogation Under 18 USC. sec. 2340-2340A." It became known as the Bybee memo, after Jay Bybee, the head of the OLC at the time.

28. The memo's most astounding statement was that federal criminal law does not apply to the president: *"Even if an interrogation method arguably were to violate Section 2340A, the statute would be unconstitutional if it impermissibly encroached on the President's constitutional power to conduct a military campaign. . . .* The demands of the Commander-in-Chief power are especially pronounced in the middle of a war in which the nation has already suffered a direct attack. . . . *Any effort to apply Section 2340A in a manner that interferes with the President's direction of such core war matters as the detention and interrogation of enemy combatants thus would be unconstitutional"* (emphasis added).

29. See "Memorandum for William J. Haynes II, General Counsel of the Department of Defense," *Re: Military Interrogation of Alien Unlawful Combatants Held Outside the United States,* March 14, 2003, available at www.usdoj.gov/olc/docs/memo-combatantsoutsideunited states.pdf. John Yoo states that he "concludes that the Fifth and Eighth Amendments do not extend to alien enemy combatants held abroad. Moreover, we conclude that different canons of construction indicate that generally applicable criminal laws do not apply to the military interrogation of alien unlawful combatants held abroad. Were it otherwise, the application of these statutes to the interrogation of enemy combatants undertaken by military personnel would conflict with the President's Commander-in-Chief power," p. 81.

30. Joining the ACLU in the suit were the Center for Constitutional Rights, Physicians for Human Rights, Veterans for Common Sense, and Veterans for Peace.

31. Faiz Shakir, Amanda Terkel, and Satyam Khanna et al., "America's Torture Disgrace," *The Progress Report,* December 22, 2008, available at www.pr.thinkprogress.org/2008/12/pr20081222 (accessed December 22, 2008).

32. Joseph E. Stiglitz and Linda J. Bilmes, *The Three Trillion Dollar War: The True Cost of the Iraq Conflict* (New York: W. W. Norton, 2008).

33. Peter Katel, "Cost of the Iraq War," *CQ Researcher* (April 2008): 363–383, 364.

34. Stiglitz and Bilmes, *The Three Trillion Dollar War,* p. 7.

35. Dave Davies, "Joseph Stiglitz on Our 'Three Trillion Dollar War,'" *Fresh Air from WHYY,* NPR, December 23, 2008, available at www.npr.org/templates/story/story.php?storyId=8701279 (accessed December 23, 2008). Other private security guards work for other corporations such as DynCorp.

36. Ibid.

37. Ibid. The years were between 1998 and 2003.

38. Katel, "Cost of the Iraq War," p. 363.

39. Project on Defense Alternatives, "Re-Envisioning Defense," p. 2.

40. Ibid., p. 3.

41. Ibid.

42. George Lakoff, *"War on Terror," Rest in Peace,* August 1, 2005, available at www .rockridgeinstitute.org/research/lakoff/gwot_rip (accessed December 29, 2008).

43. Ibid.

44. Nye coined the term "soft power" to indicate the ability to get others to want the same outcomes as you through cooperation rather than coercion. See Joseph S. Nye Jr., *Soft Power: The Means to Success in World Politics* (New York: PublicAffairs, 2004). Nye points out that soft power is the staple of daily democratic politics. The ability to achieve goals tends to be associated with the acceptance of a culture, political values and institutions, and policies that are perceived as legitimate or having moral authority. Ibid., p. 6.

45. Project on Defense Alternatives, "Re-Envisioning Defense," p. 3.

46. "Barack Obama and Joe Biden: The Change We Need: Iraq," available at www.barack obama.com/issues/iraq (accessed December 30, 2008).

47. Ibid.

48. Greg Bruno, "US Security Agreements and Iraq," Council on Foreign Relations, December 23, 2008, available at www.cfr.org/publication/16448 (accessed December 30, 2008).

49. Andrew Gray, "Pentagon Chief Gates Backs Obama Iraq Policy," Reuters, December 2, 2008, available at www.reuters.com/articlePrint?articleId=USTREB17V820081202 (accessed December 30, 2008).

50. See Senate Resolution 534 and House Resolution 921 of July 18 and 20, 2006, respectively.

51. President George W. Bush, address to US Military Academy graduates, June 1, 2000.

52. Tim Golden, "Administration Officials Split over Military Tribunals," *New York Times,* October 25, 2004, p. A1.

53. *Rasul v. Bush* (2004).

54. Daniel Williams, "Pope Urges Dialogue to Counter 'Arrogance of Power,'" *Washington Post,* January 11, 2005, p. A12.

55. President Barack Obama, inaugural address, reprinted in *New York Times,* January 21, 2009, p. 1.

56. Ibid.

57. Project on Defense Alternatives, "Re-Envisioning Defense," p. 7.

58. Tim Shorrock, "US Espionage Enters the 'Un-Rumsfeld' Era," *Asia Times,* December 8, 2007, available at www.atimes.com/atimes/Middle_East/IL08Ak05.html (accessed January 2, 2009). For example, they made it more difficult to transfer defense intelligence officers into joint "fusion" centers run by the ODNI and the Department of Homeland Security. And when subordinates under their command took contrary positions, they took action. Ibid.

59. Secretary Rumsfeld actually resigned on November 6, 2006, the day before the midterm elections, not the day after as originally suggested by President G. W. Bush. The surprising point is that Rumsfeld was pushed out of his job on the same day he suggested a de-escalation of the Iraq War. When Rumsfeld's resignation was announced on November 8, 2006, Rumsfeld's memo suggesting that progress in the war was not coming quickly enough and the United States should consider withdrawing was still secret. It was widely assumed in Washington political circles that Bush was reacting to the Republican electoral defeat on November 7, and was appointing Gates as a gesture to the Democrats. Now, it appears to be exactly the opposite. Bush was preparing for the Iraq escalation (surge) and wanted a fresh defense secretary to buy him time. Gates implemented the surge and deflected public irritation about the escalation by presenting himself as less confrontational than Rumsfeld. See Robert Parry, "Rumsfeld's Mysterious Resignation," August 17, 2007, available at www.consortiumnews.com/Print/2007/081707.html (accessed January 6, 2009).

60. Ibid.

61. David Barstow, "Behind TV Analysts, Pentagon's Hidden Hand," *New York Times,* April 20, 2008, available at www.nytimes.com/2008/04/20/us/20generals.html.

62. Ibid.

63. Ibid.

64. In fact, federal agencies in the G. W. Bush administration paid columnists to write favorable stories about the administration. They also distributed to local TV stations "hundreds of fake news segments with fawning accounts of administration accomplishments." Many in the White House, the Pentagon, and several of the military analysts believed that pessimistic war coverage was responsible for the US defeat in Vietnam. David Barstow reported that this was a major theme with Paul Vallely, a Fox News analyst from 2001 to 2007. Vallely is a retired Army general who coauthored a paper that accused US news organizations of failing to defend the nation from "enemy" propaganda during Vietnam. He advocated using domestic network TV and radio to "strengthen our national will to victory." Ibid.

Bibliography

Adams, Bruce. "The Limitations of Muddling Through: Does Anyone in Washington Really Think Anymore?" *Public Administration Review* 39, no. 3 (November–December 1979): 545–552.

Alaska Department of Transportation. "Ketchikan Gravina Island Access Project." www.dot.state.ak.us/stwdplng/projectinfo/ser/Gravina/index1.shtml.

Alexander, Karl L., Doris R. Entwisle, and Carrie S. Horsey. "From First Grade Forward: Early Foundations of High School Dropouts." *Sociology of Education* 70, no. 2 (1998): 87–107.

Almeida, Seem Cheryl, and Adria Steinberg. "Raising Graduation Rates in an Era of High Standards." In *The Obama Education Plan*. San Francisco: Jossey-Bass, 2009.

Anderson, Gerard, Uwe E. Reinhardt, Peter S. Hussey, and Varduhi Petrosyan. "It's the Prices, Stupid: Why the United States Is So Different from Other Countries." *Health Affairs* 22, no. 3 (2003): 89–105. http://content.healthaffairs.org/cgi/reprint/22/3/89.pdf.

Araghi, Farshad. "Political Economy of the Financial Crisis: A World-Historical Perspective." *Economic and Political Weekly* 43, no. 45 (November 8, 2008): 27–33.

Arnold, Roger A. *Macroeconomics*. St. Paul, MN: West, 1996.

Association of American Medical Colleges. "Medical Student Education: Costs, Debt, and Loan Repayment Facts, 2008." www.aamc.org/programs/firs/debt/debtfactcard.pdf.

Bailey, John J., and Robert J. O'Connor. "Operationizing Incrementalism: Measuring the Muddles." *Public Administration Review* 35, no. 1 (January–February 1975): 60–66.

Baker, Dean. "It's Not the Credit Crisis, Damn It!" Beat the Press Archive, November 29, 2008. http://prospect.org/csnc/blogs/beat_the_press_archive?month=11&year=2008.

Baker, Dean. "The Housing Bubble Starts to Burst." www.cepr.net/index.php/op-eds-&-columns.

Baker, Dean. "The Run-Up in Home Prices: Is It Real or Is It Another Bubble?" Center for Economic Policy Research, August 2002. www.cepr.net/index.php/publications/reports/the-run-up-in-home-prices-is-it-real-or-is-it-another-bubble.

Baker, Russell. "A Revolutionary President." *New York Review of Books* 56, no. 2 (February 12, 2009).

Bandow, Doug. "Doctors Operate to Cut Out Competition." *Business and Society Review* 58, no. 2 (Summer 1986): 4–10.

Barry, Brian, and Russell Hardin, ed. *Rational Man and Irrational Society?* Beverly Hills, CA: Sage, 1982.

Barstow, David. "Behind TV Analysts, Pentagon's Hidden Hand." *New York Times,* April 20, 2008.

Bartels, Larry. *Unequal Democracy: The Political Economy of the New Gilded Age.* Princeton: Princeton University Press, 2008.

Barzel, Yoram, and Eugene Silberberg. "Is the Act of Voting Rational?" *Public Choice* 16, no. 3 (Fall 1973): 51–58.

Beard, Charles. *An Economic Interpretation of the Constitution.* New York: Free Press, 1913; reprinted 1965.

Becker, Gary. "Crime and Punishment: An Economic Approach." *Journal of Political Economy* 76, no. 2 (March–April 1968): 169–217.

Becker, Gary. *Human Capital.* New York: National Bureau of Economic Research, 1964.

Bennett, Lance W. *News: The Politics of Illusion.* 2nd ed. New York: Longman, 1988.

Bernstein, Aaron. "Waking Up from the American Dream." *Business Week,* December 1, 2003.

Bernstein, Jared. "School's Out," American Prospect Online, March 2004. www.prospect.org.

Bernstein, Jared, and Amy Chasanov. "Viewpoints." Washington, DC: Economic Policy Institute, April 2004.

Berry, Jeffrey M. "Subgovernments, Issue Networks, and Political Conflict." In Richard Harris and Signey Milkis, ed., *Remaking American Politics.* Boulder, CO: Westview Press, 1990.

Billitteri, Thomas J. "High Speed Trains." *CQ Researcher* 19, no. 17 (May 2009): 397–420.

Bivens, Josh. "Squandering the Blue-Collar Advantage: Why Almost Everything Except Unions and the Blue-Collar Workforce Are Hurting US Manufacturing." Washington, DC: Economic Policy Institute, February 2009.

Blecker, Robert. "Haven or Hell? Inside Lorton Central Prison: Experiences of Prison Justified." *Stanford Law Review* 42, no. 3 (1990): 1149–1249.

Blendon, Robert J., et al. "Voters and Health Reform in the 2008 Presidential Election." *New England Journal of Medicine* 359, no. 19 (November 2008): 2050–2061.

Blinder, Alan. "Is History Siding with Obama's Economic Plan?" *New York Times,* August 31, 2008.

Boaz, David. "The Case of Legalizing Drugs." In Herbert Levine, ed., *Point Counter Point Readings in American Government.* 4th ed. New York: St. Martin's, 1992.

Bourdieu, Pierre, and Jean-Claude Passeron. "The School as a Conservative Force: Scholastic and Cultural Inequalities." In John Eggleston, ed., *Contemporary Research in the Sociology of Education.* London: Methuen, 1974.

Bourdieu, Pierre, and Jean-Claude Passeron. *The Inheritors: French Students and Their Relation to Culture.* Chicago: University of Chicago Press, 1979.

Bruno, Greg. "US Security Agreements and Iraq." Council on Foreign Relations, December 2008. www.cfr.org/publication/16448.

Bryk, Anthony, Valerie Lee, and Peter Holland. *Catholic Schools for the Common Good.* Cambridge: Harvard University Press, 1993.

Buchanan, James. "Politics Without Romance: A Sketch of Positive Public Choice and Its Normative Implications." In Alan Hamlin and Philip Pettit, ed., *Contemporary Political Theory.* New York: Macmillan, 1991.

Burke, John. "Disgust over Abu Ghraib, Disbelief over Guantanamo." Commentary. www.niemanwatchdog.org/index.cfm?fuseaction=background.view&backgroundid=0.

Burtless, Gary. "International Trade and the Rise in Earnings Inequality." *Journal of Economic Literature* 33, no. 2 (June 1995): 800–816.

Burtless, Gary, and Christopher Jencks. "American Inequality and Its Consequences." In Henry J. Aaron, James M. Lindsay, and Pietro S. Nivola, ed., *Agenda for the Nation.* Washington, DC: Brookings Institution, 2003.

Calavita, Kitty, Henry N. Pontell, and Robert H. Tillman. *Big Money Crime.* Berkeley: University of California Press, 1997.

Callis, Robert R., and Linda B. Cavanaugh. "Census Bureau Reports on Residential Vacancies and Homeownership." Washington, DC: US Census Bureau News, February 3, 2009.

Cannon, Lou. *Governor Reagan: His Rise to Power.* New York: PublicAffairs, 2003.

Card, David, and Alan B. Krueger. "Minimum Wages and Employment: A Case Study of the Fast-Food Industry in New Jersey and Pennsylvania." *American Economic Review* 84, no. 4 (September 1994): 772–793.

Carter, Shan, Jonathan Ellis, Farhana Hossain, and Alan McLean. "Election 2008: On the Issues: Health Care." *New York Times,* October 2, 2008. http://elections.nytimes.com/2008/president/issues/health.html.

Center on Budget and Policy Priorities. "Tax Cuts: Myths and Realities." www.cbpp.org/cms/index.cfm?f.

Century Foundation. *Class Warfare: Fact and Fiction.* New York: Century Foundation, 2007. www.tcf.org/list.asp?type=PB&pubid=90.

Century Foundation. "The New American Economy: A Rising Tide That Lifts Only Yachts." A Century Foundation Guide to the Issues, 2004. www.tcf.org/Publications/EconomicsInequality/wasow_yachtrc.pdf.

Chait, Jonathan. *The Big Con.* New York: Houghton Mifflin, 2007.

Chase, Stuart. *A New Deal.* New York: Macmillan, 1932.

Chen, Edwin. "Bush, in Pennsylvania, Hails Record Homeownership." *Los Angeles Times,* March 16, 2004.

Children's Defense Fund. *The Bush Administration: Set to Exacerbate Growing Housing Crisis for Families with Children.* Washington, DC: US Government Printing Office, January 2005.

Cho, David. "A Conversion in 'This Storm.'" *Washington Post,* November 18, 2008.

Chubb, John, and Eric A. Hanushik. "Reforming Educational Reform." In Henry J. Aaron, ed., *Setting National Priorities: Policy for the Nineties.* Washington, DC: Brookings Institution, 1990.

Chubb, John E., and Terry M. Moe. *Politics, Markets, and America's Schools.* Washington, DC: Brookings Institution, 1990.

Clinton, Bill. *My Life.* New York: Alfred A. Knopf, 2004.

Cobb, Roger W., and Charles D. Elder. *Participation in American Politics: The Dynamics of Agenda Building.* 2nd ed. Baltimore: Johns Hopkins University Press, 1983.

Coleman, Clive, and Clive Norris. *Introducing Criminology.* Portland, OR: Willan, 2000.

Coleman, James S., Thomas Hoffer, and Sally Kilgore. *High School and Beyond.* Pittsburgh: National Center for Educational Statistics, 1981.

Conally, William E., ed. *The Bias of Pluralism.* New York: Atherton, 1971.

Conetta, Carl. "Forceful Engagement: Rethinking the Role of Military Power in US Global Policy." Project on Defense Alternatives. Cambridge, MA: Commonwealth Institute, December 2008.

Congressional Budget Office. *The Outlook for Social Security.* Washington, DC: US Government Printing Office, 2004.

Cook, Phillip, et al. "The Medical Cost of Gunshot Injuries in the United States." *Journal of the American Medical Association* 282, no. 5 (August 4, 1999): 447–454.

Cooper, Mary H. "Environmental Justice." *CQ Researcher* 8, no. 23 (June 1998): 529–552.

Coughlin, Ellen. "How Rational Is Rational Choice?" *Chronicle of Higher Education,* December 7, 1994.

Currie, Elliott. *Crime and Punishment in America.* New York: Simon and Schuster, 1986.

Cushman, Robert F. *Cases in Constitutional Law.* Englewood Cliffs, NJ: Prentice-Hall, 1979.

Cutler, David M. *Your Money or Your Life: Strong Medicine for America's Health Care System.* New York: Oxford University Press, 2004.

Dahl, Robert. *Who Governs? Democracy and Power in an American City.* New Haven: Yale University Press, 1961.

Darby, Michael R. "Three-and-a-Half Million US Employees Have Been Mislaid: Or, an Explanation of Unemployment, 1934–1941." *Journal of Political Economy* 84, no. 1 (1976): 1–16.

Davies, Dave. "Joseph Stiglitz on Our 'Three Trillion Dollar War.'" NPR, *Fresh Air from WHYY,* December 23, 2008. www.npr.org/templates/story/story.php?storyId =8701279.

Davis, Kingsley, and Wilbert Moore. *Some Principles of Stratification.* Reprint Series in Social Science. New York: Columbia University Press, 1993.

Denmert, Henry. *Economics: An Understanding of the Market Process.* New York: Harcourt Brace Jovanovich, 1991.

Denzau, Arthur T., and Michael C. Munger. "Legislators and Interest Groups: How Unorganized Interests Get Represented." *American Political Science Review* 80, no. 10 (March 1986): 89–106.

Dillon, Sam. "States' Data Obscure How Few Finish High School." *New York Times,* March 20, 2008.

Dinardo, John. *Still Open for Business: Unionization Has No Causal Effect on Firm Closures.* Washington, DC: Economic Policy Institute, March 2009.

Dolbeare, Cushing N., Irene Basloe Saraf, and Sheila Crowley. *Changing Priorities: The Federal Budget and Housing Assistance, 1976–2005.* Washington, DC: National Low-Income Housing Coalition, October 2004.

Dooley, Martin, and Peter Gottschalk. "Earnings Inequality Among Males in the United States: Trends and the Effects of Labor Force Growth." *Journal of Political Economy* 92, no. 1 (1984): 59–89.

Dougherty, Kevin J., and Floyd M. Hammack. *Education and Society.* New York: Harcourt Brace Jovanovich, 1990.

Downs, Anthony. *An Economic Theory of Democracy.* New York: Harper, 1957.

Doyle, Alister. "Greenhouse Gas Jump Spurs Global Warming Fears." Reuters, October 11, 2004.

Dye, Thomas R. *Who's Running America? The Bush Era.* 5th ed. Englewood Cliffs, NJ: Prentice-Hall, 1990.

Dye, Thomas R., Harmon Zeigler, and S. Robert Lichter. *American Politics in the Media Age.* 4th ed. Pacific Grove, CA: Brooks/Cole, 1992.

Easton, David. *A Systems Analysis of Political Life.* New York: John Wiley and Sons, 1965.

Easton, David. "The New Revolution in Political Science." *American Political Science Review* 63, no. 4 (December 1969): 1051–1061.

Ebenstein, William, and Alan Ebenstein. *Great Political Thinkers: Plato to the Present.* 5th ed. Fort Worth, TX: Holt, Rinehart, and Winston, 1991.

Ehrlich, Paul R., and John Holden. "Impact of Population Growth." *Science,* March 26, 1971.

Eilperin, Juliet, and Steven Mufson. "Budget Expects Revenue from Limits on Emissions." *Washington Post,* February 26, 2009.

Elder, Charles D., and Roger W. Cobb. *The Political Uses of Symbols.* New York: Longman, 1983.

Emerson, Eric. "Relative Child Poverty, Income Inequality, Wealth, and Health." *Journal of the American Medical Association* 301, no. 4 (January 28, 2009): 425–426.

Favreault, Melissa, and Gordon Mermin. *Are There Opportunities to Increase Social Security Progressivity Despite Underfunding?* Washington, DC: The Urban Institute, 2008.

Federal Bureau of Investigation. *Uniform Crime Report 2007.* Washington, DC: US Government Printing Office, 2008. www.fbi.gov/ucr/cius2007/offense/violent_crime/murder_homicide.html.

Frank, Patrick. "America Is Not a 'Center-Right' Nation." www.opednews.com.

Frank, Robert H. *Falling Behind: How Rising Inequality Harms the Middle Class.* Berkeley: University of California Press, 2007.

Frank, Thomas. *What's the Matter with Kansas? How Conservatives Won the Heart of America.* New York: Metropolitan Books, 2004.

Friedman, Milton. *Capitalism and Freedom.* Chicago: University of Chicago Press, 1962.

Fuchs, Victor R. "Reforming US Health Care: Key Considerations for the New Administration." *Journal of the American Medical Association* 301, no. 9 (March 4, 2009): 963–965.

Fukuyama, Francis. "The End of History?" *National Interest* 16 (Summer 1989): 3–18.

Furnival, John S. *Colonial Policy and Practice.* New York: New York University Press, 1956.

Fusfeld, Daniel R. *The Age of the Economist.* 9th ed. Boston: Addison-Wesley, 2002.

Galbraith, John Kenneth. *The Culture of Contentment.* New York: Houghton Mifflin, 1992.

Gale, William G., and Peter R. Orszag. "Tax Notes." In William G. Gale and Peter R. Orszag, *Bush Administration Tax Policy: Summary and Outlook.* Washington, DC: Brookings Institution, November 2004.

Geilman, Barton. "Historians Say He Could Redefine the Presidency." *Washington Post,* January 20, 2009.

Gelbspan, Ross. "A Global Warming." *American Prospect,* March–April 1997.

Gerston, Larry N. *Making Public Policy: From Conflict to Resolution.* Glenville, IL: Scott, Foresman, 1979.

Gilder, George. *Wealth and Poverty.* New York: Basic Books, 1981.

Glaeser, Edward, and Jesse Shapiro. "The Benefits of the Home Mortgage Interest Deduction." NBER Working Paper Series, National Bureau of Economic Research, Cambridge, MA, October 2002.

Glaeser, Edward L., and Joseph Gyourko. "Two Ways to Revamp US Housing Policy," Economix, *New York Times,* December 16, 2008. http://economix.blogs.nytimes .com/2008/12/16/two-ways-to-revamp-us-housing-policy/?pa....

Golden, Tim. "Administration Officials Split over Military Tribunals." *New York Times,* October 25, 2004, p. A1.

Goldfield, Michael. *The Color of Politics: Race and the Mainspring of American Politics.* New York: The New Press 1997.

Goldsmith, Jack. *The Terror Presidency: Law and Judgment Inside the Bush Administration.* New York: W. W. Norton, 2007.

Goldstein, P. J. "Drugs and Violent Crime." In N. A. Weiner and M. E. Wolfgang, ed., *Pathways to Violent Crime.* Newbury Park, CA: Sage, 1989.

Goldstein, P. J., et al. *Drug Related Involvement in Violent Episodes: Final Report.* New York: Narcotic and Drug Research, 1987.

Goldwater, Barry. *The Conscience of a Conservative.* New York: Regnery Press, 1960.

Gonzales, Patrick, Trevor Williams, Leslie Jocelyn, Stephen Roey, David Kastberg, and Summer Brenwald. "Highlights from TIMSS 2007: Mathematics and Science Achievement of US Fourth- and Eighth-Grade Students in an International Context." National Center for Education Statistics, no. 2009–001. Washington, DC: US Department of Education, December 2008.

Goodman, Peter S. "A Fresh Look at the Apostle of Free Markets." *New York Times,* April 13, 2008.

Gordon, David M. "Capitalism, Class, and Crime in America." In Ralph Andreano and John J. Siegfried, ed., *The Economics of Crime.* New York: John Wiley and Sons, 1980.

Gray, Andrew. "Pentagon Chief Gates Backs Obama Iraq Policy." Reuters, December 2, 2008. www.reuters.com/articlePrint?articleId=USTREB17V820081202.

Great Books Online. "Respectfully Quoted: A Dictionary of Quotations." www.bartleby .com/73/753.html.

Greenhouse, Linda. "Supreme Court Changes Use of Sentence Guides." *New York Times,* January 13, 2005.

Greenhouse, Steven. *The Big Squeeze: Tough Times for the American Worker.* New York: Random House, 2009.

Greenstein, Robert, and Chad Stone. "What the 2008 Trustees' Report Shows About Social Security." Center on Budget and Policy Priorities, 2008. www.cbpp.org/ cms/index.dfm?f.

Grogger, J. T., and D. Neal. "Further Evidence on the Effects of Catholic Secondary Schooling." In W. G. Gale and Pack J. Rothenberg, ed., *Brookings-Wharton Papers on Urban Affairs.* Washington, DC: Brookings Institution, 2000.

Hambrick, Ralph S., and Debra J. Rog. "Homelessness: United States." In Neil J. Smelser and Paul B. Baltes, ed., *International Encyclopedia of the Social and Behavioral Sciences.* New York: Elsevier, 2001.

Harcourt, G. C., ed. *Keynes and His Contemporaries.* New York: St. Martin's, 1985.

Hardin, Garrett. "The Trajedy of the Commons." *Science,* December 13, 1968.

Hardin, Garrett. "Population Policy," *E: The Environment Magazine,* November–December 1990.

Harrison, Bennett, and Barry Bluestone. *The Great U-Turn: Corporate Restructuring and the Polarizing of America.* New York: Basic Books 1988.

Harvard School of Public Health. "Americans' Views on the US Health Care System Compared to Other Countries." Press release. March 20, 2008.

Harvard School of Public Health. "Most Republicans Think the US Health Care System Is the Best in the World. Democrats Disagree." Press release. March 20, 2008.

Hawthorne, Michael. "Mercury Tainted Fish on FDA Menu." *Chicago Tribune,* December 14, 2008. www.ewg.org/node/27453.

Headen, Alvin E., Jr. "Price Discrimination in Physician Services Markets Based on Race: New Test of an Old Implicit Hypothesis." *Review of Black Political Economy* 15, no. 4 (Spring 1987): 5–20.

Heckman, James J., and Paul A. LaFontaine. "The Declining American High School Graduation Rate: Evidence, Sources, and Consequences," February 2008. www.voxeu.org/index.php?q=n.

Heckman, James J., and Paul A. LaFontaine. *The GED and the Problem of Noncognitive Skills in America.* Chicago: University of Chicago Press, 2008.

Heilbroner, Robert. *The Worldly Philosophers.* 3rd ed. rev. New York: Simon and Schuster, 1967.

Heilbroner, Robert. *The Essential Adam Smith.* New York: W. W. Norton, 1986.

Heilbroner, Robert. "The Embarrassment of Economics." *Challenge: The Magazine of Economic Affairs,* November–December 1996.

Heilbroner, Robert, and Lester Thurow. *Economics Explained: Everything You Need to Know About How the Economy Works and Where It's Going.* New York: Simon and Schuster, 1998.

Heineman, Robert, et al. *The World of the Policy Analyst: Rationality, Values, and Politics.* Chatham, NJ: Chatham House, 1990.

Herbert, Frank. "Impossible, Ridiculous, Repugnant." *New York Times,* October 6, 2005.

Hill, Michael, and Peter Hupe. *Implementing Public Policy: An Introduction to the Study of Operational Governance.* Beverly Hills, CA: Sage, 2009.

Himmelstein, David, Elizabeth Warren, Deborah Thorne, and Steffie Woolhandler. "MarketWatch: Illness and Injury as Contributors to Bankruptcy." *Health Affairs: The Policy Journal of the Health Sphere* 63, no. 1 (February 2005). http://content.healthaffairs.org/cgi/content/full/hlthaff.w5.63/DC1.

Hodges, Michael. "Government Trust Fund and Deficit/Surplus Report." http://mwhodges.home.att.net/deficit-trusts.htm.

Inciardi, James A. *Criminal Justice.* 3rd ed. New York: Harcourt Brace Jovanovich, 1990.

Institute of Medicine at the National Academies of Science. "Insuring America's Health: Principles and Recommendations." www.iom.edu/?id=17848.

Jacobson, Linda. "Long-Term Payoff Seen from Early-Childhood Education." In *The Obama Education Plan.* San Francisco: Jossey-Bass, 2009.

Jans, Nick. "Asaska Thanks You." *USA Today,* May 17, 2005.

Jefferson, Thomas. *The Papers of Thomas Jefferson.* Vol. 8, edited by Julian P. Boyd. Princeton: Princeton University Press, 1953.

Jencks, Christopher. "The Homeless." *New York Review of Books,* April 21, 1994.

Jencks, Christopher S., et al. *Who Gets Ahead?* New York: Basic Books, 1979.

Jillson, Calvin C., and Cecil L. Eubanks. "The Political Structure of Constitution Making: The Federal Convention of 1787." *American Journal of Political Science* 28, no. 3 (August 1984): 435–458.

Johns, Roe J., Edgar L. Morphet, and Kern Alexander. "Human Capital and the Economic Benefits of Education." In Kevin J. Dougherty and Floyd M. Hammack, ed., *Education and Society.* San Diego: Harcourt Brace Jovanovich, 1990.

Johnson, Paige. "Reduce Teen Pregnancies to Reduce the Dropout Rate." www.carrborocitizen.com/main/2008/05/08/reduce-teen-pregnancies-to-reduce-the-dropout-rate.

Johnstone, David, with Steven Holmes. "Experts Doubt Effectiveness of Crime Bill." *New York Times,* September 14, 1994.

Joint Center for Housing Studies of Harvard University. *The State of the Nation's Housing, 2008.* Cambridge, MA: Harvard University, 2008.

Judis, John B., and Ruy Teixeira. *The Emerging Democratic Majority.* New York: Scribner, 2002.

Kaiser Family Foundation. "Health Industry Premiums Rise 6.1 Percent in 2007, Less Rapidly Than in Recent Years but Still Faster Than Wages and Inflation." www.kff.org/insurance/ehbs091107nr.cfm.

Kamin, David, and Isaac Shapiro. *Studies Shed New Light on Effects of Administration's Tax Cuts.* Washington, DC: Center on Budget and Policy Priorities, 2004.

Katel, Peter. "Cost of the Iraq War." *CQ Researcher* 18, no. 16 (April 2008): 363–383.

Keegan, Rebecca Winters. "Greenspan 'Shocked' to Find Flaws in His Free-Market Ideology." www.time.com/timespecials/2008/top10/article/0,30583,1855948_1864014_1864016.

Kelling, George L., Tony Pate, Duane Dieckman, and Charles Brown. *The Kansas City Preventive Patrol Experiment.* Washington, DC: Police Foundation, 1974.

Kelling, George L., and James Q. Wilson. "Broken Windows." *Atlantic Monthly,* March 1982. www.theatlantic.com/doc/198203/broken-windows.

Kennickell, Arthur B. "Ponds and Streams: Wealth and Income in the US, 1989–2007." Divisions of Research and Statistics and Monetary Affairs. Washington, DC: Federal Reserve Board, 2009.

Key, V. O., Jr. *The Responsible Electorate: Rationality in Presidential Voting 1936–1960.* Cambridge: Harvard University Press, 1966.

Keynes, John Maynard. *The General Theory of Employment, Interest, and Money.* New York: Harcourt Brace Jovanovich, 1966.

Kindall, Henry W., and David Pimentel. "Constraints on the Expansion of the Global Food Supply." *Ambio* 23, no. 3 (May 1994): 198–205.

Kingdon, John W. *Agendas, Alternatives, and Public Policies.* Boston: Little, Brown, 1984.

Kirk, Russell. "Is Social Science Scientific?" In Nelson W. Polsby, Robert Dentler, and Paul Smith, ed., *Politics and Social Life.* Boston: Houghton Mifflin, 1963.

Kiser, Larry, and Elinor Ostrom. "The Three Worlds of Action." In Elinor Ostrom, ed., *Strategies of Political Inquiry.* Beverly Hills: Sage, 1982.

Klockers, Carl, ed. *Thinking About Police.* New York: McGraw-Hill, 1983.

Kochan, Thomas J., and Beth Shulman. "A New Social Contract: Restoring Dignity and Balance to the Economy." Washington, DC: Economic Policy Institute, February 2007.

Korenman, Sanders, and Christopher Winship. "A Reanalysis of the Bell Curve: Intelligence, Family Background, and Schooling." In Kenneth Arrow, Samuel Bowles, and Steven Durlauf, ed., *Meritocracy and Economic Inequality.* Princeton: Princeton University Press, 2000.

KosMedia LLC. "McCain Blames I-35 Bridge Collapse on Bridge to Nowhere." www.dailyKos.com.

Kotz, Nick. *Wild Blue Yonder: Money, Politics, and the B-1 Bomber.* Princeton: Princeton University Press, 1988.

Krugman, Paul. *Peddling Prosperity: Economic Sense and Nonsense in the Age of Diminished Expectations.* New York: W. W. Norton, 1994.

Krugman, Paul. "The Death of Horatio Alger," *The Nation,* January 5, 2004.

Krugman, Paul. *The Conscience of a Liberal.* New York: W. W. Norton, 2007.

Krugman, Paul. "About the Social Security Trust Fund." *New York Times,* March 28, 2008.

Kuttner, Robert. "Must Good HMOs Go Bad?" *New England Journal of Medicine* 338, no. 21 (May 1998): 635–639.

Kuznets, Simon. "Economic Growth and Income Inequality." *American Economic Review* 45, no. 1 (March 1955): 1–28.

Lakoff, George. "'War on Terror,' Rest in Peace." www.rockridgeinstitute.org/research/lakoff/gwot_rip.

Lasswell, Harold. *Politics: Who Gets What, When, How.* Cleveland: Meridian, 1958.

Leonhardt, David. "Obama's Housing Plan: Who Will Benefit?" Economix, *New York Times,* February 18, 2009. http://economix.blogs.nytimes.com/2009/02/18/obamas-housing-plan-who-will-benefit/?p.

LeVert, Marianne. *Crime in America.* New York: Facts on File, 1991.

Levi, Michelle. "Obama Says Charitable Giving Not Affected by Tax Increases." www.cbsnews.com/blogs/2009/03/24/politicsalhotsheet/entry4890928.chtml.

Lindblom, Charles E. "The Science of 'Muddling Through.'" *Public Administration Review* 19, no. 1 (Spring 1959): 79–88.

Lineberry, Robert. *American Public Policy.* New York: Harper and Row, 1977.

Lowi, Theodore. "American Business, Public Policy, Case Studies, and Political Theory." *World Politics* 16, no. 4 (July 1964): 677–715.

Lowi, Theodore. *The End of Liberalism: The Second Republic of the United States.* New York: W. W. Norton, 1979.

Lowi, Theodore, Benjamin Gensberg, and Kenneth A. Shepsle. *American Government: Power and Purpose.* 10th ed. New York: W. W. Norton, 2008.

Luttbeg, Norman R. "Differential Voting Turnout in the American States, 1960–82." *Social Science Quarterly* 65, no. 1 (March 1984): 60–73.

Lyman, Rick, and Gary Gately. "Behind the Maryland Fires: A County in Transition." *New York Times,* January 7, 2005.

Lynch, James. "Crime in International Perspective." In James Q. Wilson and Joan Petersilia, ed., *Crime: Public Policies for Crime Control.* Oakland: ICS, 2002.

MacIntyre, Alasdair. *After Virtue: A Study in Moral Theory.* 2nd ed. Notre Dame, IN: University of Notre Dame Press, 1984.

Malthus, Thomas Robert. "An Essay on the Principle of Population." In E. A. Wrigley and D. Souden, ed., *The Works of Thomas Robert Malthus.* 6th ed., vol. 3. London: William Pickering, 1986.

Marmor, T. R. *The Politics of Medicare.* 2nd ed. New York: Aldine de Gruyter, 2000.

Marx, Karl, and Friedrich Engels. *The Communist Manifesto.* Edited by Samuel Beer. New York: Appleton-Century Crofts, 1955.

Maslow, Abraham. "A Theory of Human Motivation." *Psychological Review* 50, no. 2 (1943): 370–396.

Mauer, Marc. "Thinking About Prison and Its Impact in the Twenty-First Century." Fifteenth Annual Walter C. Reckless Memorial Lecture, Ohio State University, April 14, 2004.

McGill, Dan, Kyle Brown, John Haley, and Sylvester Schieber. *Fundamentals of Private Pensions.* 7th ed. Philadelphia: University of Pennsylvania Press, 1966.

Meisels, Samuel J. "Universal Pre-K: What About the Babies." In *The Obama Education Plan.* San Francisco: Jossey-Bass, 2009.

Mills, C. Wright. *The Power Elite.* New York: Oxford University Press, 1956.

Miron, Gary. "Strong Charter School Laws Are Those That Result in Positive Outcomes." Western Michigan University, paper presented at the AERA annual meeting, Montreal, Quebec, Canada, 2005.

Mitchell, William C. *Government as It Is.* London: Institute of Economic Affairs, 1988.

Moe, Terry. "Schools, Vouchers, and the American Public." A discussion by Terry Moe at the Brookings Center on Education Policy. www.brookings.edu/comm/transcripts/2001.

Moller, S., E. Huber, J. D. Stephens, and D. Bradley. "Determinants of Relative Poverty in Advanced Capitalist Democracies." *American Sociological Review* 68, no. 3 (2003): 22–51.

Montaigne, Michel de. *The Essays of Michel de Montaigne.* Vol. 3. Editor and translator Jacob Zeitlin. New York: Alfred A. Knopf, 1936.

Montgomery, Lori. "Recession Puts a Major Strain on Social Security Trust Fund: As Payroll Tax Revenue Falls, so Does Surplus." *Washington Post,* March 31, 2009.

Moore, Mark H. "Controlling Criminogenic Commodities: Drugs, Guns, and Alcohol." In James Q. Wilson, ed., *Crime and Public Policy.* San Francisco: Institute for Contemporary Problems, 1983.

Morgenthau, Hans J. "The Purpose of Political Science." In James C. Charlesworth, ed., *A Design for Political Science: Scope, Objectives, and Methods.* Monograph no. 6. Philadelphia: American Academy of Political and Social Science, 1966.

Morin, Richard. "America's Middle-Class Meltdown." *Washington Post,* December 1, 1991.

Moyers, Bill. *Bill Moyers Journal.* Transcript. August 29, 2008. www.pbs.org/moyers/journal/08292008/transcript4.html.

Nelson, Barbara. *Making an Issue of Child Abuse.* Chicago: University of Chicago Press, 1984.

Newman, Oscar. *Defensible Space: Crime Prevention Through Urban Design.* New York: Macmillan, 1973.

Nozick, Robert. *Anarchy, State, and Utopia.* New York: Basic Books, 1974.

Nye, Joseph S. *The Paradox of American Power.* New York: Oxford University Press, 2002.

Nye, Joseph Jr. *Soft Power: The Means to Success in World Politics.* New York: PublicAffairs, 2004.

Obama, Barack. Inaugural address. January 20, 2009.

Okun, Arthur. M. *Equality and Efficiency: The Big Tradeoff.* Washington, DC: Brookings Institution, 1975.

Organisation for Economic Co-operation and Development. *Revenue Statistics, 1965–2007.*

Padover, Saul K. *Thomas Jefferson on Democracy.* New York: Appleton-Century, 1939.

Parry, Robert. "Rumsfeld's Mysterious Resignation." August 17, 2007. www.consortiumnews.com/Print/2007/081707.html.

Parsons, Wayne. "Myths About Single Payer National Health Insurance." May 13, 2009. http://honolulu.injuryboard.com/medical-malpractice/myths-about-single-payer-national-health-insurance.aspx?googleid=262904.

Perks, Robert. *Rewriting the Rules: The Bush Administration's Assault on the Environment.* 3rd annual edition. Washington, DC: Natural Resources Defense Council, April 2004.

Peterson, Chris, and Rachel Burton. "US Health Care Spending: Comparison with Other OECD Countries." Congressional Research Service Report for Congress. Washington, DC: US Government Printing Office, September 2007.

Pew Research Center for the People and the Press. *Evenly Divided and Increasingly Polarized: 2004 Political Landscape.* Washington, DC: Pew Research Center for the People and the Press, November 2003.

Phillips, Kevin. *Arrogant Capital: Washington, Wall Street, and the Frustration of American Politics.* Boston: Little, Brown, 1994.

Phillips, Kevin. *American Dynasty: Aristocracy, Fortune, and the Politics of Deceit in the House of Bush.* New York: Viking, 2004.

Pickler, Nedra. "Obama Calls for Universal Health Care." January 2007. www.washingtonpost.com/wpdyn/content/article/2007/01/25/AR2007012500764.html.

Pope Leo XIII. *Rerum Novarum.* May 15, 1891. www.osjspm.org/majordoc_jrerum_novarum_official.aspx.

Posner, Richard. "Optimal Sentences for White Collar Criminals." *American Criminal Law Review* 17, no. 4 (Winter 1980): 409–410.

Poterba, James, and Todd Sinai. "Tax Expenditures for Owner-Occupied Housing Deductions for Property Taxes and Mortgage Interest and the Exclusion of Imputed Rental Income." Paper presented January 2008. http://real.wharton.upenn.edu/~Sinai/papers/Poterba-Sinai-2008-ASSA-fin.

Press, Bill. *Train Wreck: The End of the Conservative Revolution.* Hoboken, NJ: John Wiley and Sons, 2008.

Project on Defense Alternatives. *Re-Envisioning Defense: An Agenda for US Policy Debate and Transition.* Cambridge, MA: Commonwealth Institute, December 2008. pda@comw.org.

Putnam, Robert. "Bowling Alone: America's Declining Social Capital." *Journal of Democracy* 6, no. 1 (January 1995): 65–78.

Putnam, Robert. "The Strange Disappearance of Civic America." *American Prospect,* Winter 1996.

Rachels, James. *The Elements of Moral Philosophy.* New York: McGraw-Hill, 1986.

RAND Institute for Entrepreneurship and Public Policy. "Is the Economic Burden of Providing Health Insurance Greater for Small Firms Than for Large Firms?" http://rand.org/pubs/research_briefs//2008/RAND_RB9340.pdf.

Rattner, Steven. "Volker Asserts US Must Trim Living Standard." *New York Times,* October 18, 1979.

Rawls, John. *A Theory of Justice.* Cambridge: Harvard University Press, 1971.

Reagan, Ronald. Inaugural address. January 20, 1981.

Reich, Robert B. *The Resurgent Liberal and Other Unfashionable Prophecies.* New York: Vintage, 1989.

Reinberg, Steven. "Recession Scrambling Health Spending in US." *US News and World Report,* February 24, 2009.

Reinhardt, Uwe. "Wanted: A Clearly Articulated Social Ethic for American Health Care." *Journal of the American Medical Association* 278, no. 17 (November 1997): 1446–1447.

Reiss, Albert J., and Jeffry A. Roth, ed. *Understanding and Preventing Violence.* Washington, DC: National Academy Press, 1993.

Renzulli, Linda, and Vincent Roscigno. "Charter Schools and the Public Good." *Contexts.* www.caliber.ucpress.net/doi/abs/10.1525/ctx.2007.6.1.31.

Rice, Dorothy P., et al. "Cost of Injury in the United States: A Report to Congress, 1989." San Francisco and Baltimore: Institute for Health and Aging, University of California, and the Injury Prevention Center, Johns Hopkins University, 1989.

Riker, William H. *Liberalism Against Populism: A Confrontation Between the Theory of Democracy and the Theory of Social Choice.* San Francisco: Freeman, 1982.

Robelen, Eric W. "NAEP Gap Continuing for Charters: Sector's Scores Lag in Three Out of Four Main Categories." In *The Obama Education Plan.* San Francisco: Jossey-Bass, 2009.

Roche, John P. "The Founding Fathers: A Reform Caucus in Action." *American Political Science Review* 55, no. 4 (December 1961): 799–816.

Rosen, Yereth. "Palin, 'Bridge to Nowhere' Line Angers Many Alaskans," Reuters, September 1, 2008.

Rosenbaum, Walter A. *Environmental Politics and Policy.* Washington, DC: Congressional Quarterly Press, 2005.

Rossi, Peter. *Down and Out in America: The Origins of Homelessness.* Chicago: University of Chicago Press, 1989.

Saad, Lydia. "Perceptions of Crime Problem Remain Curiously Negative." Gallup, October 22, 2007. www.gallup.com/poll/102262/Perceptions-Crime-Problem-Remain-Curiously-Negative.aspx.

Sabatier, Paul. "Top-Down and Bottom-Up Models of Policy Implementation: A Critical Analysis and Suggested Synthesis." *Journal of Public Policy* 6, no. 2 (January 1986): 21–48.

Sabatier, Paul A. "Political Science and Public Policy." *PS: Political Science and Politics* 24 (June 1991): 145.

Sard, Barbara. "Number of Homeless Families Climbing Due to Recession: Recovery Package Should Include New Housing Vouchers and Other Measures to Prevent Homelessness." Washington, DC: Center on Budget Policy and Priorities, January 2009.

Sawhill, Isabel V., and Charles F. Stone. "The Economy: The Key to Success." In Isabel V. Sawhill and John Palmer, ed., *The Reagan Record: An Assessment of America's Changing Domestic Priorities.* Cambridge, MA: Ballinger, 1984.

Schattschneider, E. E. *The Semi-Sovereign People: A Realist's View of Democracy in America.* New York: Holt, Rinehart, and Winston, 1960.

Schlesinger, Arthur, Jr. "The 'Hundred Days' of FDR." *New York Times,* April 10, 1983.

Schultz, Theodore W. "Investment in Human Capital." *American Economic Review* 51, no. 1 (March 1961): 1–17.

Schweinhart, Lawrence J. "Creating the Best Prekindergartens." In *The Obama Education Plan.* San Francisco: Jossey-Bass, 2009.

Shafritz, Jay M. *Dictionary of American Government and Politics.* Chicago: Dorsey Press, 1988.

Shafritz, Jay M., ed. "Health Policy." In *The International Encyclopedia of Public Policy and Administration.* Vol. 2. Boulder, CO: Westview Press, 1998.

Shaiken, Harley. "Unions, the Economy, and Employee Free Choice." EPI Briefing Paper. Washington, DC: Economic Policy Institute, February 2009.

Shakir, Faiz, et al. "America's Torture Disgrace." *The Progress Report,* December 2008. http://pr.thinkprogress.org/2008/12/pr20081222.

Sherman, Lawrence. "The Police." In James Q. Wilson and Joan Petersilia, ed., *Crime.* San Francisco: ICS, 1995.

Shorrock, Tim. "US Espionage Enters the 'Un-Rumsfeld' Era." *Asia Times,* December 8, 2007. www.atimes.com/atimes/Middle_East/IL08Ak05.html.

Simon, William. *A Time for Truth.* New York: Reader's Digest, 1978.

Skidelsky, Robert J. *Maynard Keynes: The Economist as Saviour, 1920–1937.* New York: Viking Penguin, 1992.

Smith, Adam. *An Inquiry into the Nature and Causes of the Wealth of Nations,* Edwin Cannan, ed. New York: G. P. Putman's Sons, 1877; originally published 1776.

Smith, Adam. *The Theory of Moral Sentiments,* D. D. Raphael and A. L. Macfie, ed. Oxford: Clarendon, 1976.

Smith, Allen W. *The Looting of Social Security.* New York: Carroll and Graf, 2003.

Smith, Page. *A New Age Now Begins.* New York: McGraw-Hill, 1976.

Source Watch. "Grover Norquist: Conservative Activist." www.sourcewatch.org/index .php?title=Grover_Norquist.

Squires, Gregory. "Education, Jobs and Inequality: Functional and Conflict Models of Social Stratification in the United States." *Social Problems* 24, no. 4 (April 1977): 436–450.

Stanton, Mark W. "Employer-Sponsored Health Insurance: Trends in Cost and Access." US Department of Health and Human Services, Agency for Healthcare Research and Quality. www.ahrq.gov/research/empspria/empspria.htm.

Starr, Paul. "The Realignment Opportunity." *American Prospect,* December 2008.

State of Alaska. "Gravina Access Project Redirected." Press release, September 9, 2007.

Stephens, G. Ross. "Public Policy, Income Distribution, and Class Warfare." *Poverty and Public Policy* 1, no. 1 (2009). www.bepress.com/pso_poverty/vol1/iss1/art3.

Stiglitz, Joseph, and Linda Bilmes. *The Three Trillion Dollar War: The True Cost of the Iraq Conflict.* New York: W. W. Norton, 2008.

Stout, David. "Obama Outlines Plan for Education Overhaul." *New York Times,* March 11, 2009.

Stratton, Allegra, and Ashley Seager. "Darling Invokes Keynes as He Eases Spending Rules to Fight Recession." *The Guardian,* October 20, 2008. www.guardian.co.uk/politics/2008/oct/20/economy-recession-treasury-energy-housing.

Struyk, Raymond J. *Should Government Encourage Home Ownership?* Washington, DC: Urban Institute, 1977.

Suskind, Ron. *The Price of Loyalty: George W. Bush, the White House, and the Education of Paul O'Neill.* New York: Simon and Schuster, 2004.

Suskind, Ron. *The One Percent Doctrine.* New York: Simon and Schuster, 2006.

Sutherland, Edwin H. *White Collar Crime.* New York: Holt, Rinehart, and Winston, 1949.

Thomas, Helen. "Greenspan Hints at Humility." *New York Times,* October 29, 2008.

Thompson, C. Bradley. "The Decline and Fall of American Conservatism." *The Objective Standard* 1, no. 3 (Fall 2006). www.theobjectivestandard.com.

Titus, James G., and Charlie Richman. "Maps of Lands Vulnerable to Sea Level Rise." US Environmental Protection Agency, Global Warming Publications. Washington, DC: US Government Printing Office, 2008.

Tocqueville, Alexis de. "Democracy in America." Cited in William Ebenstein and Alan Ebenstein, *Great Political Thinkers.* New York: Harcourt Brace, 1991.

Truman, David B. *The Governmental Process.* New York: Alfred A. Knopf, 1971.

Tucker, Robert C., ed. *The Marx-Engels Reader.* 2nd ed. New York: W. W. Norton, 1978.

Tullock, Gordon. "An Economic Approach to Crime." In Ralph Andreano and John J. Siegfried, *The Economics of Crime.* New York: Schenkman, 1980.

Turque, Bill, and Maria Glod. "Stimulus to Help Retool Education, Duncan Says." *Washington Post,* March 5, 2009.

United Nations. *United Nations Convention Against Torture and Other Cruel, Inhuman or Degrading Treatment or Punishment.* New York: United Nations Publications.

United Nations Environment Programme. "Basic Facts and Data on the Science and Politics of Ozone Protection," August 2003. www.unep.org/ozone.

US Advisory Commission on Intergovernmental Relations. *Guide to the Criminal Justice System for General Government Elected Officials.* Washington, DC: US Government Printing Office, 1993.

US Census Bureau. *Factfinder.* http://factfinder.census.gov/home/saff/main.html?_long=en.

US Census Bureau. *Statistical Abstract.* Washington, DC: US Government Printing Office, multiple years.

US Congressional Budget Office. "Technological Change and the Growth of Health Care Spending." January 2008. www.cbo.gov/ftpdocs/89xx/doc8947/01-31-tech Health.pdf.

Verba, Sidney, Kay Schlozman, and Henry Brady. *Voice and Equality: Participation in American Politics.* Cambridge: Harvard University Press, 1996.

Viadero, Debra. "Top Students Said to Stagnate Under NCLB." In *The Obama Education Plan.* San Francisco: Jossey-Bass, 2009.

Vold, George B., and Thomas J. Bernard. *Theoretical Criminology.* New York: Oxford University Press, 1986.

Weeks, John. "Inequality Trends in Some Developed OECD Countries." In Jomo K. S., ed., with J. Baudot, *Flat World, Big Gaps: Economic Liberalization, Globalization, Poverty and Inequality.* New York: Zed Books, 2007.

Wellford, Charles F., John V. Pepper, and Carol V. Petrie, ed. *Firearms and Violence.* Washington, DC: National Research Council, 2004.

"Where They Stand." *Anchorage Daily News,* October 22, 2006.

White, Lawrence. *The Regulation of Air Pollutant Emissions from Motor Vehicles.* Washington, DC: American Enterprise Institute, 1982.

Wikelius, Kristin, et al. *National Health Insurance: Lessons from Abroad.* New York: Century Foundation Press, 2008.

Wildavsky, Aaron. *The Politics of the Budgetary Process.* Boston: Little, Brown, 1984.

Williams, Daniel. "Pope Urges Dialogue to Counter 'Arrogance of Power.'" *Washington Post,* January 11, 2005.

Wills, Gary. *Inventing America: Jefferson's Declaration of Independence.* New York: Doubleday, 1978.

Wilson, James Q. *The Moral Sense.* New York: Free Press, 1993.

Wilson, William Julius. *The Truly Disadvantaged: The Inner City, the Underclass, and Public Policy.* Chicago: University of Chicago Press, 1987.

Wolff, Edward N. *Top Heavy: A Study of the Increasing Inequality of Wealth in America.* New York: Twentieth Century Fund, 1995.

Woolhandler, Steffie, Terry Campbell, and David Himmelstein. "Costs of Health Care Administration in the United States and Canada." *New England Journal of Medicine* 349, no. 8 (2003): 768–775.

Zandi, Mark M. "Assessing President Bush's Fiscal Policies." July 2004. www.economy .com.

Index

About the Book

Now in its fourth edition, *Public Policy: Perspectives and Choices* successfully combines a clear explanation of the basic concepts and methods of the policymaking process with a keen focus on how values influence policy choices.

The authors first cover the fundamentals:

- How do issues reach the policy agenda?
- How are policies crafted and implemented?
- Who pays and who benefits?
- How is the effectiveness of a policy determined?

They then apply this foundation to a range of policy areas: the economy, welfare, education, crime, health care, housing, the environment, foreign policy, and domestic security.

The fully updated text:

- Presents complicated ideas in an accessible way
- Engages with controversial ideas that bring the study of public policy alive
- Draws on a wealth of "real world" examples
- Provides balanced consideration of liberal and conservative policy positions
- Emphasizes the essential relationship between individual self-interest and national well-being

The result is an ideal combination of theory and practice for effectively teaching public policy.

Charles L. Cochran and **Eloise F. Malone** are professors of political science at the US Naval Academy.